Historical Dictionaries of Diplomacy and Foreign Relations
Jon Woronoff, Series Editor

Historical Dictionary of U.S. Diplomacy from World War I through World War II

Martin Folly
Niall Palmer

Historical Dictionaries of Diplomacy and Foreign Relations, No. 11

The Scarecrow Press, Inc.
Lanham • Toronto • Plymouth, UK
2010

Published by Scarecrow Press, Inc.
A wholly owned subsidiary of The Rowman & Littlefield Publishing Group, Inc.
4501 Forbes Boulevard, Suite 200, Lanham, Maryland 20706
http://www.scarecrowpress.com

Estover Road, Plymouth PL6 7PY, United Kingdom

British Library Cataloguing in Publication Information Available

Library of Congress Cataloging-in-Publication Data

Folly, Martin H., 1957–
  Historical dictionary of U.S. diplomacy from World War I through World War II
/ Martin Folly, Niall Palmer.
    p. cm. — (Historical dictionaries of diplomacy and foreign relations ; no. 11)
  Includes bibliographical references.
  ISBN 978-0-8108-5606-6 (cloth : alk. paper) — ISBN 978-0-8108-7376-6
(eBook)
    1. United States—Foreign relations—1913-1921—Dictionaries. 2. United
States—Foreign relations—1921-1923—Dictionaries. 3. United States—Foreign
relations—1923-1929—Dictionaries. 4. United States—Foreign relations—
1929-1933—Dictionaries. 5. United States—Foreign relations—1933-1945—
Dictionaries. 6. World War, 1914-1918—Diplomatic history—Dictionaries.
7. World War, 1939-1945—Diplomatic history—Dictionaries. 8. World War,
1914-1918—United States—Dictionaries. 9. World War, 1939-1945—United
States—Dictionaries. I. Palmer, Niall A. II. Title. III. Title: Historical dictionary
of US diplomacy from World War I through World War II. IV. Title: Historical
dictionary of U.S. diplomacy from World War 1 through World War 2.
  E784.F65 2010
  973.91—dc22

                                                              2009036400

Printed in the United States of America

Contents

Editor's Foreword

The period from the outset of World War I to the end of World War II was among the most significant in the history of the United States. Twice it was drawn into "foreign entanglements," wars it initially thought were no concern of its own and of which it tried to steer clear, only to realize that it could not stand aside, in splendid or any other form of isolation. Each time, it geared up in record time, entered the fray massively, and was crucial to the outcome. Each war, in its own way, tested the American people and their leaders, and in each case the country came out of the conflagration not only stronger than before but stronger relative to other countries than it had ever been. This was the period when the United States became a world leader. The lessons learned during the interval between the two wars, when Americans tried vainly to ignore the rest of the world, taught the nation that it could not just stand by when certain things happened, and that intervening earlier could actually be the better solution, as long as the intervention was truly necessary.

This *Historical Dictionary of U.S. Diplomacy from World War I through World War II* is thus a crucial link in the series on American diplomacy, not only because of the wars it covers but also the period of isolationism sandwiched between them. All three phases get ample treatment in this volume, which includes numerous dictionary entries on notable persons, institutions, and events. Even those who believe that events and institutions are somehow more important than persons will have to mull over the role played by such exceptional individuals as Woodrow Wilson, Franklin D. Roosevelt, Winston Churchill, and Joseph Stalin. Along with the dictionary, which as always has pride of place, this volume also offers a substantial chronology that helps readers keep track of events, a plethora of abbreviations and acronyms in their own section, and some rather useful appendixes. This is topped off by an extensive bibliography, which can point interested readers in the right direction to learn more about any specific aspect or the period in general.

This book was written by Martin H. Folly and Niall A. Palmer. Both are British historians who specialize in U.S. history and teach it largely to students for whom the United States is a foreign country. That is certainly not a bad thing; in fact, it can have many positive aspects, in that much less is simply assumed and much more has to be pointed out and explained. Dr. Folly is a senior lecturer in U.S. and international history at Brunel University in London. His expertise is largely in U.S. foreign policy in the 1930s, World War II, and the Cold War (on which he will be producing the follow-up volume in this series). He has published widely, including several books, in particular *The United States in World War II: The Awakening Giant*. Dr. Palmer is a lecturer in politics and history at the same university. He, too, has written extensively on U.S. history, the most relevant work being *The Twenties in America: Politics and History*. As we all know, it is extremely important to learn from the past. As we tend to forget, it is just as easy to learn the wrong things as the right things. But at least knowing the past better will be a precious contribution to getting the lessons right.

Jon Woronoff
Series Editor

Acronyms and Abbreviations

AAA	Agricultural Adjustment Agency
AALL	American Association for Labor Legislation
AAUN	American Association for the United Nations
ABC	Argentina–Brazil–Chile
ABC-1	America–British–Canadian Plan 1
ABDA	American–British–Dutch–Australian Command
ACLU	American Civil Liberties Union
ACPFP	Advisory Committee on Postwar Foreign Policy
ACPFR	Advisory Committee on Problems of Foreign Relations
AEF	American Expeditionary Force
AFC	America First Committee
AFL	American Federation of Labor
AFSC	American Friends Service Committee
AMGOT	Allied Military Government
APL	American Protective League
APM	American Peace Mobilization
ARA	American Relief Administration
AUAM	American Union against Militarism
AVG	American Volunteer Group
B2H2	Ball/Burton/Hatch/Hill Resolution, 1943
BRUSA	Britain-United States of America Agreement
CBO	Combined Bomber Offensive
CBS	Columbia Broadcasting System
CCS	Combined Chiefs of Staff
CDAAA	Committee to Defend America by Aiding the Allies
CFR	Council on Foreign Relations
CIA	Central Intelligence Agency
CNO	Chief of Naval Operations
COI	Coordinator of Information

COMINCH	Commander in Chief, U.S. Navy
Comintern	Communist International
COSSAC	Chief of Staff to Supreme Allied Commander
CPD	Emergency Advisory Committee for Political Defense
CPI	Committee on Public Information
CPUSA	Communist Party of the United States
DEEFA	State Department Division of Eastern European Affairs
EAC	European Advisory Commission
Ex-Im Bank	Export-Import Bank
FBI	Federal Bureau of Investigation
FBPC	Foreign Bondholders' Protective Council
FDIC	Federal Deposit Insurance Corporation
FEA	Foreign Economic Administration
FFF	Fight for Freedom
FOR	Fellowship of Reconciliation
HUAC	House Committee on Un-American Activities
IADB	Inter-American Defense Board
IBRD	International Bank for Reconstruction and Development(World Bank)
ICAO	International Civil Aviation Organization
ICC	International Chamber of Commerce
IGR	Institute for Government Research
ILO	International Labour Organization
IMF	International Monetary Fund
IPR	Institute of Pacific Relations
ITT	International Telephone and Telegraph
IWW	Industrial Workers of the World
JCS	Joint Chiefs of Staff
KAOWC	Keep America out of War Congress
LNA	League of Nations Association
NAM	National Association of Manufacturers
NATO	North Atlantic Treaty Organization
NCLB	National Civil Liberties Bureau
NCPW	National Council for the Prevention of War
NDRC	National Defense Research Committee
NFNS	No-Frontier News Service
NKGB	Union of Soviet Socialist Republics Commissariat for State Security

NSDAP	National Socialist German Workers' (Nazi) Party
OCIAA	Office of the Coordinator of Inter-American Affairs
OEW	Office of Economic Warfare
OPM	Office of Production Management
OSRD	Office of Scientific Research and Development
OSS	Office of Strategic Services
OWI	Office of War Information
PPS	Policy Planning Staff
ROTC	Reserve Officer Training Corps
RSFSR	Russian Soviet Federated Socialist Republic
SCAEF	Supreme Commander Allied Expeditionary Force
SEC	Securities and Exchange Commission
SSA	Signals Security Agency
SWNCC	State-War-Navy Coordinating Committee
TVA	Tennessee Valley Authority
TWA	Trans-World Airlines
UAW	United Automobile Workers
UFC	United Fruit Company
UN	United Nations
UNESCO	United Nations Educational, Scientific, and Cultural Organization
UNRRA	United Nations Relief and Rehabilitation Administration
USAAF	United States Army Air Force
USIA	United States Information Agency
USSR	Union of Soviet Socialist Republics
WILPF	Women's International League for Peace and Freedom
WPP	Women's Peace Party
WRB	War Refugee Board
WRL	War Resisters League

Chronology

1913   3 November: United States demands Victoriano Huerta resign and leave Mexico. **17 November:** First vessel passes through Panama Canal.

1914   27 January: U.S. Marines land in Haiti. **1 April:** Civil government established in the Panama Canal Zone. **14 April:** U.S. warships sent to Tampico, Mexico, to enforce salute of the flag. **21 April:** U.S. Marines land at Veracruz, Mexico. **20 May:** Argentina, Brazil, and Chile (ABC powers) meet at Niagara Falls to arbitrate between U.S. and Mexico. **24 June:** U.S.–Mexico agreement signed. **28 June:** Assassination of Archduke Franz Ferdinand of Austria. **5 July:** Huerta reelected president of Mexico. **15 July:** Huerta resigns and goes into exile. **28 July:** Austria-Hungary declares war on Serbia. **1 August:** Germany declares war on Russia. **3 August:** Germany declares war on France. **4 August:** Germany invades Belgium. Great Britain declares war on Germany. United States declares neutrality. **15 August:** Panama Canal officially opens. U.S. troops withdraw from Veracruz. **3 November:** Large Republican gains in U.S. congressional elections.

1915   11 February: U.S. send notes to Britain and Germany regarding naval blockade. **18 February:** Intensive German submarine (U-boat) warfare begins. **1 March:** One American dies on British liner *Falaba*, first passenger ship to be sunk in the war. **11 March:** British blockade of Germany begins. **1 May:** American steamship (SS) *Gulflight* sunk by a U-boat without warning. **7 May:** RMS *Lusitania* sunk by U-boat; 1,198 (128 Americans) killed. **23 June:** Robert Lansing becomes secretary of state after William Jennings Bryan resigns. **27 July:** Revolution in Haiti. **28 July:** U.S. troops occupy Haiti (remain until August 1934). **19 August:** SS *Arabic* sunk by U-boat, killing two Americans. **18 September:** Germans pledge that U-boats will not attack passenger liners without warning. **25 September:** United States loans $500 million to

Britain and France. **9 October:** Latin American states recognize Venustiano Carranza as president of Mexico. **4 December:** Henry Ford's peace ship *Oscar II* commences voyage to Europe.

1916 19 January: President Woodrow Wilson's envoy, Edward House, arrives in London at start of mission to European capitals. **29 February:** German order to U-boats to sink merchant ships without warning. **9 March:** Raid by Pancho Villa on Columbus, New Mexico. **15 March:** Punitive expedition into Mexico after Villa raid. **24 March:** A U-boat sinks French ship *Sussex*, killing four Americans. Wilson sends an ultimatum to Germany to stop submarine warfare. **5 May:** *Sussex* pledge: unrestricted submarine warfare will stop if United States compels Britain to end blockade of Germany. **16 May:** U.S. forces occupy Dominican Republic (remain until 1924). **21 June:** Battle of Carrizal between United States and Mexico. **26 July:** U.S. protest against British blacklist of American companies. **4 August:** U.S. agrees to purchase Virgin Islands from Denmark. **7 November:** Woodrow Wilson reelected U.S. president. **6 December:** Lloyd George replaces Asquith as Britain's prime minister. **20 December:** Wilson sends peace note to all belligerents.

1917 31 January: Germany renounces *Sussex* pledge and announces unrestricted submarine warfare. **3 February:** United States and Germany break off diplomatic relations. **24 February:** Great Britain passes the Zimmermann telegram to the U.S. government. **26 February:** Wilson requests congressional authority to arm merchant ships. **1 March:** State Department releases the Zimmermann telegram to the press. **4 March:** Armed Ships Bill is filibustered in Senate. **8 March:** Wilson announces arming of merchant ships by executive order. U.S. troops land at Santiago, Cuba. First Russian revolution begins. **16 March:** Abdication of Russian Tsar Nicholas II. **31 March:** United States takes over Virgin Islands. **2 April:** Wilson asks Congress to declare war on Germany. **6 April:** United States declares war on Germany. **14 April:** Committee on Public Information established by Wilson. **20 April:** United States and Turkey break off diplomatic relations. **18 May:** Selective military conscription introduced in United States. **26 June:** First U.S. army division arrives in France. **9 July:** U.S. government takes control of fuel and food. **2 November:** Lansing–Ishii agreement. **5 November:** U.S. troops in first action against German army. **7 No-**

vember: Bolsheviks seize power in Russia. **7 December:** U.S. declares war on Austria-Hungary. **28 December:** Government takes control of U.S. railroads.

1918 **8 January:** Fourteen Points announced by President Wilson. **3 March:** Peace treaty of Brest–Litovsk between Germany and Russia. **29 April:** Major German offensive on Western Front ends. **16 May:** Sedition Act passed. **25 May:** U-boats first appear in U.S. waters. **6 July:** Wilson agrees to send U.S. troops to Siberia. **18 July:** Allied counterattack on Western Front. **15 August:** United States and Russia break off diplomatic relations. **4 September:** U.S. troops of Polar Bear Expedition land at Arkhangelsk, Russia. **12 September:** U.S. offensive at St. Mihiel. **3 October:** German–Austrian peace note to the United States. **12 October:** Germany and Austria agree to Wilson's terms. **4 November:** Armistice with Austria-Hungary comes into force. **5 November:** Republicans victorious in U.S. congressional elections. **9 November:** Kaiser Wilhelm II of Germany abdicates. **11 November:** Armistice with Germany signed and comes into force. **14 December:** Wilson arrives in Paris for peace conference.

1919 **3 January:** Herbert Hoover becomes director of international relief to Europe. **16 January:** Prohibition amendment ratified, making sale of liquor illegal in United States. **18 January:** Peace conference at Versailles begins. **25 January:** Peace conference adopts principle of League of Nations. **3 February:** Wilson presides over first League of Nations meeting, Paris. **4 March:** Foundation of Comintern (Third International) in Moscow. U.S. Senator Henry Cabot Lodge begins campaign to modify Treaty of Versailles. **25 March:** Paris conference adopts Wilson's League of Nations Covenant. **4 April:** Philippine Islands demand independence. **6 May:** The Paris conference assigns German colonies to other powers as mandates. **28 June:** Treaty of Versailles signed. **10 July:** Wilson presents Versailles Treaty to U.S. Senate. **14 July:** Lodge begins reading treaty aloud to Senate (finishes 28 July). **19 August:** Wilson makes concessions to Senate Committee on Foreign Relations. **4 September:** Wilson begins speaking tour. **10 September:** Treaty of St. Germain with Austria. Senators William Borah and Hiram Johnson begin tour to oppose Versailles Treaty. **25 September:** Wilson collapses from a stroke. **29 October:** International Labor Conference in Washington, D.C. **6 November:** Senate Committee on Foreign Relations proposes Lodge Reservations. **13 November:** Senator Gilbert Hitchcock's mild reservations rejected by Senate Committee on Foreign Relations. **19 November:** Senate rejects Versailles Treaty with Lodge Reservations, 39–55, then rejects treaty with no reservations, 38–53. **29 December:** Mild reservationists demand that Lodge compromise.

1920   **2 January:** Communists arrested in 33 U.S. cities. **10 January:** League of Nations comes into being. **1 February:** Britain and France declare they would accept Senate reservations. **10 February:** Senate Committee on Foreign Relations approves Versailles Treaty with Lodge Reservations. **13 February:** Robert Lansing resigns as secretary of state. **25 February:** Bainbridge Colby becomes secretary of state. **8 March:** Wilson reiterates his opposition to the Lodge Reservations. **19 March:** Senate fails to approve Versailles Treaty with Lodge Reservations, though vote is 49–35 in favor. **20 May:** Congress votes to end war with Germany in the Knox Resolution. **27 May:** Wilson vetoes Knox Resolution. **4 June:** Treaty of Trianon between Allies and Hungary signed. **2 November:** Republican Warren G. Harding elected U.S. president. **10 December:** Wilson awarded Nobel Peace Prize.

1921   **24–29 January:** Paris conference to set German reparation payments. **18 February:** U.S. representative to Reparation Commission recalled. **4 March:** Harding inaugurated as president. **25 March:** U.S. refuses Russian request to resume trade. **12 April:** Harding declares United States will play no part in League of Nations. **24 April:** United States refuses to mediate in German reparations controversy. **19 May:** Emergency Immigration Quota Act passed. **7 June:** United States withholds recognition of Mexican government. **2 July:** Congress votes to end war with Germany in the Knox–Porter Resolution. **24 August:** U.S. peace treaty with Austria signed. **25 August:** U.S. peace treaty with Germany signed. **29 August:** U.S. peace treaty with Hungary signed. German state of emergency over economic crisis. **12 November:** Washington Conference on naval disarmament and the Far East begins. **13 December:** Four-Power Washington Treaty on island possessions in Pacific signed. **29 December:** Five-Power Washington Treaty on naval disarmament signed.

1922   **1 February:** Washington conference agrees to treaties on poison gas and submarine warfare. **4 February:** Japan agrees to return Shantung to China. **11 February:** Nine-Power Treaty on Chinese independence and "open door" signed in Washington, D.C. **15 February:** First sessions of Permanent Court of International Justice (World Court), The Hague. **6 March:** United States prohibits arms sales to China. **20 March:** Harding withdraws troops from Rhineland. **16 April:** Treaty of Rapallo between Germany and Russia signed. **7 November:** Republican majority reduced in U.S. congressional elections.

1923 **1 January:** Union of Soviet Socialist Republics (USSR) proclaimed. **11 January:** France and Belgium occupy Ruhr over German reparations default. **19 January:** German passive resistance brings economy to standstill. **31 January:** Britain accepts terms for funding war debt to the United States. **2 February:** Central American republics sign treaty of friendship in Washington. **3 March:** Senate rejects proposal to join World Court. **21 March:** Secretary of State Charles Evans Hughes says United States will not recognize USSR until it accepts Russian debts and restores foreign-owned property. **25 March:** Fifth Pan-American conference opens in Santiago, Chile (ends 4 May). **26 April:** Mexico recognizes oil concessions predating 1917 in Bucareli agreements. **3 May:** Pan-American Treaty on peaceful settlement of disputes (Gondra Treaty) signed at Santiago conference. **19 June:** American–British war debt convention signed. **2 August:** Harding dies; Calvin Coolidge becomes president. **3 September:** United States recognizes government of Mexico. **8 December:** United States signs treaty of friendship and commerce with Germany.

1924 **28 February:** U.S. troops land in Honduras. **9 April:** Dawes Plan issued by Reparations Commission. **26 May:** Coolidge signs immigration bill imposing tighter quotas and excluding Chinese and Japanese. **13 July:** U.S. returns Dominican Republic to home rule.

1925 **11 January:** Frank B. Kellogg becomes secretary of state. **9 March:** Coolidge arbitrates Chilean–Peruvian dispute. **1 December:** Locarno treaties signed, stabilizing Western European frontiers.

1926 **2 May:** U.S. Marines sent to Nicaragua following Chamorro coup (remaining until 1933). **18 May:** First meeting of Preparatory Commission for Conference on Arms Reduction and Limitation in Geneva (meets until January 1931). **12 June:** Brazil leaves League of Nations. **26 June:** McNary–Haugen tariff bill defeated in Senate. **26 July:** Philippine legislature's call for referendum on independence vetoed by American governor. **28 July:** U.S.–Panama Treaty on protection of Canal Zone. **8 September:** Germany enters League of Nations.

1927   1 January: Mexican Petroleum and Land Laws restrict foreign ownership. **27 January:** Panamanian assembly refuses to ratify Panama Canal Treaty. U.S. Congress demands arbitration of petroleum dispute with Mexico. **2 May:** Geneva economic conference (to 23 May). **4 May:** United States agrees to oversee elections in Nicaragua. **20 June:** Geneva naval disarmament conference (to 4 August). French Foreign Minister Aristide Briand presents draft treaty to outlaw war, after consultation with Kellogg. **7 August:** International Peace Bridge between United States and Canada opens. **17 November:** Mexican supreme court invalidates limits on foreign oil concessions under Petroleum Law; law amended in December, improving relations with United States. **17 December:** Kellogg announces intention to negotiate treaty with France renouncing war as an instrument of foreign policy. **25 December:** Mexican congress confirms pre-1917 concessions to foreign oil companies. **27 December:** Josef Stalin victorious in power struggle in USSR.

1928   16 January: Sixth Pan-American conference opens in Havana, Cuba (ends 20 February). **13 April:** Kellogg presents plan for treaty to outlaw war to Locarno powers. **19 April:** Japan occupies Shantung. **17 July:** Assassination of Alvaro Obregon, president-elect of Mexico. **27 August:** Kellogg–Briand Pact signed in Paris. **10 September:** Argentina nationalizes oil wells. **6 October:** Chiang Kai-shek elected president of China. **6 November:** Republican Herbert Hoover elected U.S. president. **6 December:** Skirmishes between Bolivia and Paraguay over Gran Chaco. **10 December:** Pan-American conference on conciliation and arbitration opens in Washington (ends 5 January 1929). **17 December:** Undersecretary of State Reuben Clark submits memorandum on Roosevelt Corollary and U.S. intervention in Latin America. **22 December:** Committee appointed under Owen Young to reconsider reparations.

1929   5 January: Inter-American Treaty of Arbitration signed in Washington, D.C. **4 March:** Hoover inaugurated as president. **20 May:** Japan evacuates Shantung. **3 June:** Settlement of Arica–Tacna dispute involving Chile, Peru, and Bolivia. **7 June:** Young Plan for German economy presented. **24 July:** Kellogg–Briand Pact comes into force. **6 August:** Germany accepts Young Plan; Allies agree to evacuate Rhineland. **16 September:** Cease-fire signed between Bolivia and Paraguay. **29 October:** Black Thursday: prices crash on New York Stock Exchange.

1930   21 January: London naval disarmament conference begins (ends 22 April). **18 February:** Geneva tariff conference begins (ends 24 March). **17 June:** Smoot–Hawley tariff act signed by Hoover. **17 November:** Geneva economic conference begins (ends 28 November).

1931   11 May: Bankruptcy of Austrian Credit Anstalt bank starts economic collapse of Central Europe. **20 June:** Hoover announces plan for moratorium on reparations and war debts. **1 August:** U.S.–French loan to Great Britain. **11 August:** London protocol on Hoover moratorium. **12 September:** Mexico admitted into League of Nations. **18 September:** Japan besieges Mukden and begins seizure of Manchuria. **21 September:** Great Britain abandons gold standard. **16 October:** U.S. delegates attend League of Nations Council discussions on Japan. **11 December:** Japan abandons gold standard.

1932   2 January: Japan proclaims republic of Manchukuo in Manchuria. **4 January:** Japanese troops reach Great Wall at Shanhaikwan. **7 January:** Doctrine of nonrecognition of Japanese conquests announced by Secretary of State Henry Stimson. **28 January:** Japanese troops occupy Shanghai (until May). **2 February:** Geneva disarmament conference begins (ends July). **16 June:** Lausanne Conference cancels 90 percent of reparations owed by Germany. **21 July:** British Empire conference at Ottawa begins (ends 2 August) approves moderate imperial preference in tariffs. **31 July:** Chaco War between Bolivia and Paraguay begins (ends 1935). **1 September:** War between Peru and Colombia over Leticia begins (ends March 1933). **2 October:** Lytton Report to League of Nations on Manchuria. **8 November:** Democrat Franklin D. Roosevelt elected U.S. president. **9 December:** Japan invades Jehol, China. **15 December:** Mexico leaves League of Nations. **28 December:** Congress resolves against cancellation of German war debt.

1933   13 January: Congress approves Philippine independence in Hare–Hawes–Cutting Act, over Hoover's veto (rejected in October by

Philippines). **30 January:** Adolf Hitler appointed chancellor of Germany. **23 February:** Japan begins occupation of China north of Great Wall. **24 February:** League of Nations adopts Lytton report. **27 February:** Hitler suspends civil liberties after Reichstag fire. **4 March:** Roosevelt inaugurated as president. **6–9 March:** U.S. banks closed. **27 March:** Japan announces it will leave League of Nations. **1 April:** Persecution of Jews in Germany begins with national boycott of Jewish businesses. **30 April:** United States abandons gold standard. **12 June:** World Monetary and Economic Conference begins in London (ends 27 July). **3 July:** Roosevelt "bombshell" message to London Economic Conference. **25 August:** United States, Canada, Australia, and USSR sign wheat agreement. **11 October:** Latin American nonaggression pact signed in Rio de Janeiro. **14 October:** Germany leaves League of Nations. **17 November:** United States recognizes USSR. **3 December:** Seventh Pan-American conference opens in Montevideo, Uruguay (ends 26 December). **26 December:** Montevideo Convention on Rights and Duties of States signed. **28 December:** Great Britain makes last war debt payment to United States.

1934 **30 January:** Gold Reserve Act empowers U.S. president to revalue dollar. **24 March:** Tydings–McDuffie Act gives Philippines independence in 1945. **12 June:** Congress passes Reciprocal Trade Agreements Act. **2 July:** Lázaro Cárdenas elected president of Mexico. **19 August:** Hitler becomes führer of Germany. **18 September:** USSR enters League of Nations. **23 October:** London Naval Disarmament Conference begins (ends 19 December). **19 December:** Japan withdraws from 1921 and 1930 Naval Disarmament Treaties.

1935 **16 March:** Germany repudiates disarmament clauses of Versailles Treaty. **11–14 April:** Conference at Stresa establishes Italian–British–French common front against Germany. **14 June:** Chaco War ends. **18 June:** Anglo-German Naval Agreement allows Germany a navy one-third the size of Great Britain's. **13 July:** U.S.–USSR trade agreement. **31 August:** Neutrality Act approved by U.S. Congress. **15 September:** Nuremberg laws restrict Jews in Germany. **2 October:** Italy invades Abyssinia (Ethiopia). **7 October:** League of Nations declares Italy the aggressor. **19 October:** League sanctions against Italy. **15 November:** Commonwealth of the Philippines is inaugurated. **15 November:** U.S.–Canada reciprocal trade agreement. **9 December:**

Hoare–Laval agreement on Ethiopia, favoring Italy, is destroyed by public outrage in Britain and France.

1936 **1 January:** Expiration of naval limitations set in 1921 Washington treaties. **15 January:** Japan withdraws from London naval conference. **21 January:** Bolivian–Paraguayan peace treaty signed. **29 February:** Congress extends 1935 Neutrality Act to 1 May 1937 and forbids loans to belligerents. **2 March:** New U.S.–Panama treaty signed. **7 March:** German troops enter demilitarized Rhineland. **25 March:** United States, France, and Great Britain sign London naval convention. **9 May:** Abyssinia formally annexed by Italy. **2 June:** General Anastasio Somoza seizes power in Nicaragua. **15 June:** League lifts sanctions on Italy. **18 June:** Army revolt led by General Francisco Franco begins Spanish Civil War (ends 1939). **14 August:** Roosevelt gives antiwar speech at Chautauqua. **9 September:** London conference on nonintervention in Spanish Civil War. **1 November:** Benito Mussolini proclaims Rome–Berlin Axis. **3 November:** Roosevelt reelected president. **23 November:** Mexican Expropriation Law passed. **25 November:** Germany and Japan sign Anti-Comintern Pact. **1 December:** Roosevelt addresses Inter-American conference on peace at opening in Buenos Aires (conference ends 23 December). **10 December:** King Edward VIII of Great Britain abdicates so he can marry American divorcee. **12 December:** Chiang Kai-shek kidnapped at Sian. **16 December:** London protocol on nonintervention in Spain signed. Buenos Aires conference agrees nonintervention protocol calling for neutrality toward conflicts between American states. **25 December:** Chiang Kai-shek released after signing Sian agreement to cooperate with warlords and communists to expel Japan from China.

1937 **2 March:** Nationalization of oil in Mexico. **27 April:** German bomber aircraft supporting Franco destroy Spanish town of Guernica. **1 May:** Roosevelt signs Neutrality Act. **7 July:** Sino-Japanese War begins. **28–29 July:** Japanese forces take Peking and Tientsin. **6 August:** U.S.–USSR trade agreement. **5 October:** Roosevelt "Quarantine" speech in Chicago. **3 November:** Brussels conference on Far East begins (ends 24 November). **9 November:** Japanese forces take Shanghai. **17 November:** British politician Lord Halifax's visit to Hitler marks beginning of British policy of appeasement. **11 December:** Italy leaves League of Nations. **12 December:** Japanese airplanes sink USS *Panay* in Yangtze River. **13 December:** Japanese forces capture Nanking. **24 December:** Japanese forces capture Hangchow.

1938 10 January: Japanese forces enter Tsingtao. **13 March:** Germany invades Austria and incorporates it into German Reich. **19 March:** Mexico expropriates U.S. oil companies' properties. **12 August:** Germany mobilizes over Czechoslovak crisis. **7 September:** France calls up reservists. **15 September:** Britain's Prime Minister Neville Chamberlain visits Hitler at Munich. **27 September:** League pronounces Japan aggressor in China. British Royal Navy mobilizes. **29 September:** Munich conference gives Czechoslovak Sudetenland to Germany. **21 October:** Japanese forces capture Canton. **25 October:** Italy formally annexes Libya. **26 October:** Japanese forces capture Hankow. **16 November:** U.S. Ambassador Hugh Wilson recalled from Germany. **9 December:** Eighth Pan-American conference opens in Lima, Peru (ends 26 December). **24 December:** Lima Declaration on consultation between foreign ministers on security issues.

1939 4 January: Roosevelt asks Congress for $552 million for defense. **15 March:** Germany occupies remainder of Czech territory; Slovakia becomes puppet state of Germany. **21 March:** Germany annexes Memel from Lithuania. **28 March:** Franco's forces enter Madrid to end Spanish Civil War. Hitler denounces 1934 Non-Aggression Treaty with Poland. **31 March:** Britain and France guarantee Poland against attack by Germany. **1 April:** United States recognizes Franco government in Spain. **7 April:** Italy invades Albania. Spain joins Anti-Comintern Pact. **15 April:** Roosevelt asks Hitler and Mussolini to guarantee they will not attack 31 specified states. **22 May:** Hitler and Mussolini sign 10-year alliance, the "Pact of Steel." **8–11 June:** King George VI of Great Britain visits United States. **26 July:** United States announces it will abrogate 1911 trade pact with Japan. **23 August:** German–Soviet non-aggression pact signed in Moscow. **25 August:** Britain and Poland sign treaty of mutual assistance in London. **1 September:** Germany invades Poland. **3 September:** Britain, France, Australia, and New Zealand declare war on Germany. **5 September:** Neutrality proclamations by Roosevelt. **8 September:** Roosevelt proclaims state of limited national emergency. **10 September:** Canada declares war on Germany. **17 September:** Poland invaded by USSR. **23 September:** First Pan-American conference of ministers of foreign affairs opens in Panama City (ends 31 September). **29 September:** USSR and Germany partition Poland. **2 October:** U.S. Navy starts patrolling 300-mile (500-km) neutrality zone. **4 November:** Revised Neutrality Act allows cash-and-carry of munitions. **30 November:** USSR invades Finland. **14 December:** USSR expelled from League of Nations.

1940   26 January: 1911 U.S.–Japanese Trade Treaty expires. **12 March:** Finland signs peace treaty with USSR. **9 April:** Germany invades Denmark and Norway. **7 May:** U.S. Pacific Fleet deployed to Hawaii. **10 May:** Germany invades France, Belgium, and Netherlands; Winston Churchill becomes prime minister of Great Britain; Committee to Defend America by Aiding the Allies formed. **15 May:** Netherlands surrenders to Germany. **16 May:** Roosevelt asks for over $1 billion for national defense. **28 May:** Belgium surrenders to Germany. **28 May:** National Defense Advisory Committee established. **10 June:** Roosevelt's Charlottesville address. **14 June:** Paris falls to German forces. **15 June:** United States declines France's appeal for military assistance. **17 June:** USSR begins occupation of Latvia, Lithuania, and Estonia. **22 June:** France surrenders to Germany. **24 June:** Japan demands closure of Burma Road. **27 June:** USSR invades Romania and annexes Bessarabia and Northern Bukovina. **5 July:** Roosevelt invokes Export Control Act against Japan. **10 July:** Battle of Britain starts. **11 July:** Republicans Frank Knox and Henry Stimson join Roosevelt's cabinet. **18 July:** Britain halts transport of munitions to China by Burma Road. **19 July:** Roosevelt signs "Two-Ocean Navy" Naval Expansion Act. **21 July:** Second Pan-American conference of foreign ministers opens in Havana (ends 30 July). **15 August:** Informal U.S.–British staff talks, London. **23 August:** German bombing of London (the "blitz") begins. **27 August:** Roosevelt authorized to call up Army Reserve and National Guard. **30 August:** Japanese military occupation of northern Indochina begins. **2 September:** Destroyers-for-bases deal finalized. **4 September:** America First Committee formed. **16 September:** Congress passes Selective Service and Training Act. **26 September:** Roosevelt embargoes sale of scrap iron and steel to Japan. **27 September:** Tripartite Pact (Axis) signed by Germany, Italy, and Japan. **18 October:** Burma Road reopened. **5 November:** Roosevelt wins reelection for third term as president. **20 November:** United States and Britain agree to standardize military equipment and pool technical knowledge. **17 December:** Roosevelt announces Lend-Lease plan. **29 December:** Roosevelt gives fireside chat on "arsenal of democracy."

1941   6 January: Roosevelt gives "Four Freedoms" address to Congress and sends Lend-Lease bill to Congress. **16 January:** Roosevelt asks Congress for 200 new merchant ships. **24 January:** American–British–Canadian (ABC) staff talks begin in Washington (end 27 March). **30 January:** Germany announces that any ship bringing aid to Britain will be sunk. **11 March:** Lend-Lease Act passed by Congress. **10 April:** USS *Niblack* depth-charges U-boat off Iceland (first act of war between Germany and United States). **24 April:** Neutrality patrol is extended to 26 degrees west. **12 May:** Secretary of State Cordell Hull is presented with Japanese peace proposal by Ambassador Kichisaburo Nomura. **21 May:** U-boat sinks U.S. freighter *Robin Moor.* **27 May:** Roosevelt declares "unlimited national emergency." **14 June:** United States freezes German and Italian assets. **22 June:** Germany invades USSR. **28 June:** Office of Scientific Research and Development established. **7 July:** U.S. troops occupy Iceland. **26 July:** U.S. freezes Japanese assets and suspends relations with Japan. **27 July:** Southern Indochina occupied by Japan. **28 July:** Japan freezes U.S. assets. **1 August:** U.S. oil embargo against Axis states. **9–12 August:** Placentia Bay Conference, during which Roosevelt and Churchill sign Atlantic Charter. **25 August:** Britain and USSR invade and partition Iran. **1 September:** U.S. Navy takes responsibility for transatlantic convoys as far as Iceland. **4 September:** U-boat attack on USS *Greer.* **11 September:** U.S. Navy ordered to attack any vessel threatening U.S. ships or ships under their escort. **15 September:** German siege of Leningrad begins. **19 September:** German forces take Kiev. **25 September:** Victory Program presented to Roosevelt. **27 September:** First Liberty ship launched. **28 September:** Moscow Supply Conference begins (ends 10 October). **17 October:** General Hideki Tojo becomes Japanese premier. USS *Kearny* torpedoed. **31 October:** USS *Reuben James* sunk by U-boat. **10 November:** First U.S.-escorted British troop convoy sails from Nova Scotia. **13 November:** 1939 Neutrality Act revised. **20 November:** Japan's final proposals presented by Ambassador Nomura. **25 November:** Japanese troop transports sighted off Formosa en route to Malaya. **26 November:** American proposals submitted by Hull to Nomura. **27 November:** War warnings sent to Pacific commands. **29 November:** USSR begins counterattack in Moscow area. **7 December:** Japan attacks Pearl Harbor and Malaya. **8 December:** United States and Great Britain declare war on Japan. Guam, Wake Island, Hong Kong, Singapore, and Philippines bombed by Japan. **9 December:** Bangkok occupied by Japan. Japanese troops land on Tarawa and Makin in Gilbert Islands. **10 December:** Japanese troops land on Luzon. Guam surrenders. **11 December:** Germany and Italy declare war on United States. Japanese attack on Wake repulsed by U.S. Marines. **14 December:** Japan invades Burma. **16 December:** Japanese troops land on Sarawak, Borneo. **22 December:** Arcadia conference in Washington begins (ends 14 January). **24 December:** Wake Island captured by Japanese. **25 December:** Hong Kong falls to Japanese.

1942 **1 January:** United Nations Declaration signed. **2 January:** Japanese take Manila. **13 January:** U-boat offensive along U.S. east coast begins. **15 January:** American–British–Dutch–Australian command (ABDA) established. Third Pan-American conference of foreign ministers opens in Rio de Janeiro (ends 27 January). **26 January:** U.S. troops arrive in Northern Ireland. **6 February:** U.S.–Great Britain Combined Chiefs of Staff (CCS) begins to function. **7 February:** War Shipping Administration established. **14 February:** Japanese troops land on Sumatra. **15 February:** Singapore falls to Japanese. **20 February:** Japanese troops land on Timor. **27 February:** Battle of the Java Sea. **1 March:** ABDA dissolved. **8 March:** Japanese complete conquest of Netherlands East Indies. **10 March:** General Joseph Stilwell appointed chief of staff to Chiang Kai-shek. **8 April:** Anglo–American discussions in London on second front (end 15 April). **9 April:** U.S. forces on Bataan surrender. **4 May:** Battle of the Coral Sea (until 8 May). **6 May:** Corregidor falls to Japanese forces. **29 May–1 June:** USSR Foreign Commissar Vyacheslav Molotov meets with Roosevelt in Washington. **3–6 June:** Battle of Midway. **7 June:** Kiska and Attu in the Aleutians occupied by Japanese. **13 June:** Office of War Information (OWI) and Office of Strategic Services (OSS) established. **18 June:** U.S.–British Conference in Washington begins (ends 25 June). **21 June:** Fort Stevens, Oregon, shelled by a Japanese submarine. **3 July:** German forces capture Sevastopol. **4 July:** First U.S. Army Air Force (USAAF) bomber raid over Europe (Rouen). **4 August:** *Bracero* program agreed to by United States and Mexico. **7 August:** U.S. troops land on Guadalcanal, Solomon Islands. **13 September:** Battle of Stalingrad begins. **8 November:** U.S.–British landings at Casablanca, Oran, and Algiers. **16 November:** U.S. forces land on New Guinea. **2 December:** Enrico Fermi achieves first atomic chain reaction. **24 December:** French Admiral Jean Darlan assassinated in Algiers.

1943   14 January: Casablanca Conference begins (ends 24 January). **21 January:** Combined Bomber Offensive Directive issued at Casablanca. **24 January:** Roosevelt announces policy demanding unconditional surrender. **27 January:** United States mounts first air raid on Germany. **2 February:** Germans at Stalingrad surrender. **9 February:** Japanese withdraw from Guadalcanal. **14–25 February:** Battle of Kasserine. **16 March:** Climax of Battle of the Atlantic: U-boats sink 27 merchant ships in five days. **19 April:** Bermuda Conference on plight of European Jews. **11 May:** Washington Conference begins (ends 25 May). **13 May:** Axis forces in Tunisia surrender. **24 May:** U-boats withdrawn from North Atlantic. **9 July:** Invasion of Sicily begins. **19 July:** Rome bombed by Allies. **22 July:** American forces capture Palermo, Sicily. **25 July:** Mussolini overthrown. **27 July:** Allied bombing raid on Hamburg causes firestorm. **28 July:** Japanese evacuate Kiska. **10 August:** First Quebec Conference begins (ends 24 August). **17 August:** U.S. air raids on Schweinfurt and Regensburg. **8 September:** Italy surrenders. **9 September:** Americans and British land at Salerno, Italy. **10 September:** Germans occupy Rome. **25 September:** Sumner Welles forced to resign as undersecretary of state. **18–30 October:** Moscow Foreign Ministers Conference. **6 November:** Soviet forces recapture Kiev. **20 November:** U.S. Marines land on Tarawa, Gilbert Islands. **23 November:** Tarawa taken. Cairo Conference begins (ends 26 November). **28 November–1 December:** Teheran Conference. **3 December:** Second part of Cairo Conference begins (ends 7 December). **5 December:** General Dwight D. Eisenhower selected to command invasion of France (Operation Overlord). **15 December:** U.S. troops land on New Britain in the Pacific.

1944   22 January: Landings at Anzio, near Rome. **27 January:** Siege of Leningrad ends after 900 days. **31 January:** U.S. forces land on Marshall Islands. **20 February:** "Big Week" bombing operations over Germany begin. **4 June:** U.S. troops enter Rome. **6 June:** U.S.–British–Canadian Overlord landings in Normandy, France. **15 June:** U.S. forces land on Saipan, Marianas Islands. **19–20 June:** Battle of the Philippine Sea. **27 June:** Cherbourg captured by U.S. forces. **1 July:** Bretton Woods Conference begins (ends 22 July). **18 July:** Premier Tojo and Japanese cabinet resign. **27–28 July:** Honolulu Conference on Pacific strategy. **4 August:** Allied forces liberate Florence. **15 August:** Operation Dragoon landings on French Riviera. **19 August:** U.S. forces reach River Seine. **21 August:** Dumbarton Oaks Conference begins (ends 7 October). **25 August:** Paris liberated. **1–4 September:** Allies liberate Brussels and Pisa. **10 September:** Second Quebec Conference begins (ends 17 September). **11 September:** U.S. troops cross German frontier at Trier. **15 September:** U.S. troops land on Peleliu in Palau Islands. **14 October:** British forces liberate Athens. **18 October:** Roosevelt announces General Joseph Stilwell's recall from China. **20 October:** U.S. forces land on Leyte, Philippines. **23 October:** Allies recognize Charles de Gaulle as head of French provisional government. Battle of Leyte Gulf (to 25 October). **30 October:** Germans make last use of gas chambers at Auschwitz. **6 November:** Roosevelt wins fourth term as president. **24 November:** First raid on Tokyo by U.S. aircraft from Marianas. **30 November:** Edward Stettinius succeeds Cordell Hull as secretary of state. **16 December:** Start of Battle of the Bulge, Ardennes region, Luxembourg. **27 December:** German Ardennes offensive halted.

1945 **9 January:** U.S. forces land on Luzon, Philippines. **20 January:** Hungary surrenders to Allies. **26 January:** Soviet troops liberate Auschwitz. **4–11 February:** Conference at Yalta, Crimea. **13–14 February:** U.S.–British bombing of Dresden. **19 February:** U.S. forces land on Iwo Jima. **21 February:** Inter-American conference opens in Mexico City (ends 8 March). **25 February:** Firebomb raid on Tokyo. **4 March:** American forces capture Manila after month-long battle. **7 March:** U.S. forces cross River Rhine at Remagen. **8 March:** Act of Chapultepec agreed to by Inter-American conference. **9 March:** Firebomb raids on Tokyo. **16 March:** Iwo Jima captured. **1 April:** U.S. forces land on Okinawa. **6 April:** Heavy kamikaze attacks begin off Okinawa. **12 April:** Roosevelt dies; Harry S. Truman becomes president. **13 April:** Vienna captured by Soviet forces. **16 April:** U.S. forces enter Nuremberg. **23 April:** Soviet troops enter outskirts of Berlin. **25 April:** Start of San Francisco Conference. U.S. and Soviet forces meet at Torgau, Germany. **28 April:** Mussolini executed by Italian partisans. Allies capture Venice. **29 April:** U.S. forces liberate Dachau concentration camp. Germans in Italy surrender. **30 April:** Hitler commits suicide. **2 May:** Soviets take Berlin. **7 May:** Germany surrenders. **8 May:** Victory in Europe (VE-Day). **9 May:** Soviet troops occupy Prague. **25 May–7 June:** Harry Hopkins in Moscow to settle Poland issue with Stalin. **21 June:** Fighting on Okinawa ends. **26 June:** United Nations Charter signed in San Francisco. **1 July:** U.S., British, and French troops move into Berlin. **2 July:** Stettinius replaced as U.S. secretary of state by James Byrnes. **5 July:** United States and Britain recognize Polish provisional government. **16 July:** Trinity test of atomic bomb. **17 July:** Conference at Potsdam, Germany, begins (ends 2 August). **25 July:** Truman authorizes use of atomic bomb. **26 July:** Potsdam Declaration to Japan. **6 August:** Atomic bomb dropped on Hiroshima. **8 August:** USSR declares war on Japan. **9 August:** Atomic bomb dropped on Nagasaki. Further conventional bombing raids on Japan (to 14 August). **10 August:** Soviet forces enter Korea. **14 August:** Japan surrenders. **15 August:** Victory over Japan (VJ-Day). **28 August:** First U.S. troops land in Japan. **2 September:** Japanese surrender signed on board USS *Missouri*. **9 September:** Japanese forces in China surrender. **13 September:** Japanese troops in Burma surrender. **24 October:** United Nations begins operating. **20 November:** Nuremburg war crimes trials begin.

Introduction

The period 1914 to 1945 saw a great transformation in the status and role of the United States in international affairs. In 1914, while a major economic power, the United States maintained a separation from the activities of the other great powers. This was underlined when the United States asserted its neutrality as World War I broke out in 1914. By 1945, the United States had become intensely involved in world affairs, and its postwar power so dwarfed other nations that a new term was coined to describe it—superpower. U.S. foreign policy, however, did not follow a clear and consistent course toward this enlargement of power, influence, and engagement. It can be seen as falling into three distinct periods: World War I and its aftermath, when the United States sought to reshape international politics; the period from 1920 to 1940, when policy makers and the general public sought to return to political separation from the rest of the world; and then the 1941–45 period, when the United States became engaged fully and irrevocably in international affairs through its participation in World War II and a new commitment to leadership in the management of international affairs. However, during each of these periods, there were dissenting voices and much debate, so that the picture when viewed in detail presents aspects that make this pattern of development nuanced and complex. Moreover, U.S. policy toward the western hemisphere was subject to quite different lines of development, and to a lesser degree one must also distinguish between American attitudes to foreign relations across the Atlantic Ocean toward Europe and those looking westward across the Pacific Ocean to Asia.

THE ORIGINS OF U.S. FOREIGN POLICY

To understand these developments, it is first necessary to grasp the structural and ideological background to the American approach to its role in world affairs. The U.S. outlook in 1914 was shaped by geography, the U.S. Constitution, domestic politics, and the sense of the unique nature of the United States as a political and cultural entity. By 1914, the Native American population of the continental United States had been defeated, conquered, and contained. The last large area of official Indian Territory was absorbed into the state of Oklahoma in the decade before the outbreak of World War I. With the exception of these peoples, the United States was a nation of immigrants and the descendants of immigrants (in the case of many black Americans, forced immigrants). This fundamentally shaped popular attitudes toward the outside world, and often elite attitudes as well. Americans believed that they, or their ancestors, had come to the United States to begin a new way of life, and that the state they had created was a new experiment in the organization of politics and society, free from aristocratic privilege, the tyranny of the few, religious persecution, and continual warfare. America was defined by this contrast to the Old World—meaning, effectively, Europe. The founders of the republic had encapsulated this viewpoint in a few key statements that were regarded as the fixed points of America's relations with Europe. In his farewell address, George Washington, the first president, had warned of the danger to American order and stability that would be brought by becoming involved in European political conflicts. Thomas Jefferson, the third president, had expanded this dictum by cautioning solemnly against "entangling alliances." Thus was established the defining principle of American attitudes to foreign policy: the United States had no interest in, and was not affected by, events on another continent, and should at all times retain the valuable freedom of action given by its geographical distance from these events.

In 1823, this principle was given further emphasis in the Monroe Doctrine, in which President James Monroe warned European powers not to interfere in the internal affairs of the American continent. He issued this unilateral statement in the context of the struggle for independence of Latin American colonies from the Spanish and Portuguese empires. To the United States, the Monroe Doctrine became a sacred principle: the western hemisphere was for Americans. It was the concomitant of the principle of keeping out of European affairs. The doctrine gained the appearance of being an international law by the fact that the paramount naval power in the Atlantic, Great Britain, shared the opposition to further encroachments by European states into the western hemisphere, and it had the power to enforce this attitude, which the United States at this time did not. This meant, in effect, that throughout the 19th century, America's key foreign policy interest was being maintained free of cost by the British navy. This had the great advantage for the United States of freeing resources for economic development. It also meant that Americans took the Monroe Doctrine very much for granted.

The Constitution of the United States said little about foreign policy, reflecting the early belief that the United States would not be heavily involved in overseas activities. Certain powers in foreign policy were granted to the executive: the president was to appoint envoys to foreign powers and receive their reports, and the Department of State was created, which would handle these matters. As commander in chief, the president would be responsible for the deployment of American armed forces. On the other hand, Congress was given certain vital powers that constrained the president's freedom of action and were designed to ensure that foreign policy was subject to legislative oversight. Congress held the power to declare war, and the Senate had to approve ambassadorial appointments. Moreover, a two-thirds majority of the Senate was needed to ratify a treaty, meaning that crucial foreign policy powers were subject to a veto by a minority of senators. This reflected the fear of entanglements held at the start of the republic, as well as the sense that unless a large majority of educated Americans approved a foreign policy initiative, it was best to remain inactive.

Until the end of the 19th century, the United States was essentially inward looking, as it expanded across the continent toward the Pacific. As part of this process, an ideology of manifest destiny developed, which justified expansion in terms of an American civilizing mission, and a war was fought with Mexico (1845–46) to gain control of the west. American commerce began to reach out from the Pacific shores, and although the U.S. Navy remained small, it was used to effect in 1853–54 when Commodore Matthew Perry forced Japan to end its long period of isolation and allow access to American commerce. Apart from the acquisition of Alaska from Russia, there was little interest in overseas territories to accompany this expansion of trade, until the 1880s. Then, a school of thought grew up around the ideas of Captain Alfred Thayer Mahan, a naval theorist, that a great power (which the United States was rapidly becoming) needed an ocean-going navy and naval bases to protect its trading interests. With the end of westward expansion in the 1890s, many Americans felt that the nation needed to continue to grow. Others saw a need for overseas markets for growing American industrial production. Given the civilizing claims that Europeans were using to justify their latest round of imperialist activity, some argued that the United States should embrace its manifest destiny and help bring Christianity and American values to other parts of the world.

These strands of thought came together in 1898 when popular outcry, stirred up by the new mass-market newspapers as well as some economic interests, brought American involvement in Cuba's war for independence against Spain. The short Spanish–American War signaled the appearance of the United States on the world stage as a significant actor. Colonies were acquired—the Philippines, Guam, and Puerto Rico—and a protectorate over Cuba. An American-inspired coup had overthrown the ruler of Hawaii, which now became a territory of the United States.

While this phase of outright imperialism quickly faded, under President Theodore Roosevelt (1901–09) the United States asserted itself in world affairs. Roosevelt, a keen Mahanian, enlarged the navy and sent it on a world cruise—as the so-called Great White Fleet—to show America's arrival as a naval power. He also intervened in the crisis between European powers over Morocco, and he won a Nobel Prize for Peace for negotiating the end to the Russo–Japanese War in 1905. Roosevelt added a corollary to the Monroe Doctrine when he asserted the principle that advanced "civilized" powers had the duty to maintain stability and order and declared that the United States would act, with military power if necessary, in exercising this role of policeman in the western hemisphere. Roosevelt and other Mahanians had long been pressing for a canal across the Central American isthmus to ease the passage of warships between the Atlantic and Pacific Oceans. Roosevelt encouraged a revolt in northern Colombia when that state was reluctant to cooperate. The new republic of Panama granted the United States territorial rights over the canal that was finally completed in 1914.

THE UNITED STATES AND WORLD WAR I

Roosevelt's successor, William Howard Taft (1909–13), was less interested in activities outside the western hemisphere, and this also was the initial attitude of Woodrow Wilson when he became president in 1913. Wilson was a progressive who sought to reform and modernize American society and politics, all with a high moral purpose. When war broke out in Europe in August 1914, Wilson declared that the United States would be neutral in thought and deed. Shocked that the apparently civilized nations of Europe had resorted to bloodshed, Americans were confirmed in their belief in the moral superiority of the United States and thankful for the breadth of the Atlantic Ocean. With the nation containing a high proportion of recent immigrants, however, sympathies toward the belligerents were very divided.

As the European war moved into stalemate, orders for American produce and foodstuffs flooded in from the belligerents, pulling the United States out of an economic recession. This brought danger, too, for it made this trade a target as the nations at war became increasingly desperate for new ways to hit at their enemies. The United States found itself in repeated disputes over its rights as a neutral country, which as a great power it was determined to uphold. Clashes with the British over their naval blockade of Germany brought many tensions, but worse was the impact of a new weapon, the submarine. Germany sought to counterblockade Britain with its "U-boats," but to use them effectively it had to break international law, which had been drawn up before the submarine appeared. The British and French, more dependant on American trade, made greater efforts to mollify American opinion than did Germany. Britain and the United States had been rivals in the western hemisphere, but by the end of the 19th century all their disputes had been settled. They now had a sense of shared interests, as major trading and naval powers, and shared cultural connections, particularly between the governing elites. The British embarked on a skilful propaganda campaign to depict the Germans as barbarians, responsible for atrocities in occupied Belgium and in their conduct at sea. They characterized the war as one between civilization and barbarism.

At first this had little impact. However, German sinkings of civilian vessels carrying American passengers, notably the liner *Lusitania* in May 1915, began to change this. Wilson believed he had to issue stern warnings to Germany, which caused his secretary of state, Williams Jennings Bryan, to resign in protest against what he saw as a movement away from impartial neutrality. On the other hand, there were those, like ex-president Roosevelt, who argued that the United States should fully enter the war. The Germans backed down, but incidents continued, and the issue became how much affront to its neutrality would the United States tolerate before taking action. This was complicated by the attitudes of the large number of Americans of German or Irish origin, who were hostile to fighting on the side of Britain.

Wilson sought a way out of this dilemma by sending his close friend Colonel Edward House to Europe to try to negotiate an end to the intensely destructive war. The proposal was "peace without victory." After two years of warfare, neither side was inclined to accept anything but full victory—if for no other reason than that the defeated side could be made to pay the huge costs the war was incurring. House's mission failed, and Wilson was running out of options. He fought and won the 1916 U.S. presidential election with the slogan "he kept us out of war," claiming that his policy was one of peaceful preparedness. Privately, he knew that after previous ultimata, further German actions could easily precipitate war. In January 1917, the Germans, believing that the collapse of Russia meant they could win the war in 1917, declared a policy of unrestricted submarine warfare. Britain leaked a telegram they had intercepted from the German undersecretary for foreign affairs, Alfred Zimmermann, containing a plan for Mexico to enter the war if the United States did so, promising that Mexico would receive back some of the territories lost in the 1840s. This caused a great outcry among Americans. When U.S. vessels were sunk by U-boats, Wilson saw no option but to ask Congress for a declaration of war. This came on 6 April 1917, though the nation can hardly be said to have entered the war united.

Wilson kept the United States at some political distance from the other nations fighting Germany. To avoid any appearance of accepting the secret treaties they had made disposing of enemy territory, the United States remained an "associate," not an ally. Wilson proposed a new set of war aims, both in order to get around these treaties but also to give Americans a sense that they were fighting a war for a worthwhile purpose. Propaganda demonized the enemy, coordinated by George Creel's Committee on Public Information. Spy scares intensified feelings, and there were outbreaks of vigilantism against those of "enemy" ethnicity. The Espionage and Sedition Acts limited traditional rights of freedom of speech and encouraged the idea that there were traitors in the United States, identifiable by their political views and national origins. At the same time, the administration encouraged the idea that the war was a crusade—it would be a war to end all wars and make the world safe for democracy. American participation was justified if the war resulted in a new world order that brought permanent peace. The aim had therefore shifted from peace without victory to a radical progressive peace through total victory.

Wilson encapsulated these ideas in his famous "Fourteen Points" address in January 1918. Partly these were a response to the even more radical ideas for a new world order coming from the Bolshevik regime that had just seized power in Russia. Partly they were to give a moral gloss to the cause of America and its associates. The central point for Wilson was his plan for a League of Nations. This world organization would be a forum for settling disputes. Nations would disarm, and any nation committing aggression rather than agree to the League's arbitration would be subject to condemnation by world opinion. Wilson argued that empires must be dismantled (though his specific proposals only related to enemy empires), and nations must be allowed to choose their own governments. This was the principle of self-determination of peoples.

The United States was not ready to send substantial forces to Europe's battlefield until 1918, but when they arrived, they provided a welcome freshness to the jaded Allied forces. The Germans knew they had to win before American power came fully to play, and when their offensive was halted, the high command looked to get out of the war before the German home front collapsed, short of food after years of blockade. The German Kaiser abdicated amid naval mutiny and hunger riots, and the new republican government sued for peace on the basis of the Fourteen Points. The firing ceased on 11 November 1918.

THE TREATY OF VERSAILLES AND
THE FIGHT FOR THE LEAGUE OF NATIONS

Determined to shape the peace settlement, Woodrow Wilson became the first incumbent U.S. president to travel to Europe, where he was met by adoring crowds and feted everywhere. The Republicans had just gained control of the U.S. Senate in the 1918 elections, but Wilson's delegation to the peace conference in Paris did not include any members of Congress from that party. This was to cost him dear. The negotiations in Paris lasted a long time and tested Wilson's skills. His fellow leaders were by no means committed to every aspect of the Fourteen Points. Wilson was forced to compromise on a number of issues, notably the French insistence on large reparations payments from Germany and the written admission of sole war guilt by Germany that provided the justification for them. Wilson believed such concessions were balanced by the agreement to include reference to the League of Nations in each treaty. Wilson hoped that the League could in time rectify whatever flaws emerged from the process of compromise at the conference.

These compromises were less understood back in the United States, and Wilson had to journey back to Paris to renegotiate some clauses. He still faced a tough battle to gain the two-thirds majority in the Senate necessary for the ratification of the Treaty of Versailles. Republicans did not wish to hand Wilson a personal success, and there was considerable personal animosity between the president and Henry Cabot Lodge, the chair of the Senate Committee on Foreign Relations. Taking Lodge to Paris would have given him greater understanding of the process of negotiating with other sovereign powers and would have made it more a bipartisan effort—but it is unlikely that Lodge and Wilson could actually have worked together in such a way. Lodge proposed a set of reservations to qualify American accession to the treaty. More extreme opponents of the treaty in the Senate, the 16 "irreconcilables," objected to the implication of an entangling commitment to future action enshrined in Article 10 of the League covenant. Others had profound objections to other parts of the treaty. What bound them together was a fixed determination not to compromise. There were also more mild reservationists within Wilson's party. If Wilson had been prepared to accommodate Lodge, the treaty may well have gained the necessary majority. However, he ordered Democrats to vote against the Lodge reservations, and in return, Republicans rejected the original treaty and the mild reservations. A majority of senators supported the treaty (and League) in some form. Thus, while blame for its failure has tended to be ascribed to the irreconcilables, who consistently voted against it, the treaty could have been approved had Wilson and Lodge been able to compromise.

Wilson, profoundly impressed by the adulation of the crowds in Europe, decided to appeal directly to the American people. He intended that the 1920 presidential election would serve as a referendum on the treaty, and he embarked on a nationwide speaking tour, shadowed by the irreconcilables. His health suffered from the exertion and he suffered a debilitating stroke. This reduced his effectiveness as president in his last year in office and may have contributed to his stubbornness in refusing to move in Lodge's direction. Therefore, although Lodge and many of his followers were not outright opponents of the League, and although their reservations about American freedom of action would have fitted in with the way that the League subsequently operated, the United States never did join the League, nor did it ratify the Treaty of Versailles. It made its own peace with Germany in 1921 and was therefore formally uncommitted to any of the agreements that had been settled in Paris regarding territorial changes, reparations, or security guarantees to France and Belgium.

U.S. FOREIGN POLICY IN THE 1920s

Critics writing after World War II tended to see the 1920s and 1930s as an era of isolationism. However, while some aspects of the isolationist impulse are certainly common to both decades, Americans in the 1920s liked to think they were simply putting America first, and felt they were justified in doing so. Scholars in recent years have preferred terms like "independent nationalism" or "unilateralism" to "isolationism" in describing the 1920s. These terms draw attention to the key point—the emphasis on freedom of action. This was seen as not only a viable option, given America's geographical position and economic self-sufficiency, but also an imperative, given widespread contemporary views concerning the harmful effects of having departed from America's traditional policies by entering World War I.

The key characteristics of U.S. foreign policy in the 1920s were fourfold. They were shared widely across the political spectrum. First, the United States was determined to remain neutral in any future European war. Second, it was determined to avoid "foreign entanglements"—whether bilateral alliances or involvement in any multilateral arrangements that made commitments to future action. Third, this preference for distancing from the outside world was diplomatic and political, not commercial or cultural. This was a time of great American commercial expansion, and with it came the spread of American culture, notably in the form of music and film. Fourth, the American mission was to be delivered by example, not by direct proselytization. There would be no more "crusades for democracy."

Certainly Americans' sense of the exceptional nature of the United States as a political and social entity had not been diminished—far from it. However, that nationalism had acquired a rather jingoistic, exclusivist nature during the war. In the 1920s, while eagerly selling their culture overseas, Americans sought to erect barriers to exclude supposedly harmful elements from entering the United States. If anything, the World War I experience had reinforced notions of the corruption of the Old World, and now it acquired a new form in the guise of bolshevism. This dangerous political movement was identified with foreigners. During 1919–20, the first American "red scare" took place, in which radicals were arrested and some were deported. In 1921, immigration quotas were introduced. This departure from the tradition of welcoming immigrants reflected the inward-looking tendencies of the postwar era, drawing on nativist and racist elements and reflecting public anxiety over job losses during the sharp recession into which the nation's economy plunged after 1919. The United States ceased to present itself to the world as a haven for the persecuted. Instead, immigration quotas were an attempt to maintain a certain ethnic balance, dating back to the time before the great immigration of 1890–1914. Chinese and Japanese were excluded altogether, and other nationalities were allowed in on the basis of very restrictive quotas based on the proportion of that ethnicity in the population in 1890.

In a similar vein, Congress imposed high tariffs on the import of foreign goods, protecting American manufacturers from competition. At the same time, there was determined insistence that the nations that borrowed money from the United States during the war should repay it, although the tariff policies made it difficult for them to earn dollars with which to do so. American financial orthodoxy saw no reason to help them out—though there was, ironically, more willingness to deal with the plight of the former enemy—the Dawes (1924) and Young (1929) plans provided a solution to the problems Germany was facing in attempting to pay its war reparations to Britain and France. When Britain suggested linking cancellation of reparations to cancellation of war debts, however, the United States refused.

Americans after 1920 acted as though they had made a clear decision to reject membership of the League of Nations, and U.S. politicians were wary of giving any signs that they were acting collectively with other states. For a time, Secretary of State Charles Evans Hughes ignored any correspondence from the League. Yet the decision had been far less clear-cut in 1919–20. The final time it had voted on the Treaty of Versailles and U.S. membership in the League, the Senate had produced a majority in favor. However, Wilson's strategy of regarding the 1920 presidential election as a "solemn referendum" on League membership catastrophically backfired. The Republican platform was deliberately vague on the subject, and the League was not the major issue of the election, which was predominantly fought on issues of domestic politics. After the event, however, the election was generally depicted as the rejection of the League by American voters.

Those who had previously been the firmest supporters of the concept turned their attentions to other means of preventing war, notably international disarmament. Women's organizations, having successfully achieved the vote, turned their focus toward these issues. There were those who argued that the United States had a vital interest in being active in international organizations, in order to advance the cause of peace, but while some continued to lobby in favor of the League, most focused on a more subsidiary but seemingly achievable objective, American membership in the World Court. The Harding administration became an enthusiastic advocate of the court and seemed willing to confront Senate isolationists over the issue. President Harding's sudden death, however, deprived the campaign of its strongest domestic advocate. Calvin Coolidge, though also in favor of World Court membership, perceived no groundswell of voter or media support for it and was disinclined to push hard on the issue for fear of provoking a Republican split in Congress.

Disillusion concerning World War I continued to exercise a profound influence on attitudes throughout the interwar era. The 1919 Paris peace conference appeared to many Americans to confirm that what they had been told was a war for democracy had been used by their associates as a war to increase their empires. There was a rapid reaction against the German war guilt clause: writers in the 1920s argued that all European powers had been equally to blame. Disillusioned veterans tended to be harsher in their opinions of former allies than of the enemy. The

United States was more sympathetic to German economic problems in the 1920s than to those of France—European attempts to have war debt repayments reduced were seen as attempts by these large empires to play Americans for fools. The French occupation of the Ruhr in 1923 received a hostile reaction in the United States, and the French desire for an American security guarantee, to which Wilson had agreed at Paris, but which had never been considered by the Senate, was continually ignored throughout the 1920s. Overall, even Wilsonians had been convinced by the experience of the peace conference that Americans could not remake the world according to a progressive vision, nor could they undo centuries of European history.

Another major factor in shaping American attitudes toward involvement in world affairs was a reaction against the sheer horror of warfare that World War I provoked. Societies for disarmament and the outlawing of war proliferated. They were strongly supported by churches, feeling guilty about their support for the war in 1917. Moreover, both liberals and conservatives looked back to the wartime experience in the domestic sphere and drew negative conclusions. To conservatives, war had provided a pretext for the expansion of government: not only in an increase in the bureaucracy, but more significantly in increased intervention in the economy. Liberals reacted against the aggrandizement of executive power, concluding that the war had provided an excuse for persecution of radicals and restriction of freedom of speech, and had produced ugly manifestations of super-patriotism and racism. All reacted against the exaggerated propaganda that had been produced by the Creel committee, and the conclusion was widespread across the political spectrum that foreign wars were a serious threat to American values and liberties. Washington and Jefferson, it was felt, were vindicated.

The foreign policy attitudes produced by these powerful feelings were often criticized in the 1940s and 1950s for leading the United States to turn its back on its responsibilities as a world power. Revisionists in the 1960s asserted that the United States was not in fact so isolationist as realists had claimed, pointing to disarmament activity and to commercial expansionism. Certainly, Americans believed they should isolate themselves from political "entanglements." This took precedence over action to preserve economic stability. While Americans agreed it was desirable that the world be accessible to U.S. trade and business, they did not believe that the United States should become politically involved, outside the western hemisphere, to ensure it. Republicans, in power throughout the decade, sought a low-cost foreign policy that would allow them to reduce taxation and federal government spending. They were ready to put domestic constituencies above international considerations, even when they might have a negative impact on American economic activity.

This was particularly reflected in war debts policy—President Calvin Coolidge's response, "They hired the money, didn't they?" was widely shared—and in the increasingly high tariffs. Congressional tariff policies protected domestic American industry but provoked reciprocal responses in countries to which Americans wished to export, harming agriculture in particular. By reducing the Europeans' ability to sell in the American market, they also seriously impeded economic recovery in the region that was America's largest market. Such policies were popular at home, however, and even when presidents perceived the dangers and vetoed tariff increases, Congress overrode them. Americans failed to see how the growth of U.S. power (and the decline of others as a result of the war) meant that in America's own interests there were certain constraints on its actions, and that to ignore them would be to risk harmful consequences. Americans, however, despite warnings by a handful of economists, thought they had the option to do what they wanted, and that whatever might happen in the outside world, it would not damage U.S. vital interests or domestic development.

The consequence of these attitudes in actual foreign policy terms are that, though the United States was engaged in dynamic economic expansion, moving into new markets and creating great demand for its products in existing markets, the major policy initiatives were in the fields of disarmament. Peace activists persuaded Secretary of State Hughes and President Harding to host a disarmament conference in Washington, D.C., in 1921. During World War I, the United States had embarked on a program of naval expansion. The fear in 1915 was that if Britain were to be defeated, the shield provided by British naval dominance of the Atlantic would disappear. It thus intended to build up the U.S. Navy. A battleship building program had begun, and although battleships were not the most important naval weapon in the war, they were a potent (and expensive) symbol of a nation's power. After the war, all the victorious powers embarked on similar programs. A new naval arms race was under way, notably between the United States, Britain, and Japan.

Worried in particular about Japanese ambitions (and concerned about being faced with a Japanese–British combination), the Harding administration was ready to respond to the campaign by disarmament activists. The result was a number of treaties that established American naval parity with Great Britain. Capital shipbuilding was limited in overall tonnage and in size of individual ships. The agreements covered battleships, battle cruisers, and aircraft carriers but left other types of warships free of restrictions, an omission that allowed a continuance of the naval arms race and necessitated further (and increasingly fruitless) conferences. Japan was given a ratio that fixed it as the third naval power behind Britain and the United States. The argument was that Japan would have all its strength in one ocean, the Pacific, while the other two powers operated in two or more oceans. The British were forced to abrogate their 1902 treaty with Japan. These measures were seen in Tokyo as deep humiliations, and taken with immigration restrictions, they led to a profound souring of U.S.–Japanese relations.

The other great foreign policy initiative in the 1920s produced the Pact of Paris in 1928, commonly known as the Kellogg–Briand Pact. U.S. Secretary of State Frank B. Kellogg deflected renewed French requests for a Franco–American security treaty by taking up an idea advanced by pacifist groups in the United States. He proposed a multilateral treaty that outlawed all war. The pact included no provisions for enforcement nor penalties for infraction. It was simply a statement of hope, and it resonated not just with Americans but worldwide. It was eventually signed by all but five of the independent nations of the world. It has often been derided as a piece of foolish idealism, reflective of the unrealistic optimism of the time. It did, however, subsequently provide a basis in international law by which the aggressors in World War II could be tried. At the time, its unworldliness was underlined when in the course of the negotiations the United States and Britain added qualifying statements that excepted war in self-defense and war in defense of territories vital to a state's survival—thus making an exception for the two main reasons usually given for a nation going to war. Kellogg was awarded a Nobel Peace Prize for his achievement.

THE GOOD NEIGHBOR?
U.S. RELATIONS WITH LATIN AMERICA

U.S. foreign policy toward Latin America during 1914–45 falls into two phases, though movement from one phase to the other was gradual, through a long transition. The first period saw a continuation of U.S. approaches to the region as defined by the Roosevelt Corollary. The second was characterized by the Roosevelt administration's much publicized Good Neighbor policy, in which the United States sought to modify its ways of dealing with change and stability in the region without seriously modifying the attitude that it was the United States' "own backyard."

During the presidency of Woodrow Wilson, American intervention in Latin America continued to take an overtly military form, although the president characterized it in high moral terms. Mexico was of special interest, given its long land border with the United States. U.S. troops intervened in Mexico in 1914, but Wilson told Mexican press correspondents in 1915 that American motives were entirely moral and altruistic. Relations with Mexico were often tense through most of this period, up until 1942. Wilson responded to raids by Pancho Villa into the United States in 1916 with a punitive expedition led by General John Pershing. In February 1917, under U.S. pressure, Mexico adopted a new constitution, a bicameral legislature, and a democratically elected president. However, from 1924, Mexico was effectively ruled by military dictators. The principal American concern was to protect the privileged position of American oil companies.

The same approach was evident in dealings with states in the Caribbean and in Central and South America. Panama was a special case because of the canal, completed in 1914. The Panama Canal, and the zone it ran through, remained under direct United States control. The canal was of vital strategic importance, as it allowed the U.S. Navy and American trading vessels to pass between the Atlantic and Pacific much faster than previously, when they had to go around Cape Horn. The stability of Panama was therefore of utmost significance, and the United States reserved the right to intervene in case of disorder. By extension, islands in the Caribbean were regarded as key to the defense of the canal, and the United States applied the same principle. It acquired the Virgin Islands from Denmark in 1917, for $25 billion, to supplement its existing presence in Puerto Rico. Under the Platt Amendment (1902), the United States had asserted its right to intervene in Cuba, the Caribbean island closest to the U.S. mainland. In addition to their strategic importance, these Caribbean islands were of great interest commercially, being sources of significant crops such as sugar and fruit.

The U.S. government had traditionally shown itself ready to intervene to ensure stable political and economic conditions in these territories. The Roosevelt Corollary depicted this as acting in the interest of regional order and the protection of civilized values, but a driving force was the protection of commercial activities of American businesses, notably the maintenance of discriminatory privileges in tariffs and markets. Intervention was most often triggered when there were threats by nationalist groups to retract concessions or to reform landownership. The Wilson administration continued this policy and was ready to use military force. U.S. marines occupied Haiti in 1915 and the Dominican Republic in 1916, in response to internal political instability. Thus the Theodore Roosevelt policy of policing of the region was maintained.

This policy remained in place well into the 1920s. In 1926, a coup by General Chamorro in Nicaragua aroused a violent response and marines were sent to protect American interests. They returned intermittently until 1933. U.S. troops left the Dominican Republic in 1924 but remained in Haiti until 1934. However, there was a movement away from this heavy-handed military intervention, in line with the Republican administrations' preference for a low-risk, low-cost foreign policy. While strongly favorable toward the interests of American corporations active in Latin America, the governments of Harding, Coolidge, and Hoover looked to build a more cooperative relationship with their southern neighbors. A key stage in this development was the State Department's Clark memorandum (1928), in which the Roosevelt Corollary was rejected. The United States would no longer claim the right to intervene militarily in Latin American states. The administration put more effort into the Pan-American Union, which had originally been no more than a forum for U.S. dominance but was now to be an agency to further mutual cooperation between equals.

This approach was maintained by the Franklin Roosevelt administration, though by coining a new name for it, the Good Neighbor policy, it was depicted as a new initiative. The new secretary of state, Cordell Hull, had as his prime foreign policy goal the development of trade, in the form of reciprocal trade agreements that could bypass the prohibitive tariffs Congress had imposed. Trade, Hull believed, was the key not only to prosperity but to peace: nations that enjoyed good trading relations did not go to war with each other. As a necessary accompaniment to negotiating such agreements, Hull made an explicit announcement at the Pan-American Conference in Montevideo in 1933 that the United States was no longer claiming the right to intervene, except under certain circumstances. At successive conferences, this pledge was made stronger and hedged with fewer qualifiers.

While this undoubtedly marked a new phase in relations between the United States and its southern neighbors, substantial U.S. involvement continued, and the Roosevelt administration still sought to influence political and economic developments in the region. If military intervention had been eschewed, active political subterfuge and heavy pressure using economic weapons continued. This was evident in the case of Cuba, where U.S. envoy Sumner Welles, a close friend of the president, took an active part in engineering the overthrow of the Ramón Grau San Martín government, which appeared ready to expropriate American resources, and supported the coup by Fulgencio Batista. The United States revoked the Platt Amendment but retained the major naval base at Guantanamo Bay with full sovereignty, giving it an easy access point for intervention in Cuban affairs.

Latin American republics remained in an ambiguous relationship to the United States at the end of the 1930s—economically dependent on trade with the United States, suspicious of U.S. power, ruled by regimes that owed their own power to their relationship with the United States, but always having to deal with forces within their states that sought to modify that relationship. As the crisis in Europe intensified, the issue of security came to prominence. U.S. policy makers were sensitive to the possibilities of Nazi penetration into Latin America as a new threat to the Monroe Doctrine and were aware that some of the very rulers they had put in power had fascistic inclinations. Some states, notably Argentina, had close relationships with Fascist Italy and with the Spain of Francisco Franco. The United States therefore increased its efforts to develop good relations and to draw the region together with feelings of solidarity against the outside world. The administration stressed that the Atlantic was relatively narrow between west Africa and Brazil, and that the security interests of all the American republics were the same. They had some success in drawing the region into adopting the idea of a Neutrality Zone in 1939, and in progressively extending that zone eastward. The American states made increasingly strong statements of commitment to hemispheric defense, in the Panama Declaration in 1939 and the Act of Havana in 1940.

The real test of the Good Neighbor policy came in the Mexican oil crisis of 1938–42. Mexican dictator General Lázar Cárdenas introduced social reforms in 1938, including land redistribution and nationalization of the oil companies. Ultimately, a settlement was reached, with World War II giving a strong impetus to resolve the issue. Relations improved with the Mexican declaration of war on Germany and Japan in May 1942 and with the *bracero* agreement, which provided access for Mexican farm workers to the American labor market. Most Latin American states eventually entered World War II (Argentina was a notable exception until the very end of the war). Their role was mostly the provision of resources, though some provided fighting forces. The most prominent contribution came from Brazilian troops, who fought in Italy against the Germans. The United States actively sought increased coordination in security matters between the republics, in the process binding the American states closer to the United States, especially in the military sphere.

FOREIGN POLICY IN THE 1930s

While Americans in the 1920s may not have thought of themselves as isolationist, during the next decade many favored the term, seeing it to describe the wisest approach in a world of increasing and bewildering dangers. However, the word became overused—and this has persisted in subsequent commentaries on the period—notably by becoming synonymous with neutralism and pacifism, which were different though related phenomena.

One of the chief consequences of the Great Depression was the curtailment of international trade. Thus one of the central elements of U.S. involvement in international affairs, commerce, was no longer a strong draw toward the independent nationalism characteristic of the 1920s. The other main focus of American internationalist activity, disarmament, continued to attract some interest, though the kind of arrangements sought in the London and Geneva Naval Disarmament Conferences figured less prominently on pacifist agendas. Pacifism grew in strength, but its main focus was less the avoidance of involvement in wars by general disarmament, more a determination to isolate the United States from conflicts that appeared unavoidable in other parts of the world. The fact was that aggressor nations were showing themselves uninterested in disarmament.

The idea remained that munitions manufacturers were guilty of conniving at war, but the emphasis shifted from the impersonal and universal idea that arms races cause wars to a more personalized one, that arms dealers caused American involvement in World War I. This idea gained strength from a swing in public opinion against the business sector in the context of the continuing economic depression, and from historical revisionism concerning the causes of World War I. This revisionism questioned the Versailles verdict that the Germans bore sole war guilt. The failure of Britain, France, and other countries to maintain their war debt payments fed into a feeling that all the European participants had been to blame. Innocent and naïve Americans had been duped by them (especially by the cunning British), and by those Americans who stood to make fortunes from involvement in the war, or who stood to lose vast investments if the Allies should be defeated. These were popularized as the "merchants of death." A congressional committee was convened to investigate these charges, headed by Senator Gerald P. Nye of South Dakota. The committee questioned bankers and industrialists but could not make any specific charges stick. Still, the general notion retained its strength and resulted in passage of the Neutrality Act in 1935.

Underlying these measures to insulate the United States from being drawn into a war was a broad current of isolationism that ran parallel to pacifism. There has been much discussion of the nature, origins, and extent of 1930s isolationism and the ways in which it differed from the attitudes of the 1920s. After World War II, realists in particular saw isolationism as a deluded and ignorant attitude that overlooked true American interests. They tended to treat it in their analyses as a pathology, needing special investigation. In fact, while some population groups and regions were stronger than others and more enduring in adherence to the precepts of isolationism, its basic tenets were accepted widely across the spectrum of American politics, ethnicities, and regions. It was only the pace of Nazi expansionism in Europe that caused some Americans to reassess the wisdom of the attitude—but one should not allow the excesses of the most extreme supporters of isolationism in 1940–41 to mask the way that it drew very strongly on core American cultural and political traditions, and how its fundamental assumptions, notably that of U.S. invulnerability, retained their potency right up to the Japanese attack on Pearl Harbor in December 1941.

There were key distinctions between the attitude of the 1930s and that which had prevailed in the 1920s. The change in mood might be summarized as a movement from "We have no pressing interest in world affairs" to "We have a pressing interest in keeping separate from world affairs." The fundamental assumption at the heart of this attitude had two aspects: first, that a foreign war could not involve vital national interests, only those of certain individuals or concerns, and second, that war could not be a solution to anything, and neither could the threat of war. The lesson of World War I was that war could bring only chaos, devastation of property, and the loss of cherished liberties. It could not bring any kind of positive outcome, so it should be avoided at all costs. Only when events in Europe and Asia changed some people's attitudes toward these assumptions did opinion shift. It is worth noting that the general pessimism so endemic during the Depression years tended to bring people to see activism in world affairs as synonymous with becoming engaged in war. Neutralists and pacifists argued that there were only two alternatives: full disengagement, or war. President Franklin D. Roosevelt was to struggle to gain acceptance that there was a third alternative: engagement in order to prevent war. But given the mood of revulsion at national crusades, and pessimism about the chances of affecting developments elsewhere on the planet, such notions were unpopular with public opinion, the media, and professional policy makers, and Roosevelt showed only intermittent commitment to the idea.

ROOSEVELT AND THE NEUTRALITY ACTS

When Franklin D. Roosevelt won election to the presidency in November 1932, all thoughts were on domestic issues, with the unraveling of the banking system precipitating further rises in unemployment and intensifying the Great Depression that had begun in 1929–30. By the time Roosevelt took office in March 1933, 20 percent of the labor force was unemployed, and still more workers were either working part-time hours or had had their wages so reduced that they could not support themselves and their families. But Roosevelt had confidence in his own ability and offered morale-boosting statements like "We have nothing to fear but fear itself." President Hoover had attempted to get Roosevelt to agree to prolong a moratorium on war debt payments, but Roosevelt was unsympathetic to the idea of finding international solutions to the Depression. He was committed to send a delegation to the London Economic Conference that Hoover had helped organize, but in the middle of it he sent a further envoy, Ray Moley, with the message that the United States was withdrawing from the gold standard and saw no function for such meetings until world trade had recovered. Even if he did not share the vague feelings of many Americans that the Depression was the fault of foreigners, Roosevelt seemed in accord with the fundamentally isolationist (and exceptionalist) approach of the American people.

By 1934, Roosevelt's New Deal had produced improvements in public morale, and much temporary relief to the unemployed, but the jobless totals remained stubbornly high, and for all the reforms to the financial system and involvement of business people in bodies like the National Industrial Recovery Agency, the economy remained stagnant and many continued to work less than a full workweek. Roosevelt was beginning to see part of the problem to be resistance to reform among the wealthier classes, and he was happy to encourage Senator Nye's investigations into munitions makers and bankers. As the investigations could make no specific assignment of guilt, energies were refocused toward legislating against the possibility of such conspiracies in the future.

Support for neutrality legislation came from a number of quarters. Those who remained internationalist were anxious that the United States not undermine measures the League of Nations might take, such as economic sanctions against an aggressor. The original idea for a neutrality act, the Burton resolution, came from internationalists, to supplement the Kellogg–Briand Pact. Henry Stimson, when secretary of state under Hoover, had been keen for such legislation at the time of the Bolivian–Paraguayan Chaco War and the Japanese invasion of Manchuria. The United States could have applied sanctions without any appearance of following League instructions. These internationalists wanted powers to limit American trade with belligerents to be discriminatory, so that they could be used against an aggressor, and discretionary, with the power to implement them resting with the president.

On the other hand, pacifist isolationists sought impartial and mandatory embargoes in order to isolate the United States from war, not deter it or affect its outcome. For them, discriminatory embargoes would raise exactly the problems of partiality that they saw as having drawn the United States into World War I. They were deeply hostile to the arms trade and wanted to avoid all involvement in war. The Nye investigations had drawn attention to the rise in profits of financiers like J. P. Morgan during World War I, and these people were determined to prevent such developments happening again. They supported a ban on loans to belligerents, embargoes on trade with them (some argued for them to cover trade in all items, some for just trade in war materials), and restrictions on travel by Americans into war zones.

Traditional neutralists opposed restrictions on commerce and advocated traditional neutral rights to trade. They wished to reinforce American neutrality but argued that the United States was drawn into World War I by a failure to maintain that neutrality. Some in the business sector supported these ideas, being opposed to the introduction of any trade quotas or restrictions. President Roosevelt wished for a revision of what neutrality meant, and what rights the United States would insist upon, to ensure that doing so did not lead to war. He favored discretionary authority being granted to the president. He was therefore less than satisfied with the outcome, which reflected some concern in Congress to restrain presidential initiative, as well as the activities of business. As the 1935 Neutrality Act was finally framed, the only presidential discretion lay in his having the duty to declare when a state of war existed somewhere. Once he did, the act would come into force. All arms shipments to belligerents would be forbidden (though shipments of strategic materials like oil, steel, and chemicals would be allowed). U.S. citizens would travel on belligerent ships at their own risk.

These measures were tested almost immediately, when Italy invaded Abyssinia (Ethiopia). It quickly became evident that their effect was to advantage the aggressor, for the Italians had been free to stockpile materials in advance of their planned aggression. It also exposed as fallacious the idea that Americans might not find their sympathies involved in a foreign war. Roosevelt appealed to American business (especially oil companies) to apply a "moral embargo" against Italy, but at a time when all foreign trade was precious, this fell largely on deaf ears.

The Neutrality Act was up for renewal in 1936, and it was continued for another year, with little attempt to deal with the way it had been shown to work in practice—reflecting that most Americans were largely happy with the protection it appeared to give from being drawn into faraway conflicts. It was strengthened by adding a prohibition of loans to belligerents.

In the context of the ongoing civil war in Spain, which had broken out in June 1936, the act was revised again in 1937 and made permanent. It was expanded to cover civil wars. Fears that the spread of war would hamper the delicate revival of American commerce led to considerable debate about the issue of trade embargoes. Financier Bernard Baruch and others advanced the "cash-and-carry" idea, and this was incorporated in the legislation. In order to prevent American ships from being caught up in war, belligerents would be allowed to trade with American companies in items other than munitions, but they would have to carry them from American ports in their own vessels. To avoid issues of loans and debts, they would have to pay in cash. Americans could therefore reap whatever profits were to be made from a war situation without risking the United States being drawn into the conflict.

ROOSEVELT AND THE EUROPEAN CRISIS

U.S. foreign policy initiatives in the first two years of the Roosevelt administration were mainly limited to Hull's pursuit of reciprocal trade agreements and the Good Neighbor policy. The exception was Roosevelt's negotiations with Foreign Commissar Maxim Litvinov of the Union of Soviet Socialist Republics (USSR), which brought U.S. recognition of the Soviet regime. Apart from that, Roosevelt devoted little time to foreign affairs.

This began to change as crises developed in Europe. When the Spanish Civil War broke out, Roosevelt made a clear statement of American neutrality. Americans who wished to do more for the republican government in Spain had to go as private individuals or as volunteers in the international brigades. Roosevelt's infrequent statements suggested his primary concern was to prevent localized conflicts from spreading. This was underlined in a major speech he made on 5 October 1937 in Chicago, in the heartland of isolationism. Roosevelt suggested that war was like a contagion, and that the proper way to deal with it was by a quarantine. The implication was that the United States would join with other peace-loving nations in isolating an aggressor.

It is unclear whether Roosevelt was trying to move the United States toward participation in collective security and a more active role in world affairs with the application of economic sanctions against aggressors. He did not follow his speech with any concrete proposals. Roosevelt later said he felt that he was leading where no one was following, and that he had to wait for public opinion to catch up before attempting to engage the United States more actively in the preservation of peace. At the time, however, he did nothing to educate public opinion regarding the need for the United States to do so. Roosevelt scholars debate whether he had at this time become persuaded that the United States was threatened by developments in Europe. The quarantine speech suggested that he was, but the lack of any subsequent action indicates that this was not high on his list of priorities.

Roosevelt was effectively a passive spectator of the further European crises in 1938, which concerned the annexation of Austria by Germany in March 1938 and the Czechoslovak crisis later in the year that brought Europe close to war. Roosevelt's contribution went no further than suggestions for international conferences to solve the crises, qualified by indications that the U.S. role would be observatory and that the United States would give no guarantee of any settlement. It has been argued that Roosevelt's ability to intervene was tightly circumscribed by the mood in the United States. Over and above the neutrality legislation, the United States had entered a renewed economic recession that demanded his attention, and there were high-profile demonstrations of public concerns about being drawn into foreign crises. When American sailors were killed in an attack on the gunboat USS *Panay* by Japanese airplanes in China, there was an outcry that they had been in a war zone at all, aggravated when it was suggested their ship was there to protect the interests of an American oil company. Then there was the proposal for a constitutional amendment (the Ludlow amendment) that would mean Congress could not declare war without a national referendum. Congress refused to give up this power, but the tone of the public debate left the president in little doubt of feelings about intervention.

This situation continued in 1939 as the European crisis gathered pace. Roosevelt could do nothing but send messages urging restraint and negotiation, and this rendered the United States an irrelevancy in the unfolding crisis. American introversion was demonstrated in the attitude toward victims of the crisis: there was little inclination to make exceptions to the immigration quotas to accommodate Jewish refugees from Nazi persecution. Although it resulted from a Roosevelt initiative, the 1938 Evian conference on refugees was a story of evasion of action by all concerned.

What Roosevelt could do was use the continuing crisis to achieve a measure of American rearmament—many isolationists did not object to naval expansion, and important decisions were made in 1938 with regard to the modernization of the U.S. Navy and the initiation of the designs for weapons systems that ultimately were to be crucial to victory in World War II. It seems clear that Roosevelt was deeply troubled by the rise of Nazism in Germany. He had a long-standing distrust of German militarism and could foresee a threat to U.S. interests were Germany to dominate the continent of Europe. It might shut out American business with its policy of autarky and extend this to South America, and it might threaten the British ability to control the Atlantic sea lanes. Liberal opinion was beginning to question whether America could ignore who was in power in Europe. But when war broke out in Europe on 1 September 1939, there was no doubt that the United States, shocked once more by a European plunge into war, would be neutral, even if opinion regarding the protagonists was less disengaged than it had been in 1914.

THE ROAD TO WAR WITH GERMANY

Germany invaded Poland on 1 September 1939. On 3 September, Britain and its dominions Australia and New Zealand (followed by Canada on 10 September) and France declared war on Germany. President Roosevelt declared that the United States would remain neutral in deed, but in contrast to Wilson's equivalent announcement in 1914, he distinguished between actions and thoughts. This has been seen as an indication that Roosevelt inclined toward the Allies (as Britain, France, and Poland were known) and was even then preparing the way for American intervention in the war. There are those who see the American road to war from this point as a straight one. What isolationist critics saw as a devious conspiracy to involve the United States in war, supporters have seen as Roosevelt's firm commitment to the cause of freedom represented by the Allies, as he plotted a gradual course of increasing involvement, drawing a reluctant American people step by step to realize that their sympathies and interests were involved in the outcome of the war, and that they could not remain aloof from the struggle against German dictator Adolf Hitler.

To view the stages by which the United States entered the war as a progressively deeper involvement is to oversimplify matters, and to ascribe to Roosevelt both a single-mindedness of purpose and a clarity of objective that are probably misplaced. It is a more persuasive analysis, and more in keeping with Roosevelt's character and mode of working politically, to see him as largely operating in the short-term, principally driven by a concern to manage domestic politics. He clearly wished for an Allied victory, for a number of reasons, but it is unlikely that in September 1939 he thought it could be achieved only by direct American intervention. Roosevelt's views are very hard to establish definitively, and it is not easy to determine at what point he became certain that the United States would have to go to war. Many of his military advisors, notably Admiral Harold Stark, the chief of naval operations, reached that viewpoint in November 1940. It seems likely, however, that at least until the summer of 1941, Roosevelt hoped that American actions could be limited to "all aid short of war," involving the supply of munitions and other materials, together with pressure in the Pacific to keep Japan from attacking valuable Allied resources in Southeast Asia. His policy initiatives do not conform to the "straight line" thesis, for he wavered and backtracked, and while there is some credibility to the argument that he was forced to do so by domestic politics, this also seems to have stemmed from a lack of an overall strategy and an inherent opportunism that had characterized Roosevelt's conduct of the presidency since taking office in 1933.

When the neutrality legislation was first enacted in 1935, Roosevelt had preferred that embargoes be applied in a discretionary manner. This had not been approved, but Roosevelt understood that the realities of sea power and geography meant that Britain and France would be able to gain much better access to resources than Germany. Roosevelt pressed, however, for the legislation to be modified. He had first floated this idea earlier in 1939, only to withdraw when opposition emerged. He revived it in the fall, seeking for the cash-and-carry provision to be extended to munitions. He argued that this was the best way for the United States to avoid involvement in the war, implying strongly that victory for the

Allies was in America's interest, though ostensibly the cash-and-carry provision would apply equally to all belligerents. The debate in Congress saw the alignment of opinion around this question that would persist until December 1941, as some agreed with Roosevelt's cautious and tacit support for the Allies while others resisted any measure that might seem unneutral. The measure was passed. The resultant flood of orders was extremely welcome to an American economy still seriously underperforming—there remained 10 million unemployed at the start of 1940.

The defeat of France in May–June 1940 precipitated a number of further initiatives. One was an increase in the tempo of America's own rearmament. This gained support from a considerable section of isolationist opinion that was not pacifist, but argued that the United States should concentrate on making itself impregnable. These "Fortress America" arguments had first emerged in the mid-1930s. They represented a departure from the basic assumption that America was safe and isolated by geography from unpleasant events in the rest of the world. But the response was purely defensive and drew on the themes of American exceptionalism and the menace from foreigners that were commonplace in isolationist thought generally. Advocates supported expenditure on the navy, and naval expansion had begun in 1938. The navy was seen as a defensive weapon, and the U.S. Army remained small and underequipped. In 1940, the United States had the 18th largest army in the world, smaller than that of Romania. Roosevelt indeed weakened it in the summer of 1940 by allowing it to be scoured for equipment to pass on to the Allies. Further naval building was approved in the ambitious Two Ocean Navy Act. This was to be interpreted by the Japanese as a mortal threat, though it was probably impelled at this point by the anxiety that the British and French fleets might fall into German hands, giving them control of the Atlantic. As far as the army went, rearmament was a more sensitive issue, as army expansion carried an implication that it might be deployed overseas. Roosevelt allowed others to put forward the idea of a draft and only supported the idea when it was clear that it would pass through Congress. The 1940 Selective Service Act drafted a proportion of young American males for a year's military training, though it did not address the severe shortages of equipment.

Roosevelt also acted to broaden his administration, to try to avert opposition along purely party lines—a particular danger during an election year. He took into his cabinet two high-profile and nonisolationist Republicans, former secretary of state Henry Stimson as secretary for war, and Frank Knox, vice presidential candidate in 1936, as secretary for the navy. Pressure groups began to be increasingly organized and vocal on all sides of the debate—either in favor of greater American aid for the British, or in favor of building up American defenses and not diverting materials to a lost cause in Britain. It was also argued that the United States would best defend democracy by keeping well out of conflict. Those of an anti-British persuasion, such as many Irish-Americans, lent vociferous support to the latter arguments.

Roosevelt, having decided to run for a third term, steered a careful course designed to avoid alienating all but extremist opinion. This was made difficult by the plight of Great Britain, and by Prime Minister Winston Churchill's firm belief that only American help could bring ultimate victory. Churchill bombarded Roosevelt with appeals, couched in terms appealing to American interests. Roosevelt sought to encourage Churchill while not committing to anything that was too risky in domestic political terms. The immediate British need was for naval escort vessels. The United States had a surplus of these, in the form of ships of World War I vintage. Roosevelt came to an arrangement with Churchill, which avoided directly giving warships to a belligerent, a deeply unneutral act, by negotiating an exchange of the ships for 99-year leases on bases on British territory in the western hemisphere, from Newfoundland to Trinidad. He was able to represent this destroyers-for-bases deal as an addition to American strength and a stage in the dismantling of the British empire, seeking thereby to appeal to Fortress America advocates and to anti-British opinion. Although the warships were not of high quality, Churchill saw this as a significant step toward U.S. involvement in the war, and isolationists read it the same way. Days after the deal was announced, isolationists coalesced their activities within a single organization, the America First Committee (AFC). The AFC commenced an effective program of lobbying, attacking this unneutral behavior, and accusing Roosevelt of leading the United States deliberately into war. They argued that Britain would be defeated, and claimed that Roosevelt was acting like a dictator in bypassing Congress, having made the agreement in his capacity as commander in chief.

Concurrently with these developments, the United States was improving its relations with Mexico and drawing the Latin American countries together in the Act of Havana. The consequence was a wide neutral zone extending out into the Atlantic, which the U.S. Navy was to patrol, though it was unclear what measures it would take if it encountered German warships.

Roosevelt's opponent in the 1940 presidential election, Wendell Willkie, was no isolationist and initially soft-pedaled on foreign policy issues. However, as Roosevelt built up a comfortable lead in the opinion polls, the issue began to be raised, and Roosevelt was drawn into stating that "American boys" would not be sent to fight in any foreign wars. This was not hypocrisy, for Roosevelt believed at this point that the policy of aid to the Allies short of war would be sufficient, although military planners, engaged in revising America's war plans, reached a different conclusion. American public sympathies toward the British had begun to rise, in admiration of the successful battle of Britain and in particular in response to the German bombing of London, which began in September 1940. Roosevelt's line therefore chimed in with their own attitudes.

Having won the election in November, Roosevelt was confronted by Churchill with the British financial situation, which was close to collapse. Forbidden under the Debt-Default Act and the Neutrality Act from borrowing in American money markets, Britain had been forced to liquidate many of its assets in the United States, on very unfavorable terms, in order to fund purchases of American materials. Most Americans, Roosevelt included, were skeptical that the vast British empire was really in such dire straits—the image of the cunning British making suckers out of naïve Americans died hard.

However, Churchill's increasingly frank statements made an impact, and Roosevelt took an initiative that turned out to be world changing. First, he spelled out to Americans in a "fireside chat" on 29 December 1940 how American interests were tied up with others' struggle for freedom. America, he said, should be the "arsenal of democracy"—supply the arms that would allow others to win the fight that would preserve American, as well as their own, freedom. Soon afterward, in a slight flight of Wilsonianism, Roosevelt appealed to Americans' sense of moral exceptionalism, saying that America's aim was that from this war should emerge a world based on four freedoms—freedom from fear and from want, and freedom of speech and of religion. Thus he implied that those actually fighting in the war, primarily for their own survival, were doing so in pursuit of American values. This was just preparing the ground. Roosevelt's key proposal was Lend-Lease. To overcome the problem of finance for aid short of war, and to bypass the prohibition on loans, Roosevelt's plan was to lend the items needed by the Allies, with payment to be arranged later. He used the analogy of the fire hose: when your neighbor's house is on fire, you loan him your hose, he said; you do not haggle about the price. If it is damaged, you can talk about compensation when the fire is out.

An epic political battle followed. Critics argued that it was not the loan of a fire hose but, as Republican Senator Robert Taft put it, a piece of chewing gum—you would not want it returned after use. It was therefore a straight giveaway, not a loan. Democrat Senator Burton Wheeler particularly aroused Roosevelt's fury by saying that it resembled the New Deal's agricultural policy (which had subsidized farmers to kill livestock), in that it would "plow under every fourth American boy." Isolationists argued that giving such aid to Britain would inevitably drive Germany to war with the United States, and that this was exactly what Roosevelt intended. In fact, it was not—Roosevelt sincerely thought that by removing all restraints on access to American production, he would guarantee British victory. It would also, by expanding American industry to deal with the orders (paid for by the government in the short term), bring prosperity to the American economy for the first time since 1929. Fortress America enthusiasts complained that American armaments should go to arm American forces first. Voting on the Lend-Lease Act in Congress on 11 March 1941 split generally on party lines, giving Roosevelt victory. Initially Lend-Lease was granted to Britain and China—but there would be some delay before the American economy would actually be geared up to meeting the increased demand it created.

The following months saw U.S. policy toward the war in Europe follow an inconsistent course. Some argue that Roosevelt was treading carefully, in view of the continuing vociferousness of the AFC. It is not clear, however, that Roosevelt intended taking further steps. There were those in the administration, such as Knox, who believed the United States should take more decisive action. A fresh lobby group, Fight for Freedom, was set up by those frustrated with the policy of aid short of war. Thus, Roosevelt was criticized from two opposite directions, though majority public opinion inclined to the president's view, which was argued in public by the Committee to Defend America by Aiding the Allies.

Roosevelt moved to send troops to replace British forces occupying Iceland, and he extended the American neutrality zone to reach halfway across the Atlantic. He would not, however, order the U.S. Navy to escort convoys of foreign ships or proceed beyond the neutrality zone. He agreed to meet with Churchill off the coast of Newfoundland in August, but while they reached an agreement on general war aims, the Atlantic Charter, Churchill left disappointed that he had failed to draw Roosevelt further into the war. They had also discussed the new dimension to the war brought by the German invasion of the Soviet Union on 22 June 1941. Roosevelt's aide Harry Hopkins had visited the Soviet leader, Josef Stalin, and reported that the Soviets, despite heavy defeats, were resolved to fight on. Americans had no taste for aiding what they saw as a godless regime, and it was not until November 1941 that Lend-Lease was extended to the Soviets.

When the extension of Selective Service beyond its duration of a year was approved in the House of Representatives by only one vote, Roosevelt adopted even greater caution, but his policies began to produce effects that developed a momentum of their own. The warships in the Atlantic had been placed in an unsustainable position, escorting ships but not empowered to take action. Incidents began to multiply, and as had happened with Woodrow Wilson, the president was drawn along by events he could not control. However, unlike Wilson, Roosevelt appears to have been more eager to use them to advance a line of policy, and it seems likely that by September 1941, Roosevelt had come to the conclusion that Lend-Lease alone was not enough. He was still not envisaging a land war, but he could see that it made no sense to supply Britain with materials and then do nothing to prevent them being destroyed by German submarines. The United States therefore moved toward an undeclared naval war, partly by Roosevelt's exercise of his commander-in-chief powers, partly by manipulating some of the incidents that arose, while being careful to ignore others so as not to push the situation too far. Hitler did the same. Historical records show that there were far more confrontations and incidents in the Atlantic than were reported to the public. Those that were reported were used to intensify American involvement and, for the navy, give some clarity to the situation.

An attack on the USS *Kearny* in September produced what later became known as the "shoot on sight" order, though Roosevelt was not that explicit at the time. Loss of life when the USS *Greer* was torpedoed in October and then when the USS *Reuben James* was sunk gave Roosevelt grounds to ask for revision of the Neutrality Act to allow arming merchant ships and other measures. The situation then stabilized as each side avoided pushing the issue to its logical conclusion. The U.S. Navy was now engaged in active and aggressive operations against German submarines and was sharing intelligence with Britain and Canada. In this intelligence cooperation in particular, the United States was acting like a belligerent.

But still war did not come to the United States. Some claim that Roosevelt was waiting for a clear act of aggression to unite the country. But many incidents in the Atlantic could have fulfilled this purpose, had Roosevelt wished to exploit them. Possibly he was playing for time. He had called earlier for military planners to draw up not only strategies to fight a war against the Axis powers, but also a Victory Program of the necessary forces and production that would be required. This was not fully finished by December. Possibly he was waiting for the final result. More likely, he was still hoping that a land war for the United States would not be necessary, and that an undeclared naval war would be sufficient U.S. involvement. Even after the Japanese attacked Pearl Harbor and the United States declared war against Japan, the reluctance to engage in a land war prevailed as the U.S. Navy looked to shift forces to the Pacific. The situation was clarified when Germany and Italy declared war on the United States on 11 December 1941.

THE CRISIS IN U.S.–JAPANESE RELATIONS

U.S.–Japanese relations are conventionally depicted as deteriorating as a consequence of the Washington treaties of 1921–22. In fact, they remained reasonably good through the 1920s. While many officers of the Japanese navy saw the ratios agreed to in Washington as a humiliation, and regretted the loss of the alliance with Britain, the treaty relieved Japan of a naval arms building program that it could ill afford, especially after the disastrous Tokyo earthquake of 1923. American immigration restrictions on the Japanese were also seen as insulting, but Japan continued to be the United States' best customer in Asia, because Japanese modernization depended on imports from the United States. Relations really began to deteriorate when Japanese policy in China altered in 1931. Japan had sought to follow the policy applied by western nations and secure a sphere of influence in China. In 1931, the Japanese army occupied Manchuria, and Japan subsequently established a puppet state, Manchukuo, under the former emperor of China. The annexation was condemned by the League of Nations, though no action was taken. The Hoover administration announced a policy of nonrecognition of Manchukuo—the Stimson Doctrine. No sanctions were applied, however, and Japan continued to be a major customer for American oil, scrap metal, and advanced engineering.

But Japan had now identified itself to many Americans as a threat to long-standing U.S. interests in China. These interests were more in terms of sympathy and future hopes for trade and missionary achievements than present economic reality, and during the 1930s, U.S. policy was to avoid confrontation over China. The American ambassador in Tokyo, Joseph C. Grew, recommended that the best way to influence the Japanese was to remain on good terms with them. The American response was therefore muted when Japan invaded China proper after the Marco Polo Bridge incident in 1937. When the USS *Panay* was sunk by Japanese airplanes, the Roosevelt administration was ready to accept the Japanese apology and compensation.

The position was profoundly altered by the course of the war in Europe. The fall of France and the Netherlands in May and June 1940 left their colonial possessions in the East very vulnerable. The Japanese were stuck in a war in China that had brought vast conquests but was dragging on with no sign that the Chinese would come to terms. The resources of the Dutch East Indies and French Indochina would make a big difference. This was especially important with a change in American policy toward trade with Japan.

Roosevelt had not activated the Neutrality Act in 1937. Neither side had declared war, which meant the United States could supply China with war materials but also that Japan continued able to buy vital materials from the United States, which found itself supporting a war effort of which it disapproved. Within the State Department, officials, notably Stanley Hornbeck, argued that the Japanese could be restrained by a tougher diplomatic line. The United States gave notice that it would terminate its 1911 commercial treaty with Japan. Export of some strategic materials to Japan was halted in July 1940. The United States could argue that it needed the materials for its own rearmament and for supplying Britain, but this and the plans to enlarge the navy seemed a threatening move to the Japanese. They put pressure on the British to close the Burma Road supply route to the Chinese and persuaded French officials to allow them to occupy northern Indochina. In September, Japan joined the Axis pact. This agreement with Germany specified that the signatories would go to the aid of each other if attacked by a power they were not at present at war with. This appeared to be directed at the United States.

Britain was dependent on its Asian territories for vital supplies, notably rubber, and deterring a Japanese attack seemed to the Roosevelt administration to be one way that the United States could help the British war effort without offending isolationists. Measures were introduced to strengthen the defenses of the Philippines, and the Pacific Fleet was moved to Pearl Harbor in Hawaii as a deterrent. In July 1941, after Japan moved into southern Indochina, the administration tightened the embargoes imposed after Japan joined the Axis pact. All Japanese assets in the United States were frozen. In practice, this became indistinguishable from a full embargo, including most crucially oil. In August, when Roosevelt met Churchill in Placentia Bay, they agreed on the seriousness of the Japanese threat but approved a policy of "Germany first": Japan was to be treated firmly, but a breach was to be avoided. Germany, as the stronger Axis power, should be dealt with first.

The oil embargo was regarded in Japan as a very serious threat. If maintained, it would bring the army and especially the navy to a standstill within two years and would seriously impede their offensive capability long before that. A dual strategy was formulated, to attempt to negotiate an end to the embargo, while preparing for offensive action to seize oil and other resources in the Dutch East Indies and Southeast Asia should this fail. Negotiations with the United States dragged on. A second negotiator was sent to Washington, but the United States was convinced that a hard line would bring a Japanese retreat. Hull insisted on Japanese withdrawal from China as a condition for lifting the embargo. A request from Japanese Premier Funimaro Konoye for a personal meeting with Roosevelt was rejected, resulting in Konoye's replacement with the more belligerent General Hideki Tojo. Although defenses in the Philippines would not be ready until March 1942, Hull did not feel that concessions should be made to buy time. Talks became increasingly sterile. The last chance was the idea of a modus vivendi, but Chinese leader Chiang Kai-shek would not accept it, and the Japanese decided that they had to activate their second option, which was to seize the resources for themselves. In the belief that the United States would intervene, a preemptive strike on the U.S. Pacific Fleet was incorporated in the plan.

At dawn on 7 December 1941, Japanese aircraft from six aircraft carriers launched a devastating surprise attack on the fleet at Pearl Harbor and crippled it, though they failed to destroy the port facilities, and the American aircraft carriers were elsewhere. The manner of attack united the nation behind Roosevelt's ringing declaration that this was "a date that would live in infamy." He added that what would ultimately matter was not who fired the first shot, but who would fire the last.

U.S. POLICY IN WORLD WAR II

The means by which the United States entered World War II, through a surprise attack on U.S. territory, profoundly shaped American public attitudes to the war and to American foreign relations. Pearl Harbor brought a shift that endured long after the war was over. It confirmed what Roosevelt had been saying since at least June 1940: the United States could not isolate itself from political developments on other continents. No longer did the oceans appear to give the United States invulnerability. In the short term, Pearl Harbor also filled Americans with a burning desire for complete victory. The nation entered the war united.

It is not the place here to discuss in detail the U.S. military and economic contributions to Allied victory. Suffice it to say that 16 million men and women served in uniform, and 292,000 were killed. The United States ended the war with the largest navy, the largest strategic air force, and the second largest army. American industrial productivity had armed the Allies through the mechanism of Lend-Lease, which had crucially removed all issues of finance from the equation, for the duration of the war. Foreign policy during the war was concerned with two main areas (though they overlapped): managing relations with the nations with whom the United States was fighting, and planning for the postwar world.

In the first area, the president took the lead. Roosevelt conducted relations with his main allies personally. His relations with Cordell Hull were cordial but distant, and he did not trust the State Department to conduct policy according to his own preferences. Most particularly, he sensed accurately that the policy he adopted toward the USSR, of building goodwill and avoiding contention, was viewed with misgivings in the State Department, particularly by its cohort of Soviet specialists. Roosevelt therefore sidelined the department as much as possible, using special envoys to conduct relations when personal contact was not possible. Roosevelt's objectives with regard to his Soviet ally were twofold: keep the USSR fighting in the war until Germany was defeated, and persuade the Soviet leadership to cooperate in his plans for maintaining a stable and lasting peace after the war.

Roosevelt had supported U.S. membership in the League of Nations in 1920 and had been a member of Woodrow Wilson's administration. Since then, a commitment to internationalism had not been apparent in his attitudes to foreign policy. There is some debate regarding the degree to which Roosevelt was an ardent believer in an international organization as a mechanism for world peace. In his public pronouncements, he committed himself to it, and he worked hard to achieve U.S. membership in a new organization to replace the League. He clearly believed that American absence from the organization had weakened it and may have contributed to the onset of World War II. However, it is likely that Roosevelt's principal purpose for the United Nations was as a vehicle to maintain the American people's readiness to be involved in world affairs, and to ensure that there was no return to isolationism after the war. It is likely that he saw it also as a means to draw the Soviet Union out of the isolation that it had experienced before World War II, within a framework of international self-restraint.

Roosevelt as a politician had a strong inclination to pragmatic solutions, and to dealing with the realities of political power. This side of him was in evidence in his private dealings with Stalin and Churchill, which differed markedly from his pronouncements in public. The solution to international disorder that he proposed to his "Big Three" colleagues was what he called the "four policemen": the four great powers—the United States, Great Britain, the Soviet Union, and China—

would act in concert to preserve peace, maintaining armaments while others were disarmed. Implicit in this, and in Roosevelt's statements to Stalin regarding the Soviet right to "friendly governments" on their borders, was the existence of spheres of influence, even if Roosevelt preferred these spheres to be open to commerce and political contacts. In public, the official American stance was firmly against any such spheres (while maintaining that the Monroe Doctrine was still a fixed point in international politics).

Up until the Teheran conference in November 1943, the first full meeting of the "Big Three," Roosevelt avoided raising political issues with Stalin, and he attempted to build an atmosphere of trust and good-will by Lend-Lease aid. His announcement in January 1943 that nothing short of unconditional surrender would be required of the Axis was designed to avoid contention over terms to be offered to enemy states, and to keep the alliance operating on a basic common aim of total victory. At Teheran, the United States and Britain committed themselves to what Stalin had been demanding above all other things, an invasion of German-occupied Western Europe. From this point on, Roosevelt has been seen as attempting to develop a more mutual pattern of give and take with Stalin, though he was prepared to compromise or defer to the Soviet leader on many issues. This was largely because of a concern that lasted past the Yalta conference in February 1945, to get the large Soviet army into the war with Japan, once the war with Germany was over. There were great fears that Japan could be defeated only by invasion of the Japanese home islands, and that the Japanese way of war would mean a high casualty rate. Soviet participation was therefore seen as highly valuable, and at Yalta, Roosevelt offered Stalin concessions in China, in return for his promise to do so. Stalin, for his part, agreed to free elections in the European countries his forces were liberating, but he afterward failed to adhere to this "Declaration on Liberated Europe." Whether Roosevelt would have made a large issue of this is uncertain, as he died on 12 April 1945, with the war still unfinished.

Roosevelt's successor, Harry Truman, was not aware of the differences between Roosevelt's public and private utterances, nor of Roosevelt's way of managing affairs according to short-term opportunity. He viewed the agreements with the Soviets at face value and turned for advice to people in the State Department and the ambassador in Moscow, Averell Harriman, whose advice Roosevelt had ignored.

They advised a harder line, pressing the Soviets to keep to the letter of their agreements. However, with the United States still seeking Soviet involvement in the new United Nations organization, established at the San Francisco conference in June 1945, as well as in the final stages of the war against Japan, Truman alternated between hard and conciliatory postures. Most notably, he dispatched Roosevelt's confidant Harry Hopkins to Moscow, where he reached a compromise settlement on the contentious Polish issue in early June 1945. It has been widely suggested that Truman's decision to use the atomic bomb against Japan was shaped by his concern to demonstrate American power to the Soviets, and to bring them to keep to their agreements. While he and some of his advisors, such as Secretary of State James F. Byrnes, did see the bomb as a welcome element in their relationship with the Soviets, the question of whether to use the bomb was never considered in quite the way that would make that the clinching argument.

In relations with the other great ally, Britain, Roosevelt's policy was quite different. He had no need to conciliate Britain. He shared the views of many Americans that a desirable outcome to the war would be the demise of the European empires, including that of Great Britain. Churchill strongly resisted Roosevelt's pressures on this subject. There was some tension over the issue of Indian independence, but the Americans had more success in drawing the British into their plans for a redesigned international economic system. This was established at the Bretton Woods conference in 1944 and amounted to a reorientation of international finance around the U.S. dollar. Concurrent with this, American trade was penetrating into many areas previously dominated by Britain, whose merchant shipping and commerce had suffered badly in the war. Relations with Britain over war strategy were also tense, as the British leaders preferred an indirect strategy involving operations in the Mediterranean, while American strategists wished to invade France as early as possible. The British had their way in 1941–43, as they had combat experience and more forces in the field—and also because Roosevelt was keen to get involved anywhere in Europe, to keep the American public from paying all their attention to the Pacific theater. Mediterranean operations were possible sooner than Western European ones. Once the balance of military force shifted, the Americans were successful in orienting strategy in the direction they wanted, which had the advantage for Roosevelt and Hopkins of drawing closer to the Soviets.

American relations with China in the war were shaped initially by an exaggerated estimate of Chinese military power and political cohesion, which slowly faded away. There was a highly effective pro-China lobby in the United States, headed by publisher Henry Luce, and Chiang Kai-shek and his wife were extremely popular figures, encapsulating many long-standing American hopes about China's future as a democratic state and market for American goods. Roosevelt hoped that China could act as trustee for former European colonies, but as it turned out, Chiang was not strong enough to assert control over his own country, let alone territories further afield.

The United States emerged from World War II as a superpower, possessing not only military might, which would soon be demobilized, but having demonstrated industrial power that dwarfed that of the rest of the world. The engineering and scientific feat of producing the atomic bomb demonstrated this fact starkly. Americans had come to the conclusion that isolation was impossible in the modern world. They were committed to the task of remodeling the defeated enemy nations as liberal democracies and participating in the new world organization to preserve peace. Some were already apprehensive that the war had unleashed a new menace, in the form of the Soviet Union, but for most Americans that was an issue to be faced once the war was over. The appearance and some of the substance of the wartime alliance that Roosevelt planned would persist into the peace: the four dominant powers would help manage the world as permanent members of the UN Security Council. The alliance was still intact when the final conference of World War II met in Potsdam in defeated Germany in July 1945. The Cold War was still to come.

The Dictionary

– A –

ABC-1 PLAN. Military planners from the United States, **Great Britain**, and Canada conducted a series of highly secret strategic talks in Washington, D.C., between 24 January and 27 March 1941, during **World War II**. This breach of U.S. neutrality would have given **isolationists** powerful ammunition had knowledge of the talks leaked out. The planners considered various scenarios. The ABC-1 plan followed U.S. plan Rainbow 5, which outlined strategy should the three powers find themselves at war with both **Japan** and **Germany**. Operations against Japan would be limited to defending strategically vital areas until Germany was defeated. The reasoning was that Germany, being the stronger, could fight on without Japan and was more likely to produce dangerous new weapons, including an atomic bomb. ABC-1 was approved by President **Franklin D. Roosevelt** and British Prime Minister **Winston Churchill** at their **Placentia Bay meeting** in August 1941.

This and other instances of prior cooperation between the military organizations, which are usually loath to share intelligence and planning, made the construction and working of the wartime Western alliance much smoother once the United States was fully drawn into the war. They also probably reduced the time it took for the United States to get fully mobilized. The Pearl Harbor attack, however, undermined commitment to the "Germany first" strategy within the U.S. military, especially the **U.S. Navy**. To move U.S. troops into the European theater, Roosevelt endorsed Churchill's plan to invade French North Africa (Operation **Torch**). *See also* RAINBOW PLANS.

ABC POWERS CONFERENCE (1914). The ABC Powers Conference was a meeting in Niagara, Canada, on 20 May 1914 intended to calm relations between the United States and **Mexico** following the U.S. fleet's action in bombarding and occupying the Mexican port of **Veracruz** in April. The ABC powers were **Argentina, Brazil,** and Chile. The U.S. representatives at the conference included Joseph R. Lamar, associate justice of the Supreme Court. The conference led to a commission to mediate future disputes in an effort to avoid military conflict. *See also* LATIN AMERICA; ROOSEVELT COROLLARY; WILSON, WOODROW.

ABRAHAM LINCOLN BRIGADE. U.S. volunteers fighting on the republican side during the **Spanish Civil War** joined the International Brigades in two battalions, the George Washington Battalion and the Abraham Lincoln Battalion. Both of these were part of the XV International Brigade. In the United States, the term "Abraham Lincoln Brigade" came to be applied indiscriminately to both units. U.S. volunteers also served in the John Brown Anti-Aircraft Battery and in hospital units. The battalions were organized in early 1937, with about 450 members, and took part in several battles. Some 2,800 Americans ignored a State Department ban on travel to Spain and joined the fight. Over a hundred served in medical units. The **League of Nations** Non-Intervention Committee banned foreign volunteers in February 1937. The two units were withdrawn from battle in early 1938 and the survivors repatriated. As they were inadequately trained and poorly commanded, their casualty rate was high. More than 700 Americans died in the conflict. Many were members of left-wing groups, including the **Communist Party of the United States.** In the post–**World War II** era, all veterans of the International Brigades tended to be regarded as communists, but many who had gone to Spain with pronounced left-wing views had returned disillusioned by communist efforts to take over the Spanish republican movement.

ACHESON, DEAN (1893–1971). A Yale graduate, Dean Acheson trained at Harvard Law School, was private secretary to Supreme Court Justice Louis Brandeis (1919–21), and then practiced law in Washington, D.C., until President Franklin D. Roosevelt appointed him undersecretary of the treasury in 1933. Although a lifelong Democrat, the conservative Acheson broke with Roosevelt when the president took the United States off the gold standard. He became a strong internationalist when war broke out in Europe in 1939.

Acheson was an admirer of the British empire and strongly advocated aid to Great Britain. In 1941, he was appointed assistant undersecretary for economic affairs at the State Department. He has often been held responsible for extending the freeze on Japanese assets that was imposed after Japan's occupation of southern Indochina in July, to include oil. The resulting full embargo of oil exports to Japan, which Roosevelt retrospectively approved, was a major step in the road to war between Japan and the United States. Acheson played an important role at the Bretton Woods economic conference in 1944. President Harry S. Truman made him undersecretary at the State Department in 1945. Acheson was to be a major architect of U.S. Cold War containment policy under Truman, serving as secretary of state from 1949 to 1953.

ADAMS, CHARLES FRANCIS (1866–1954). A descendant of President John Quincy Adams, banker Charles Adams was a mayor of Quincy, Massachusetts (1896–97), and secretary of the navy in the administration of U.S. President Herbert Hoover (1929–33). Adams fought for continued U.S. naval parity with Great Britain during the 1930 London Naval Disarmament Conference and defended U.S. naval strength against budget cutbacks during the early 1930s. He retired from politics at the end of the Hoover administration.

ADDAMS, JANE (1860–1935). The prime motivator behind the settlement house movement that began in the 1890s, Addams founded Hull House, a refuge for destitute workers and their families in Chicago. She later gained national recognition as a **progressive** campaigner for the rights of women, African Americans, and labor. A committed **pacifist**, Addams helped organize the **Women's Peace Party** in 1915 and campaigned against U.S. participation in **World War I**. The International Congress of Women, which she helped establish, tried to end the war through diplomacy. This activism made her unpopular with the American press, leading to her expulsion from the Daughters of the American Revolution.

In 1920, Addams became the first president of the **Women's International League for Peace and Freedom** and assisted in the creation of the American Civil Liberties Union (ACLU). She was awarded the Nobel Peace Prize in 1931. *See also* AMERICAN UNION AGAINST MILITARISM; WALD, LILLIAN.

ADVISORY COMMITTEE ON POSTWAR FOREIGN POLICY (ACPFP). A secret committee established by Secretary of State **Cordell Hull** on 12 February 1942, the ACPFP developed policy recommendations for the president regarding the postwar period. In effect the successor to the **Advisory Committee on Problems of Foreign Relations**, it also took on some of the functions performed by the State Department's **Division of Special Research**. It was proposed to Hull by **Leo Pazvolsky** and **Norman Davis**, who had been members of the earlier committee.

A number of ACPFP subcommittees dealt with economic, territorial, political, and international organization matters, and after four sessions, Hull abolished the main committee, retaining the subcommittees under the direction of Pazvolsky. Members of the main committee had included Hull as chair, Pazvolsky, **Sumner Welles, Dean Acheson**, Army Chief of Staff General **George C. Marshall, Alger Hiss**, Vice President **Henry Wallace, Philip Jessup, Archibald MacLeish**, and **Harry Dexter White**. Experts were recruited from the **Council on Foreign Relations**, including **Hamilton Fish Armstrong, Myron Taylor, Benjamin Cohen, James Shotwell**, and **Anne O'Hare McCormick. Clark Eichelberger** of the **League of Nations Association** was a member of the international organizations subcommittee.

By 1943, the importance of the committees had declined and the main work was performed by a smaller group, the Informal Political Agenda Group, comprising Hull, Welles, Davis, Taylor, Pazvolsky, and **Isaiah Bowman**, and by Pazvolsky's Divisions of Political Studies and Economic Studies. These had superseded his Division of Special Research on 1 January 1943.

ADVISORY COMMITTEE ON PROBLEMS OF FOREIGN RELATIONS (ACPFR). Secretary of State **Cordell Hull** created the ACPFR on 27 December 1939 after his assistant **Leo Pazvolsky** convinced him of the need to consider problems of peace and reconstruction that would arise at the end of **World War II**. It was originally called the Committee on Problems of Peace and Reconstruction, and like many other committees that Hull established, it was to experience renaming, reorganization, abolition, and then reformation. The original chair was Undersecretary of State **Sumner Welles**. There were 15 members, including **Norman Davis** and George Rublee from outside the State Department. Pazvolsky headed the economics subcommittee, and other members were **Adolf Berle**, **Stanley Hornbeck**, and Herbert Feis. The committee came up with a plan for a revised **League of Nations** based on regional blocs and possessing a police force. The ACPFR's existence was sensitive, given U.S. neutrality at the time, and it was abolished in the summer of 1940. *See also* ADVISORY COMMITTEE ON POSTWAR FOREIGN POLICY.

ALIEN REGISTRATION ACT (1940). *See* SMITH ACT.

ALLEN, DEVERE (1891–1955). A **pacifist** Christian socialist, Allen advocated nonviolent resistance to war. While at Oberlin College in 1917, he produced the journal *Radical Patriot* and was influenced by the views of Leyton Richards of the Fellowship of Reconciliation (FOR). He was among the pacifists, social workers, and liberal Christians who advocated programs for the promotion of peace education, **disarmament**, neutrality legislation, international cooperation, and antimilitarism during and after **World War I**. These included people like **Oswald Garrison Villard** and **Norman Thomas** and such organizations as the **Women's International League for Peace and Freedom** (1919) and the **National Council for Prevention of War** (1922).

Allen led the Young Democracy movement in 1918 and edited its journal. It suffered in the Red Scare raids (Palmer raids) in 1919–20, and in 1921 the journal merged with the major pacifist journal, *The World Tomorrow*, founded in 1918 by FOR. Allen was managing editor from 1921 and editor 1925–31. He worked with Villard at the *Nation* from 1931 to 1932 but returned to *The World Tomorrow* when Villard opposed his plan to run for the Senate as a socialist. Under Allen's editorship, *The World Tomorrow* presented opinions on race relations, education, sex, and prison reform as well as antimilitarism. Allen published *The Fight for Peace* in 1930, eloquently expressing the nonviolent philosophies of FOR and the **War Resisters League** and providing the first history of the American peace movement. He was a key member of the Socialist Party in the 1930s. After *The World Tomorrow* folded in 1934, he concentrated on his No-Frontier News Service (NFNS), a center for exchanging information between international peace organizations and propagating their message. The NFNS published the periodical *World Events* (1933–39).

As an active organizer and publicist, Allen was a key member of the peace movement in the interwar years. He became a Quaker in 1941. He found himself in disagreement with many members of the Socialist Party when he refused to modify his pacifism to support armed action to help the republicans in the **Spanish Civil War**. Allen collaborated with Socialist leader Norman Thomas in the **Keep America out of War Congress** (KAOWC) from 1938 to 1941 because he was opposed to the draft and war preparedness on the grounds of his pacifism, not because he accepted **isolationism**. To accommodate Latin American sensibilities about their boundaries, NFNS was renamed Worldover Press in 1942. It continued to function until Allen's death in 1955.

ALLIED MILITARY GOVERNMENT (AMGOT). The AMGOT was the administration put in place by the United States and **Great Britain** in Italian territory liberated from **Germany** during **World War II**. With no role assigned to the **Union of Soviet Socialist Republics**, the AMGOT set the precedent that those nations conducting military occupations would be predominantly responsible for political affairs in the territories that they liberated, for a time span determined by the occupying powers themselves, and shaping relations with civilian authorities as suited their immediate military needs.

ALSOS MISSION. A cooperative project to gain nuclear **intelligence** in **World War II**, the Alsos Mission involved the Office for Scientific Research and Development and the **U.S. Navy** and U.S. Army. It arose out of concern that **Germany** would build an **atomic bomb**. The Alsos Mission collected information on German atomic research and sent teams to Europe at the end of the war to take over German research facilities and capture scientists.

AMERICA FIRST COMMITTEE (AFC). An **isolationist** pressure group, the AFC was created in response to the increasing arms shipments to **Great Britain** under the **cash-and-carry** policy during **World War II**. Yale law student R. Douglas Stuart organized the Emergency Committee to Defend America First in July 1940. On 4 September, following the government's **destroyers-for-bases** deal, it was reestablished on a broader footing as the Committee to Defend America First, commonly called the America First Committee or just America First. It was the most active and effective isolationist group campaigning against increasing U.S. involvement in the war in 1940–41. Its founders were convinced that President **Franklin D. Roosevelt** was deliberately and unconstitutionally leading the United States into the war.

The AFC was chaired by Sears, Roebuck chair **Robert E. Wood**. Stuart became executive secretary. Support came from disparate groups, including **pacifists**, pro-Nazi and German American groups, supporters of **fortress America**, anti-British groups such as Irish Americans, and communists under orders from Moscow to oppose the war (until June 1941, when **Germany** attacked the **Union of Soviet Socialist Republics**). Its leading figures included conservative Senator **Robert Taft**, **progressive** Robert La Follette, former New Dealer Hugh Johnson, advertising executive Chester Bowles, and Chicago financier Sterling Morton. It was largely funded by **Henry Ford**. Its message was promulgated stridently by the newspapers of **William Randolph Hearst** and Colonel Robert McCormick's ultra-isolationist *Chicago Tribune*.

The AFC was strongest in Chicago and the Midwest but had supporters across the nation. Its most popular speaker was **Charles Lindbergh**, who joined the executive committee in April 1941. Lindbergh argued that because Great Britain was bound to be defeated, U.S. resources should be devoted to America's defense. Support for Britain would also run the risk of the United States being drawn into war as in 1917. American values, it was argued, would best be protected by keeping out of any possible connection to the conflict. No other state would attack the United States if it was well armed. The main principles of the AFC were thus that the United States could not be successfully attacked by any foreign power but must build up its own defense, that democracy in the United States could only be preserved by keeping out of the war, and that the policy of "aid short of war" was not an acceptable compromise but would weaken national defense and draw the United States into the conflict.

At its height in 1941, the AFC had a membership of 850,000 in 450 chapters and an income of $370,000 from donations. Rallies featuring Lindbergh, journalist **John T. Flynn**, socialist leader **Norman Thomas**, or Congressmen **Gerald P. Nye**, **Hamilton Fish**, and **Burton K. Wheeler** drew large crowds. Although it did not manage to defeat Roosevelt on any specific measures, its presence acted as a restraint on his actions and shaped some of his caution regarding issues like the draft and naval deployments. The AFC was to lose some of its credibility when speakers, including Lindbergh, verged into crude anti-Semitism, but it remained a significant pressure group until the **Japanese** attack on **Pearl Harbor**, after which it was quickly disbanded. *See also* KEEP AMERICA OUT OF WAR CONGRESS.

AMERICAN–BRITISH–DUTCH–AUSTRALIAN COMMAND (ABDA). A joint command formed on 15 January 1942, ABDA used combined Allied forces to defend the "Malay Barrier" against advancing Japanese forces during **World War II**. Overall command went to British General Archibald Wavell, whose responsibilities ranged over a huge area and involved forces grouped together in an ad hoc manner. Such an arrangement had been discussed in the weeks before **Japan** launched its assaults in December 1941, but little planning had been undertaken. ABDA was further handicapped by the unavailability of reinforcements.

The forces hastily thrown together proved no match for the highly trained and well-equipped Japanese, who enjoyed little local numerical superiority. The major engagements were at sea, where forces under Dutch Admiral Karel Doorman proved unable to even slow down the Japanese advance into the Dutch East Indies. Most of ABDA's naval forces were destroyed in the Battle of the Java Seas on 27 February and in other engagements at this time. ABDA had ceased to exist as a command in the field before it was formally disbanded on 1 March 1942. *See also* COMBINED CHIEFS OF STAFF; WASHINGTON CONFERENCE (1941–42).

AMERICAN CENTURY. A famous editorial in *Life* magazine by owner **Henry Luce** published on 7 February 1941, the "American

Century" argued that the United States should take an active role in world affairs. Americans, Luce argued, should not be afraid to exercise power. They should look to advance U.S. interests, which would be to the benefit of all peace-loving peoples. *See also* WALLACE, HENRY AGARD.

AMERICAN EXPEDITIONARY FORCE (AEF). U.S. military force deployed to Europe in 1917–18 by President **Woodrow Wilson**, the AEF was created to support the Allied Powers against **Germany** and Austria-Hungary in **World War I**. Although **France** and **Great Britain** envisaged U.S. troops reinforcing existing Allied divisions under foreign commanders, the American Expeditionary Force's commanding general, **John J. Pershing**, insisted on complete operational independence. This restriction was relaxed early in 1918, as AEF troops aided Allied armies in repulsing German offensives at Cantigny (May 1918), Belleau Wood (June 1918), and the Second Battle of the Marne (July 1918). The St. Mihiel offensive (September 1918) was the first completely independent AEF assault. Pershing continued to mount offensives up to the day the armistice went into effect (11 November 1918).

By the last months of the war, the combined total of AEF combat troops and support personnel exceeded 2 million. The size of American infantry divisions (around two-and-a-half times larger than most other combat units) and of its air support (estimated at 45 squadrons by November 1918) hastened the collapse of the **Central Powers**. AEF forces were racially segregated. Some 367,000 African Americans were accepted for the draft, and around 100,000 of these went to France with the AEF. Around 42,000 saw active combat, the rest being assigned to labor battalions or other supporting roles. *See also* BAKER, NEWTON DIEHL; PREPAREDNESS CAMPAIGN.

AMERICAN PEACE MOBILIZATION (APM). A communist peace group, the APM was founded in 1940 as a successor to the American League for Peace and Democracy, a communist front organization dissolved when the Nazi–Soviet pact was signed in August 1939. Following the policy of the **Union of Soviet Socialist Republics** to agitate against U.S. aid to **Great Britain**, it held a nonstop peace demonstration outside the White House, but this was abruptly terminated on 21 June 1941 after about six weeks. With the German invasion of the Soviet Union the next day, the APM, like the **Communist Party of the United States**, reversed its line and advocated all-out aid to the Allies, renaming itself American People's Mobilization. In 1948, the APM was listed as a communist front organization on the U.S. attorney general's list of subversive organizations.

AMERICAN PROTECTIVE LEAGUE (APL). A citizen volunteer body organized during **World War I** by a group of Chicago business leaders, the APL assisted federal government departments in the identification and arrest of pro-German spies across the United States. APL volunteers also formed security patrols around munitions factories and helped track down suspected draft dodgers. Based in Washington, D.C., it liaised mainly with the Justice Department.

The **Woodrow Wilson** administration believed the APL could compensate for the lack of military **intelligence** investigators on the home front. The organization had no centralized control system, and no programs for the coordination of activities or training of members. Some groups, such as the Four Minute Men, were affiliated with the APL while working under the direction of George Creel's **Committee on Public Information**. APL units tended to apply their own, often biased assessments of national security threat levels. Consequently, actions both random and unconstitutional were often taken against already unpopular political or social minority groups, such as socialists, **pacifists**, union activists, or German Americans. The Justice Department broke up the APL in 1919, shortly after the end of World War I.

AMERICAN RELIEF ADMINISTRATION (ARA). Established to help coordinate distribution of food and medical supplies in Europe after **World War I**, the ARA was headed by **Herbert Hoover**, former director of the **Commission for Relief in Belgium** (and future secretary of commerce and U.S. president). The ARA played an important role in combating famine and typhus in the 1921–22 **Volga Famine Relief Effort**.

AMERICAN SHOOTING SEASON. Starting in January 1942, six or so German submarines were deployed from Cape Hatteras to the St.

Lawrence to wreak havoc upon U.S. coastal shipping in a period that German submariners called the "American shooting season" or the "second happy time." They were unwittingly aided by U.S. Admiral **Ernest King**'s decision not to introduce coastal convoys, the lack of blackout of ships or towns, and radio indiscipline. German U-boats sunk 1.25 million tons of shipping in three months until the introduction of effective countermeasures drove them back into the mid-Atlantic and the Caribbean in March 1942. A full interlocking system of coastal convoys from the Caribbean to Canada was not in place until May 1942. *See also* UNITED STATES NAVY; WORLD WAR II.

AMERICAN UNION AGAINST MILITARISM (AUAM). A **pacifist** group based in New York, the AUAM was originally formed as the Anti-Militarism Committee in 1915 and renamed the American Union Against Militarism in 1916. Its main aim was to counter the **Woodrow Wilson** administration's **preparedness campaign** and discourage increases in military expenditure. Founder members included women's rights and peace activist **Jane Addams**. AUAM activists did not confine their activities to opposing U.S. entry into **World War I** but also campaigned against militarism in general. They were involved in efforts to prevent a U.S. war with **Mexico** in 1916. In October 1917, a split in AUAM ranks over the organization's tactics and direction led to the establishment of the **National Civil Liberties Bureau** (NCLB), which became the American Civil Liberties Union (ACLU) in January 1920. *See also* WOMEN'S PEACE PARTY.

AMERICAN VOLUNTEER GROUP (AVG). A unit of American fighter pilots also known as the Flying Tigers, the AVG fought in defense of nationalist **China** during **World War II**. The group was founded by General **Claire Chennault**, an advisor to **Chiang Kai-shek**, and was given much adulatory publicity by the pro-Chiang press of **Henry Luce**. Chennault gained Chiang's agreement that volunteers from the U.S. Army and **U.S. Navy** could operate in China against the forces of **Japan**. From September 1941, about 100 pilots and 200 ground crew were recruited and trained at a British airfield in Burma. Three squadrons were formed and trained in the use of Chennault's tactics for aerial warfare. They fought the Japanese in Burma and patrolled from Kunming in China. The AVG distinguished itself in the air battle over Rangoon in February 1942 and went on to operate in defense of Chinese cities. The AVG was intended to be incorporated into Chennault's new China Air Task Force, which was part of the 10th U.S. Army Air Force, but most of the pilots returned home when their contracts expired in July 1942.

ANAPALA PACT (1924). An agreement negotiated by U.S. State Department envoy **Sumner Welles** and representatives of the governments of Guatemala, El Salvador, and **Nicaragua** in 1924, the Anapala Pact blocked the supply of arms and ammunition to the rebel forces of General Tiburcio Carrias, who was fighting against the U.S.-backed government of Honduras, led by President Rafael Guttierez.

ANARCHIST ACT (1918). Passed by the U.S. Congress on 16 October 1918 (amended in June 1920), the Anarchist Act expanded the range of groups whose entry into the United States was proscribed or restricted under the terms of the 1917 **Immigration Act**. The new measure included aliens deemed to be potentially subversive, including anarchists.

ANTI-COMINTERN PACT (1936). In the Anti-Comintern Pact between **Japan** and **Germany** signed on 25 November 1936, the two powers expressed their hostility toward international communism, and in effect toward the **Union of Soviet Socialist Republics (USSR)**. It was part of Nazi foreign policy advisor Joachim von Ribbentrop's plan to shape a foreign policy alignment based on anticommunism. Japan received German recognition of its conquests resulting from the **Manchurian Crisis** (1931–32) in return for its signature. Italy acceded to the pact in 1937. The pact caused Soviet leader **Josef Stalin** to intensify his internal tyranny, and simultaneously to step up the USSR's quest for **collective security** with the Western European powers. Initially, many Americans welcomed this sign of Japan's determination to stand up against the USSR's expansionism in the Far East.

ANTI-DUMPING ACT (1916). The Revenue Act of 1916 (also known as the Anti-Dumping Act) was a trade statute permitting private claims to be brought against any businesses importing goods into the United States at prices deemed to heavily undercut the price levels set by home producers.

ANVIL, OPERATION. *See* DRAGOON, OPERATION.

ARABIC. A White Star liner from **Great Britain**, the *Arabic* was torpedoed in the Atlantic Ocean on 19 August 1915 by a German submarine. Two U.S. citizens were among the 44 dead. The administration of President **Woodrow Wilson** considered suspending diplomatic relations with **Germany** over the incident, but a prompt apology from Germany's ambassador, Johann von Bernstorff, together with an assurance from the German government that passenger ships would henceforth be unharmed unless they resisted interception, temporarily calmed the situation. Advocates of U.S. neutrality during **World War I** regarded the German pledge as a guarantee that U.S. lives and rights of free naval passage were secure. *See also LUSITANIA; SUSSEX.*

ARCADIA MEETING. *See* WASHINGTON CONFERENCE (1941–1942).

ARDENNES. In the heavily forested and hilly Ardennes region of Luxembourg and eastern Belgium came a surprise thrust by German tanks in 1940 that decisively won the battle against France during **World War II**. In December 1944, it was the scene of another surprise attack, operation Autumn Mist, part of the Battle of the **Bulge**, the largest land battle for U.S. forces in Europe in World War II.

ARGENTIA. *See* PLACENTIA BAY MEETING.

ARGENTINA. One of the larger South American republics, Argentina often contested U.S. influence in order to assert its status as a regional power. Between 1900 and 1930, the main focus of U.S. policies toward Argentina was to expand commercial opportunities and secure Argentine legislation that protected U.S. patents, allowed free movement of individuals and capital, and provided open markets for U.S. produce. Argentine leaders welcomed the commerce-based emphasis of relations—there had been bitterness during the 19th century over U.S. tariffs against Argentine wool, which had ended only in 1893. But they remained sensitive to signs that the United States was seeking to dominate the Pan-American Union established in 1890. Argentina was strongly nationalistic and a reluctant participant in the pan-American venture.

With a large population of Spanish and Italian origin, Argentina had close cultural connections to Europe, reinforced by economic ties, and it remained neutral in **World War I**. During the 1930s, Argentina resisted the U.S. attempt to develop pan-Americanism into security coordination. At the conferences of **Buenos Aires** (1936), **Lima** (1938), **Panama** (1939), and **Havana** (1940), Argentina blocked the adoption of any binding commitments to hemispheric defense. Relations with the United States became increasingly strained when it maintained this stance after U.S. entry into **World War II** in December 1941. The regime of Acting President Ramón Castillo had sympathies with the **Axis** powers, particularly Italy. At the **Rio de Janeiro Conference** in January 1942, Argentina continued to resist U.S. schemes for hemispheric defense coordination and led the opposition to the U.S. proposal that all the republics should break off relations with the Axis.

In June 1943, Castillo was overthrown by a coup by the United Officers Group. Elements of the army were strongly pro-Axis and relations with the United States became even more strained. Eventually, in January 1944, diplomatic relations were broken with **Germany** and **Japan**. In February, General Edelmiro Julian Farrell became president, and Colonel Juan Domingo Perón was an increasingly powerful member of the junta, with a strong following from labor. The United States would not recognize Farrell's government, though Ambassador **Norman Armour** remained in Buenos Aires for a time. Argentina was not invited to the conference on war and peace at Chapultepec in Mexico City in February 1945, though a section of Latin Americanists in the State Department led by **Nelson Rockefeller** hoped it would be possible to draw Argentina in. Accordingly, **Mexico** invited Argentina to sign the **Act of Chapultepec**. Seeing that the war was ending, Argentina signed the act and declared war on Germany on 27 March 1945, promising also to purge itself of fascist influences. On 9 April, the United States and the other republics recognized Farrell's regime.

There was controversy at the 1945 **San Francisco Conference** regarding Argentine membership in the **United Nations**. Despite misgivings by President **Harry S. Truman** and members of the U.S. delegation, including **Arthur Vandenberg** and **Tom Connally**, a compromise was struck whereby Argentina was allowed to attend the conference in return for **Latin American** acceptance that two of the constituent republics of the **Union of Soviet Socialist Republics** should receive separate seats. Argentina had thus formally reentered the system of inter-American cooperation, but there continued to be deep misgivings about the Farrell regime and its slowness to remove fascist elements. New U.S. Ambassador **Spruille Braden** expressed these feelings strongly, and further controversy was to erupt in 1945–46 when Braden, now undersecretary for Latin American affairs, tried to prevent the election of Perón by publicizing the "Blue Book," a State Department document that labeled wartime Argentina as pro-Nazi. Perón used the incident as evidence of U.S. interference in Argentine politics and probably gained votes as a result of Braden's action. Perón adopted a neutral stance in the first years of the Cold War, before economic problems made better relations with the United States imperative.

ARIZONA, USS. A U.S. battleship launched in 1914, the *Arizona* was bombed during the first wave of the **Pearl Harbor** attack by Japanese forces during **World War II**. The *Arizona* blew up in a massive explosion, with the loss of 1,103 of the 1,400 on board at the time. The ship was partially salvaged during the war, but the bulk of the wreck remains where it sank. It was dedicated as a national shrine on 30 May 1962, a permanent memorial to those who died at Pearl Harbor.

ARMOUR, NORMAN (1887–1982). Born in England of American parents, Norman Armour graduated from Princeton and from Harvard Law School and had posts in Austria (1912) and **France** (1915–16) before formally entering the Foreign Service. He was second secretary in the embassy in Petrograd (St. Petersburg), **Russia**, from 1916 until the Bolsheviks came to power after the **Russian Revolution**. Armour escaped using a fake passport and helped Princess Myra Koudacheff escape. They were married in Brussels in 1919.

Armour served in Belgium, the Netherlands, and Uruguay before being posted to the State Department (1922–24). He then served in **Japan** (1925–28) and France (1928–32). In 1932, he was minister to Haiti, where he worked on the termination of the U.S. occupation. He was minister to Canada (1935–38) and ambassador to Chile (1938–39) and **Argentina** (1939–44). He pressed Argentina not to support the **Axis** powers during **World War II**, and Argentina broke off relations with the Axis on 26 January 1944, but a new government was then formed led by Edelmiro Julian Farrell and dominated by elements of the army, which was pro-Axis. The United States refused to recognize the new government, although Armour remained in Buenos Aires until June 1944. He was acting chief of the Division of Latin American Affairs in the State Department, served as ambassador to Spain in 1945, and then retired but ended his retirement to be assistant secretary for political affairs in the State Department in 1947–48. He later served as ambassador to Venezuela (1950–51) and Guatemala (1954–55). In 1954, he defended the State Department against accusations by the anticommunist Senator Joseph McCarthy. The *New York Times* once called Armour "the perfect diplomat." *See also* BRADEN, SPRUILLE; LATIN AMERICA.

ARMS CONTROL. *See* DISARMAMENT AND ARMS CONTROL.

ARMSTRONG, HAMILTON FISH (1893–1973). Foreign policy expert Hamilton Fish Armstrong was named after his great uncle Hamilton Fish, who was secretary of state to President Ulysses S. Grant. Following graduation from Princeton, Armstrong joined the staff of the *New Republic* magazine but enlisted in the army in 1917. He was military attaché to the Serbian war mission in the United States and in November 1918 was posted to Belgrade as assistant military attaché. Discharged from the army in June 1919, he joined the *New York Evening Post* as special correspondent for Eastern Europe. Deeply interested in foreign affairs, he became involved with the new **Council on Foreign Relations** (CFR). In 1922, he became managing editor of the CFR's journal, *Foreign Affairs*, and later its editor (1928–72). He was executive director of the CFR (1922–28) and remained a director until 1972.

Armstrong met many U.S. and world leaders and served on many committees, including the President's Advisory Committee on Refugees, as a trustee of the Woodrow Wilson Foundation, and three times as a delegate to the International Studies Conference. During **World War II**, Armstrong served on the State Department **Advisory Committee on Postwar Foreign Policy** (1942–44). In 1944, he became special assistant to the U.S. ambassador in London, with the rank of minister, and in 1944–45 was special advisor to Secretary of State **Edward R. Stettinius**. He worked on drafting the charter of the **United Nations** and at the 1945 **San Francisco Conference** was a senior advisor with the U.S. delegation.

Armstrong was a prolific writer. Among his publications are *Can We Be Neutral?* (1936) co-authored with **Allen W. Dulles**, *"We or They": Two Worlds in Conflict* (1937), *When There Is No Peace* (1939), *Can America Stay Neutral?* (1939) also with Dulles, and *Chronology of Failure* (1940).

ARNOLD, HENRY HARLEY (1886–1950). In **World War II**, "Hap" Arnold was made deputy chief of staff for the U.S. Army Air Force (USAAF) in 1941. He set up the 8th USAAF in **Great Britain** in 1942 and in March 1942 was made commander of the U.S. Army Air Force. He organized and trained the largest air force in the world: 2.5 million people and 95,000 aircraft. He received the Distinguished Service Medal in September 1942 for undertaking a 77-hour, non-stop flight from Brisbane to San Francisco. Arnold also served on the **Joint Chiefs of Staff** and **Combined Chiefs of Staff**. With his promotion in March 1943, he became the first full general of the USAAF. In December 1944, he was made a five-star general.

ARSENAL OF DEMOCRACY. U.S. President **Franklin D. Roosevelt** used the phrase "arsenal of democracy" in his fireside chat of 29 December 1940 to denote the U.S. role in the defeat of Nazi **Germany** during **World War II**. Roosevelt identified the success of **Great Britain** and its allies as vital to U.S. national security and claimed that they were fighting for the values that Americans cherished—but the American contribution to their victory would be the production of arms for them to use, rather than actual fighting. The policy reflected public opinion of the time, which favored aid to the

Allies, but not entry into the war. *See also* COMMITTEE TO DE-
FEND AMERICA BY AIDING THE ALLIES; FIGHT FOR FREE-
DOM COMMITTEE; FOUR FREEDOMS; LEND-LEASE.

ATHERTON, RAY (1883–1960). Ray Atherton graduated from Harvard in 1905, worked in banking, studied architecture in Paris for
four years, then joined the Foreign Service. Early postings were to
Tokyo (1917–19), Peking (1919–21), the **Philippines** (1921), and
Athens (1923), with service in the State Department (1922–23 and
1924). Atherton was temporary ambassador to Greece (1923–24) and
first secretary and subsequently counselor at the London embassy
(1924–37). He was an advisor at the 1930 and 1935–36 **London
Naval Disarmament Conferences** and was minister to Bulgaria
(1937–39) and Denmark (1939–40). He was also acting chair of the
Wheat Advisory Commission, London, in 1939.

As head of the State Department's Division of European Affairs
in 1940–43, Atherton received the notification from the German Embassy on 11 December 1941 that was in effect a declaration of war.
In 1943, Atherton was briefly minister to the exiled Luxembourg
government in Canada and then served as minister and later ambassador to Canada (1943–48).

ATLANTIC CHARTER. A statement of fundamental principles for
the postwar world, the Atlantic Charter was agreed to by U.S. President **Franklin D. Roosevelt** and British Prime Minister **Winston
Churchill** at the **Placentia Bay** meeting of 9–12 August 1941, during **World War II**. It was later adopted as the war aims of the Allies
in the **United Nations Declaration**.

The charter was a set of general principles rather than specific aims.
Its eight points affirmed commitment to **collective security**, freedom
of the seas, national self-determination (people should be free to
live under governments "of their own choosing"), and liberalization
of **trade**. The "aggressor nations" would be disarmed, pending the
establishment of a general system of security. The signatories denied
any ambition to add to their territory. By agreeing to joint aims with
a belligerent, the United States had symbolically broken with its isolationist policy and signaled its unneutrality in the conflict.

The vague generalities of the charter obscured disappointments on both sides. The British failed to get a commitment to U.S. membership in a new world organization. They merely obtained an endorsement of a "wider and permanent system of general security." The U.S. desire for a commitment to free trade came up against British concern to protect their system of imperial preference; free access to trade and raw materials was endorsed, but "with due respect for existing obligations." On reading these words, Secretary of State Cordell Hull was "keenly disappointed." Churchill made clear that commitment to self-determination was in no sense a promise to dismantle the British empire.

The Atlantic Charter was widely publicized as showing the shared commitment of the Allies to the fight for essential liberties. A month later, the **Union of Soviet Socialist Republics** acceded to the charter, though indicating it did not accept the precise wording. The 13 other nations at war with the Axis at that time also endorsed the document, and it was specifically referred to in the **United Nations Declaration**. However, the document was not in any way a definite plan, and no procedures were proposed at Placentia Bay or subsequently for its implementation or enforcement, nor was it referred to at subsequent conferences. Its principal value was as a propaganda document, signaling at the time of its signature that there was growing U.S.–British collaboration, and giving a positive alternative to the New Order schemes of **Germany** and **Japan**. *See also* BRETTON WOODS CONFERENCE; DECLARATION ON LIBERATED EUROPE.

ATOMIC BOMB. A weapon developed during **World War II**, the atomic bomb uses the massive energy released by nuclear fission. When radioactive isotopes, such as Uranium 235, are bombarded with neutrons, a chain reaction is initiated, producing a huge explosion. Scientists working in the **Manhattan Project** produced two different types of atomic bomb in World War II. The plutonium bomb was tested on 16 July 1945 near Alamogordo, New Mexico, generating an explosive power equivalent to about 20,000 tons of TNT. Such a bomb, nicknamed "Fat Man," was used on **Nagasaki** on 9 August 1945. The uranium bomb was not tested; nicknamed "Little Boy," it was detonated for the first time over **Hiroshima** on 6 August 1945.

Controversy continues as to whether the bombs were necessary to end the war with **Japan** or whether Japan would have surrendered before an invasion of the Japanese homeland took place. Some argue that the bombs were dropped to demonstrate U.S. power to the **Union of Soviet Socialist Republics** and to try to moderate its behavior. Others argue that President **Harry S. Truman** and his advisors were mainly concerned to end the war as quickly as possible and made the decision to use the atomic bombs on military grounds. *See also* AL-SOS MISSION; BUSH, VANNEVAR; CONANT, JAMES BRYANT; FERMI, ENRICO; GROVES, LESLIE; OPPENHEIMER, JULIUS ROBERT; STIMSON, HENRY LEWIS.

AVIATION, CIVIL. An international convention signed in Paris in 1919 was the first international arrangement dealing with civil aviation. The rapid development of airplanes during and after **World War I** and their potential for the transport of people, goods, and mail raised novel challenges for international relations and intricate legal questions concerning airspace. A pan-American convention on civil aviation was adopted at the 1928 **Havana Conference** to deal with issues raised by the increasing number of flights that crossed national borders. By the end of the 1930s, however, although there had been some progress on international flight regulations, most nations were very protective of their own airlines and granted very few facilities to those of others.

No agreement had yet been reached that permitted aircraft to fly nonstop over the territory of one country en route to another. The United States had been a pioneer of long-distance civil air flights because of the size of the nation, coupled with its economic integration. American airlines, such as Pan-American, were pioneers of international scheduled flights. The United States was particularly anxious therefore to remove political barriers to the exploitation of the potential of commercial aviation—it was in a sense simply an aspect of the drive for freedom of **trade** and a liberal economic order advocated by Secretary of State **Cordell Hull**, his advisor **William Clayton,** and others, and encapsulated in the 1944 **Bretton Woods** agreements.

The matter was dealt with at the 1944 **Chicago Conference**. The International Civil Aviation Organization was created, though it did not come into operation until 1947. International standards for signals and navigation were established. It was harder to agree on the economics of aviation: U.S. preference for a free market came up against the preference of **Great Britain** for regulation. The result was a compromise, but it still provided the basis for the rapid expansion of civil aviation after **World War II**.

AXIS POWERS. The Axis is the name commonly given to the cooperation of Nazi **Germany** and Fascist Italy after Italian dictator Benito Mussolini spoke of a "Rome–Berlin Axis" on 1 November 1936. It was supplemented by the **Anti-Comintern Pact** between Germany and **Japan** on 25 November 1936, which was joined by Italy in 1937. On 22 May 1939, a formal treaty was signed between Germany and Italy, the "Pact of Steel." In September 1940, Germany, Italy, and Japan signed the **Tripartite Pact**, and the three were commonly known in **World War II** as the Axis powers, together with their smaller allies and satellites. It was a loose alliance, with little coordination of strategy, though there was a small amount of technological and **intelligence** exchange, and Italian forces fought under German command in North Africa and in the **Union of Soviet Socialist Republics**. Ironically, one of the unintentional effects of the Axis benefited the Allies: because the United States was reading Japan's diplomatic correspondence through Operation **Magic**, the reports of Japan's envoys in Berlin were an important source of information on the political and economic situation in Nazi-controlled Europe.

– B –

BACKDOOR TO WAR THEORY. Some historians and political critics of President **Franklin D. Roosevelt** immediately after **World War II** advanced the claim that the disaster of **Pearl Harbor** was not a result of the United States being taken by surprise, but was connived at by the president as a way of getting into war against **Germany**, something that his provocative acts in the Atlantic Ocean had failed to do. They argued that he thus found a "backdoor to war," a way to avoid the nation's strong **isolationism**. The claim was based on the absence of crucial U.S. aircraft carriers from Pearl Harbor on the day of the attack, and on claims that Operation **Magic** had provided details of the plan for **Japan**'s attack.

The backdoor theory was generally rejected at the time, as it seemed ludicrous that a president would enter a war by sacrificing major warships. There was also a powerful argument that the Japanese attack made a war with Germany less likely, not more. The theory was revived by some revisionist historians in the 1960s, notably by Bruce Russett. With the growing interest in **intelligence** and enthusiasm for conspiracy theories, the idea has had a number of adherents since the 1980s. It is also claimed that **Winston Churchill** played a major part in the conspiracy by keeping back vital intelligence to ensure that the United States was drawn into the war to save the British empire. But the theorists have not been able to show that there was unambiguous evidence of Japan's intention to attack Pearl Harbor, or that the failure to act effectively was deliberate rather than the result of errors fueled by overconfidence and mistaken assumptions about the Japanese.

BAKER, NEWTON DIEHL (1871–1937). Newton Baker was secretary of war (1916–21) in the Woodrow Wilson administration and a strong supporter of the appointment of General **John J. Pershing** as commander of the **American Expeditionary Force** (AEF) in **World War I**. Baker oversaw the military conscription system which eventually mobilized 4,355,000 American citizens during the war. On the domestic front, he authorized the use of American troops in Washington, D.C., and in Mobile, Chicago, and other cities to quell race riots in 1919. He was a member of the delegation accompanying President Wilson to the 1919 **Paris Peace Conference** and was a prominent supporter of U.S. membership in the **League of Nations**, having helped to draft its founding charter.

In 1921, Baker retired from politics and resumed his law practice until invited by President-elect **Herbert Hoover** to serve as a U.S. representative at the **World Court**. When deadlock threatened the 1932 Democratic national nominating convention in Chicago, Baker was considered as a potential compromise candidate and was reputedly the rival most feared by supporters of the eventual nominee, New York Governor **Franklin D. Roosevelt**. The Roosevelt administration later invited Baker to chair a congressional committee examining the state of the U.S. Army Air Corps (1934).

BALCH, EMILY GREENE (1867–1961). Peace campaigner and writer Emily Greene Balch was among the first graduates of Bryn Mawr in 1889. She studied at the Sorbonne in Paris and at Berlin University, and she founded the Denison House settlement in Boston in 1892 and the Boston Women's Trade Union League in 1905. She completed ground-breaking research on eastern and southeastern European immigrants and became a professor of economics and sociology at Wellesley College in 1913.

After **World War I** broke out in 1914, Balch became committed to the cause of peace. In 1915, she was a founding member of the **Women's International League for Peace and Freedom** (WILPF) at The Hague. She campaigned against U.S. entry into the war in the **Women's Peace Party**, meeting with President **Woodrow Wilson** to argue her case. She served on a congressional delegation to **Russia** and Scandinavia to promote mediation in the conflict and was a member of the Neutral Conference for Continuous Mediation in Stockholm in 1915.

Wellesley terminated Balch's contract in 1918 because of these activities and her associations with the Women's Trade Union League, and she became an editor for the liberal magazine the *Nation*, as well as secretary of the WILPF. Balch became a Quaker in 1921. She visited Haiti in 1926 and urged the ending of the U.S. occupation. She also campaigned in favor of the **League of Nations** and on issues such as **disarmament**, drug control, and internationalization of waterways and aviation. In the 1930s, she campaigned for aid for refugees from Nazi **Germany**. She was secretary of the WILPF in Geneva (1919–22), president of the U.S. section of the WILPF (1928–33), joint chair of the WILPF international executive committee (1929–32), honorary international secretary (1934–35), and honorary president (1937–61).

Horrified by Nazi Germany, Balch modified her **pacifism** and supported the U.S. effort during **World War II**, while pressing for long-term internationalist solutions. She won a Nobel Peace Prize in 1946 in recognition of her work with the WILPF. She was only the second

U.S. woman to win this prize, after **Jane Addams**, with whom she had campaigned. *See also* DETZER, DOROTHY.

BANK FOR INTERNATIONAL SETTLEMENTS (BIS). A banking institution established as a result of the **Young Plan** (1929), the BIS was originally conceived as a central clearing house for reparations and debt repayments. The bank continued into the 21st century as an institution encouraging cooperation and coordination among international banks.

BARUCH, BERNARD (1870–1965). Financier and presidential advisor Bernard Baruch was wealthy by the age of 30 as a result of successful speculation on Wall Street. During **World War I**, Baruch was chair of the War Industries Board (1918–19) and advised on national defense and mobilization of the economy. He was an economic advisor to President **Woodrow Wilson** at the 1919 **Paris Peace Conference** and helped shape the economic provisions of the **Treaty of Versailles**.

Baruch coordinated U.S. strategy at the 1933 **London Economic Conference** and had hoped to be appointed secretary of state by President **Franklin D. Roosevelt**. Baruch was a close friend of Hugh Johnson's and had a significant following in Congress that Roosevelt had to take into account. However, Baruch was not a New Dealer and his influence with Roosevelt faded by 1936. Eleanor Roosevelt was on better terms with him and agreed with him that the United States needed to rearm in the face of the fascist threat. Baruch was one of the originators of the **cash-and-carry** modification of the 1937 **Neutrality Act**.

Baruch was touted by the press to mastermind U.S. preparedness as war started in Europe in 1939, but Roosevelt kept him at arm's length. Baruch believed Roosevelt should move faster and put greater effort into rearming the United States in 1940–41 and because of this criticism, remained excluded from policy making. As a result of his experience in World War I, Baruch pressed that there should be a war resources administrator with centralized control of the economy, but this idea did not appeal to Roosevelt, who preferred to work through a number of competing agencies. After the United States entered the war, Baruch was special advisor to fellow South Carolinian **James**

F. Byrnes. In 1943, he authored a report on postwar reconversion of the economy. After the war, Baruch was representative to the United Nations Atomic Energy Commission and formulated the Baruch plan for international control of atomic energy.

BATISTA Y ZALDIVAR, FULGENCIO (1901–1973). Dictator of **Cuba** in 1934–44 and 1952–58, Fulgencio Batista was a sergeant in the Cuban army and participated in the coup against President **Gerardo Machado** in July 1933. He then led the "Sergeant's Revolution" on 5 September 1933 that made Ramón Grau San Martín president. He promoted himself to colonel and was encouraged by U.S. Ambassador **Sumner Welles** to conspire against Grau, whom Welles regarded as too radical. Cuban army leaders agreed and in January 1934 Batista seized power. Although not officially president at first, Batista established himself as dictator, building a fascistic corporate state until 1937 when he allowed political parties to form. He received support from the United States, which abrogated the **Platt Amendment** and provided loans through the **Export-Import Bank**. Cuban sugar imports to the United States were given a favorable tariff in the **Jones–Costigan Act**.

In a free election in 1939, Batista was elected president. He retired from office in 1944 and went to live in the Dominican Republic. He returned to power in Cuba by means of a coup in 1952 and established a one-party dictatorship, with close connection to the American Mafia. He lost support, even of his own army, because of his corruption and oppression. After a three-year insurgency, he was overthrown by Fidel Castro. Batista left for exile in the Dominican Republic on 31 December 1958.

BATTALION OF DEATH. Journalists and financiers campaigning against U.S. membership of the **League of Nations** in 1919–20 gained the nickname "battalion of death." *See also* BORAH, WILLIAM EDGAR; IRRECONCILABLES.

BERLE, ADOLF A. (1895–1971). Lawyer Adolf Berle served in army **intelligence** in **World War I** and was part of the U.S. delegation to the 1919 **Paris Peace Conference**. He subsequently became involved in New York politics and was a member of the "brains trust" that advised Governor **Franklin D. Roosevelt**. When Roosevelt became president in 1933, Berle was appointed assistant secretary of state, but he advised on a wide range of issues, including the economic recession in 1937. Berle favored government planning and control rather than outright antitrust measures. He served as ambassador to **Brazil** in 1945–46. During President John F. Kennedy's administration in the 1960s, he chaired a task force on **Latin America**.

BERLIN, TREATY OF (1921). A separate peace treaty signed between the United States and **Germany** on 25 August 1921, the Treaty of Berlin brought a formal end to the state of hostilities that had existed between the two nations since April 1917. The separate peace settlement was needed because the U.S. Senate had failed (in 1919 and 1920) to ratify the **Treaty of Versailles**. The Berlin Treaty was signed by President **Warren G. Harding** on 2 July 1921 and came into effect on 26 November. *See also* KNOX–PORTER RESOLUTION; ST. GERMAIN, TREATY OF; TRIANON, TREATY OF.

BIDDLE, ANTHONY JOSEPH DREXEL, JR. (1897–1961). The son of a millionaire, Anthony Drexel Biddle Jr. served in the U.S. Marine Corps during **World War I**. He was then involved in the shipping business before being appointed minister to Norway (1935–37). Subsequently, he was ambassador to **Poland** (1937–43), witnessing **Germany**'s invasion. He then moved to London with the exiled Polish government. From 1941 to 1943, he was also minister and later ambassador to other allied governments in exile in London, from Norway, Belgium, Yugoslavia, Greece, Czechoslovakia, and the Netherlands. He was ambassador to Spain in 1961.

BIDDLE, FRANCIS BEVERLEY (1886–1968). Born in Paris, **France**, Francis Biddle was the son of a law professor and received a law degree from Harvard. In 1935, President **Franklin D. Roosevelt** made him chair of the National Labor Relations Board. In 1939, he became a circuit judge for the Court of Appeals and in 1940 became U.S. solicitor general. From 1941 to 1945, Biddle was attorney general. Although a civil libertarian, Biddle was responsible on 7 December 1941 for issuing instructions to the **Federal Bureau of Investigation** to arrest enemy aliens, which was the precursor of

Federal Order 9066, providing for the internment of Japanese Americans during **World War II**. Roosevelt's successor, President **Harry S. Truman**, asked Biddle to resign but appointed him to be a judge at the **International Military Tribunal** at Nuremberg, which tried Nazis for war crimes. Biddle was a member of the American Civil Liberties Union and, after the war, of Americans for Democratic Action.

BIG THREE. The United States, **Great Britain**, and the **Union of Soviet Socialist Republics** were the three major Allies in the struggle against the **Axis** powers in **World War II** and were commonly known as "the Big Three." The term was also frequently applied to their three leaders, **Franklin D. Roosevelt**, **Winston Churchill**, and **Josef Stalin**. *See also* GRAND ALLIANCE; MOSCOW CONFERENCE; POTSDAM CONFERENCE; TEHERAN CONFERENCE; YALTA CONFERENCE.

BLISS, TASKER HOWARD (1853–1930). Tasker Bliss served in Puerto Rico in the 1898 Spanish–American War and then was collector of customs in Havana, **Cuba** (1899–1902). He participated in the negotiation of the treaty with Cuba in 1902. He subsequently served as president of the Army War College and as commander in Luzon, **Philippines**. In 1915, he became the U.S. Army's assistant chief of staff. In this position, he oversaw mobilization of the army for **World War I**.

Bliss served as chief of staff of the army from 1917 to 1918. On his retirement, President **Woodrow Wilson** kept him in his rank of full general, and he was appointed to the Allied Supreme War Council in **France**. Bliss was a delegate to the 1919 **Paris Peace Conference**. He supported U.S. membership in the **League of Nations**. After retirement in 1919, he was governor of the Soldier's Home in Washington, D.C.

BOHLEN, CHARLES EUSTIS (1904–1974). Charles "Chip" Bohlen graduated from Harvard in 1927 and entered the Foreign Service in 1928. He was trained by **Robert F. Kelley** in analysis of the **Union of Soviet Socialist Republics** (USSR) and was posted to Moscow in 1934–35 and 1938–41, succeeding to his friend **George F. Kennan**'s position in the embassy. Bohlen was appointed liaison between the State Department and the White House during **World War II**. He acted as interpreter for President **Franklin D. Roosevelt** at the 1943 **Teheran Conference** and accompanied Roosevelt to the 1945 **Yalta Conference**. Unlike Kennan, he came to accept Roosevelt's belief that a friendly cooperative relationship could be achieved with Soviet leader **Josef Stalin**.

After the war, Bohlen was a counselor at the State Department, and his views moved back toward being more critical of the Soviet Union. He became ambassador to the USSR in 1953, despite opposition by Senator Joseph McCarthy. But Secretary of State **John Foster Dulles** believed Bohlen to be associated with appeasement of Stalin at Yalta and moved him to the **Philippines** in 1957. He was subsequently ambassador to **France** (1962–68) and deputy undersecretary of state (1969).

BOHR, NIELS (1885–1962). Danish nuclear physicist Niels Bohr won the Nobel Prize for Physics in 1922. Bohr was the leading nuclear physicist of the interwar period. He escaped from occupied Denmark to Sweden in September 1943 and was instrumental in gaining sanctuary for most of Denmark's Jews in Sweden. In the United States, Bohr worked as an advisor on the **Manhattan Project**. In 1944, he attempted to persuade U.S. President **Franklin D. Roosevelt** and British Prime Minister **Winston Churchill** to invite the **Union of Soviet Socialist Republics** to join in atomic research during the war. He hoped this would lead to the internationalization of atomic weapons and avoid a postwar arms race. Churchill and Roosevelt rejected the advice at the 1944 **Quebec Conference** and resolved to keep information of the project from their Soviet ally, concluding the 1944 **Hyde Park Agreement** soon afterward. Churchill regarded Bohr as a security risk as a result of this proposal, and he was placed under surveillance, although Bohr was not suggesting the actual passing of nuclear secrets to the Soviet Union. *See also* OPPENHEIMER, JULIUS ROBERT.

BOLERO, OPERATION. Operation Bolero was the buildup of U.S. troops and materiel for the invasion of Europe in **World War II**. When the United States entered the war, the agreed strategy was the updated **Plan Dog** approved by U.S. President **Franklin D. Roosevelt** and British Prime Minister **Winston Churchill** at the 1941 **Placentia Bay Conference**. This plan set the priority of defeating **Germany** first. U.S. Army planners believed the way to do this would be through an attack on German-held northern **France**. In early 1942, Army Chief of Staff **George C. Marshall** presented to Roosevelt a plan for the amassing of U.S. forces in **Great Britain** for an invasion of France within the year. Marshall argued that the need was to confront Germany quickly, before turning to defeat **Japan**.

In April 1942, Marshall and presidential aide **Harry Hopkins** traveled to London to develop the plan but met strong opposition from the British military, who believed it would be impossible in 1942. This clash over fundamental strategy was to be the central issue in relations between the United States and Britain through to the end of 1943. Although Roosevelt stated in June 1942 to Vyacheslav Molotov, commissar for foreign affairs of the **Union of Soviet Socialist Republics**, that they were urgently addressing the need for a **second front**, the British remained adamant. The result was that at the June 1942 **Washington Conference**, Roosevelt overruled the **Joint Chiefs of Staff** and agreed to Operation **Torch**, so that U.S. troops would be engaged against German troops as soon as possible. The invasion of France was to take place in 1943, as Operation Round-up. The buildup of U.S. forces in Britain was to be Operation Bolero. Bolero had originally been the U.S. Army's codename for Great Britain as a theater of war.

A combined U.S.–British committee was set up to plan this unprecedented movement of troops, weapons, supplies, and aircraft, with sections in both London and Washington, D.C. The committee drew up plans to transport and accommodate 1,147,000 troops by the end of March 1943. However, Bolero proceeded more slowly than expected, hampered by the need to defeat German submarines in the Atlantic and by delays in completing Operation Torch. After the January 1943 **Casablanca Conference**, the rate of buildup of U.S. troops under Bolero was increased and a planning staff (named COSSAC) was established. However, the decision taken at Casablanca to invade Sicily in Operation **Husky** meant that Round-up was postponed to 1944, though this was not explicitly accepted by Marshall, or communicated to the Soviet government, until the summer of 1943. The invasion was renamed Operation **Overlord**. Under Bolero, a total of over 1.5 million U.S. troops and 250,000 Canadians was assembled in Great Britain for this operation by June 1944. *See also* GRAND ALLIANCE.

BORAH, WILLIAM EDGAR (1865–1940). A leading attorney in Idaho, William E. Borah served in the U.S. Congress as a **progressive** Republican in 1907–40. Nicknamed "the Lion of Idaho" and "the Great Opposer," Borah supported the antitrust campaigns of Presidents **Theodore Roosevelt** and **William Howard Taft**. In foreign policy, he parted company with the administration of **Woodrow Wilson** and was the principal leader of the Senate's **Irreconcilables**, opposing ratification of the **Treaty of Versailles** and U.S. participation in the **League of Nations**. The basis of Borah's opposition was his hostility to entangling alliances: as he put it in 1919, "America has arisen to a position where she is respected and admired by the entire world. She did it by minding her own business."

Borah supported the advancement of world peace through conventional forms of international dialogue, including bilateral treaties and cultural links, but he deeply distrusted the establishment of supranational bodies such as the League. He contended that European and American concepts of democracy were incompatible and refused to attend a meeting with President Wilson to discuss possible avenues of compromise. Borah feared that U.S. membership, with or without the **Lodge reservations**, would undermine America's sovereign right to defend its own territory and interests. He spearheaded the nationwide campaign against membership in 1919, gathering press support and financial backing from multimillionaire business leaders such as **Andrew W. Mellon**. His backers were nicknamed the "**battalion of death**."

Borah chaired the **Senate Committee on Foreign Relations** in 1924–33, succeeding **Henry Cabot Lodge**. During his tenure, he organized resistance to tentative efforts by the **Calvin Coolidge** administration to secure U.S. membership of the **World Court**. Somewhat ironically, Borah was an enthusiastic supporter of the **Kellogg–Briand Pact**, a multinational, collaborative effort aiming to abolish war through international cooperation and mediation. He favored recognition of the **Union of Soviet Socialist Republics** and had unofficial contacts with the Soviet government. In 1931, Borah declared his support for revision of the Treaty of Versailles and the **Treaty of Trianon**, which was also produced at the 1919 **Paris Peace Conference** and dealt with Hungary. In 1932, he opposed the revocation of **war debts** as a means to cure the Great Depression. Borah attempted to secure his party's nomination for president in 1936; having failed, he refused to endorse the Republican candidate.

BOWMAN, ISAIAH (1878–1950). Born in Ontario, Canada, Isaiah Bowman gained a Ph.D. in geography from Yale in 1909. He taught geography at Yale (1905–15) and was director of the American Geographical Society (1915–35). He went on three expeditions to South America between 1907 and 1913. Bowman was chief territorial advisor to President **Woodrow Wilson** at the 1919 **Paris Peace Conference**. He became a director of the newly founded **Council on Foreign Relations** (CFR) in 1921. He was on the executive committee of the National Research Council (1919–29) and then chair (1933–35). He was president of Johns Hopkins University (1935–48), president of the International Geographical Union (1931–35), and vice president of the National Academy of Sciences (1940–45).

Bowman was chair of the CFR's War and Peace Studies territorial group before and during **World War II**, and he was vice president of the CFR in 1945–49. A territorial advisor to the State Department during the war, Bowman served on the **Advisory Committee on Postwar Foreign Policy** and the Informal Political Agenda Group. He was a contributor to U.S. planning with regard to the structure of the future **United Nations**.

BRACERO **PROGRAM (1942–1964).** A labor agreement between the United States and **Mexico**, the *bracero* program was devised during **World War II**, when the induction of men into the military, together with the internment of 112,000 Japanese Americans, who mostly worked in the agricultural sector, created a serious shortage of farm workers in the western United States. The *bracero* agreement was reached with the Mexican government in 1942. It brought 200,000 workers, known as *braceros*, into the United States on temporary work visas. Most were laborers on fruit or grain farms, though some went into construction and worked on the railroads. Initially, Texas was excluded as a destination for the *braceros*, as the State Department feared that attitudes to Hispanic laborers there might provoke a diplomatic incident with Mexico and threaten the **Good Neighbor** policy. The *bracero* arrangement was mutually satisfactory for both the United States and Mexico and continued long after the end of the war.

BRADEN, SPRUILLE (1894–1978). Spruille Braden graduated from Yale in 1914 and was involved in various business ventures in Chile from 1914 to 1925. He was a delegate to the 1933 **Montevideo Conference** and led the U.S. delegation to the **Chaco War** peace negotiations (1935–38). He was ambassador to Colombia (1939–42) and **Cuba** (1942–45), where he was on bad terms with **Fulgencio Batista**. Similarly, while ambassador in Buenos Aires, **Argentina**, from May to September 1945, he attracted the enmity of the regime of Edelmiro Fennell and Juan Perón by publicly siding with its opponents and publicizing the State Department's "Blue Book" assessment that Argentina was pro-Nazi. Braden was withdrawn and made assistant secretary of state for American Republic Affairs, a post he held until he returned to private business in 1947. *See also* MESSERSMITH, GEORGE STRAUSSER; ROCKEFELLER, NELSON ALDRICH.

BRANDEGEE, FRANK BOSWORTH (1864–1924). Lawyer Frank Brandegee was elected to the House of Representatives from Connecticut in 1902 and became a senator in 1905. He served on the Senate Committee on Panama and the Committee on Interoceanic Canals (1911–13). One of the Senate **Irreconcilables** who opposed U.S. membership of the League of Nations, he exerted pressure on the **Senate Committee on Foreign Relations** chair **Henry Cabot Lodge** to resist compromise with the **Woodrow Wilson** administration. Brandegee was chair of the Senate Judiciary Committee when he committed suicide on 14 October 1924. *See also* ROUND ROBIN; VERSAILLES, TREATY OF.

BRAZIL. Occupying almost half of the South American continent, Brazil has been a rival of the United States for influence in **Latin America**. During the 19th century, relations were generally friendly but distant. They grew more cordial after the Brazilian military overthrew the monarchy in 1889 and established a republic. Brazil sought a close relationship with the United States, supported it in the 1898 war with Spain, and backed the **Roosevelt Corollary** and U.S. policies toward **Mexico** and Panama. In 1906, Brazil became the first Latin American state to exchange envoys with the rank of ambassador with the United States. But the United States did not meet the Brazilian desire to create a special relationship, preferring to treat all Latin American states equally.

Once **World War I** broke out in Europe in 1914, U.S. businesses seized the opportunity to challenge the dominance of **Great Britain** in the Brazilian market. U.S. officials sought Brazilian manganese and rubber for U.S. industry, and coffee and sugar exports to the United States increased. By 1918, the United States controlled over 40 percent of Brazil's foreign trade.

After the United States entered the war in April 1917, a determined effort was made to induce Brazil to join the war as well. Brazil did so, and subsequently supported President **Woodrow Wilson** at the 1919 **Paris Peace Conference**. Wilson, however, did not give any special regard to Brazilian viewpoints in return. After the war, more U.S. attention was devoted to getting cooperation from **Argentina**, which had remained neutral, and little importance was attached to Brazil, which was seen as backward and unimportant. Despite levels of trade, there was no inclination to give Brazil any special treatment in economic matters.

Unlike the militaries in other Latin American countries at this time, the Brazilian military maintained close contacts and good relations with U.S. armed forces. The military regarded itself as a nation-building force, with the emphasis on order and security. U.S. policy makers primarily sought a stable Brazil, and thus were in accord with the attitudes of the Brazilian armed forces, the most influential element in Brazilian politics. The United States had long regarded domestic order as the most important issue in Brazil and supported the authoritarian regime of President Getulio Vargas, which ruled Brazil in 1930–45 and 1951–54. U.S. officials claimed that although it was a dictatorship, it was rooted in popular support.

The rise of the power of **Germany** and **Japan** in the 1930s brought increased U.S. interest in developing solidarity with the states of South America. The administration of **Franklin D. Roosevelt** supplemented its declared **Good Neighbor** policy with an increasing emphasis on shared hemispheric security interests. Brazil's support was sought for U.S. initiatives. The Brazilian military was pressed to replace **Axis** suppliers with U.S. companies. After 1939, cut off from Europe, Brazil depended increasingly on U.S. military equipment and training. The joint Brazilian–U.S. Defense Commission coordinated defense policies, effectively bringing Brazil more tightly under U.S. leadership.

After the United States entered **World War II**, Brazil was again pressed to follow suit as an example for the other Latin American states. Vargas had little choice but to cooperate with the United States once communications with Europe became interrupted by the war. Brazil hosted the 1942 **Rio de Janeiro Conference** and declared war on Germany soon afterward. The pretext was that Brazilian vessels had been sunk by German submarines. Unlike other Latin American states, Brazil went so far as to send an expeditionary force to fight the **Axis** in Europe. However, after the war, the United States still preferred to develop a hemispheric policy rather than focus on a special relationship with Brazil, while pressing once again for Brazil to set an example in anticommunism in the early Cold War and in support for U.S. policies in the 1950–53 Korean War. *See also* BERLE, ADOLF; CAFFERY, JEFFERSON; GIBSON, HUGH S.

BRETTON WOODS CONFERENCE (1944). The international economic conference held 1–22 July 1944 at Bretton Woods, New Hampshire, during **World War II**, aimed to reform the international economic system to avoid the problems that had spread and prolonged the Great Depression. The conference has also been seen as a deliberate attempt by the United States to assert its financial preeminence and to advance the process of reducing the European colonial empires. Its major result was in effect to shift the center of the financial world from London to New York. It led to the establishment of a new international monetary system featuring the **International Monetary Fund** (IMF) and International Bank for Reconstruction and Development (the IBRD or **World Bank**). The agreements were signed by 45 nations. The exchange rate was fixed against the price of gold and the dollar, which assumed a position of preeminence among world currencies previously held by the currency of **Great Britain**, the pound. The system remained in place until 1973. *See also* GOLD STANDARD.

BRITAIN–UNITED STATES OF AMERICA AGREEMENT (BRUSA). In June 1943, the United States and **Great Britain** signed BRUSA, which dealt with collaboration on **intelligence** matters. The two powers agreed to exchange decrypted enemy messages, though not the raw, undecrypted intercepts. The United States took responsibility for Japanese messages and Britain took responsibility for German and Italian communications. The two powers had been cooperating on intelligence matters since late 1940, notably in the **Ultra-Magic deal**, and the agreement was a formalization of what had developed incrementally over two years. Sharing intelligence is a major act of interstate cooperation, and this collaboration during **World War II** more than anything else indicates the closeness and the mutual trust at the heart of U.S. relations with Britain, despite differences on a range of political and strategic matters. *See also* MAGIC, OPERATION; SIGNALS INTELLIGENCE.

BROOKINGS INSTITUTION. A public policy organization and think-tank, the Brookings Institution originated in the Institute for Government Research (IGR) founded by a group of reformers to analyze and advise on public policy at a national level. One of the founders, Robert S. Brookings (1850–1932), was a business leader and philanthropist from St. Louis, and one of the original trustees of the Carnegie Endowment for International Peace. During **World War I**, he served as a member of the War Industries Board and the Allied Purchasing Commission. Brookings later founded the Institute for Economic Research (1922) and the Robert Brookings Graduate School (1924), which merged with the IGR to form the Brookings Institution in 1927. In the 1920s, the organization assisted **Charles G. Dawes** in his role as budget director and numbered among its members **Herbert Hoover**, **William H. Taft**, and **Elihu Root**.

In the 1930s, the Brookings Institution was commissioned by President **Franklin D. Roosevelt** to do a large-scale study of the causes of the economic depression. Its president, Harold Moulton, came to oppose the New Deal on the grounds that it would not solve the problems of the Great Depression. During **World War II**, the institution studied mobilization and issues connected to the planning of the **United Nations**. The Brookings Institution has become a study center on foreign policy and various aspects of public policy. In

1948, it was heavily involved in the formulation of the organizational aspects of the European Recovery Program (Marshall Plan).

BROWDER, EARL (1891–1973). American communist Earl Browder joined the Socialist Party at the age of 15. Like most socialists, he believed **World War I** was an imperialist war and opposed U.S. participation. He was imprisoned under the **Espionage Act** in 1917 for opposing the draft. Released in 1918, he was rearrested for his opposition to the war, and he served in jail until 1920.

Browder joined the **Communist Party of the United States** (CPUSA) in 1921 and operated for a time in the 1920s as a Communist International (Comintern) activist in **China**. He edited the party's newspaper and rose to become general secretary in 1930 and president in 1932, after **William Z. Foster** suffered a heart attack. From the mid-1930s, Browder was a recruiter of espionage agents for the **Union of Soviet Socialist Republics** (USSR). He ran for U.S. president in 1936, gaining 80,195 votes, having failed to persuade socialist **Norman Thomas** to run on a joint ticket. Browder favored a popular front approach and consequently supported the New Deal, while arguing that it should go further. In 1940, he was jailed for having traveled to the USSR under a false passport and was forbidden to travel the country to campaign in the 1940 election, in which he gained only 46,251 votes.

Browder was released from jail when the United States joined **World War II**. The Soviet Union was now a U.S. ally, and the CPUSA supported the war effort. He came to advocate a popular front strategy more strongly, and in 1944 he declared that communism and capitalism could peacefully coexist. After condemnation by French communist Jacques Duclos, he was expelled from the party in 1946 and was replaced by Foster. Browder continued to oppose the blindly pro-Soviet line of the CPUSA and criticized the party in hearings held by Senator Joseph McCarthy in 1950.

BRUSSELS CONFERENCE (1937). The international conference held in Brussels, Belgium, 3–24 November 1937, tried to bring an end to the aggression by **Japan** in the **Sino–Japanese War**, using the 1921 Five Power Treaty as a basis. As a follow-up to his October **quarantine** speech, President **Franklin D. Roosevelt** sent delegates, led by **Norman Davis**, but presented no firm initiatives, and the conference failed to come up with any agreements. Only the **Union of Soviet Socialist Republics** favored actual reprisals against Japan. The U.S. attitude of avoidance of involvement was clearly evidenced in the USS *Panay* incident the following month.

BRYAN, WILLIAM JENNINGS (1860–1925). William Jennings Bryan was elected to the U.S. House of Representatives from Nebraska in 1890. He used his rhetorical skills and populist stands on the issues of free silver, antibossism, and support for agriculture and labor to develop strong national support. He received the nomination of the Democratic Party for the presidency in 1896, 1900, and 1908. Despite being defeated three times for the presidency (by William McKinley in 1896 and 1900 and by **William H. Taft** in 1908), the "Great Commoner" retained considerable influence inside the party and was appointed secretary of state by President **Woodrow Wilson** (1913). Although not opposed to the extension of American influence in **Latin America**, he consistently opposed increases in military spending and any signs of "the paralyzing influence of imperialism" or international entanglements beyond the American hemisphere. This stance drew support from the **isolationist** wing of the Democratic Party but strained relations with the more **internationalist** President Wilson after the outbreak of **World War I**.

As secretary of state, Bryan focused particularly on Central American affairs. He sought to protect American influence and investments in the region, albeit through less militaristic means than those used by previous administrations. On 5 August 1914, he signed the **Bryan–Chamorro Treaty**, an agreement with the government of Nicaragua granting the United States perpetual rights over future canal construction in the region.

Bryan's departure from the State Department in 1915 was prompted by a disagreement with Wilson over the tone of U.S. communications with **Germany** in the wake of the sinking of the *Lusitania* (7 May 1915). Bryan advocated minimizing the risk of further American deaths by discouraging U.S. citizens from traveling on ships carrying munitions to or from a war zone. This warning would be combined with protests to **Great Britain** over the effects of its naval blockade. Instead, Wilson, with the support of Secretary of War

Lindley Garrison and presidential advisor **Edward House**, wrote a strongly worded note warning Germany that the United States would take "any necessary act" to protect American lives. Bryan resigned in protest (8 June 1915), accusing the president of compromising U.S. neutrality. Bryan's action was heavily criticized in some sections of the Democratic and Republican parties and in the nation's press.

Bryan continued to use his influence inside his party to restrain Wilson's interventionist impulses, arguing that the **Central Powers** could mistake a vigorous **preparedness** program for aggressive intent, thus escalating tensions and provoking misunderstandings which would make conflict inevitable. In 1916, Wilson's public support for the concept of a new international arbitration system as a mechanism for preventing future world conflicts drew Bryan's qualified support. Though committed to nonviolent conflict resolution, he remained an isolationist at heart. Although he had initially supported the **League to Enforce Peace** (also endorsed by Wilson in the summer of 1916), he came to suspect it of excessively internationalist designs. Bryan's antiwar views were echoed in Congress by Senators **Robert M. La Follette** and **George Norris**. Bryan's political influence declined after his resignation, though he remained a respected figure nationally and within the Democratic Party. His final public appearance was at the 1925 Scopes "Monkey Trial" in Dayton, Ohio, where his statements against the theory of evolution attracted widespread press criticism. He died within days of the trial's conclusion.

BRYAN–CHAMORRO TREATY (1914). This treaty between the United States and Nicaragua was signed on 5 August 1914 by U.S. Secretary of State **William Jennings Bryan** and General Emiliano Chamorro. The negotiations had started during the presidency of **William H. Taft** (1909–13). Under its terms, the United States secured perpetual rights over any future canal constructed in Nicaragua. This helped it to capitalize for a longer period on its ownership of the Panama Canal by forestalling the construction by rival powers of faster routes elsewhere. The treaty also permitted the United States to build a naval base in the Gulf of Fonseca and gave it a renewable 99-year lease on two islands in the Caribbean. In return, the Nicaraguan government was to receive a payment of $3 million, which it badly needed to repair the damage from its recent civil war.

El Salvador and Costa Rica, perceiving a potential threat to their security interests, challenged the legality of the treaty in the **Central American Court of Justice**. The United States lost the case, but the **Woodrow Wilson** administration ignored the ruling, provoking accusations of U.S. economic imperialism. On 14 July 1970, the United States and Nicaragua signed a convention terminating the provisions of the treaty.

BRYCE REPORT (1915). Published in 1915, the report was the work of the Committee on Alleged German Outrages, which was created at the request of **Great Britain** to investigate charges of brutality leveled against **Germany** after its forces overran Belgium in 1914, during **World War I**. It was headed by James Bryce, a former British ambassador to the United States (1907–13) and author of *The American Commonwealth* (1888), a classic 19th-century study of American government and society. Bryce's participation added weight to the final report, a detailed account of alleged German atrocities that exacerbated anti-German sentiment in the United States. Later historians questioned the report's balance. *See also LUSITANIA*.

B2H2 RESOLUTION. *See* CONNALLY RESOLUTION.

BUCARELI AGREEMENTS (1923). In the Bucareli Agreements between the United States and **Mexico**, the **Warren G. Harding** administration offered the government of **Alvaro Obregon** full diplomatic recognition in return for the assurance that U.S. property rights in Mexico would be recognized and respected. (The agreements were named for the conference location: Avenida Bucareli in Mexico City.) Foreign rights to ownership of Mexican oil had been revoked in 1918 by President **Venustiano Carranza**, using powers granted to the Mexican government under a new constitution adopted the previous year. Carranza's removal in 1920 gave the United States the opportunity to use diplomatic recognition as a bargaining chip to protect its business interests. The agreements were negotiated by Secretary of State **Charles Evans Hughes** and approved by President Harding shortly before his death. They guaranteed legal title to all U.S. properties developed before the 1917 constitution came into force. **Calvin Coolidge**, who succeeded Harding on 2 August 1923, endorsed the agreements and formally recognized the Obregon government on 31 August 1923. The agreements provided only a temporary solution to a long-term problem. *See also* CALLES, PLUTARCO ELIAS; MEXICAN OIL EXPROPRIATION CONTROVERSY.

BUCK, PEARL S. (1892–1973). American novelist Pearl Buck wrote many books set in **China**, where she had been raised and where she worked as a Christian missionary. Her best-selling trilogy *The Good Earth* (1931), *Sons* (1932), and *A House Divided* (1935) increased the American public's idealized view of China and its sentimental attachment to **Chiang Kai-shek**'s nationalist regime. Buck depicted the Chinese as noble peasants in the early stages of China's transformation into a democracy. *The Good Earth*, which received a Pulitzer Prize, was made into a popular film in 1937. In 1938, Buck became the first American woman to receive the Nobel Prize for Literature.

BUENOS AIRES CONFERENCE (1936). Suggested by U.S. President **Franklin D. Roosevelt**, the Inter-American Conference for the Maintenance of Peace met in Buenos Aires, **Argentina**, 1–23 December 1936 to discuss ways of ensuring peace in the western hemisphere, with both the recent **Chaco War** and developing tensions in Europe and Asia in mind. A convention was agreed on for maintaining peace, with procedures for consultation established. The participating republics stated in the Declaration of Principles of Inter-American Solidarity and Cooperation that any act that breached the peace in the region was the concern of them all. They affirmed that territorial conquest was proscribed, and no acquisition of territory by violence would be recognized. Most significantly, the United States delegation, led by Secretary of State **Cordell Hull**, joined in the condemnation of intervention in the internal or external affairs of another state and of the forcible collection of debts, thus further elaborating on the abandonment of the **Roosevelt Corollary** and confirming the commitment to the **Good Neighbor** policy. All disputes between signatories would be resolved by arbitration or through the institutions of international justice. An attempt by Hull to get the conference to issue a condemnation of European fascism led to clashes with the president of the conference, Foreign Minister Carlos Saavedra Lamas of Argentina, and nothing was done in this regard. *See also* MONTEVIDEO CONFERENCE (1933).

BULGE, BATTLE OF THE. On 16 December 1944, at a time when the Allies assumed **World War II** was almost won, **Germany** launched a surprise attack initiating the Battle of the Bulge. In Operation Autumn Mist, Germany threw its armored reserves in a desperate gamble to penetrate the American line, capture fuel, and then thrust on to Antwerp, the Allies only operational port. Fog grounded Allied aircraft, and complacency meant **intelligence** was ignored. German forces in U.S. uniforms caused chaos, and the Germans made rapid initial progress. They were held up by stiff resistance from units of the 101st Airborne Division at Bastogne and the 7th Armored Division at St. Vith, who were in the area to recuperate. Failure to take Bastogne or capture the petrol dumps gave time for Allied forces under British Field Marshal Bernard Montgomery to the north and American General George Patton to the south to regroup, counterattack, and defeat this last German offensive in the west. A timely reminder of the fight still left in the German forces, with the river Rhine still to cross, the battle influenced the cooperative spirit between the Allies at the **Yalta Conference**. However, Montgomery caused friction in the U.S.–British alliance by claiming publicly that he had rescued the Americans.

BULLITT, WILLIAM CHRISTIAN (1891–1967). Originally a journalist from Philadelphia, Bullitt joined the State Department in 1917 after working as a correspondent in Europe covering **World War I**. He was a delegate at the 1919 **Paris Peace Conference** and was sent by President **Woodrow Wilson** on a fact-finding mission with journalist Lincoln Steffens to **Russia**. Bullitt went beyond his brief and, convinced that **Vladimir Ilyich Lenin**'s Bolshevik government would last, made an agreement whereby Allied troops would evacuate Russia and Lenin would make territorial concessions to end the Russian civil war. Back in Paris, the British refused to agree and Wilson would not back Bullitt. Already dissatisfied with Wilson's concessions to the Allies at Paris, Bullitt resigned. He later wrote that he resolved to go to the beach and "watch the world go to hell." He testified against the **Treaty of Versailles** to the Senate.

Bullitt maintained his interest in Russia and in early 1933 met Foreign Commissar Maxim Litvinov of the **Union of Soviet Socialist Republics** (USSR) in London. They unofficially agreed that opening relations was in the interests of both sides, especially with regard to common interests in the Far East. When President **Franklin D. Roosevelt** wished to negotiate the recognition of the USSR in October 1933, the **Litvinov Agreement**, he turned to the ambitious Bullitt, who was generally considered a friend of Russia. Bullitt was made special assistant to Secretary of State **Cordell Hull** but was effectively Roosevelt's personal envoy. He made the first contacts with the head of the Soviet Information Bureau in Washington, D.C. After recognition, Bullitt was appointed the first United States ambassador to the USSR. He went to Moscow known as a liberal, even radical figure, and well-inclined toward his hosts; he returned in 1935 embittered by the experience. He had suffered difficult living conditions, hostility from Soviet bureaucrats, and spies among his domestic staff, and he believed the Soviets were breaking the recognition agreements. The purges that began in 1935 intensified his feelings. His embassy officials, including **George Kennan** and **Loy Henderson**, influenced him with their hard-line views.

Bullitt became ambassador to **France** in 1936 and served there until the fall of France to **Germany** in 1940. He became one of Roosevelt's special envoys, going to Africa and the Middle East (1941–42), then was special assistant to the secretary of the navy. Now a staunch anticommunist, in January 1943 he wrote the first of a series of memoranda to Roosevelt recommending a tough stance toward the Soviet Union. This set him at odds with Roosevelt's policies regarding the **Grand Alliance**, and his alienation from the president was completed when he played a role in getting **Sumner Welles** dismissed. After failing to be elected mayor of Philadelphia, Bullitt worked with the Free French, becoming a major in the Free French army and receiving the Croix de Guerre from **Charles de Gaulle**. After the war, he became a Republican and was a critic of the **Harry S. Truman** administration for the loss of **China** to communism. A book on Woodrow Wilson that he co-authored with Sigmund Freud in the 1920s, using psychoanalysis in a highly critical portrait, was published in 1967.

BURKE-WADSWORTH ACT (1940). *See* SELECTIVE TRAINING AND SERVICE ACT.

BUSH, VANNEVAR (1890–1974). Vannevar Bush was a professor of electrical engineering at the Massachusetts Institute of Technology (1923–32), then vice president and dean of engineering (1932–38). He developed a network analyzer of electrical networks and an analog computer. As president of the Carnegie Institution (1939–55), he gave scientific advice to the U.S. government. On 12 July 1940, Bush suggested to President **Franklin D. Roosevelt** that there was a need for closer liaison between scientists and the government: if the United States entered **World War II**, researchers, business, and the military would need to cooperate. Roosevelt made Bush chair of the **National Defense Research Committee** (NDRC).

During the war, the NDRC was subsumed into a broader-based Office of Scientific Research and Development (OSRD), of which Bush was the director. In the OSRD, he oversaw the development of military technology, integrating the work of scientists and engineers with the needs of the armed forces, when previously there had been little respect for scientists among the military. Bush transformed the way that the government viewed scientific research, and he became a well-known public figure. One journal called him "the man who may win or lose the war." He was involved with programs developing radar, proximity fuses, and drugs such as penicillin. Bush initially did not think that atomic weapons would be available in World War II but changed his mind at the end of 1941 and was instrumental in establishing the **Manhattan Project**. He chose the army to run the project, as he had had bad experiences with the **U.S. Navy**'s attitude to scientists. Bush warned Secretary of War **Henry L. Stimson** in 1944 of the dangers of an atomic arms race if there was not free international exchange of research; the United States in such a race could only expect to maintain its lead for a short time. Even so, Bush favored the use of the **atomic bomb** when it was completed.

After the war, Bush worked unsuccessfully to secure civilian dominance of research for the military. Each service preferred to direct its own research and development, leading to great duplication. He returned to MIT (1955–71) and was the author of *Modern Arms and Free Men* (1985). He is seen as one of the early theorists of what later became hypertext, the basis for the Internet. *See also* COMPTON, ARTHUR HOLLY; CONANT, JAMES BRYANT.

BYRNES, JAMES F. (1879–1972). Born in Charleston, James F. Byrnes was a lawyer in South Carolina and then a Democratic member of the U.S. House of Representatives (1911–25). In 1930, he was elected to the U.S. Senate. Although some aspects of the New Deal were too radical for him, he supported President **Franklin D. Roosevelt** and played a significant role in securing Roosevelt's nomination for a third presidential term in 1940, during **World War II**. He left the Senate to become a Supreme Court justice (1941–42) but was then invited by Roosevelt to take a role in organizing the home front as director of the Office of Economic Stabilization (1942–43). When demand grew for an agency to have overall organizational direction of the domestic war effort, Byrnes was appointed to head it. As director of the Office of War Management (1943–45), to many Americans, especially the press, Byrnes was a kind of "assistant president" for the home front—though it is clear that Roosevelt did not like him being described that way and ensured that Byrnes's powers were limited.

Byrnes was disappointed to be passed over when **Harry S. Truman** was selected as Roosevelt's running-mate in 1944, but he accompanied Roosevelt to the **Yalta Conference** in February 1945. When Truman became president in April 1945, he made Byrnes secretary of state, but relations between the two could often be tense, as Byrnes believed he should have been president. He was closely involved in the deterioration of relations with the **Union of Soviet Socialist Republics** (USSR) after the war. Byrnes was an exponent of "atomic diplomacy," and his comments about the utility of the **atomic bomb** in conducting relations with the Soviet Union have been taken as evidence that the bomb was dropped in order to intimidate the Soviets as well as bring the war with **Japan** to a rapid conclusion.

As secretary of state until the end of 1946, Byrnes played a central role in the negotiations regarding the postwar peace settlement in the Council of Foreign Ministers and in the growing tensions with the USSR that ultimately became the Cold War. His Stuttgart speech in September 1946 was a major first step in the postwar revival of western Germany. As governor of South Carolina (1951–55), Byrnes took a conservative viewpoint on civil rights issues.

– C –

CAFFERY, JEFFERSON (1886–1974). After two years of practicing law, Jefferson Caffery entered the Foreign Service in 1913. He served in minor posts in Caracas, Stockholm, Teheran, Madrid, and Athens. He was counselor at the Tokyo embassy (1923–25) and in Berlin (1925–26), then minister (head of mission) in El Salvador (1926–28) and Colombia (1928–33). He was ambassador to **Cuba** (1934–37), **Brazil** (1937–44), **France** (1944–49), and Egypt (1949–55). Caffery developed good relations with **Fulgencio Batista** in Cuba and was instrumental during **World War II** in persuading the government of Brazil to depart from its neutrality policy and side with the United States. *See also* BRADEN, SPRUILLE.

CAIRO CONFERENCES (1943). Two conferences were held in Cairo, Egypt, before and after the **Big Three** meeting at **Teheran**. The first, 22–26 November 1943, was a preliminary summit for U.S. President **Franklin D. Roosevelt** and Prime Minister **Winston Churchill** of **Great Britain** before the Teheran Conference. They mainly discussed the Far East, and it was the only major wartime conference attended by **Chiang Kai-shek** of **China**. It was agreed that **Japan** would be deprived of all its acquisitions since 1894, and it was reiterated that Japan would be required to surrender unconditionally. This was embodied in the Cairo Declaration.

At the second conference, 4–6 December 1943, Churchill and Roosevelt agreed that General **Dwight D. Eisenhower** would be the supreme commander of Operation **Overlord**. They also met with the president of Turkey but failed to persuade him that Turkey should enter the war.

CALLES, PLUTARCO ELIAS (1877–1945). As president of **Mexico** (1924–28), Plutarco Calles introduced new agrarian and educational legislation, but his support for anticlerical reforms sparked revolts organized by the radical Cristeros. Passage of the Alien Land Law and Petroleum Law (1925) reignited disputes with the United States over oil and land rights and prompted President **Calvin Coolidge** to send his friend and advisor **Dwight W. Morrow** to Mexico in 1927. The subsequent Calles–Morrow Agreement forestalled the confiscation of lands owned by Standard Oil and other U.S. companies, thus avoiding the disastrous economic consequences of a withdrawal of American investment. Still in office when president-elect Obregon was assassinated, Calles appointed Emilio Portes Gil as president but remained a powerful figure behind the scenes, engineering the rise and fall of three presidents before attempting to regain the office himself in 1935. He was defeated by Lázaro Cárdenas and left the country, returning as a private citizen in 1941. *See also* BUCARELI AGREEMENTS; MEXICAN OIL EXPROPRIATION CONTROVERSY.

CALVO DOCTRINE. Devised by Argentinean judge Carlos Calvo during the first Pan-American Conference (1889), the Calvo Doctrine stated that foreign investors in dispute with the government of a host country should appeal matters affecting commercial property and rights to the judiciary of the host country, not to their home government. Calvo believed this rule was essential not only to prevent businesses operating with special privileges and against the laws of the host country, but also to remove a pretext for external powers such as the United States to resort to diplomatic or military intervention. The Calvo Doctrine was often invoked by **Mexico** against the United States during the 1920s. *See also* BUENOS AIRES CONFERENCE; CALLES, PLUTARCO ELIAS; GOOD NEIGHBOR POLICY; MONTEVIDEO CONFERENCE.

CARRANZA, VENUSTIANO (1859–1920). Venustiano Carranza was president of **Mexico** from 1917 to 1920. He organized the successful rebellion in 1914 against the regime of **Victoriano Huerta**, in concert with **Alvaro Obregon**, Emiliano Zapata, and **Francisco "Pancho" Villa**. He was proclaimed a rebel by Villa and Zapata after he refused to support the decision of a constitutional convention to establish an interim presidency under Eulialo Gutierrez. Supporters of Carranza and Obregon later routed the forces of Villa and Zapata, and Carranza was elected president of Mexico in March 1917. He favored a radical approach to improving social conditions, involving nationalization of any lands or property deemed appropriate by the government. This, combined with Carranza's opposition to the **Monroe Doctrine** as a charter for U.S. interference in **Latin America**, increased tensions with the United States. Forbidden by law to seek a second term in 1920, he tried to prevent the election of Obregon by running his own candidate, the Mexican ambassador to the United States, Ignacio Bonillas. A campaign of harassment and intimidation sparked an armed insurrection by Obregon's supporters. Carranza fled the capital but was captured and killed on 20 May 1920. *See also* BUCARELI AGREEMENTS.

CASABLANCA CONFERENCE (1943). The Casablanca Conference, 14–24 January 1943, was a meeting between U.S. President **Franklin D. Roosevelt** and Prime Minister **Winston Churchill** of **Great Britain**, along with their military staffs. Premier **Josef Stalin** of the **Union of Soviet Socialist Republics** was invited, but he declined on the grounds that he was too involved with the conduct of the battle at Stalingrad. There was much debate on future strategy. The British view prevailed that the forces fighting in North Africa should be further utilized in an invasion of Sicily (Operation **Husky**). U.S. Army Chief of Staff General **George C. Marshall** maintained that the step after that should be the invasion of northern **France**. The Allies agreed on the **Combined Bomber Offensive**. At the end of the conference, Roosevelt issued his statement on **unconditional surrender**. Roosevelt met Free French leader **Charles de Gaulle** for the first time, but attempts to ease friction between the United States and the Free French, and between different factions of the Free French, were not wholly successful. *See also* BOLERO, OPERATION; GRAND ALLIANCE; SECOND FRONT.

CASH-AND-CARRY. One of the objections to the 1935 **Neutrality Act** was that it would harm U.S. commerce by restricting trade with belligerent nations and preventing U.S. ships from entering war zones. A solution proposed by **Bernard Baruch** and incorporated in the revised 1937 act was the cash-and-carry policy: trade in nonmunitions with belligerents would be allowed, on a strictly cash basis, thus avoiding the growth of a pattern of loans and **war debts** such as had developed in **World War I**. Belligerents would also be required to carry the goods away from the United States in their own vessels, thereby avoiding risk to U.S. ships. This meant that American business would not be deprived of the opportunities presented by the increased needs of nations at war but would not risk being drawn into war by the commerce involved. Under pressure from President **Franklin D. Roosevelt**, cash-and-carry was extended to include munitions in the Neutrality Act of November 1939. *See also* ARSENAL OF DEMOCRACY; LEND-LEASE.

CASTILLO–KNOX TREATY (1911). This treaty between **Nicaragua** and the United States was finalized by Secretary of State Philander C. Knox on 6 June 1911 and signed by the U.S. and Nicaraguan governments in August 1914, but it was never formally ratified by the U.S. Senate. It gave the United States broad rights of intervention in Nicaraguan affairs to protect U.S. interests (particularly by preventing construction of any new canal undermining the advantage held by the United States with the existing Panama Canal) in return for a payment of $15 million to the Nicaraguan government. The 1914 **Bryan–Chamorro Treaty**, which superseded it, served the same purpose but contained no blanket intervention clause. *See also* LATIN AMERICA.

CASTLE, WILLIAM (1879–1963). William Castle was born in Honolulu; his father had represented the king of Hawaii in Washington, D.C. Castle was assistant dean at Harvard University (1904–13) and in 1917 became communications director for the American Red Cross. After **World War I**, he entered the State Department as a special assistant and later was chief of the Division of Western European Affairs (1921–27). He was made assistant secretary of state in 1927. In 1930, Castle briefly served as U.S. ambassador to **Japan**. During the 1930 **London Naval Disarmament Conference**, he was a special envoy to persuade Japanese hard-liners that the negotiated treaties were in their interests, but he had little success. In 1931, he became undersecretary of state.

Castle conducted most of the negotiations concerning **war debts** and the **Hoover moratorium** that took place in 1931–32. He was a friend of President **Herbert Hoover** and of many members of the **Senate Committee on Foreign Relations**, putting him in the inner circle of policy making. He favored international cooperation and supported the **Stimson Doctrine** on nonrecognition of **Japan**'s conquests in Manchuria. He opposed recognition of the **Union of Soviet Socialist Republics**, a state which he regarded as a threat to peace.

When **Franklin D. Roosevelt** became president in 1933, Castle left the State Department. He was overseer at Harvard College (1935–41), opposed Roosevelt's New Deal, and became a strong supporter of **isolationism**. Unlike most other noninterventionists in 1939–41, whose attention was drawn to events in Europe, Castle's focus was mainly on avoiding involvement in conflict in Asia.

CENTRAL AMERICAN COURT OF JUSTICE. Established in 1907 at the suggestion of the United States and **Mexico**, the court was intended to maintain peace and mediate disputes between the states of Central America. Problems in defining the scope of the court's powers and in restraining interference from governments of the member states led to its dissolution in spring 1918. The concept of a regional court was revived after **World War II**.

CENTRAL POWERS. Austria-Hungary and **Germany,** the Central Powers, were allied against the Entente powers of **Great Britain, France**, and **Russia** at the start of **World War I**. In 1915, Bulgaria and Turkey joined the Central Powers.

CENTURY GROUP. An interventionist, activist organization, the Century Group was formed in July 1940, during **World War II**, to lobby for an immediate U.S. declaration of war on **Germany**. It was named after the club in New York City where the group met. The fear was that **Great Britain** would soon be defeated and its navy fall into German hands, and that Germany would then proceed on a mission of world conquest. Leading members were **Lewis Douglas**, Admiral **William Standley**, Bishop Henry Hobson, Francis P. Miller, and Herbert Agar. The lobby group used news releases and personal contacts to influence public opinion. Douglas organized liaison with the much larger **Committee to Defend America by Aiding the Allies**, though their aims were not identical. The Century Group was one of the originators of the idea of the **destroyers-for-bases** deal to overcome congressional objections to giving Britain something for nothing.

CHACO WAR (1933–1935). Chaco was disputed territory between Bolivia and Paraguay at the foot of Andes. When rumors of oil in Chaco caused clashes in 1928, the issue was referred to the **League**

of **Nations**, but the arbitration convention of August 1929 was rejected by both countries. Paraguay withdrew from negotiations in Washington, D.C., in 1931, and war broke out in Chaco in July 1933. Paraguay was victorious and a truce was agreed to in June 1935, after about 100,000 casualties. An agreement at the 1936 **Buenos Aires Conference** provided for arbitration by six Latin American presidents, who on 10 October 1938 awarded most of Chaco to Paraguay, though guaranteeing Bolivia access to the Atlantic by way of the Paraguay River.

CHAMBERLAIN, ARTHUR NEVILLE (1867–1940). Neville Chamberlain, a member of **Great Britain**'s Conservative Party, rose to chancellor of the exchequer (1931–37) and then prime minister (1937–40). Attempting to negotiate with the leader of **Germany, Adolf Hitler**, in an effort to prevent what became **World War II**, Chamberlain conceded to what initially seemed reasonable demands that Germanic peoples be united in one state and that the harsher aspects of the **Treaty of Versailles** be revised. This policy culminated in a meeting at Munich in September 1938, when Chamberlain and the prime minister of **France,** Eduard Daladier, agreed with Hitler and Italian dictator Benito Mussolini to concede Czechoslovak territory to Germany. Such concessions were seen by many as appeasement that only encouraged Hitler. Chamberlain believed that American **isolationism** and the **Neutrality Acts** meant that he could not expect any U.S. support, and he dismissed as irrelevant President **Franklin D. Roosevelt**'s suggestions of multinational conferences. Chamberlain preferred face-to-face negotiations on a bilateral basis.

After German troops marched into Prague in March 1939, Chamberlain reversed course. Concluding that he could not trust Hitler, he issued security guarantees to **Poland**, Romania, and Greece. Germany invaded Poland on 1 September 1939, and after Hitler failed to respond to a British ultimatum, Britain declared war on 3 September. Chamberlain remained prime minister until May 1940, though not an enthusiastic war leader. After a disastrous campaign in Norway, he lost support from some in his own party and stood down. His successor, **Winston Churchill**, formed a coalition government. Chamberlain remained leader of his party and a member of the war cabinet until he had to retire due to ill health in September 1940.

CHAPULTEPEC, ACT OF (1945). The Inter-American Conference on War and Peace held in Mexico City in March 1945, during **World War II**, produced the Act of Chapultepec (8 March 1945). This was adopted by 20 American republics and signed for the United States by Secretary of State **Edward R. Stettinius**. It was a move toward a regional defense alliance, which was to be finalized two years later in the Rio Treaty. The agreement called for joint action against aggression against any state in the region, including by another American state. They would act collectively in their own defense, until the world organization could take effective action. The arrangement was constructed around U.S. leadership and supply of weaponry, and it contrasts with U.S. opposition to the creation of spheres of influence in other parts of the world. The conference was limited to the states at war with the **Axis** powers. **Argentina** adhered to the agreement after its declaration of war at the end of March 1945. *See also* INTER-AMERICAN DEFENSE BOARD; ROCKEFELLER, NELSON ALDRICH.

CHARLOTTESVILLE ADDRESS (1940). This speech by President **Franklin D. Roosevelt** at the University of Virginia at Charlottesville on 10 June 1940 was largely in response to the impending defeat of **France** by **Germany**. Roosevelt stated that the majority of the American people now believed that a victory in **World War II** by the **Axis** powers would be a threat to democracy in the western hemisphere. He made his most explicit attack on **isolationism** to date, saying that if the Axis won, the United States would be a "lone island in a world dominated by the philosophy of force." This would be a "nightmare prison," with America "handcuffed, hungry, and fed through the bars from day to day by the contemptuous, unpitying masters of other continents."

These strong words, however, were not followed by proposals of decisive intervention. Roosevelt limited himself to requesting $10.5 billion from Congress to build up American defenses, a proposal that would appeal to **fortress America** isolationists as well as to interventionists. He did announce that the United States would make resources available to the Allies fighting the Axis. In order to gain time for U.S. industry to produce what was required, the United States needed **Great Britain** and France to maintain their resistance.

Roosevelt did not, however, suggest going to the direct assistance of the Allies. As a result of the speech, stocks of surplus army materials were made available for purchase by Britain and France under the **cash-and-carry** provision. On 14 June, Roosevelt signed the 1940 "11 percent" Naval Expansion Act. Twelve days after the speech, France signed an armistice with Germany. A month later, Congress approved the **Two-Ocean Navy Act**. *See also* ARSENAL OF DEMOCRACY; DESTROYERS-FOR-BASES DEAL.

CHAUTAUQUA SPEECH (1936). In this speech by President **Franklin D. Roosevelt** on 14 August 1936 at Chautauqua, New York, he eloquently stated his hatred of war. He suggested that peace was endangered by the quest for profit. This was in line with his presidential campaign of that year, which attacked big business. Roosevelt supported the **Neutrality Act** in the speech and said, "If we face the choice of profits or peace, the nation will answer—must answer—we choose peace." The United States, he said, sought no territory, opposed imperialism and arms races, and sought to be a **good neighbor**. Coming during the opening stages of the **Spanish Civil War**, the speech demonstrated the determination of the Roosevelt administration to remain isolated from conflict. *See also* NYE COMMITTEE; QUARANTINE SPEECH.

CHENNAULT, CLAIRE LEE (1890–1958). In **World War I**, Claire Chennault was a pioneer of fighter tactics by the U.S. Army Air Force. He retired from the army in 1937 with the rank of colonel. He went to **China** and organized the air force for **Chiang Kai-shek's** nationalist government, which was fighting the invasion by **Japan**. In 1941, he formed the **American Volunteer Group** (AVG) for American pilots wishing to help defend China. With U.S. entry into **World War II**, he was recalled to duty as a brigadier general, and the AVG was transformed into the China Air Task Force; from March 1943, it was the 14th U.S. Army Air Force.

Chennault came to disagree with General **Joseph Stilwell**, nominally his commanding officer, about the role of the army in China. Chennault thought China should be the basis for the U.S. strategic bombing offensive against Japan, and that the army's main function was guarding its air bases. The Japanese overran most of the bases in their Ichi-Go offensive in 1944, causing bitter disputes with Stilwell. Now a major general, in July 1945 Chennault resigned in protest against the disbandment of the joint American–Chinese wing of the Chinese Air Force. *See also* SINO–JAPANESE WAR (1937–45).

CHIANG KAI-SHEK (JIANG JIESHI) (1887–1975). Chinese nationalist leader and professional soldier Chiang Kai-shek was chief of staff to the leader of the Chinese Revolution, Sun Yat-sen (Sun Zhongshan), and succeeded him as leader of the nationalist movement, the **Kuomintang** (Guomindang) in 1925. Chiang, a staunch anticommunist, led the Chinese government from 1928 until 1949. Most of his period in power was spent fighting for control against local warlords, the Chinese Communist Party, and **Japan**. Chiang saw the communists as the greater threat to **China**—he anticipated that Japan would overstretch itself in China. Others wished to focus on the foreign invader, and in December 1936 Chiang was kidnapped by rebel officers in Sian (Siking). A compromise was reached whereby Chiang returned to his capital, Nanking (Nanjing), and the communists incorporated their forces into the nationalist ones so that together they would fight Japan.

After the Japanese capture of Nanking in December 1937, Chiang retreated inland, following a policy of trading "space for time" in the hopes eventually of receiving sufficient aid from the United States to regain control of his country. He was based at Chungking (Chonqqing) throughout **World War II** and was both head of government and commander in chief of the armed forces, taking the title of generalissimo. Chiang's regime was corrupt and inefficient, but he was immensely popular in the United States, especially with the **Henry Luce** press, and was featured on the cover of *Time* and *Life* five times during the war, more than any other individual. He was converted to Christianity in 1930 by his wife, Soong Mei-ling, who enjoyed as much if not greater popularity in the United States.

President **Franklin D. Roosevelt** intended that Chiang's China should be the fourth great power and should oversee decolonization in Asia. They met at the **Cairo Conference** in 1943. By 1944, Chiang's failure to use Allied supplies to take the offensive against Japan and his poor relations with his American chief of staff, General **Joseph Stilwell**, meant that Roosevelt cooled a little in his expectations and was prepared to concede Chinese territory to the **Union of Soviet Socialist Republics** in return for its engaging Japan. Confident that the Americans would defeat Japan, Chiang was husbanding his resources for a future conflict with the communists. Civil war reemerged in China after World War II, and by 1948 Chiang was effectively defeated. In December 1949, he and his remaining supporters retreated to Formosa (Taiwan), where they claimed to be the government of all China. The United States recognized them as such, allowing Taiwan to hold the Chinese permanent seat on the **United Nations** Security Council until after Chiang's death. *See also* BUCK, PEARL S.; CHENNAULT, CLAIRE LEE; DIXIE MISSION; FOUR POLICEMEN; HURLEY, PATRICK; SINO–JAPANESE WAR; YALTA CONFERENCE.

CHICAGO CONFERENCE (1944). The rapid development of aircraft technology in **World War II**, and U.S. aspirations to expand its commercial activities internationally, led to a strong desire to set international standards and regulations for civil **aviation**, and beyond that to establish principles that allowed international airlines to operate between sovereign states. The United States discussed the issue with its allies in early 1944, and 52 states sent delegates to the International Civil Aviation Conference in Chicago in November and December. The resulting Convention on International Civil Aviation established the International Civil Aviation Organization (ICAO), which came into operation once 26 nations had ratified the convention—this was not done until 4 April 1947.

The main issues addressed by the conference were legal and technical arrangements concerning navigation signals, landing rights and the like, and the broader issues of the economics of civil aviation. The United States advocated free competition for airlines, with the ICAO's remit limited to technical matters. **Great Britain** wished for the ICAO to be concerned with regulation, so that it could allocate routes, fix rates, and regulate the frequency of flights. In a compromise, the ICAO was to maintain order in the air and technical standardization. Its economic role was limited, but it was empowered to avoid waste through excessive competition. The convention affirmed states' sovereign rights over the airspace over their territory, though leaving unclear how high into the stratosphere this extended. Scheduled flights can only be made through this airspace with permission. Subsidiary agreements, the International Air Services Transit Agreement, and the International Air Transport Agreement (Five Freedoms agreement), which were not accepted by all parties, established rights of transit and emergency landing, and freedom to carry goods and passengers between countries that were not the aircraft's homeland. The ICAO, based in Montreal, Canada, became a specialized agency of the **United Nations** in October 1947.

CHINA INCIDENT. *See* SINO–JAPANESE WAR.

CHINA. From the start of the 20th century until 1931, U.S. policy toward China was defined by the **open door** principles of free access for American commerce and opposition to the development of exclusive spheres of influence by other powers. Chinese **immigration** to the United States had been halted in 1882, but Americans had developed a sentimentalized attachment to China itself. It was seen as an area of opportunity for Christian missionary work and for the expansion of markets for American manufacturers. China was believed to have the potential to become a democratic republic along American lines. U.S. activities in China, as in other parts of Asia, largely took the form of government-encouraged private loans and initiatives, in addition to missionary activities.

The United States found itself increasingly opposed to **Japan**'s ambitions in China and attempted to circumscribe them in the Five Power Treaty agreed on at the 1921 **Naval Disarmament Conference** in Washington, D.C. However, there was no desire to get embroiled officially in Chinese affairs, though events like the 1927 **Nanking Incident** had that effect. A trade treaty in 1928 gave China most favored nation status with regard to **tariffs**. By 1930, 500 U.S. companies were investing $155 million in China, though this was only 1 percent of total U.S. foreign investments, and trade with Japan was double that with China.

When Japan occupied Manchuria in the 1931–32 **Manchurian Crisis**, the U.S. response was passive disapproval, enunciated in the **Stimson Doctrine**. American popular attitudes toward China were sympathetic, encouraged by the writings of **Pearl S. Buck**, but sentiments of **pacifism** and **isolationism** meant there was little support for active intervention. This attitude prevailed with the outbreak of the **Sino–Japanese War** in July 1937 and the USS *Panay* incident in December. Shanghai fell to Japan in November after devastating bombing of civilians. The capital, Nanking (Nanjing), fell in December 1937, followed by extensive massacres and rapes. President **Franklin D. Roosevelt** had delivered his **quarantine speech** in October but made no concrete proposals. At the November **Brussels Conference**, U.S. delegates did not press for blockades or embargoes of Japan.

This changed in 1940 with a shift in State Department policy associated with **Stanley K. Hornbeck**. Japan's expansionism was to be contested. Publisher **Henry Luce** and others stepped up pro-**Chiang Kai-shek** reporting. Chiang, who had become a Christian in 1930, was widely regarded in the United States as a democratic Chinese nationalist and modernizer, and U.S. flyers joined the **American Volunteer Group** to come to his aid. China was named as a first recipient of **Lend-Lease** along with **Great Britain**. Congress voted a $500,000 loan in February 1942. The State Department wanted to go further and build American strategy around extensive aid to Chiang and military operations in China. Roosevelt was keen for China to be regarded as the fourth great power alongside the United States, Great Britain, and the **Union of Soviet Socialist Republics** (USSR) and had hopes that China could spearhead the process of decolonization of the European empires in Asia. However, he was cautious about building military strategy around China. General **Joseph Stilwell** was sent to assist the Chinese struggle, but few U.S. troops were deployed there, and China was low on the list of priorities for supplies. This was partly because the route to China was a difficult one, involving flights over the Himalayas. Roosevelt played up support for China domestically, and U.S. domestic opinion continued to be very enthusiastic about Chiang, and his wife, Soong Mei-ling, became a national celebrity in her own right, boosted by the Luce press. Roosevelt met Chiang at the 1943 **Cairo Conference** and painted a rosy picture to him of China's future role. Roosevelt promised in the Cairo Declaration that China would receive back all territory lost to Japan since 1894.

While this was generally popular with the American public, opinion was shifting within the government. There was a suspicion that

Chiang was reserving his strength for a future conflict with the communists, because he believed the United States could defeat Japan without Chinese help. When Stilwell urged reforms of Chiang's army and criticized the endemic corruption, relations between them became very bitter. Vice President **Henry Wallace** went to China on a mission in June 1944 and came away recommending an increase in contacts with the communists led by Mao Zedong, on the grounds that they were doing more to defeat Japan. By this time, U.S. strategy was no longer based on operations from China, though some bombing missions were flown by General **Claire Chennault**'s forces. A further Roosevelt envoy, **Patrick Hurley**, took Chiang's side, contested the opinions of the **Dixie Mission** to the communists, and secured Stilwell's replacement.

By this point, Roosevelt was lukewarm about a Chinese role in decolonization and was prepared at the 1945 **Yalta Conference** to make concessions affecting Chinese sovereignty to Soviet leader **Josef Stalin**, without informing Chiang. By the end of **World War II**, the China policy of the U.S. government was uncertain and contradictory. It was still committed to Chiang, but with deep reservations in many quarters concerning his democratic credentials and ability to secure victory over the communists. U.S. aid to him continued, but not in sufficient quantities to guarantee his victory, nor with any safeguards to ensure it was used effectively. Conversely, the China lobby headed by Henry Luce continued to be a vociferous presence in American public discourse. *See also* DAVIES, JOHN PATON; GAUSS, CLARENCE EDWARD; JOHNSON, NELSON TRUSLER; SERVICE, JOHN STEWART.

CHURCHILL, WINSTON S. (1874–1965). British Prime Minister Winston Churchill's mother was American, and he had a deep interest in the United States, though he had seldom visited it before his conferences there during **World War II**. Although he served in most of the high political offices in **Great Britain**, by the 1930s Churchill was in the political wilderness, opposing mainstream opinion in his own party on issues like self-government in India, the abdication of King Edward VIII, and the need for rearmament in the face of the growing power of Nazi **Germany**. He returned to office on the outbreak of World War II in September 1939 as First Lord of the

Admiralty. In this post, Churchill not only supervised naval operations but opened direct correspondence with President **Franklin D. Roosevelt**.

Churchill became prime minister of a coalition government on 11 May 1940, after military disasters in Norway. He pursued a determined policy of fighting on against Germany despite the defeat of **France**, and he devoted much effort to gaining U.S. support in the form of armaments, concluding the **destroyers-for-bases deal** in September 1940. He assiduously pressed and cajoled Roosevelt, and eventually his pleas that Britain was running out of funds prompted Roosevelt's **arsenal of democracy** speech and proposal of **Lend-Lease**. Churchill met Roosevelt in August 1941 at the **Placentia Bay meeting** for their first proper conversations. After U.S. entry into the war, Churchill sought close cooperation between the Allies, while seeking to ensure his strategic vision prevailed involving operations in the Mediterranean rather than a **second front** in France. His ability to shape Allied strategy lasted until the 1943 **Teheran Conference**, when Roosevelt and **Josef Stalin** of the **Union of Soviet Socialist Republics** (USSR) forced from him a firm commitment to Operation **Overlord**.

Churchill was increasingly aware of declining British power and the possible ambitions of the Soviet Union. He sought to arrange spheres of activity with Stalin in October 1944 and to gain acceptance that France should share in the occupation of Germany, in order to balance Soviet power. He unsuccessfully pressed on Roosevelt and later President **Harry S. Truman** that German territory should be bargained for Soviet fulfillment of agreements made at the **Yalta Conference**. Churchill left in the middle of the **Potsdam Conference** in July 1945 after losing the British general election. In 1946, he warned of the descent of the "Iron Curtain" and pressed for a renewal of the Anglo–American alliance that he saw as central to the preservation of world peace. Churchill served again as prime minister from 1951 to 1955.

CLARK, GRENVILLE (1882–1967). A lawyer from New York, Grenville Clark was a founder of the Military Training Camps Association in **World War I**. He was one of the authors of the Burke–Wadsworth bill in 1940 that became the **Selective Training and Service Act**.

Clark believed in limiting national sovereignty as a way to world peace. He wrote *A Federation of Free Peoples* (1939), co-authored *World Peace through World Law: Two Alternative Plans* with Louis B. Sohn (1958), and was an activist on civil rights issues.

CLARK, JAMES BEAUCHAMP (1850–1921). "Champ" Clark, a lawyer from Missouri, served as a Democratic member of the U.S. House of Representatives (1893–95, 1897–1921). He was speaker of the House (1911–19) and the initial front-runner for the Democratic Party nomination for president in 1912. He consistently led **Woodrow Wilson** in the convention balloting but could not attain the two-thirds majority required by party rules. Clark helped steer Wilson's legislation through the House but later provoked dissension in the Democratic Party by opposing Wilson's decision to seek a **declaration of war** against **Germany** in April 1917. His son, **Joel Bennett Clark**, was a senator.

CLARK, JOEL BENNETT (1890–1954). Bennett Clark, a lawyer from Missouri, was the son of **James Beauchamp Clark**. He was parliamentarian of the U.S. House of Representatives (1913–17), a colonel in the U.S. Army in **World War I**, and a U.S. senator (1931–45). Clark made a strident demand in the Senate in January 1944 that Emperor **Hirohito** of **Japan** should be executed as a war criminal. Failing to be renominated for the Senate in 1944, he then served as a judge on the U.S. Court of Appeals.

CLARK, JOSHUA REUBEN (1871–1961). Lawyer J. Reuben Clark worked in the Justice Department during **World War I** and became undersecretary of state in 1928. In 1930, he was appointed ambassador to **Mexico** and served for three years, retiring from regular government service in 1933. *See also* CLARK MEMORANDUM.

CLARK MEMORANDUM (1928). Produced during the administration of President **Calvin Coolidge** by Undersecretary of State **J. Reuben Clark**, this memorandum asserted that the United States had no inherent right to intervene militarily in **Latin America**. The memo was subsequently published as an official document by the administration of President **Herbert Hoover**. It represented a formal repudiation of the **Roosevelt Corollary** to the **Monroe Doctrine**, and it restated the original intent of the latter that U.S. military action would be triggered *only* by European armed intervention in Latin America. Some historians claim that the memorandum originated not with Clark but from a confidential memorandum to U.S. embassies in Latin America from Secretary of State **Frank B Kellogg**, which contended that the Monroe Doctrine should not be construed as a catch-all excuse for intervention. *See also* CALVO DOCTRINE; GOOD NEIGHBOR POLICY; MONTEVIDEO CONFERENCE.

CLAY, LUCIUS DUBIGNON (1897–1978). Soldier Lucius Clay was an expert in procurement during **World War II**. Clay was responsible for the enlargement of hundreds of airports in the United States, and he was sent to **Brazil** to organize the same there in 1942. He was made chair of the Army Procurement Campaign in 1942. Clay worked on logistics in Normandy after Operation **Overlord** and in 1945 was made director of war mobilization. He served as military governor of the U.S. zone in **Germany** after World War II and was promoted to four-star general in 1947. Clay had been keen on cooperation with the **Union of Soviet Socialist Republics** (USSR), but experience quickly made him pessimistic. When the Soviets blockaded Berlin in 1948, he recommended breaking through with tanks. Truman refused but set up the Berlin Airlift with Clay in command. Clay retired from the army in May 1949, after the blockade was lifted.

CLAYTON, WILLIAM LOCKHART (1880–1966). In 1904, William Clayton was a founder of Anderson, Clayton, and Co. in Oklahoma City; under Clayton's influence, it became a major player in the international cotton trade. Clayton became known as "Mr. Cotton," or "the greatest cotton merchant in the world." During **World War I**, he was a member of the Cotton Distribution Committee of the War Industries Board.

Clayton was a Democrat who disapproved of President **Franklin D. Roosevelt**'s agricultural policy but supported his and Secretary of State **Cordell Hull**'s views on **trade**. In 1940, Clayton became an unpaid assistant to **Nelson Rockefeller** at the **Office of the Coordinator of Inter-American Affairs**. He was vice president of the **Export-Import Bank** (1940–42) and then assistant secretary of commerce, in which position he directed the purchase of strategic materials to keep them out of **Germany**'s hands in **World War II**, and he developed the policy for international civil **aviation**. He was administrator of the Surplus War Property Administration (1944) before becoming assistant secretary of state for economic affairs in December 1944. Clayton was a committed advocate of free trade and was the major driving force for it after the retirement of Hull. He was on the Interim Committee that advised Secretary of War **Henry Stimson** on the **atomic bomb**. He was economic advisor to President **Harry S. Truman** at the 1945 **Potsdam Conference**.

After the war, Clayton was undersecretary of state for economic affairs, an office specifically created for him, and was influential in pressing for the reduction of trade barriers and in constructing the General Agreement on Tariffs and Trade (GATT). Clayton was alternate governor of the **World Bank** (1946–49) and closely involved in the formulation of the Marshall Plan of economic aid for Europe. He retired from the State Department in October 1947 but remained active in international affairs, chairing the U.S. delegation to the 1948 **United Nations** conference on trade and employment in Havana. As vice chair of the Atlantic Union (1949–61), he promoted international trade as an antidote to communism. He also became heavily involved in charitable work in Houston, Texas, where he lived. *See also* BRETTON WOODS CONFERENCE (1944).

CLEMENCEAU, GEORGES (1841–1929). Nicknamed "the Tiger," Georges Clemenceau was mayor of Montmartre and interior minister before becoming prime minister of **France** (1906–09, 1917–20). He argued for a strong defense posture against **Germany**. In November 1917, he formed a coalition cabinet, becoming both premier and minister of war. With the support of President Raymond Poincaré, he pressed for harsh terms to be imposed on Germany at the 1919 **Paris Peace Conference**, including punitive **reparations** and the return of Alsace-Lorraine to France. Although he had a good working relationship with Prime Minister **David Lloyd George** of **Great Britain**, Clemenceau regarded U.S. President **Woodrow Wilson** as naively idealistic. He was dissatisfied with the terms of the **Treaty of Versailles** and believed that a second great war with Germany was inevitable. Defeated in the January 1920 French elections, he retired from active politics.

COHEN, BENJAMIN VICTOR (1894–1983). Lawyer Benjamin Cohen was a member of **Franklin D. Roosevelt**'s "brains trust" of advisors and a framer of much of the New Deal legislation. As an unpaid counsel for the Office of War Mobilization, he drafted the legal opinion that expedited the **destroyers-for-bases** deal of September 1940. He drafted the **Lend-Lease** bill, House Resolution 1776, in 1941. Cohen served as economic advisor to the U.S. embassy in **Great Britain** during **World War II**, then worked with **James F. Byrnes** in the Office of Economic Stabilization. Cohen was on the drafting team for the U.S. delegation's proposals at the 1944 **Dumbarton Oaks Conference** and was a delegate to the **United Nations** (1947–52). He was also active in the American Zionist movement.

COLBY, BAINBRIDGE (1869–1950). Lawyer Bainbridge Colby was a New York State assemblyman (1901–2), an unsuccessful Republican candidate for the U.S. Senate (1914, 1916), and a commissioner on the U.S. Shipping Board (1917–19). He was a surprise appointment as secretary of state in March 1920 to replace **Robert Lansing**: he had been a **progressive** Republican for most of his career and had only switched sides to vote for the Democratic President **Woodrow Wilson** in 1916. Colby pushed hard in Congress for ratification of the **Treaty of Versailles** without reservations. Toward the end of the Wilson presidency, he made a goodwill tour of **Latin America** in an effort to repair the damage done to America's image by **dollar diplomacy** and military interventions. Colby also indicated that the **Roosevelt Corollary** to the **Monroe Doctrine** might in the future be reexamined and restricted. After the Wilson presidency, Colby and the former president established a law partnership. Colby continued to practice law after Wilson's death in 1924. An early supporter of President **Franklin D. Roosevelt** in the 1930s, he eventually became a critic of the New Deal.

COLLECTIVE SECURITY. Multilateral cooperation to ensure peace and security was a popular goal at the end of **World War I**, and collective security was a key concept in the formation of the **League of Nations**. The term was much used during the 1930s as the threat of war increased in Europe and Asia, sometimes in the quest for effective action by the League, and sometimes by those seeking multilateral cooperation as an alternative to League inactivity.

The goal of collective security is to build a system that replaces arms races and balance-of-power politics with collective action. Participating nations agree to two obligations: to refrain from the use of military force against other members of the system, and to use force against members who breach that first obligation. In the 1930s, advocates of collective security saw it as an alternative to an arms buildup but were concerned with the threat of aggression from states outside the collective security group, such as **Germany**. Collective security advocates sought what is provided by a military alliance but wanted an alternative to such military arrangements. Partly because of this paradox, and partly because of distrust of the motives of the **Union of Soviet Socialist Republics** when it began urging collective security after 1935, the government of **Great Britain** under Prime Minister **Neville Chamberlain** sought accommodation with the potential aggressor through appeasement, rather than reliance on toothless collective security measures. The United States had kept its distance from collective security since the Senate's failure to ratify the **Treaty of Versailles**.

Japan's attack on **Pearl Harbor** brought a shift in attitudes, and many Americans came to believe that international peace and security could be obtained only through a collective security system. The idea had already been endorsed in a general way in the 1941 **Atlantic Charter**. The Senate in the 1943 **Fulbright** and **Connally resolutions** favored collective security. Article 1 of the 1945 **United Nations Charter** makes clear that the organization was intended to "take effective collective measures for the prevention and removal of threats to the peace." *See also* BRUSSELS CONFERENCE.

COMBINED BOMBER OFFENSIVE (CBO). A plan originating with U.S. Army Air Force General Ira C. Eaker for a combined offensive by British and American bombers against **Germany** during **World War II**, the CBO was established in the Casablanca Directive of 21 January 1943, issued at the **Casablanca Conference**. The stated objective was the progressive destruction of the German military, economic, and political system and the undermining of the morale of the German people until their capacity for resistance was fatally weakened. The plan was amended in the Pointblank Directive issued by the **Combined Chiefs of Staff** in June 1943, giving priority to the destruction of German fighter aircraft. The 1943 **Quebec Conference** officially abandoned the specific targeting of German morale.

The CBO suffered heavy losses in its initial campaigns and only began to make progress when long-range escort fighters were available in early 1944. In the "Big Week" of 20–26 February 1944, German air strength was substantially eroded by the casualties inflicted on the pilots. This was a vital precondition for the success of Operation **Overlord** in June 1944 and the subsequent destruction of German oil and transportation industries by the bombers. *See also* DRESDEN.

COMBINED CHIEFS OF STAFF COMMITTEE (CCS). At the **Washington Conference** (Arcadia) in December 1941, the United States and **Great Britain** agreed to have regular meetings of the chiefs of their armed forces to facilitate joint strategy. This was regularized as the Combined Chiefs of Staff Committee. The CCS met in Washington, D.C., throughout **World War II** and during major conferences elsewhere. The United States was represented by Army Chief of Staff **George C. Marshall**, commander of the Army Air Force General **Henry Arnold**, chief of the Naval Staff Admiral **Ernest King**, and chief of staff to the president Admiral **William D. Leahy**—these four also constituted the new U.S. **Joint Chiefs of Staff** (JCS). The British were represented by their chiefs of staff or deputies permanently stationed in the United States, headed by General John Dill. When he died in 1944, Dill was honored by becoming the first foreigner to be buried in Arlington Cemetery.

The CCS was the forum for the major British–American strategic disputes of the war, notably regarding the choice between operations in the Mediterranean or the invasion of **France**, and strategy in the China–Burma–India theater, but was ultimately a vital element in the successful integration of the fighting effort of the Western Allies, principally because of the willingness on both sides to respect each other's views and to accept the final decisions of the committee. At times, these decisions were subject to considerable modification by President **Franklin D. Roosevelt** and Prime Minister **Winston Churchill**. The committee continued after the end of the war, but lack of interest on the U.S. side led to its meeting rarely, and its agenda was taken up with insignificant issues. It was effectively revived with the creation of the North Atlantic Treaty Organization (NATO) in 1949. *See also* GRAND ALLIANCE; SECOND FRONT.

COMMERCIAL AGENCY AGREEMENT (1915). This agreement between **J. P. Morgan**'s company and the government of **Great Britain** during **World War I** gave the former broad powers to arrange and supervise all aspects of arms and munitions sales to Britain, **Russia**, and **France**, including financial transactions and shipping. The House of Morgan undertook purchases for Allied governments amounting to over $3 billion in 1915–17. Close cooperation between U.S. manufacturers and Allied buyers under this agreement enabled British quality control inspectors to monitor and advise on production techniques in U.S. arms factories. It also greatly increased Britain's financial dependence on the United States. *See also MERCHANTS OF DEATH*; NYE COMMITTEE; WAR DEBTS.

COMMISSION FOR RELIEF IN BELGIUM. Created in October 1914 and headed by future U.S. president **Herbert Hoover**, the relief commission aimed to meet the growing threat of starvation in Belgium, which had been occupied by **Germany** during the early weeks of **World War I** and could not import vital food supplies due to the Allied blockade. Over four years, the commission organized the delivery of more than 5 million tons of food, to over 2,500 cities and towns. It set up a rationing system and raised over $1 billion in donations and government grants. The fund eventually had its own flag, trains, and designated factories. Hoover gained international fame as a humanitarian and dynamic organizer, which set him on the path to cabinet office in 1921 and the U.S. presidency in 1929. *See also* UNITED NATIONS RELIEF AND REHABILITATION ADMINISTRATION; VOLGA FAMINE RELIEF EFFORT.

COMMITTEE ON FOREIGN RELATIONS. *See* SENATE COMMITTEE ON FOREIGN RELATIONS.

COMMITTEE ON PUBLIC INFORMATION (CPI). The Committee on Public Information was established by the federal government to oversee U.S. propaganda efforts during **World War I**. President **Woodrow Wilson**, worried that public opinion was divided over

U.S. entry into the war, selected journalist and newspaper proprietor George Creel to chair the committee to deal with this problem.

The CPI's governing body (Creel and the secretaries of war, state, and the navy) met only once during the war. Creel saw the CPI's role as a vital part of the war effort. He argued that this war, unlike previous conflicts, was not purely a military struggle but a global contest between starkly opposed values and ideologies. The scale of the conflict, he contended, mandated an unprecedented and centrally coordinated propaganda effort to strengthen resolve at home and boost troop morale in Europe. The CPI was, for Creel and his supporters, "the voice created to plead the justice of America's cause before the jury of Public Opinion." It sent thousands of volunteer speakers across the country and distributed millions of posters, full-page newspaper ads, and pamphlets (the Red, White, and Blue Books) to homes, newspaper offices, and workplaces explaining U.S. war aims and emphasizing the superiority of America's moral arguments.

CPI speakers were nicknamed the "Four Minute Men" because they were trained to deliver talks lasting no more than four minutes. They would appear at movie theaters to remind audiences of the importance of economizing at home, writing supportive letters to U.S. troops abroad, and staying alert to the dangers of sabotage. Creel also ensured that schools, universities, and farms received a constant stream of propaganda materials. Military equivalents of the Four Minute Men bolstered troop morale in Europe and were particularly active when **Russia**'s withdrawal from the war early in 1918 prompted fears of a wave of antiwar sentiment in the trenches.

The CPI's activities raised accusations that the administration sought to muzzle the press, indoctrinate the public, and suppress free speech. The resumption of normal partisan politics in late 1918 caused Creel to clash with the Republican 66th Congress, which quickly shut off CPI funds and launched an investigation into its finances. Negative images of the CPI, especially its heavy-handed rhetoric and its encouragement of hyper-patriotism and vigilantism, would profoundly affect approaches to government propaganda in **World War II**. *See also* OFFICE OF WAR INFORMATION.

COMMITTEE TO DEFEND AMERICA BY AIDING THE AL-LIES (CDAAA). Also known as the White Committee, the Committee to Defend America by Aiding the Allies was active from May

1940 to October 1942. The group was formed by Kansas City newspaper editor **William Allen White, Clark M. Eichelberger** of the **League of Nations Association**, and others active in Eichelberger's **Nonpartisan Committee for Peace through Revision of the Neutrality Law**, such as banker **Thomas Lamont** and peace activist and public health specialist Frank Boudreau. Its original aim was to shape public opinion in favor of aid to the Allies: **Great Britain, France**, and other countries in Europe fighting Nazi **Germany** during **World War II**. The CDAAA argued that if sufficient U.S. aid was supplied, this would keep the United States out of war.

White served as national committee chair until January 1941, when he retired through a combination of ill health and disagreement over strategy. He was succeeded by Ernest W. Gibson, and then in spring 1941 by Eichelberger. The national committee was based in New York City, with local and state chapters in every state and U.S. territory. There were also special divisions for women, youth, labor, artists, scientists, and the like. The committee communicated through newsletters, flyers, advertisements, radio spots, and rallies. It was mainly supported by fund-raising activities and donations.

The CDAAA never supported a **declaration of war**, though it was generally supportive of moves by the **Franklin D. Roosevelt** administration to provide more aid to Great Britain, such as the **destroyers-for-bases** deal, **Lend-Lease**, and revision of the **Neutrality Acts**. After September 1940, it campaigned against the **America First Committee**. Members who felt by the spring of 1941 that aid alone was not enough to ensure U.S. national security broke away to form **Fight for Freedom**, but CDAAA remained close to the views of the administration and the president until the attack on **Pearl Harbor**.

After the United States entered the war, the CDAAA merged with the Council for Democracy to form an organization called Citizens for Victory: To Win the War, To Win the Peace. The aim was to focus on issues of the postwar peace, but effectiveness as a lobby group was lost without the unifying issue and with members engaged in more urgent tasks related to the war effort. The organization officially dissolved in October 1942.

COMMITTEE TO DEFEND AMERICA FIRST. *See* AMERICA FIRST COMMITTEE.

COMMUNIST PARTY OF THE UNITED STATES (CPUSA). The CPUSA was founded in 1919 by former members of the Socialist Party who had been expelled for supporting the Bolshevik revolution. They included Elizabeth Gurley Flynn, Claude McCay, John Reed, and **William Z. Foster**. By August 1919, the party had 60,000 members while the Socialist Party had 40,000. This growth worried President **Woodrow Wilson**, and the result was the Red Scare orchestrated by Attorney General A. Mitchell Palmer and his assistant J. Edgar Hoover.

The first chair of the CPUSA, James Cannon, attended the meeting of the Communist International (Comintern) in Moscow in 1928. He was subsequently expelled for criticizing the rise to power of **Josef Stalin** in the **Union of Soviet Socialist Republics** (USSR), to be succeeded by Foster. Foster gained the CPUSA's best general election result ever in 1932 with 102,991 votes, though this was much less than **Norman Thomas** gained for the Socialists. Foster was succeeded by **Earl Browder** in 1932. The CPUSA's foreign policy line followed the direction laid down by the Comintern. From 1935, it followed the "popular front" line of cooperating with other antifascist forces. The CPUSA supported the New Deal and in this period gained its widest membership, including many intellectuals and artists drawn by the strength of its hostility to fascism. In 1936, it helped organize the International Brigades (**Abraham Lincoln Brigade**) to fight in the **Spanish Civil War**.

In August 1939, as a consequence of the Nazi–Soviet pact, the CPUSA opposed any move toward war or aid to **Great Britain** and **France**. Many members left at this time because of what they saw as a betrayal of the antifascist cause that had attracted them to the party during the 1930s. In June 1941, the line was reversed again when **Germany** invaded the Soviet Union. The CPUSA became a fervent supporter of the war and opposed labor strikes that might undermine the war effort. It vociferously supported Soviet demands for a **second front**.

Browder believed U.S.–USSR cooperation would outlast the war and in 1944 attempted to abolish the party in preparation for what he thought would be greater involvement in mainstream politics. He set up the Communist Political Association instead. The growth of Cold War tensions brought his replacement in 1945 by Foster, as the

CPUSA once again fell in line with the direction of Soviet foreign policy. Membership of the party had peaked at 75,000 during the war, but it was later subject to legal attacks under the Aliens Registration Act (**Smith Act**), and its leaders were tried and jailed. By 1957 membership had fallen to 10,000, though the party continued in existence. *See also* VENONA PROJECT.

COMPTON, ARTHUR HOLLY (1892–1962). Arthur Compton won a Nobel Prize for Physics in 1927 for his work on X-ray particle scattering. In 1941, he and **Vannevar Bush** helped revitalize the U.S. **atomic bomb** program. Compton took charge of the Office of Scientific Research and Development's S-1 committee investigating the properties of uranium. Compton appointed **J. Robert Oppenheimer** as the committee's main theorist. The committee's work came under the authority of the U.S. Army in summer 1942 as the **Manhattan Project**.

Appointed in 1941 to be chair of the National Academy of Sciences Committee to Evaluate Use of Atomic Energy in War, Compton had been organizing the work on plutonium at Chicago University since December 1941, with the target of perfecting a bomb by January 1945. In December 1942, the team at Chicago, led by **Enrico Fermi**, achieved a chain reaction in their work to create plutonium. This led to the building of reactors at Hanford, Washington, that made the plutonium for the **Nagasaki** bomb. Compton played a significant role in the government decision to use the atomic bomb in 1945, a story he told in his book *Atomic Quest* (1956). After the war, he was chancellor of Washington University, St. Louis (1946–53). Compton was president of the American Physical Society (1934), the American Association of Scientific Workers (1939–40), and the American Association for the Advancement of Science (1942).

CONANT, JAMES BRYANT (1893–1978). James B. Conant gained a Ph.D. in chemistry from Harvard in 1916 and worked in the Chemical Warfare Service in **World War I**. He returned to Harvard to teach chemistry and became its president in 1933. He was a Republican opposed to the New Deal but did not agree with the **isolationism** of many in the party. When **World War II** began, he advocated aid to the Allies and worked to enlist scientists in war preparations through the **National Defense Research Committee**. He was closely involved in liaising with **Great Britain** over atomic research and was active in the Office of Scientific Research and Development and the **Manhattan Project**. He was associated with the decision in June 1945 that the **atomic bomb** should be dropped on a sizable Japanese city with war-making facilities—this turned out to be **Hiroshima**. Conant was an advisor to the Atomic Energy Commission (1946–62) and a major defender of the decision to drop the bomb, on the grounds that it shortened the war and reduced casualties. He was high commissioner in Western **Germany** (1953–55), ambassador to the Federal Republic of Germany (1955–59), and subsequently involved in educational reform in the United States.

CONNALLY, THOMAS TERRY (1877–1963). Lawyer Tom Connally served in the Texas Volunteer Infantry in the 1898 Spanish–American War and the U.S. Army in **World War I**. A Democratic member of the U.S. House of Representatives (1916–29), he served on the House Foreign Affairs Committee and was a critic of U.S. policy in the Caribbean. Connally then served in the Senate (1929–53).

Although originally a supporter of President **Franklin D. Roosevelt**, he moved to the right under the influence of Texan oil magnates and became one of Roosevelt's sharpest critics in Congress on domestic affairs. He supported Roosevelt's foreign policy, however, and assisted the passage of the 1941 **Lend-Lease Act**. Connally served on the **Senate Committee on Foreign Relations** and chaired the committee from 1941 to 1947, sponsoring the **Connally Resolution** (November 1943) concerning U.S. participation in an international organization. He also chaired the Committee of Eight that liaised on foreign policy between the Senate and the administration. He was vice chair of the U.S. delegation to the 1945 **San Francisco Conference** and U.S. representative at the first and second sessions of the **United Nations** in 1946. He supported the formation of the North Atlantic Treaty Organization and generally endorsed the foreign policy of President **Harry S. Truman**.

CONNALLY RESOLUTION (1943). In October 1943, following on from the **Fulbright Resolution**, the B2H2 resolution was introduced in the Senate, named after its four sponsors: Joseph Ball (R-Minn.), Harold Burton (R-Ohio), Carl Hatch (D-N.M.), and Lister Hill (D-Ala.). It proposed a commitment to U.S. membership in an international organization with police powers. A fierce debate followed, revolving around the issues of the fundamental nature of the organization, the extent to which the police powers could be allowed to impinge on national sovereignty, and whether the Senate would be giving a blank check to the president in negotiating the details of such an organization. Senator **Claude Pepper** argued that the Senate might be committing itself to an arrangement that endorsed imperialism. **Tom Connally**, chair of the **Senate Foreign Relations Committee**, proposed an alternate resolution that merely advised that the United States should be a member of a postwar "international authority" of "free and sovereign nations." Further debate erupted over the meaning of these vague words and over the U.S. role in the postwar world.

Connally proposed a Committee of Eight to circumvent difficulties between the White House and Senate, such as had erupted in 1919 over the **Treaty of Versailles**. The more he was pressed, the more he became sensitive to criticism. The B2H2 group argued strongly in favor of a crusading **internationalism**. On the other side, conservatives, led by **Robert Taft** of Ohio, questioned the whole concept, asking who would police the police power. Republican **Arthur Vandenberg** of Michigan, only recently converted from **isolationism**, took a lead in formulating a compromise. Vandenberg followed a line suggested by President **Franklin D. Roosevelt**, essentially endorsing what had been agreed to at the recent 1943 **Moscow Conference** of foreign ministers: regarding **World War II**, there would be no separate peace, and the United States would cooperate with its allies in securing a just peace. The resolution declared the need for an international organization, based on sovereign equality, which the United States should join, "to prevent aggression and to preserve the peace of the world." The proviso was added, however, that while the Senate recognized the necessity for such an organization, any treaty made to give effect to this resolution was subject to the consent of the Senate, two-thirds of the senators present concurring.

The resolution, still known as the Connally Resolution, was approved on 5 November 1943 by a vote of 85–5. The Senate thus reflected growing public (and bipartisan) enthusiasm for a world organization and encouraged the administration to engage in negotiations to that end, while reserving to the Senate the ultimate say on U.S. membership. *See also* COLLECTIVE SECURITY; DUMBARTON OAKS CONFERENCE; UNITED NATIONS.

CONVENTION ON INTERNATIONAL CIVIL AVIATION. *See* CHICAGO CONFERENCE.

COOLIDGE, CALVIN (1872–1933). The 30th president of the United States, Calvin Coolidge practiced law in Northampton, Massachusetts, was elected to the state senate in 1914, became lieutenant governor in 1915, and was elected governor in 1918. He gained national fame for his stern response to the 1919 Boston Police strike. In a telegram to labor leader Samuel Gompers, Coolidge wrote, "There is no right to strike against the public safety by anyone, anywhere, any time." His confrontation with Gompers made him popular with delegates to the 1920 Republican national convention, who defied their party leadership and nominated Coolidge for vice president. The ticket of **Warren G. Harding** and Calvin Coolidge won a landslide victory against Democrats **James M. Cox** and **Franklin D. Roosevelt**. Coolidge maintained a low profile as vice president, presiding over the U.S. Senate and attending cabinet meetings. He succeeded to the presidency on the death of Harding on 2 August 1923.

Coolidge made few significant changes to Harding's conservative domestic policy but was less inclined than his predecessor to confront congressional opposition. Consequently, the payment of cash bonuses to veterans of **World War I** (vetoed by Harding in 1922) was passed over Coolidge's veto in 1924. In the same year, Congress passed the **National Origins Act**, imposing strict limitations on immigration quotas, despite the president's misgivings. Coolidge displayed little interest in foreign policy, delegating decisions to the State Department whenever possible. He appointed **Frank B. Kellogg**, a wealthy lawyer with no significant background in diplomacy, to succeed **Charles Evans Hughes** as secretary of state after the latter's resignation in 1925. The choice disappointed many Washington observers, who considered Kellogg unqualified.

The most notable treaty of the Coolidge–Kellogg period, the **Kellogg–Briand Pact** (1928), was a well-meaning but futile effort to outlaw war between the major powers. Coolidge and Kellogg privately considered the pact naïve but endorsed it due to pressure from foreign diplomats, domestic antiwar lobbying groups, and an influential combination of **isolationists** and **progressives** in Congress led by Senator **William E. Borah**. Coolidge also appeared only half-heartedly committed to the 1927 **Naval Disarmament Conference** in Geneva. Some European diplomats and press later criticized the administration's apparent lack of preparation. Coolidge also disappointed European governments by his comparative inflexibility over **war debt** repayments.

In **Latin American** affairs, Coolidge shared Harding's distaste for the imperialistic interventionism of Presidents **Theodore Roosevelt** and **Woodrow Wilson** but continued his predecessor's efforts to protect American lives, property, and investments, particularly in **Mexico**. During the first half of the Coolidge period, U.S.–Mexico relations deteriorated markedly due to disputes over Mexican intentions toward Nicaragua, debt repayments, and implementation of the **Bucareli Agreements**. Coolidge's choice of an old college classmate, **Dwight Morrow**, as ambassador to Mexico proved a turningpoint. Morrow's diplomacy enabled the United States and Mexico to resolve differences over American property rights.

In Nicaragua, the political situation had also deteriorated by the mid-1920s. Political instability accompanying the removal of the anti-U.S. **Emiliano Chamorro** erupted into civil war after Mexican intervention on the side of the Nicaraguan liberals and their general, Jose Moncada. Coolidge made another successful choice of emissaries, instructing **Henry L. Stimson**, previously secretary of war in the **William H. Taft** administration, to travel to Managua and "clean up that mess." Stimson persuaded Moncada to accept the authority of President Adolfo Diaz (who had succeeded Chamorro), pending fair elections to be held in 1928 under U.S. supervision. The agreement was known as the Peace of **Tipitapa**. Elections were held successfully, but a rebellion led by **Augusto Sandino** continued until 1934, when Sandino was killed.

In both Mexico and Nicaragua, long-term problems remained after the end of the Coolidge administration, but some historians praise the president for his use of personal emissaries and for continuing the cautious and conciliatory policies introduced by Harding and Hughes.

Coolidge's foreign policy, like Harding's, was constrained by domestic political circumstances. Congressional isolationists maintained their defiant opposition to "internationalist" policies, and the president was unable to move in foreign policy making with the freedom and confidence of Roosevelt and Wilson. Further, the American public had no taste for imperialistic operations in Latin America or participation in ambitious international organizations. **Dollar diplomacy** and mediation remained viable options but required skill and patience in their implementation. Harding had chafed at the constraints, but Coolidge's more passive personality enabled him to accept and work within them, bringing a toned-down style and outlook to U.S. foreign policy during the 1920s.

COUGHLIN, CHARLES E. (1891–1979). Born in Canada, Father Charles Coughlin, a Roman Catholic priest in Michigan, was one of the first people in American politics to use the radio to put their message across. More than 40 million listened to his broadcasts in the 1930s. At first, he supported President **Franklin D. Roosevelt**'s New Deal but later argued that the Great Depression was caused by the uncontrolled activities of capitalists, and he sought more radical reforms than Roosevelt was making. His populist message attacked capitalists, communists, and Roosevelt, whom he saw as the tool of the other two groups. Roosevelt sent **Joseph Kennedy**, a Catholic, to attempt to silence him, but the attacks increased in vehemence. Coughlin set up the Christian Front, which proposed schemes of "social justice" in opposition to the New Deal, some of which stemmed from his admiration for German dictator **Adolf Hitler** and Italian Fascist ruler Benito Mussolini and were often tinged with anti-Semitism. He supported **isolationism** and was an advocate for the **America First Committee**.

COUNCIL OF NATIONAL DEFENSE. *See* PREPAREDNESS CAMPAIGN.

COUNCIL ON FOREIGN RELATIONS. The Council on Foreign Relations was formed in 1921 from a merger of the American Institute of International Affairs and various groups supporting the **League of Nations**. Its main aim was to educate the American public on foreign policy issues from an **internationalist** perspective. Its membership was limited to 650, drawn from leading figures in politics, academia, commerce, law, and journalism, and it came to be seen as an elitist organization. Leading founding members included General **Tasker H. Bliss**, **Norman Davis**, and financier **Thomas Lamont**. The council began to publish the journal *Foreign Affairs* in 1922 and its annual report *The United States in World Affairs* in 1931. *See also* ARMSTRONG, HAMILTON FISH.

COX, JAMES MIDDLETON (1870–1957). James M. Cox served two terms as a **progressive** governor of Ohio (1913–15, 1917–21) before being chosen as the Democratic Party's nominee for the presidency in 1920. Incumbent Democratic President **Woodrow Wilson** was reported to have dismissed Cox's nomination as "a joke," despite the latter's pledge to campaign strongly for U.S. membership in the **League of Nations**. The Democrats selected Assistant Navy Secretary **Franklin D. Roosevelt** as Cox's running mate. Both were heavily defeated in the election of 1920. In 1933, after becoming president, Roosevelt made Cox a delegate to the 1933 **London Economic Conference**.

CROWLEY, LEO T. (1889–1972). From very humble origins as a railroad worker's son in Wisconsin, Leo Crowley rose to be a successful banker by the end of the 1920s. Despite engaging in irregular practices that led to his losing the presidency of his bank, Crowley became the most influential figure in behind-the-scenes Democratic Party politics in Wisconsin. He was involved in New Deal efforts to solve farm and banking problems in Wisconsin and worked closed with the agencies of **Jesse Jones** and **Henry Morgenthau**.

In 1934, President **Franklin D. Roosevelt** appointed Crowley chair of the Federal Deposit Insurance Corporation (FDIC). Despite misgivings by Morgenthau, Roosevelt overlooked Crowley's past financial misdemeanors because of his skill as an administrator, his standing with conservatives, and his influence in politics in the Midwest. Crowley worked hard as a "fixer" for Roosevelt and formed a vital link to conservative opinion as the liberal mood faded in the later 1930s. In 1939, Crowley became chair (later president) of the Standard Gas and Electric corporation.

During **World War II**, Crowley was a protégé of **James F. Byrnes**. In 1942, he was made alien property custodian with Byrnes's support and against Morgenthau's opposition. In 1943, he gained more influence when Secretary of Commerce Jesse Jones and Vice President **Henry Wallace** were in conflict over control of overseas economic operations. At Byrnes's suggestion, Crowley was made head of a new Office of Economic Warfare (OEW). Later in 1943, he was made head of the Foreign Economic Administration (FEA), which included OEW and the administration of **Lend-Lease**. Crowley thus became an important figure in the economic aspects of the war effort and in planning postwar economic policy.

Crowley gained congressional extension for Lend-Lease, but the FEA was large and hard to manage, and many administration liberals were unhappy with his conservatism. There were also accusations of conflict of interest because of his position at Standard Gas. His position weakened politically, but he remained head of the FDIC and FEA. His most controversial action concerned termination of Lend-Lease in August 1945. He favored ending the program quickly at the end of the war, as did conservatives and many others in Congress. He has been blamed for the way this was done on 15 August 1945, when ships at sea bound for **Great Britain** and the **Union of Soviet Socialist Republics** (USSR) were recalled. This issue seriously soured U.S.–Soviet relations. However, it is generally acknowledged that President **Harry S. Truman** later unfairly blamed Crowley for being solely responsible for this action. After the war, Crowley was head of the Chicago, Milwaukee, St. Paul & Pacific Railroad, served on the Civil Rights Commission, and continued to advise the FDIC.

CUBA. Following the war of 1898 between the United States and Spain, Cuba became effectively a protectorate of the United States. The 1901 **Platt Amendment**, the 1902 Cuban constitution, and the 1903 treaty gave the United States important rights of intervention in Cuban affairs and a permanent naval base on Cuban territory, at Guantánamo Bay. Cuba had long been closely tied economically to the United States, and independence was followed by a large increase in U.S. economic penetration. The United States gained a preeminent position in the sugar, mining, and tobacco industries. By the 1930s, it dominated Cuban trade and was the controlling element in banking, transportation, and utilities. There were armed interventions by the United States in 1906, 1912, and 1917, in response to insurrections that damaged U.S.-owned property. The highly visible U.S. presence was so powerful in the economic, political, and cultural fields that it inevitably became the focus of discontent and nationalist feeling. The Platt Amendment provided a direct target for such agitation.

During the early 1930s, economic depression and repressive policies led to a revolution against dictator **Gerardo Machado y Morales**, but anti-American sentiments were also a contributory factor. This was reflected in the decrees of the successor government of Ramón Grau San Martín. The United States was prepared therefore, through Ambassador **Sumner Welles**, to connive at Grau's overthrow.

The new power in Cuba was **Fulgencio Batista y Zaldívar**, who saw himself as a defender of order and property. The Platt Amendment was abrogated in 1934, changing the formal terms of the U.S. relationship with Cuba; the only clause retained was the possession of the Guantánamo base. With Batista in power, U.S. privileges and power would continue. In return, the 1934 **Jones–Costigan Act** lowered tariffs on imports of sugar from Cuba. Cuba was guaranteed the sale of approximately 2 million tons in the U.S. market. About 42 percent of sugar production was controlled by U.S. businesses. Much of the rest of the Cuban infrastructure was U.S.-owned, and Cuban trade was dominated by the relationship to the United States. Cuba remained in fact, if not in name, a protectorate of the United States. *See also* DETZER, DOROTHY; DOLLAR DIPLOMACY; GOOD NEIGHBOR POLICY; JOHNSON, HIRAM WARREN; UNDERWOOD, OSCAR WILDER.

CUDAHY, JOHN CLARENCE (1887–1943). John Cudahy graduated from Harvard and the University of Wisconsin Law School. He served in **France** during **World War I** and was in the force that took part in the U.S. intervention in **North Russia** in 1918–19. In the interwar years, he was a successful property developer. A Democrat, he was appointed by President **Franklin D. Roosevelt** to be ambassador to **Poland** in 1933, was transferred to Ireland in 1937, and was then ambassador to Belgium and Luxembourg from January to July 1940. He witnessed **Germany**'s invasion of those countries in May 1940.

Cudahy conducted a personal interview with German leader **Adolf Hitler** during this time.

CUMMINS, ALBERT BAIRD (1850–1926). *See* IRRECONCIL-ABLES.

– D –

DANIELS, JOSEPHUS (1862–1948). Josephus Daniels studied law in North Carolina before embarking on a career as a newspaper propri-etor and editor. His *News and Observer* became a force in southern politics and a vocal supporter of segregation and the Democratic Party. As a reward for his support for **Woodrow Wilson**'s presi-dential candidacy in 1912, Daniels was made secretary of the navy (1913–21). His deputy was **Franklin D. Roosevelt**, who proved considerably more energetic in the post than Daniels and more en-thusiastic in support of U.S. entry into **World War I**. Daniels's most notable achievements were overseeing naval expansion during the war (particularly in production of submarines and destroyers), ban-ning alcohol in the officers' mess, permitting women to serve in the navy, and establishing training schools on ships. In 1933, Roosevelt, now president, made Daniels ambassador to **Mexico**. Despite initial unpopularity with Mexicans because of his role in the 1914 attack on the port of **Veracruz**, Daniels helped smooth relations and remained in this post until 1941. *See also* MEXICAN OIL EXPROPRIATION CONTROVERSY.

DANISH WEST INDIES, ACQUISITION OF (1917). Negotiations to acquire the islands of St. Thomas, St. John, and St. Croix, close to Puerto Rico in the Caribbean Sea, began during the American Civil War and continued for 50 years. Congress rejected the purchase of the islands from Denmark in 1867, and the Danish parliament failed to ratify a deal made in 1902.

The completion of the Panama Canal in 1914 raised U.S. interest in the islands, and the outbreak of **World War I** that year created apprehensions concerning **Germany** gaining control of them. The United States threatened to occupy the islands if Denmark refused to sell them. The islanders were not polled on the issue, though generally they seem to have favored the change because they expected to become full U.S. citizens. A treaty was concluded on 31 March 1917, under the supervision of Secretary of State **Robert Lansing**, providing for the purchase, at a cost of $25 million. The territory was renamed the U.S. Virgin Islands. The inhabitants of the islands were denied U.S. citizenship for 10 years and governed, under a continuance of Danish colonial laws, by the **U.S. Navy** for 14 years. Since then, they have been democratically governed locally but are not fully represented in the U.S. Congress.

DARLAN, JEAN XAVIER FRANÇOIS (1881–1942). François Darlan distinguished himself as a commander in the French navy in **World War I**. He rose to admiral, executive head of the navy (1933–39), and then commander in chief. After the surrender of **France** in 1940, during **World War II**, Darlan's mistrust of **Great Britain** was intensified by the British attack on French warships at Mers-el-Kebir. Having assured the British that the French fleet would not allow itself to be taken over by **Germany**, he was affronted that the British doubted his word. He joined the French government based in Vichy as minister of marine and became foreign minister in February 1941. He was also vice premier, minister of information, and minister of the interior, and from August 1941 was minister of defense as well. He was willing to collaborate with the Germans and concluded the Paris Protocols in May 1941, granting Germany military concessions in Africa and the Middle East. Darlan failed to get much from Germany in return and the protocols remained unratified. He was replaced in April 1942 by Pierre Laval, though he remained commander in chief of the armed forces.

Darlan was in Algiers when the United States and Britain attacked French North Africa in Operation **Torch** (8 November 1942). After extensive negotiations with **Robert Murphy**, Darlan agreed to cooperate with U.S. forces and ordered French forces not to fire on them. Germany responded to Torch by occupying the Vichy areas of France, and Darlan regarded this as releasing him from his oaths of loyalty to the Vichy government. Darlan undertook to work with the Allies and was made high commissioner for French North Africa. This arrangement made the military operation much easier but raised concerns among many in the United States with regard to the ethics of making deals with someone seen as a collaborator with the Nazis. Darlan was assassinated on 24 December 1942 by a French royalist. The broader issue that arose from the incident was a contributory factor in Roosevelt's decision to announce three weeks later at the **Casablanca Conference** that the Allies would require **unconditional surrender** from their **Axis** enemies.

DAVIES, JOHN PATON (1908–1999). John Paton Davies was born in **China** of missionary parents. He joined the Foreign Service in 1933 and was posted to China. In February 1942, during **World War II**, he was made political attaché to General **Joseph Stilwell**. In 1944, Davies helped create the U.S. Army Observation Group, known as the **Dixie Mission**, which was the first official contact between the United States and the Chinese communists. Davies believed such efforts could counter Soviet influence with the communists and might help them develop into an acceptable alternative to **Chiang Kai-shek**'s nationalists. Davies was one of the "China hands" who recommended that the United States should deal directly with the Chinese communists as well as with Chiang Kai-shek. They argued that the communists were agrarian-based and by no means subservient to Moscow, but ignoring them might drive them in that direction. They predicted civil war would resume after the war and were unimpressed with the ability of Chiang's regime to defeat the communists.

After Stilwell's departure in October 1944, Davies found himself at odds with **Patrick Hurley**, who became ambassador to China in November 1944. Hurley wished to unify communists and nationalists under Chiang's presidency, while Davies believed that Chiang was not worth backing, that the communists were likely to win in China, so the United States should develop good relations with them. As a result of this disagreement, during which Hurley accused Davies of being a communist, Davies left China in January 1945. He served in the U.S. embassy in Moscow. After the war, he was on the policy planning staff at the State Department and with the high commission in **Germany**. He was serving in the embassy in Peru when McCarthyite accusations of disloyalty led to his dismissal in 1954, despite his having been cleared. Senator Joseph McCarthy had identified

Davies and the other "China hands" as having "lost China" to the communists. *See also* SERVICE, JOHN STEWART.

DAVIES, JOSEPH E. (1876–1958). A native of Wisconsin, Joseph Davies trained as an attorney, served as chair of the Federal Trade Commission (1915–16), and was an economic advisor to President **Woodrow Wilson** at the 1919 **Paris Peace Conference.** From 1933, Davies acted as counsel for **Rafael Trujillo,** dictator of the **Dominican Republic,** and was leader of the influential "Dominican lobby" in the United States that was composed of business leaders, lawyers, and legislators. Davies married Marjorie Merriwether Post, the General Foods heiress, in 1935.

A personal friend of President **Franklin D. Roosevelt's,** Davies was ambassador to the **Union of Soviet Socialist Republics** (USSR) from 1936 to 1938. He was appointed to the post on the basis of his political skills, loyalty to Roosevelt, and his wife's financial standing and social skills. Although present during the purges by Soviet dictator **Josef Stalin,** Davies was determined to see only good things in his hosts, much to the frustration of embassy officials like **George Kennan, Loy Henderson,** and **Charles Bohlen.** Davies reported that those accused by Stalin in the show trials were guilty, which was against the opinion of his officials. They were later also to complain that he spent much of his time socializing on his yacht or collecting art treasures.

Davies was ambassador to Belgium and minister to Luxembourg from 1938 to 1939. During **World War II,** he was a special assistant to Secretary of State **Cordell Hull,** though he was more important as a member of Roosevelt's circle of trusted informal advisors. When the United States and Soviet Union became allies, Davies was feted as a prophet of Soviet–American friendship. *Mission to Moscow,* his account of his ambassadorship, was a best-seller and was made into a movie in 1943, starring Walter Huston, but it was so flattering of Stalin that it embarrassed even the Soviets. Roosevelt used Davies as an occasional wartime envoy, and **Harry S. Truman** sought advice from him upon taking office as president, balancing somewhat the anti-Soviet views he received from **Averell Harriman** and the State Department.

DAVIS, DWIGHT FILLEY (1879–1945). Dwight Davis fought in the 138th Infantry Regiment of the U.S. Army in the 1918 Meuse–Argonne offensive during **World War I**. He later became director of the War Finance Corporation and served as secretary of war (1925–29) in the administration of **Calvin Coolidge**. Davis argued, largely without success, for increases in the military budget. When **Herbert Hoover** became president in 1929, Davis was made governor general of the **Philippines**, a post he held until 1932. During **World War II**, he served as director general of the Army Specialist Corps. Davis was also the founder of the international Davis Cup tennis competition.

DAVIS, JOHN WILLIAM (1873–1955). Lawyer John Davis represented West Virginia in the U.S. House of Representatives (1911–13) and took part in negotiations in Berne, Switzerland, between the United States and **Germany** for the release of prisoners of war in September 1918. He served as U.S. ambassador to **Great Britain** (1918–21) and was a compromise Democratic nominee for the presidency in 1924, when the two principal candidates deadlocked after 103 convention ballots. Davis was soundly defeated by President **Calvin Coolidge** and subsequently retired from politics.

DAVIS, NORMAN H. (1878–1944). Financier Norman Davis organized the Trust Company of **Cuba** in 1905. He was made undersecretary of state by President **Woodrow Wilson** in 1920. He left the State Department in 1921, in disagreement over the movement toward **isolationism**. Davis was a founder of the **Council on Foreign Relations** in 1921. During the 1920s he campaigned for U.S. membership in the **League of Nations** and the **World Court** and in favor of **disarmament**. He was a delegate to the 1927 Geneva Economic Conference and the 1932 **Geneva Disarmament Conference** and was appointed ambassador-at-large by **Franklin Roosevelt** in 1933. He led the U.S. delegation to the 1935 **London Naval Disarmament Conference** and the 1937 **Brussels Conference**. Between 1938 and his death, he headed the American Red Cross.

DAWES, CHARLES GATES (1865–1951). Charles Dawes rose to prominence during the William McKinley administration as comptroller of the currency (1898–1901) and acquired a reputation as a skilled organizer and motivator. Between periods of government service, he worked on the staff of General **John J. Pershing**, taking responsibility during **World War I** for procurement and distribution of essential supplies to the **American Expeditionary Force** in Europe in 1917–18.

President **Warren G. Harding** appointed Dawes as the first head of the new Bureau of the Budget (later the Office of Management and Budget), where he embarked on drastic cost-cutting and reorganization measures, estimated to have reduced federal government expenditure by $1.8 billion in the first 12 months. Harding is rumored to have considered replacing his vice president, **Calvin Coolidge**, with Dawes. Dawes's initiative and drive made him a logical choice to head the committee assembled to design a solution to the German **reparations** and hyperinflation crisis of 1923–24. As a result of the committee's proposal, popularly known as the **Dawes Plan**, Dawes received the 1925 Nobel Peace Prize.

The 1924 Republican National Convention chose Dawes for its vice presidential candidate, after the position had been declined by Senators **William E. Borah** and Frank O. Lowden. His relations with President Coolidge were strained, and his relations with the Senate, over which he presided, never recovered from his tactless inaugural address, in which he attacked Congress for preserving the seniority system and other procedures he considered arcane and undemocratic. He left office in March 1929 to become ambassador to **Great Britain** and was a delegate to the 1930 **London Naval Disarmament Conference**. His last significant government work came as the first head of the **Herbert Hoover** administration's Reconstruction Finance Corporation. Dawes stayed only a few months, long enough to oversee the distribution of $700 million in loans to struggling companies. He left politics to pursue a business career.

DAWES PLAN (1924). In 1923, **Germany** announced that it could not meet its punitive **reparations** bill (set in 1921 at $33 billion) imposed after **World War I**. Hyperinflation had cut the value of Germany's currency to an equivalency of 4 trillion marks to one American dollar by late 1923. In response, French and Belgian troops occupied the Ruhr region, further escalating international tensions. Secretary of State **Charles Evans Hughes** argued that the United States could not ignore the crisis, since European governments were more or less dependent on reparations payments from Germany in order to meet their own financial obligations to the United States. He proposed a committee to examine the problem. Chaired by former U.S. Budget Director **Charles G. Dawes**, the committee included delegates from **Great Britain**, Belgium, the United States, **France**, and Italy.

Under the committee's proposed Dawes Plan, a new schedule of debt repayments was drawn up requiring payment of $50 million in 1925, rising gradually to $500 million by 1929. These levels represented substantial reductions from the annual $2 billion demanded under the original terms of the **Treaty of Versailles**. An additional loan from the United States of $200,000 was designed to bolster German industrial recovery. The plan also established a new Reichsbank, stabilized Germany's currency, and proposed a phased withdrawal of French and Belgian troops from occupied territory. In the short term, the plan was successful, but the German government continued to argue that repayments were crippling economic recovery. The Dawes Plan was superseded in 1929 by the **Young Plan**. *See also* LAUSANNE CONFERENCE; WAR DEBTS.

DEBT DEFAULT ACT (1934). Also known as the Johnson Act after its sponsor, Senator **Hiram Johnson**, the Debt Default Act tackled the issue of **war debts**. It forbade loans to nations in default of repayment of loans given in **World War I**. It was a response to the fact that all the European states had ceased payment as a result of economic collapse, and it reflected a belief that foreigners were to blame for the economic depression in the United States. It was produced by the same public mood that produced the **Nye Committee** investigations—a sense that the United States had been duped into World War I and was now being duped again. As a result of the act, loans to **Great Britain** and **France** were impossible when **World War II** broke out in September 1939, and ultimately President **Franklin D. Roosevelt** came up with the ingenious solution of **Lend-Lease**. The act also impeded the negotiation of a postwar reconstruction loan with the **Union of Soviet Socialist Republics**, a significant element in the cooling of relations at the end of the war. *See also* DEBT FUNDING ACT; EXPORT-IMPORT BANK.

DEBT FUNDING ACT (1922). Passed by the U.S. Congress on 9 February 1922, the Debt Funding Act established a World War Foreign Debt Commission to oversee repayment of the $10.35 billion in **war debts** owed to the United States by its wartime allies and by the new states created from the collapsed Russian and Austro-Hungarian empires. The act laid down guidelines for negotiation, set an overall interest rate (4.25 percent), and set a final deadline for repayment (15 June 1947). **Great Britain** and other former European allies contended that outright cancellation of the debts would speed European economic recovery, stimulate trade, and prevent a worsening of the postwar trade imbalance between America and Europe.

The administration of **Woodrow Wilson** refused to consider the option but the administration of **Warren G. Harding** proved more pragmatic. It largely ignored the 1922 act in its negotiations with the British government. Talks between U.S. Treasury Secretary **Andrew Mellon** and British Chancellor of the Exchequer Stanley Baldwin in January 1923 resulted in interest rates of 3.3 percent for the first 10 years and 3.5 percent for a further 52 years. Great Britain would thus discharge its financial obligations by 1985. The agreement was approved by the Senate, over protests by **isolationist** Senator **Hiram Johnson** that the United States would be regarded as an "international sucker." Secretary Mellon argued that the agreement with Britain, and later similar agreements with 14 other nations, constituted "the most favorable settlements that could be obtained short of force." *See also* DAWES PLAN; DEBT DEFAULT ACT; LAUSANNE CONFERENCE.

DECLARATION OF NEUTRALITY (1914). President **Woodrow Wilson** issued a declaration of U.S. neutrality on 19 August 1914 as European powers entered **World War I**. It denounced the war "with which we have nothing to do, whose causes cannot touch us." The president requested that American citizens not take sides and remain unbiased "in thought as well as in deed." It expressed the hope that the United States would be able to continue to enjoy the rights of neutrals, particularly in maritime **trade**. *See also* BALCH, EMILY GREENE; BRYAN, WILLIAM JENNINGS; DECLARATION OF WAR (1917); *LUSITANIA*.

DECLARATION OF WAR (1917). During **World War I**, the threat to American shipping from German submarines and **Germany**'s support for a war by **Mexico** on the United States led President **Woodrow Wilson** to appear before Congress on 2 April 1917 to request a formal declaration of war on Germany and its allies. Wilson warned that American property and lives were in grave peril and that "armed neutrality" was no longer a viable option. He expressed deep regret at having to lead the nation into "the most terrible and disastrous of all wars" but represented the coming struggle as a campaign to "make the world safe for democracy" and expressed the hope that its outcome would be the establishment and protection of the rights of free peoples and small nations across the world. On 4 April, the Senate passed the war declaration 82–6. Two days later, the House of Representatives followed suit. The president's address was widely praised, but he later commented, "My message today was a message of death for our young men . . . how strange it seems to applaud that." Congress formally declared war on Austria-Hungary in December 1917. *See also* FOURTEEN POINTS; RANKIN, JEANNETTE PICKERING; ZIMMERMANN TELEGRAM.

DECLARATIONS OF WAR (1941). After the Japanese attack on **Pearl Harbor** during **World War II**, the U.S. Congress declared war on Japan, with two dissenting votes in the House, on 8 December 1941. One of those voting against the declaration was **Jeanette Rankin**, who had also voted against the 1917 **declaration of war**. After **Germany** and Italy declared war on the United States, Congress recognized a state of war with Germany and Italy on 11 December 1941, and with Bulgaria, Hungary, and Romania on 5 June 1942.

DECLARATION ON LIBERATED EUROPE (1945). The Declaration on Liberated Europe was an agreement between the United States, the **Union of Soviet Socialist Republics** (USSR), and **Great Britain** at the **Yalta Conference** in February 1945 during **World War II**. It originated with the U.S. State Department, though the final statement was less specific than the department proposed. It committed the signatories to aid the economic and political recovery of liberated and former **Axis** states in Europe, to carry out measures of relief, to form broadly representative interim governments made up of democratic elements, and to facilitate "where necessary" the holding of free elections. In effect, it was a reassertion of the principles of the **Atlantic Charter**. Soon after the conference, the declaration became the focus for a deterioration in Allied relations, as the USSR acted unilaterally in the countries in Eastern Europe that it liberated, applying a very narrow definition of "democratic" that excluded many individuals and parties favored by the United States. The situation was aggravated by severe restrictions placed on U.S. and British observers in these countries. *See also* BIG THREE; GRAND ALLIANCE; POLAND.

DE GAULLE, CHARLES ANDRÉ JOSEPH MARIE (1890–1970).
French military and political leader Charles de Gaulle was one of the prophets of modern armored warfare in the 1930s. In May 1940, during **World War II**, he commanded a unit of the French army in an action against the advancing German army that nearly made a crucial breakthrough at Montcornet. He was then appointed undersecretary for defense, and he was the only significant member of the French government to leave the country at the time of **France**'s surrender on 22 June 1940, in order to carry on resistance. In London, he declared himself the leader of the "fighting French."

At first, de Gaulle had few forces at his disposal, but he comported himself as the personification of France. He was endorsed by Prime Minister **Winston Churchill** of **Great Britain**, though with reservations, and his relationship with President **Franklin D. Roosevelt** was tense. The United States maintained diplomatic relations with the official French government in Vichy until November 1942, which made de Gaulle's official position uncertain. The seizure by Free French forces of two French islands off the Newfoundland coast, **St. Pierre and Miquelon**, prompted a crisis, as he had not cleared the action with Roosevelt. In turn, Roosevelt and Churchill's preference for making deals with other French leaders made de Gaulle suspicious of them. He was not informed of Operation **Overlord** until after the event. However, Free French forces were given the honor of being the first to enter liberated Paris, and given de Gaulle's political following, the Allies had to treat him as leader of the provisional French government.

De Gaulle resigned in 1946 but returned to leadership during the Algerian crisis in 1958 and was president of the French Fifth Republic until 1968. His policies were designed to restore France as a great power and involved distancing France from the United States and Great Britain. At least partly, this derived from de Gaulle's continuing resentment at the way they had treated him during the war. *See also* CASABLANCA CONFERENCE.

DESTROYERS-FOR-BASES DEAL. On taking office as prime minister of **Great Britain** during **World War II**, **Winston Churchill** stressed to President **Franklin D. Roosevelt** that much of the materiel being bought from the United States under the **cash-and-carry** system was being sunk by German submarines, and therefore escort vessels were needed. He repeated his plea in July. Roosevelt was extremely cautious about taking such an unneutral step as transferring **U.S. Navy** warships to the British, but he encouraged others, such as the **Century Group**, to begin putting forward a plan by which this could be done without a vote in Congress. The result was that Roosevelt made an executive agreement under his powers as commander in chief to transfer to Great Britain 50 old destroyers not required by the navy in return for 99-year, rent-free leases on bases in British possessions in Newfoundland, the Bahamas, Jamaica, St. Lucia, Trinidad, Antigua, and British Guiana.

Roosevelt was able to claim that this destroyers-for-bases deal enhanced U.S. national security, which would appeal to **fortress America** enthusiasts, and also that it represented a move in the dismantling of British imperial power in the New World, which would appeal to **isolationists**. However, many isolationists saw the plan as Churchill did, as a big step toward linking the United States with the British war effort. They attacked the circumvention of Congress as typical of Roosevelt's "executive dictatorship." The finalizing of the deal on 2 September 1940 was the impetus for the foundation of the **America First Committee**.

DETZER, DOROTHY (1893–1981). Writer and social activist Dorothy Detzer traveled in the Far East after graduating from high school in Indiana and then lived at **Jane Addams**'s Hull House in Chicago. In 1919, she spent a year in Austria as part of the relief operation organized by the American Friends Service Committee and followed that with two years in **Russia** as a famine relief administrator for the committee. Her work and the loss of her twin brother in **World War I** brought her to the cause of **pacifism**. When she returned to the United States in 1924, she became secretary of the U.S. section of the **Women's International League for Peace and Freedom** (WILPF).

As a lobbyist, Detzer was influential in the setting up of the **Nye Committee** in 1934. She also campaigned against exploitative activities by U.S. businesses in Africa, receiving the Order of African Redemption from the Liberian government in 1933 in recognition of these activities. She lobbied for recognition of the **Union of Soviet Socialist Republics** and for the end of U.S. claims to intervene in **Cuba** under the **Platt Amendment**. Detzer supported the **Neutrality Acts** and campaigned for U.S. neutrality as the crisis in Europe and Asia developed in the late 1930s. She was a member of the governing committee of the **Keep America out of War Congress**. Detzer resigned as secretary of WILPF in 1946 and worked as a freelance foreign correspondent thereafter.

DEVIL THEORY. The "devil theory" was advanced in the early 1930s as part of revisionism concerning U.S. involvement in **World War I**. The "devils" were usually either the government of **Great Britain**, American munitions makers, or Wall Street financiers—or a conspiracy of all three. The British were said to have duped Americans into the war by exaggerated atrocity propaganda and overstating the morality of their own objectives. Arms manufacturers and bankers were said to have been in collusion with the British, or to have fooled Americans into believing they were fighting for democracy whereas they were drawn into war to protect investments and profits.

The devil theory played into antibusiness feeling that developed as a result of the Great Depression, together with a tendency to scapegoat foreigners, building on a long-standing disillusionment with the British dating back to the 1919 **Paris Peace Conference**, if not even further back in American history. The tangible results were the **Debt-Default Act** and the **Nye Committee** hearings, as well as initial skepticism about atrocity stories in **World War II**. *See also* COMMERCIAL AGENCY AGREEMENT; DISARMAMENT; HANIGHEN, FRANK CLEARY; LUDLOW AMENDMENT; *MERCHANTS OF DEATH*.

DEWEY, JOHN (1859–1952). As a teacher of philosophy at Columbia University (1904–30), John Dewey advocated education based
on practical experience not authoritarianism. He had supported U.S.
entry into **World War I**, but during the 1920s, Dewey combined his
internationalism with support of **pacifism**. He opposed officer training programs in schools and the 1940 **Selective Training and Service Act**. Dewey was a strong believer that war could be prevented
by being outlawed, as was done in the 1928 **Kellogg–Briand Pact**.

DEWEY, THOMAS E. (1902–1971). Lawyer Thomas E. Dewey
was district attorney for New York City (1937–41) and governor of
New York State (1943–54). He was famous for the prosecution of
Mafia boss Lucky Luciano and acquired the nickname "gangbuster."
Dewey was the unsuccessful Republican candidate for the presidency
in 1944 and 1948. He represented northeastern business elements
in the Republican Party and offered a more liberal alternative to
Republican leaders such as **Robert A. Taft**. Dewey had failed to
win the nomination in 1940 partly because of his **isolationism** when
Germany was overrunning Western Europe in **World War II**. By
1944, Dewey's views had altered, as they had for many liberal Republicans, and he had become a firm supporter of U.S. membership
in the **United Nations**.

In his 1944 campaign, Dewey criticized inefficiencies and alleged
communist tendencies in the **Franklin D. Roosevelt** administration
but avoided foreign policy issues. After the war, Dewey supported
measures such as the Marshall Plan and the Truman Doctrine, in opposition to conservative isolationists in his party. Having narrowly
been defeated in 1948, he played a key role in securing **Dwight D.
Eisenhower** the presidency in 1952 in preference to Taft. *See also*
VANDENBERG, ARTHUR HENDRICK.

DIAZ, ADOLFO (1875–1964). President of **Nicaragua** Adolfo Diaz
first assumed office in 1911, after the resignation of President Juan
Jose Estrada. The conservative Diaz appealed to the United States
for military aid when a liberal revolt broke out in 1912. U.S. marines
helped quash the rebellion but a detachment remained in the country
for over a decade. Diaz was elected to a full term, although liberal
groups refused to recognize his government's legitimacy. He retired

in 1917 but became president again in 1926, after a failed coup by General Emiliano Chamorro prompted another direct intervention by the United States. Diaz confronted a second liberal revolt during his second term but accepted an agreement—the **Peace of Tipitapa**—brokered by the United States on 12 May 1927, which saw Diaz step down as president the following year to be replaced by Jose Maria Moncada in 1929. Diaz eventually left Nicaragua, settling first in the United States and later in Costa Rica. *See also* COOLIDGE, CALVIN; ROOSEVELT COROLLARY; STIMSON, HENRY LEWIS.

DIES, MARTIN (1900–1972). Lawyer Martin Dies was elected to the U.S. House of Representatives as a Democrat from Texas in 1930; his father had also been in the House. Dies was originally a New Dealer but came to oppose President **Franklin D. Roosevelt**'s plan. In 1937, along with Samuel Dickstein, Dies founded the **House Committee Investigating Un-American Activities**. Dies was the first chair, and it was commonly known as the Dies Committee. It later became the House Committee on Un-American Affairs (commonly abbreviated to HUAC) on a permanent basis in 1946. Ostensibly its targets were equally fascists and communists, but Dies was most interested in exposing communists and those who were their unwitting stooges. Methods of inference and guilt by association appeared early in the history of the committee. Dies unsuccessfully sought a Senate seat in 1941. His exposure of communist infiltration into unions in the Congress of Industrial Organizations (CIO) led the CIO to campaign against Dies in Texas, and Dies withdrew from his campaign for reelection in 1944. Dies's book *The Trojan Horse in America* (1940) was an attack on communist subversion. Dies served in the House again from 1953 to 1959. *See also* COMMUNIST PARTY OF THE UNITED STATES; SMITH ACT.

DISARMAMENT AND ARMS CONTROL. The term "disarmament" is sometimes used synonymously with "arms control," though the two terms are not interchangeable. In the period following **World War I**, "disarmament" referred to reduction of arms, as seen in the restrictions on German armed forces contained in the **Treaty of Versailles,** and to arms control measures such as the Five Power Treaty, which set limits on the building of certain classes of warships. Since this involved at the time the downsizing of fleets to meet the agreed ratios, this also involved acts of disarmament as well, though essentially it was about preventing arms increases and setting force levels, rather than bringing about decreases.

The movements for disarmament and arms control sprang from a strong belief in some quarters that the arms race between the major powers, especially the naval race between **Germany** and **Great Britain**, had been a cause of World War I, and that arms cause wars. The **collective security** ideas behind the concept of the **League of Nations** were designed to encourage nations to disarm. Advocates for disarmament tended to focus on specific weapons systems, the existence of which made states feel insecure. The idea was that if those weapons systems were eliminated, then states would feel secure and have no cause to go to war.

In the United States in the 1930s, advocacy of disarmament gained strength in association with revisionist views on U.S. entry into World War I that produced the **devil theory** and attacks on arms manufacturers in books such as *The Merchants of Death*. Those who advocated **pacifism** were therefore joined by those with specific hostility to arms manufacturers, and by those who saw entry into World War I as a mistake and were drawn to **isolationism** as a result. Apart from producing the **Neutrality Acts**, this coalition of opinions combined with economic realities to keep the size of the U.S. Army small. Naval expenditure was also curtailed, but this came to an end in 1938 with **Carl Vinson**'s Naval Expansion Act: the **U.S. Navy** was acceptable to many isolationists as a defensive force, and the building of warships provided employment.

During **World War II**, there was less talk of disarmament as the principal means to preserve peace. At the 1941 **Placentia Bay meeting**, U.S. President **Franklin D. Roosevelt** and British Prime Minister **Winston Churchill** agreed that aggressor nations should be disarmed, but also that the victor nations should stay armed to preserve the peace until such time as a viable international settlement was in place. Thus, disarmament was spoken of only in terms of the treatment of the defeated enemy. The implications of Roosevelt's **four policemen** concept and creation of the Security Council in the **United Nations** were that the victorious great powers would remain armed. The United Nations itself was given powers to raise military forces from its members. After World War II, the focus of disarmament activists shifted principally to the issue of the **atomic bomb**. *See also* ATLANTIC CHARTER; LONDON NAVAL DISARMAMENT CONFERENCE (1930); LONDON NAVAL DISARMAMENT CONFERENCE (1935–36); NATIONAL COUNCIL FOR THE PREVENTION OF WAR; NAVAL DISARMAMENT CONFERENCE (1921); NAVAL DISARMAMENT CONFERENCE (1927); RAPIDAN CONFERENCE (1929).

DIVISION OF SPECIAL RESEARCH, STATE DEPARTMENT. The Division of Special Research was established on 3 February 1941 to prepare studies of issues that might arise in the period following the end of **World War II**. Like the earlier **Advisory Committee on Problems of Foreign Relations**, it reflected an eagerness on the part of some in the State Department that the United States, although neutral, should play an active role in shaping the postwar settlement, and a conviction that the United States would have the power and influence to do so. The war seemed an opportunity to reengage the United States with world affairs as well as to correct some of the flaws in the prewar international system. Secretary of State **Cordell Hull** sympathized with this approach. There was also a desire to begin this task of reshaping while the war was proceeding. The division was headed by **Leo Pazvolsky**. It collated statements on postwar issues made by the Allied and neutral governments, and it considered issues like the future of the **League of Nations**. In January 1943, the division was replaced by the Division of Political Studies and the Division of Economic Studies, both superintended by Pazvolsky. Much of the postwar planning shifted to the **Advisory Committee on Postwar Foreign Policy** and then to the Informal Political Agenda Group. *See also* BRETTON WOODS CONFERENCE; CONNALLY RESOLUTION; DUMBARTON OAKS CONFERENCE.

DIXIE MISSION. In 1944, during **World War II**, a U.S. Army observation group known as the Dixie Mission was sent to Yenan in northern China to make contact with the Chinese communists led by Mao Zedong, who were fighting against the occupation by **Japan**. The mission lasted from 22 July 1944 to 11 March 1947. The army group was commanded by Colonel David Barrett, and the diplomatic section was headed by **John S. Service**. A leading member was diplomat **John Paton Davies**, who had proposed the mission to **Joseph Stillwell** as a means of countering potential Soviet influence in China. It was initially opposed by **Chiang Kai-shek**, but he finally agreed to it as part of a deal struck with Vice President **Henry Wallace**, in which the United States promised to send a replacement for Stillwell as Chiang's liaison with President **Franklin D. Roosevelt**.

The mission's reports presented a positive outlook on the communists, both as a wartime ally against Japan and in terms of downplaying their Marxism and presenting them as merely agrarian reformers. The Dixie Mission hosted **Patrick Hurley** (1944) and **George Marshall** (1946) on their missions to improve relations with the communists. Hurley blamed his failure to reconcile the nationalists and communists on Service, Davies, and other members of the Dixie Mission. They were to become the targets for the hostility of the "China lobby" in the postwar period that criticized U.S. failure to support Chiang Kai-shek. Consequently, many of the members of the mission were the subjects of accusations of being soft on communism made by Senator Joseph McCarthy in the early 1950s.

DODD, WILLIAM EDWARD (1869–1940). William Dodd, from North Carolina, gained a Ph.D. from the University of Leipzig, **Germany** (1900), and was a professor of history at the University of Chicago (1908–33). He was a Jeffersonian liberal and an expert on the American South. Dodd was a supporter of Wilsonian **internationalism** and helped President **Woodrow Wilson** prepare for the 1919 **Paris Peace Conference**.

Dodd was ambassador to Nazi Germany from June 1933 to December 1937, and his diary from that period is a key historical source. Dodd was second choice for the job after **Newton Baker** turned it down. He was given the post because of his German connections and his Wilsonian ideals. In the face of the excesses of the **Adolf Hitler** regime, Dodd maintained a public face of integrity, refusing to join the diplomatic corps at the Nazi Nuremberg rallies. He was not a skilled diplomat, however, and the State Department found his stiff Wilsonianism unhelpful in the conduct of foreign policy. At the time, his criticism of Nazism was not welcomed in the State Department, and Secretary of State **Cordell Hull** regarded him as "somewhat insane." He was brought home for discussions, sent back to Berlin, and then immediately relieved of his post. *See also* GILBERT, PRENTISS BAYLEY; SMITH, TRUMAN; WILSON, HUGH ROBERT.

DOLLAR DIPLOMACY. As a characterization of U.S. foreign policy, the term "dollar diplomacy" has positive and negative connotations. To **William H. Taft**, during whose presidency (1909–13) the term became popular, the linkage of diplomacy and economic incentives was preferable to armed intervention. "Substituting dollars for bullets," Taft argued, fostered stability and closer commercial and political ties, to the benefit of all involved. His secretary of state, **Philander C. Knox**, believed domestic instability and economic or armed intervention by foreign powers in **Latin America** and the Caribbean could be successfully forestalled by the expansion of U.S. business investment in the region. The administration therefore encouraged U.S. bankers to rescue the economy of Honduras and expand their influence in Haiti and **Nicaragua**.

Similar policies were pursued by the Republican administrations of the 1920s. The Democratic administration of **Woodrow Wilson**, less convinced of the moral justification for dollar diplomacy, refused to back **J. P. Morgan**'s $125 million loan for Chinese railroad construction, which had been arranged by Knox, on the grounds that the loan's terms threatened to compromise **China**'s administrative independence. Wilson's administration was not consistent on this issue, however, and brought heavy economic and military pressure to bear on **Mexico** and other Latin American countries in defense of U.S. economic and political interests. Despite some successes, dollar diplomacy failed to prevent instability in the Caribbean, Latin America, or China and was often criticized as simply an economic manifestation of imperialism. *See also* CLARK MEMORANDUM; EXPORT-IMPORT BANK; GOOD NEIGHBOR POLICY; MONROE DOCTRINE; ROOSEVELT COROLLARY.

DOMINICAN REPUBLIC. Dominican President Ramon Caceres was assassinated in 1911, and a series of unstable regimes followed, leading to national bankruptcy. In May 1916, President **Woodrow Wilson** dispatched U.S. marines to restore order and bring financial stability and democracy. The marines imposed martial law and governed the country for eight years. The financial system was reformed and run by Americans, and roads and other domestic infrastructure were improved. The occupation was unpopular, however, and armed resistance broke out in rural areas of the Dominican Republic. After his election in 1920, President **Warren G. Harding** negotiated withdrawal, which was completed in 1924, though the United States continued to administer the Dominican customs until 1940. *See also* TRUJILLO, RAFAEL.

DONOVAN, WILLIAM (1883–1953). New York lawyer William Donovan fought in **World War I** and later became a confidant of **Franklin D. Roosevelt's**. Roosevelt appointed Donovan head of the Office of the Coordinator of Information (COI) in July 1941, during **World War II**, in response to a memorandum by Donovan that emphasized the need for a central organization of **intelligence**, for psychological warfare, and for "black" propaganda (misinformation of the enemy). "Wild Bill" Donovan was an energetic, unorthodox figure who had little patience with conventional bureaucracies. As head of the COI, he had conflicts with other agencies, notably the **Federal Bureau of Investigation**, but Roosevelt rated him highly and appointed him head of the **Office of Strategic Services** (OSS) in July 1942.

Donovan shaped the OSS in line with his own ideas, and his relationship with the president ensured that his agency was able to resource the wide range of activities he envisaged for the organization. He was on less good terms with President **Harry S. Truman**, and Donovan's arguments that the OSS's expertise should not be dispersed after the war were ignored; it was abolished in September 1945.

DOUGLAS, LEWIS WILLIAMS (1894–1974). Lewis Douglas was a lieutenant in the U.S. Army (1917–19) in **World War I**. He then worked in his father's mine before becoming an academic at Amherst College. He was in the Arizona legislature (1923–25) and was a Democratic member of the U.S. House of Representatives (1927–33). On 7 March 1933, he was appointed director of the budget by President **Franklin D. Roosevelt**, but he came to oppose the deficit spending element of the New Deal and resigned in 1934. Douglas became vice president of the American Cyanamid company and then an academic at McGill University in Canada. He was an influential member of the **Century Group**, founded in 1940, and he was an **internationalist** who supported the Republican **Wendell Willkie** in the 1940 election. During **World War II**, Douglas took charge of the War Shipping Administration, responsible for the production of **Liberty Ships** (1942–44). After the war, he served as ambassador to **Great Britain** (1947–53).

DRAGOON, OPERATION. A military operation planned to take place simultaneously with operation **Overlord**, Operation Dragoon was originally codenamed Anvil. Allied forces would land on the French Mediterranean coast and advance up the Rhône valley. The principal objective was to prevent German forces in southern **France** from moving against the main landings in Normandy, and also to obtain use of French Mediterranean ports, particularly Marseilles. Anvil was agreed to at the 1943 **Teheran Conference** over the objections of Prime Minister **Winston Churchill** of **Great Britain**. The British preferred to use Allied forces in this theater to attack further in Italy, or to move northeast up into the Adriatic. Soviet Premier **Josef Stalin** backed Anvil at the conference. The operation was delayed by lack of landing craft and other logistical problems and finally took place on 15 August, two months after the Normandy landings, and by that point had been renamed Dragoon. *See also* SECOND FRONT.

DRESDEN. A historic city in eastern Germany, Dresden was the target for massive day and night bombing raids by U.S. and British aircraft in Operation Thunderclap, 13–14 February 1945, during **World War II**. The raids are controversial because the war was so close to its end and no obvious military targets were involved. At least 35,000 people were killed, mostly civilians, and many were refugees fleeing the advancing armies of the **Union of Soviet Socialist Republics** (USSR). After the war, British Prime Minister **Winston Churchill** fueled the controversy by voicing his disgust with the raids (having been a strong supporter of strategic bombing). But the mission had been requested by the Soviets to disrupt German movements on their front, and Dresden was a significant road junction. Many similar raids had been carried out as part of the **Combined Bomber Offensive** on small and poorly defended historic towns such as Lübeck as well as the larger cities, and on strategic targets like oil refineries and ball-bearing factories. *See also* GRAND ALLIANCE.

DULLES, ALLEN WELSH (1893–1969). Diplomat and **intelligence** operative Allen Dulles was the son of a Presbyterian minister. He and his brother, **John Foster Dulles** were nephews of Secretary of State **Robert Lansing** and grandsons of another secretary of state. Dulles graduated from Princeton in 1916 and joined the diplomatic service. He served in Vienna, Berne, Paris, Berlin, and Istanbul, and in 1922 he was made chief of the Division of Near Eastern Affairs in the State Department. He left the department to complete a law degree at George Washington University in 1926 and worked at the same New York international corporate law firm as his brother. In this role, he did much business in **Germany** and made many contacts.

In 1941, Dulles was appointed by **William Donovan** to head New York operations for the Coordinator of Information. After the **Office of Strategic Services** (OSS) was set up under Donovan, Dulles was made station chief for Europe, based in Berne, Switzerland, from November 1942. He developed contacts with German resistance groups and garnered intelligence about German jet fighter planes. He was involved in March 1945 in the discussions with SS General Karl Wolff regarding surrender of German forces in Italy, which led to accusations from Soviet leader **Josef Stalin** that the United States was conducting separate peace negotiations.

After **World War II**, Dulles served as OSS Berlin station chief for six months until the OSS was abolished. He was involved with the new Central Intelligence Agency (CIA) from its foundation in 1947. He oversaw Operation Paperclip, which resettled Nazi scientists in the United States and put them to work for the U.S. Army, protecting them from investigation. In 1953, Dulles became the first civilian head of the CIA. He was fired from the position by President John F. Kennedy after the Bay of Pigs fiasco in 1961. He later was a member of the Warren Commission investigating Kennedy's assassination.

DULLES, JOHN FOSTER (1888–1959). Lawyer John Foster Dulles, brother of **Allen Welsh Dulles**, was a nephew of Secretary of State **Robert Lansing**. He was educated at Princeton, the Sorbonne

(Paris), and George Washington Law School. He was secretary to his grandfather John W. Foster (a former secretary of state) at the second Hague Conference in 1907 and became a prominent international lawyer in New York. Dulles was an advisor to president **Woodrow Wilson** at the 1919 **Paris Peace Conference** and a delegate on the Reparations Commission and on the Supreme Economic Council. Opposed to excessive **reparations** demands, he became known for his advocacy of Christian virtues in foreign policy. He was a delegate at the 1933 Berlin Debt Conference and became a well-known figure among foreign policy makers. On the U.S. team for the 1945 **San Francisco Conference**, he subsequently served at a number of **United Nations** General Assemblies, and he became secretary of state under President **Dwight D. Eisenhower** (1953–59).

DUMBARTON OAKS CONFERENCE (1944). A series of international talks held at Dumbarton Oaks House in Georgetown, near Washington, D.C., the conference met between August and October 1944. Representatives of the United States, **Great Britain**, **China**, and the **Union of Soviet Socialist Republics** debated the structure of an international organization to replace the **League of Nations**. The main topic of contention was the Security Council and the veto powers of its permanent members. No agreement on this subject was reached, and it had to be referred to the meeting of the leaders of the **Big Three** powers at the **Yalta Conference** in February 1945.

The importance of the Dumbarton Oaks Conference was the basic consensus that a new organization was needed and also the incorporation into its structure of President **Franklin D. Roosevelt**'s idea of the **four policemen**, through the acceptance of the principle of great power management of the organization through the Security Council. The final details of the new **United Nations** were not settled until the **San Francisco Conference** in April 1945. *See also* ATLANTIC CHARTER; CONNALLY RESOLUTION; GRAND ALLIANCE; INTERNATIONALISM; UNITED NATIONS CHARTER; UNITED NATIONS DECLARATION.

DURBROW, ELBRIDGE (1903–1997). Elbridge Durbrow graduated from Yale University in 1926 and went on to study international law, economics, and finance at Stanford University, the University of Chicago, The Hague, the École Libre des Sciences Politiques in Paris, and at Dijon, **France**. He entered the Foreign Service in 1930 as vice consul in Warsaw, **Poland**. He received training in analysis of the **Union of Soviet Socialist Republics** (USSR) and was posted to Bucharest, Romania, in 1932. In 1934, he went to Moscow as an economics expert. Like other diplomats in the Moscow embassy, such as **Loy Henderson**, he developed a profound dislike for the Soviet regime. He was transferred to Naples, Italy, in 1937, and to Rome in 1940. In 1941, he was made assistant to Henderson, who was in charge of the Soviet desk in the State Department Division of European Affairs.

During **World War II**, Durbrow hoped that closer relations with the United States would cause the Soviet Union to moderate its expansionist ambitions, but as the Red Army advanced, he warned of Soviet intentions in Eastern Europe, masked by its use of popular front governments. In 1944, Durbrow became chief of the reconstituted Division of Eastern European Affairs and was a strong advocate of nonrecognition of the regimes the USSR established in Romania, Bulgaria, and Hungary. He was a delegate at the 1944 **Bretton Woods Conference**. After the war, he was counselor in Moscow, minister in Rome, and in 1957 became ambassador to South Vietnam. From 1961 to 1965, he was a U.S. representative with the North Atlantic Treaty Organization. *See also* BOHLEN, CHARLES EUSTIS; KENNAN, GEORGE FROST; THOMPSON, LLEWELLYN E.

– E –

EDGE ACT (1919). Passed by the Republican-controlled Congress of 1919–21, the Edge Act permitted U.S. banks to jointly fund foreign trade operations by American businesses by combining their capital investments. It also allowed U.S. corporations to undertake foreign banking operations. Corporations operating in this way were chartered by the U.S. Federal Reserve and known as "Edge corporations." *See also* EDGE, WALTER EVANS.

EDGE, WALTER EVANS (1873–1956). Walter Edge was twice elected governor of New Jersey (1917–19, 1944–47). While a member of the U.S. Senate (1919–29), he sponsored the **Edge Act**, permitting international banking operations by U.S. banks. He served as U.S. ambassador to **France** from 1929 to 1933.

EICHELBERGER, CLARK MELL (1896–1980). Clark Eichelberger served with the army in **France** in **World War I**, was later in Geneva at the **League of Nations**, and then became a lecturer on international affairs (1922–27). In 1928, he became director of the Midwest branch of the **League of Nations Association** (LNA) and in 1934 became its national director. When the LNA changed in 1945 to the American Association of the United Nations (AAUN), he remained as executive director (1945–64). Eichelberger was a founder of the Commission to Study the Organization of Peace (CSOP) in 1939 and was its director (1939–64), chair (1964–68), and executive director (1968–74).

Eichelberger also founded, with **William Allen White**, the **Committee to Defend America by Aiding the Allies** (CDAAA), a successor to their earlier pressure group, the **Nonpartisan Committee for Peace through Revision of the Neutrality Law**, and he was involved in other organizations advocating international cooperation. Eichelberger became national chair of the CDAAA in spring 1941. He was a consultant to the League of Nations secretariat in 1938 and to the **San Francisco Conference** in 1945. He was a member of the committee that produced the working draft of the **United Nations Charter**.

EINSTEIN, ALBERT (1879–1955). Physicist Albert Einstein was born in **Germany** but became a naturalized Swiss in 1905. His first special theory of relativity (1905) and general theory of relativity (1915–16) revolutionized concepts of physics. He was director of the Kaiser Wilhelm Institute of Physics at Berlin (1914–33), but Nazi anti-Semitism caused him to emigrate to the United States. He became a U.S. citizen in 1940 and was a professor at Princeton University. He became concerned that German nuclear physicists might succeed in building an **atomic bomb** and was asked by other nuclear physicists to communicate this to the U.S. government. In August 1939, he wrote a letter to President **Franklin D. Roosevelt** warning of German acquisitions of uranium in the former Czechoslovakia and the potential of atomic power as the basis of a weapon. Roosevelt eventually responded by initiating the **Manhattan Project**. After World War II, Einstein advocated international control of atomic weapons through the **United Nations**. In 1953–54, he publicly protested against the methods of McCarthyite investigations.

EISENHOWER, DWIGHT D. (1890–1969). Born in Denison, Texas, and raised in Kansas, Dwight Eisenhower graduated from West Point in 1915. His main talents were organizational, and his career was mainly as a staff officer. In 1930–35, he was assistant secretary of war and then chief of staff to General **Douglas MacArthur**. He was in the **Philippines** with MacArthur from 1936 to 1939. He was appointed chief of the War Plans Division in February 1942, during **World War II**. In May 1942, Eisenhower was sent to **Great Britain** but failed to convince the British of the possibility of invading German-occupied **France** that year. The eventual alternative was Operation **Torch**, and Eisenhower was appointed commander of the Allied forces. While not a great strategist, Eisenhower had valuable strengths as the leader of a multinational coalition, and he gained a reputation for absolute impartiality in dealing with the volatile personalities and politics involved in his command. He commanded the invasion of Sicily (Operation **Husky**) in July 1943 and of Italy in September 1943.

President **Franklin D. Roosevelt** appointed Eisenhower supreme commander of the Allied Expeditionary Force for the invasion of France in June 1944 (Operation **Overlord**). British General Bernard Montgomery commanded the ground forces on the day, but it was Eisenhower's responsibility to give the order to go ahead with the operation. He rated its chances of success at 50–50. Eisenhower took active command on 1 September 1944. He accepted Montgomery's disastrous plan for a quick advance over the Rhine, Operation Market-Garden. After it failed, Eisenhower resolved on a slower but less risky broad front strategy.

Generally, Eisenhower managed to keep the more flamboyant commanders, like General George Patton, under restraint, and he maintained good collaborative relations among the Allies. Despite the setback in the **Battle of the Bulge**, Eisenhower's forces were on the River Elbe by the second week of April 1945. Fearing that diehard Nazis would base themselves in the Bavarian Alps, he diverted Patton southward and reached agreement with Premier **Josef Stalin** of the **Union of Soviet Socialist Republics** (USSR) that the Soviet forces would be the ones to take Berlin. British Prime Minister **Winston Churchill** complained that Eisenhower was intruding into political matters, but Eisenhower responded that he was dealing with matters of military coordination with a fellow supreme commander, and he was backed by the **Joint Chiefs of Staff** and by President **Harry S. Truman**. His agreement with Stalin meant that Patton's forces halted on entering Czechoslovakia, and it was left to Soviet forces to liberate Prague.

After the war, Eisenhower was army chief of staff (1945–48), president of Columbia University (1948–51), and supreme commander of North Atlantic Treaty Organization forces in Europe (1951–52). He was elected 34th president of the United States in November 1952 and completed two terms in office, presiding over domestic affluence and Cold War tensions with the Soviet Union and the People's Republic of **China**.

EMERGENCY ADVISORY COMMITTEE FOR POLITICAL DEFENSE (CPD). Set up at the **Rio de Janeiro Conference** of American republics in January 1942, the CPD was to study and coordinate measures by individual states to counter subversion in the western hemisphere. The committee could only recommend actions to the governments; it could not undertake activities itself. The CPD was chaired by the Uruguayan representative and met in Montevideo. Other committee members came from **Argentina, Brazil,** Chile, **Mexico,** Venezuela, and the United States. *See also* INTER-AMERICAN DEFENSE BOARD.

EMERGENCY AGRICULTURAL TARIFF ACT (1921). A measure to raise **tariffs** passed by Congress in May 1921, the legislation responded to demands from U.S. agricultural interests for assistance. Extra duties were applied to wheat, sugar, wool, meat, and other farm products imported from abroad. The measure was rushed through Congress within weeks of the beginning of the new Republican administration of President **Warren G. Harding.** Conservative Republicans controlled Congress and saw protectionist measures as a way to steer the nation out of a severe postwar recession. President **Woodrow Wilson** had earlier vetoed a similar measure. *See also* TRADE.

EMERGENCY QUOTA ACT (1921). Signed by President **Warren G. Harding** in May 1921, the Emergency Quota Act (also known as the Immigration Quota Act) was a landmark in American **immigration** policy. An overall annual limit for immigrant numbers was set at 357,000, and a quota was established for each nationality equivalent to 3 percent of the total numbers settled in the United States at the time of the 1910 census. The act effectively ended the "open door" immigration policy and reflected heightened racial and ethnic tensions in the United States during the first quarter of the 20th century. It was also partly motivated by a deep economic recession that pushed up unemployment rates in 1920–22. The act was strongly supported by the American Federation of Labor (AFL) and the American Legion (representing war veterans), who argued that the American job market needed protection from the expected postwar flood of cheap labor. This argument proved more persuasive for members of Congress than the claim by the National Association of Manufacturers (NAM) that long-term economic benefits would accrue from retaining the open immigration policy. *See also* NATIONAL ORIGINS ACT (1924).

ENGELBRECHT, HELMUTH CAROL (1895–1939). Journalist Helmuth Engelbrecht earned a Ph.D. from Columbia University and wrote a study of German idealist philosopher Johann Gottlieb Fichte (1933). He was associate editor of **Devere Allen**'s **pacifist** journal *The World Tomorrow* in 1933, when he met **Frank Hanighen** at the offices of Dodd, Mead publishers. With a mutual interest in the abuses of the munitions industry, they collaborated in writing the influential *The Merchants of Death* (1934).

ESPIONAGE ACT (1917). Passed by Congress in June 1917, the Espionage Act mandated fines, prison terms of up to 30 years, and in extreme cases execution for anyone convicted of attempting to incite mutiny in the armed services of the United States, attempting to obstruct recruitment, or compromising national security through disclosure of information concerning government or industry. Many conscientious objectors, **pacifists**, and socialists were jailed under this act, including Emma Goldman, John Reed, and Socialist Party leader Eugene V. Debs, who was arrested for making a speech denouncing the act in 1918.

EUROPEAN ADVISORY COMMISSION (EAC). A proposal by British Foreign Minister Anthony Eden at the 1943 **Moscow Conference** during **World War II** led to the establishment of the European Advisory Commission in London in late 1943. The commission was to draw up armistice and surrender terms to be applied to the **Axis** powers, and it was to formulate arrangements for postwar occupation and control of their territories. **Great Britain** was represented by a Foreign Office official, the United States and the **Union of Soviet Socialist Republics** (USSR) by their ambassadors. The idea of the commission was to reach agreements away from the confusion and politics of high-level conferences, but the United States and USSR were not prepared to delegate much authority to their representatives, and progress was painfully slow. Eventually, arrangements were drawn up for occupation zones in **Germany** and Austria, which were then subject to approval by the **Big Three** leaders at the 1945 **Yalta** and **Potsdam Conferences**.

The work of the EAC meant that when the victorious armies met in the middle of Germany in May 1945, they had already agreed on their relative areas of occupation, which prevented a great deal of confusion and potential confrontation. Because the Western Allies had to withdraw from certain areas they had occupied, turning them over to the USSR, there has been some controversy. At the time, British Prime Minister **Winston Churchill** favored holding on to these territories as a bargaining chip to get better behavior by the USSR with regard to **Poland**. However, President **Harry S. Truman** and General **Dwight D. Eisenhower** were adamant that the agreements should be adhered to. *See also* GRAND ALLIANCE.

EVIAN CONFERENCE (1938). Held in France 6–15 July 1938, the Evian Conference was convened at the instigation of U.S. President **Franklin D. Roosevelt** to discuss the problem of Jewish refugees. Thirty-two nations took part, but the conference failed to agree on any action. Participants were mostly at pains to indicate that their countries could not possibly accommodate any more refugees. The U.S. representative was **Myron C. Taylor**, a businessman, serving as a personal envoy from Roosevelt, rather than a regular diplomat. Taylor stated that the immigration quota for Austria and **Germany** under the **National Origins Act** was available but promised nothing more. The International Committee on Refugees was set up to encourage permanent settlement of refugees, but it received no support subsequently and fell into abeyance. *See also* MORGENTHAU, HENRY; WAR REFUGEE BOARD.

EXPORT-IMPORT BANK. An independent government agency, the Export-Import Bank (Ex-Im Bank) was established to finance and insure foreign purchases of U.S. goods where no other funding is available because of credit risk. The bank was created under presidential executive order 6581 on 2 February 1934 with two main purposes: to serve as the government's agent in trading with the **Union of Soviet Socialist Republics** (USSR) and to compensate for the inability of the commercial banking sector to fund export activities as a result of the Great Depression.

The idea originated with the chief of the State Department Division of Eastern European Affairs, **Robert F. Kelley**, following U.S. recognition of the **Union of Soviet Socialist Republics** (USSR) in 1933. Kelley was concerned to stop the Soviet state trading agency from playing U.S. exporters against each other, and he hoped this would provide leverage to ensure the Soviets came to an agreement on the Kerensky debts issue. The executive order was prepared under the guidance of **William C. Bullitt**, and one of the drafters was **Warren L. Pierson**, special counsel for the Reconstruction Finance Corporation, which had previously given loans to U.S. businesses looking to trade with the USSR.

On 9 March 1934, executive order 6638 established the second Export-Import Bank, which would handle **trade** with **Cuba**. The United States believed it could do business with the new regime established under the auspices of **Fulgencio Batista**. In July 1934, this second bank was enlarged to do business anywhere in the world except the Soviet Union.

By January 1935, negotiations on the Soviet debts had stalemated, and in June 1935 the two banks were merged, largely because the first bank was doing no business. The banks already shared a president, **George Peek**, who was also special advisor on foreign trade. But Peek, taking a statist approach, disagreed with Secretary of State **Cordell Hull**'s **Reciprocal Trade Act**. The dispute led to his resignation in November 1935, and the post was offered to **Jesse Jones**, who served for two months on a temporary basis but refused a permanent position. Warren Pierson was appointed in February 1936.

Pierson developed the bank along business lines, though it continued also to be an instrument of U.S. foreign policy. **Walton Moore** and Kelley, assistant secretaries of state, were both in positions of authority, on the board of trustees and executive committee respectively. Pierson visited **China** in 1937 and later traveled extensively in South America. The bank provided the financing that built the Burma Road in 1938. In December 1938, the bank loaned $25 million to the Universal Trading Corporation, set up by Chinese business interests in the United States to buy and sell Chinese goods. This was depicted as a commercial move, but both **Japan** and President **Franklin D. Roosevelt**'s critics recognized the political dimensions of the move.

When the bank's charter was up for renewal in Congress in early 1939, Hull and Jones defended it in terms of its utility to U.S. foreign policy. The bank became identified with Roosevelt's foreign policy, no more so than in **Latin America**, where it provided some of the funds that allowed the "Rich Neighbor" aspect of the **Good Neighbor** policy. The bank was active in complex projects to improve Latin American export capabilities, while at the same time it sought to draw countries like **Brazil** away from their traditional economic ties to **Germany**. While Latin America accounted for roughly 20 percent of U.S. exports at this time, over 60 percent of Export-Import Bank authorizations were directed to the region.

Roosevelt shifted the Ex-Im Bank bureaucratically a number of times, though Pierson attempted to keep its procedures consistent. In 1939, it was placed in the Federal Loan Agency. In 1942, Roosevelt transferred it to the Department of Commerce. In July 1943, it became part of the Office of Economic Warfare (OEW), headed by **Leo Crowley**, who also succeeded Jones as chair of the Ex-Im's board of directors. In September 1943, Crowley was put in charge of the Foreign Economic Administration, with the OEW (still including the bank) and the Office of **Lend-Lease** Administration under him. Pierson resigned as president on 31 March 1945 and was succeeded by Wayne C. Taylor.

In July 1945, the Export-Import Bank Act established the bank on a permanent basis. Congress insisted on its being an independent governmental agency, not dependent on any government department. The act abolished the 1934 **Debt-Default Act** (Johnson Act). In 1946, the bank acted as a precursor to the Marshall Plan by providing over $2 billion in loans to be used in the reconstruction of Europe. With the International Bank for Reconstruction and Development (the **World Bank**) not ready yet to provide loans, the Ex-Im Bank was the only institution equipped to provide the credits and loans required for immediate postwar reconstruction. *See also* DOLLAR DIPLOMACY.

– F –

FAYMONVILLE, PHILIP RIES (1888–1962). After graduating from Stanford University, Philip Faymonville trained at the U.S. Military Academy, emerging as an ordnance officer. Gifted in **intelligence** work and fluent in Japanese, he began to learn Russian in 1916. Faymonville served as chief ordnance officer and judge advocate in the U.S. forces undertaking the **Siberian Intervention** of 1918–20. He subsequently served as military attaché in **Japan**. Faymonville was convinced that **Russia**, and later the **Union of Soviet Socialist Republics** (USSR), was a natural ally for the United States against what he saw as the major threat in the Far East, Japan. He supported recognition of the USSR in 1933, when he was at the U.S. War College and also senior military aide to the White House. He was picked by **William C. Bullitt** to join the staff of the new embassy in Moscow, where he established good relations with his Soviet counterparts. He shared the views of Bullitt's successor as ambassador, **Joseph E. Davies**, and was at odds with Foreign Service officials in the embassy, notably **Loy Henderson**. Faymonville was military attaché in Moscow from 1934 to 1939 and was then appointed to minor posts because of his views, which were regarded as too pro-Soviet by the U.S. Army.

This situation changed after the German attack on the Soviet Union in **World War II**, and Faymonville's expertise was now in demand. He was appointed director of the new Soviet supply section in the Division of Defense Aid Reports of the **Lend-Lease** Administration in July 1941. Faymonville was active in improving the flow of aid to the USSR, under the direction of **Harry Hopkins** and Major General James H. Burns. In September, at Hopkins's request, Faymonville went with **Averell Harriman** to Moscow for the 1941 **Moscow Conference** on the supply situation. He remained in Moscow as the representative of the Soviet supply section. He was independent of the embassy and came into conflict once more with Foreign Service officials and the military attaché because of his more accommodating attitude to the Soviet Union. This attitude conformed with that of President **Franklin D. Roosevelt** at this time, who preferred to bypass the embassy. As a consequence, Faymonville became known as "the Red General" (he was an acting brigadier general). In 1943, Roosevelt decided to deal with the personality clashes in Moscow by appointing Harriman as ambassador, and Faymonville and others were withdrawn. Faymonville served out the rest of his military career in the Ordnance Division, retiring in 1948. *See also* GRAND ALLIANCE.

FEDERAL BUREAU OF INVESTIGATION (FBI). The FBI is the principal investigative arm of the Department of Justice. It was founded in 1908 as the Bureau of Investigation, initially to deal with interstate commerce issues. Its role was expanded in **World War I** to cover espionage, sedition, sabotage, and draft-law evasion. It was renamed the Federal Bureau of Investigation in 1934. The FBI's jurisdiction is domestic, but under J. Edgar Hoover, director from 1924 to 1972, it took a broad view of its counterespionage role. During **World War II**, the FBI successfully operated against German spy rings in the United States. To mollify Hoover over the creation of the **Office of Strategic Services**, the FBI's responsibilities were extended by President **Franklin D. Roosevelt** to cover counterespionage in the western hemisphere, which Hoover interpreted broadly to include the gathering of **intelligence** and combating what he defined as subversion. The FBI was therefore an instrumental part of the wartime policy of reshaping the **Good Neighbor policy** around the coordination and management of security and defense issues with the Latin American republics, as seen also in the establishment of the **Inter-American Defense Board**. *See also* EMERGENCY ADVISORY COMMITTEE FOR POLITICAL DEFENSE.

FERMI, ENRICO (1901–1954). Italian-born physicist Enrico Fermi lectured in mathematical physics in Italy until 1938, when he emigrated to the United States to escape Benito Mussolini's Fascist regime, which had passed anti-Semitic laws (Fermi's wife was Jewish). He had just been awarded the Nobel prize for physics. By this time, he was the world expert on neutrons, and he was a professor of physics at Columbia University from 1938 to 1942. Fermi performed a key set of experiments concerned with chain reactions and in December 1942 made the first controlled atomic chain reaction in a Chicago stadium. He became an important member of the **Manhattan Project**, and his work was particularly crucial in producing the plutonium bomb. Fermi became an American citizen in 1944. From 1946 until his death in 1954, he was a professor at the Institute for Nuclear Studies at the University of Chicago. *See also* ATOMIC BOMB; COMPTON, ARTHUR H.; CONANT, JAMES B.

FIGHT FOR FREEDOM COMMITTEE (FFF). A breakaway group from the **Committee to Defend America by Aiding the Allies** (CDAAA), the FFF was established in April 1941 to lobby for full U.S. entry into **World War II** on the side of **Great Britain**. Its members were frustrated at the inconsistencies in President **Franklin D. Roosevelt**'s policies and believed that aid short of war would not bring Allied victory. Roosevelt had said in his **arsenal of democracy** fireside chat that Britain was fighting for freedom and defending American security, and the FFF thought it was unworthy of the United States to limit its role to providing arms with which others would fight. The CDAAA supported aid short of war, while the FFF pressed for full U.S. involvement. The FFF also acted as a counterweight to the **America First Committee**.

FISH, HAMILTON, III (1888–1991). A grandson of Secretary of State Hamilton Fish (1869–77), Hamilton Fish III was elected to the

New York State Assembly as a progressive in 1914. During **World War I**, he served in the U.S. Army in **France** as a white officer of the African American 369th Regiment, and he received the Croix de Guerre. In 1920, he was elected to the House of Representatives as a Republican and served there until 1945. He opposed the New Deal of his onetime friend President **Franklin D. Roosevelt** and proposed a number of anticommunist measures. His House Resolution 180 set up what became known as the Fish Committee, investigating people and organizations suspected of communist activities, including the American Civil Liberties Union. The committee favored tighter **immigration** laws, to keep communists out of the United States.

In 1939, Fish led the U.S. delegation to the Interparliamentary Union Congress in Oslo and associated himself with Foreign Minister Joachim von Ribbentrop of **Germany**. He said German claims to Danzig were just and on his return to the United States engaged in anti-Semitic propaganda. He was a staunch supporter of **isolationism** and strongly opposed the movement toward intervention in **World War II**. Repudiated by Republican presidential candidate **Thomas Dewey**, he was defeated in the congressional election of 1944 as part of the turn in public opinion against isolationism. Fish's father and his son, both called Hamilton, also served in the House of Representatives. *See also* COMMUNIST PARTY OF THE UNITED STATES; DIES, MARTIN.

FIVE-POWER TREATY. *See* NAVAL DISARMAMENT CONFERENCE.

FLETCHER, HENRY PRATHER (1873–1959). A distant cousin of President William McKinley, Henry Fletcher served as one of **Theodore Roosevelt**'s Rough-Riders in 1898. After diplomatic postings in **Cuba**, **China**, and Portugal, he was minister and later ambassador to Chile (1910–16) and was ambassador to **Mexico** (1917–19), Belgium (1922–24), Luxembourg (1923–24), and Italy (1924–29). He was involved in the 1921 **Naval Disarmament Conference** in Washington, D.C., as an undersecretary of state (1921–22). In 1930, he was made chair of the U.S. Tariff Commission, serving until the end of 1931. He was a delegate to the 1944 **Dumbarton Oaks** and **Bretton Woods Conferences**. He also served as chair of the National Committee of the Republican Party (1934–36).

FLYNN, JOHN THOMAS (1882–1964). John T. Flynn studied law at Georgetown University but switched to journalism and became a reporter on financial affairs with the *New York Globe* in 1920. He went on to become a freelance in 1923 and wrote for *Collier's Weekly*, *Harper's Magazine*, and the liberal *New Republic*, though his views were to move to the right. Flynn supported **Franklin D. Roosevelt** for the presidency in 1932 but criticized the New Deal as a vast increase in government intervention that would develop a corporatist society along the lines followed by the fascist movement of Benito Mussolini in Italy. Flynn believed that one aspect of this policy was a readiness to go to war, and in 1936 he depicted Roosevelt as a war monger and a "born militarist." Flynn acted as advisor to the 1934 **Nye Committee** and wrote most of its reports. In September 1940, he was a founder of the **America First Committee** (AFC). He was active in the AFC's publicity campaigns.

During **World War II**, Flynn continued to criticize Roosevelt, publishing *The Truth about Pearl Harbor* in 1944 and accusing Roosevelt of leading the country toward fascism in *As We Go Marching*. He continued these attacks after the war. In the article *Why the Americans Did Not Take Berlin* in 1948, he accused Roosevelt of making a deal with Premier **Josef Stalin** of the **Union of Soviet Socialist Republics** at the 1945 **Yalta Conference**, giving Stalin a free hand in Eastern Europe. Flynn was a strong supporter of Senator Joseph McCarthy's anticommunist campaigns in 1950–54. His continued opposition to military spending and to any military interventions overseas, however, tended to separate Flynn from other members of the right wing in U.S. politics.

FORD, HENRY (1863–1947). A pioneer of mass production in the automobile industry, business leader Henry Ford chartered the vessel *Oscar II* on a peace voyage in November–December 1915 in an attempt to end **World War I**. Ford joined a party of unofficial peace "negotiators" who sailed to Europe in an attempt to mediate an end to the conflict. Ford had earlier claimed the sinking of the *Lusitania* had been a plot by international financiers to drag the United States into the war. The very public failure of the mission damaged his previously popular reputation.

In 1918, Ford unsuccessfully ran for the Senate as a Democrat, campaigning in favor of U.S. entry into the **League of Nations**. Ford was becoming anti-Semitic and blamed Jews for his defeat in this election. A series of articles published in his newspaper, the *Dearborn Independent*, alleged the manipulation of world affairs by an international Jewish conspiracy. Ford closed the paper, renouncing its anti-Semitic tones, in 1927. Ford took advantage of opportunities that opened up in the 1920s to do business in the **Union of Soviet Socialist Republics** (USSR). He made a loss building cars in the USSR, but his mass production methods had a profound impact on Soviet planners.

Ford became hostile to labor unions and lost his early reputation as an enlightened employer. He opposed the New Deal in the 1930s and depicted a United Automobile Workers (UAW) strike in 1937 as the beginnings of a red revolution. Despite his personal opposition to U.S. entry in **World War II**, Ford supported the war effort and made his peace with the UAW as war orders flooded in. Ford built the huge Willow Run plant near Detroit to build bombers, and it has been estimated that his corporation produced more munitions in World War II than did Italy. *See also* AMERICA FIRST COMMITTEE; WOMEN'S PEACE PARTY.

FORDNEY–MCCUMBER TARIFF ACT (1922). Under the **tariff** act sponsored by Michigan Representative Joseph W. Fordney and Senator Porter McCumber of North Dakota, duties on goods imported from abroad were raised significantly. Agricultural produce like rye, wheat, beef, and lamb were affected, as well as textiles, chemicals, jewelry, and dyes, all of which saw protection barriers raised sharply. The act also empowered the president to raise or lower tariffs by up to 50 percent in line with rises or falls in production costs. Though popular with contemporary American voters, the act has since been criticized for taking a myopic view of international **trade** relations. Historians argue that it weakened European postwar economic recovery during the 1920s. *See also* EMERGENCY AGRICULTURAL TARIFF ACT; SMOOT–HAWLEY TARIFF ACT.

FOREIGN BONDHOLDERS' PROTECTIVE COUNCIL. A private nonprofit agency created by President **Franklin D. Roosevelt** by executive order in 1933, the council was to help U.S. citizens collect on defaulted foreign bonds. It negotiated settlement of defaults on about $2 billion of foreign government bonds in the hands of American investors. It was most active during the 1930s and during the 1970s and 1980s.

FOREIGN POLICY ASSOCIATION. A nonpartisan, nonprofit body founded in 1918, the Foreign Policy Association was dedicated to increasing American public awareness and knowledge of foreign policy issues. It forms part of the World Affairs Councils of America, which has member institutions in most states of the United States.

FOREIGN SERVICE ACT (1924). Landmark legislation passed by the 68th Congress, the Foreign Service Act is also known as the Rogers Act after its sponsor, Representative John J. Rogers of Massachusetts. Before 1924, career diplomacy was usually the preserve of independently wealthy or well-connected individuals who, although possessing little diplomatic experience, could afford to live and work as diplomats without a government salary. The Rogers Act created a new department which merged the consular service with the diplomatic corps into a new body. Congress set aside funds to ensure that all Foreign Service officials would be paid according to a scale. All applicants were required to take entrance examinations, and promotion through the ranks of the service would be strictly by merit. The tradition of leaving officials in post on a long-term basis, often resulting in laziness or corruption, was also ended. After passage of the Rogers Act, all diplomatic assignments were time-limited and rotated. *See also* MOSES–LINTHICUM ACT.

FORTRESS AMERICA. Favored by some **isolationists**, the fortress America concept arose during the 1930s as crises escalated in Europe and Asia. Its proponents argued that the United States needed to re-arm. The object was to reinforce the protection given to the United States by the oceans, reduce U.S. reliance on the navy of **Great Britain** as first line of defense in the Atlantic, and prevent interventionists from arguing that the poor state of U.S. defenses necessitated alliances or even the dispatch of forces overseas.

Fortress America enthusiasts were distinguished from others who favored isolationism by their support for rearmament and their recognition that crises overseas might have an impact on U.S. security.

They were thus particularly ready to support expansion of the **U.S. Navy** from 1938, and development of the B-17 bomber, which was originally intended as an antishipping weapon. Once **World War II** broke out in Europe, fortress America enthusiasts argued that instead of sending munitions to other nations, this equipment should be used to strengthen American defenses (national and hemispheric). *See also* AMERICA FIRST COMMITTEE; LINDBERGH, CHARLES; TWO OCEAN NAVY ACT.

FOSDICK, RAYMOND B. (1883–1972). A student of **Woodrow Wilson** at Princeton University, Raymond Fosdick was secretary and auditor to the National Democratic Committee in 1912 although he was a Republican. Fosdick had a number of public service posts in New York until appointed special representative of the War Department in **France** in 1917, during **World War I**. He was responsible for administering the prohibition of alcohol in the army, and he headed the Commission on Training Camp Activities of the Council of National Defense, which sought to uplift troop morality. He was an aide to General **John J. Pershing** at the 1919 **Paris Peace Conference** and undersecretary of the **League of Nations** (1919–20), relinquishing the post when the Senate failed to ratify the **Treaty of Versailles**. He returned to public service in 1933 on the Liquor Study Committee. From 1936 to 1948, he was president of the Rockefeller Foundation.

FOSTER, WILLIAM ZEBULON (1881–1961). An unskilled worker in a variety of jobs, William Foster joined the Socialist Party in 1901 and was active in the Industrial Workers of the World (IWW). He attended the International Union Conference in Budapest in 1911. Foster favored working within the established labor union movement. He left the IWW and organized workers in the meatpacking industry in Chicago.

In 1921, at the invitation of **Earl Browder**, Foster traveled to Moscow to attend the conference of the Red International of Labor Unions (Profintern), and on his return he joined the **Communist Party of the United States** (CPUSA). He was the party candidate in the presidential elections of 1924, 1928, and 1932. He became CPUSA general secretary in 1928. Throughout his life, he was a committed Stalinist, and under his leadership the CPUSA followed the line dictated from Moscow through the Communist International (Comintern). After a heart attack, he was replaced as party chair by Earl Browder in 1932. In 1945, he regained the leadership of the CPUSA and reasserted Stalinist orthodoxy. Foster consistently aligned with the **Union of Soviet Socialist Republics** and refused to allow any criticism of its record on human rights or its foreign policy. He was indicted under the **Smith Act** in 1948 but escaped the trial of CPUSA leaders because of ill health. He retired from the leadership in 1957.

FOUR FREEDOMS. In his State of the Union address to Congress on 6 January 1941, President **Franklin Roosevelt** summarized what the United States stood for in the world arena by talking about four basic freedoms: freedom from want, freedom from fear, freedom of religion, and freedom of speech. As was often the case with Roosevelt, these words were delivered without a plan for them to be the central theme of propaganda that they later became. He proposed no concrete action then or later to advance them. It fell to others to popularize them. Indeed, when the populist artist Norman Rockwell drew representations of the four freedoms, these were first rejected by the government for use as propaganda tools. But after they appeared in the *Saturday Evening Post* and were received with enthusiasm by public opinion, they were adopted to form a poster campaign for the sale of war bonds. Rockwell's illustrations became the most famous representation of Roosevelt's words. For many Americans, the four freedoms were an encapsulation of what they were fighting for in **World War II**. *See also* ATLANTIC CHARTER, UNITED NATIONS DECLARATION.

FOUR POLICEMEN. President **Franklin Roosevelt** proposed that the four Great Powers should act as policemen in the immediate period following **World War II**, maintaining the peace and disarming other states. While Roosevelt publicly supported **Woodrow Wilson**'s idea of a democratic world order built around an international organization (having been a member of Wilson's administration and endorsing the **League of Nations** plan), in private conversations with the leaders of the **Union of Soviet Socialist Republics** (USSR) and **Great Britain**, Roosevelt revealed a preference for power politics. In late May 1942, in Washington, D.C., Roosevelt first raised the idea with the USSR commissar for foreign affairs, Vyacheslav Molotov. He suggested that the United States, USSR, Britain, and **China** (if it had an established central government) should act as policemen of the peace. The implication was that they would each disarm states in their vicinity (not only the aggressor nations) and effectively manage peace by keeping their own spheres peaceful. Molotov and Premier **Josef Stalin** welcomed this concept. Although it went against both his public statements and his often-voiced hostility to the idea of "spheres of influence," Roosevelt reverted to the idea in his first meetings with Stalin, at the 1943 **Teheran Conference**. In a modified form, it was realized in the Security Council concept in the **United Nations**. *See also* DISARMAMENT.

FOUR-POWER TREATY. *See* NAVAL DISARMAMENT CONFERENCE (1921).

FOURTEEN POINTS (1918). In an address to a joint session of the U.S. Congress on 8 January 1918, President **Woodrow Wilson** presented 14 specific proposals for restructuring the international order after an armistice. The president described the motives which had prompted the United States to enter **World War I**: self-defense, and the desire to see the world made safe "for every peace-loving nation which, like our own, wishes to live its own life, determine its own institutions, be assured of justice and fair dealing by the other peoples of the world as against force and selfish aggression."

Points 1–3 of Wilson's program focused on issues of transparency and freedom of movement. He called for "open covenants of peace, openly arrived at" to avoid the entangling, often informal or secret alliances that had complicated the foreign relations of the great European empires. He also urged "absolute freedom of navigation upon the seas" and "the removal, so far as possible, of all economic barriers and the establishment of an equality of **trade** conditions among all the nations consenting to the peace." Exceptions to the latter were allowed when cooperative action in restricting shipping was needed to enforce existing agreements.

Points 4–5 aimed to allay future tensions by calling for the world's arsenals to be "reduced to the lowest point consistent with domestic safety" while nations should work toward an "absolutely impartial adjustment of all colonial claims." Wilson argued that the settlement of sovereignty issues should be based on the principle that "the interests of the populations concerned must have equal weight with the equitable claims of the government whose title is to be determined."

Point 6 dealt with the turmoil in revolutionary **Russia** which continued to concern the State Department. Two months earlier, the Bolshevik party had seized power in Russia, stifled its feeble democracy, and begun peace negotiations with **Germany**. Wilson called for "a settlement of all questions affecting Russia as will secure the best and freest cooperation of the other nations of the world in obtaining for her an unhampered and unembarrassed opportunity for the independent determination of her own political development and national policy and assure her of a sincere welcome into the society of free nations under institutions of her own choosing." At first sight, this appeared to be an olive branch to the ideologically hostile Bolshevik leadership, particularly as Wilson noted that the "treatment accorded Russia by her sister nations in the months to come will be the acid test of their good will." The somewhat enigmatic wording, however, suggests the president was offering something less than an outright acceptance of Bolshevism as the free choice of the Russian people.

Points 7–9 called for the restoration of Belgian sovereignty and the invaded portions of French territory, noting the importance of a final settlement of the question of control over the Alsace-Lorraine region. Readjustment of the Italian borders was also mandated "along clearly recognizable lines of nationality." Points 10–11 called for the evacuation of occupied territory in Romania, Montenegro, and Serbia, with a guarantee of Serbian access to the sea and of autonomous development for the peoples of the collapsing Austro-Hungarian empire. The explosive question of Balkan relations was to be "determined by friendly counsel along historically established lines of allegiance and nationality."

Point 12 dealt with the disintegrated Ottoman Empire, Turkish sovereignty, and the opening of the Dardanelles as a free shipping route. Point 13 asserted the need for an independent state of **Poland** which, as with other territorial dispensations under the Fourteen Points, "should be guaranteed by international covenant."

Point 14 asserted the need to cement the new world order through the creation of a "general association of nations" capable of creating and sustaining "mutual guarantees of political independence and territorial integrity to great and small states alike." It was on this last point that the viability of his program for world peace rested. In defending it, he would face intense political opposition at home. **Isolationists** viewed it as the first step toward creation of a world government. Even those conceding the need for a voluntary association of nations feared that U.S. membership could compromise its sovereignty and freedom of action. Despite the positive reception that Wilson's speech received, it also marked the beginning of a long conflict between his administration and isolationists of both parties. The latter were disturbed by what they perceived as a messianic tone and his assertion that "the world's peace . . . is our program; and that program, the only possible program."

Some also considered the proposals overambitious and unrealistic. Wilson's call for "open covenants," for example, struck some observers as naïve. Few believed the governments of **Great Britain** and **France**, once victorious, would willingly surrender territory or weaken their naval or military power. Further, while the president invited a democratic Germany to "accept a place of equality among the peoples of the world," the French government argued for harsh reparations terms. Nonetheless, when armistice talks began in November 1918, it was on the assumption that the principles embodied in the Fourteen Points would form the foundation of the postwar settlement. Despite these obstacles, President Wilson remained confident that his program would be accepted. He saw the Fourteen Points as a cohesive program based on "the principle of justice to all peoples and nationalities, and their right to live on equal terms of liberty and safety with one another, whether they be strong or weak." Inevitably, given his character and beliefs, it was also an idealistic program which sought to adapt and project onto the world stage the fundamental **progressive** principles on which he believed American democracy to be based. *See also* LEAGUE OF NATIONS; PARIS PEACE CONFERENCE; RUSSIAN REVOLUTIONS; VERSAILLES, TREATY OF.

FRANCE. U.S. relations with France cooled in the late 19th century, largely as a result of French interference in the affairs of **Mexico** in the 1860s. In addition, French expansionism in Indochina brought it into a degree of conflict with the **open door** policy. The United States therefore had no strong inclination to support France when **World War I** broke out in 1914. Conversely, President **Woodrow Wilson**'s attempts to negotiate a "peace without victory" seemed an affront in France, which saw itself as fighting a just war to regain French territory. Relations naturally improved after the United States entered the war, and France then had better access to loans from American financial institutions to stave off its economic difficulties.

France did not share Wilson's idealistic vision of a new international order, and Prime Minister **Georges Clemenceau** sought a settlement at the 1919 **Paris Peace Conference** that kept **Germany** weak and promised German resources for French reconstruction. In spite of their many disagreements, Wilson was prepared in March 1919 to offer a security treaty between the United States and France. When this was lost with the failure of the Senate to ratify the **Treaty of Versailles**, it reinforced French determination to squeeze **reparations** out of Germany. When Germany defaulted on its payments in 1923, France occupied the Rhineland, an action widely condemned in the United States, and President **Warren G. Harding** withdrew U.S. troops from the area, where they had been enforcing demilitarization. The United States suspected that France sought to dominate Europe, while the French believed that U.S. **disarmament** initiatives would further weaken France, when it was already crippled by the war. France was also unhappy that its navy was ranked equal with that of Italy at the 1921 **Naval Disarmament Conference** in Washington, D.C.

After the **Dawes Plan** restructured reparations payments, the French economy benefited from German economic recovery. Aristide Briand became foreign minister in 1925, and relations improved between Germany and France with the conclusion of the Treaty of **Locarno**. Following a suggestion by Professor **James T. Shotwell**, Briand sought a treaty with the United States in which each country renounced the possibility of war with the other, as a means of improving Franco–American relations. U.S. reluctance to enter a purely bilateral treaty led eventually to the 1928 **Kellogg–Briand Pact**, a multilateral agreement that outlawed war as an instrument of foreign policy. France, however, continued to be dissatisfied with disarmament proposals, feeling deeply insecure as Germany recovered. It was able to form alliances only with smaller countries, such as Czechoslovakia and Yugoslavia in the Little Entente, since France's former counterweight to Germany, **Russia**, was now under communist rule.

In the 1930s, the United States kept itself disengaged from European affairs. Hopes were raised in France by the 1937 **quarantine speech** by President **Franklin D. Roosevelt**, only to be dashed when no initiative followed it. While Roosevelt maintained a neutral stance when France went to war with Germany in September 1939, the revision of the **Neutrality Act** in November allowed France to place large orders for aircraft and other munitions with U.S. manufacturers. Many Americans were shocked by Germany's defeat of France in June 1940. The U.S. government, suspicious of **Charles de Gaulle** and his claim to speak for the true fighting spirit of France, preferred to maintain as close relations as possible with the new government of France based at Vichy. Admiral **William Leahy** was appointed as a high-profile ambassador, and Roosevelt hoped to keep France from collaborating too closely with Germany, and in particular from giving Germany use of the French navy. Relations with de Gaulle worsened after the **St. Pierre and Miquelon** affair, which the administration chose to see as an affront to the **Monroe Doctrine**.

When U.S. forces landed in French North Africa in Operation **Torch**, Roosevelt made determined efforts to sideline de Gaulle in favor of first Admiral **François Darlan** and then General Henri Giraud. De Gaulle, however, commanded far more support among the Free French armed forces and in the resistance movement in France. Although de Gaulle was excluded from the early stages of Operation **Overlord**, Free French forces were given the opportunity to liberate Paris, and de Gaulle's triumphal entry made clear that he was the French leader the United States would have to deal with. Partly because of his suspicions of de Gaulle's ambitions, Roosevelt did not share Prime Minister **Winston Churchill** of **Great Britain**'s aim of restoring France as a great power. Churchill managed to persuade him and Premier **Josef Stalin** of the **Union of Soviet Socialist Republics** at the 1945 **Yalta Conference** to allow France a zone of occupation in Germany, carved out of the British and U.S. zones, and a seat on the Allied Control Commission for Germany.

Roosevelt also backed away from his aim of divesting France of its empire in Asia. He had planned that **China** would act as a trustee responsible for bringing Indochina to independence, but by the end of 1944 he had lost faith in China's ability to carry out this task and was persuaded by Britain to accommodate French wishes and support their return to their colonies. This meant reneging on engagements made by the **Office of Strategic Services** with the Vietnamese independence movement led by Ho Chi Minh. U.S. relations with France were to improve in the later 1940s, with the disappearance of de Gaulle from power and with the onset of the Cold War, in which France appeared as a useful ally both in Western Europe and in Asia. *See also* BULLITT, WILLIAM CHRISTIAN; CAFFERY, JEFFERSON; EDGE, WALTER EVANS; HERRICK, MYRON TIMOTHY.

FREEDOM HOUSE. A nongovernmental research and advocacy organization, Freedom House was established in 1941 by **Wendell Willkie**, George Field, Dorothy Thompson, Herbert Bayard Swope, and Eleanor Roosevelt, with the intention that it be an advocate for democracy around the world and a response to the threat of fascism. While independent, it receives approximately 80 percent of its funding from U.S. government grants. During **World War II**, it urged the government to adopt policies that advanced human rights both at home and overseas.

FULBRIGHT RESOLUTION (1943). On 21 September 1943, the U.S. House of Representatives approved a resolution introduced by J. William Fulbright of Arkansas that favored creation of "international machinery" with sufficient power "to establish and maintain a just and lasting peace." The resolution also supported U.S. participation, in accordance with its constitutional practices. The Senate concurred, though a further resolution was to emerge from a Senate debate on the subject in November. The Fulbright resolution gave expression to the growing belief in the country during **World War II** that the United States needed to embrace **internationalism** and even **collective security** in the interests of its own national security and that U.S. absence from the **League of Nations** had contributed to the causes of the war. *See also* CONNALLY RESOLUTION; DUMBARTON OAKS CONFERENCE; SAN FRANCISCO CONFERENCE.

– G –

GAUSS, CLARENCE EDWARD (1887–1960). Diplomat Clarence Gauss entered the Foreign Service in 1906 and served almost exclusively in **China**. He was vice consul and consul in Shanghai (1912–16), Amoy (1916–20), and Tsinan (1920–23). Gauss was then consul general in Mukden (1923–24), Tsinan (1924–26), Shanghai (1926–27), Tientsin (1927–31), and Shanghai again (1935–37). He had a short spell in Paris in 1935. He was virtual head of the Shanghai international settlement when the **Sino–Japanese War** broke out in 1937. He was minister to Australia (1940–41) and then ambassador to China through most of **World War II** (1941–44). During that time, he was effectively superseded as a channel of communication with the Chinese government by the U.S. military mission and by General **Joseph Stillwell**. Despite all his service in China, Gauss never learned Chinese.

GENEVA DISARMAMENT CONFERENCE (1932). Following the 1930 **London Naval Disarmament Conference**, the **League of Nations** Preparatory Commission on Disarmament, meeting in Geneva, called for further reductions in arms, this time also addressing land weapons and armies. The Geneva conference began on 2 February 1932 to look at general disarmament. Concerned at the cost of armaments to national economies, U.S. President **Herbert Hoover** proposed elimination of all offensive weapons, and then, when that failed, proposed a reduction of 30 percent in such munitions. The conference adjourned without agreement in June 1932, meeting again from February to June 1933 and in October 1933. The conference was dissolved permanently in April 1934 without having agreed to any reductions.

GENEVA NAVAL CONFERENCE (1927). *See* NAVAL DISARMAMENT CONFERENCE (1927).

GENEVA PROTOCOL (1925). An agreement banning the use of gas and bacteriological warfare, the Geneva Protocol resulted from the Conference for the Supervision of the International Traffic in Arms held in Geneva in 1925. The U.S. **Senate Committee on Foreign Relations** failed to ratify this agreement after heavy pressure from lobbyists representing the chemical industry. In the 1930s, President **Franklin D. Roosevelt** used executive powers to announce a general policy that the United States would not make first use of poisoned gas in warfare.

GEORGE VI (1895–1952). King of **Great Britain** George VI succeeded his brother Edward VIII in 1936 after the latter abdicated in order to marry the American divorcee Wallis Simpson. George had served in the British navy in **World War I**, fighting at the battle of Jutland. In 1939, he made a landmark tour of the United States and Canada to raise public perceptions of Great Britain and counter American and Canadian **isolationism**. The royal couple received an enthusiastic response from the American public, visited the New York World's Fair, and stayed with President **Franklin D. Roosevelt**. During **World War II**, the British royal family remained in residence in London, refusing to evacuate in the face of German bombing. His daughter Elizabeth, who served in the British army in the war, succeeded him in 1952 as Elizabeth II.

GEORGE, WALTER FRANKLIN (1878–1957). Lawyer Walter George was an associate justice on the supreme court of Georgia (1917–22) and a Democratic member of the U.S. Senate (1922–57), where he chaired the **Senate Committee on Foreign Relations** in 1940–41 and 1955–57. He initially took an **isolationist** line when **World War II** started, but he supported **Lend-Lease** to **Great Britain**. As chair of the Senate Finance Committee (1941–47), George helped steer through legislation that financed the U.S. war effort. Considered one of the Senate's best public speakers, he was president pro tempore of the Senate in 1955–57. After his retirement from the Senate, he served for six months as ambassador to the North Atlantic Treaty Organization.

GERMAN-AMERICAN BUND. The bund was an organization of German Americans that was dominated by American Nazis, led by **Fritz Kuhn**. It promoted anti-Semitic and anticommunist propaganda in rallies, magazines, and leaflets, and its members were

strident admirers of **Adolf Hitler** of **Germany**. The group opposed
U.S. intervention in **World War II** and cooperated with **isolationist** groups, such as the Christian Front organized by Father **Charles
Coughlin**. Its membership at its peak was around 25,000, including
8,000 uniformed storm troopers. It organized youth camps modeled
on the Hitler Youth. A Madison Square Garden rally in February
1939 attracted 20,000 people. The **House Committee Investigating
Un-American Activities** investigated the Bund in 1939 and found it
had clear ties to the German Nazi government. Kuhn was imprisoned
for embezzlement from his own organization in 1939. Its leaders
were interned on the U.S. entry into World War II, and the organization was banned by the federal government. *See also* GREAT
SEDITION TRIAL; ISLANDS FOR WAR DEBTS COMMITTEE;
VIERECK, GEORGE SYLVESTER.

GERMANY. From the late 19th century, U.S. relations with the German government of Kaiser Wilhelm II had been difficult. This was
often due to the unpredictability of Wilhelm, who veered erratically
between exaggerated expressions of respect for American economic
and military power and suspicions that U.S. diplomats were innately
sympathetic toward **France** and **Great Britain**. The administration
of President **Theodore Roosevelt** was compelled to move carefully
in handling crises in the **Dominican Republic** (1904) and Morocco
(1905), which involved German financial and strategic interests.

   The outbreak of **World War I** was met with an outward response
of determined neutrality from the administration of President **Woodrow Wilson**, but the German government suspected, with some justification, that the sympathies of many members of the U.S. government lay with the Allied powers. Germany's doubts were intensified
by the perceived lack of even-handedness by the United States in
dealing with threats to U.S. mercantile interests arising from the war.
The resignation of **William Jennings Bryan** in 1915, on the issue
of President Wilson's strongly worded protest at the sinking of the
Lusitania, further aggravated German suspicions, as did the efforts
of some private American companies in supplying arms and financial
aid to France and Great Britain. Despite this, Wilson succeeded for
more than two years in keeping America out of the conflict. U.S.
neutrality finally broke down under the weight of unrestricted Ger-

man submarine activity and the publication of the **Zimmermann telegram** in March 1917, revealing an attempt by German officials to interest **Mexico** in territorial gains inside the United States in the aftermath of a German victory.

The arrival of the **American Expeditionary Force** on the European continent in 1917–18 hastened the collapse of the German government and the end of World War I. America welcomed the establishment of Germany's new Weimar Republic under the moderate socialist Friedrich Ebert. After the U.S. Senate rejected the **Treaty of Versailles**, the two nations signed the **Treaty of Berlin** on 25 August 1921, putting a formal end to the hostilities that had ceased with the armistice of 11 November 1918, and confirming the **Knox–Porter Resolution** already signed by President **Warren Harding** on 2 July 1921. Germany signed the border-stabilizing **Treaty of Locarno** (1925), joined the **League of Nations** in 1926, and acquiesced in the **Kellogg–Briand** Pact (1928), thus demonstrating its willingness to play an active role in establishing collective security in the postwar world.

During the 1920s, U.S.–German relations were mainly concerned with problems caused by the post-1918 economic slump and heavy reparations demands. The U.S.-initiated **Dawes Plan** (1924) restored a degree of fiscal stability to the ravaged German economy by rescuing the reichsmark and rescheduling war debt repayments. The **Young Plan** (1929) further adjusted repayments to aid economic recovery. Loans to Germany remained a problem for U.S. politicians during the 1920s. The U.S. Department of Commerce reluctantly approved loans to German agriculture and to steel and chemicals firms, despite protests from domestic lobbies that it was subsidizing foreign competition. The New York stock market crash of October 1929 had severe repercussions for the struggling German economy, as short-term credit facilities were withdrawn and investment was drastically reduced. The global economic depression placed more pressure on the already fragile democracy of the Weimar Republic.

After Nazi leader **Adolf Hitler** became chancellor of Germany, U.S. diplomats such as Ambassador **William Dodd** (1933–37) made public their dislike of Nazi excess. It is not clear that these were instigated by the U.S. government. U.S. inaction in the face of growing German acts of persecution of Jews and breaches of the **Treaty of**

Versailles reflected the country's **isolationism** and what public opinion would allow at the time. With the exception of the October 1937 **quarantine speech**, President **Franklin D. Roosevelt** made little attempt to influence public opinion, and the administration paid little attention to reports coming from Germany from Dodd or military attaché **Truman Smith**. There was little conviction in initiatives to help Jews, such as the 1938 **Evian Conference**, though Ambassador **Hugh Wilson** was withdrawn in protest at the attacks on Jews in the *Kristallnacht* in 1938. Roosevelt on occasion proposed multilateral conferences to address the growing crisis in Europe but indicated that the United States could not guarantee any arrangements reached. He thus effectively excluded the United States from influence on events there. He voiced some approval for the efforts of British Prime Minister **Neville Chamberlain** to find a negotiated settlement instead of war in September 1938.

It is, however, fairly certain that Roosevelt saw Hitler as a menace to U.S. interests in the long term, and he began to work to counter **Axis** influence in **Latin America** with the 1938 **Lima declaration**. Hitler saw the United States as ultimately an enemy of his "thousand-year Reich," but until 1941 he did not regard it as an immediate threat. He ridiculed Roosevelt in public speeches, and the Nazi policy of autarky gradually closed the parts of Europe that Germany controlled to U.S. commerce. But some U.S. corporations continued to do business with Nazi Germany until the **declaration of war** in December 1941.

When **World War II** broke out in Europe in September 1939, Roosevelt proclaimed that the United States would be neutral but not "blind to the facts." He clearly favored a victory for Britain and France, and he initially believed this could be achieved without direct U.S. intervention. Over the next two years, U.S. aid to the Allies developed by incremental steps, each of which was intended to be sufficient. As Roosevelt's rhetoric toward Germany became more critical, Hitler's personal hostility toward Roosevelt grew. However, while U.S. warships acted in a quasi-belligerent fashion in the Atlantic while escorting convoys, Hitler resisted the provocation. Roosevelt seemed satisfied that such an anomalous state of affairs (which the **U.S. Navy** found deeply unsatisfactory) was serving his purpose of effective aid to Britain. He used incidents such as the sinking of USS *Reuben James* to gain approval in the United States for more explicitly warlike activity but still held off from seeking a declaration of war from Congress.

After **Japan**'s attack on **Pearl Harbor**, most of Roosevelt's cabinet believed that a declaration of war on Germany would not be possible, now that the U.S. was at war with Japan. The only exception was Secretary of War **Henry Stimson**. Roosevelt made some remarks critical of Germany in a fireside chat, and on 11 December Hitler broke diplomatic relations with the United States in a splenetic speech to the Reichstag and declared war.

During World War II, there was much debate on the future treatment of Germany. Opinion ranged between singling out only Nazi leaders for punishment or dealing radically with the German state and people as a whole. The latter approach was most starkly indicated in the 1944 **Morgenthau Plan** that would have dismantled German industry. There was agreement, however, that **reparations** should be avoided, and that except for a separate Austria, it was best not to dismember the German state unless it came spontaneously from within. It was agreed that Austria should be separated once more from Germany. Germany was to be occupied by the four major powers—the United States, Great Britain, the **Union of Soviet Socialist Republics**, and **France**—but treated as one unit for economic purposes. Such matters were the subject of considerable dispute among the victors of World War II, and the failure to agree on the future of Germany at the 1945 **Potsdam Conference** and later meetings was a major cause of the breakdown in the wartime **Grand Alliance** and the onset of the Cold War. *See also* CLAY, LUCIUS DUBIGNON; EUROPEAN ADVISORY COMMISSION; HOUGHTON, ALANSON BIGELOW; JCS 1067; KIRK, ALEXANDER COMSTOCK; LAUSANNE CONFERENCE; LINDBERGH, CHARLES; PLAN DOG; SHIRER, WILLIAM LAWRENCE.

GIBSON, HUGH SIMONS (1883–1954). Diplomat Hugh Gibson worked alongside **Herbert Hoover** at the **Commission for Relief in Belgium** and subsequently undertook posts at the U.S. embassies in London and Paris. Sent as minister to **Poland** by President **Woodrow Wilson** in 1919, he wrote a controversial report questioning the extent of anti-Semitic violence there. Gibson was a supporter of the **League of Nations** and **World Court** and a firm believer in the professionalization of America's diplomatic service by ending the appointment of wealthy partisan donors. After turning down an appointment as undersecretary of state in the administration of President **Calvin Coolidge**, Gibson represented the United States in Switzerland (1924–27). Under President **Franklin D. Roosevelt**, he served as ambassador to **Brazil** (1933–36) and Belgium (1927–33, 1937–38). During and after **World War II**, he was involved in the organization of food relief in Europe, working closely with former President Herbert Hoover. *See also* FOREIGN SERVICE ACT; UNITED NATIONS RELIEF AND REHABILITATION ADMINISTRATION.

GILBERT, PRENTISS BAYLEY (1883–1939). Prentiss Gilbert was in the U.S. Army in **World War I** before joining the State Department. After a number of appointments in Washington, D.C., including chief of the Bureau of Current Intelligence, he was appointed consul in Geneva, Switzerland, in 1930. Gilbert's main responsibility was reporting on the activities of the **League of Nations**. Since 1928, a staff of observers had been maintained at the Geneva consulate, though it was only with Gilbert's appointment that their actual function was acknowledged. By 1932, of the staff of seven consuls and vice consuls, five had as their sole duty the observation of the League.

With the outbreak of the **Manchurian Crisis** in 1931, the League invited the United States to have a nonvoting observer at its council meetings, to associate the United States with League efforts in the crisis, and Gilbert was appointed by President **Herbert Hoover**'s administration to participate regarding U.S. obligations under the **Kellogg–Briand Pact**. **Isolationists** in the United States were highly suspicious, but Hoover maintained a distinct separation between U.S. policy and the decisions of the League. Gilbert's official attendance at sessions of the League council did produce slightly closer relations between the League and the United States. In 1937, Gilbert was appointed to the embassy in Berlin, **Germany**, and acted as chargé d'affaires after ambassador **Hugh Wilson** was withdrawn in protest over *Kristallnacht* in 1938. Gilbert died in Germany in 1939.

GOLD RESERVE ACT (1934). The Gold Reserve Act was passed by the U.S. Congress on 31 January 1934, requiring all gold and gold certificates held in the Federal Reserve to be vested in the Treasury. The measure followed from Executive Order 6102 issued by President **Franklin D. Roosevelt** on 5 April 1933, which made it a crime for private citizens to own gold except jewelry. This was intended to stop hoarding, which was seen as limiting circulation of currency and therefore consumption and investment. The order had been enacted under the 1917 **Trading with the Enemy Act**. These measures were an attempt to deal with a perceived cause of the Great Depression. They came after the United States and other nations withdrew from the **gold standard**. The consequent instability of convertibility of currencies seriously impeded world **trade** and aggravated the economic depression. The 1933 **London Economic Conference** was intended to confront this issue on an international basis, but it was undermined by Roosevelt's determination to pursue a national solution to the Depression.

GOLD STANDARD. The gold standard was the system of currency valuation used by all major nations from the latter part of the 19th century onward. There were bitter debates in the United States during the 19th century regarding whether to base the currency on gold alone or on gold and silver. In 1900, the United States was unequivocally committed to gold in the Gold Standard Act. Under the international gold standard, countries fixed the value of their domestic currencies in terms of a specified amount of gold. Currency and other financial instruments could be freely converted into gold at a fixed price.

During **World War I**, most major states went off the gold standard in order to fund their war expenditures by paper money not linked to exchangeability into gold. After the war, **Germany** lost its gold in **reparations** and was unable to return to the gold standard. Other nations gradually readopted the gold standard from about 1925 onward. The onset of the Great Depression put the system in jeopardy. On 21 September 1931, **Great Britain** withdrew from the gold standard, effectively devaluing the British pound. Many currencies were tied to the pound, and the devaluation at first stimulated **trade**. However, most countries then followed suit and withdrew from the gold standard. Currencies devalued, and the absence of a regular and predictable system of international exchange produced a serious decline in international trade, further aggravating the global economic depression.

The 1933 **London Economic Conference** was intended to address this problem, but the lack of interest in a revival of the gold standard on the part of U.S. President **Franklin D. Roosevelt** meant that it failed to do so. Instead the United States sought bilateral arrangements under the 1934 **Reciprocal Trade Agreements Act**. In 1944, the **Bretton Woods Conference** established a modified system of exchange based on fixed rates that allowed governments to sell gold to the U.S. Treasury at $35 an ounce. The system lasted until 1971, when the link between gold and currency valuations was ended. *See also* GOLD RESERVE ACT.

GOMPERS, SAMUEL (1850–1924). Labor leader Samuel Gompers was born in London, England; his parents had recently emigrated from the Netherlands. The family moved to New York when Gompers was 13. He followed his father's trade as a cigar maker and became involved in organizing workers. He was a founding member of the American Federation of Labor (AFL) in 1886, serving as its president in 1886–94 and from 1896 to his death. Gompers was hostile to socialism and Marxism and sought by organization and collective bargaining to improve material conditions for workers, not to challenge capitalism or the U.S. political and economic system. The AFL represented the skilled workers in American industry. Although employers were not sympathetic to labor organization of any kind, Gompers became a major public figure, and to a degree he was accepted by them. Gompers opposed unrestricted **immigration** on the grounds that it brought in cheap labor that decreased wages, and he opposed any immigration from Asia. The AFL was active in securing the 1921 **Emergency Quota Act** and the 1924 **National Origins Act**, severely restricting immigration.

Unlike more radical unionists, Gompers and the AFL supported U.S. entry into **World War I**. Gompers became a member of the Council of National Defense, and the relationship between the skilled unions and the Democratic Party was strengthened. President **Woodrow Wilson** took Gompers to the 1919 **Paris Peace Conference** as a labor advisor, and Gompers played an instrumental part in the creation of the **International Labour Organization**.

GONDRA TREATY (1923). The Treaty to Avoid or Prevent Conflicts between the American States, signed at the **Santiago Conference**

on 3 May 1923, is known as the Gondra Treaty after its author, Paraguayan diplomat Manuel Gondra. The treaty provided for inter-American conflict resolution and established a "cooling off period" as an alternative to **disarmament**. All disputes that could not be settled by diplomacy should be submitted to a commission of inquiry; one was based in Washington, D.C., and another in Montevideo, Uruguay. Each would have five members—the three senior heads of diplomatic mission from American countries and a representative from each side in the dispute. The commission would investigate facts and report within a year. The parties would only make preparations for war six months after the commission reported. The report would not, however, have the authority of an arbitration award, and inquiries could only take place if the parties in a dispute cooperated. The effectiveness of the arrangement therefore depended on tempers cooling off during the period of 18 months following the initiation of the commission process. The Gondra Treaty was ratified by 20 of the 21 signatories (**Argentina** was the exception), but it was never invoked. *See also* PAN-AMERICAN CONFERENCE ON CONCILIATION AND ARBITRATION.

GOOD NEIGHBOR POLICY. U.S. President **Franklin D. Roosevelt** continued and extended the approach to **Latin America** initiated by Presidents **Warren G. Harding**, **Calvin Coolidge**, and **Herbert Hoover**, wherein the United States abandoned its practice of armed intervention to overturn revolutionary governments and protect American economic interests. The policy got its name from Roosevelt's statement in his first inaugural address (1933) that he would follow "the policy of the good neighbor." In 1928, Roosevelt had written of the need to end "intervention by United States in the internal affairs of other nations."

The growing strength of nationalism in Latin America and the threat of boycotts to **trade** induced Secretary of State **Cordell Hull** to support a nonintervention resolution at the seventh Inter-American Conference (**Montevideo Conference**) in 1933. Hull, however, qualified this considerably by reserving the rights to intervene that were allowed by the "law of nations as generally recognized." At the 1936 **Buenos Aires Conference**, the commitment to nonintervention was extended to "indirect" as well as "direct" intervention, though the

United States did not abandon the policy of using political and economic pressure to shape events throughout the hemisphere. The United States had recently intervened indirectly in **Cuba** but had repealed the **Platt Amendment** regarding the extent of U.S. dominance there. The United States withdrew from Haiti and the **Dominican Republic**, so that by 1935 no U.S. troops were in Latin America except in bases in Cuba and Panama. The new policy was demonstrated in responses to the **Mexican oil expropriation controversy** that began in 1938. Despite an outcry from conservatives and corporations, Roosevelt eschewed armed intervention and used Ambassador **Josephus Daniels** to broker a deal between the government of **Mexico** and the oil companies.

The main gain from the Good Neighbor policy was an upsurge in trade with the area: U.S. exports rose from $244 million in 1933 to $642 million in 1938. The increasing dominance of U.S. capital in the area led some to dub this the "rich neighbor" policy. It also increasingly took the form toward the end of the decade of a drawing together of the American nations to resist possible **Axis** penetration. The Declaration of Inter-American Solidarity that Roosevelt secured when he attended the 1936 Buenos Aires Conference provided for consultation when the hemisphere was menaced from outside. The results when **World War II** began were the 1939 **Panama Declaration** and the 1940 Act of **Havana** and, after the war, the establishment of the Organization of American States. *See also* CLARK MEMORANDUM; EXPORT-IMPORT BANK; INTER-AMERICAN DEFENSE BOARD; ROCKEFELLER, NELSON ALDRICH; WELLES, SUMNER.

GORE–McLEMORE RESOLUTION (1916). A congressional measure sponsored by Oklahoma representative Thomas P. Gore and Texas representative Atkins J. McLemore during **World War I**, the resolution stated that American citizens should "forbear to exercise the right to travel as passengers on any armed vessel of any belligerent power." President **Woodrow Wilson** opposed the measure and it was defeated in Congress in 1916. The resolution was intended to reduce the risk that further incidents similar to the sinking of the *Lusitania* would drag the United States into the war. *See also ARABIC*; NEUTRALITY ACTS; *SUSSEX*.

GRAND ALLIANCE. The partnership of the United States, Great Britain, and the **Union of Soviet Socialist Republics** during **World War II** is sometimes called the Grand Alliance, a term coined by British Prime Minister **Winston Churchill** after the war. Because of the ideological differences that separated these **Big Three** powers, tensions arose over many issues, notably future political arrangements in Eastern Europe, especially **Poland**, and over the timing of the **second front** in Western Europe. However, strategy and supplies (through **Lend-Lease**) were coordinated, and the alliance held together to achieve its prime objective, the defeat of the **Axis** powers. On 1 January 1942, **China** joined with the Big Three to create a formal alliance set forth in the **United Nations Declaration**.

During the war, the leaders of the Big Three met together on three occasions, at the **Teheran, Yalta,** and **Potsdam Conferences**, and established a number of joint bodies, such as the **European Advisory Commission**. Some worked well, but political differences sometimes produced stalemate. This was especially true for the control commissions set up in the liberated states of Europe in the wake of the Yalta **Declaration on Liberated Europe**. President **Franklin D. Roosevelt's** **unconditional surrender** policy provided a strong bond in the alliance, as a basic shared war aim, but it was under increasing strain as Allied forces entered Axis-held territory in 1944–45, with Italy and Poland the main sources of tension. Hopes that the Grand Alliance would last into the postwar era to provide the foundation for peace, in accordance with Roosevelt's **four policemen** concept, were to be dashed, as ideological and geopolitical differences emerged to create the Cold War. *See also* FAYMONVILLE, PHILIP RIES; HARRIMAN, W. AVERELL; HOPKINS, HARRY LLOYD; KENNAN, GEORGE FROST; MOSCOW CONFERENCE (1941); MOSCOW CONFERENCE (1943).

GREAT BRITAIN. At the start of the 20th century, U.S.–British relations were generally cordial. There were no longer any major issues on which the two nations clashed, and their shared history, language, and **trade** relations reinforced common political interests in many parts of the world, notably with regard to the **open door** policy in **China**. President **Woodrow Wilson's** administration was generally anglophile, and on the outbreak of **World War I**, the British government headed by Herbert H. Asquith saw good relations with the United States to be vital. However, tensions grew over the British naval blockade of the **Central Powers**, which led to interference with U.S. shipping. Wilson issued a sharp protest about British violation of neutral rights on 30 March 1915. However, he regarded the invasion of Belgium to be evidence of **Germany**'s expansionist aims and came to see German submarine warfare, which threatened lives, to be far worse than the blockade, which threatened property. Property matters could be settled after the end of the war.

Britain became the largest U.S. trading partner and its greatest debtor as a result of U.S. loans during the war. Britain worked very hard to project its image in the United States and to damage German standing, spreading alarming atrocity stories. A British **intelligence** coup enabled the leak of the **Zimmermann telegram** at the start of March 1917, soon after the German declaration of unrestricted submarine warfare on 31 January 1917. U.S. entry into the war followed in April.

To distinguish the United States from the war aims of Britain and **France**, Wilson kept the United States an "associated power" rather than an ally. U.S. forces under General **John J. Pershing** were not integrated with those of the other powers. There was cooperation with Britain at a political and economic level, though the British did not fully endorse all of the **Fourteen Points**. At the 1919 **Paris Peace Conference**, Wilson and British Prime Minister **David Lloyd George** were generally in agreement, though Lloyd George was under great domestic pressure to agree to a punitive peace. Wilson's proposal for a **League of Nations** emerged from discussions with the British, headed by Wilson's envoy **Edward M. House** and from lobbying by both American and British pressure groups, such as the American **League to Enforce Peace**. Britain and the United States agreed on most European issues, such as frontiers, though they disagreed on **reparations** and on policies toward **Japan**'s requests for territory in the Far East. Britain was still allied to Japan at this time.

In the interwar period, U.S. British relations deteriorated, soured by the immense **war debt** Britain owed the United States: a sum approaching $4 million. Britain pressed for the debt to be reduced or cancelled in recognition of their common cause in the war and the fact that British financial resources were having to be used to service the debt rather than fund national recovery or international **trade**. Presidents **Warren G. Harding, Calvin Coolidge,** and **Herbert Hoover** took the line popular with U.S. taxpayers that the money should be repaid in full.

In spite of these continuing economic tensions, Britain and the United States agreed on the need for control of the arms race. Britain supported the U.S. line at the 1921 **Naval Disarmament Conference** in Washington, D.C., and was prepared to sacrifice the Anglo–Japanese alliance. In doing so, Britain tacitly accepted that British interests in the Far East would have to be protected by the **U.S. Navy,** where previously they had been taken care of by the alliance with Japan. Britain could no longer afford to station significant naval forces there itself.

The global economic depression led Britain to leave the **gold standard** in September 1931, and subsequently to default on its debts. President **Franklin D. Roosevelt** did not share Hoover's view that the depression should be solved internationally, and he followed a policy of economic nationalism, mitigated only by Secretary of State **Cordell Hull**'s pursuit of reciprocal trade agreements. U.S. attitudes of **pacifism** and **isolationism,** the **Neutrality Acts,** and the **Debt Default Act** all contributed to a distant relationship between Britain and the United States during the 1930s. The sense that the United States could not be counted on to become involved in European affairs was a contributory element in the pursuit of a policy of appeasement of German dictator **Adolf Hitler** by British Prime Minister **Neville Chamberlain.**

Britain declared war on Germany on 3 September 1939 because it had guaranteed **Poland** against attack by Germany. The United States remained neutral, but Roosevelt came to the conclusion that a German victory would not be in the interests of the United States. Germany's autarkic economic approach would exclude U.S. commerce from Europe. Germany was also suspected of attempting to gain an economic foothold in **Latin America,** in contravention of the **Monroe Doctrine.** And if a British defeat left the Germans in control of the British navy, this would be a potential threat to U.S. security. Roosevelt, believing that an Allied victory could be achieved by opening up access to U.S. industrial production, worked for revision of the Neutrality Act in fall of 1939. He also sought measures to improve American defenses in the 1940 **Two-Ocean Navy Act.**

By the summer of 1940, Britain's major allies had been defeated by Germany, and Prime Minister **Winston Churchill** sought direct U.S. involvement, not just American resources. Roosevelt procrastinated, partly because of the strength of isolationism (and some popular anti-British feeling) and partly because he did not believe Britain to be as weak as it actually was. The September 1940 **destroyers-for-bases deal** gave Britain 50 old destroyers in return for valuable bases. Churchill regarded it as an important step with regard to a public U.S. commitment to British survival, but Roosevelt probably did not have a plan at that point to go any further, even before taking into account the evident strength of the newly formed **America First Committee**.

After Roosevelt secured reelection in November 1940, Churchill managed to convince him that Britain would soon be unable to pay for the resources it needed. Faced with British collapse and the cessation of orders that had revitalized the depression-hit U.S. economy, Roosevelt devised the **Lend-Lease** system. He also declared to the U.S. public that Britain was fighting for the same values that the United States held dear, and that the role of the United States in this struggle should be to become the **arsenal of democracy**. The expanded supply of war materials to Britain was accompanied by highly secret acts of cooperation—notably the sharing of **signals intelligence** and the **ABC talks** on strategic planning. Roosevelt accepted Churchill's argument that it was wasteful if Lend-Lease materials were granted only to be lost to German submarines, and he gradually expanded the role of the U.S. Navy beyond that of neutrality patrols. He also authorized the occupation of Greenland and Iceland. In August 1941, he met Churchill at **Placentia Bay**, and they agreed on basic war aims in the **Atlantic Charter**. By this point, the United States and Britain were in effect allies, though the United States was still a nonbelligerent.

Once Japan's attack on **Pearl Harbor** and Hitler's declaration of war brought the U.S. **declarations of war**, U.S.–British relations were shaped by issues of strategic planning. At the **Washington Conferences** held during 1941–43, and in the **Casablanca Conference** and **Quebec Conference** in 1943, deep differences were evident regarding priorities. Nonetheless, their close cooperation was symbolized in the creation of the **Combined Chiefs of Staff**. They integrated their military units and command structures, and they pooled their work on the **atomic bomb** and intelligence activities. This level of cooperation was a key contribution to the success of the **Grand Alliance** against the **Axis** powers.

Differences of viewpoint were evident over political and economic issues: notably over U.S. plans for a liberal economic world order that required the breaking open of closed imperial trading blocs, and more generally over the future of the British empire. This latter was one of the few issues over which Roosevelt and Churchill openly disagreed. Many U.S. planners overestimated British strength and regarded Britain as likely to be the great postwar economic rival of the United States. The 1944 **Bretton Woods Conference** agreements were designed to end Britain's established dominance of the world financial system, and as with earlier conditions attached to the **Master Lend-Lease agreements**, the British had no choice but to acquiesce. Britain hoped for Lend-Lease to be continued after the war, to aid reconstruction and avoid a repetition of the damage caused by the World War I war debts issue. However, Lend-Lease ended at the end of the war, and Great Britain was forced to negotiate a loan with disadvantageous terms. Two years later, the United States had to devise an ambitious plan of aid, the European Recovery Program (Marshall Plan), to help the devastated British and European economies. These difficulties aside, however, **World War II** set in place a close relationship between the United States and Great Britain that has endured, even if it has not always amounted to Churchill's concept of the "special relationship." *See also* BOLERO, OPERATION; BRITAIN–UNITED STATES OF AMERICA AGREEMENT; COMMERCIAL AGENCY AGREEMENT; GEORGE VI; GREY, EDWARD; HINES PAGE, WALTER; KENNEDY, JOSEPH PATRICK; MORGAN, JOHN PIERPONT, JR.; OVERLORD, OPERATION; RAPIDAN CONFERENCE; ULTRA-MAGIC DEAL; WINANT, JOHN GILBERT.

GREAT SEDITION TRIAL (1944). On 17 April 1944, during **World War II**, the trial began of 30 people for violations of the **Smith Act**. This became known as the Great Sedition Trial. Among the defendants were **George Viereck** and **Gerald Smith**. They were accused of being part of an international Nazi conspiracy on the basis of their **isolationist** and pro-fascist viewpoints. The prosecution had difficulty showing actual intent to overthrow the government. On 29 November 1944, a mistrial was declared after the death of the judge. The trial has been seen as a "show-trial" that set freedom of speech against the needs of national security, and in this instance, the government was unable to establish successfully the precedence of the latter over the former. *See also* GERMAN-AMERICAN BUND; HOUSE COMMITTEE INVESTIGATING UN-AMERICAN ACTIVITIES; REYNOLDS, ROBERT RICE.

GREER, USS. The *Greer* incident was an important stage on the road toward full U.S. involvement in **World War II**. The destroyer USS *Greer* was escorting a convoy southwest of Iceland on 4 September 1941 when it was attacked by a German submarine. The *Greer* then took active measures against the submarine. President **Franklin D. Roosevelt** considered the incident an act of "piracy" and an unprovoked attack on a warship of a neutral nation. He declared that American ships had a right to engage in active defense within the U.S. defense perimeter as defined by Roosevelt himself. They would now chase down sonar contacts. Any German or Italian warships that entered this zone did so at their own risk. This **shoot-on-sight order** clarified the situation for the **U.S. Navy**, which had been patrolling without orders to shoot. However, it was only implied that they would open fire, not stated explicitly. The effect was that the U.S. Navy was now waging an undeclared war against the German navy in the North Atlantic. See also *REUBEN JAMES*, USS.

GREW, JOSEPH C. (1880–1965) A Harvard graduate, Grew entered the Foreign Service in 1904. After a number of postings, he was a delegate at the 1919 **Paris Peace Conference** and 1922–23 Lausanne Conference. He served as undersecretary of state (1924–27) and was ambassador to Turkey (1927–32) and **Japan** (1932–41). Grew was influential in shaping America's nonconfrontational stance to Japan in the 1930s, and his reports in 1940 concerning the need for a tougher stance were influential in shaping President **Franklin D. Roosevelt**'s policy in 1940–41. Grew was in favor of accepting the request of Japanese Prime Minister Funimaro Konoye for a summit meeting with the president in the fall of 1941, which he believed would halt the slide to war. After a brief internment in Japan during **World War II**, he was returned to the United States, where he served in the State Department. He was regarded by some in 1945 as soft on Japan because he advocated the retention of the Emperor **Hirohito**. He briefly served as acting secretary of state in 1945 and then retired. *See also* HORNBECK, STANLEY KUHL.

GREY, EDWARD (1862–1933). Sir Edward Grey served as foreign secretary of **Great Britain** from 1905 to 1916. His preference for informal "understandings" over formal treaties was often criticized during his tenure. Some historians believe it contributed to the diplomatic misunderstandings and miscalculations that preceded the outbreak of **World War I**. He retired in May 1916 but served as a special emissary to the United States in 1919–20, attempting to break the congressional deadlock over ratification of the **Treaty of Versailles**. Grey later advised the British government that the Senate's refusal to rubber-stamp the treaty should not be mistaken for hostility to the **League of Nations** itself. He suggested that the long tradition of executive–legislative rivalry, combined with U.S. reluctance to become entangled in international affairs, meant that ratification was predictably difficult but not impossible. The **Lodge reservations**, he added, could reassure the American public that national sovereignty was not compromised by membership in the League. The White House was reportedly incensed at Grey's statement, since it contradicted the Wilson administration's claim that the Allies would never accept add-ons to the treaty. British Prime Minister **David Lloyd George** felt obliged to avoid damaging relations with President **Woodrow Wilson** by denying that Grey had carried a secret cable supporting the views of reservationist senators. In his later years, Grey (made Viscount Grey of Fallodon in 1916) served as leader of the House of Lords. *See also* HOUSE, EDWARD MANDELL.

GROVES, LESLIE R. (1896–1970). The son of a minister, Leslie R. Groves served in the U.S. Army with the Quarter-Master General's Construction Department before **World War II**. In 1942, he was placed in command of the **Manhattan Project**. Groves was responsible for organizing many of the scientists and facilities for the construction of the **atomic bomb**. While some scientists had moral reservations, Groves strongly advocated to President **Harry S. Truman** the use of the bomb on Japanese cities in 1945 to hasten **Japan**'s surrender. He argued that the $2 billion cost of the project would be hard to justify if the bomb was not used when it was available. Groves retired from the army with the rank of lieutenant general in 1948 and became a vice president of Remington Rand.

GUADALCANAL, BATTLE OF (1942). Guadalcanal, an island at the southern end of the Solomon Islands chain in the southwest Pacific, was the site of a crucial **World War II** battle. The island was occupied by **Japan**'s forces on 6 May 1942, as part of a plan to interdict lines of communication between Hawaii and Australia. On 7 August 1942, U.S. marines landed on the island and captured the airfield that was being built there. They named it Henderson Airfield after a marine pilot who died at the battle of **Midway**. Japan landed forces to regain the island and fierce fighting raged until 7 February 1943.

Guadalcanal was the first major U.S. land victory against Japan and was in many ways the turning point of the Pacific War. It demonstrated American resolve and fighting abilities to the Japanese, who had underrated these. It also initiated the brutal and unforgiving combat that characterized not just the rest of the Solomons campaign, which lasted another year, but the whole Pacific War. A series of intense naval battles took place in the waters around Guadalcanal that resulted in heavy losses on both sides. One of the waterways leading to the island was known as "Ironbottom Sound" because of all the ships sunk there. The battles demonstrated the superiority of the **U.S. Navy** at a time when numbers were about equal and before the massive reequipment through the **Two-Ocean Navy Act**.

GUOMINDANG. *See* KUOMINTANG.

– H –

HANIGHEN, FRANK CLEARY (1899–1964). Peace activist and journalist Frank Hanighen, a Harvard graduate, worked as a foreign correspondent in Europe for the *New York Post* and the *Philadelphia Record*. He was subsequently Washington correspondent for *Common Sense* and an editorial assistant with publishers Dodd, Mead. He wrote a number of books, the most famous being **The Merchants of Death** (1934) with **Helmuth Engelbrecht**, an exposé of the international armaments trade. While it did not find U.S. manufacturers to be among those most culpable, the book, together with George Seldes's more sensationalistic *Iron, Blood, and Profits*, directly influenced the establishment of the **Nye Committee**. Hanighen was active in the **America First Committee** and was still writing pieces favoring **isolationism** in the late 1940s. From 1944, Hanighen was joint editor of a conservative foreign policy review, *Human Events*, which was partly funded by **Robert E. Wood**. *See also* DEVIL THEORY; DISARMAMENT AND ARMS CONTROL; NEUTRALITY ACTS; PACIFISM.

HARDING, WARREN GAMALIEL (1865–1923). The 29th president of the United States, Warren G. Harding had a reputation as a reliable party man. He had supported President **William H. Taft** against the **progressive** challenge of former President **Theodore Roosevelt** in the 1912 election, though both lost to Democrat **Woodrow Wilson**. In 1914, Harding was elected to the U.S. Senate (R-Ohio), and he gave the keynote address to the 1916 convention that nominated **Charles Evans Hughes**. Harding's nomination for the presidency at the Republican convention in 1920 arose after the two leading contenders deadlocked in the balloting.

During the campaign, Harding's reputation as a conciliator made it possible to smooth over the party's divisions on the issue of **League of Nations** membership. He had been a member of the **Senate Committee on Foreign Relations** and was part of the delegation that visited President Wilson at the White House on 19 August 1919 to question him over the terms of the **Treaty of Versailles**. He supported U.S. membership in the League but insisted on acceptance of the **Lodge reservations**. Harding thus straddled the issue, reassuring **isolationists** such as **Hiram Johnson** that he would not accept membership on President Wilson's terms, while promising **internationalists** such as Taft and Hughes that he would seek constructive engagement with the international community.

Harding was elected president in a landslide on 2 November 1920, with **Calvin Coolidge** as vice president. U.S. foreign policy continued to be hampered by tensions between the isolationist and internationalist blocs in Congress. Isolationists were disappointed at Harding's appointment of the self-described "qualified internationalist" Charles Evans Hughes as secretary of state but delighted when, in April 1921, the president permanently shelved the League question, arguing that the domestic political climate made passage of the treaty impossible. However, he supported U.S. membership in the **World Court**, setting his administration on a collision course with senators such as Johnson and **William Borah**. Members sympathetic to the League were encouraged by this new dispute. Nebraska Senator **Gilbert Hitchcock** saw World Court membership as a chance to gain entry to the League "on the installment plan."

Throughout his tenure, President Harding supported the expansion of international **trade** and cultural links and the establishment of bilateral treaties to preserve peace. In July 1921, he signed the **Knox–Porter Resolution**, which ended the official state of hostility with **Germany**. He refused diplomatic recognition to the **Union of Soviet Socialist Republics** (continuing Wilson's policy) unless the Soviet government pledged to abide by international legal and diplomatic conventions and guarantee the security of U.S. citizens and their property. Despite this, he approved the **Volga famine relief effort** coordinated in 1921–22 by Secretary of Commerce **Herbert Hoover**. Harding also permitted Treasury Secretary **Andrew Mellon** to relax some of the pressure on **Great Britain** over **war debt** repayment schedules.

In an effort to prevent future arms races (while simultaneously displaying Harding's commitment to an active world role for the United States), the administration invited delegates from European nations, **China**, and **Japan** to the 1921 **Naval Disarmament Conference** in Washington, D.C., to discuss armaments limitation and specific territorial issues. The U.S. approach to the conference, from the appointment of a bipartisan U.S. delegation to the ambitious proposals presented by Secretary Hughes at the first session, was innovative but failed to resolve international tensions.

In **Latin America**, the administration worked to reverse the imperialistic image of the United States. It pursued negotiations with the post-revolutionary government of **Mexico**, resulting in the 1923 **Bucareli Agreements**. The U.S. State Department also arbitrated boundary disputes between Costa Rica and Panama (1921) and Peru and Chile (1922). American forces withdrew from **Cuba** and laid preparations for withdrawal from the **Dominican Republic**. The Colombian Treaty was finalized (April 1921), providing for the payment of reparations to Colombia for America's role in the 1903 Panamanian Revolution (**Thomson–Urrutia Treaty**). With policies that were less high-handed, more flexible, and more constructive than those pursued by the United States during the previous 30 years, the foundation was laid for the **Good Neighbor policy** of **Franklin D. Roosevelt** in the 1930s.

In June 1923, Harding began a tour of the western United States as the opening gambit in his campaign for reelection. A principal theme of his speeches was World Court membership. In Missouri, the president declared, "My passion is for justice over force. My hope is in the great Court. My mind is made up." However, Harding fell ill and died in San Francisco (2 August 1923). Revelations of corruption among his associates tarnished Harding's posthumous image. Moreover, the collapse of conservative and isolationist political influence in the United States between 1929 and 1941 (caused by the Great Depression and **World War II**) appeared to discredit the economic and foreign policies of all three administrations of the 1920s. Although Harding has often been depicted as an ignorant isolationist with no aptitude for foreign affairs, he is now seen more as a pragmatic moderate steering a middle course between the high-handed approach of Wilson and the disengagement of Coolidge. Against determined opposition from isolationists in Congress, he continued to prod his party and the nation toward an active world role through World Court membership, **disarmament** talks, and increased trade and cultural links.

HARE–HAWES–CUTTING ACT (1933). The first law for decolonization of the **Philippines** was the 1933 Hare–Hawes–Cutting Act.

The 1916 **Jones Act** had stated that the United States would grant the Philippines independence at some point, and by the 1930s U.S. sugar and dairy companies were pushing for independence, so that the islands' cane sugar and coconut oil would be subject to import restrictions. Similarly, labor organizations pressed for it so that Filipinos would fall under the immigration quotas. The Hare–Hawes–Cutting Act was passed by Congress in December 1932 but vetoed by President **Herbert Hoover**. On 13 January 1933, the act was passed over the president's veto. It provided for independence in 1945, while reserving U.S. rights to military bases and U.S. review of decisions made by Filipino courts. It imposed quotas and tariffs on Filipino exports. The Philippine Senate rejected the act in October 1933, and the issue was later taken up in the **Tydings–McDuffie Act**.

HARRIMAN, FLORENCE (1870–1967). Suffragist and diplomat Florence Jaffray Hurst married J. Borden Harriman, a cousin of **Averell Harriman's**, in 1889. Her husband was a banker in New York, but she became a reforming social activist and campaigner for women's right to vote. She campaigned for **Woodrow Wilson** in 1912, and he appointed her to the first U.S. Commission on Industrial Relations. Harriman was widowed in 1914, and on the outbreak of **World War I** founded the Committee of Mercy to help women and children impoverished by the war. On U.S. entry into the war, she organized the Women's Motor Corps of the Red Cross in **France**. In 1917–19, she was chair of the National Defense Advisory Commission's Committee on Women in Industry. She participated in the 1919 **Paris Peace Conference** and returned a strong supporter of the **League of Nations** and other world peace organizations.

Harriman served on the Democratic National Committee from 1920 to the 1950s and in 1922 was the founder and first president of the Women's National Democratic Club. In 1937, President **Franklin D. Roosevelt** appointed her minister to Norway. Harriman was present when **Germany** invaded Norway on 9 April 1940, and her military attaché, Captain Robert M. Losey, was the first American serviceman to be killed in **World War II**. She assisted with the evacuation of American citizens and members of the Norwegian royal family to Sweden. Back in the United States, and a private citizen again, Harriman assisted in the unsuccessful bipartisan campaign to get **Wendell Willkie** elected governor of New York in 1942.

In 1944, Harriman wrote one of the first books on the death camp at Auschwitz. In 1952, she helped with the unsuccessful campaign of Averell Harriman for the Democratic presidential nomination. In 1963, President John F. Kennedy gave her a Citation of Merit of Distinguished Service.

HARRIMAN, W. AVERELL (1891–1986). Averell Harriman inherited his father's railroad empire and proceeded to make his own fortune in railroads, banking, and venture capitalism. He invested in the Soviet market in the 1920s, in manganese as well as railroads. He was a strong supporter of **Franklin D. Roosevelt** and became an administrator and special assistant in the National Recovery Administration (1934–35). He was chair of the Business Advisory Council (1937–39), and he owned *Today* magazine with Vincent Astor from 1935 until 1937, when it merged with *Newsweek*.

In 1941, Harriman was made chief of the Materials Branch and Production Division of the Office of Production Management. Harriman was one of Roosevelt's circle of informal advisors and became a close confidant during **World War II**, entrusted with sensitive missions to major U.S. allies. He attended the **Placentia Bay** conference in August 1941. His auspicious diplomatic career began when Roosevelt appointed him to London in 1941, both as **Lend-Lease** representative and as a special envoy to Prime Minister **Winston S. Churchill** of **Great Britain**. He formed a close relationship with Churchill, and a liaison with his daughter-in-law, Pamela Churchill.

In October 1941, Harriman went with Lord Beaverbrook to attend the 1941 **Moscow Conference** and negotiated the first protocol of supplies of munitions and other materials to the **Union of Soviet Socialist Republics** (USSR). When Roosevelt wished for a higher profile ambassador in Moscow, and one closer to his own views, he appointed Harriman in October 1943. Harriman was present at the **Teheran** and **Yalta Conferences** as well as Churchill's two visits to Moscow in 1942 and 1944. His attitudes soured as a result of the hostile attitude that **Josef Stalin**'s regime manifested toward foreigners, even allies, and became convinced that a firmer policy was required. He was not advocating a break but argued that the Soviets appreciated hard bargaining and could not be softened by shows of goodwill. Harriman, himself, however, was inconsistent in his practice of this precept.

After Roosevelt's death, Harriman eagerly pressed his views on the new president, **Harry S. Truman**. It is likely that Harriman's advice to be firmer influenced Truman's demeanor in his first meeting with the Soviet commissar for foreign affairs, Vyacheslav Molotov, in April 1945, as well as the general tone of U.S.–Soviet interactions.

Harriman was ambassador to Britain (1946) and secretary of commerce (1946–48). He served as governor of New York (1954–58) and was an ambassador-at-large (1961) in the John F. Kennedy administration. He was a representative at the Paris peace talks with North Vietnam in 1968. Harriman was a major figure in the foreign policy making elite well into the 1980s. He later married Pamela Churchill, who went on to serve as a U.S. ambassador in her own right.

HARVEY, GEORGE (1864–1928). Journalist and diplomat George Harvey played a key role in nominating **Woodrow Wilson** for the presidency in 1912, but he grew disillusioned with Wilson's policies during **World War I**. In 1919–20, he worked to bolster support for the Senate **Irreconcilables** who opposed U.S. membership of the **League of Nations**. He lent his support to the 1920 candidacy of Republican **Warren G. Harding** and was appointed ambassador to **Great Britain** by Harding in 1921. He resigned in 1923.

HAVANA, ACT OF (1940). The second pan-American meeting of foreign ministers took place in Havana, Cuba, on 21–30 July 1940, during **World War II**. The American republics affirmed in a declaration known as the Act of Havana (30 July) that they would act jointly or individually in their own defense and to defend the continent, and this would include taking over any European colonies in the hemisphere that were threatened by aggression. At the same meeting, they established the Inter-American Commission on Territorial Administration to guard the sovereignty of the states of the western hemisphere. These decisions reflected concern that the war in Europe would spread into the region through actions between the belligerents, or by **Axis** attempts to take over territories owned by conquered states such as **France** and the Netherlands. Trusteeships would be formed rather than allow **Germany** to take over these territories. The U.S. State Department had already warned in the **Nontransfer Corollary to the Monroe Doctrine** on 17 July that it would not recognize transfers of sovereignty of American territory from one non-American power to another. *See also* PANAMA DECLARATION; ST. PIERRE AND MIQUELON AFFAIR.

HAVANA CONFERENCE (1928). The sixth International Conference of American States, held in Havana, **Cuba**, 16 January–20 February 1928, was notable for former Secretary of State **Charles Evans Hughes**'s fierce denunciation of anti-U.S. sentiment and defense of U.S. intervention in **Latin America** in order to protect the lives of American citizens. Hughes also helped to block an effort by some Latin American delegations to reduce the influence of the **Pan-American Union** and ban intervention in the affairs of other states. *See also* CLARK MEMORANDUM; ROOSEVELT COROLLARY.

HAVANA CONFERENCE (1940). *See* HAVANA, ACT OF.

HEARST, WILLIAM RANDOLPH (1863–1951). Publisher William Randolph Hearst made his name pioneering sensationalistic "yellow journalism" in his *New York Journal* in the 1890s. His papers catered to a working-class readership, attacked the British empire, and helped stir up "yellow peril" fears of **immigration** from Asia. Hearst exploited issues like the revolution in **Cuba** to boost his circulation. He was deeply ambitious, served two terms in Congress (1903–7), and received 263 convention votes for the Democratic presidential nomination in 1904. He opposed U.S. involvement in **World War I** and membership in the **League of Nations**.

By 1930, he controlled a vast publishing empire of over 20 newspapers and magazines while amassing an enormous art collection and building an ornate mansion at San Simeon, California. The Great Depression depleted his fortune, and he helped **Franklin D. Roosevelt** gain the presidential nomination in 1932. Hearst interviewed **Germany**'s dictator **Adolf Hitler** in 1934. He broke with Roosevelt by 1935 over New Deal policies toward business and over foreign policy. He lost touch with his working-class readership and was overtaken by more innovative publishers, like **Henry Luce**. Hearst backed **isolationism** in 1940 and was a vociferous anticommunist in the 1940s, despite having advocated recognition of the **Union of Soviet Socialist Republics** during the 1920s. The motion picture *Citizen Kane* (1941) was loosely based on his life.

HENDERSON, LOY (1892–1986). Loy Henderson was a member of the 1919 Inter-Allied Commission to **Germany** for repatriation of prisoners of war following **World War I** and a member of the American Red Cross Commission to Europe in 1919–21. He entered the Foreign Service in 1922, serving as vice consul in Dublin until joining the Division of East European Affairs in the State Department in 1925. Henderson was one of the young officials trained as experts on Eastern Europe and the **Union of Soviet Socialist Republics** (USSR) by **Robert F. Kelley**. He served as third secretary to the legation in the Baltic States at Kovno, Tallinn, and Riga in 1927–30, where the prime occupation was observing developments in the USSR, since the United States had no diplomatic representation inside the Soviet Union. After another term in the Division of East European Affairs in 1930–34, Henderson became second secretary at the newly established embassy in Moscow in 1934. He rose to be first secretary and acted as chargé d'affaires after Ambassador **William C. Bullitt** left. Like the other Foreign Service professionals at the embassy, such as **George F. Kennan**, Henderson was unhappy with Bullitt's replacement, **Joseph P. Davies**, believing he was too uncritical of dictator **Josef Stalin**'s acts of terror.

In 1938, Henderson was recalled to Washington, D.C., to be assistant chief of the Division of European Affairs in the State Department. In 1942, probably because of his hostile attitude to the Soviet Union, which was now a U.S. ally, he was first made inspector of diplomatic missions, then ambassador to Iraq (1943–45). After **World War II**, Henderson served as director of Near Eastern and African Affairs and played an influential role in early American Cold War policy. He was then ambassador to India and Iran. After his retirement in 1961, he was a professor of international relations. *See also* BOHLEN, CHARLES EUSTIS; DURBROW, ELBRIDGE; FAYMONVILLE, PHILIP RIES.

HERRICK, MYRON TIMOTHY (1854–1929). A governor of Ohio (1904–6), Myron Herrick was appointed ambassador to **France** in

1912 by President **William H. Taft**. He won praise in France for helping to prevent panic in Paris as **Germany**'s army advanced in 1914. After an unsuccessful campaign for the U.S. Senate in 1920, he returned as ambassador (1921–29) at the request of President **Warren G. Harding**. He worked to reduce France's **war debt** burden from **World War I** and to strengthen U.S.–French relations.

HILL, DAVID JAYNE (1850–1932). Diplomat David Jayne Hill served as assistant secretary of state (1898–1903), minister to Switzerland (1903–5), minister to the Netherlands (1905–7), and ambassador to **Germany** (1908–11). An advocate of **preparedness** and U.S. entry into **World War I**, he spoke out strongly against U.S. membership in the **League of Nations** and **World Court**. He later wrote several studies of U.S. foreign policy.

HINES PAGE, WALTER (1855–1918). Editor of the *Atlantic Monthly* (1898–99) and *World's Work* (1900–13), Walter Hines Page was a southern **progressive** and an early supporter of the presidential candidacy of **Woodrow Wilson**. He was rewarded with appointment as ambassador to **Great Britain** (1913–18). After August 1914, with the outbreak of **World War I**, he strongly supported the cause of Britain and its allies but became frustrated by the Wilson administration's stance of neutrality. The friction did not improve even after the U.S. **declaration of war** on **Germany** in April 1917. Hines Page died shortly after retiring from his post in 1918.

HIROHITO, EMPEROR (1901–1989). Hirohito succeeded his father, Taisho, as emperor of Japan on 25 December 1926. His reign was known as the Showa era. Hirohito had traveled in Europe in 1921 and had acquired a concept of constitutional monarchy based on a meeting with King George V of Great Britain. He favored close relations with Great Britain and the United States. In the early years of his reign, he voiced some opposition to hard-line policies against China and supported the agreements reached at the 1930 London Naval Disarmament Conference, which some Japanese officers regarded as a humiliation.

Becoming vulnerable to attacks from hard-liners, Hirohito chose to emphasize the emperor's aloofness from policy making and decided he must defer to cabinet decisions, as a constitutional monarch in the European mold. He thus accepted the Japanese army's actions in the Manchurian Crisis (1931) and in the Sino–Japanese War. This remained true with regard to the attack on Pearl Harbor in 1941, though some have held that without the emperor's rather cryptic haiku poem, the Japanese high command would not have proceeded with the plan.

Hirohito acted as a patriotic head of state during World War II, doing what he could to achieve Japanese victory while following his interpretation of his constitutional role: he would express his personal views, but often in a way that was cryptic or deliberately framed in nonpolitical terms, and he would defer to cabinet decisions. His one major intervention was accepting the need to surrender after atomic bombs were used on Hiroshima and Nagasaki in August 1945. After the war, the United States decided to retain Hirohito as emperor and not to put him on trial for war crimes, seeing his utility as a unifying national force that would make the task of occupation much easier. He became more of a ceremonial figurehead, in the style of modern constitutional monarchs. He visited Europe again in 1971 and the United States in 1975. *See also* UNCONDITIONAL SURRENDER.

HIROSHIMA. The Japanese city of Hiroshima was the target of the first **atomic bomb** used in warfare. The bomb, a uranium bomb code-named "Little Boy" and the product of the **Manhattan Project**, was dropped from the B-29 bomber, *Enola Gay*. It detonated about 500 meters over the center of the city on the morning of 6 August 1945. There were some military and naval installations in the general area, and President **Harry S. Truman**, on announcing the mission, described it as a military target. While similar Japanese cities had been subjected to area bombing since March 1945, Hiroshima and four other cities were spared this earlier bombing in order to provide an appropriate target for the atomic bomb. Hiroshima was selected largely because of its geography—the flat terrain enhanced the destructive force. An area of 5 square miles (13 square kilometers) was completely devastated, and 62 percent of the buildings in the city were destroyed. Out of a population of 320,000, an estimated 118,000 died as a result of the bomb by August 1946. Longer-term radiation effects and other consequences have since raised this figure over 140,000. *See also* NAGASAKI.

HISS, ALGER (1904–1996). After graduating from Johns Hopkins University and Harvard Law School, Alger Hiss worked with justices Felix Frankfurter and Oliver Wendell Holmes before becoming an attorney for various New Deal agencies, notably the Agricultural Adjustment Administration. He worked with the **Nye Committee** in 1934. He and his brother Donald entered the State Department in 1936. He was special assistant to the director of the Office of Far Eastern Affairs and in 1944, during **World War II**, became special assistant in the Office of Special Political Affairs, which worked on postwar planning. In this office, he acted as executive secretary at the 1944 **Dumbarton Oaks Conference**. Hiss attended the meetings at the 1945 **Yalta Conference** that discussed the **United Nations** organization and opposed the demands of **Josef Stalin**, leader of the **Union of Soviet Socialist Republics** (USSR), for 16 separate places for Soviet republics in the United Nations.

Hiss was secretary-general of the 1945 **San Francisco Conference**. He then became director of the Office of Special Political Affairs. He left the State Department in 1946 and was president of the Carnegie Endowment for International Peace. He was then subject to accusations of having been a member of the **Communist Party of the United States** in the 1930s and of having passed secret materials to the Soviets. He was convicted of perjury in 1950 and served a 44-month jail sentence. Debate persisted as to whether Hiss was actually a spy. There is significant, though not definitive, evidence in the materials decoded by the **Venona project** that he was the spy codenamed Ales.

HITCHCOCK, GILBERT M. (1859–1934). Lawyer Gilbert Hitchcock was a Republican U.S. senator for Nebraska in 1911–23. A member of the **Senate Committee on Foreign Relations**, he was a strong supporter of the **preparedness** policies of President **Woodrow Wilson**. He introduced Wilson's war resolution on the floor of the Senate in April 1917 and argued in favor of acceptance of the **Treaty of Versailles**. In 1919, to assist the cause of the administration during debates over the treaty, Hitchcock proposed the five **Hitchcock reservations** to counter those proposed by Senator **Henry Cabot Lodge**. These were limited in scope and interpretive in nature, however, and were voted down in the Senate. Hitchcock remained adamant that senators should support the president and vote down the treaty with the **Lodge reservations** attached.

HITCHCOCK RESERVATIONS (1919). Conditions for acceptance of the **Treaty of Versailles**, the Hitchcock reservations were proposed by Senator **Gilbert M. Hitchcock**. Supporters, known as "mild reservationists," were criticized by Senator **William Borah**, a leading treaty opponent, for taking positions virtually indistinguishable from those already taken by President **Woodrow Wilson**. Hitchcock's proposals reinforced an existing treaty stipulation that domestic concerns (including **immigration** and **tariff** legislation) fell outside the remit of the **League of Nations**. He also sought to reassure Americans that if the United States withdrew from the League, it, and not the League, would be the "sole judge as to whether its obligations . . . have been performed." Further, advice offered by the League to member nations regarding its naval and military forces "is merely advice which each member nation is free to accept or reject." The Hitchcock reservations also reiterated the inviolability of the **Monroe Doctrine**. They were voted down in the Senate on 19 November 1919. *See also* IRRECONCILABLES; LODGE RESERVATIONS.

HITLER, ADOLF (1889–1945). Austrian-born dictator of **Germany** Adolf Hitler served in a Bavarian regiment in **World War I** and in 1919 joined the tiny German Workers Party. His charismatic and demagogic leadership transformed it into the National Socialist German Workers Party (NSDAP), or Nazi Party. In 1923, he was jailed after an unsuccessful coup attempt in Munich. While in jail, he wrote *Mein Kampf* ("My Struggle"), expounding his social and political theories, revolving around the ideas of the superiority of the Aryan "master race" and its mission to acquire "living space." With the outbreak of the global economic depression, his simplistic explanations of Germany's social and economic problems attracted support by offering scapegoats for Germany's problems in the injustices of the 1919 **Treaty of Versailles** and what he claimed was a vast "Jewish-Bolshevik conspiracy." The

Nazis became the largest party in the Reichstag (parliament) and Hitler became chancellor in January 1933, placed in power by conservatives who believed they could dispense with him once he had defeated the communists. Instead, Hitler established a dictatorship after the contrived burning of the Reichstag and became Fuhrer (leader) on the death of President Hindenburg in 1934. Now head of state, he gained the loyalty of the German army after eliminating the more radical of his own followers.

Hitler proceeded to regain by gradual steps what Germany had lost under the Treaty of Versailles, beginning with the remilitarization of the Rhineland in 1936, followed by union with Austria in 1938 and the annexation of Bohemia and Moravia in March 1939. Germany's invasion of **Poland** in September 1939 sparked **World War II** in Europe. In the next two years, Germany conquered most of Europe and established a New Order, the central features of which were economic exploitation in favor of Germany, excluding foreign **trade** where possible, and the eradication of the Jewish population. The latter was carried out in a series of policies culminating in the "final solution"—mass extermination.

Hitler's views of the United States were shaped by his racial attitudes. He saw the United States as industrially powerful but corrupted by being racially mixed and dominated by Jewish capitalist interests. He believed President **Franklin D. Roosevelt** was the tool of these interests. He did not regard the United States as an immediate threat but saw that a final U.S.–German conflict was inevitable. Although provoked by the increasing involvement of U.S. warships in action against German submarines in the fall of 1941, Hitler did not at that time seek war with the United States, involved as he was in war with the **Union of Soviet Socialist Republics**. However, when **Japan**, a partner in the **Axis** alliance, attacked at **Pearl Harbor**, he declared war on the United States. It is probable that he hoped to aid Japanese operations by involving the United States in a war on two fronts and calculated that German submarines could prevent the United States from intervention in the war in Europe until he had secured victory there. He undoubtedly underestimated the speed and extent to which the United States was able to mobilize its economy and its armed forces for war, and his racial assumptions led him to seriously underrate the military prowess of the United States. The submarines did enjoy great short-term success in the **American shooting season**, but ultimately U.S. entry in the war was a major contribution to his defeat. He committed suicide in his bunker in Berlin on 30 April 1945. *See also* DECLARATION OF WAR (1941); SHOOT-ON-SIGHT ORDER.

HOLT, RUSH DEW (1905–1955). High school teacher and liberal Democrat Rush Holt was elected U.S. senator for West Virginia in 1934, taking his seat in 1935 when he gained the age of 30. He was an idiosyncratic senator who alienated his liberal and labor support by his criticism of the New Deal. A staunch noninterventionist and neutralist, he opposed any U.S. actions that might bring involvement in war, such as loans to belligerents. The basis of his views was **pacifism**, and this led him to a strong **isolationist** stance. He was influenced by the findings of the **Nye Committee** and made addresses under the auspices of the **National Council for Prevention of War**. He delayed passage of **Carl Vinson**'s 1938 Naval Expansion Act in the Senate for two weeks. Holt failed to gain renomination from his party in 1940. He spoke widely for the **America First Committee** during 1941. He subsequently served in the state legislature.

HOOVER, HERBERT CLARK (1874–1964). The 31st president of the United States, Herbert Hoover was a mining engineer and self-made millionaire. He rose to prominence helping the U.S. ambassador to **Great Britain**, **Walter Hines Page**, arrange for the safe return home of U.S. citizens stranded in Europe at the outbreak of **World War I**. Consequently, Hoover was appointed head of the **Commission for Relief in Belgium**, which spent more than $1.5 billion aiding civilians in Belgium and northern parts of **France** after the German invasion. In 1917, he was appointed by President **Woodrow Wilson** as U.S. Food Administrator with the task of reducing waste and inefficiency in food production and consumption. Hoover's efforts helped to triple U.S. food exports to Allied countries. As secretary of commerce during the **Warren G. Harding** and **Calvin Coolidge** administrations (1921–29), he reinforced his reputation for activity, administrative efficiency, and media awareness. The resultant expansion of Commerce Department power led to territorial clashes with the State Department, which suspected Hoover of manipulating international commerce in order to influence foreign policy.

Having acquired the nicknames of "the Great Engineer" and "the Great Humanitarian," Hoover's election to the presidency in 1928, at the height of 1920s prosperity, was virtually a foregone conclusion. His one-term presidency, however, was dominated by the effects of the stock market crash in October 1929. Hoover lost his reputation for innovation and dynamism through his apparent unwillingness to use government powers to their fullest extent to combat the Great Depression. In foreign policy, he was more inclined to **internationalist** viewpoints than his predecessor, Coolidge, though he did not make any fresh attempt to gain U.S. membership in the **League of Nations**. He encouraged U.S. cooperation with the **World Court** and sent delegates to the April 1930 **London Naval Disarmament Conference**, which set new limits on cruiser and battleship production. The initial impetus for the conference had come from his **Rapidan Conference** with Prime Minister Ramsay MacDonald of Great Britain. Hoover also took an interest in the early sessions of the **Geneva Disarmament Conference** in 1932. He disavowed the **dollar diplomacy** of previous administrations and hastened the withdrawal of U.S. troops from Haiti and **Nicaragua**. Under his administration, the State Department published the **Clark Memorandum** eliminating the **Roosevelt Corollary** as a key element of American policy in **Latin America**.

Hoover also pushed the pace of professionalization in the diplomatic service begun by the 1924 **Foreign Service Act** (Rogers Act), by replacing many political appointees with career diplomats. Convinced that the 1928 **Kellogg–Briand Pact** was too weak to succeed in its aims of abolishing war, he tried, without success, to push for a strengthening amendment. During Hoover's tenure, the 1930 **Smoot–Hawley Tariff Act** was passed by Congress, partly in response to the dire conditions confronting America's farmers. This replaced the 1922 **Fordney–McCumber Tariff Act**. Though sympathetic to the farmers' plight, Hoover was initially reluctant to sign Smoot–Hawley. His fear that it would provoke retaliatory measures abroad, harming prospects for economic recovery from the Depression, were quickly realized. In an effort to stimulate recovery, he announced the **Hoover Moratorium** in 1931, offering a year's relief from payment of **war debts** by America's wartime allies.

In January 1932, responding to **Japan**'s September 1931 invasion of Manchuria and the subsequent **Manchurian Crisis**, the administration announced the **Stimson Doctrine** (after Secretary of State **Henry L. Stimson**), which refused to recognize Japanese territorial gains. Defeated by Democrat **Franklin D. Roosevelt** in the 1932 presidential elections, Hoover remained active in politics and became a critic of Roosevelt's domestic and foreign policies. After **World War II**, he was sent to Europe by President **Harry S. Truman** to monitor food relief distribution and also chaired commissions on reorganization of the executive branch of the government.

HOOVER MORATORIUM. On 20 June 1931, the administration of President **Herbert Hoover** announced a moratorium on the payment of **reparations** by former enemies of the United States during **World War I** and also on the repayment of **war debts** owed by wartime allies such as **Great Britain** and **France**. The proposal was welcomed by European governments, since it had the potential to reduce pressure on national economies in a time of deepening economic depression. It met with some opposition in the U.S. Congress, however. Some members believed the nation's own economic problems could be reduced or even cured by increasing rather than slowing the pace of debt and reparations repayments. Advocates of a cash bonus for American war veterans argued that immediate repayment by foreign debtors would enable the federal government to fully fund the bonus without a tax increase, thus giving a massive cash stimulus to the economy. In December 1931, Congress formally approved the moratorium. By the end of 1932, however, it was clear that the moratorium was too short and the economic deterioration too grave for it to have made any real impact on the world economy. *See also* LAUSANNE CONFERENCE; LONDON ECONOMIC CONFERENCE.

HOPKINS, HARRY LLOYD (1890–1946). Presidential advisor Harry Hopkins was trained as a social worker. He became President **Franklin D. Roosevelt**'s closest confidant and a key advisor during the New Deal and **World War II**. Hopkins, who had worked with Roosevelt in New York when Roosevelt was governor, was appointed federal emergency relief administrator in 1933. He was best known for his commitment to providing employment through federal works programs in the Civil Works Administration and Works Progress Administration, which he headed (1935–38).

Hopkins was secretary of commerce (1938–40) and lived in the White House during World War II when supervising the **Lend-Lease** program. Roosevelt used him for special missions to Prime Minister **Winston Churchill** in **Great Britain** and to Premier **Josef Stalin** of the **Union of Soviet Socialist Republics** from 1941 onward. His friendship with Churchill was significant in forging the close U.S.–British wartime working relationship. Hopkins acted as advisor at the **Casablanca, Teheran,** and **Yalta Conferences.** Although very ill, he went on one final mission to Stalin in June 1945, at the request of President **Harry S. Truman,** and reached an accommodation on the issue of the government of liberated **Poland** that was essentially a modification of the Yalta conference agreement, in Stalin's favor.

HORNBECK, STANLEY KUHL (1883–1966). Stanley Hornbeck was a Rhodes scholar in **Great Britain** (1904–6), the first from Colorado. At the University of Wisconsin, he studied Far Eastern politics under Paul Reinsch, a strong advocate for the **open door** policy. In 1909, Hornbeck went to teach in **China.** A **progressive,** he was a supporter of the Chinese Revolution of 1911. In 1913, based in Mukden, Manchuria, he wrote a study of the open door policy for the Carnegie Endowment for International Peace. His four years in China convinced him of China's internal instability and vulnerability to foreign pressure, and the danger to China from **Japan.** Hornbeck returned to academic posts in Wisconsin and at Harvard. He was a member of President **Woodrow Wilson**'s group of advisors known as the **Inquiry** and attended the 1919 **Paris Peace Conference.**

Hornbeck was a technical expert in the State Department Office of the Economic Advisor (1921–24), head of the Division of Far Eastern Affairs (1928–37), then special advisor to Secretary of State **Cordell Hull** (1937–44), and he has been seen as an important influence in moving U.S. policy toward more assertive opposition to Japanese expansion in China. Hornbeck was a keen advocate of improved U.S. relations with China. As a counter to the recommendations of the ambassador in Japan, **Joseph C. Grew,** Hornbeck recommended throughout the 1930s a policy of economic pressure on Japan.

Hornbeck disagreed with Grew and Eugene Dooman at the Tokyo Embassy over the proposal by Prime Minister Funimaro Konoye of Japan in August 1941 that he should meet President **Franklin D. Roosevelt**. The U.S. rejection of the proposal, on Hornbeck's advice, has been seen as a crucial element in the demise of Konoye's government and the rise of the war party under General **Hideki Tojo**. Hornbeck believed Japan would never dare to go to war with the United States, and he was the author of Hull's note of 26 November 1941 that required Japan to withdraw from Indochina and China as a condition for resumption of U.S. oil shipments. Hornbeck served as U.S. ambassador to the Netherlands in 1944–47 and was the author of eight books.

HOT SPRINGS CONFERENCE (1943). Delegates from a number of **United Nations** countries met at Hot Springs, Virginia, 8 May–3 June 1943, to discuss international food and agricultural issues. The Interim Commission of Food and Agriculture was established. This body formulated a plan for the Food and Agricultural Organization, which was affiliated with the United Nations, to act as an advisory agency on production and technical matters.

HOUGHTON, ALANSON BIGELOW (1863–1941). Alanson Houghton of New York was a Republican member of the U.S. House of Representatives in 1919–22. He served on the House Foreign Affairs Committee before being appointed ambassador to **Germany** (1922–25) by President **Warren G. Harding**. He was appointed ambassador to **Great Britain** (1925–29) by President **Calvin Coolidge**. After being defeated in a bid for election to the U.S. Senate in 1928, Houghton went into business but kept involved in world events through his work for the American Peace Society.

HOUSE COMMITTEE INVESTIGATING UN-AMERICAN ACTIVITIES. In 1934, the House of Representatives set up the Special Committee on Un-American Activities Authorized to Investigate Nazi Propaganda and Certain Other Propaganda Activities (McCormack–Dickstein Committee). The purpose was to investigate an alleged plot to blow up the White House, the "Business Plot." The committee extensively investigated fascist and anti-Semitic organizations in the

United States, largely driven by the concerns of its vice chair, Samuel Dickstein (D-N.Y.). It held investigations in six cities and gathered a large amount of evidence concerning the dissemination of foreign and subversive propaganda. In May 1938, the House Committee Investigating Un-American Activities was created with a broader remit, to investigate Nazi activity and the Ku Klux Klan. It was chaired by **Martin Dies** (D-Tex.) until 1944, with Dickstein as vice chair. Soviet documents later revealed that Dickstein was on the payroll of an **intelligence** agency of the **Union of Soviet Socialist Republics** from 1937 to 1940, which hoped thereby to gain information on fascist anti-Soviet organizations.

The Dies Committee was also interested in communist activities, and the affiliations of many of its members with the Ku Klux Klan meant that investigations of the KKK were soon set aside—the Klan was characterized as "an American institution." While there was some investigation of pro-Nazi activities among German American organizations, the focus of the committee was increasingly on investigating alleged communist infiltration of New Deal agencies like the Federal Theater Project.

Dies was succeeded as chair of the committee by Edward Hart (1944–45) and John Wood (1945–46). In 1946, it was made a standing committee as the House Committee on Un-American Activities (commonly abbreviated as HUAC), by which time its sole focus was on communism. It was prominent in the anticommunist movement of the late 1940s and early 1950s, particularly in connection with the **Alger Hiss** case, and with its investigations into Hollywood in 1947. The committee was renamed the Internal Security Committee in 1969 and abolished in 1975. *See also* COMMUNIST PARTY OF THE UNITED STATES; GERMAN-AMERICAN BUND; SMITH ACT.

HOUSE, EDWARD MANDELL (1858–1938). A political advisor to President **Woodrow Wilson**, Edward House (often referred to as "Colonel House," an unofficial designation) served as a roving ambassador to Europe in 1915–16, during **World War I**. His tendency to act without consulting the State Department nearly caused a diplomatic rift in 1916 when Foreign Secretary **Edward Grey** of **Great Britain** delivered the "House-Grey memorandum" to Prime Minister Herbert Asquith. This confidential memorandum, dated 22 February 1916, reported that House, in conversation with Grey, stated the United States would probably enter the war against **Germany** unless the **Central Powers** accepted an offer of mediation by the Wilson administration. House did not, in fact, have Wilson's prior agreement in giving such an assurance to Grey, and its rejection by the British government saved the president considerable embarrassment. Though House helped Wilson draft the **Fourteen Points** and accompanied him to the 1919 **Paris Peace Conference**, he disagreed with his intransigence over **League of Nations** membership, arguing for compromise over the **Lodge reservations**. He rapidly lost his influence within the administration. In 1932, he was an unofficial foreign affairs advisor to Democratic presidential nominee **Franklin D. Roosevelt**.

HOUSE-GREY MEMORANDUM. *See* HOUSE, EDWARD MANDELL.

HUERTA, VICTORIANO (1854–1916). After usurping power in the February 1913 coup that resulted in the execution of President Francisco Madero, Victoriano Huerta became the leader of **Mexico**. The coup had the active support of U.S. ambassador Henry Lane Wilson but the administration of **Woodrow Wilson** refused to recognize Huerta, recalled the ambassador, placed an embargo on arms shipments, and encouraged rebellion by **Venustiano Carranza** and **Francisco ("Pancho") Villa** in the north and Emiliano Zapata in the south. In April 1914, U.S. troops were dispatched to occupy the port of **Veracruz**. Unable to contain the Carranza and Villa forces, Huerta resigned on 15 July 1914 and fled the country. He eventually settled in the United States, where he was later arrested for conspiring to regain power with the aid of German agents.

HUGHES, CHARLES EVANS (1862–1948). Charles Evans Hughes was a Wall Street lawyer before becoming governor of New York in 1907. He was appointed to the Supreme Court by President **William Howard Taft** in 1910 but resigned in 1916 to campaign for the Republican presidential nomination. He countered the Democrats' effective campaign slogan "He kept us out of war" by claiming that President **Woodrow Wilson**'s neutrality policy at the start of **World**

War I was compromised by anglophilism. Hughes was unable to bridge the gap between **progressives** and conservatives in the Republican Party, and lukewarm support from California's progressive governor, **Hiram Johnson**, cost Hughes the state's electoral votes and the election.

Hughes was appointed secretary of state by President **Warren G. Harding** in 1921, over the protests of Republican **isolationists** in the Senate, who suspected Hughes, correctly, of having **internationalist** leanings. During his tenure, after the failure of the Senate to ratify the **Treaty of Versailles**, the United States concluded a separate peace treaty with **Germany**, permanently shelved the question of U.S. membership in the **League of Nations**, and sought more stable and cooperative relations with **Latin America**. Policies in Latin America emphasized the peaceful encouragement of **trade** links and stable, democratic government—seeking to distance the administration from the military interventionism of President **Woodrow Wilson** and the aggressive nationalism of President **Theodore Roosevelt**. These tactics foreshadowed the **Good Neighbor policy** promoted by President **Franklin D. Roosevelt** in the 1930s. Hughes favored U.S. membership of the **World Court** (Permanent Court of International Justice) and a flexible policy toward **reparations** and **war debt** repayments. Probably his greatest accomplishment came with the 1921 **Naval Disarmament Conference** in Washington, D.C., which concluded the most significant agreements on naval arms limitations of the interwar era.

President **Herbert Hoover** appointed Hughes chief justice of the Supreme Court in 1930. A notable ruling by the Hughes Court affecting international relations came in *United States v. Curtiss–Wright Export Corporation* (1936), when the Court supported the president's constitutional right to restrict U.S. exports of military equipment to Bolivia. Hughes's tenure was most notable, however, for its 1937 confrontation with President Franklin Roosevelt over the Court's striking down of large parts of the New Deal as unconstitutional. Roosevelt considered packing the court with liberal appointees but decided against the idea, and the Court later endorsed other key New Deal laws, thus ending the deadlock. By the time of his retirement in 1941, Hughes's conservative political and judicial views had become unfashionable in the new liberal era.

HULL, CORDELL (1871–1955). After serving in the Tennessee state legislature, Cordell Hull became a Democratic member of the U.S. House of Representatives (1907–21, 1923–31) and a senator (1931–33). He served the longest term of any U.S. secretary of state, from 1933 to 1944, following his appointment by President **Franklin D. Roosevelt**. A key figure in the **progressive** wing of the party, he was one of the most popular Democrats in the country.

Hull believed that liberalizing **trade** was the way that peace could be assured, since, he argued, nations that trade with each other do not go to war with each other. In the context of Congress's attachment to high **tariffs**, Hull sought to enlarge trade through **reciprocal trade agreements** throughout the 1920s, and he saw this as his principal mission when he became secretary of state. He negotiated tariff reductions with **Great Britain** and **France** in 1934–35. He used **Sumner Welles** to negotiate reciprocal trade agreements in **Latin America**. As part of the **Good Neighbor policy**, Hull advocated withdrawal of troops from Central America and encouraged the repeal of the **Platt Amendment** that allowed intervention in **Cuba**.

Welles was appointed undersecretary of state in 1937, ostensibly to reduce Hull's workload but also to represent Roosevelt's preferences in foreign policy within the State Department. Hull, who favored the aging **Walton Moore** for the post, saw this as an affront, and this belief was strengthened when the press attributed the leading role in foreign affairs to Welles rather than to Hull. Hull blamed Welles for leaks to the press and was annoyed when he was sent by Roosevelt to Europe in early 1940 in an attempt to mediate peace during **World War II**. Roosevelt left relations with non-European powers to Hull, though Hull had little interest or expertise in noncommercial matters. In 1941, Hull handled the negotiations with **Japan** that resulted in stalemate. Hull had accepted the viewpoint of **Stanley Hornbeck** that Japan had to be treated firmly. After stating his position, essentially a demand that the Japanese relinquish their conquests in **China**, Hull was not interested in further discussion.

After the United States entered the war, Roosevelt handled relations with the major allies himself, using personal envoys rather than State Department officials. Hull managed to convince Roosevelt that issues in Welles's personal life made him a political liability and secured his removal from the State Department in 1943. Hull was sidelined frequently due to ill health—he suffered from tuberculosis—and was not among Roosevelt's inner circle of advisors.

Hull played a role in wartime international affairs with his participation in the 1943 **Moscow Conference**, though Roosevelt excluded him from **Big Three** meetings. Hull devoted himself to the establishment of the **United Nations** and superintended the **Dumbarton Oaks Conference** in 1944. He retired on 27 November 1944 and received the Nobel Peace Prize in 1945 for his work on the United Nations. *See also* CLAYTON, WILLIAM LOCKHART; PAZVOLSKY, LEO.

HURLEY, PATRICK (1883–1963). Born in Choctaw Indian Territory, Patrick Hurley served in the U.S. Army in **World War I**, reaching the rank of major general. He then became active in Republican Party politics and served as secretary of war (1929–33) in President **Herbert Hoover**'s administration. During **World War II**, Hurley served in the **Philippines** area before filling a number of diplomatic roles, as minister to New Zealand, and as President **Franklin D. Roosevelt**'s special envoy to Moscow, the Middle East, Afghanistan, and **China**, where he arranged the meeting of **Chiang Kai-shek** with Roosevelt at the **Cairo Conference** in December 1943. He attended the 1943 **Teheran Conference**.

Hurley returned to China in August 1944 as Roosevelt's personal representative, with orders to ease relations between Chiang and General **Joseph Stilwell**. His sympathies were with Chiang, and he succeeded in getting Stilwell replaced. He was appointed ambassador in November 1944. Hurley was hostile to State Department officials such as **John Paton Davies** and **John Stewart Service**, whom he regarded as too pro-communist. He opposed the concessions made to the **Union of Soviet Socialist Republics** at Chinese expense at the 1945 **Yalta conference**, but having failed to convince Roosevelt or President **Harry S. Truman** that they would result in a communist China, he resigned in November 1945. He was convinced that State Department officials had undermined his efforts. After the war, he ran three times for the Senate but was not elected. *See also* DIXIE MISSION.

HUSKY, OPERATION. The Allied invasion of Sicily 10 July 1943, Husky was the first major successful amphibious operation by the

Allies in the European theater during **World War II**. There were also some problems in the mission, which in the long run were useful lessons regarding the complexities of inter-Allied operations. U.S. forces under General George Patton occupied Messina in July to complete the operation, though the bulk of the German forces escaped to Italy. Husky precipitated Italian dictator Benito Mussolini's removal from office by the Italian Fascist Grand Council. The aid of the Mafia in New York was enlisted to help with certain **intelligence** aspects of the operation. *See also* CASABLANCA CONFERENCE; SECOND FRONT.

HYDE PARK AGREEMENT (1941). President **Franklin D. Roosevelt** and Prime Minister William Mackenzie King of Canada issued a joint statement of principles on 20 April 1941 at Roosevelt's home at Hyde Park, New York. This Hyde Park Agreement built on the spirit of the 1940 **Ogdensburg Agreement**. Roosevelt and King effectively removed the U.S.–Canadian border in matters of defense production during **World War II**. Canada was in financial difficulties, as it normally funded its **trade** deficit with the United States through a surplus in trade to **Great Britain**. Canada could no longer convert its British pounds into U.S. dollars. Under the Hyde Park Agreement, $400 million in U.S. orders was promised to Canada. **Reciprocal trade** would establish a balance. Unlike Great Britain, Canada was not required to divest itself of its investments in the United States as a condition. By the end of the war, Canada's trade deficit with the United States had disappeared, and Canada had drawn closer to the United States in economic relations as well as in defense relations as provided for under the Ogdensburg Agreement.

HYDE PARK AGREEMENT (1944). Following the 1944 **Quebec Conference** during **World War II**, Prime Minister **Winston Churchill** of **Great Britain** spent two days at the home of President **Franklin D. Roosevelt** at Hyde Park, New York. They discussed the **Manhattan Project** to develop the **atomic bomb**, in which British and Commonwealth scientists and engineers were participating. On 19 September, Churchill and Roosevelt initialed an agreement that atomic research should be kept secret, including from their ally the **Union of Soviet Socialist Republics**, and no international agreement on the use of atomic weapons should be sought. They agreed that when the bomb was available, its use against **Japan** might be considered. Finally, Churchill and Roosevelt agreed that full collaboration on atomic power should continue between the two countries for military and commercial purposes after the defeat of Japan, unless ended by joint agreement.

However, no copy of the 1944 Hyde Park Agreement seems to have been kept in the State Department, and in 1946 Congress passed the MacMahon Act forbidding the sharing of atomic research with any other state, in breach of this agreement. The British had kept a copy, but it was not until the 1950s that President **Dwight D. Eisenhower** was prepared to return to the terms of the 1944 agreement. In the meantime, Britain had developed its own atomic project, in place of the joint one envisioned by Churchill and Roosevelt. *See also* BOHR, NIELS.

– I –

IMMIGRATION. Although early in its history the United States had an open door policy toward immigrants, restrictions began to be applied after U.S. entry into **World War I**. A literacy test was imposed in 1917. The intense wartime patriotism, combined with a tendency to associate labor unrest and political extremism with recent immigrants, produced fears among some Americans that traditional values were endangered by unrestricted immigration. The belief that certain national groups made "better Americans" was reflected in the measures that followed.

The total number of immigrants was restricted in the 1921 **Emergency Quota Act**. People were let in on the basis of 3 percent of the number of each nationality already in the United States in 1910. This worked in favor of nationalities that had been migrating into the United States for a long time, such as British, Irish, and German, and against "new" immigrants from countries such as Italy, Spain, **Poland**, and **Russia**. The 1924 **National Origins Act** reduced the quota to 2 percent of the population in 1890. From 1927, the total annual immigration would be 150,000, distributed proportionately according to the ethnic composition of the population in 1920. Immigration from the western hemisphere was largely untouched by the 1924 act, but ad hoc restrictions were imposed in the 1930s under the provision that excluded individuals who would be a drain on public funds. Labor shortages in **World War II** brought an end to this, and migration was encouraged in the *Bracero* **agreement** with **Mexico**, in a controlled form.

Attitudes toward immigration have often been associated with the same set of ideas as **isolationism** in foreign relations at this time. Nevertheless, ending of the open door era did not prevent hundreds of thousands of new immigrants arriving at Ellis Island. The U.S. population grew from 106 million in 1920 to 120 million in 1929, and a major reason was immigration. *See also* GOMPERS, SAMUEL; IMMIGRATION ACT.

IMMIGRATION ACT (1917). The Immigration Act passed by Congress on 5 February 1917 defined controversial new categories of exclusion among emigrants seeking to enter the United States — particularly those deemed "feeble-minded," "professional beggars," and "persons of constitutional psychopathic inferiority." Alcoholics, anarchists, and polygamists were also to be refused entry, as were those found to be suffering from or exhibiting symptoms of "a loathsome or dangerous contagious disease." A literacy test was included for all persons over the age of 16, and the entry tax was raised to $8 per person. The act was most controversial for banning all immigration from an Asiatic "Barred Zone," which comprised a large area of East Asia and the Pacific islands. The act was passed by Congress over the veto of President **Woodrow Wilson**.

IMMIGRATION QUOTA ACT. *See* EMERGENCY QUOTA ACT.

INQUIRY, THE (1917–1919). The Inquiry was a group of specialist advisors gathered in New York by **Edward M. House**, at the request of President **Woodrow Wilson**, to study the economic, political, social, and territorial problems that would confront the United States and the world in the aftermath of **World War I** and in drawing up a treaty of peace. Members included the historian E. S. Corwin, Columbia University Professor **James T. Shotwell**, and journalist **Walter Lippmann**. The team was also instrumental in preparing data for

Wilson's **Fourteen Points** speech (January 1918). By the time of the 1919 **Paris Peace Conference**, some 2,000 reports had been drawn up by over 150 members of the Inquiry. Some were considered too academic or complex to be of use in treaty negotiations; some proposals for resolution of territorial disputes were criticized as too simplistic. Members of the Inquiry were ultimately disappointed by their lack of influence in Wilson's decision making. *See also* HORN-BECK, STANLEY KUHL; LEAGUE TO ENFORCE PEACE.

INSTITUTE OF PACIFIC RELATIONS (IPR). The Institute of Pacific Relations was set up in 1925 to promote better relations among countries of the Pacific Ocean or Pacific Rim. The nonpartisan organization used mutual contacts, education programs, and research. Its major publication was *Pacific Affairs*. Individual national councils were represented on the Pacific Council, which directed the IPR's affairs. The central office was in Hawaii (1925–33), and then New York City. The U.S. branch raised much of the funding and published the important *Far Eastern Survey*.

The IPR was founded on Wilsonian ideals regarding the need to promote liberal democracy in the world, and it gained significant funding from the Rockefeller Foundation and the Carnegie Corporation. However, it had members with far left views, such as **Communist Party of the United States** member Frederick Vanderbilt Field, the executive secretary of the American Council, and Edward C. Carter, the IPR secretary general. Many other members were later revealed by the **Venona project** to be communists or collaborators with Soviet **intelligence** agencies. IPR members were closely involved with the editorial team of the journal *Amerasia*, which was investigated by the **Federal Bureau of Investigation** in 1946 for passing secret information to foreign agents. Many of the experts on Chinese affairs, known as the "China Hands," were members of the IPR, and as Chinese communists became successful in the Chinese civil war, they recommended that the United States should open contacts with Mao Zedong to keep **China** from falling into the Soviet orbit.

During the 1950s, the nonpartisan standing of the IPR was challenged by Senator Joseph McCarthy, who alleged that it had communist leanings and attacked the former editor of *Pacific Affairs*, Owen

Lattimore. The "China lobby," which was supportive of **Chiang Kai-shek**, claimed the China Hands had undermined U.S. policy toward China, producing a communist victory, and that the IPR was a communist front organization. The attacks undermined the credibility of the IPR, which folded due to lack of funds in 1960. *See also* MAGIC, OPERATION; PURPLE, OPERATION; SERVICE, JOHN STEWART; SIGNALS INTELLIGENCE; ULTRA-MAGIC, OPERATION; VENONA PROJECT.

INTELLIGENCE. The gathering of intelligence before the 20th century was primarily the province of diplomats and the military, and there was usually no interface between them. During the 20th century, all major states developed specialized intelligence gathering agencies and attempted, with varying degrees of success, to build bureaucratic structures that coordinated their activities and pooled their product. In the United States, there has tended to be a political resistance to certain forms of intelligence gathering as unworthy of a democratic nation, and some forms have been seen as a threat to domestic political liberties.

During **World War I,** the European belligerents developed their intelligence capabilities, incorporating new activities such as aerial reconnaissance and the interdiction of radio and telegraphic messages. The United States tended to lag behind states like **Great Britain** in these developments as a result of its later entry into the war and opinions on some practices. After the war, these attitudes became stronger, expressed forcefully in Secretary of War **Henry Stimson**'s statement that "gentlemen do not read others' messages." The U.S. armed services developed their code-breaking capabilities but did not coordinate their activities, nor did they interact with the State Department or the **Federal Bureau of Investigation** (FBI). The FBI gathered domestic intelligence and took upon itself the role of counterintelligence against foreign penetration.

This divided situation continued during **World War II.** Efforts to coordinate these activities, in the **State-War-Navy Coordinating Committee,** were not very effective. New agencies, notably the **Office of Strategic Services**, only made the picture more complicated. Institutional rivalries and the need for secrecy meant the problem persisted into the postwar era and defied the attempts of reformers, for instance in the 1947 National Security Act. Nonetheless, intelligence gathering played an increasingly important role in U.S. foreign policy making during and after World War II. *See also* BRITAIN–UNITED STATES OF AMERICA AGREEMENT; HISS, ALGER; KENT, TYLER; MAGIC, OPERATION; PEARL HARBOR; SIGNALS INTELLIGENCE; VENONA PROJECT; WHITE, HARRY DEXTER; ZIMMERMANN TELEGRAM.

INTER-ALLIED CONFERENCE (1917). Held in Paris between the United States and its **World War I** associates, the 1917 conference sought to resolve problems in the coordination of transport and supply of food and fuels. It also canvassed views on the creation of a permanent supranational body for mediating postwar disputes. **Edward M. House** led the U.S. delegation.

INTER-AMERICAN CONFERENCE (1942). *See* RIO DE JANEIRO CONFERENCE.

INTER-AMERICAN CONFERENCE FOR THE MAINTENANCE OF PEACE. *See* BUENOS AIRES CONFERENCE.

INTER-AMERICAN CONFERENCE ON WAR AND PEACE (1945). *See* CHAPULTEPEC, ACT OF.

INTER-AMERICAN DEFENSE BOARD (IADB). Following the **Rio de Janeiro Conference** in January 1942, the Inter-American Defense Board was established in March 1942. Its purpose was to coordinate defense planning for the western hemisphere during **World War II**. Undersecretary of State **Sumner Welles** assured the U.S. War Department that the IADB would not be used by **Latin America** to press for U.S. munitions that were needed for the war. Nor would it be an executive body or interfere with existing bilateral military arrangements. Its importance was therefore largely political. In the State Department view, it was intended to foster the spirit and practice of regional cooperation. The IADB met in Washington, D.C., and was an important step in the formation of a regional collective defense organization under U.S. leadership. It came to deal with exchange of **intelligence** and standardization of training and material. At the time of the signature of the 1945 **Act of Chapulte-pec**, the IADB was recognized as the military organ of the developing Inter-American system, until such time as a permanent agency was established. The IADB became that permanent body in 1947, when the Organization of American States was established. *See also* EMERGENCY ADVISORY COMMITTEE FOR POLITICAL DEFENSE; HAVANA, ACT OF.

INTER-AMERICAN SOLIDARITY AND COOPERATION, DECLARATION OF PRINCIPLES OF. *See* BUENOS AIRES CONFERENCE.

INTERNATIONAL BANK FOR RECONSTRUCTION AND DEVELOPMENT. *See* WORLD BANK.

INTERNATIONAL LABOUR ORGANIZATION (ILO). The International Labour Organization was founded in 1919 as an agency of the **League of Nations**, under the **Treaty of Versailles**. The ILO was the product of 19th-century reform movements that sought social justice for the world's working classes. Its purpose was to seek improvements in labor conditions around the world. The idea behind the incorporation of this in the treaty was that social stability would be enhanced by raising the standard of living, and it reflected concerns about the spread of communism on the part of the powers at the 1919 **Paris Peace Conference**. A major role in framing the proposal was played by **Samuel Gompers** of the American Federation of Labor (AFL).

The first meeting of the ILO took place in Washington, D.C., on 19 October 1919, with U.S. Secretary of Labor William B. Wilson in the chair. However, the failure of the Senate to ratify the Treaty of Versailles meant that the United States could not continue as a member of the organization. It was not until June 1934 that Congress approved U.S. membership. The ILO met in London, therefore, until headquarters were established in Geneva in July 1920. It began with 45 member states. The ILO has representation not just from governments but from employers and workers as well. The first director general was French, the second British, and the third American, **John G. Winant** (1938–41).

During **World War II**, the ILO was based in Montreal, Canada, returning to Geneva in 1946. Its founding principles were reasserted in the Philadelphia Declaration on 10 May 1944. The ILO was recognized as having been one of the more effective elements of the League of Nations, and after World War II it was retained as the first specialized agency to be linked to the **United Nations**. It did much useful work in the 1950s and 1960s concerning migrant workers and was awarded the Nobel Prize for Peace in 1969.

INTERNATIONAL MILITARY TRIBUNAL (NUREMBERG TRIALS) (1945–1946). The **London Charter** of August 1945 provided the basis for the military tribunal that tried Nazi war criminals after **World War II**, following from a proposal by Samuel Rosenman, legal advisor to President **Franklin D. Roosevelt**, and approved by Secretary of War **Henry Stimson**, Secretary of State **Edward Stettinius**, and Attorney General **Francis Biddle**. The trials were held in Nuremberg, **Germany**, from November 1945 to October 1946. Each of the four occupying powers provided a justice. The U.S. chief prosecutor was **Robert Jackson**. Eighteen of the 21 surviving defendants were found guilty; 12 were condemned to death. The tribunal set important precedents for international law with regard to the definition of war crimes. The key indictment of "waging aggressive war" was at least partly made possible by the 1928 **Kellogg–Briand Pact**. A similar trial for the Far East was conducted in Tokyo from January 1946 to November 1948. *See also* MOSCOW CONFERENCE; TOJO, HIDEKI.

INTERNATIONAL MONETARY FUND (IMF). The International Monetary Fund (IMF) was designed at the 1944 **Bretton Woods Conference** and formally established on 27 December 1945. It was an attempt to solve the problems caused by currency fluctuations. The framers had in mind the competitive devaluations of the early 1930s as nation after nation came off the **gold standard**. The damage to world commerce that followed convinced many economists that currency stabilization was essential if international economic stability was to be achieved.

During **World War II**, officials from the United States and **Great Britain** discussed means by which countries with ailing currencies could be assisted. British representatives, led by economist John Maynard Keynes, favored an interventionist organization. U.S. officials were more cautious and sought safeguards that would prevent excessive lending and ensure that the organization was constrained by clear rules, and this was reflected in the organization that emerged from Bretton Woods. The **Union of Soviet Socialist Republics** refused to join.

The IMF began to operate in 1946. Voting within the IMF is weighted according to contribution, giving the United States the major influence. Between 1946 and 1971, the IMF maintained the Bretton Woods system of fixed-rate dollar and gold-based international finance. After 1971, when currencies were allowed to float, the IMF played a significant role in making loans to economies in difficulties, while imposing stringent conditions. *See also* WORLD BANK.

INTERNATIONALISM. Internationalism was essentially the view that peace in the world could be achieved by **collective security**, and that the United States should be an active participant in world affairs, either out of material interest or moral responsibility. In the period 1914–45, internationalism primarily took the form of support for U.S. membership in an international organization of sovereign states. President **Woodrow Wilson** attempted to put internationalist principles into practice with the incorporation of the covenant of the **League of Nations** in the peace treaties reached at the 1919 **Paris Peace Conference**. Following the U.S. failure to ratify the **Treaty of Versailles**, Americans holding internationalist views devoted their energies during the 1920s to causes such as **disarmament**. While most Americans inclined more toward **isolationism** in the interwar period, internationalism came back into fashion during **World War II**, and Wilsonian ideals were embraced in the **Fulbright** and **Connally Resolutions** in Congress in 1943, approving U.S. membership in a new international organization. The result was the establishment of the **United Nations** at the 1945 **San Francisco Conference**.

IRRECONCILABLES. The Irreconcilables were 16 U.S. senators who, during debates over ratification of the **Treaty of Versailles** in 1919–20, firmly opposed U.S. membership in the **League of Nations**. Their political backgrounds varied. Some were conservative, some **progressive**. Some believed in unilateral intervention where necessary but argued that the League would compromise the independence of U.S. foreign policy and was therefore unconstitutional. Others preferred a general policy of **isolationism** to prevent the United States from being dragged into further international conflicts. Some Irreconcilables remained influential in Congress, particularly within the Republican Party, during the 1920s, guarding against the **internationalism** of League supporters or adherents to the cause of U.S. membership in the **World Court**, or against any sign of revived presidential interest in international cooperation. The Irreconcilables included **William E. Borah, Philander C. Knox, Frank Brandegee**, Albert B. Cummins, Albert B. Fall, William S. Kenyon, **Hiram Johnson**, and Miles Poindexter.

ISLANDS FOR WAR DEBTS COMMITTEE. Set up in 1939 ostensibly to campaign for the repayment of **war debts** from **World War I**, the committee advocated that **Great Britain** and **France** surrender their colonial possessions in the western hemisphere in lieu of monetary payments. However, the organization was a front for the distribution of pro-German propaganda by **George Sylvester Viereck**. Using it and the Make Europe Pay War Debts Committee, Viereck persuaded **isolationist** and anti-British members of the U.S. Congress to enter his materials in the *Congressional Record* and then distribute them under the congressional franking privilege. Thus German propaganda was being circulated in the United States at the expense of U.S. taxpayers. *See also* FISH, HAMILTON; REYNOLDS, ROBERT RICE.

ISLE OF PINES TREATY (1925). Under this treaty, the United States handed control of the Isle of Pines to **Cuba**, concluding a long dispute between the United States and Cuba over ownership of the island, which lies 63 miles (100 kilometers) to the south of Cuba itself. In July 1903, the Hay–Quesada Treaty had conceded Cuba's ownership rights, but the United States had failed to give up control, largely due to pressure from some in the State Department and military who claimed the island served as a key operations base for protecting U.S. interests in the region. The 1903 agreement was finally ratified on 13 March 1925.

ISOLATIONISM. U.S. isolationism reflected a reluctance to intervene in or engage with international affairs on a diplomatic, political, or economic basis. It involved opposition to intervention in war outside the Americas, notably in Europe, as well as hostility to alliances and to membership in international security organizations. The United States had a deep-rooted distaste for "foreign entanglements" stemming from early 19th-century threats of armed aggression from **Great Britain** and other European powers. From the later nineteenth century , isolationism also served as an expression of anti-imperialism, as many Americans grew concerned at the nation's acquisition of territories and protectorates outside of the continental United States.

Isolationism is less a compact ideology than an instinct, expressed in different ways and with differing degrees of severity. Such instincts are not limited to one part of the political spectrum. It was not unusual for conservatives and **progressives** in Congress to find common cause in an isolationist stance during the early 20th century. Neither were isolationist instincts restricted to the Republican Party. The battle over ratification of the **Treaty of Versailles** in 1919 found a significant number of Democrats with doubts about U.S. membership in the **League of Nations,** and interwar isolationism was similarly to be found in both parties.

Isolationism is not the same as **pacifism**, as isolationists will support unilateral armed intervention at times. The fundamental aim is the preservation of U.S. freedom of action. During 1919–41, isolationism was founded upon a strong sense of the invulnerability of the United States to outside attack and a belief that intervention in **World War I** had been against U.S. vital interests. However, U.S. foreign policy during the 1920s and 1930s was not dominated by pure isolation from world affairs. Comparatively few 20th-century isolationists rejected *all* involvement in international institutions, rules, or conflicts. Members of Congress representing districts dominated by powerful agricultural or coal and steel interests, for example, supported high **tariffs** against foreign imports in the early-mid 20th century but were not necessarily opposed to League, **World Court**, or **United Nations** membership. The *nature* and *context* of the proposed involvement tended to dictate the level and type of isolationism. Thus, Senator **William Borah** led Senate isolationists against League membership in 1919 but also played a leading role in persuading the U.S. government to call a **disarmament** conference in 1921 and to join an international peace movement by signing the **Kellogg–Briand Pact** in 1928. Similarly, the shelving of the League issue by President **Warren G. Harding** was more an act of political expediency than an expression of isolationist belief, since Harding publicly argued for stronger international trading links, multilateral disarmament treaties, and World Court membership. Throughout the 19th and 20th centuries, American politicians, diplomats, and military leaders adhered to the **Monroe Doctrine** regarding **Latin America** and pledged direct U.S. intervention in response to any attempt by a foreign power to attack, militarily or economically, any Latin American nation.

In the 1930s, isolationism combined with neutralism and pacifism to produce the **Neutrality Acts** and the U.S. response to the USS *Panay* incident, in which the major American concern was to avoid being dragged into war. Isolationism was also evident in the **Debt Default Act** of 1934 and congressional opposition to membership in the World Court in 1935. As the crisis intensified in Europe in the late 1930s, isolationists organized together with pacifists in the **National Council for the Prevention of War** and the **No Foreign Wars Committee**. The most popular isolationist organization was the **America First Committee**, founded in September 1940 to oppose U.S. involvement in **World War II**. By no means all isolationists were pacifists: many were **fortress America** enthusiasts who supported American rearmament and preparedness but opposed aid to Great Britain. Isolationism was strongest in the Midwest, among traditionally anti-British groups such as Irish Americans. But at its height in the mid-1930s, isolationism was evident across the United States and was not limited to any class, region, or ethnic group.

The Nazi aggression in Europe brought many liberals to move away from isolationism, leaving its core support more narrowly conservative. After the attack on **Pearl Harbor** on 7 December 1941, isolationism was largely discredited, and in 1943 Congress supported U.S. participation in a world organization in the **Fulbright** and **Connally Resolutions**. Residual isolationism reappeared after World War II, mainly among Europhobe conservative Republicans, notably Senator **Robert A. Taft**, but disappeared as the Cold War intensified.

IWO JIMA, BATTLE OF (1945). A small volcanic island in the Bonin Islands Group, Iwo Jima was a target for U.S. forces in **World War II** as it could provide a useful airfield for fighter support for bombers flying against **Japan** from the Mariana Islands. U.S. marines landed on 19 February 1945, and the severity of the fighting that followed before the island was fully in American hands on 26 March gave a sharp warning of the likely cost of an attack on the Japanese mainland. This gave increased incentive to find an alternative way of achieving a Japanese **unconditional surrender**, such as the **atomic bomb**, which was nearing completion, or the involvement of the **Union of Soviet Socialist Republics** in the Pacific War. Some 60,000 marines and 800 warships were deployed to take Iwo Jima, and over a third of the marines were killed or wounded. The 22,000 Japanese soldiers manned strongpoints such as Hill 382 and Bloody Gorge and fought to the last man. The raising of the U.S. flag over Mount Suribachi was the subject of one of the most iconic photographs of World War II, though the photograph was of the second flag-raising: the first occurred while the place was still under fire. *See also* OKINAWA, BATTLE OF.

– J –

JACKSON, ROBERT HOUGHWOUT (1892–1954). Before becoming a Supreme Court justice, lawyer Robert Jackson was general counsel to the Treasury Department's Bureau of Internal Revenue (1934–36), assistant attorney general (1936–38), solicitor general (1938–40), and attorney general (1940–41). He was a strong defender of the legality of the New Deal. President **Franklin D. Roosevelt** rated him highly and in 1941 appointed him to the Supreme Court. Jackson is regarded by many as one of the great Supreme Court justices of the 20th century. After **World War II**, he was given a leave of absence to act as U.S. chief prosecutor at the **International Military Tribunal** in Nuremberg, **Germany**, having helped draw up the tribunal's **London Charter**. He resigned after the first trial and returned to the Supreme Court, on which he remained until his death.

JAPAN. U.S. relations with Japan in the first decade of the 20th century were primarily shaped by two issues: **China** and **immigration**.

Hostility in California toward Japanese immigrants had led to the 1907 Gentlemen's Agreement in which Japan agreed to halt migration of Japanese laborers from Hawaii to the mainland in return for a promise to end discrimination against those who had already settled in the United States. In Asia, Japan's defeats of China (1894–95) and **Russia** (1904–5) had left Korea and Manchuria under effective Japanese control. Japan had emerged as the country most likely to threaten the **open door** policy. This was evident after the outbreak of **World War I**. Japan began to take advantage of post-revolutionary chaos in China to carve out an expanded sphere of influence, notably with the Twenty-One Demands of January 1915. Japan had joined the war on the Allied side on 23 August 1914 and proceeded to seize **Germany**'s Pacific island possessions and its leased territories on China's Shantung (Shandong) peninsula. Japan's demands, and the Sino–Japanese Treaty that followed, gave Japan dominance over the Chinese economy.

President **Woodrow Wilson**, preoccupied with events in Europe and **Mexico**, responded that the United States did not recognize these arrangements and stood by the open door principle, but he took no action. After the United States entered World War I, relations with Japan improved. The **Lansing–Ishii** agreement of 2 November 1917 recognized Japan's special interest in China, while Japan stated its acceptance of the open door. At the 1919 **Paris Peace Conference**, Wilson agreed to Japanese control of Shantung in order to get Japan into the **League of Nations** but then affronted the Japanese by refusing to allow the racial equality clause they proposed to be incorporated into the League covenant.

U.S.–Japanese relations improved in the 1920s, largely as a result of a liberalization in Japanese politics. Japanese leaders, perceiving U.S. industrial power, settled for a policy of accommodation and economic growth, rather than territorial expansion. Thus, Japan's diplomats at the 1921 **Naval Disarmament Conference** accepted the limits on warship building in the Five Power Treaty, going against opinion in sections of the Japanese navy. They accepted a smaller ratio for Japan in return for the United States limiting itself, which meant Japanese local naval superiority in the western Pacific was assured. Japan was unhappy at having to give up its treaty with **Great Britain**, and having to return Shantung to China and withdraw troops from Siberia. The Five Power Treaty guaranteed China's integrity and sovereignty, and it formalized the open door as an international agreement. The treaty also asserted the status quo elsewhere in the region, including the level of fortifications of bases. During the 1920s, Japan became a major U.S. trading partner: 40 percent of Japanese trade went to the United States. However, anti-Japanese feeling continued in California, among some naval officers, and in the press owned by **William Randolph Hearst**. The Japanese exclusion clause in the **National Origins Act** of 1924 closed off any further Japanese immigration. The Japanese were deeply insulted by the anti-Asian tone of this legislation.

The global economic depression hit Japan severely. The high U.S. **Smoot–Hawley** tariff (1930) aggravated Japan's economic problems. At the same time, Chinese nationalists led by **Chiang Kai-shek** were showing ambitions toward reasserting Chinese control of Manchuria. Officers in the Japanese army of Kwantung responded by contriving the Mukden incident (September 1931). In the **Manchurian Crisis** that followed, Japan occupied the region. Japanese naval forces took aggressive action in the **Shanghai Incident** (January 1932). These actions were initiated by junior officers in the field but subsequently endorsed in Tokyo, which moved to create the puppet state of Manchukuo, headed by the former Chinese emperor, Pu Yi. Only Germany and Italy were to recognize this state; the United States in the **Stimson Doctrine** followed a policy of nonrecognition. President **Herbert Hoover**'s belief that economic sanctions would lead to war meant that no other action was taken. During the Shanghai Incident, the small U.S. Asiatic fleet had been deployed to Shanghai at Secretary of State **Henry Stimson's** request, and **Joseph C. Grew** was appointed as ambassador to Japan. Grew came to the conclusion that taking a vociferous moral stance without backing it up with the threat of force only encouraged Japanese militants.

These militants were increasingly taking control in Japan as the depression saw the collapse of liberal government and the rise of ultra-patriotism. Military officers became the dominating force in government, and moderates often suffered assassination if they protested. Ideas began to be propagated of an East Asian "co-prosperity sphere"—ostensibly economic cooperation among states to be liberated from European colonialism, but in fact a mask for imperialism by Japan. Plans were launched in 1936 to militarize Japanese society and assert hegemony in China, and the navy forced a withdrawal from the Five Power Treaty and from agreements reached at the 1930 **London Naval Disarmament Conference**. They demanded a drive southward to acquire bases and the resources in which Japan was deficient, which included virtually everything needed by an industrial state.

In this tense situation, an incident in July 1937 at the Marco Polo Bridge outside Peking (Beijing) began the second **Sino–Japanese War** (1937–45). Peking soon fell, Shanghai was heavily bombarded again, and the capital Nanking (Nanjing) was captured with great bloodshed (known as the "Rape of Nanking") in December. Chiang Kai-shek retreated to Chungking (Chongqing). Japan secured control of all the major Chinese ports over the next 18 months, with the exception of those in European hands. In the U.S. State Department, official **Stanley K. Hornbeck** advised that Japan should be opposed, but President **Franklin D. Roosevelt** followed Grew's advice and avoided a confrontation that he could not back up with force, the **U.S. Navy** being considerably inferior in the region. Thus, when the USS *Panay* was sunk by Japanese airplanes on 12 December 1937, Roosevelt was ready to accept the Japanese apology and indemnity. U.S. public opinion was supportive of this policy of noninvolvement, despite sympathies for China. The policy convinced Japanese military leaders that the United States lacked the will to defend its interests or principles in Asia.

Until 1940, U.S. policy was inconsistent. On the one hand, **trade** continued with Japan, providing many materials that aided Japan's war machine, such as airplane engines, scrap metal, and oil. On the other, Chinese silver was purchased in large amounts, enabling China to purchase American weapons. Such transactions were permissible as the **Neutrality Acts** were not activated. Secretary of State **Cordell Hull** pressed U.S. aircraft manufacturers to carry out a "moral embargo" on sales to Japan, in place of the statutory embargo.

The situation changed during **World War II**. Japan was initially impressed by the stance taken by **France** and Great Britain in declaring war on Nazi Germany in September 1939. However, Japan's respect for the power of the imperial states was destroyed by the sweeping German successes in the summer of 1940. The defeat of

France and the Netherlands left their Asian colonies very vulnerable. At the same time, U.S. policies began to take a clearer line: Hull announced the abrogation of the 1911 U.S.–Japan Treaty of Commerce and Navigation. European weakness prompted Roosevelt to move the Pacific Fleet to **Pearl Harbor** as a deterrent. The 1940 "11 percent" Naval Expansion Act and the **Two-Ocean Navy Act** were clear signals to Japan that the United States sought to reverse its naval inferiority in the Pacific. Japan's naval superiority now had a fixed duration. Grew began to recommend that a harder line would persuade Japan to halt its expansion in China. On 25 July, Roosevelt announced an embargo on the export of high-grade scrap metal and petroleum products to Japan, claiming that they were needed domestically because of war orders from Great Britain. For their part, Japan's military leaders saw a way out of their stalemate in China by coercing the French authorities, the collaborationist regime at Vichy, to allow them to station troops in northern Indochina. Together with pressure on the British that brought the temporary cessation of supplies to China along the Burma Road, this was an attempt to squeeze China into agreeing to terms.

In September 1940, Japan concluded the **Tripartite Pact** with Germany and Italy. Each power agreed to support the other if it was attacked by a power with which it was not yet at war. When it joined the pact, Japan claimed that it had the right to take supplies of rubber, oil, rice, and tin from the European possessions in Southeast Asia. On 26 September 1940, Roosevelt responded to the pact by including all scrap iron and steel in the embargo. In the United States, the Tripartite Pact was seen as directed specifically at America. This feeling was magnified when Japan concluded a nonaggression pact with the **Union of Soviet Socialist Republics** in April 1941.

The United States and Japan were now on collision course. The United States took the line that Japan had to withdraw from China as a condition of negotiations, and the administration was now firmly of Hornbeck's view that being tough with the Japanese was the best way to get them to back down. This would also have the effect of helping Britain by keeping Japan away from vital resources in Southeast Asia. There was much less domestic pressure to avoid war with Japan than with Germany: **isolationists** paid little attention to the Pacific and most Americans assumed Japan was not a dangerous opponent. Japanese militarists thought the same about the United States. Few Japanese leaders thought the United States would risk war over China or Southeast Asia. The long negotiations between Hull and Japanese representatives, Ambassador Kichisaburo Nomura and envoy Saburo Kurusu, quickly became futile. When Japanese forces moved into southern Indochina on 23 July 1941, Roosevelt ordered that all Japan's assets in the United States be frozen. This amounted to a full embargo, and Assistant Secretary of State **Dean Acheson** gave orders that made clear this included all oil shipments. Japan's military and naval forces had only an 18-month supply of oil, and their operations would be severely restricted long before then.

Roosevelt agreed with Prime Minister **Winston Churchill** of Great Britain at the **Placentia Bay meeting** in August 1941 that Japan was a lesser threat than Germany, but that it was wise to avoid a breach in relations until the war with Germany was won. It thus seemed necessary to make concessions to buy time. In September 1941, Premier Funimaro Konoye of Japan proposed a summit meeting with Roosevelt, but the Americans insisted such a meeting could only follow agreement on the key issues. The rejection of Konoye's suggestion led to his replacement by General **Hideki Tojo** in October. Tojo ordered plans for war to be made, and he set a deadline for diplomacy to succeed by the start of December or Japan would have to take action to seize the resources it needed for its war effort. With Hull demanding a withdrawal from China before the oil embargo could be lifted, diplomacy produced no breakthrough. Hull rejected the last Japanese proposal on 25 November. On 7 December 1941 (Hawaiian time), Japan launched its assaults against the British empire in the Far East and attacked U.S. forces in the **Philippines** and at Pearl Harbor to prevent them from intervening. On 8 December, Congress declared war on Japan.

The conflict lasted until Japan surrendered on 15 August 1945, following the use of the **atomic bomb** against **Hiroshima** and **Nagasaki**, though the turning points, the battles of **Midway** and **Guadalcanal**, took place in 1942. Japan fought tenaciously, if without much chance once the full weight of U.S. industrial power and naval superiority was turned against it. By the end of the war, Japan had resorted to suicide attacks (*kamikaze*), and U.S. bombers and submarines had reduced the Japanese economy, its transportation systems, and many of its towns and cities to ruins.

After the formal surrender on 2 September 1945, General **Douglas MacArthur** took charge of Japan. Some Japanese leaders were tried in the Tokyo international military tribunal (war crimes trials), but Emperor **Hirohito** was allowed to stay on the throne, and Japan was remodeled as a demilitarized capitalist liberal democracy. The occupation was ended in the 1951 Treaty of San Francisco, and Japan became a valued U.S. ally and economic rival. *See also* IWO JIMA, BATTLE OF; OKINAWA, BATTLE OF.

JAPANESE EXCLUSION CLAUSE. *See* NATIONAL ORIGINS ACT.

JCS 1067. A document issued by the **Joint Chiefs of Staff** in September 1944, JCS 1067 provided guidance for the treatment of **Germany** after its surrender in **World War II**. Germany was to be treated as a defeated nation, with the minimum amount of rehabilitation aid provided, sufficient only to prevent disorder and disease. Nazi sympathizers were to be arrested and a denazification process initiated. However, the U.S. representatives in Germany, General **Lucius Clay** and **Robert Murphy**, believed that the severity of this policy was unwise, and that the result would be unemployment at a time when European economic recovery depended on Germany's skilled industrial workforce being productive. Agreements made at the August 1945 **Potsdam Conference** revised U.S. policy toward Germany, allowing administrators more scope for encouraging economic activity. In July 1947, the more permissive JCS 1779 replaced JCS 1067, reflecting changing attitudes toward the need to encourage German industrial activity and the developing context of Cold War tensions. *See also* EUROPEAN ADVISORY COMMISSION; MORGENTHAU, HENRY; MORGENTHAU PLAN.

JESSUP, PHILIP CARYL (1897–1986). A Yale graduate, Philip Jessup taught diplomacy and international law at Columbia University. In 1943, during **World War II**, he joined the State Department's foreign relief and rehabilitation office and from 1943 to 1944 was assistant secretary general of the **United Nations Relief and Rehabilitation**

Administration (UNRRA). He was a delegate at the 1944 **Bretton Woods Conference**. After the war, he served in the **United Nations** General Assembly and was U.S. delegate on the Security Council during the debate on the Berlin blockade (1948–49). From 1961 to 1970, he was a judge at the International Court of Justice at The Hague.

JOHNSON ACT (1934). *See* DEBT DEFAULT ACT.

JOHNSON, HIRAM WARREN (1866–1945). Politician Hiram Johnson was the candidate for vice president on **Theodore Roosevelt**'s "Bull Moose" third-party ticket in 1912. As governor of California (1911–17), Johnson pursued **progressive** policies such as the eight-hour workday for women and children and pure food laws, but he was also known for his hostility to immigration from **Japan**. His 1919 call, "Let us be Americans again!" struck a chord with voters disillusioned by war and suspicious of foreigners. Johnson, unlike some of his progressive contemporaries, opposed not only the commitment to **internationalism** inherent in U.S. membership in the **League of Nations** but most other types of formal international cooperation. Although President **Warren G. Harding** is rumored to have offered him the vice presidency in 1920, Johnson became Harding's chief opponent when the president attempted to negotiate America's entry into the **World Court** in 1923.

As a Republican member of the U.S. Senate (1917–45), Johnson chaired various committees with foreign policy connections, including the Committee on Cuban Relations, the Committee on Commerce, the Committee on Immigration, and the Committee on Territories. In his last years, he backed the New Deal domestic agenda of President **Franklin D. Roosevelt** but retained his **isolationist** instincts. He sponsored the **Debt Default Act** (1934), forbidding further U.S. loans to countries in default of **war debt** payments, and he opposed U.S. membership in the **United Nations**. *See also* IRRECONCILABLES.

JOHNSON, NELSON TRUSLER (1887–1954). After service in **China** as an interpreter and a consular official, Nelson Johnson became head of the State Department Division of Far Eastern Affairs in 1925. In 1929, he returned to China as minister, later ambassador, to the government of **Chiang Kai-shek**. Johnson consistently recommended that U.S. policies encourage the reestablishment of order in China and the sovereignty of the Chinese republic. He therefore opposed U.S. participation in punitive measures desired by **Great Britain** after incidents in Canton and Hankow, and likewise in response to the 1927 **Nanking Incident**. He favored a better **tariff** arrangement and an end to extraterritoriality in cities like Shanghai. Johnson was influential in shaping Secretary of State **Henry Stimson**'s response to the **Shanghai Incident** of 1932, and his recommendations were followed in Stimson's letter to Senator **William Borah** reaffirming the **Stimson Doctrine** in February 1932.

Later in the 1930s, Johnson's influence declined somewhat as policy followed the recommendations of Ambassador **Joseph C. Grew** in Tokyo. Johnson became concerned about **Japan**'s expansionism, but his proposals fell short of U.S. intervention. He thought the United States should reconsider the decision to grant independence to the **Philippines** in the **Tydings–McDuffie Act**. By the end of the decade, he believed that the Chinese resistance, and what he saw as successful organization of the state by Chiang, warranted U.S. support. Johnson was replaced in February 1941, but his subsequent reports were influential on the granting of **Lend-Lease** and other aid to China. He was ambassador to Australia (1941–45) and later secretary general of the Far Eastern Commission. *See also* GAUSS, CLARENCE; HORNBECK, STANLEY KUHL.

JOHNSON–REED ACT (1924). *See* NATIONAL ORIGINS ACT.

JOINT CHIEFS OF STAFF COMMITTEE (JCS). The U.S. Army and **U.S. Navy** before **World War II** tended to be rivals for a very limited defense budget, and this spilled over into other aspects of their activities, most significantly **intelligence** operations. This has been seen as a contributory factor in the U.S. unpreparedness for the **Pearl Harbor** attack. Army and navy chiefs of planning had met together in the Joint Board since **World War I**, but it had no independent authority to enforce decisions. Partly as a result of the intelligence failure over Pearl Harbor, and partly because of the needs to interact with **Great Britain**, which had such an organization in place, the chief of staff to the president, Admiral **William D. Leahy**, began to chair a committee made up of General **George C. Marshall**, Admiral **Ernest King**, and General **Henry "Hap" Arnold**, from the Army, Navy, and Army Air Force respectively. The membership remained the same throughout the war.

Initially, there were ad hoc meetings to provide input from the U.S. side into the U.S.–British **Combined Chiefs of Staff Committee** that was established in February 1942. Under Leahy's leadership, this became more regularized by July 1942. However, the Joint Chiefs of Staff Committee, as it came to be known, was not formally constituted until the National Security Act of 1947.

Unlike the British system, no joint staffs or organizations for planning, intelligence, or supply were established below this top level during World War II, so that JCS meetings were often the place where differences between the armed forces had to be confronted. At the early inter-Allied conferences, this could lead to arguments between the American chiefs during discussions with their British counterparts, who were more accustomed to reaching unanimous agreement prior to such meetings. Bitter disagreements emerged because the army and navy tended to view the war quite differently, with the navy placing far greater emphasis on the Pacific theater, and within that theater being at odds with the army over the appropriate line of advance. President **Franklin D. Roosevelt** was unwilling to provide consistently firm direction on these issues, though he overrode JCS objections in 1942 when he decided to agree to the British proposal of Operation **Torch**. The JCS organization became permanent, and was equipped with a full supporting organization, only with the reorganization and unification of the armed services structures in the National Security Act, and then in the revisions to it in 1949, which established the Department of Defense.

JONES ACT (1916). The Philippine Autonomy Act, known as the Jones Act after its sponsor, Representative William Atkinson Jones, replaced the 1902 Philippine Organic Act, which had been introduced shortly after the U.S. takeover of the islands and provided for the creation of a legislature, extended all provisions of the U.S. Bill of Rights to the Philippines, and disestablished the Catholic Church. The Jones Act reiterated the U.S. intention to grant full independence to the **Philippines** and altered legislative arrangements to increase the degree of Filipino self-government. The U.S. governor general, however, retained his veto over legislation, and U.S. appointees continued to dominate the Filipino supreme court. The outlines laid down by the Jones Act remained in force until the mid-1930s. *See also* HARE–HAWES–CUTTING ACT; TYDINGS–MCDUFFIE ACT.

JONES–COSTIGAN ACT (1934). Passed on 9 May 1934, the Jones–Costigan Act set quotas and prices for sugar production along the lines of the New Deal's Agricultural Adjustment Act. It was significant for foreign affairs because it set quotas regarding imports of sugar. In particular, it addressed the problems faced by the sugar industry in **Cuba**. It gave a guaranteed, and increased, share in the U.S. market: from 25.4 percent in 1933 to 31.4 percent in 1940, at a preferential **tariff** set 20 percent lower than that paid by other foreign producers. At the same time, an agreement under the 1934 **Reciprocal Trade Agreements Act** gave preferential rates for other Cuban agricultural products; in return, over 400 U.S.-produced items were given favorable rates in the Cuban market. These measures reflected the new stage in U.S.–Cuban relations following the rise of **Fulgencio Batista**: a more mature relationship with the abrogation of the **Platt Amendment**, but the Cuban economy was tied inextricably to the U.S. market, and development of an independent Cuban manufacturing industry was stifled.

JONES, JESSE HOLMAN (1874–1956). Successful in the building business in Houston, Texas, Jesse Jones was invited by President **Woodrow Wilson** to be secretary of commerce. Jones preferred to remain in private business but later served as director general of military relief for the American Red Cross in **World War I**. Jones served in the Reconstruction Finance Corporation under President **Herbert Hoover**, and President **Franklin D. Roosevelt** appointed him to the board of the **Export-Import Bank** (1936–43). Jones refused an offer to be president of the bank. He acted as an important intermediary between business and the administration and was responsible for saving many companies from financial failure.

During **World War II**, Jones was administrator of the Federal Loan Agency (1939–45) and secretary of commerce (1940–45). He was disappointed to be passed over as vice presidential candidate in favor of **Henry Wallace** in 1940 and became more aligned with anti-Roosevelt forces in the Democratic Party. Jones's jurisdiction overlapped with Wallace's responsibility for economic warfare, and they clashed frequently. Wallace regarded Jones's approach as too conservative. Roosevelt asked Jones to resign in February 1945, and Wallace replaced him as secretary of commerce. Jones refused other posts, and newspapers that he owned withheld support from Democratic Party candidates.

JONES–SHAFROTH ACT (1917). Signed into law by President **Woodrow Wilson** on 2 March 1917, the Jones–Shafroth Act, sponsored by Representative William Atkinson Jones and Senator John Franklin Shafroth, granted citizenship rights to all Puerto Ricans, established regular elections and manhood suffrage, and divided the institutions of Puerto Rican government along lines similar to those in the United States. There were limitations, however, to this extension of democracy. The U.S. Congress reserved the right of veto over any legislation passed by the new Puerto Rican legislature, control of fiscal policy remained with the United States, and the governor of Puerto Rico continued to be an appointee of the U.S. president rather than elected by Puerto Rican voters.

– K –

KEARNY, USS. The torpedoing of the destroyer USS *Kearny* on 17 October 1941, while on escort duty in the North Atlantic, took the United States a stage further toward full involvement in **World War II**. Eleven American sailors were killed and 22 wounded. This was the first time in the undeclared naval war that U.S. service members' lives had been lost. President **Franklin D. Roosevelt** called German submarines "rattlesnakes of the Atlantic" and used the incident to press for alteration of the 1939 **Neutrality Act** to allow the arming of American merchant ships and the abolition of the "carry" provision to allow American vessels to carry **Lend-Lease** supplies all the way to **Great Britain**. However, it was the sinking of the USS *Reuben James* on 31 October that finally brought this about.

KEEP AMERICA OUT OF WAR CONGRESS (KAOWC). Early in 1938, the **pacifist** Keep America out of War Committee was formed by the **National Council for the Prevention of War (NCPW)**, the American Friends Service Committee (AFSC), the Fellowship of Reconciliation (FOR), the **Women's International League for Peace and Freedom (WILPF)**, the Peace Committee of the General Conference of American Rabbis, World Peaceways, and the Commission for World Peace of the Methodist General Conference. At the National Anti-War Congress in May 1938, the name was changed to the Keep America out of War Congress. It had a joint six-point program to supplement the efforts of the individual member organizations, representing aims on which these diverse groups could agree.

The main aims were to keep U.S. ships and people out of war zones, a referendum on war (similar to that proposed by **Louis Ludlow**), and social justice. The KAOWC opposed conscription and mobilization of industry for arms production. A leading organizer was the socialist **Norman Thomas**, and its emphasis was generally left-wing, though it was prepared to cooperate with the **America First Committee** and other anti-interventionist organizations. Also on the organizing committee were **Dorothy Detzer** and Mildred Scott Olmsted of the WILPF, **A. J. Muste** and Abraham Kaufman of the **War Resisters League**, Ray Newton of the American Friends Service Committee, **Frederick J. Libby** of the NCPW, and **Devere Allen**. Thomas declared that the intention was to "arouse the American people to the dangers with which the president and his administration are confronting us." Like America First, the KAOWC saw itself as a lobby group to restrain the government. In 1942, the organization changed its name to the Provisional Committee toward a Democratic Peace, and later that year to the Post War World Council. *See also* ISOLATIONISM.

KELLEY, ROBERT FRANCIS (1894–1976). Educated at Harvard and at the Sorbonne, Paris, Robert Kelley was in the U.S. Army (1917–22) and served as assistant military attaché in Denmark and Finland, and then military observer in the Baltic states. In 1922, he joined the Foreign Service. He was vice consul in Calcutta, India

(1923–24) then became a member of the Russian Division in the State Department, which had been set up in 1919 following the **Russian revolutions**. Kelley, fluent in Russian, developed the division as a center of study of the newly formed **Union of Soviet Socialist Republics** (USSR), gathering expertise from the likes of Samuel Harper of Chicago University, one of the first academic experts on the subject.

In 1924, the Russian Division was made part of the Division of Eastern European Affairs (DEEA), with Kelley as assistant chief (1925–26) and then chief (1926–37). He focused the division almost exclusively on analysis of the USSR. Under his tutelage, the State Department's first generation of Soviet specialists was trained in their anti-Bolshevik attitudes, including **George Kennan, Charles Bohlen**, and **Loy Henderson**. He insisted they immerse themselves in Russian culture and language, which brought them mostly into contact with White Russians in exile from the USSR. Kelley was also a trustee of the **Export-Import Bank** from 1934 to 1937.

In 1937, the DEEA became just one part of a new Division of European Affairs headed by **J. Pierrepont Moffat**, and Kelley became counselor at the embassy in Ankara, Turkey (1937–45). He left the State Department in 1945 and helped create Amcomlib, which oversaw the first broadcasts to the communist bloc by Radio Liberty in 1951. He worked on Radio Liberty until 1967.

KELLOGG, FRANK BILLINGS (1856–1937). Lawyer Frank Kellogg served as special counsel for President **Theodore Roosevelt** in antitrust cases and was president of the American Bar Association (1912–14). While serving as a Republican Senator for Minnesota (1917–23), Kellogg supported President **Woodrow Wilson** in his efforts to get the **Treaty of Versailles** ratified by Congress. He was the U.S. representative at the Pan-American **Santiago Conference** in 1923 and was appointed ambassador to **Great Britain** later the same year. In this capacity, he attended the conference on war **reparations** which led to the **Dawes Plan**.

Upon the retirement of **Charles Evans Hughes** in 1925, Kellogg was named secretary of state by President **Calvin Coolidge**. Despite reluctantly acquiescing to armed intervention in **Nicaragua** in 1926, Kellogg generally shared Hughes's preference for peaceful diplomacy, with agreements reached through quiet, painstaking negotiation. During his four-year tenure at the State Department, the United States signed some 80 treaties with foreign nations, a record that encouraged groups favoring **internationalism** and **pacifism**, still frustrated at U.S. failure to join either the **League of Nations** or the **World Court**, to press for new cooperative initiatives.

Kellogg's most memorable achievement, for which he was later awarded the Nobel Peace Prize, was the Pact of Paris, known as the **Kellogg–Briand Pact**, which arose from an initiative by Foreign Minister Aristide Briand of **France**. The French government proposed to outlaw the use of armed force in relations between France and the United States. Publicity surrounding the proposal caused it to gather momentum and requests for inclusion by other nations. Despite their private skepticism, Kellogg and President Coolidge eventually steered through Congress what had become, by August 1928, a 62-nation treaty. Kellogg retired at the end of the Coolidge administration, becoming an associate judge on the World Court.

KELLOGG–BRIAND PACT (1928). On 6 April 1927, French Foreign Minister Aristide Briand called for a new Franco–American friendship treaty to outlaw the use of armed force in any dispute between the two nations. The call was supported by American **pacifist** groups and religious organizations and quickly broadened into a proposal for a multilateral treaty outlawing the use of war for the settlement of international disputes. Secretary of State **Frank B. Kellogg** and President **Calvin Coolidge** both preferred less ambitious, bilateral agreements but bowed to popular pressure after the idea received support from **William E. Borah**, the powerful **isolationist** chair of the **Senate Committee on Foreign Relations**. Borah stipulated, however, that the United States would not be legally bound to take military action against signatory nations which violated the agreement. The Pact of Paris, commonly known as the **Kellogg–Briand Pact**, was signed on 27 August 1928. It was ratified by the Senate (85–1) on 15 January 1929. It outlawed war as an instrument of foreign policy, though the clauses added by the United States and **Great Britain** excepting self-defense and defense of territories of vital interest were deemed by some to undermine the treaty's effectiveness.

Historians generally regard the pact as a grandiose but futile gesture doomed to failure by the lack of enforcement provisions. Columbia University Professor **James T. Shotwell**, who had helped plant the idea with Briand in the first place, argued the treaty was "negative" in focusing only on the renunciation of war, rather than pursuing "positive" measures to replace war as a policy instrument. Shotwell assisted President **Herbert Hoover** in proposing an amendment that signatory nations would refuse to recognize the legitimacy of any territory seized by military force, withdraw diplomatic recognition from the offending power, and set up impartial commissions to mediate disputes. The idea was abandoned when it became clear the League of Nations would consider this an interference with **League of Nations** authority. *See also* INTERNATIONAL MILITARY TRIBUNAL.

KENNAN, GEORGE FROST (1904–2005). Diplomat George Kennan studied history at Princeton and in 1926 joined the Foreign Service. Early postings were to Geneva (1927), Hamburg (1927–28), Tallinn (1928–29), and Riga (1931–33). He studied Russian at the University of Berlin (1929–31) and was a participant in **Robert F. Kelley**'s immersion program for training young State Department officials for service relating to the **Union of Soviet Socialist Republics** (USSR). Kennan served at the embassy in Moscow as third secretary (1934–37) and witnessed USSR dictator **Josef Stalin**'s show trials. Like the other Kelley-trained officials who served in Moscow, **Loy Henderson** and **Charles Bohlen**, he saw no possibility for meaningful cooperation with the Soviet Union under any circumstances. He was moved to the Russian desk of the Department of European Affairs at the State Department (1937–38), then posted to Prague (1938–39) and Berlin (1939–41). He was interned in **Germany** when the United States entered **World War II**. He was released in April 1942 and assigned to Lisbon.

In 1944, he returned to Moscow as counselor of the embassy and at times served as chargé d'affaires. Kennan influenced Ambassador **Averell Harriman** in his growing skepticism toward the USSR, which in turn influenced the attitudes of **Harry S. Truman** when he became president in April 1945. Kennan's assessments of Soviet motivations in his Long Telegram of March 1946 and his "Mr. X" article of July 1947 were key contributions to the development of the postwar U.S. policy of containment. He was recalled to head the new Policy Planning Staff (PPS) established to coordinate analysis within the State Department in April 1947. In time, he came to disagree with aspects of the policy, notably the movement toward a militarized approach, and policy toward **China**, and he resigned from the PPS in December 1949. He was ambassador to the USSR from May to December 1952, when a controversy with the Soviet government meant he had to relinquish the post. He was ambassador to Yugoslavia (1961–63) and a productive author on **Russia** and the USSR.

KENNEDY, JOSEPH PATRICK (1888–1969). Joseph P. Kennedy, the father of U.S. President John F. Kennedy (1961–63), made his fortune on the stock exchange as a speculator and investor and by the late 1950s was among the 15 richest people in the country. He supported **Franklin D. Roosevelt**'s campaign for president in 1932 with large amounts of money and in return was made chair of the new Securities and Exchange Commission (SEC). He was a reformer, drawing on his extensive knowledge of the markets. Kennedy then took charge of the Maritime Commission in 1935.

Kennedy was a strong supporter of the New Deal and was instrumental, with other prominent Catholic Americans, in prevailing upon the Vatican to silence the criticisms of Father **Charles Coughlin** in 1936. Kennedy urged Roosevelt to keep a distance from the **Spanish Civil War**, arguing that many Catholic Democratic supporters favored the right-wing Francisco Franco. In 1938, Kennedy's support was rewarded with the prestigious posting of ambassador to **Great Britain**. Kennedy firmly supported Prime Minister **Neville Chamberlain**'s policy of appeasement toward Nazi **Germany**. He argued that a second world war would be even more horrendous than the first. He twice unsuccessfully sought an interview with German dictator **Adolf Hitler** to head off such a catastrophe, without State Department sanction.

With Roosevelt's policy moving toward aid to the Allies during **World War II**, Kennedy found himself at odds with the president and resigned in November 1940. Kennedy's son Joe had opposed Roosevelt's renomination, and relations between Kennedy and the president had badly deteriorated. But Kennedy did support Roosevelt's campaign, and he advocated aid to Britain in 1941, giving his support to **Lend-Lease** before Congress and on the radio. Kennedy had no role, however, in wartime administration. In the postwar period, he formed close relations with the controversial anticommunist Senator Joseph McCarthy and used all his influence to secure the presidency for his second son, John, Joe having died on a bombing mission during the war.

KENT, TYLER (1911–1988). The son of a diplomat, Tyler Kent was born in **China**. He joined the Foreign Service in 1934 and was posted to Moscow, where he came under suspicion of espionage and was transferred to London to work as a cipher clerk in 1939. In February 1940, Kent came into contact with Anna Wolkoff and other members of the anti-Semitic Right Club. Kent showed them copies of correspondence between President **Franklin D. Roosevelt** and **Winston Churchill**. These documents were then passed on to German **intelligence** via the Italian embassy. When approached by British intelligence, Ambassador **Joseph P. Kennedy** waived Kent's diplomatic immunity. On 20 May 1940, when the police raided his apartment, they found copies of 1,929 classified documents. After a secret trial, Tyler was sentenced to seven years imprisonment under the British Official Secrets Act. In December 1945, he was deported to the United States. The Kent affair was kept very quiet because of the potential embarrassment to the Roosevelt administration if the extent of the correspondence with Churchill was revealed while the United States was still neutral. Kent later became editor of a newspaper connected to the Ku Klux Klan, though the **Federal Bureau of Investigation** continued to suspect he was actually an agent for the **Union of Soviet Socialist Republics**.

KING, ERNEST J. (1878–1956). Commander in chief of the **U.S. Navy** during **World War II**, Ernest King had joined the navy in 1897 and served in the Spanish–American War (1898). He was involved in the occupation of **Veracruz** in 1914. He gained experience with both surface and submarine vessels, and he learned to fly in 1927. He commanded the aircraft carrier USS *Lexington* (1930–32). Now a rear-admiral, he was made chief of the Bureau of Aeronautics in 1933 and subsequently commanded naval air forces. He was made vice admiral in 1938 and admiral in February 1941, when he became commander in chief of the Atlantic Fleet. He was in command for the undeclared naval war waged with German submarines in the fall of 1941.

On 30 December 1941, King was made commander in chief of the U.S. Navy and on 18 March 1942 was made chief of naval operations as well, replacing Admiral **Harold Stark**. King was an abrasive personality and a capable but controversial commander. He saw the Pacific theater as the main interest of the navy. King once complained that the Pacific got only 15 percent of Allied resources when it deserved 30 percent. He begrudged diversion of resources, such as landing craft and long-range aircraft, to Europe. He disliked the British. This may have been one of the reasons for his slowness in adopting coastal convoys and blackouts on U.S. entry into **World War II**, which resulted in the German U-boats' **American shooting season**. As commander in chief of the navy, King served on the **Joint Chiefs of Staff Committee** throughout the war. He was the second admiral to be promoted to five-star rank, the newly created one of Fleet Admiral, on 15 December 1944, and was junior in the navy only to Admiral **William Leahy**. He retired in December 1945 but served as an advisor to the secretary of the navy in 1950.

KING–CRANE COMMISSION (1919). The American Section of the Inter-Allied Commission on Mandates in Turkey was an investigative body set up by the administration of President **Woodrow Wilson** to determine conditions in the collapsed Ottoman empire and assess the potential for creating a lasting peace in the Middle East. It was commonly known as the King–Crane Commission, as it was headed by Henry King, a professor of theology, and Chicago industrialist Charles R. Crane. The commission's report favored more active U.S. involvement in the region, but its recommendations were not taken up by the Wilson administration or its successors.

KIRK, ALEXANDER COMSTOCK (1888–1979). Alexander Kirk graduated from Harvard Law School, studied at the École Libre des Sciences Politiques in Paris, then joined the Foreign Service. His early service during **World War I** was in Berlin, Constantinople, and The Hague. He was secretary to Secretary of State **Robert Lansing**

at the 1919 **Paris Peace Conference**, and he served as counselor in the embassy in Rome from 1930 to 1937. After a brief appointment as consul general to Singapore, he was appointed counselor in the embassy in Moscow in 1938. He served as chargé d'affaires after the departure of **Joseph P. Davies**. In April 1939, he was transferred to **Germany** to fulfill the same role at the embassy in Berlin. Ambassador **Hugh Wilson** had been recalled after the anti-Semitic persecutions of *Kristallnacht* the previous fall.

Kirk was thus in Germany at the start of **World War II**, serving until October 1940. While there, he maintained discreet contacts with elements of the aristocratic resistance to dictator **Adolf Hitler**. Kirk was appointed minister to Egypt in 1941. He took responsibility for representation to the Greek government in exile in Cairo from 1943 and was also representative to Saudi Arabia in 1941–43. In April 1944, Kirk became ambassador to the government of liberated Italy. In September, succeeding **Robert Murphy**, he was also political advisor to the supreme Allied commander in the Mediterranean theater. He retired in 1946.

KNOX, PHILANDER CHASE (1853–1921). Lawyer Philander Knox was an influential member of the cabinets of Presidents William McKinley, **Theodore Roosevelt** (as attorney general, 1901–5), and **William H. Taft** (as secretary of state, 1909–11). He made an abortive bid for the Republican presidential nomination in 1908. As secretary of state, he promoted **dollar diplomacy** as a tool for fostering economic and political stability in **Latin America** while protecting U.S. business interests in the region. The policy was also applied to American business activity in **China**. Knox also introduced organizational reforms in both the State Department and diplomatic service. As a Republican Senator for Pennsylvania (1917–21), he attacked the Democratic administration of President **Woodrow Wilson** for its advocacy of U.S. membership in the **League of Nations**. Knox became a prominent member of the group of Senate **Irreconcilables** who rallied opposition to the **Treaty of Versailles**. Briefly considered a contender for the presidency in 1920, Knox gave a lukewarm endorsement to the candidacy of Senator **Warren G. Harding**. Knox died in Washington, D.C., on 12 October 1921, shortly after steering the **Knox–Porter Resolution** through Congress. *See also* ROUND ROBIN.

KNOX–PORTER RESOLUTION (1921). A joint resolution of Congress passed in 1921, the Knox–Porter Resolution terminated the state of hostilities between the United States and **Germany** that had existed since April 1917. At the end of **World War I**, Congress did not pass a formal suspension resolution. President **Woodrow Wilson** vetoed the first attempt by Pennsylvania Senator **Philander C. Knox** to push the resolution through in 1920, contending that no independent action should be taken outside the terms of the **Treaty of Versailles**, which the president still hoped would be ratified by Congress. In spring 1921, President **Warren G. Harding** declared the question of U.S. membership in the **League of Nations** to be closed, prompting Knox to reintroduce his motion. A separate version was pushed through the House of Representatives by Stephen G. Porter. On 1 July 1921, the final resolution cleared Congress. Separate peace treaties were later concluded with Austria and Hungary. President Harding signed the Knox–Porter Resolution on 2 July 1921, thus bringing a formal end to World War I. *See also* BERLIN, TREATY OF.

KNOX, WILLIAM FRANKLIN (1874–1944). Journalist and publisher Frank Knox was secretary of the **U.S. Navy** during **World War II**. Knox fought with the Rough Riders in the Spanish–American War (1898) and made the acquaintance of **Theodore Roosevelt**. He enlisted in the U.S. Army for **World War I** at the age of 43. By 1927, he was general manager of all **William Randolph Hearst**'s daily newspapers. He managed the *Chicago Daily News* from 1931 to 1940, using it to attack President **Franklin D. Roosevelt**'s New Deal. A **progressive** Republican, Knox ran for vice president in 1936.

Knox supported measures of naval rearmament following the occupation of Austria by **Germany** in 1938. His editorials supported Roosevelt's foreign policy and especially the modification of the **Neutrality Act** in 1939. He called for a bipartisan cabinet, and in July 1940 Roosevelt appointed him secretary of the navy. When fellow Republicans criticized him for accepting the post, he replied that he was an American first and a Republican afterward.

Knox took a public line supporting aid for **Great Britain** in 1940–41, at odds with **isolationists** in his party and more definite than Roosevelt was in public. He was active in garnering support in Congress for both the **destroyers-for-bases** deal, which he helped design, and **Lend-Lease**. During World War II, he visited war fronts in the Pacific and European theaters. He presided over the building of the two-ocean navy and its increase to over 3 million personnel. Knox was a firm advocate of close Allied cooperation, visiting **Brazil** in 1942 when that country entered the war, and working hard to develop the U.S–British alliance, touring Britain in 1943 to foster good relations. When he died in 1944, the U.S. Navy was by far the largest in the world.

KUHN, FRITZ (1896–1951). An American Nazi and leader of the **German-American Bund**, Fritz Kuhn had fought in the German army in **World War I**. He moved to **Mexico** and then the United States after the war, becoming a U.S. citizen in 1934. In 1939, he was prosecuted by New York District Attorney **Thomas Dewey** for embezzlement of $14,000 from the German-American Bund. During **World War II**, Kuhn was interned in Texas and in 1945 was deported to **Germany**.

KUOMINTANG (GUOMINDANG). The nationalist party in **China**, the Kuomintang was headed by **Chiang Kai-shek** after the death in 1925 of the father of the Chinese Revolution, **Sun Yat-sen**.

– L –

LA FOLLETTE, ROBERT M. (1855–1925). Politician Robert M. La Follette, who served as a member of the U.S. House of Representatives (1885–91), governor of Wisconsin (1901–6), and U.S. senator (1906–25), was the best-known **progressive** politician in the United States during the first quarter of the 20th century. Though a Republican, he was often in conflict with the party's conservative, pro-capitalist policies. He created resentment among party managers by opposing "boss politics" and demanding electoral reforms that would curb party influence at the state level. La Follette was one of the principal opponents of U.S. entry into **World War I**, claiming the United States was being tricked into war in order to boost the profits of big business, particularly arms manufacturers. Like Secretary of State **William Jennings Bryan**, La Follette also suspected the administration of pro-British sympathies. His opposition to the 1917 **declaration of war** (he was one of six senators to vote against it) earned him the bitter hostility of the American press and many of his colleagues. Later, he opposed ratification of the **Treaty of Versailles**. La Follette ran for president as an independent in 1924 and won the electoral votes of his home state and nearly 5 million votes nationwide.

LAMONT, THOMAS (1870–1948). Banker Thomas Lamont was a partner in the J. P. Morgan company with **John Pierpont Morgan Jr**. He owned the *New York Evening Post* from 1918 to 1922 and served as one of the two Treasury Department representatives in the U.S. delegation to the 1919 **Paris Peace Conference**. Lamont went on a semiofficial mission to **Japan** in 1920 to safeguard U.S. economic interests in East Asia. He did not, however, support a tough response to Japan in the **Manchurian Crisis** (1931).

Lamont sympathized with fascism in Italy and in 1925 arranged a $100 million loan to dictator Benito Mussolini. He went on special missions to several countries, including **China** and **Mexico**, to negotiate loans and give financial advice. He was a delegate to the 1933 **London Economic Conference**. Lamont was a member of the **League of Nations Association** and as an **internationalist** was involved with the **Nonpartisan Committee for Peace through Revision of the Neutrality Law** and the **Committee to Defend America by Aiding the Allies**. He was acting head of J. P. Morgan during the 1929 Wall Street crash and was elected chair of the company in 1943. After **World War II**, he made a large donation toward the restoration of Canterbury Cathedral in **Great Britain**.

LANDIS, JAMES MCCAULEY (1899–1964). The son of missionaries, James Landis was born in **Japan**. He was a student of Felix Frankfurter at Harvard Law School and served on the Federal Trade Commission (1933–34), the Securities and Exchange Commission (1934–37), and as a regional and then national director for the Office of Civilian Defense (1941–43). He was director of Economic Operations in the Middle East, based in Cairo, Egypt (1943–45). After **World War II**, he was chair of the Civil Aeronautics Board (1946–47). He was legal counsel for **Joseph P. Kennedy**, and he was dean of Harvard Law School (1938–46).

LANE, ARTHUR BLISS (1894–1956). Arthur Bliss Lane graduated from Yale and from the École de l'Isle, France. In 1917, he was private secretary to Ambassador Thomas Nelson Page in Italy. After serving in minor diplomatic posts in London, Paris, Berne, and Warsaw, Lane was minister to Nicaragua (1933–36), the Baltic states (1936–37), Yugoslavia (1937–41), and Costa Rica (1941). While in Yugoslavia, he encouraged the young king, Peter, to resist **Germany**. During **World War II**, he protected U.S. citizens and property after Germany occupied Belgrade. Lane was ambassador to Colombia (1942–44) and to **Poland** (1944–47). He reported from Poland on breaches of the 1945 **Yalta Conference** agreements by the **Union of Soviet Socialist Republics** and criticized what he saw as U.S. appeasement of the Soviets. He subsequently became a critic of the U.S. policy of containment and an advocate of a more forward policy of liberation.

LANSING, ROBERT (1864–1928). Lawyer Robert Lansing was an advisor to the State Department and had served occasionally as acting secretary of state when he succeeded **William Jennings Bryan** as secretary of state in June 1915. His appointment was recommended by **Edward M. House**, who argued that President **Woodrow Wilson** needed a secretary of state with "not too many ideas of his own." Lansing, however, showed clear sympathies for the Allied cause during **World War I**, working to secure financial loans on generous terms for **Great Britain** and **France**.

In December 1916, when Wilson offered U.S. mediation between the warring powers, Lansing told journalists that this was not a "peace note" but a last effort to avoid U.S. entry into the war. The comment undermined the administration's pose of studied neutrality and weakened the president's confidence in Lansing. In 1918, Lansing privately criticized some aspects of Wilson's **Fourteen Points** speech to Congress as unrealistic. His personal relations with the president were also strained by Wilson's increasing tendency to bypass the State Department and use personal emissaries to conduct negotiations.

Wilson excluded Lansing from the detailed negotiations conducted at the 1919 **Paris Peace Conference**. During negotiations, the secretary of state, in conversation with U.S. conference delegate **William C. Bullitt**, expressed his private doubts over **League of Nations** membership. Bullitt later testified before the **Senate Committee on Foreign Relations** that Lansing had called the League "useless." In February 1920, Wilson accused Lansing of disloyalty for holding informal cabinet meetings without the president's knowledge during Wilson's illness. Lansing resigned immediately. After retiring from public life, Lansing wrote several books on U.S. law and diplomacy. *See also* LANSING–ISHII AGREEMENT.

LANSING–ISHII AGREEMENT (1917). Under the treaty between the United States and **Japan** negotiated by Secretary of State **Robert Lansing** in 1917, the United States recognized Japanese interests in **China** in return for a Japanese pledge not to obstruct freedom of **trade** in the region—essentially a recognition of the **open door policy**. Both nations agreed to refrain from seeking special rights in China, to respect Chinese sovereignty, and to ensure that other nations acted with similar restraint.

LATIN AMERICA. U.S. relations with Latin America underwent major changes during 1914–45. In 1904, President **Theodore Roosevelt** had declared in the **Roosevelt Corollary** to the **Monroe Doctrine** that the United States would act as an international police power in the Caribbean and neighboring territories, to protect U.S. interests, particularly the Panama Canal, and prevent disorder. This was the guiding principle during the presidency of **Woodrow Wilson**. In effect, a number of territories became U.S. protectorates, notably **Cuba**, Panama, **Nicaragua**, Haiti, and the **Dominican Republic**. The United States intervened in **Mexico** following the 1910 revolution, as U.S. corporations appealed to Wilson to protect their interests and he sent troops south of the border twice. Even so, the 1917 Mexican constitution endorsed nationalistic principles and the expropriation of foreign-held property.

World War I strengthened the U.S. trading position with Latin America, because it cut contact between the republics and European markets and investors. Where previously most U.S. commercial activity had been in Central America and the Caribbean, now ties rapidly grew with South America too. The unchallenged nature of U.S. hegemony encouraged the Republican administrations of the 1920s to move toward a less overtly interventionist policy. Troops were withdrawn from the Dominican Republic, and attempts were made through ambassador **Dwight Morrow** to improve relations with Mexico. The Roosevelt Corollary was set aside in the **Clark Memorandum** of 1928. The **Franklin D. Roosevelt** administration continued and enlarged upon this approach, dubbing it the **Good Neighbor policy**. In gradual stages, the United States renounced its claim to the right to intervene with military force, beginning with the statement made at the 1933 **Montevideo Conference**, confirmed and clarified at the 1936 **Buenos Aires Conference**. At the same time, the United States continued to exert powerful influence through diplomatic, political, and economic means, as seen for instance in the encouragement of the rise to power of **Rafael Trujillo** in the Dominican Republic, and of **Fulgencio Batista** in Cuba.

By the end of the 1930s, the U.S. government was becoming concerned once more about threats to its hegemony from Europe—this time from the fascist powers. Efforts were made, beginning at the 1938 **Lima Conference**, to draw the Latin American countries together in cooperation against penetration from outside the hemisphere, under the guise of an increased emphasis on Pan-Americanism and "hemispheric solidarity." Although **Argentina** in particular resisted these efforts, the United States was successful in persuading the Latin American states to join it in isolating the hemisphere from the war in 1939–41, and then, when the United States joined **World War II**, in drawing most of them into some form of participation in it. They were promised help with industrialization and modernization as incentives. This process began at the 1942 **Rio Conference**. Only Chile and Argentina resisted this movement.

The State Department was divided on how to deal with this matter. The "Latin Americanists," headed by **Sumner Welles**, and including in their number **George Messersmith** and **Nelson Rockefeller**, favored a conciliatory policy to preserve the Good Neighbor image.

The "internationalists," led by Secretary of State **Cordell Hull** and including **Spruille Braden**, put Allied unity first and were thinking in global rather than regional terms. They favored putting economic and political pressure on recalcitrant republics to get them to sign up to U.S. methods and goals. While the compromise agreement at the Rio Conference was a success for the Latin Americanists, subsequently the demise of Welles and the military coup in Argentina strengthened the hands of the internationalists. The United States refused to recognize the Argentine government of Edelmiro Farrell in February 1944. Argentina was excluded from the conference on war and peace at Chapultepec in March 1945. Nelson Rockefeller was now in charge of Latin American affairs at the State Department and managed to broker an arrangement that paved the way for Argentina to rejoin inter-American cooperation. Argentina entered the war at the end of March 1945 and subscribed to the **Act of Chapultepec**.

Chile was one of the more democratic of the American republics, but it had long-standing economic links to **Germany** and a significant German emigrant population. Although it accepted the resolutions of the Rio Conference, it refused to sever relations with the **Axis**. As a result, **Lend-Lease** agreements remained uncompleted. Chile was also under pressure to restrain Nazi agents believed to be spying on Allied shipping. On 20 January 1943, the Chilean senate narrowly voted to break relations. The government refused to declare war on Germany, though it did declare war on **Japan** on 12 February 1945. Two days later, it signed the **United Nations Declaration**.

Institutions established during the war, such as the **Inter-American Defense Board**, were the beginnings of the security cooperation formalized in the 1947 Rio treaty and the increased role of the Organization of American States. *See also* BRYAN–CHAMORRO TREATY; CALVO DOCTRINE; DOLLAR DIPLOMACY; EXPORT-IMPORT BANK; GONDRA TREATY; HAVANA, ACT OF; JONES–COSTIGAN ACT; JONES–SHAFROTH ACT; MCCOY, FRANK ROSS; MEXICAN OIL EXPROPRIATION CONTROVERSY; OFFICE OF THE COORDINATOR OF INTER-AMERICAN AFFAIRS; PANAMA DECLARATION; PAN-AMERICAN UNION; PITTMAN ACT; PLATT AMENDMENT; ROWE, LEO STANTON; SHEFFIELD, JAMES ROCKWELL; THOMSON–URRUTIA TREATY; UNITED FRUIT COMPANY; WHITE, FRANCIS.

LAUSANNE CONFERENCE (1932). The Lausanne Conference, 16 June–9 July 1932, was an attempt to deal with the continuing issue of German **reparations** payments following **World War I**. After the respite provided by the 1929 **Young Plan**, reparations were again an issue because of the effects of the global economic depression in Europe. Delegates from **Germany**, **Great Britain**, **France**, and **Japan** agreed to reduce reparations payments to one final payment of 3,000 million marks, in the form of bonds to be issued when world economic conditions improved. A condition of the agreement, however, was that payment of **war debts** to the United States would be deferred. The failure of the U.S. Congress to agree to reduce or cancel the debts meant that the Lausanne agreement never came into force. The delegates also agreed to hold the **London Economic Conference** in 1933. *See also* HOOVER MORATORIUM.

LEAGUE OF NATIONS. During **World War I**, a number of political leaders and groups proposed the creation of an international organization to maintain peace, and thereby replace the system of highly armed alliances that had, it seemed, brought about the war. Groups such as the **League to Enforce Peace** had been advocating such a concept for some time, and President **Woodrow Wilson**'s envoy **Edward M. House** had discussed it with **Great Britain**. Wilson made formation of a league of nations one of his **Fourteen Points**, and he saw it as the cornerstone of a new way of conducting international affairs, through openness, democracy, and arbitration, rather than through secret treaties and arms races. It was on Wilson's insistence that the covenant of the League of Nations was included in each of the five treaties drawn up at the 1919 **Paris Peace Conference**.

The League was established with its headquarters at Geneva, Switzerland. Its first secretary general was British diplomat Eric Drummond (1919–32). The United States was not a member because of the failure of the U.S. Senate to ratify the **Treaty of Versailles**. **Germany** was a member from 1926 to 1933 and the **Union of Soviet Socialist Republics** (USSR) from 1934 to 1940. **Brazil** (1926), **Japan** (1933), and Italy (1937) left the organization after certain of their actions were condemned. The League had some success in organizing postwar reconstruction and in settling international disputes arising from the 1919 treaties, but it possessed no military force and relied on the cooperation of members and nongovernmental economic enterprises to apply its main weapon against an aggressor, which was the boycott of **trade** and other forms of sanctions.

The League lost much credibility through its failure to restrain Japan in the **Manchurian Crisis** (1931). Its Lytton Commission condemned Japan but failed to formulate any effective action. In 1935, little was done in response to the Italian invasion of Ethiopia. The League was the focus for belated attempts by the USSR to engage in **collective security** in 1935–39 but was essentially irrelevant in the crises in 1938–39 that culminated in the outbreak of **World War II** in Europe. The League had more success in its nonpolitical and socioeconomic activities: overseeing the mandate system and maintaining organizations like the **International Labour Organization** (ILO). The League continued to function from Geneva throughout World War II, though largely ignored after the last great political debate, which saw the expulsion of the Soviet Union for its attack on Finland in December 1939. Its nonpolitical activities, notably the ILO, were absorbed into the **United Nations** in April 1946.

LEAGUE OF NATIONS ASSOCIATION. In January 1923, the American Association for International Cooperation merged with the League of Nations Nonpartisan Committee to form the League of Nations Nonpartisan Association. It was renamed League of Nations Association in 1929. The aim of the organization was to promote world peace, specifically by engaging in public information activities to present a positive image of the **League of Nations** to the public in the United States and to work toward U.S. entry into the League. It used public meetings, films such as *Hell and the Way Out*, radio programs, and petitions. After **World War II**, it was renamed the United Nations Association. *See also* EICHELBERGER, CLARK; PACIFISM.

LEAGUE TO ENFORCE PEACE. An organization established in New York in 1915 by some members of the New York Peace Society, the league promoted the idea of an international organization dedicated to peaceful resolution of disputes through arbitration. It supported U.S. membership in the **League of Nations** but was divided on the question of the **Lodge reservations**. The League's first president, **William H. Taft**, later unsuccessfully attempted to prod the Republican Party toward a more internationalist stance. The League to Enforce Peace lost influence after President **Warren G. Harding** shelved the issue of U.S. membership in the League of Nations in 1921. *See also* PACIFISM.

LEAHY, WILLIAM D. (1875–1959). A naval officer and chief of staff to Presidents **Franklin D. Roosevelt** and **Harry S. Truman** during **World War II**, Leahy had served in the Spanish–American War (1898), the Philippine insurgency (1899–1902), the Boxer Rebellion (1900), and the U.S. occupation of Nicaragua in 1912. During **World War I**, he earned the Navy Cross and worked for a time closely with Franklin Roosevelt, who was then assistant secretary of the navy. In January 1937, he succeeded Admiral **William Standley** as chief of naval operations and served in that post until August 1939. When he retired, Roosevelt said to him, "Bill, if we have a war, you're going to be right back here helping me run it."

Leahy served as governor of Puerto Rico from September 1939, working to prepare military bases but following a policy of nonintervention in local politics. He was nicknamed *Almirante Lija* ("Admiral Sandpaper"), a play on his last name, but was one of the more tolerant governors of the island. Leahy was appointed ambassador to the French government at Vichy in November 1940, arriving in **France** in January 1941. It was hoped that he might persuade the defeated French to reenter World War II, but he achieved nothing in this respect. He was recalled in April 1942 as a protest against Vichy collaboration with the Nazis.

President Roosevelt wanted a senior military figure to liaise with armed forces chiefs, and on 6 July 1942, Leahy was appointed to the new post of chief of staff to the commander in chief and acted as chair of the **Joint Chiefs of Staff Committee** throughout World War II. He briefed the president daily and drafted much of his correspondence relating to strategic matters. Leahy attended most of the major wartime Allied conferences and alternated with his counterpart from **Great Britain** in chairing the U.S.–British **Combined Chiefs of Staff Committee**.

Leahy was appointed the first full fleet admiral on 15 December 1944 (equivalent to a five-star general). He criticized the use of the

atomic bombs in August 1945 as barbaric but was to be a committed Cold War warrior. Leahy was an intimate advisor at the very center of power from 1942 to his resignation in March 1949, playing a vital role in the development of U.S. strategic and international policy.

LEND-LEASE. Following his declaration in a fireside chat in December 1940 that the United States should be the **arsenal of democracy**, President **Franklin D. Roosevelt** proposed Lend-Lease aid to Allied nations in **World War II**. He was responding to the increasing inability of **China**, **Great Britain**, and others fighting the **Axis** powers to pay for munitions and other materials. Under Lend-Lease, the president would be authorized to supply weapons to any state whose defense he identified to be vital to the defense of the United States. The materials would be returned after the war or paid for in goods or cash.

Isolationists bitterly opposed Lend-Lease when it was introduced in Congress as House Resolution 1776, "An Act to Promote the Defense of the United States." The great debate on intervention in the war reached a climax over this proposal, which isolationists like Senators **Robert A. Taft** and **Burton K. Wheeler** asserted would mean direct involvement in the war. Roosevelt claimed it would keep the United States out of the war by enabling the Allies to win. A Gallup poll showed public opinion to be in favor of Lend-Lease by two to one. On 11 March 1941, Congress approved the Lend-Lease Act by a vote of 60–30 in the Senate and 200–165 in the House.

The first appropriation was $7 billion allocated to Great Britain and China. The final amount of Lend-Lease aid was more than $50 billion. Britain and its empire received $32 billion. Lend-Lease did draw the United States closer to war and did identify it closely with the Allied cause, though it did not itself bring direct involvement. Its major significance was that in 1941–45, it made U.S. industrial production a major factor in the defeat of the Axis by removing financial obstacles to the transfer of U.S.-made arms. Although Congress was initially reluctant to supply Lend-Lease to the **Union of Soviet Socialist Republics** (USSR), $1 billion was authorized in November 1941, and eventually $7 billion was provided. This was a small proportion of total Soviet needs but included trucks, jeeps, and railroad locomotives that gave the Soviet army greater mobility than their

German opponents. It also provided for boots and enough processed meat (Spam) to feed the Soviet army.

Both Britain and the Soviet Union hoped Lend-Lease would continue into the postwar reconstruction period, but it was terminated on the day **Japan** surrendered. Its contribution to victory in World War II, however, was significant. *See also* CROWLEY, LEO T.; MASTER LEND-LEASE AGREEMENTS; MOSCOW CONFERENCE (1941).

LEVINSON, SALMON O. (1865–1941). By 1914, Indiana attorney Salmon Levinson had made his fortune in the law and turned to peace advocacy. He was the main sponsor of a proposal that war be made illegal under international law. He tried, and failed, to get this provision incorporated in the covenant of the **League of Nations** at the 1919 **Paris Peace Conference**. As a consequence, he became a severe critic of both the League and the **World Court** (Permanent Court of International Justice). Levinson worked with **Philander C. Knox** and **William E. Borah** but had no better success at the 1921 **Naval Disarmament Conference**, nor in linking the issue with the **war debts** and **reparations** questions. He formed the American Committee for the Outlawry of War to take the idea directly to the public. Levinson was influential with **James Shotwell** in bringing about the proposals that produced the **Kellogg–Briand Pact** in 1928 between **France** and the United States. In the late 1930s, Levinson advocated arbitration as the solution to the **Sino–Japanese War**. *See also* PACIFISM.

LIBBY, FREDERICK JOSEPH (1874–1970). Peace activist Frederick Libby, a theologian and pastor, traveled widely in the Middle East and East Asia before **World War I**. He did relief work with the American Friends Service Committee (1918–20) and joined the Society of Friends (Quakers) in 1921. From 1921 to his death in 1970, Libby was executive secretary of the **National Council for the Prevention of War**. *See also* PACIFISM.

LIBERTY BONDS. During **World War I**, many Americans purchased bonds known as Liberty Bonds. Much of the income from the bonds went abroad in U.S. loans to its allies and to new states created after the breakup of the empires of **Russia** and Austria-Hungary.

LIBERTY SHIPS. In 1940, **Great Britain** ordered 60 merchant ships in the United States to replace war losses. In order to produce them quickly, the ships were built by welding rather than riveting. They were basic, rather ugly, but functional vessels. Henry Kaiser, who was from the construction industry, was given the task of building them, and he introduced mass production techniques to the building of ships for the first time, cutting the completion time by a third. The design was adopted for the ships subsidized under the **Merchant Marine Act** as well. The first 14 were launched in September 1941, when they were given the name Liberty Ships to boost their public image, which had been tarnished by their makeshift appearance. By 1943, three were being finished every day, with an average construction time of 42 days. A total of 2,710 were made during the war, as were a tanker version (the T10) and a larger freighter, the Victory ship. This phenomenal achievement was one of the crucial contributions of the U.S. economy to Allied victory in **World War II**.

LIMA CONFERENCE (1938). The Eighth International Conference of American States met in Lima, Peru, on 9–26 December 1938. The Lima Conference reaffirmed the sentiments of the 1936 **Buenos Aires Conference** regarding inter-American solidarity and respect for each other's sovereignty. The Lima Conference went a small stage further in solidifying the U.S. movement away from policies of intervention by agreeing that there would be no forcible collection of international debts. The U.S. delegation was concerned about the increased level of **Axis** trade with and propaganda in **Latin America**, and Assistant Secretary of State **Adolf Berle** set out to form a "north-south axis" to ensure unity in resisting this penetration. The "southern cone" republics, **Argentina**, Uruguay, and Chile, resisted this, but the majority of other delegates agreed to a generalized agreement, though this was someway short of the quasi-alliance sought by Berle and Secretary of State **Cordell Hull**. The agreement was contained in the **Lima Declaration** issued on 24 December. *See also* GOOD NEIGHBOR POLICY.

LIMA DECLARATION (1938). Issued by the **Lima Conference** on 24 December 1938, the declaration was a generalized statement of solidarity among the American republics and contained a fairly weak commitment to consult in the event of a threat to "the peace, security, or territorial integrity" of any signatory. Opposition to foreign intervention (by implication from outside the hemisphere) was affirmed. It was some way short of the measures the United States hoped for, which were intended to allow the United States to coordinate, and thereby control, the relations of the republics of **Latin America** with the **Axis** powers. *See also* HAVANA, ACT OF; PANAMA DECLARATION.

LINDBERGH, CHARLES (1902–1974). Aviator Charles Lindbergh achieved fame on 25 May 1927 as the first person to fly solo across the Atlantic Ocean. Lindbergh toured Central America from December 1927 to February 1928 to promote goodwill between the United States and the republics. In **Mexico**, he met Anne Morrow, daughter of ambassador **Dwight Morrow**, and they later married. They were in the news in 1932 because of the kidnapping and murder of their baby son.

After moving to England in 1935, Lindbergh visited **Germany** a number of times. He was involved in testing aircraft for the German air force and received a medal from Nazi leader Hermann Göring. He returned to the United States in 1939.

Lindbergh emerged as a prominent spokesman for **isolationism** during **World War II**. In the summer of 1940, he voiced his opinion that **Great Britain** would be defeated. He had been very impressed with German air power and believed the United States would be best served by conserving its resources for its own defense. He also argued that it did not matter to the United States which country was victorious in Europe. Lindbergh was the most popular spokesperson for the **America First Committee**, but he made some anti-Semitic remarks that somewhat tarnished his image. After the United States entered the war, he flew some combat missions in the Pacific and retired as a colonel. *See also* SMITH, TRUMAN.

LIPPMANN, WALTER (1889–1974). Educated at Harvard University, journalist Walter Lippmann had a talent for lucid expression of complex ideas. His work as a propagandist in **World War I** led him to conclude the public could not understand complicated political issues, and his writings on public opinion, which have been seen as the foundation of the public relations profession, assume irrationality and partiality in the masses. Lippmann founded *New Republic* in 1914 and later wrote for the *New York World* (1921–31) and *Herald Tribune* (from 1931). During World War I, he became secretary of the **Inquiry**, charged with preparing the postwar U.S. negotiating position. However, he broke with President **Woodrow Wilson** at the end of the war, believing that plans for self-determination of peoples as promised in the **Fourteen Points** would lead to chaos in Central and Eastern Europe. During the 1930s, Lippmann responded to the rise of fascism with the idea of a Western alliance built around U.S.–British solidarity. He supported moves toward **collective security** in **World War II**. After the war, he opposed the policy of containment and instead recommended consolidating an Atlantic community.

LITVINOV AGREEMENT (1933). The first major foreign policy initiative of President **Franklin D. Roosevelt** was recognition of the **Union of Soviet Socialist Republics** (USSR) in 1933. After opening contacts through the informal intermediary activities of **William C. Bullitt**, an agreement was negotiated with the Soviet foreign commissar, Maxim Litvinov, in November 1933. Under the Litvinov Agreement, the United States recognized the Soviet government in return for an agreement that neither country would conduct propaganda in the other, or work to undermine its governmental system. Roosevelt disarmed potential criticism from religious groups by getting Litvinov to agree that Americans in the USSR would have religious freedom. The difficult issue of the repayment of **war debts** incurred by **Russia**'s tsarist and Kerensky regimes was left for future negotiation, though a start was made with a Soviet pledge that they would pay between $70 million and $150 million.

The rationale for recognizing the Soviet Union was pragmatic. Some American business leaders, including Armand Hammer, **Henry Ford**, and **Averell Harriman**, were already doing business in the USSR, and in the context of the Great Depression, many entrepreneurs saw great potential for future business with a rapidly industrializing state largely unaffected by the world economic downturn.

There were also strategic calculations: the Soviet Union might be a useful partner in restraining **Japan**'s expansion in East Asia. Bullitt was appointed first U.S. ambassador to the USSR. As it turned out, little expansion of **trade** happened, and the Soviet Union failed to keep its side of the bargain with regard to curtailing espionage activities in the United States and covert support for communist infiltration of the U.S. labor movement. The debts were not repaid. *See also* COMMUNIST PARTY OF THE UNITED STATES; RUSSIAN REVOLUTIONS; SMITH ACT.

LLOYD GEORGE, DAVID (1863–1945). Liberal politician David Lloyd George became prime minister of **Great Britain** in 1916 after criticism of the conduct of **World War I** undermined Prime Minister Herbert Asquith. Lloyd George prosecuted the war effort with greater vigor and centralized planning in the hands of the war cabinet. At the 1919 **Paris Peace Conference**, he considered the French delegation to be too severe in its attitude to a postwar settlement but supported the punitive **reparations** payments that were eventually agreed. He thought the **Fourteen Points** outlined by President **Woodrow Wilson** were naïve and based on an unrealistic assessment of the international political environment. Lloyd George's coalition government fell in 1922, after the Conservative Party withdrew its support.

LOCARNO, TREATY OF (1925). Negotiated in Geneva on 5–16 October 1925 and signed in London on 1 December 1925, the Locarno Treaty was a series of agreements. The first guaranteed the common borders of **Germany**, Belgium, and **France**, as already laid down by the **Treaty of Versailles**. The Rhineland was declared a neutral zone, with Germany agreeing to seek border changes by arbitration only. Additional mechanisms were created to mediate disputes between France, Germany, **Poland**, and Czechoslovakia, though these were not designed to nullify the authority of the **League of Nations** or the Treaty of Versailles. Most importantly, the German Weimar Republic avoided the same kind of recognition of the permanence of the Versailles German frontiers in the east that they agreed to for those in the west. Nonetheless, the agreements paved the way for Germany to join the League in 1926. Optimistically regarded as an important safeguard for world peace, the treaties, like the 1928 **Kellogg–Briand Pact**, were disregarded by **Adolf Hitler** in the 1930s.

LODGE, HENRY CABOT (1850–1924). A U.S. senator for Massachusetts (1893–1924), Henry Cabot Lodge was a conservative Republican who helped draft the Organic Act of the **Philippines** (1902) and served as a close advisor to President **Theodore Roosevelt**. Lodge opposed many of the domestic policies of President **Woodrow Wilson** but supported the temporary centralization of economic and political authority by the executive during **World War I**. Lodge's anger at Wilson's partisan campaign tactics during the 1918 congressional midterm elections and the president's refusal to invite any senior Republicans to join the U.S. delegation to the 1919 **Paris Peace Conference** caused a rift that was to have a lasting impact on U.S. foreign policy. Congress reverted to Republican control after 1918, and Lodge, now chair of the **Senate Committee on Foreign Relations** (1919–24), called for changes to the **Treaty of Versailles** before Senate ratification. He argued that U.S. membership in the **League of Nations** threatened to undermine American national sovereignty.

Despite pleas from moderates of both parties that Wilson accept a compromise, the president believed the proposed **Lodge reservations** weakened U.S. commitment to international cooperation and the future authority and credibility of the League. Wilson also insisted he could not honorably return to Europe to present these new conditions to other signatory powers. He instructed his supporters to vote the treaty down when eight of the reservations were added in February and March 1920. Despite his disdain for the president, Lodge showed, at least in private, some willingness to compromise and believed that the row over League membership could have been avoided had Wilson taken a bipartisan delegation to Paris or kept Congress informed during negotiations.

The battle over the League ruined Wilson's career but also tainted Lodge's. Though probably the best-known Republican in the country by 1920, he was too controversial to be seriously considered as a candidate for the party's presidential nomination. His authority quickly began to erode. As chair of the 1920 Republican convention, he failed to impose order on the delegates or to prevent **Calvin**

Coolidge's nomination for the vice presidency. Lodge was also unable to control Republican President **Warren G. Harding**, despite rumors that he had led a cabal which conspired to place Harding in the White House as a Senate puppet.

Lodge's prestige still enabled him to lead Senate debates over the **Knox–Porter Resolution** (1921), introduce the **Thomson–Urrutia Treaty** (1921), and exercise influence at the 1921 **Naval Disarmament Conference** in Washington, D.C., but he lost clashes with Harding over cabinet appointments and cash bonuses for war veterans. The president also discounted Lodge's opposition to U.S. membership in the **World Court**. By the time of his death, Lodge had published several biographies of leading American historical figures such as Daniel Webster and Alexander Hamilton. *See also* HITCHCOCK RESERVATIONS; ROUND ROBIN.

LODGE RESERVATIONS. The Lodge reservations were a series of 14 proposals put forward by Senator **Henry Cabot Lodge** as amendments to the **Treaty of Versailles** which had been concluded on 28 June 1919 at the **Paris Peace Conference**. They included a stipulation that Congress would retain its right to declare war or withhold such declaration, as granted under Article I of the U.S. Constitution, and demanded written assurance that the **Monroe Doctrine** would continue to be "interpreted by the United States alone." Other reservations gave Congress the right, by concurrent resolution, to terminate U.S. membership at any time and the right to ignore any commitment made by **League of Nations** members to arms limitation if that commitment was considered by Congress to threaten American security or harm its long-term interests. Lodge also proposed that the United States demand retention of "full liberty of action" in matters affecting relations between **China** and **Japan**. President **Woodrow Wilson**, in a letter to Senator **Gilbert M. Hitchcock**, argued that Lodge's proposals did not "provide for ratification but, rather, for nullification of the treaty." He urged that "all true friends of the treaty will refuse to support the Lodge resolution."

The Lodge reservations were approved by the **Senate Committee on Foreign Relations** on 6 November 1919. In accordance with Wilson's instructions, Democratic senators voted against them, and on 19 November the Senate rejected the treaty with reservations and then the treaty with no reservations. On 10 February 1920, the committee again approved the treaty with the reservations. Wilson repeated his opposition, and this, and the votes of the **Irreconcilables**, was enough to prevent the treaty gaining the necessary two-thirds majority. The vote on 19 March 1920 was 49–35.

LONDON CHARTER (1945). On 8 August 1945, the charter of the **International Military Tribunal** was issued in London. The London Charter (also known as the Nuremberg Charter) declared that three categories of crimes committed by the European **Axis** powers during **World War II** would be tried: war crimes, crimes against peace, and crimes against humanity. Representing the United States on the drafting body, the **European Advisory Commission**, was **Robert H. Jackson**. The initial authority for the declaration derived from a Statement on Atrocities issued by the 1943 **Moscow Conference**. The procedures for the Nuremberg trials were laid down. There would be trial before judges rather than a jury, and hearsay evidence would be allowed. Obedience to orders would not necessarily be allowed as mitigation for punishment. Defendants would be allowed to cross-examine witnesses and would have the right of appeal to the Allied Control Council.

LONDON ECONOMIC CONFERENCE (1933). President **Herbert Hoover** believed that stabilizing international currencies would be a significant step toward dealing with the Great Depression. He induced **Franklin D. Roosevelt**, his victorious opponent in the 1932 election, to agree that the United States would attend the World Monetary and Economic Conference that he had arranged to take place in London to attempt this. Roosevelt believed that the solution to the problem was domestic, but he sent Secretary of State **Cordell Hull** and Senator **Key Pittman** to join delegates from 64 nations for the conference held 12 June–24 July.

Abandonment of the **gold standard** had led to wild currency fluctuations that made international commerce so risky and unpredictable that many businesses had simply abandoned such **trade**. The conference was supposed also to address the issue of **war debt** payments after the end of the **Hoover moratorium** and to seek to reduce trade barriers. Pittman and Hull soon quarreled. Pittman, from a silver-producing state, did not support the gold standard, and Hull was only interested in **tariff** reduction. Roosevelt dispatched **Raymond Moley** to settle their differences, but then on 3 July sent his "bombshell" telegram rejecting any scheme for fixing currency rates until a majority of nations had stable, balanced budgets. International measures would thus only follow domestic, national ones. The conference collapsed in disarray. There was to be no currency stabilization arrangement, apart from informal arrangements in 1935 regarding valuation by **Great Britain**, the United States, and **France**, until the **Bretton Woods** agreements in 1944.

LONDON NAVAL DISARMAMENT CONFERENCE (1930). After the failure of the 1927 **Naval Disarmament Conference** at Geneva, the naval building race continued, and U.S. relations with **Great Britain** deteriorated. To improve matters, the prime minister of Great Britain, Ramsay MacDonald, visited Washington, D.C., in the fall of 1929. At the **Rapidan Conference**, his suggestion of further naval talks met with the approval of President **Herbert Hoover**, and MacDonald invited the other Big Five powers (**Japan**, **France**, Italy, and the United States) to London.

The conference lasted from 22 January to 22 April. The U.S. delegation was led by Secretary of State **Henry Stimson** and included Secretary of the Navy **Charles Adams** and two senators, Joseph Robinson, a Democrat, and David Reed, a Republican, together with Ambassadors **Charles Dawes** and **Dwight Morrow**. As at Geneva, the discussions were difficult. France and Italy resented the lower ratios they had been given at the 1921 **Naval Disarmament Conference** in Washington, D.C., and refused to agree to new ratios. Agreement was reached on new rules for submarine warfare. The ratios for capital ships belonging to Japan, Britain, and the United States were retained and extended to cover heavy cruisers, newly defined as carrying guns above 6.1 inches. There was to be a six-year holiday in capital ship building.

The arrangements were generally greeted favorably in the United States as a small step toward **disarmament**. Some naval officers claimed it weakened the ability of the United States to defend the **Philippines** against Japan. Hoover had wished for more but recommended acceptance of the London agreement to the Senate. In actuality, the treaty was more about arms control than disarmament, as some of the limits were set above current tonnage. The United States was able to build some additional ships under the treaty, which provided some employment during the Great Depression.

Senators who were inclined to **isolationism** were suspicious of any presidential agreement and demanded to see all the conference papers to be sure there were no secret agreements. Hoover refused, as **Warren G. Harding** had done in 1922, but was able to satisfy the Senate that there were no such agreements. Senators still inserted a clause in their approval stating they were not bound by any secret agreement. The debate reflected isolationist aversion to any international commitment, even one designed to lessen the dangers of war, because of the implication that it somehow committed the United States to future actions. The principal concern of senators remained what it had been at the time of the debate on **League of Nations** membership: that nothing should restrict the freedom of action of the Senate in overseeing foreign policy matters.

LONDON NAVAL DISARMAMENT CONFERENCE (1935–1936). In 1934, **Japan** indicated its intention to withdraw from the naval disarmament arrangements made at the 1921 **Naval Disarmament Conference** in Washington, D.C., and the 1930 **London Naval Disarmament Conference**. The provisions made at Washington and extended at London were anyway due to expire in 1936. The United States, **Great Britain**, and Japan met in London for the second London Naval Conference from 9 December 1935 to 25 March 1936. They were unable to reach agreement when Japan demanded that it should be given parity in any new agreement with the United States and Britain. Japan left the conference on 15 January 1936. The United States and Britain together with **France** then made a new naval treaty in which the size of warships was restricted, though their numbers were no longer regulated. Rules regarding submarine warfare made at the 1930 London Conference were confirmed.

LONDON NAVAL TREATY (1936). *See* LONDON NAVAL DISARMAMENT CONFERENCE (1935–1936).

LONG, BRECKINRIDGE (1881–1958). Lawyer Breckinridge Long of Missouri became third assistant secretary of state in 1917 during

President **Woodrow Wilson**'s administration. He lost two election bids for the U.S. Senate in 1920 and 1922. He was appointed U.S. ambassador to Italy (1933–36) by President **Franklin D. Roosevelt**. After returning to the United States, he worked again in the State Department, assuming responsibility for immigrant visas. Long is considered by many historians to have held strong anti-Semitic views and to have deliberately obstructed Jewish immigration during **World War II**. He retired in 1944.

LUCE, CLARE BOOTHE (1903–1987). In 1930, writer Clare Boothe became an editorial assistant at *Vogue* magazine and was managing editor of *Vanity Fair* (1931–34). In 1935, she married her second husband, publisher **Henry Luce**. She wrote a number of successful plays, including *The Women* (1936) and *Kiss the Boys Goodbye* (1938). In 1940, she reported for her husband's *Life* magazine from Western Europe and **Great Britain**. In 1941, she visited **China** with her husband. During **World War II**, she went to Africa, China, India, and Burma as a war journalist. She interviewed British General Harold Alexander in the Middle East and **Chiang Kai-shek** and General **Joseph Stilwell** in China.

Clare Boothe Luce was elected to the U.S. House of Representatives (R-Conn.) in 1942. Her maiden speech was an attack on **Henry Wallace**'s **internationalist** approach to foreign policy. She frequently spoke out against President **Franklin D. Roosevelt**'s foreign policy and in favor of desegregation of the armed forces. In favor with Republican Party **isolationists**, she was given a position on the Military Affairs Committee.

In 1946, Luce became a Roman Catholic and retired from Congress. She returned to writing and became well-known as a strident anticommunist. She was ambassador to Italy (1953–57), the first woman to be U.S. ambassador to a major country, and briefly ambassador to **Brazil** (1959). Luce also served on the president's Foreign Intelligence Advisory Board (1981–83).

LUCE, HENRY (1898–1967). Publisher Henry Luce was born in **China**, the son of missionaries. He was educated in China, **Great Britain**, and at Yale University. Luce then became a journalist and with Briton Hadden founded the newsmagazine *Time*, first published in 1923. Luce was business manager and, when Hadden died in 1929, became editor in chief. *Time* built up a circulation of 3 million readers. Luce started the business magazine *Fortune* in 1930 and the illustrated weekly *Life* in 1936. He produced the influential *March of Time* series of newsreels for cinema, with a radio version as well. Time, Inc., was the largest magazine publisher in the world by the 1950s.

Luce was an influential member of the Republican Party and a committed anticommunist. He was a central member of the China lobby, and used his journals to garner U.S. support for the nationalist regime of **Chiang Kai-shek**. In particular, he was responsible for projecting positive images of Chiang and his wife Soong Mei-ling. Harboring ambitions to be a secretary of state, Luce wrote the **American Century** editorial for *Life* published on 7 February 1941, setting out his vision of an assertive U.S. foreign policy. *See also* LUCE, CLARE BOOTHE.

LUDLOW AMENDMENT. In January 1938, **Louis Ludlow** introduced into the U.S. House of Representatives a proposal for an amendment to the U.S. Constitution seeking to limit presidential freedom of action in foreign policy even further than the **Neutrality Acts**. It would have required a national referendum before any declaration of war. Ludlow had been advocating this since 1935, but it had failed even to be reported out from the House Judiciary Committee. Even members of Congress who favored restraining President **Franklin D. Roosevelt** did not wish to limit their own power over the declaration of war in this manner. After public enthusiasm for Ludlow's book *Hell or Heaven*, the proposal came before the full Congress, but in January 1938 it was narrowly defeated in the House of Representatives, 209–188. *See also UNITED STATES V. CURTISS–WRIGHT EXPORT CORPORATION.*

LUDLOW, LOUIS (1873–1950). Louis Ludlow (D-Ind.) served in the U.S. House of Representatives in 1928–48 and introduced a war referendum amendment for the U.S. Constitution in 1935. It was not reported out of the House Judiciary Committee. His book *Hell or Heaven* (1937) gained 75 percent public support for the **Ludlow Amendment**, which required a national referendum before any declaration of war, but it was defeated in Congress in January 1938. Ludlow worked on other measures, including arms limitations, a proposal for a referendum on peacetime conscription, and a resolution to mediate the European conflict. Following **World War II**, Ludlow advocated an international peace referendum, a ban on atomic weapons, and a cabinet-level department of peace and goodwill in the U.S. government.

LUSITANIA. A British Cunard liner, the *Lusitania* was torpedoed by a German submarine off the southern Irish coast on 7 May 1915. It sank in 18 minutes with the loss of nearly 1,200 lives, including 128 Americans. Responding to criticism of the attack, **Germany** pointed out that the *U-20*, which sank the *Lusitania*, fired only one of the two torpedoes it possessed, which left unexplained the cause of a second explosion that ripped open the ship's hull after the first torpedo struck the opposite end of the boat. They argued that the second blast was caused by secretly stockpiled ammunition destined for **Great Britain**. They also claimed that the *Lusitania* had deliberately entered an "exclusion zone" despite a warning by the German navy that "vessels flying the flag of Great Britain or any of her allies are liable to destruction in those waters" and that civilian passengers choosing to board such ships or travel such routes "do so at their own risk." The British government denied the *Lusitania* had been transporting munitions and claimed the sinking was further evidence of German "barbarity." *See also LUSITANIA* NOTES.

LUSITANIA **NOTES (1915).** The administration of President **Woodrow Wilson** responded to the loss of 128 American lives during the 7 May 1915 sinking of the Cunard liner *Lusitania* by sending a series of diplomatic messages to **Germany**. The first *Lusitania* note, drafted mainly by Wilson and Secretary of State **William Jennings Bryan**, was sent on 13 May 1915 and called for "just, prompt, and enlightened" action to prevent a repetition of the incident by ceasing attacks on commercial vessels.

Germany's response was deemed only partially satisfactory and prompted a second note on 9 June. This repeated the claim that Germany had acted illegally, and that the presence or absence of munitions on board the *Lusitania* was "irrelevant" to the U.S. argument that the safe passage on the seas of citizens from neutral countries must be respected. Secretary Bryan's resignation (June 1915) was prompted by his belief that Wilson, through this diplomatic correspondence, was using the *Lusitania* incident to lay the groundwork for the United States to enter the war on the side of the Allies.

On 21 July 1915, the president, still dissatisfied with the German government's unwillingness to abandon unrestricted submarine warfare, dispatched a third note demanding adherence to the "accepted practices of regulated warfare." He warned that a further attack by the German navy involving U.S. citizens would be regarded as "deliberately unfriendly" by Washington.

The notes were partially successful. When the sinking of the SS *Arabic* on 19 August 1915 also resulted in American casualties, Germany apologized and temporarily suspended its strategy.

– M –

MACARTHUR, DOUGLAS (1880–1964). A graduate of the U.S. Military Academy at West Point, Douglas MacArthur was commissioned an engineer in 1903 and served in Tokyo in 1905, where his father was official military observer. MacArthur served with the army in **France** during **World War I**, distinguishing himself at the second battle of the Marne (1918) and becoming the youngest divisional commander in the **American Expeditionary Force**. General MacArthur was U.S. Army chief of staff from 1930 to 1935 and was responsible for breaking up the July 1932 Bonus Army protest in Washington, D.C., with excessive force. On retirement from the post, he was seconded to command military forces in the **Philippines**.

When **Japan** attacked the Philippines in December 1941, during **World War II**, MacArthur and the U.S. forces had to retreat into the Bataan peninsula. In March 1942, he was withdrawn to Australia to take command of Allied forces in the southwest Pacific. An overbearing character with a genius for self-promotion, and little skill in handling allies, MacArthur fought a successful campaign involving island hopping and amphibious assaults in the Solomon Islands and New Guinea. He was involved in disputes over strategy with Admiral **Chester Nimitz** but secured President **Franklin D. Roosevelt**'s approval of his promised return to the Philippines. The campaign opened with the Battle of Leyte Gulf in October 1944, and fighting was still continuing in the Philippines when Japan surrendered. MacArthur presided over the official surrender ceremony on 2 September 1945 and was appointed commander of the occupation forces in Japan (1945–51). He managed the rehabilitation and reshaping of Japan in autocratic style. In 1950, he took command of **United Nations** forces in the Korean War, until dismissed by President **Harry S. Truman** in 1951.

MACHADO Y MORALES, GERARDO (1871–1939). Cuban dictator Gerardo Morales was a general in **Cuba**'s war for independence against Spain in the 1890s. An industrialist and member of the political elite, he was elected president of Cuba in 1925. He attempted to modernize the economy and diversify away from sole dependence on the sugar trade with the United States. His methods became increasingly despotic, and he gained enemies on both left and right. While emphasizing nationalistic objectives, he did not oppose U.S. investment, and it soared to $1.5 billion by 1929. When the global economic depression hit Cuba and sugar prices plummeted, aggravated by the **Smoot–Hawley tariff**, his tyranny became increasingly murderous through roving death squads. Resentments grew, and the United States came to see Machado as a liability. Newly appointed U.S. Ambassador **Sumner Welles** recommended armed intervention, but President **Franklin D. Roosevelt** would only send warships to patrol the coast. Welles encouraged Cuban veterans and army leaders to topple Machado. He was overthrown and left office on 12 August 1933, taking exile in Florida. *See also* BATISTA, FULGENCIO.

MACLEISH, ARCHIBALD (1892–1982). A Yale graduate, writer Archibald MacLeish published his first book of poetry in 1917. He served in the army in **France** in **World War I** and took part in the second Battle of the Marne in 1918. MacLeish trained as a lawyer but continued to write poetry. He was editor of *Fortune* magazine (1929–38) and won a Pulitzer Prize in 1932. Along with **John Dewey** and Lewis Mumford, MacLeish formed the League for Independent Political Action, looking for alternatives to the discredited capitalist system. In 1936, he urged the U.S. government to support the republicans in the **Spanish Civil War** and, along with Lillian Hellman, John Dos Passos, and Ernest Hemingway, sponsored a documentary film about the war, *The Spanish Earth*. His radio play *The Fall of the City* (1937) commented on fascism in Europe, attracting a wide audience in the United States.

In 1939, MacLeish was appointed librarian of Congress by President **Franklin D. Roosevelt**, though some right-wing members of Congress objected, claiming, inaccurately, that he was a communist. J. Parnell Thomas of the **House Committee Investigating Un-American Activities** coined the phrase "fellow-traveler" with reference to MacLeish. In fact, MacLeish was a liberal humanist, close to the views of Roosevelt in many ways, and suspected by those on the far left as well as those on the right. At the Library of Congress, MacLeish revived and modernized the organization. In addition, Roosevelt made him director of the Office of Facts and Figures in 1941, one of a number of propaganda agencies during **World War II**. It had little authority and was merged into the **Office of War Information** in 1942, with MacLeish becoming assistant director (1942–43).

J. Edgar Hoover, chief of the **Federal Bureau of Investigation**, thought MacLeish was appointing too many left-wingers and was suspicious of his antifascism and support for the Soviet war effort. MacLeish resigned from the Library of Congress in 1944, but Roosevelt then appointed him assistant secretary of state for cultural and public affairs (1944–45). The appointment passed in the Senate by a 43–25 vote, with 28 abstentions. His job was to promote the concept of the **United Nations** organization to the American people. On becoming president, **Harry S. Truman** terminated the post. In 1945, MacLeish headed the U.S. delegation to the first organizational meeting of the United Nations Educational, Scientific, and Cultural Organization (UNESCO) and was assistant head of the delegation to UNESCO in 1946. Retiring from public service, MacLeish became a professor of rhetoric and oratory at Harvard University in 1949. During the 1950s, he strongly defended himself and others in the face of attacks by Joseph McCarthy, writing his play *The Trojan Horse* (1952) on the subject.

MADERO, FRANCISCO (1873–1913). A liberal reformer, Francisco Madero became the president of **Mexico** in 1911, ending the 35-year rule of dictator Porfirio Diaz. Madero was overthrown on 18 February 1913 in a coup by forces loyal to General **Victoriano Huerta**. Under the terms of a deal said to have been worked out at the U.S. Embassy with the collaboration of Ambassador Henry Lane Wilson, Madero was to be sent into exile. Instead, he was seized from detention and killed on 22 February 1913.

MAGIC, OPERATION. On 23 September 1940, during **World War II**, Colonel William Friedman of the U.S. Army broke the code of **Japan**'s encryption machine **Purple**. The joint army–navy operation that followed was called Operation Magic. Its principal achievement was the decoding of Japan's diplomatic signals traffic. Three tracking stations intercepted signals between Tokyo and all Japanese embassies around the world. Magic provided information concerning Japanese intentions and activities, and reports from the Japanese embassy in Berlin supplied vital information about **Germany**'s war effort and strategy. It did not give clear indication of the **Pearl Harbor** attack in December 1941, though it did give advance warning that Japan was going to deliver an ultimatum and was going to initiate military operations. *See also* SIGNALS INTELLIGENCE; ULTRA-MAGIC DEAL.

MAKE EUROPE PAY WAR DEBTS COMMITTEE. *See* ISLANDS FOR WAR DEBTS COMMITTEE.

MANCHURIAN CRISIS (1931–1932). On 18 September 1931, soldiers of **Japan**'s Kwantung army in Manchuria who were garrisoning the railway outside the capital, Mukden, claimed to have confronted some Chinese saboteurs. The Kwantung army had long sought to take control of Manchuria from **China**. The province was important as a barrier against Soviet communism and as a source for important raw materials such as coal and iron. Over half of all Japanese foreign investments were in the province. The United States had recognized Japan's prominence there through the 1908 Root–Takahira and 1917 **Lansing–Ishii** agreements.

Secretary of State **Henry Stimson** regarded the Japanese action in the Mukden Incident as an attack on the **open door policy** and a breach of the agreements reached at the 1921 **Naval Disarmament Conference** in Washington, D.C., but did not want the United States to get involved. On 24 September, he urged Japan and China to cease hostilities. The **League of Nations**, with American observer **Prentiss Gilbert** present, passed resolutions for peace and sent a commission under Lord Lytton. The Japanese seized all of Manchuria in a few months and in February 1932 created a puppet state called Manchukuo, with the last Chinese emperor, Pu Yi, as its ruler. Because of the danger of war, President **Herbert Hoover** rejected the idea of economic sanctions, though Japan's dependence on U.S. oil would have made them effective. Instead, the United States followed a policy of nonrecognition of Manchukuo. This **Stimson Doctrine** (7 January 1932) was met with the **Shanghai Incident**: a Japanese attack on Shanghai, where there were many foreigners, including U.S. troops.

Stimson restated the policy in an open letter to Senator **William E. Borah** on 23 February. The letter condemned the breach of the open door and the **Kellogg–Briand Pact** and threatened an increase in U.S. naval strength in the Pacific. The Japanese did not remain in Shanghai but did entrench themselves in Manchuria. After the Lytton Commission mildly condemned Japan's actions, it withdrew from the League of Nations. Stimson's policy of nonrecognition achieved nothing, but the United States had neither the power nor will to act in the region and did not wish to cooperate too closely with the League.

MANHATTAN PROJECT. During **World War II**, the secret development of the **atomic bomb** was known as the Manhattan Project. Physicist **Albert Einstein** wrote to President **Franklin D. Roosevelt** on 11 October 1939 warning that **Germany** could produce an atomic bomb using nuclear fission in the foreseeable future. Roosevelt set up a commission, which learned of progress being made in **Great Britain**, and in December 1941 it recommended a full-scale American effort. The British scientists were short of resources and agreed to merge their research and relocate to the United States. With them came a number of refugee scientists from occupied Europe, making this truly an international project.

A large community of workers on the project, "the Manhattan Engineering District," was established at Oak Ridge, Tennessee, in August 1942. The project was initially administered by the Office of Scientific Research and Development under **Vannevar Bush** but was then transferred to the War Department and put under the command of Colonel (later Lieutenant General) **Leslie Groves**. Other facilities were established at Los Alamos, New Mexico, developing the bomb itself under the scientific leadership of **J. Robert Oppenheimer**, and at Hanford, Washington, exploring the manufacture of plutonium, a synthetic alternative to uranium. At Oak Ridge, the main work on separating out sufficient quantities of Uranium 235 was carried out.

In December 1942, **Enrico Fermi** successfully separated out plutonium at the University of Chicago. The project culminated in the detonation of the first atomic weapon in the Trinity Test (16 July 1945) and the dropping of the uranium bomb on **Hiroshima** (6 August 1945) and the plutonium bomb on **Nagasaki** (9 August 1945). The project cost $2 million and involved over 600,000 people. It was a triumph not only of applied science but also engineering, and could only have been done at this time in the United States, given the resources and expertise required. *See also* COMPTON, ARTHUR HOLLY; CONANT, JAMES BRYANT.

MARCO POLO BRIDGE INCIDENT (1937). *See* SINO–JAPANESE WAR.

MARSHALL, GEORGE CATLETT (1880–1959). A graduate of the Virginia Military Institute in 1901, George C. Marshall fought in **France** in **World War I** and was chief of operations, U.S. First Army, at the Battle of St. Mihiel (13–18 September 1918). After serving as chief of staff to General **John Pershing** (1921–24), Marshall served three years in **China** (1924–27). Marshall trained what would be the army's future high command at Fort Benning Infantry School, Georgia, where he was assistant commandant (1927–32), and wrote the infantry training manual that was to be used in **World War II**. After a number of field commands, he became a staff officer in the War Department in July 1939.

As U.S. Army chief of staff (1939–45), Marshall was primarily responsible for the organization of U.S. military efforts during World War II. He raised the U.S. Army personnel from 200,000 to more than 8.5 million, the largest army in U.S. history. Marshall was a formidable administrator, with a strong work ethic and a formal, unbending personality. Prime Minister **Winston Churchill** of **Great Britain** called him "the true organizer of victory." President **Frank-**

lin D. **Roosevelt** considered him for the command of Operation **Overlord** but decided he could not do without him in Washington, D.C. Marshall participated in all the major wartime international conferences. He was promoted to general of the army in December 1944. In December 1945, he went on a diplomatic mission to China to try to end the civil war.

Marshall, secretary of state from 16 January 1947 to 7 January 1949, was most famous for his initiative that led to the Marshall Plan of economic aid to Western Europe. He was also instrumental in the creation of the North Atlantic Treaty Organization and the organization of the Berlin airlift. He later served as secretary of defense (1950–51). He received the Nobel Prize for Peace in 1951 for the creation of the Marshall Plan.

MASTER LEND-LEASE AGREEMENTS (1942). After the United States entered **World War II**, agreements were reached for the effective pooling of resources between the Allies. On 23 February 1942, the Master Mutual **Lend-Lease** Agreement was signed by the United States, **Great Britain**, Australia, and New Zealand. Subsequently, master agreements were concluded with 11 other Allied nations. Under the agreements, the United States was the main supplier of materials, though it was also a recipient, notably of raw materials, bases, and services, under "reverse lend-lease." As a result of concern about the **war debts** problems that followed **World War I**, the agreements provided that the arrangements "shall be such as not to burden commerce between the two countries but to promote mutually advantageous economic relations between them and the betterment of worldwide economic matters."

The agreements also noted that the signatories would "join with the United States in working toward some of the economic conditions which are a prerequisite to a secure peace." Even at this stage of the war, U.S. policy makers were seeking to gain commitments from their Allies with regard to the establishment of the American concept of a liberal world economic order. In return for the materials it needed, Britain was in effect required to endorse a global **open door policy** constituting a multilateral world economic order, with its system of imperial trade preferences opened up. Moreover the Master Lend-Lease Agreement imposed strict limits on the accumulation in London of foreign exchange and gold. This would seriously affect Britain's prospects for postwar economic recovery, which depended on imports of raw materials and food, let alone its ability to be a genuine **trade** rival of the United States. The stringency of this was lessened somewhat in arrangements made at the 1944 **Bretton Woods Conference** that allowed for some trade restrictions should a crisis develop in the British economy.

The master agreement with the **Union of Soviet Socialist Republics** (USSR) was signed on 11 June 1942, supplementing the arrangements entered into in the supply protocol agreed by **Averell Harriman** at the 1941 **Moscow Conference**. In return for U.S. supplies, the Soviet Union agreed that articles or information would not be transferred to another state without agreement of the U.S. president. The agreement was to continue until a date agreed on by the parties, with unconsumed materials to be returned after the war, if desired by the supplier. The termination of Lend-Lease shipments immediately after the war with **Japan** ended was to be a discordant end to a successful agreement. *See also* CROWLEY, LEO T.

MATTHEWS, HARRISON FREEMAN (1899–1986). A graduate of Princeton University and the École Libre des Sciences Politiques in Paris, Freeman Matthews entered the Foreign Service in 1924 and served in Hungary (1924–26) and Colombia (1926–29). He was assistant chief of the State Department Division of Latin American Affairs during the transformation of U.S. policy to **Latin America** following the **Clark Memorandum**, and he was first secretary in the embassy in **Cuba** (1933–37), first secretary in the embassy in **France** (1937–1941), and temporarily ambassador to Spain (1939). During **World War II**, he was counselor in the embassy in London (1941–43), then chief of the State Department Division of European Affairs (1943–44). It was renamed Office of European Affairs in 1944, with Matthews as director (1944–47). In 1945, he acted as State Department representative on the Combined Civil Affairs Commission of the **Combined Chiefs of Staff**. After the war, Matthews was ambassador to Sweden (1947–50), the Netherlands (1953–57), and Austria (1957–62), and deputy undersecretary of state (1950–53).

MCCLOY, JOHN J. (1895–1989). Lawyer and diplomat John Mc-Cloy had an interest in international finance. He traveled extensively in Europe in the 1920s, and believed the demand for **reparations** from **Germany** to be unwise and unfair. He developed extensive contacts in Nazi Germany in the 1930s. McCloy was made assistant secretary for war in 1941. He was given responsibility for the issue of Japanese American residents on the west coast and was instrumental in formulating the policy of removal and internment. After the war, McCloy became president of the **World Bank** (1947–49). In 1949, he replaced **Lucius Clay** as high commissioner for Germany (1949–53) and was responsible for the release of Alfred Krupp and other German industrialists imprisoned for their association with Nazi crimes. He was chair of Chase Manhattan Bank (1953–60) and the Ford Foundation (1958–65), and he served on the Warren Commission investigating the assassination of President John F. Kennedy.

MCCORMICK, ANNE O'HARE (c. 1882–1954). Born in **Great Britain** and educated in the United States, Anne O'Hare McCormick was associate editor for the *Catholic Universe Bulletin*. She married an importer, Francis McCormick, and accompanied him on many journeys abroad. In 1921, she volunteered to be a freelance contributor of foreign news stories for the *New York Times*. She provided the first detailed reports from Italy of the rise of Benito Mussolini and the Fascist movement. She interviewed many leading figures, including **Germany**'s leader **Adolf Hitler**, **Josef Stalin** of the **Union of Soviet Socialist Republics**, Prime Minister **Winston S. Churchill** of **Great Britain**, Popes Pius XI and Pius XII, and President **Franklin D. Roosevelt**. In 1936, McCormick became the first woman appointed to the editorial board of the *New York Times*, and in 1937 she won a Pulitzer Prize for her dispatches from Europe. She was the first woman to win this honor and was now one of the country's leading foreign correspondents. In 1939, she reported from 13 countries as the crises leading to **World War II** mounted. During the war, she served on the **Advisory Committee on Postwar Foreign Policy**. After the war, she was a member of the U.S. delegation to the first United Nations Educational, Scientific, and Cultural Organization (UNESCO) conference. She continued as an active journalist until her death.

MCCOY, FRANK ROSS (1874–1954). A West Point graduate, Frank McCoy began his career under **Leonard Wood** in **Cuba** in the Spanish–American War (1898) and worked with Wood in Cuba after the war to establish democratic reforms. He then served in the **Philippines** during the Filipino insurgency. McCoy was part of a group called "the Family," which gathered in a house on H Street in Washington, D.C., before **World War I** and were united by enthusiasm for the interventionist imperialist rhetoric of **Theodore Roosevelt**. Many rose to prominent positions in the foreign policy hierarchy, most notably **Joseph C. Grew** and Willard Straight. McCoy saw further service in **Mexico**, before distinguishing himself in **France** in World War I. He rose to the rank of major general.

McCoy had a long career as a roving troubleshooter for presidents from Theodore Roosevelt to **Herbert Hoover**. He undertook postwar missions in Turkey, Armenia, and the Philippines. Most notably, he was given the task of supervising the 1928 elections in **Nicaragua**. His legislation to ensure free and fair elections (known as *la ley McCoy*) was voted down by the Nicaraguan Congress but implemented by executive order of President **Adolfo Diaz** on 21 March 1928. He and **Henry Stimson** organized the Nicaraguan National Guard after the 1927 **Peace of Tipitapa**.

McCoy served on the **League of Nations** Lytton Commission investigating the 1931 **Manchurian Crisis**. He was involved in mediating between Bolivia and Paraguay during the **Chaco War**. He was president of the pro-interventionist Foreign Policy Association before **World War II** and was appointed by his close friend Stimson to serve on the commission investigating the attack on **Pearl Harbor**. His final appointment was as chair of the Far Eastern Commission (1945–49), set up after World War II to decide the future of **Japan**.

MCCUMBER, PORTER JAMES (1858–1933). Lawyer Porter McCumber, a U.S. senator (R-N.D.) from 1899 to 1923, was co-author of the 1922 **Fordney–McCumber Act** which significantly raised U.S. **tariff** levels. He was appointed to the International Joint Commission by President **Calvin Coolidge** in 1925 to adjudicate disputes arising from shared water boundaries between the United States and Canada.

MCNUTT, PAUL VORIES (1891–1955). Paul McNutt graduated from Indiana University, where he was a friend of **Wendell Willkie**'s. McNutt gained a degree at Harvard Law School in 1916 and joined the U.S. Army in 1917 but did not serve in **France**. In 1919, he began teaching at Indiana Law School. He opposed **pacifism** and as dean of the school supported compulsory military training on campus. In 1928–29, he was national commander of the American Legion. In 1932, he was elected governor of Indiana as a Democrat. He legalized beer sales in advance of the repeal of Prohibition, expanded welfare reform, and was prepared to use the national guard against striking miners.

President **Franklin D. Roosevelt** rewarded McNutt for his support in the 1936 election by appointing him high commissioner to the **Philippines**. The role was largely ceremonial, but McNutt acted to get Jewish refugees from Europe admitted when they were unable to enter the United States. He was skeptical about the speed of the movement toward independence set out under the 1934 **Tydings–McDuffie Act**, believing the Philippines could not defend themselves.

McNutt returned to the United States in 1939 to head the Federal Security Administration, which handled social security matters. He was ambitious to run for president in 1940 but was prevented by Roosevelt's decision to run for a third term. He was passed over as vice presidential candidate in favor of the liberal **Henry Wallace**. McNutt was given responsibility for defense-related health and safety programs, and in 1942 he became head of the War Manpower Commission as well. In May 1942, the War Research Service, a secret part of the Federal Security Administration, undertook research into biological warfare. It was abolished in 1944. At end of **World War II**, McNutt returned to the Philippines as high commissioner. In 1946–47, he was the first U.S. ambassador to the republic of the Philippines. He subsequently chaired the Philippine–American Trade Council.

MELLON, ANDREW WILLIAM (1855–1937). Multimillionaire Andrew Mellon was the longest-serving secretary of the treasury in American history (1921–32). His conservative fiscal policies, emphasizing economy in government and sharply reduced tax rates, enabled him to drastically reduce the national debt. With Chancellor of the Exchequer Stanley Baldwin, Mellon negotiated the rescheduling of **war debts** incurred during **World War I** by **Great Britain**. An agreement reached on 19 January 1923 allowed Britain's $4.5 billion war debt to be paid off in installments over 62 years. Interest rates were set at 3 percent for the first 10 years and 3.5 percent thereafter. These terms ignored the much tougher conditions set out by Congress in the 1922 Debt Refunding Act, which Mellon and President **Warren G. Harding** considered too stringent. Mellon subsequently presided over the refunding of the war debts of other European nations.

Mellon's Revenue Acts during the 1920s reduced taxation rates and took many low-income Americans out of the tax system altogether, but some criticized his policies for increasing the unequal distribution of wealth in the United States. After the stock market crash of October 1929, Mellon came under attack for refusing to alter his conservative attitudes to fiscal management, which critics argued had worsened the effects of the Great Depression for ordinary Americans. Mellon briefly served as ambassador to Great Britain (1932–33).

MERCHANT MARINE ACT (1936). This act established the U.S. Maritime Commission and set targets for the size of the merchant marine, which was to be capable of carrying all domestic waterborne commerce and a substantial proportion of foreign commerce. Its vessels should be American and its crews properly trained. It was to be available as a naval auxiliary in time of war. Subsidies were provided to help the merchant marine compete with foreign counterparts. *See also* LIBERTY SHIPS.

THE MERCHANTS OF DEATH. A best-seller by **Helmuth Engelbrecht** and **Frank Hanighen** published in 1934, *The Merchants of Death* was a detailed exposé of the international armaments trade. It assembled a mass of data to demonstrate the malign influence of munitions manufacturers on the outbreak of **World War I**. Going beyond the generalizations of **disarmament** advocates who claimed that arms races by their nature produced conflict, it pointed the finger directly at specific agencies that, it claimed, had had an interest in provoking and maintaining the war. Its main targets were European companies like Krupps of **Germany** and Vickers of **Great Britain**. It did not find U.S. manufacturers among the most culpable. Along with more sensationalistic works, like George Seldes's *Iron, Blood, and Profits*, it fit in with a developing public mood that combined distaste for big business with an acceptance of **devil theories** about U.S. entry into the war. It influenced the establishment of the **Nye Committee** and passage of the **Neutrality Acts**. See also MORGAN, JOHN PIERPONT.

MESSERSMITH, GEORGE STRAUSSER (1883–1960). A graduate of Delaware State College, George Messersmith joined the consular service in 1915, beginning with a posting at Fort Erie. After service at Curaçao and Antwerp, he was consul general at Antwerp (1926–27), Buenos Aires (1929), and Berlin (1930–34). In **Germany**, his hostility to **Adolf Hitler**'s party earned him the nickname "terror of Nazi Germany." In the State Department, the length of his missives earned him the name "Forty-page George." Messersmith was a perceptive reporter on economic and political affairs, and this brought his transfer from purely consular duties. Messersmith was minister to Austria (1934–37) and then worked in the State Department as assistant secretary of state for departmental administration, until becoming ambassador to **Cuba** in 1940. He was moved to **Mexico** as ambassador in 1942 and to **Argentina** in 1946. The fallout from the Blue Book controversy involving **Spruille Braden**, and his own disagreements with Braden, brought an end to his ambassadorship in 1947. Messersmith was unusual among U.S. diplomats of the period for his non-Ivy League background and for having risen through the consular service.

MEXICAN OIL EXPROPRIATION CONTROVERSY (1938–1941). In 1938, when U.S. oil companies operating in **Mexico** were resisting strikes by workers demanding higher wages, Mexican president Lázaro Cárdenas intervened and nationalized the property of all foreign oil companies. Secretary of State **Cordell Hull** and professional diplomats in Mexico City responded toughly. This did not amount to military intervention, which had been publicly disowned at the 1936 **Buenos Aires Conference**, but involved economic coercion. U.S. purchases of Mexican silver would be reduced. Oil companies refused to sell equipment to Mexico or carry Mexican oil in their tankers. Standard Oil of New Jersey spread propaganda that Cárdenas was a communist.

However, the ambassador to Mexico, **Josephus Daniels**, convinced President **Franklin D. Roosevelt** that Cárdenas was a committed Democrat engaged in New Deal–style reforms. Roosevelt agreed to merely seek compensation. Increasing demand for Mexican oil from the **Axis** powers gave a further incentive to reach a settlement that would improve relations with Mexico, and this became more imperative as the United States edged closer to involvement in **World War II**. Negotiations lasted until 1941. The deal finally struck involved concessions on both sides and signaled a new, more mature U.S.–Mexican relationship. The United States conceded that Mexico owned the raw materials on its own territory, and Mexico agreed to pay for the property that had been expropriated. The **Export-Import Bank** gave a $30 million loan. Mexico agreed in 1944 to pay $24 million plus 3 percent interest in compensation for the property expropriated from U.S. oil companies in 1938. *See also* *BRACERO* AGREEMENT; GOOD NEIGHBOR POLICY.

MEXICO. The United States maintained a tense relationship with Mexico for much of 1914–45, during which successive U.S. administrations veered between impartial mediation efforts, direct military intervention, and **dollar diplomacy**. This partly reflected the civil and political instability which plagued Mexican politics and society, particularly in the first quarter of the 20th century, after the Mexican Revolution. Regime change in Mexico was often accompanied by violence or civil war, as with the assassinations of President **Francisco Madero** (1913) and President-elect **Alvaro Obregon** (1928) and the military insurrection against the usurping regime of **Victoriano Huerta** (1913–14). Guerrilla warfare conducted by Emiliano Zapata and **Pancho Villa** in 1914–23 also created continued turbulence, with Villa's activities provoking the U.S. government into sending a military expedition across the border in an effort to capture him in 1916–17.

U.S. reactions to or involvement in Mexican affairs often created resentment and brought accusations of imperialism. Huerta's seizure of power in 1913 had allegedly been aided by U.S. ambassador Henry Lane Wilson, and the overthrow of Huerta was achieved with U.S. backing. The United States also intervened militarily at **Veracruz** in 1914, after an incident involving U.S. naval personnel brought the two nations to the brink of war. Further mistrust was generated by the **Zimmermann telegram** of 1917, revealing that Mexico had been offered territorial gains inside the United States in the event of war between the United States and **Germany**.

From the 1920s, the danger of war or armed intervention receded gradually. U.S. policy was dictated by its determination to protect either its business interests or the lives of U.S. civilians. This was still a cause of friction between the United States and Mexico in 1917–23, when radical Mexican leftist politicians proposed a new constitution that threatened the property rights of U.S. oil developers. The U.S. government, under Presidents **Woodrow Wilson** and **Warren G. Harding**, insisted on adherence to established conventions of guaranteeing the security of the life, liberty, and property of foreign citizens. The tensions were resolved by diplomatic rather than military means with the **Bucareli Accords** (1923) but subsequently reappeared with passage of the Mexican Alien Land Law and Petroleum Law in 1925. These pieces of legislation appeared to jeopardize U.S. business interests and seemed likely to provoke a withdrawal of American business, with potentially harmful consequences for the Mexican economy. Again, diplomatic means were used to defuse tensions. President **Calvin Coolidge** appointed **Dwight Morrow** to negotiate a settlement with President **Plutarco Calles** which guaranteed the rights of Standard Oil and other companies.

Although satisfactory to the U.S. State Department, such compromises rarely satisfied left-wing and nationalist groups in Mexico who resented what they regarded as the subservience of Mexican governments to the demands of U.S. capitalism. During the 1930s, President **Franklin D. Roosevelt**, recognizing the implications of an upsurge of nationalism in **Latin America**, pursued a **Good Neighbor policy**, the foundations for which had been laid by Republican presidents of the 1920s. The softer approach was evident in 1938, when President Lázaro Cárdenas nationalized the Mexican oil industry. Although right-wingers in the U.S. Congress demanded swift intervention, the administration merely sought a compensation deal for U.S. oil companies. Concerns by the U.S. government to coordinate Latin American defense activities and counter economic activities of the **Axis** powers in the region were a strong impetus for an improvement in U.S.–Mexican relations. The *Bracero* **agreement** and the resolution of the **Mexican Oil Expropriation Controversy** (1938–41) were indications of a more mature and mutually advantageous attitude, at least at the political level. *See also* CHAPULTEPEC, ACT OF; LIMA CONFERENCE; SHEFFIELD, JAMES ROCKWELL.

MEYER, EUGENE ISAAC (1875–1959). Financier and publisher Eugene Meyer was a Yale graduate who became a successful speculator on the New York Stock Exchange. In 1920, he formed the Allied Chemical and Dye Corporation, later Allied Chemicals, a forerunner of Honeywell. Meyer worked as head of the War Finance Corporation during **World War I** and attended the 1919 **Paris Peace Conference**. He was made chair of the Federal Farm Loan Board in 1927, and in 1930 President **Herbert Hoover** made him chair of the board of governors of the Federal Reserve System. He held the office until May 1933. Meyer favored government help to businesses hit by the Great Depression, and he became chief of the Reconstruction Finance Corporation. He left this office when **Franklin D. Roosevelt** became president.

In 1933, Meyer bought the bankrupt *Washington Post* and made it into a newspaper of quality, though it did not show a profit until the 1950s. Meyer served as the first president of the **World Bank** from June to December 1946. He chaired the *Washington Post* until his death. His daughter Katharine Meyer Graham followed him as the *Post*'s publisher.

MIDWAY, BATTLE OF (1942). The battle for Midway Island is generally regarded as the turning point in the Pacific War during **World War II**. When **Japan**'s forces attempted to take Midway Island, a westerly outlier of the Hawaiian Islands, their main objective was drawing the U.S. Pacific Fleet into a decisive battle. But American code breakers at **Pearl Harbor** were able to pinpoint the target of the Japanese operation, so the much smaller U.S. forces were able to avoid the trap. Instead, partly due to radar and partly due to luck, they were able to find the major Japanese aircraft carriers and sink three of them in half an hour on the morning of 5 June 1942, and a fourth later that day. The Japanese navy suffered a setback from which it never recovered. The United States lost one carrier, USS *Yorktown*, but U.S. industrial superiority meant that it was far better placed to make good the losses. Japan's hopes for victory rested on decisive victories before the United States could bring its industrial production to bear, and the failure at Midway, followed by the long attrition of the Solomons campaign that began with the **Battle of Guadalcanal**, sealed its fate.

MOFFAT, JAY PIERREPONT (1896–1943). Diplomat and historian Jay Pierrepont Moffat served in the embassy in the Netherlands (1917–19), the legation in **Poland** (1919–21), and the embassy in Tokyo (1921–23). He served as ceremonial officer in the White House (1925–27), was then posted to Switzerland (1927–31), and was consul general in Australia (1935–37). From 1937 to 1940, Moffat was chief of the State Department's new and important Division of European Affairs. In June 1940, Moffat was appointed ambassador to Canada. He died in post in 1943. He was married to the daughter of ambassador **Joseph C. Grew**.

MOLEY, RAYMOND CHARLES (1886–1975). Political economist Ray Moley taught at Columbia University from 1923 to 1954. He was an economic advisor to Governor Alfred E. Smith of New York and was a major figure in the group of advisors to Smith's successor, **Franklin D. Roosevelt**, who were known as the brains trust. Moley wrote many of Roosevelt's presidential election speeches. When Roosevelt became president, Moley was appointed assistant secretary of state. Roosevelt sent him to the 1933 **London Economic Conference**, which was already under way, to deliver his "bombshell message," which derailed international efforts at finding a monetary solution to the Great Depression. Moley felt humiliated at being used this way. He left the administration, became a Republican, and worked with **Wendell Willkie**, Roosevelt's opponent in the 1940 presidential election.

MONROE DOCTRINE (1823). Announced by President James Monroe, though drafted by Secretary of State John Quincy Adams, the Monroe Doctrine was a unilateral statement by the United States government in 1823 asserting the autonomy of the western hemisphere and warning European powers against any attempts to gain, or regain, territory in the Americas. This statement became one of the fixed points of U.S. foreign policy through the 19th century and well into the 20th. It was a key doctrine both as a foundation for U.S. **isolationism** and as an assertion of a U.S. role as protector and guarantor of the republics of **Latin America**. This aspect of the doctrine was elaborated upon in the 1904 **Roosevelt Corollary**.

Although the corollary was rejected in the 1928 **Clark memorandum**, the Monroe Doctrine continued to be regarded by most Americans as an essential principle of international affairs, indeed as an unwritten international law. Thus, in 1940–41, President **Franklin D. Roosevelt** could characterize **Germany**'s activities in Latin America during **World War II** as a breach of the Monroe Doctrine in his drive to gain popular support for aiding the Allies and to counter **isolationist** arguments that the European conflict had no impact on U.S. interests. *See also* HAVANA, ACT OF; MONTEVIDEO CONFERENCE; NONTRANSFER COROLLARY TO THE MONROE DOCTRINE.

MONTEVIDEO CONFERENCE (1933). The Seventh International Conference of American States was held at Montevideo, Uruguay, on 2–26 December 1933. The conference is notable for the declaration by Secretary of State **Cordell Hull** on 15 December enlarging on the declaration of the **Good Neighbor policy** made by President **Franklin D. Roosevelt** on 4 March 1933. Hull gave a public disavowal of armed intervention in the affairs of other American states. He also called for a reduction in **tariffs**.

On 26 December, the Montevideo Convention on the Rights and Duties of States was signed. This set out a definition of statehood that has become widely accepted as an international benchmark, though it merely restated what was customary practice in international law. Article 8 declared that "no state has the right to intervene in the internal or external affairs of another." Nineteen states signed the convention (the United States, **Brazil**, and Peru did so with reservations). Of the attendees, only Bolivia did not sign. The agreement came into force on 26 December 1934. The conference also attempted mediation in the **Chaco War** but achieved only a short-lived armistice. *See also* LATIN AMERICA; MONROE DOCTRINE.

MOONEY, JAMES D. (1884–1957). Trained as an engineer, James Mooney served (although over-age) in **France** in **World War I**. He joined the General Motors Corporation (GMC) and was president of its overseas operations. In this role, he traveled extensively and forged contacts with government officials and politicians. He became involved unofficially in international affairs and believed that methods of negotiation developed in corporate management were superior to those of professional diplomats. Mooney received the German Order of Merit of the Eagle from German leader **Adolf Hitler** in 1938, and he used his contacts in **Germany** in 1939 to arrange economic talks between **Joseph P. Kennedy** and Helmuth Wohltatt from the German Office of the Four Year Plan.

In December 1939, with the outbreak of **World War II**, Mooney had two discussions with President **Franklin D. Roosevelt** in which the president agreed that neutral third-party mediation could bring the warring powers in Europe together and end the conflict. As Roosevelt's informal envoy, Mooney had discussions in March 1940 with Nazi leaders Hermann Göring and Adolf Hitler, dealing with U.S.–German relations. This was unconnected with **Sumner Welles**'s mission to Europe at this time, and it was typical of Roosevelt's use of informal envoys. Nothing came of the talks, except that Mooney was later accused of pro-German leanings. During the war, Mooney worked in the Bureau of Aeronautics and the office of the Chief of Naval Operations. After the war, he returned to his corporate career with GMC and Willys-Overland Motors.

MOORE, JOHN BASSETT (1860–1947). John Moore was a law clerk in the State Department (1896–91), an assistant secretary of state, and then professor of law at Columbia University (1891–1924). He represented the United States on a number of important international commissions: notably on The Hague Tribunal (1912–38) and as the first U.S. judge on the **World Court** (1921–28). Moore, however, was an **isolationist** and argued that the United States should not join alliances, and that neutrality, rather than alliance blocs and **collective security**, would tend to keep wars localized and minor. Moore was thus an advocate for the **Moore–Pepper reservation** that effectively prevented the United States from joining the World Court, even though he served on it. He wrote a number of the standard textbooks on international law.

MOORE, ROBERT WALTON (1859–1941). Walton Moore received a law degree from the University of Virginia in Charlottesville, was a member of the Virginia senate (1887–90), and was president of the Virginia Bar Association in 1911. He represented southern companies in cases before the Interstate Commerce Commission, and in 1918–19 was assistant general counsel to the U.S. Railroad Administration. He served as a Democrat in the U.S. House of Representatives in 1919–31. Moore was a supporter of the New Deal, and President **Franklin D. Roosevelt** rewarded him by appointing him assistant secretary of state in September 1933. In 1937, Moore was the preferred candidate of Secretary of State **Cordell Hull** to be undersecretary. When Roosevelt appointed his friend **Sumner Welles**, Moore was given the newly invented title of counselor in the State Department. He was 78 at the time, and though the post had no specified duties, he remained in it until his death.

MOORE–PEPPER RESERVATION. The Moore–Pepper reservation was the last of five conditions set on U.S. membership in the **World Court** by Congress in 1925–26. It was promoted by **John Bassett Moore**, an American jurist already serving as a judge on the court, and Pennsylvania Senator George Wharton Pepper. The condition stipulated that "the Court shall not . . . without the consent of the United States, entertain a request for an advisory opinion touching any dispute or question in which the United States has or claims an interest." The Moore–Pepper reservation was the only one of the five conditions set by Senate **isolationists** that the World Court's existing members did not accept. Therefore, U.S. membership in the World Court was prevented.

MORGAN, JOHN PIERPONT (1867–1943). Financier John Pierpont Morgan Jr. was the son of banker J. Pierpont Morgan. He was prominent in international financial activities in **World War I**, making the first wartime loan to **Russia**, to the sum of $12 million. In 1915, he loaned $50 million to **France**. His company provided the facilities through which **Great Britain** and France made all their purchases of U.S. munitions. Orders were made worth over $3 billion, from which Morgan's company took a 1 percent commission. A syndicate organized by Morgan of over 2,000 banks provided a loan of $500 million to Great Britain, France, and Russia. In 1915, he was injured in an assassination attempt that was a protest against the export of weapons.

In 1920, Morgan gave his residence in London for use as the U.S. embassy. He was involved in helping a number of countries issue bonds after the war, and he served on the **Charles Dawes** committee on German **reparations** in 1924 and at the reparations conference of 1929. Morgan's activities in World War I became the subject of public criticism in the early 1930s in books such as *The Merchants of Death*, and he was required to testify to the **Nye Committee**. While it did confirm the large financial ties of Morgan's company to the Allies during the war, and the profits it had made, the specific charges that the United States was dragged into the war to protect these investments could not be sustained.

MORGENTHAU, HENRY (1891–1967). Secretary of the Treasury Henry Morgenthau was a friend of Eleanor's and **Franklin D. Roosevelt**'s from 1913. Having studied agriculture at Cornell University, during **World War I** he worked for the Farm Administration. In 1929, when Roosevelt became governor of New York, he made Morgenthau chair of the state Agricultural Committee. In 1933, President Roosevelt appointed Morgenthau governor of the Federal Farm Board. In December 1933, when Treasury Secretary William Woodin retired because of ill health, Morgenthau succeeded him. Morgenthau was an orthodox economist and disapproved of the high-spending aspect of the New Deal, but he was deeply loyal to Roosevelt.

During **World War II**, Morgenthau fought against the inclinations of the State Department to do nothing about the World Jewish Congress's plan to fund help for European Jews out of blocked Swiss bank accounts. In January 1944, he succeeded in bringing the issue to the attention of Roosevelt, who established the **War Refugee Board** in the Treasury Department. Although too late to make much of an impact, the board brought an increasing number of Jews into the United States—possibly as many as 200,000.

Morgenthau was a leading participant in the **Bretton Woods Conference** that established a new international economic order. Later in 1944, he formulated the **Morgenthau Plan** for the future treatment of **Germany**, with the assistance of his deputy **Harry Dexter White**. The plan proposed the "pastoralization" of Germany. It was initially regarded favorably by Roosevelt and Prime Minister **Winston Churchill** of **Great Britain** but was dropped after attracting strong opposition from within the U.S. and British governments and from the American press. However, Treasury officials were given key roles in the U.S. zone of occupation in Germany and followed Morgenthau's line not to promote any German economic rehabilitation. They continued to have an impact until 1947. Morgenthau was not on good terms with President **Harry S. Truman**, who disliked the plan and would not take him to the **Potsdam Conference**. Morgenthau left office on 22 July 1945. He continued to campaign for a harsh settlement for Germany. Morgenthau later became a financial advisor to Israel.

MORGENTHAU PLAN. The Morgenthau Plan for the postwar treatment of **Germany** was proposed by Treasury Secretary **Henry Morgenthau** in 1944. It was drafted by his deputy **Harry Dexter White**, who was an agent of the **Union of Soviet Socialist Republics** (USSR), and it has been claimed that the severity of the plan reflected **Josef Stalin**'s desire to create a weak Germany that could not resist Soviet expansionism. The plan, however, fit Morgenthau's own deeply anti-German feelings and for a time chimed in with President **Franklin D. Roosevelt**'s inclination to blame the war on German militarism rather than Nazi ideology. The plan was for German industry to be dismantled and for Germany to be reduced to a level of subsistence agriculture, thereby removing all danger of its threatening world peace. Germany was to have no armed forces and no way of defending itself against attack. This radical solution to the "German problem," as an alternative to dismemberment of the German state, appealed to Roosevelt and Prime Minister **Winston Churchill** of **Great Britain**, and at the 1944 **Quebec Conference** they approved a version of it that included the parts on pastoralizing the German economy.

The State Department was not involved in its formulation and opposed the plan. Many newspapers were critical, and public opinion, while wishing for severe treatment of German war criminals, found the proposal too vindictive, and also potentially expensive. The State Department (and British Foreign Office) objected that this would lead to a massive financial burden for the victorious powers, as well as planting the seeds of a future German nationalist movement. The plan was quietly dropped. At the 1945 **Yalta Conference**, dismemberment, not Morgenthau's pastoralization, was considered the punitive option for Germany. However, German propaganda minister Josef Goebbels referred to the Morgenthau Plan to reinforce the case against **unconditional surrender** and persuade the German people to fight to the end. Goebbels claimed the Allies would turn the whole of Germany into a potato field.

Morgenthau retained his attachment to the plan, and when Treasury officials were assigned to assist in the occupation of Germany, they were instructed to interpret the occupation plan **JCS-1067** in the harshest manner, and to work against rebuilding German industrial strength. They continued to do this until the economic stagnation of the Western occupation zones proved such a drain on U.S. and British resources that occupation policies were changed in 1946–47, and steps were taken toward the managed revival of West German economic self-sufficiency.

MORROW, DWIGHT WHITNEY (1873–1931). Businessman and lawyer Dwight Morrow was appointed ambassador to **Mexico** by President **Calvin Coolidge** and served from 1927 to 1930. He succeeded in partially overcoming the hostility felt by the Mexican government of **Plutarco Calles** toward the United States. Morrow engaged in "ham and eggs diplomacy"—breakfasting and traveling with the Mexican leader on several occasions. Morrow persuaded Calles to scale back his campaign against the Catholic Church in Mexico and to rescind the 1925 Petroleum Law, which threatened the confiscation of U.S. oil developments in the country. He was also sent by Coolidge as a delegate to the 1928 **Havana Conference** and by President **Herbert Hoover** as a delegate to the 1930 London **Naval Disarmament Conference**. Morrow was elected to the U.S.

Senate (R-N.J.) in November 1930 but died within months of beginning his first term. *See also* GOOD NEIGHBOR POLICY.

MOSCOW CONFERENCE (1941). In this first conference between the United States and the **Union of Soviet Socialist Republics** (USSR) during **World War II**, **Averell Harriman**, the **Lend-Lease** representative in London, represented the United States, accompanied by Lord Beaverbrook, minister of supply of **Great Britain**. The aim of the meeting, which took place in Moscow 28 September–10 October 1941, was to assess Soviet material requirements for their struggle with **Germany**. At this point, Congress had not approved the extension of Lend-Lease to the USSR, so leadership of the delegation fell to Beaverbrook. His approach was to avoid any suggestion of bargaining, believing that the main objectives of the mission were raising Soviet morale, convincing them of Allied support and assuaging their suspicions, for no materials could actually arrive before the crucial battle for Moscow reached its climax in December. Beaverbrook made huge offers of munitions and other materials. A supply protocol was easily agreed on but set up many problems in inter-Allied relations when it proved difficult to meet the unrealistic figures. The Soviets were supposed to provide shipping, though in practice this fell exclusively on the Allies. *See also* BIG THREE; MASTER LEND-LEASE AGREEMENTS.

MOSCOW CONFERENCE (1943). During **World War II**, foreign ministers of the major Allies met in Moscow 18–30 October 1943 to prepare the agenda for a full-scale **Big Three** meeting. This was the only conference between the three major allies attended by Secretary of State **Cordell Hull**. The conference was notable for the unusually accommodating demeanor of the foreign commissar of the **Union of Soviet Socialist Republics** (USSR), Vyacheslav Molotov, signaling a Soviet commitment to cooperation. The Soviets were principally concerned to discuss the **second front**, while Hull and Foreign Secretary Anthony Eden of **Great Britain**, wanted to discuss political issues.

Little actual agreement was reached, except to establish a **European Advisory Commission** in London to work out plans for issues such as the temporary occupation zones in **Germany**. There was also agreement that war criminals would be put on trial, and that Austria would be separated from Germany. The USSR hinted that it would be prepared to join the war against **Japan** once Germany was defeated, in return for certain concessions in the Far East. Hull showed little interest in most of these issues, with the exception of discussions on a future world organization, which were inconclusive. *See also* LONDON CHARTER; TEHERAN CONFERENCE.

MOSES–LINTHICUM ACT (1931). On 23 February 1931, the U.S. Congress passed the Moses–Linthicum Act, a revision of the 1924 **Foreign Service Act**. It addressed issues arising from that act, and it sought to coordinate the diplomatic and consular elements of the Foreign Service and regularize promotions policy. It was a further step in professionalizing the service and separating it from the vagaries of party politics. Ambassadorial appointments and other diplomatic roles were still frequently given, however, to nonprofessionals.

MUKDEN INCIDENT. *See* MANCHURIAN CRISIS.

MUNRO–BLANCHET TREATY (1932). Although the U.S. ambassador to Haiti, Dana G. Munro, and the Haitian foreign minister, Albert Blanchet, reached an agreement in 1932, it was never formally ratified. Under the terms of the deal, the last U.S. marine detachment would be withdrawn from Haiti at the end of 1934 and the country would regain much of the control it lost over its economic policy following the U.S. occupation. The agreement was ultimately rejected by the National Assembly of Haiti.

MURPHY, ROBERT DANIEL (1894–1978). Diplomat Robert Murphy served in consular posts in Berne (1917–19), Zurich (1921), Munich (1921–25), Seville (1925), and Paris (1930–40). He was counselor to the embassy in Paris when the city fell to **Germany** in **World War II**, and he was for a short while chargé d'affaires with the Vichy government of **France** in 1940. He was appointed presidential envoy (with rank of minister) to French North Africa (1940–42), and was political officer to General **Dwight D. Eisenhower**'s forces in Operation **Torch**. President **Franklin D. Roosevelt** had instructed him to gather information for the landings, but Murphy instead became closely involved in the negotiations with Admiral **François Darlan** in Algiers that prevented significant French resistance to the landings. He subsequently served with Eisenhower as chief civil affairs officer and political advisor. He was co-chair of the North African Economic Board (1942–44), sat on the Allied Control Commission for Italy (1942–43), and was a political advisor for Germany (1944–45).

Murphy attended the 1945 **Potsdam Conference** and in the postwar period was regarded as a leading diplomatic troubleshooter. He was political advisor to General **Lucius Clay** in Germany (1945–49), then served as ambassador to Belgium (1949–52) and **Japan** (1953–54). He next served in the State Department, becoming undersecretary of state for political affairs in 1959. He was an advisor to Presidents John F. Kennedy, Lyndon B. Johnson, and Richard M. Nixon.

MURROW, EDWARD R. (1908–1965). Journalist Edward R. Murrow attended Stanford and Washington Universities and graduated from Washington State College in 1930. He was assistant director of the Institute of International Education (1932–35) and then joined the Columbia Broadcasting System (CBS) as director of talks and education (1935–37). Murrow served as director of the CBS European Bureau, based mainly in London, from 1937 to 1946. He was responsible for hiring and training a number of notable American correspondents, including **William L. Shirer**, **Eric Sevareid**, Howard K. Smith, and Richard C. Hottelet. He set up the first live broadcasts from Europe with Shirer in 1937. During **World War II**, Murrow's rooftop radio reports from London during the German bombing blitz of 1940–41 were highly influential in moving American public opinion toward sympathy with the plight of **Great Britain** and modifying U.S. **isolationism**.

After the war, Murrow was CBS vice president and director of public affairs (1946–47), returning to radio broadcasting with his *Hear It Now* series. Murrow was also successful with the television series *See It Now* and *Person to Person*. His broadcast criticisms of Senator Joseph McCarthy in 1954 were influential in turning congressional and public opinion against the senator's anticommunist excesses. Murrow was head of the U.S. Information Agency in 1961–64. He received nine Emmy awards for his television work.

MUSTE, ABRAHAM JOHANNES (1885–1967). Socialist activist A. J. Muste was born in the Netherlands and came to the United States when he was six. He was raised in the Calvinist Dutch Reformed Church and became a minister in 1909. Muste voted for socialist presidential candidate Eugene Debs in 1912. Feeling restrained by the strictness of his church, he switched to Congregationalism in 1914. When war broke out in Europe in 1914, Muste took a **pacifist** stance. In April 1918, he was forced out of his pastorship in Newtonville, Massachusetts, after he condemned the futility of war at a time when the congregation was mourning a leading member who had been killed in **World War I**. Muste became attracted by the philosophies of the Quakers, and in 1918 he joined the fledgling American Civil Liberties Union and became a Quaker minister. He was active in labor affairs, was general secretary of the Amalgamated Textile Workers of America (1920–21), and taught at Brookwood Labor College (1921–33).

Muste served in the 1920s as chair of the religious pacifist Fellowship of Reconciliation (FOR) but was moving toward a more radical and overtly political stance. He founded a socialist movement, the Conference for Progressive Labor Action (1929), which amalgamated with a Trotskyist group into the Worker's Party (1933). After a meeting with communist leader Leon Trotsky in Norway in 1936, Muste renounced Marxism and moved back to Christian pacifism. He was a close friend of **John Dewey** and **Norman Thomas**, and he served on the national committee of the **War Resisters League**. He was active in the **Keep America out of War Congress**, which advocated against U.S. involvement in **World War II**. From 1940 to 1953, Muste was executive director of FOR and was instrumental in the formation of the Congress on Racial Equality in 1943. He was later a mentor of Martin Luther King Jr. and led protests against the Vietnam War in the 1960s.

– N –

NAGASAKI. On 9 August 1945, the Japanese city of Nagasaki was the target of the second **atomic bomb** used by the United States during **World War II**. The plutonium bomb, code-named Fat Man, was dropped over the suburbs after the primary target was obscured by clouds. It detonated 500 meters above the ground. Fat Man was more powerful than the bomb dropped on **Hiroshima**, but it was not dropped on the city center, and Nagasaki is surrounded by mountains, so although the radius of destruction of buildings was greater, a lesser amount was totally devastated: 2.6 square miles (6.7 square kilometers). Approximately 73,900 people were killed out of a population of 270,000. *See also* MANHATTAN PROJECT.

NANKING INCIDENT (1927). U.S. naval vessels on the Yangtze River in **China** fired on forces of the Chinese **Kuomintang** at Nanking (Nanjing) on 24 March 1927. The nationalist Kuomintang forces, opposed to the influence in China of the United States, **Great Britain**, and **Japan**, were attacking foreigners in the city. Several Americans were wounded, and one was killed. In April, the United States, Britain, and Japan sent protest notes to the nationalist foreign minister demanding compensation for the attacks and punishment of the military commanders responsible. The U.S. government also closed several consulates, but Secretary of State **Frank Kellogg** refused to consider more direct military retaliation. The following year, the administration of **Calvin Coolidge** officially recognized the nationalist Chinese government.

NATIONAL CIVIL LIBERTIES BUREAU (NCLB). In October 1917, members of the **American Union against Militarism** (AUAM) who were dissatisfied with the organization's tactics and direction established the NCLB. Focusing on domestic rather than foreign policy, the NCLB challenged censorship laws and defended antiwar activists charged with bolshevism or treason. Its first secretary was Roger Nash Baldwin. In January 1920, with the AUAM having lost most of its influence, the NCLB was renamed the American Civil Liberties Union (ACLU).

NATIONAL COMMITTEE ON THE CAUSE AND CURE OF WAR (1924–1943). In 1924, nine women's organizations met together to consider coordinating their activities and agreed to lobby for U.S. membership in the **World Court** (Permanent Court of International Justice). They named the coalition the National Committee on the Cause and Cure of War and chose suffragist Carrie Chapman Catt as chair. The committee held annual conferences until 1941, when lack of funds prevented it from meeting. It was not officially **pacifist** but held many meetings to further the abolition of war, and it worked to promote peace and international cooperation. At its height, the committee claimed to represent 5 million women. It supported **disarmament** and the 1930s **Neutrality Acts**. It became defunct with U.S. entry into **World War II** but reemerged in 1943 as the Women's Action Committee for Victory and Lasting Peace.

NATIONAL COUNCIL FOR PREVENTION OF WAR. In September 1921, the National Council for Limitation of Armaments was founded in Washington, D.C., by 17 national **disarmament** organizations. It was to operate as a clearinghouse to help these organizations work together. **Frederick Libby** was made executive secretary. The council lobbied in favor of the 1921 **Naval Disarmament Conference** in Washington, D.C. The organization changed its name in January 1922 to the National Council for Reduction of Armaments, and in the fall of 1922 it was established as a permanent organization, the National Council for Prevention of War. Its threefold program was limitation of armaments, a **progressive** world organization, and worldwide peace education. It operated in every state and disseminated information among its constituent organizations. It became probably the most significant peace organization in the United States.

The council's first lobbyist was **Jeanette Rankin**, a former member of the House of Representatives. It urged peaceful settlement of the dispute with **Mexico** in 1927, supported the **Kellogg–Briand Pact** and membership in the **League of Nations** and the **World Court**, and lobbied against enlargement of the **U.S. Navy**. It assisted the investigation of arms manufacturers by the **Nye Committee** (1934–35). By 1936, the council's journal, *Peace Action*, had a circulation of 25,000. In the late 1930s, the council supported neutrality and the **Ludlow Amendment**, participating in the campaign of the **Keep America out of War Congress**. During **World War II**, it lobbied for aid to displaced persons and for fair treatment of enemies in war crimes trials. It has been calculated that Libby raised over $2 million for the movement between 1921 and his retirement in 1954.

The council officially existed until 1971 but was mostly inactive after Libby retired. *See also* PACIFISM.

NATIONAL DEFENSE ACT (1916). Signed into law by President **Woodrow Wilson** on 3 June, the 1916 National Defense Act brought state militias more closely under federal control and allowed the president of the United States to call on them to reinforce the U.S. Army in times of emergency. The act also provided for the reorganization of all state militias, allowing them to be structured in the same way as the national forces. Additionally, National Guard members received federal payment, and a Reserve Officer Training Corps (ROTC) was set up to provide military training to college students. The move was part of the **preparedness campaign** conducted by Wilson during **World War I**, but it met with opposition from antiwar groups and from **progressives**, who feared military expansion would come at the expense of domestic reform.

NATIONAL DEFENSE ACT (1920). The 1920 National Defense Act was passed by the U.S. Congress on 4 June. It formalized many of the structural changes made to the U.S. Army by the demands of U.S. involvement in **World War I**. A new Air Service and Chemical Warfare Service were created, and the War Department was given the job of planning for mobilization in the event of war. Maximum strength levels were set for different sections of the army and navy, although these were still to be dependent upon congressional appropriations (which were cut, rather than increased, during the 1920s).

NATIONAL DEFENSE RESEARCH COMMITTEE. The National Defense Research Committee was established in June 1940, with **Vannevar Bush** as chair. Its purpose was to coordinate activities of scientists and engineers in developing weapons systems and other technology of war. Its establishment was part of President **Franklin D. Roosevelt**'s moves in the summer of 1940 toward increased preparedness for war and the modernization of U.S. armed forces and their capabilities. The committee later became part of the Office of Scientific Research and Development.

NATIONAL NAVAL VOLUNTEERS. The National Naval Volunteers were created by the Naval Reserve Force Act of 29 August 1916, in order to improve U.S. naval preparedness. A properly equipped, federally controlled naval militia had been in existence only since February 1914, and it was severely limited as a potential fighting force, since it could only be called into action to repel an invasion of U.S. territory. The new National Naval Volunteers, supervised by Navy Secretary **Josephus Daniels**, boosted the numbers of trained and semitrained recruits the president could call on in the event of a crisis. One year after its inception, the volunteers force numbered over 10,000. *See also* NATIONAL DEFENSE ACT (1916); UNITED STATES NAVY.

NATIONAL ORIGINS ACT (1924). Sponsored by Representative Albert Johnson, the 1924 National Origins Act was intended to tighten restrictions imposed by the 1921 **Immigration Quota Act**. The measure aimed to reduce the overall limit for **immigration** to 157,000 per annum by 1927. The 3 percent quota imposed in 1921 was reduced to 2 percent, and the starting point for assessment of immigration rates by different regional and ethnic groups became the census of 1890 rather than that of 1910. Southern and Eastern European immigration was thereby further restricted. Immigrants from **Mexico** and the **Philippines** were exempted from the provisions of the act, since they proved a valuable source of cheap labor.

The most controversial aspect of the act was an "exclusion clause" barring Japanese immigrants, who were classed as "aliens ineligible for citizenship." The clause was little more than a sop to anti-Japanese sentiment rife in the United States in the 1920s and 1930s, particularly on the west coast, where Japanese immigration was particularly resented by the white population. The clause harmed U.S. relations with **Japan**, which had been slowly improving in the wake of Japan's support for the Allies during **World War I** and substantial American business aid to Tokyo after the 1923 earthquake. Despite some private concerns about its long-term impact on U.S. relations with Japan, President **Calvin Coolidge** signed the act, noting "America must be kept American."

NAVAL DISARMAMENT CONFERENCE (1921). When President **Warren G. Harding** took office on 4 March 1921, his administration faced conflicting pressures from **isolationist** and **internationalist** factions in Congress. Both factions desired international stability and the prevention of a renewed naval arms race. Internationalists advocated U.S. participation in the **League of Nations** and **World Court** in order to achieve these goals. Isolationists preferred bilateral and multilateral treaties negotiated separately with no threat, real or perceived, to U.S. sovereignty. Pressure from both sides for a major **disarmament** initiative resulted in Harding's invitation to **Great Britain**, **France**, **Japan**, **China**, Belgium, the Netherlands, Italy, and Portugal to attend a naval disarmament conference in Washington, D.C. Harding avoided the mistakes made by **Woodrow Wilson** in connection with the 1919 **Paris Peace Conference** by including members of the opposition Democratic Party in the official U.S. delegation to the conference, as well as notable skeptics such as Senators **Henry Cabot Lodge** and **Elihu Root**.

Harding formally opened the conference on 12 November 1921 and subsequently left negotiations in the hands of Secretary of State **Charles Evans Hughes**. Hughes surprised delegates and reporters by presenting a radical American proposal for a Five Power Treaty, involving scrapping 15 U.S. battleships and shelving construction of a further 15, a total of 845,740 tons of capital ships (battleships and battle cruisers). He invited the British delegation to scrap 23 capital ships for a total of 583,000 tons. Japan would be required to scrap 10 of its older vessels and 7 new ones. Naval tonnage after the cuts would be set at ratios of 5:5:3 for Great Britain, the United States, and Japan. French and Italian naval forces would have a maximum 175,000 tons each. Production of replacement tonnage would be restricted to ensure that each country stayed within these limits, but replacements would only be permitted after a 10-year moratorium on battleship construction. Tonnage restrictions were also to be placed on aircraft carriers, with Britain and the United States permitted 135,000 tons each.

The Japanese delegation accepted the 5:5:3 ratio unenthusiastically, since it appeared to cement existing U.S.–British supremacy on the seas while terminating old agreements between Japan and Britain. However, some in the Japanese navy and government recognized that the agreement left Japan with local superiority in East Asian waters although the United States had the potential industrial power to outbuild all its rivals.

Hughes's proposals took the conference by surprise, captured press attention, and increased the pressure on delegates to demonstrate a genuine commitment to disarmament. A separate Four Power Treaty committed the United States, Great Britain, Japan, and France to respect each other's territorial rights and acquisitions in the Pacific and to resolve differences through negotiation. The U.S. arranged a further deal with Japan to ensure continued American use of international cable facilities on the Pacific island of Yap. In the Nine Power Treaty, the United States, **China**, Great Britain, France, Japan, Belgium, the Netherlands, Italy, and Portugal pledged respect for Chinese sovereignty, fair trading arrangements, and support for Chinese efforts to stabilize their nation in return for the Chinese government's pledge to respect the rights of foreign nationals to pursue commercial activities inside China.

When the conference closed on 6 February 1922, the major powers had agreed for the first time to restrain naval armaments production, scale back existing arsenals, and enact a framework of legally binding agreements to prevent future tensions leading to war. Some critics pointed out that the continued production of naval destroyers and submarines and the destructive capacity of air force and army weaponry had not been addressed. Setting a 10,000 ton limit on the size of cruisers in practice meant each power now sought to build ships right up to that limit, and a "cruiser race" began. **Hiram Johnson** protested that the Four Power Treaty had been negotiated behind closed doors.

Johnson, **William E. Borah**, and other Senate critics faced a dilemma. Lodge and Root, both powerful and respected within the Republican Party and both cynical about any attempt to tie the United States into a formal international body like the League of Nations, had been part of the U.S. delegation. Their imprimatur on the agreements made it difficult for Johnson to rally opposition. Further, as Borah had consistently argued that separate, interlocking agreements were more workable and preferable for the United States, they would find it hard to attack the accords without inadvertently proving the claim of internationalists that only the League of Nations could be effective in securing world peace.

In the long term, the 1921 Naval Disarmament Conference failed to prevent the resumption of a competitive arms race or to reduce tensions in the Pacific. It was, nevertheless, an important development in postwar American foreign policy and the first of a series of efforts by the Harding and **Calvin Coolidge** administrations designed to stabilize international affairs and reduce the risk of war. Though the conference and later initiatives such as the **Kellogg–Briand Pact** (1928) were attacked as naïve or unworkable, there were very few practical alternatives available to administrations of the 1920s. *See also* LONDON NAVAL DISARMAMENT CONFERENCE (1930); NAVAL DISARMAMENT CONFERENCE (1927); UNITED STATES NAVY.

NAVAL DISARMAMENT CONFERENCE (1927). Although the United States remained outside the **League of Nations**, it continued to express interest in bilateral and multilateral treaties designed to reduce international tensions, bolster peace, or constrain the growth of military forces and arsenals. By 1926, **Great Britain** had built, or was in process of building, 54 new cruisers and **Japan** had 25. The U.S. government had permitted construction of only 6. Even this modest increase had concerned President **Calvin Coolidge**, who was attempting to cut back domestic government spending. In total, the British governments of Prime Ministers Stanley Baldwin and Ramsay MacDonald approved the construction of more than 150 new ships, far outstripping the 40 authorized by the U.S. government. Japan's construction rate also exceeded that of the United States.

As pressure built in Congress for a new shipbuilding program to match or exceed British production levels, it became clear that a new naval arms race threatened. A desire to avoid the expense, as well as the danger, of unrestrained competition undoubtedly underlay Coolidge's 1927 initiative for a conference. Prospects for agreement, however, were less promising than they had been in the 1921 **Naval Disarmament Conference**. From late 1926, a League of Nations Preparatory Commission had been meeting in Geneva to lay the groundwork for a comprehensive naval disarmament conference. In February 1927, Coolidge invited Great Britain, Japan, Italy, and **France** to open negotiations with U.S. diplomats in Geneva, but France and Italy declined, preferring to commit themselves solely to the League's initiative.

Only the United States, Britain, and Japan were at the table for the opening session of the conference on 20 June 1927 in Geneva. The American delegation sought to extend the 5:5:3 ratio of the Five Power Treaty to cover smaller vessels, but negotiations stalled over the total cruiser tonnage to be allowed to each nation. After the conference's opening session, only second-tier diplomats remained to continue negotiations. The deliberations failed to hold press or public attention and quickly lost momentum. After two months, the conference ended without agreement. Shortly afterward, Coolidge bowed to congressional pressure for a substantial increase in U.S. naval construction. *See also* LONDON NAVAL DISARMAMENT CONFERENCE (1930); UNITED STATES NAVY.

NAVAL EXPANSION ACT (1938). *See* VINSON, CARL.

NAVAL EXPANSION ACT (1940). *See* TWO-OCEAN NAVY ACT.

NEUTRALITY ACTS. First proposed in the wake of the **Nye Committee** investigations, the Neutrality Acts represented more generally the growth of **pacifism** in the United States and the widespread public belief that involvement in **World War I** had been a mistake. The acts sought to ensure that the United States was not drawn into war because of the commercial activities and commitments of American businesses or individuals. The implication was essentially that no national interest would be involved in such conflicts in other parts of the world. This was one of the central tenets of **isolationism**.

The main provision of the 1935 Neutrality Act was a ban on **trade** in war materials, broadly interpreted, with any belligerent, once the president had proclaimed that a state of war existed. Any U.S. vessels entering the declared war zone would do so at their own risk, and the same applied to those choosing to travel on belligerent vessels. The aim was to avoid a similar crisis to that which followed the sinking of the *Lusitania* in 1915. No loans would be allowed to belligerents (the 1934 **Debt Default Act** had already prevented loans to most European states). President **Franklin D. Roosevelt** was not opposed to the tenor of this legislation but would have preferred presidential discretion whether to apply the trade embargo equally to all belligerents. Congress, however, believed that it was not in the interest of the United States to aid any side in a conflict, whether victim or aggressor. Congress also wanted to limit presidential freedom of action and reassert congressional control regarding the issue of going to war at a time when the New Deal was greatly expanding domestic federal authority.

The Italian invasion of Ethiopia in October 1935, just two months after passage of the act, revealed its inherent bias in favor of aggressors, who could stockpile materials before attacking. Roosevelt's attempts to get voluntary embargoes met little response at a time of economic recession. One consequence was that when **Japan** renewed its aggression in **China** in 1937, Roosevelt did not declare that this was a war. The ironic result was an increase in U.S. trade with Japan. The Neutrality Act was renewed for a year in 1936; the main change was that its provisions extended to include civil wars, in response to the outbreak of the **Spanish Civil War**.

In 1937, in response to concerns that the legislation would damage American commerce, a suggestion by **Bernard Baruch** was adopted, which became known as **cash-and-carry**. Belligerents could buy nonwar materials from U.S. producers but were required to pay cash and had to ship the goods themselves from U.S. ports. On 4 November 1939, after a sharp debate in Congress, cash-and-carry was extended to munitions in the 1939 Neutrality Act. On 13 November 1941, in response to the sinking of the USS *Reuben James*, this act was effectively repealed when it was ruled that merchant ships could enter war zones and could be armed. **Lend-Lease** had already made the cash-and-carry proviso irrelevant. *See also* NONPARTISAN COMMITTEE FOR PEACE THROUGH REVISION OF THE NEUTRALITY LAW.

NICARAGUA. U.S. relations with Nicaragua were complex and often antagonistic during the first decades of the 20th century. In 1912, conservative President Adolfo Diaz appealed for U.S. assistance in putting down a liberal insurrection. President **William H. Taft**'s administration sent 2,700 marines into the country in August 1912. A small detachment remained in the country until 1925, helping to train the Nicaraguan army and national guard.

In November 1925, moderate conservative President Carlos Solorzano was overthrown by right-wingers supporting Emiliano

Chamorro, who claimed Solorzano's election had been rigged. Solorzano and his liberal vice president, Juan Sacasa, fled the country. Fighting broke out, with pro-Sacasa liberals appealing for intervention from **Mexico**'s leftist government under **Plutarco Elias Calles**. U.S. President **Calvin Coolidge**, aware that Calles was hostile to American influence in the region, became concerned for U.S. lives and business interests. He sent more marines to Nicaragua in May 1926. Chamorro was pressured to step aside in favor of Diaz in order to halt hostilities and prepare for fresh elections. The conflict escalated as Sacasa returned from exile in December 1926 to form a rebel liberal government. Coolidge sent a further marine detachment in January 1927 but now feared being dragged into a civil war with the United States arming the Diaz regime while Mexico armed Sacasa's general, Jose Maria Moncada. Coolidge also came under attack from **isolationists** in Congress, while Secretary of State **Frank B. Kellogg** aroused contempt among **progressives** by suggesting this was all a communist plot to infiltrate **Latin America**.

President Coolidge dispatched **Henry L. Stimson** to Managua to mediate between the warring factions. On 12 May 1927, agreement was reached in the **Peace of Tipitapa**. Diaz was to complete his term, and the United States would organize elections—a task assigned to **Frank B. McCoy**. U.S. marines would train a national guard. Moncada won the election, and the United States selected Anastasio Somoza Garcia to head the national guard.

Although the immediate crisis was defused, a new rebellion was almost immediately launched by liberal General Augusto Sandino, who rejected the peace agreement as a manifestation of U.S. imperialism. By 1933, the rebellion had been suppressed by Nicaragua's national guard and U.S. occupation forces. U.S. forces withdrew following the inauguration of Juan Sacasa, successor to Moncada. In 1934, General Sandino was assassinated by the national guard. Its leader, Somoza, seized control of the liberal party and overthrew Sacasa, becoming president in 1937 and establishing a military dictatorship. *See also* GOOD NEIGHBOR POLICY; LATIN AMERICA; ROOSEVELT COROLLARY.

NIMITZ, CHESTER W. (1885–1966). Admiral Chester Nimitz was chief of the Bureau of Navigation (1939–41) and commander of the

U.S. Pacific Fleet (1941–45). Nimitz's faith in the **signals intelligence** provided by his code breakers and his readiness to base his plans on their insights were major factors in the U.S. victory in the key Battle of **Midway** during **World War II**. Nimitz was responsible for the conduct of naval operations in the central Pacific that were a major part of the defeat of **Japan**. He was often in dispute with General **Douglas MacArthur**, who preferred a southwest Pacific strategy, in which the **U.S. Navy** would mostly play a supporting role. Nimitz was chief of naval operations (1945–47).

NINE-POWER TREATY. *See* NAVAL DISARMAMENT CONFERENCE (1921).

NONPARTISAN COMMITTEE FOR PEACE THROUGH REVISION OF THE NEUTRALITY LAW. A pressure group, the Nonpartisan Committee endorsed President **Franklin D. Roosevelt**'s argument in the fall of 1939 that U.S. national security required revision of the **Neutrality Acts** so that aid could be provided to belligerent countries whose victory would serve U.S. interests. The committee was set up at Roosevelt's suggestion by **Clark Eichelberger** of the **League of Nations Association** and newspaper editor **William Allen White**, to counter **isolationist** claims that revision of neutrality legislation would involve the United States in a European war. Its membership was **internationalists** and anglophiles, such as **James Shotwell**, **Thomas Lamont**, and Nicholas Murray Butler. It demonstrated the effectiveness of national pressure groups by helping to secure congressional approval for revision of the neutrality legislation in November 1939. This extended the **cash-and-carry** provision to munitions. When Roosevelt commented that the American people needed some education on the issues of the war without feeling they were being dragged into it, prominent members of the Nonpartisan Committee formed the **Committee to Defend America by Aiding the Allies**.

NONTRANSFER COROLLARY TO THE MONROE DOCTRINE. On 17 June 1940, during **World War II**, the State Department announced to all European governments that the United States would not recognize the transfer of any territory in the western hemisphere from one non-American power to another non-American power. This reflected concern that **Germany** would seek to gain control of colonies of **France** and the Netherlands in the Americas after having defeated those countries in the war. *See also* HAVANA, ACT OF; LATIN AMERICA; MONROE DOCTRINE; ST. PIERRE AND MIQUELON AFFAIR.

NORMALCY. In May 1920, speaking in Boston during his campaign for the presidency, **Warren G. Harding** claimed that the United States needed "not nostrums but normalcy." The expression was picked up by reporters and later became a catch-all definition for the policy program of the Harding administration. Harding's own definition of normalcy—a return to moderation and balance in domestic politics and the economy, as well as in America's international duties and activities—was superseded after his death by a more negative interpretation stressing the abandonment of **progressive** reforms at home, the determined pursuit of material gain, lax regulation of large corporations, suppression of workers' protests, and an **isolationist** foreign policy that opposed U.S. membership of the **League of Nations** and **World Court**.

NORRIS, GEORGE W. (1861–1944). A progressive Republican from Nebraska, George Norris served in the U.S. House of Representatives (1903–13) and the Senate (1913–43). Norris voted against U.S. entry into **World War I** in April 1917, contending that American bankers and arms manufacturers had a vested interest in conflict rather than peace. He also voted against passage of the **Treaty of Versailles** and U.S. membership in the **League of Nations**. Norris became more closely aligned with Democrats in Congress in the 1920s and 1930s, co-sponsoring the 1934 Norris–LaGuardia Act, which protected the rights of workers to join unions. He lost his reelection bid in 1942 and retired from politics.

NORTH RUSSIA, INTERVENTION IN (1918–1919). In August 1918, the United States joined with **Great Britain** and other states to send troops to **Russia**. Their ostensible purpose was to defend U.S. interests, citizens, and property, but they were drawn into taking sides in Russia's civil war. The United States and its associates were antagonistic to the Bolsheviks after they withdrew from **World War I** in the Treaty of Brest–Litovsk. Some British and U.S. naval personnel had landed in the arctic ports of Murmansk and Arkhangelsk in March 1918 to prevent arms supplies that had been provided by the Allies from falling into **Germany**'s hands. Reinforced in the summer, they soon were engaged in combat with the Bolsheviks and assisting the tsarist forces. Some 5,760 U.S. troops were deployed in what was known as the Polar Bear Expedition. They were commanded by Colonel G. E. Stuart and suffered 144 casualties. After a failed offensive, and with declining support at home, the U.S. forces were withdrawn in June 1919. *See also* RUSSIAN REVOLUTIONS; SIBERIAN INTERVENTION.

NYE, GERALD PRENTICE (1892–1971). An editor and then owner of newspapers in North Dakota from 1916, Gerald P. Nye was a supporter of **progressive** leader **Robert La Follette** and the agrarian reform movement. Having failed to be elected to the House of Representatives in 1924, Nye was appointed to the Senate in 1925 to replace a deceased incumbent. He served until 1944. Nye was among those who exposed corruption by President **Warren G. Harding**'s secretary of the interior, Albert Fall, in the Teapot Dome scandal.

Nye opposed the New Deal, but President **Franklin D. Roosevelt** encouraged his investigation of the role of arms manufacturers in U.S. involvement in **World War I**. This was formalized in the establishment of the **Nye Committee**. Nye was convinced that involvement in the war had damaged farmers' interests, and he blamed Wall Street, big business, and international bankers. In 1936, Nye stated that "these bankers were in the heart and center of a system that made our going to war inevitable." Nye favored the **Neutrality Acts**, which he believed would avoid participation in a war that would harm U.S. interests. The legislation also would limit urban production rather than the agricultural interests that Nye represented.

Nye later was an outspoken proponent of **isolationism** and accused Roosevelt of provoking the *Panay* incident in December 1937. He was an active campaigner for the **America First Committee**. In September 1941, Nye accused the Hollywood film industry of being biased in favor of intervention in **World War II**. In hearings organized by Nye and Senator **Burton K. Wheeler**, Hollywood's counsel, **Wendell Willkie**, ridiculed Nye by demonstrating he had not seen most of the movies he was attacking. On the day that **Japan** attacked **Pearl Harbor**, Nye told an America First meeting that this was part of a plot by **Great Britain** and "we have been maneuvered into this by the president." Nevertheless, he voted for the **declaration of war**. Nye suffered a sweeping electoral defeat in 1944. He later worked for the Federal Housing Authority and the Senate Committee on Aging.

NYE COMMITTEE. In the 1930s, **pacifism** and antiforeign and antibusiness sentiments were strong in the United States as a result of the Great Depression, European nations' default on **war debt** repayments, and concern that business interests had led to U.S. involvement in **World War I**. In February 1934, Senator **Gerald P. Nye** called for an investigation of the munitions industry by the **Senate Committee on Foreign Relations**. The chair, **Key Pittman**, did not like the idea and referred it to the Military Affairs Committee. The proposal was combined with one from Senator **Arthur Vandenberg** concerning reduction of war profiteering, and a Munitions Investigating Committee was established, usually known as the Nye Committee. Other members included James P. Pope, Homer T. Bone, **Walter F. George**, Warren Barbour, and **Joel B. Clark**. Journalist **John T. Flynn** acted as an advisor and wrote most of the committee's reports.

Public hearings began on 4 September 1934. The original purpose was to investigate claims made in books like *The Merchants of Death* that munitions makers and bankers, in collusion with **Great Britain**, had tricked the United States into war to defend their investments and to make profits. Leading business figures, like **John Pierpont Morgan Jr.** and Pierre Du Pont, were questioned before the committee in 93 high-publicity hearings that ended early in 1936. The committee reported that the lobbying by the munitions industry was linked to the U.S. entry into the war, but it could not find evidence of an actual conspiracy. However, the focus of the committee broadened into an examination of the causes of war and of legislative methods to prevent the United States from once again being pulled into a foreign war. The eventual result was the 1935 **Neutrality Act**. *See also* DEVIL THEORY.

– O –

OBREGON, ALVARO (1880–1928). General Alvaro Obregon fought to depose the military dictatorship of **Victoriano Huerta** in **Mexico**. In alliance with Venustiano Carranza, he also organized the military campaign against Pancho Villa, and he served as Mexico's secretary of war from 1916 until March 1917, when Carranza became president. Obregon backed leftist plans to curb the power of the Catholic Church, protect workers' rights, and assume control over petroleum reserves, all of which underpinned the new constitution of 1917. He became president of Mexico in December 1920, having forced Carranza to flee the country after the latter's abortive effort to dictate the choice of his own successor.

Relations with the United States during Obregon's tenure were tense, marked by Mexican charges that U.S. oil companies planned to strip the nation of its economic and mineral assets. The United States feared that a radical leftist government would nationalize the oil industry and seize its assets. Obregon eventually negotiated a settlement of the issue of petroleum reserve rights with the administration of President **Warren G. Harding**. The 1923 **Bucareli Agreements** ensured that foreign investors who had worked to develop petroleum-rich land before the 1917 Constitution came into effect would be exempted from government takeovers. In 1924, Obregon was succeeded as president by **Plutarco Elias Calles**. With removal of the constitutional provision restricting presidents to one term in office, Obregon was elected in 1928. On 17 July, while still president-elect, he was assassinated at an open-air restaurant.

OFFICE OF STRATEGIC SERVICES (OSS). The Office of Strategic Services was the main U.S. **intelligence** organization during **World War II**. The OSS was established by presidential military order on 13 June 1942, with the unorthodox and adventurist **William Donovan** as head. The United States had no central agency for collection and analysis of national security intelligence before this point. Donovan had been made Coordinator of Information in July 1941 and had become involved in propaganda, intelligence, sabotage, espionage, and postwar planning. This had brought rivalries with other organizations, notably the armed services and the **Federal Bureau**

of Investigation (FBI). Propaganda was made the responsibility of the new Office of War Information in June 1942, and the OSS was established as the body to collect and oversee analysis of strategic information. Donovan also operated "special services," as specified by the Joint Chiefs of Staff (JCS).

The OSS was thus an operational agency, involved in sabotage, liaison with resistance groups, and subversive activities, as well as the gathering of intelligence. It also engaged in counterintelligence against other nations' security services. The largest part of the organization was the Research and Analysis Branch, directed by historian William L. Langer, which produced weekly reports used widely throughout the government.

The OSS operated separately from intelligence operations run by the U.S. Navy, U.S. Army, and FBI. Charged with providing analysis of strategic information to the JCS, the OSS also focused on covert operations in Europe and Asia and running networks of agents in countries occupied by the Axis. Its operatives were recruited from a wide range of often unorthodox backgrounds, and it had close links to academia. At the height of its activities, the OSS employed over 12,000 people.

The OSS maintained agents in Germany and provided good field intelligence to U.S. forces in Europe but was distrusted by other branches of the government, such as the FBI and the army, because of its unorthodoxy. General Douglas MacArthur refused to allow it to operate in his areas of command in the southwest Pacific. Donovan was prepared to cooperate with anyone fighting the Axis, which led to accusations that many OSS operatives were pro-communist. But at the end of the war, Allen Dulles, the OSS bureau chief in Berne, Switzerland, was seeking means to restrict expansion by the Union of Soviet Socialist Republics (USSR). In April 1945, he engaged in controversial peace talks with German generals commanding in Italy, causing a dispute with Soviet premier Josef Stalin.

In September 1945, as a result of bureaucratic jealousies, accusations of left-wing or pro-British bias, and misgivings about the role of a secret intelligence organization in peacetime, President Harry S. Truman ordered the OSS to be dismantled. Some of its researchers were transferred to the Interim Research and Intelligence Service in the State Department, but most of the OSS's experts left government service. Its permanent peacetime successor, the Central Intelligence Agency, was established in 1947.

OFFICE OF THE COORDINATOR OF INTER-AMERICAN AF-FAIRS (OCIAA). In August 1940, during **World War II**, President **Franklin D. Roosevelt** established the Office of the Coordinator of Commercial and Cultural Relations between the American Republics. It was renamed the Office of the Coordinator of Inter-American Affairs in 1941. Its head was **Nelson Rockefeller**. The aim was to increase inter-American cooperation in economic matters. A principal focus of the agency was to dissuade U.S. firms from dealing with pro-Nazi organizations in **Latin America**, and in other ways to combat Nazi commercial activities there. It received information from the **Federal Bureau of Investigation** and **intelligence** from agents of **Great Britain**.

Rockefeller organized a large-scale effort to replace European influence in Latin America with that of the United States. At the center was a massive propaganda effort which spent $140 million over five years and employed a staff in the United States of 1,200 people. OCIAA supported cultural exchanges and media programs. Shortwave radio broadcasts were soon supplemented with newsreels and then full-length Hollywood films and cartoons from the Walt Disney organization. In each country, it organized coordinating committees, made up largely of expatriate businesspeople and connected to the **Office of Strategic Services**. Rockefeller gained tax deductions in 1942 for companies' advertising revenues in Latin America, followed by newspaper and radio revenues. Rockefeller left at the end of 1944 and was replaced by Wallace K. Harrison. The agency was renamed Office for Inter-American Affairs in 1945. In August, the propaganda activities were transferred to the State Department, and in April 1946 the office was abolished.

OFFICE OF WAR INFORMATION (OWI). A government agency established by President **Franklin D. Roosevelt** in 1942, the OWI coordinated activities of war information and propaganda bodies. It was directed by well-known radio broadcaster Elmer Davis. While it was established in response to complaints that information was being handled by too many agencies (at least five by 1942), it did not replace all these agencies, nor was Davis able fully to control them. Thus, while the OWI became the main instrument for government propaganda, the problems of confused lines of policy and responsibility remained, and one must conclude that this was the way Roosevelt liked it.

After the **World War I** experience of the **Committee on Public Information**, there was considerable public and congressional anxiety about government involvement in propaganda. The government claimed that it was intending to deal in information, not propaganda, but given the needs of total warfare and the voluntary nature of much of the U.S. domestic war effort, persuasive methods were regarded as vital. Messages concerning the need to conserve materials, observe secrecy, work in war industries, and buy war bonds were conveyed through all means available—radio, posters and billboards, newsreel films, and tours by movie stars. The OWI's impact on overseas propaganda was largely indirect. Its Bureau of Motion Pictures had some influence on Hollywood's films, and these were distributed widely in Allied and liberated territories. Propaganda in **Latin America** was the responsibility of the **Office of the Coordinator of Inter-American Affairs**. OWI budgets were severely trimmed in 1943. The OWI was disbanded on 15 September 1945.

OGDENSBURG CONFERENCE (1940). U.S. President **Franklin D. Roosevelt** met with Canadian Prime Minister William Mackenzie King at Ogdensburg, New York, on 17–18 August 1940, during **World War II**. The result was the creation of the **Permanent Joint Board on Defense**, though there was no formal agreement. Roosevelt was concerned about Canadian vulnerability should **Great Britain** be defeated by **Germany**, and in effect he committed the United States to the defense of Canada. This was the main topic to be dealt with by the joint board.

OKINAWA, BATTLE OF (1945). The largest of the Ryukyu Islands, Okinawa was a major battle site during **World War II**. It had been part of the empire of **Japan** since 1895 and was the first Japanese territory attacked by the United States that had a significant civilian population. After intensive air attacks beginning on 23 March 1945, amphibious landings took place on 1 April, in Operation Iceberg.

Some 120,000 Japanese troops were stationed on the island in strong defenses. They suffered 103,000 casualties. The United States lost 12,500 and suffered serious shipping losses from *kamikaze* suicide planes. The island was not fully secured until 21 June. Okinawa was intended to be the base for the invasion of Japan, but the fierceness of Japanese resistance fueled fears of high casualties in such an operation and influenced the decision to use the **atomic bomb**.

OPEN DOOR POLICY. In the fall of 1898, President William McKinley stated that the United States favored an "open door" with regard to access to the markets of **China**. In 1899, Secretary of State John Hay issued the "open door notes" to the other major powers, asking for formal approval of the principle that all trading nations should have equal access to all parts of China. This was a response to the political and economic disarray in China, and the fear that the European imperial powers would divide China into exclusive spheres of influence. The notes also sought recognition of China's territorial integrity. The aim was to keep all of China open to U.S. commerce, negating the advantages enjoyed by those powers that had already begun establishing spheres of influence. None of the powers endorsed Hay's proposal.

The open door became the central U.S. foreign policy principle with regard to China, and by extension to other parts of the world. It was the foundation for America's advocacy of free **trade** and its opposition to closed trading blocs. The policy brought the United States into conflict with the policies of **Japan** in China from 1915 onward, though this was temporarily set aside in the 1917 **Lansing–Ishii agreement**, and it was a major topic of discussion at the 1921 **Naval Disarmament Conference** in Washington, D.C.

The open door has been seen as a guiding principle of much of 20th-century U.S. foreign policy. It tended to be applied mainly in regions where the United States faced serious competition. In areas where the United States already economically dominated, such as **Latin America**, the principle was rarely invoked, and measures were taken to keep competitors out. *See also* MASTER LEND-LEASE AGREEMENTS; TARIFFS.

OPPENHEIMER, JULIUS ROBERT (1904–1967). Nuclear physicist J. Robert Oppenheimer graduated in physics from Harvard, then studied at the Cavendish Laboratory at Cambridge University and at the University of Gottingen, which was the world center of advanced nuclear physics research. From 1928, Oppenheimer worked jointly at the California Institute of Technology and University of California at Berkeley. He did important work in astrophysics, nuclear physics, spectroscopy, and quantum theory, and he pioneered the concept of black holes.

When **World War II** broke out, Oppenheimer became involved in development of the **atomic bomb** and worked with **Vannevar Bush** and **Arthur Compton** to focus on uranium. In 1942, when the **Manhattan Project** was established under army supervision, General **Leslie Groves** selected Oppenheimer to be scientific director. In this capacity, he managed over 3,000 staff and took a major role in supervising the solution of technical and mechanical issues. He organized the work at Los Alamos, New Mexico, that culminated in the first nuclear explosion, the Trinity test at Alamogordo on 16 July 1945. Oppenheimer supported the use of the atomic bomb against Japanese cities as a means of ending the war.

After the war, Oppenheimer was chair of the General Advisory Committee of the Atomic Energy Commission (1947–52). He initially opposed development of the hydrogen bomb, largely because it seemed impractical. Once it became a realistic possibility, he supported it, fearing that other nations would develop it, even if the United States did not. In 1953, he was accused of communist sympathies, and his security clearance was removed. Oppenheimer certainly had left-wing views and connections in the **Communist Party of the United States**, but there was no evidence that he had compromised any of the secrets of the Manhattan Project, and the scientific community was generally shocked by his treatment. Some rehabilitation took place when he was given the Atomic Energy Commission's **Enrico Fermi** award in 1963 at the express wish of President John F. Kennedy.

ORANGE, WAR PLAN. Plan Orange was one of a series of contingency war plans and scenarios drawn up by U.S. military planners during the interwar period. In the plans, countries were referred to by a color: the United States was Blue, **Great Britain** was Red, **Mexico** was Green, **Germany** was Black, **France** was Gold, **Japan** was Orange, and so on. Under Plan Orange, the United States would hold its western Pacific bases in the **Philippines** and elsewhere and deprive Japan of supplies while the Pacific Fleet mobilized. The fleet would then sail west, relieve the bases, and engage the Japanese navy in a decisive battle. Japan would then be blockaded until it surrendered. The Japanese also planned for a decisive naval battle, but both sides underestimated the impact of the new technology of submarines and aircraft.

Existence of these secret plans did not imply any intention to wage war with these countries; most militaries in the world engaged in similar practices. Some of the scenarios were used simply as staff exercises and were periodically updated by junior officers as part of their training. Others, however, were regarded as of importance owing to the existence of real or latent tensions and were the subject of consideration by senior planners. Plan Orange, war with Japan, fell into this category, and elements of the plan were incorporated into U.S. strategy during **World War II**. However, all the color plans were officially superseded in 1939 by the **Rainbow Plans**, which assumed the United States would more likely be involved in a two-ocean or multiple-front war with combinations of enemy nations. *See also* PLAN DOG.

ORGANIC ACT OF PUERTO RICO (1917). *See* JONES–SHAFROTH ACT.

OVERLORD, OPERATION. The **World War II** assault on German-held Normandy beaches on 6 June 1944 by forces of the United States, **Great Britain**, and Canada was called Operation Overlord. U.S. forces had been built up in Britain under Operation **Bolero** since 1942. Overlord was under the overall command of U.S. General **Dwight Eisenhower**, though on the day, ground forces were under the command of British General Bernard Montgomery. Parachute troops opened the assault with landings on the flanks of the operational area before dawn. The French resistance responded to coded radio messages and sabotaged German approach routes. A complex deception plan had convinced **Adolf Hitler** that the main attack would come near Calais, and he believed for some time that the Normandy landings were a diversion.

The troops struggled ashore on five beaches, codenamed Juno, Sword, Omaha, Gold, and Utah. The U.S. troops met the stiffest resistance at Omaha beach. The Allies had preponderance of firepower from their naval forces and air superiority, but the early days saw hard battles to get off the beaches and achieve the objectives. British forces struggled to take Caen, and American forces found it heavy going in the Normandy hedgerows and sunken lanes.

A breakout was eventually obtained in Operation Cobra, and German forces, after an ill-advised offensive toward Avranches, were almost encircled in the Falaise Gap. Allied forces, particularly the U.S. Third Army commanded by General George Patton, then sped eastward. Paris was liberated on 22 August 1944, and the Germans were pushed back to take their stand in front of the Rhine.

Overlord was a complex operation and a tribute to the cooperative spirit built up between the Allies as well as their technological ingenuity, especially shown in the ways they tackled the crucial problem of supplying large armies occupying a small beachhead and without a major port to handle the vast amounts of food, fuel, and munitions that had to be shipped across the English Channel. A usable port was not available until the approaches to Antwerp were finally cleared in November. Some supplies could come through Marseilles after **Operation Dragoon**, but the major achievement was the construction of two artificial ports, called Mulberries, installed on the Normandy beaches. At times a touch-and-go operation, for all the Allied superiority on sea and in the air, Overlord was crucial for paving the way to eventual victory in Europe.

– P –

PACIFIC WAR (1941–1945). *See* WORLD WAR II.

PACIFISM. Pacifism is the rejection of war. It is often associated with a broader opposition to all violence. The term was coined in 1901 in Europe to describe the goal of replacing war between nations with the management of interstate relations by international organizations and law. Peace movements had existed in the United States since the 17th century. The oldest extant organization in 1900 was the American Peace Society, formed in 1828. Between 1900 and 1914, 45 more organizations were started, notably the Carnegie Endowment for International Peace (1910), **Jane Addams**'s International Welfare Organization (1904), and **Elihu Root**'s American Society of International Law (1906). With the outbreak of **World War I**, a women's peace parade took place in New York City on 29 August 1914, organized by **Lillian Wald** and **Fanny Garrison Villard**.

During World War I, pacifism took on the narrower meaning of an individual's rejection of war. In the United States, there were groups with long-standing pacifist traditions, notably the Quakers (Society of Friends) and the Anabaptists (Mennonite and Amish). In 1915, the Fellowship of Reconciliation (FOR) was founded to campaign against war, followed by the American Friends Service Committee (1917) and the Mennonite Central Committee (1920), with similar aims. Organizations like the **Women's Peace Party** lost support after U.S. entry in the war in 1917. Most antiwar activism in 1917–18 was done by socialists. Many pacifists focused on ensuring that there would be no more war after this one was won.

The destructiveness of World War I produced a large growth in the numbers of Americans committed to pacifism. Many had been **progressive**s and social reformers, such as Jane Addams, **Dorothy Detzer**, and **Frederick Libby**. Many were socialists, such as **Norman Thomas**, **Devere Allen**, and **A. J. Muste**. Many groups were formed, reflecting the varying philosophical bases for pacifism and differences on the methods that would achieve permanent peace. Some, like the Carnegie Endowment for International Peace, placed their hopes in the creation of world institutions. Others, like FOR and the **War Resisters League**, sought to end war by individual actions of nonviolence. **Salmon Levinson** organized the American Committee for the Outlawry of War in the belief that war could be banned. In 1921, a significant number of pacifist groups formed the **National Council for Prevention of War** as an umbrella group to coordinate activities on which they could all agree. In 1923, publisher Edward Block sponsored a competition for a peace plan: he received 20,000 entries.

It has been estimated that by 1935 over 5 million Americans were members of pacifist organizations, making them a significant element in national politics. After the achievement of female suffrage in 1919, many women activists had turned to pacifism as their main cause. Pacifists tended to incline toward **internationalism**, seeking international cooperation as the alternative to the settlement of disputes by war. Thus, while pacifism shared some attitudes with **isolationism**, and with neutralism, these movements were distinct. Pacifists were strong supporters of **disarmament** measures, such as the 1921 **Naval Disarmament Conference**, and of the 1928 **Kellogg–Briand Pact**. They were influential in the formation of the **Nye Committee** and the passage of the **Neutrality Acts**. They strongly opposed the drift of the United States into war in 1940–41, comprising the main support of the **Keep America out of War Congress**. During **World War II**, pacifists threw their weight behind U.S. membership in the proposed **United Nations**. *See also* LEAGUE OF NATIONS ASSOCIATION; LEAGUE TO ENFORCE PEACE; RANKIN, JEANNETTE PICKERING; WAR RESISTERS LEAGUE; WOMEN'S INTERNATIONAL LEAGUE FOR PEACE AND FREEDOM.

PACT OF PARIS (1928). *See* KELLOGG–BRIAND PACT.

PANAMA CANAL TREATY (1926). The United States completed the Panama Canal in 1914 and retained control of the zone through which it ran. Defense of this zone was regarded as a vital U.S. security interest, as the canal was deemed essential for speedy transoceanic movement of the **U.S. Navy**, which did not yet have a two-ocean capability. On 28 July 1926, the United States signed a treaty with Panama to protect the canal in time of war. According to the treaty, if the United States entered a war, Panama would also regard itself as at war. During peacetime, the United States would be permitted to conduct military maneuvers on Panamanian territory. The treaty was regarded by many Panamanians as an affront to their sovereignty.

PANAMA CONFERENCE (1939). Foreign ministers of American states met in Panama City 23 September–3 October 1939 to agree on a joint response to the outbreak of **World War II** in Europe. Most of the states asserted their neutrality. The exception was Canada, which was not a member of the **Pan-American Union** and was already at war with **Germany**. However, the states demonstrated a pro-Allied bias: the United States persuaded the other states to reduce trade with the **Axis** and to ship key strategic war materials to the United States instead. The conference issued the **Panama Declaration** establishing a hemispheric neutral zone. A committee for economic coordination was also created.

PANAMA DECLARATION (1939). Issued at the 1939 **Panama Conference** held early in **World War II**, the Panama Declaration established a 300-mile neutral security belt around the western hemisphere, except for Canada. No belligerent naval operations were to be allowed within the zone. The zone would be enforced by patrols by the U.S. Atlantic Fleet. *See also* HAVANA, ACT OF.

PAN-AMERICAN CONFERENCE ON CONCILIATION AND ARBITRATION (1928–1929). A conference of American states was held in Washington, D.C., from 10 December 1928 to 5 January 1929, to formulate a system of peaceful arbitration of disputes between the states of **Latin America**, to build on the arrangements made at the 1923 **Santiago Conference** in the **Gondra Treaty**. The conference resulted in two multilateral agreements which came into force in December 1929.

PAN-AMERICAN UNION. Originally designated the Commercial Bureau of American Republics (1890) and then the International Bureau of American Republics (1902), the organization took the name Pan-American Union in 1910. Its main aim was to assist all American republics in the development of their social, economic, and cultural policies, through advice, supervision, judicial action, or arbitration. The underlying ideal was pan-Americanism—a sense of unity and common purpose among the nations of the Americas. The organization's effectiveness in **Latin America** was often undercut, however, by a combination of regional instability, differing priorities, U.S. military action, and **dollar diplomacy**. In 1948, it became the Organization of American States.

PANAY, **USS.** The gunboat USS *Panay* was attacked on 12 December 1937 by Japanese aircraft while patrolling on the Yangtze River in **China**. On 11 December, the *Panay* had taken on board American citizens fleeing the attack on Nanking (Nanjing) by **Japan**. The ship was sunk. Three American crew members were killed, and 43 sailors and 5 civilians were wounded.

The *Panay* was displaying a large U.S. flag, but Japan claimed the attack was an accident, and the United States accepted an apology and an indemnity of $2.2 million. Much of the public outrage was directed at the fact that the *Panay* was originally stationed in China to protect the interests of an oil company. This reaction demonstrated the strength of American **isolationism** at this time. Japan was probably testing U.S. responses, and concluded that for all its statements of sympathy for China, the United States would not take action to halt the Japanese invasion of China. Coming only two months after President **Franklin D. Roosevelt**'s **quarantine speech**, the *Panay* incident revealed the lack of U.S. commitment to opposing aggression, and even more the lack of public support for such a policy, contrasting dramatically with responses to similar events earlier in U.S. history such as the attacks on the *Maine* in 1898 and the *Lusitania* in 1915. *See also* BRUSSELS CONFERENCE; SINO–JAPANESE WAR; STIMSON DOCTRINE.

PARIS PEACE CONFERENCE (1919). Representatives from 32 nations met at the Palace of Versailles, outside Paris, on 18 January 1919 to discuss peace terms after the 11 November 1918 armistice had ended **World War I**. The victorious nations (**Great Britain**, the United States, Italy, **France**, and **Japan**) refused to invite a delegation from **Russia** (which had withdrawn from the war and signed a separate peace in 1918) or from the defeated **Central Powers (Germany**, Austria-Hungary, Bulgaria, and Turkey). The United States was represented by President **Woodrow Wilson**, a Democrat, who chose to exclude Republican members of Congress from the U.S. delegation. This proved politically unwise, as the Republicans had gained control of both houses of Congress in the November 1918 elections, and the president needed the approval of the **Senate Committee on Foreign Relations** for any treaty reached at Paris.

Wilson aimed to establish a peace settlement based on the **Fourteen Points** he had outlined to Congress in January 1918, but French Premier **Georges Clemenceau**, British Prime Minister **David Lloyd George**, and Italian Premier Vittorio Orlando regarded some elements of the program as unworkable, and they were more concerned with territorial redistribution and financial recompense. Orlando eventually walked out of the conference when unable to secure hoped-for territorial gains. Japan was disappointed when it failed to secure endorsement for a "racial equality" amendment to the treaty or to gain permanent possession of the Shantung territory in **China** previously under German control.

The final settlement deprived Germany of around 10 percent of its territory. It was forced to give up its overseas territories and pay **reparations** (initially set at $6.6 billion). Restrictions were placed on the future size of its army and naval forces. The region of Alsace-Lorraine was returned to French control and the Rhineland was demilitarized. The Saarland came under the supervision of the **League of Nations**, the new international organization designed to maintain stability, peace, and security for which Wilson had pushed strongly. The city of Danzig became a "free city" under joint League of Nations and Polish control, while much of Upper Silesia was ceded to **Poland**. This, combined with its loss of colonies, deprived the nascent German republic of much-needed markets and raw materials. Combined with its heavy new financial burden, the settlement undermined the potential for an economically viable or politically stable nation to emerge from the wreckage of imperial Germany.

Further territorial adjustments were made permitting ethnic groups once part of the old Ottoman empire to form their own states in response to Wilson's call for "self-determination" for free peoples. Five separate treaties were eventually produced by the conference, separately covering the conditions to be imposed on each defeated nation and each named after a Paris suburb—Versailles for Germany, **St. Germain** for Austria, **Trianon** for Hungary, Neuilly for Bulgaria, and Sevres for Turkey.

After protracted negotiations over smaller details, the conference finally adjourned on 21 January 1920. Many critics believe the Paris peace negotiations were mismanaged, particularly due to the desire of Britain, Italy, and France to extract revenge and economic benefits from the peace terms and to Wilson's failure to use U.S. influence to achieve a more practical, less punitive settlement. *See also* BERLIN, TREATY OF.

PAZVOLSKY, LEO (1893–1953). Born in **Russia**, Leo Pazvolsky emigrated to the United States in 1905. He reported on the 1919 **Paris Peace Conference** for the *New York Tribune*, and for the *Baltimore Sun* on the **1921 Naval Disarmament Conference** in Washington, D.C. After editing a number of journals concerned with Russian affairs, he joined the **Brookings Institution** in 1922. He studied in Geneva, Switzerland (1932–33) and then worked as an economist in the Bureau of Foreign and Domestic Commerce (1934–35) and in the State Department Division of Trade Agreements (1935–36). Pazvolsky joined the **Council on Foreign Relations** in 1938, and he and **Norman Davis** were its main links to the State Department. He was a Wilsonian **internationalist**.

Pazvolsky was a special assistant to the secretary of state from 1936 to 1946. In 1939, the State Department's **Advisory Committee on Problems of Foreign Relations** was set up on his suggestion. After the committee was abolished, he was made director of the Division of Special Research in February 1941. In 1943, it was split into the divisions of Political and Economic Studies, both of which he supervised while at the same time being executive officer of the **Advisory Committee on Postwar Foreign Policy**. He was a member of the delegation to the 1944 **Dumbarton Oaks Conference** and is best known for his work in drawing up the details of the **United Nations** (UN). He and Secretary of State **Cordell Hull** pressed successfully for a global approach to the organization, rather than one based on regional structures, as favored by **Sumner Welles** and Prime Minister **Winston Churchill** of **Great Britain**.

In 1945, Pazvolsky was a delegate to the conference in **Mexico** that drew up the **Act of Chapultepec**, and to the **San Francisco Conference** where the UN was created. He was president of the first session of the Preparatory Commission of the United Nations. In 1946, he was a member of the U.S. delegation to the UN. He was director of the Brookings Institution from 1946 until his death in 1953.

PEARL HARBOR. In May 1940, the U.S. Pacific Fleet was transferred from its bases on the west coast of the United States to the U.S. naval base at Pearl Harbor, Hawaii, where it was to act as a deterrent against aggression by **Japan**. It was believed that the shallowness and layout of the harbor would prevent any effective air attack on "Battleship Row." When general warnings to be on the alert were received from General **George Marshall** at the end of November 1941, the main danger anticipated was from sabotage. The U.S. Army, responsible for the defense of the base, grouped its aircraft in the center of its airfields as a precaution, making them vulnerable to air attack.

The Japanese *Kido Butai* carrier strike force had sailed across the northern Pacific undetected, and on Sunday 7 December 1941 (Hawaiian time) it launched its attack at dawn, achieving complete surprise. With the loss of only 29 Japanese aircraft, the two strikes sank 5 of the Pacific Fleet's 7 battleships and destroyed 188 aircraft on the ground; 2,403 were killed. Japan's triumph was qualified, however, by the complete failure of simultaneous midget submarine attacks and the fortuitous absence from Pearl Harbor of the Pacific Fleet's three aircraft carriers. Moreover, fuel and repair facilities were not targeted, so Pearl Harbor was able to continue to function as a forward base. This meant that U.S. warships avoided the long journey back to the United States for repairs. All but two of the sunken battleships were refloated and repaired—the *Arizona*, which blew up, was left as a monument. The surprise nature of Pearl Harbor stirred the American people as nothing else could and was a major factor in American determination to achieve total victory over Japan in **World War II**.

PEEK, GEORGE NELSON (1873–1943). After working for the John Deere company and serving on the War Industries Board in **World War I**, George Peek was president of the Moline Plow company from 1919 to 1923, and then president of the American Council of Agriculture. As a result of his business interests, Peek became an advocate of agrarian issues. A Republican, he supported McNary–Haugenism, which advocated requiring the U.S. government to buy farm surplus. When the Republican administrations failed to provide an export subsidy for farmers, he switched to the Democrats.

President **Franklin D. Roosevelt** appointed Peek to head the Agricultural Adjustment Agency (AAA) in 1933. After a few months, he resigned in disagreement with the AAA's view of farm surpluses. Roosevelt made him a foreign trade advisor and president of the **Export-Import Bank**. Peek disagreed with Secretary of State **Cordell Hull** over the **Reciprocal Trade Agreements Act** and resigned in 1935. He rejoined the Republicans and supported Alfred Landon in the 1936 election. Peek inclined to **isolationism**, as did many from the farming states. He became a principal speaker for the **America First Committee** and a member of its national committee.

PEPPER, CLAUDE D. (1900–1989). Lawyer Claude Pepper served in the U.S. Senate (D-Fla.) from 1936 to 1944. Pepper was a firm supporter of President **Franklin D. Roosevelt**. When he sponsored the 1941 **Lend-Lease** Bill in the Senate, his effigy was burned outside the Capitol by **isolationist** women protestors during the debate on the bill. Pepper was defeated in 1950 and returned to law practice. He was elected to the House of Representatives in 1962 and served there until his death. Pepper was awarded the Presidential Medal for Freedom in 1989, four days before he died.

PERMANENT COURT OF INTERNATIONAL JUSTICE. *See* WORLD COURT.

PERMANENT JOINT BOARD ON DEFENSE. This U.S.–Canadian committee to discuss joint defense problems was established at the **Ogdensburg Conference** in August 1940. It was an advisory committee in two national sections. Each section had a civilian chair and members from military and foreign services. It was an important stage in the development of U.S.–Canadian defense cooperation and outlived **World War II**.

PERMANENT MANDATES COMMISSION. Established in 1919 under **League of Nations** control, the commission was to oversee the administration of mandated territories around the world after **World War I**. These were territories already under the supervision of a colonial power (**Great Britain**, for example, was exercising authority over Iraq and Palestine at this time). The oversight function of the commission did not imply direct League control over the territories but the interposition of a structured legal process and the requirement for colonial powers to adhere to predetermined standards in handling the territories. The commission was responsible for reporting conformity to or breaches of these standards to the League council, on the basis of evidence submitted in annual reports by the colonial powers. The system was revised and updated into trusteeships after **World War II**. *See also* KING–CRANE COMMISSION.

PERSHING, JOHN JOSEPH (1860–1948). A West Point graduate, John J. "Black Jack" Pershing saw action in 1898 in **Cuba** during the Spanish–American War. As a result of heroism shown while serving in the **Philippines**, he was awarded the Distinguished Service Cross. He commanded the punitive force which invaded **Mexico** in 1916 in response to a raid on the town of Columbus, New Mexico, by the rebel forces of **Pancho Villa**. Pershing's unit failed to capture Villa and withdrew in 1917.

After the United States joined **World War I**, General Pershing was appointed commander in chief of the **American Expeditionary Force** (AEF). His appointment was opposed by some politicians, including Senator **Henry Cabot Lodge** (who lobbied in favor of General **Leonard Wood**). Pershing faced the tremendous task of organizing the AEF and formulating battle strategy while resisting pressure from America's European associates for the integration of U.S. "doughboys" with existing army units of other countries. Pershing initially refused, declaring, "We came American. We shall remain American and go into battle with Old Glory over our heads." However, he permitted some American troops to fight with British and French army units at Cantigny and Belleau Wood (May–June 1918). On 12 September 1918, Pershing led the first independent American attack of the war—the battle of the St. Mihiel salient. Pershing kept his forces engaged aggressively right up to the cease-fire on 11 November 1918.

Appointed chief of staff of the U.S. Army in 1921, he retired from the army in 1923. Generally reluctant to express political opinions, he was known to be critical of the **Treaty of Versailles**, believing that the terms imposed on **Germany** were too lenient. His autobiography was awarded the 1932 Pulitzer Prize for history.

PHILIPPINE INDEPENDENCE ACT (1934). *See* TYDINGS–MCDUFFIE ACT.

PHILIPPINE ISLANDS. A large archipelago of islands in the Pacific off the coast of mainland Asia, the Philippines were Spanish colonies until acquired by the United States in the Spanish–American War of 1898. After fierce debate in the United States, it was decided to annex them, and they represented the largest effort by the United States at conventional colonialism. The Philippines were well endowed in important resources and occupied a key strategic position. A bitter war (1900–2) against Filipino nationalists, who were formerly allies in the war against Spain, meant the experience soon went sour.

In 1916, the **Jones Act** provided for an elected Philippine senate; local government was already largely in the hands of Filipinos. The executive power remained in U.S. hands. This changed with the 1934 **Tydings–McDuffie Act**, which set a date for full independence and created the Philippine Commonwealth, to last for 10 years before full independence. Manuel Quezon became president in 1935.

When **Japan** began expanding into **China**, the United States started to build air bases in the Philippines, notably on Luzon. American plans to deter the Japanese from advancing against the British and Dutch empires were based on building up a bomber force on Luzon, and knowledge of this was a significant factor in the Japanese belief in 1941 that they had to cripple American forces by a surprise attack. Otherwise, they feared that the United States would act to hinder their operations against their main target, the Dutch East Indies.

Although U.S. air forces were not scheduled to be ready until March 1942, Secretary of State **Cordell Hull** took a hard line with the Japanese in November 1941. When negotiations broke down, Japan opted for war. Twelve hours after the **Pearl Harbor** attack, American bombers on Luzon were caught by surprise on the ground and destroyed. The Japanese invaded the islands, and U.S. and Filipino forces, commanded by General **Douglas MacArthur**, conducted a fighting retreat onto the Bataan peninsula, until forced to surrender in May 1942. The Philippines were occupied by the Japanese, and they set up a puppet administration, but resistance flourished. In October 1944, MacArthur made good his promise to return, following U.S. victory in the Battle of Leyte Gulf. The fighting to liberate the Philippines was still continuing at the time of the Japanese surrender in August 1945. The United States granted the Philippines independence in 1946. *See also* HARE–HAWES–CUTTING ACT.

PHILLIPS, WILLIAM (1878–1968). Graduating from Harvard Law School in 1903, William Phillips joined the Foreign Service and served in London and Peking (Beijing). He was first chief of the new Division of Far Eastern Affairs in the State Department (1908–9), subsequently returning to London. Phillips was assistant secretary of state (1917–20), minister to the Netherlands and Luxembourg (1920–22), undersecretary of state (1922–24), ambassador to Belgium (1924–27), minister to Canada (1927–29), and again undersecretary of state (1933–36).

In 1936, he was appointed ambassador to Italy to improve relations after the 1935 Ethiopian crisis. He resigned in October 1941. Phillips then headed the London office of the **Office of Strategic Services**. In October 1942, he was appointed the president's representative in India. He was strongly in favor of Indian independence, which embittered his relations with the British. Phillips was made special advisor on European politics to General **Dwight D. Eisenhower** in 1943 and retired in 1944. He was briefly called back to service as special assistant to Secretary of State **Edward Stettinius** in 1945. After **World War II**, he served on the Anglo-American Committee on Palestine and on a mediation mission to settle the frontier between Thailand and French Indochina.

PIERSON, WARREN LEE (1896–1978). Warren Pierson served as an artillery lieutenant in France in **World War I**, then graduated from Harvard Law School in 1922. Beginning in 1933, Pierson served as counsel to the Reconstruction Finance Corporation, where he became acquainted with **Jesse Jones**. In 1934, he was made counsel to the new **Export-Import Bank**. He was president of the bank from February 1936 to March 1945. Pierson was instrumental in establishing the business practices of the bank. He traveled to **China** and to **Latin America** and was responsible for the extensive loans made by the bank to encourage development in these areas. After **World War II**, Pierson was chair of Trans-World Airlines (TWA) and headed the U.S. council of the International Chamber of Commerce (ICC). He served as president of the ICC from 1955 to 1957. He represented the United States on the tripartite commission on German debts in London (1951–52), and in the 1960s he chaired the Citizens Committee for International Development.

PITTMAN ACT (1940). On 16 June 1940, during **World War II**, the U.S. Congress passed the Pittman Act, which authorized the sale of munitions to any American republic. Provisions followed on 26 September 1940 that authorized the **Export-Import Bank** to lend the republics up to $500 million and permitted them to purchase up to $400 million worth of munitions for their defense. These programs were taken over by the **Lend-Lease** Administration after March 1941. *See also* LATIN AMERICA.

PITTMAN, KEY (1872–1940). Key Pittman studied law but joined the Klondike gold rush in 1897 and worked as a miner before returning to the law. He served in the U.S. Senate (D-Nev.) from 1913 until 1940. As a politician from a silver-mining state, Pittman advocated hard currency measures. He sponsored the 1919 Pittman Act on silver coinage. As chair of the **Senate Committee on Foreign Relations** (1933–40), he was one of the leaders of the U.S. delegation to the 1933 **London Economic Conference**. His main interest there was securing a decision that the great powers would purchase large amounts of silver to replace paper currency. His concern was mainly in advancing the cause of Nevada silver miners, not monetary economics. When chair of the Foreign Relations Committee, he took a moderate **isolationist** line. During **World War II**, Pittman sponsored the 1940 **Pittman Act** allowing the sale of munitions to any American republic.

PLACENTIA BAY MEETING (1941). On 9–12 August 1941, during **World War II**, U.S. President **Franklin D. Roosevelt** had his first meetings with Prime Minister **Winston Churchill** of **Great Britain**. They met on warships (USS *Augusta* and HMS *Prince of Wales*) anchored in Placentia Bay, off the port of Argentia in Newfoundland. The United States had recently taken up the lease of a base at Argentia under the **destroyers-for-bases deal**. The meeting, code-named Operation Riviera, was highly secret; so far as the U.S. public was concerned, Roosevelt was on a fishing trip.

The meeting marked an important stage in the transition of the United States from a neutral to a nonbelligerent ally of Great Britain, as Roosevelt, Churchill, and their staffs discussed war plans in the event of the United States entering the war. Most importantly, they agreed to a strategy of dealing with **Germany** first, essentially endorsing the **ABC-1** agreements reached earlier in the year by their military planning staffs. They agreed that, if possible, **Japan** should be dealt with firmly, but that a breach in relations should be avoided while the British war with Germany continued. A joint note to Japan was drafted, threatening it with joint action if it continued to act aggressively. The note was considerably watered down from the original proposed by Churchill, though Secretary of State **Cordell Hull**, who was not present at the meeting, regarded it as "dangerously strong."

Having just visited Moscow, **Harry Hopkins** reported on the determination of the **Union of Soviet Socialist Republics** (USSR) to resist the German invasion. A joint note was sent to Soviet Premier **Josef Stalin** proposing a three-power conference; this eventually took place as the 1941 **Moscow Conference** on supply matters. Roosevelt agreed to a set of general war aims with Churchill, known as the **Atlantic Charter**, and this meeting has been seen as marking the firm reentry of the United States into the leading role in world affairs that had been abdicated after 1919.

PLAN DOG. In the fall of 1940, during **World War II**, U.S. military planners set out to adapt the existing contingency plans for strategy in the event that the United States entered the war. Admiral **Harold R. Stark**, chief of naval operations, produced a memorandum for the Joint Planning Board of the two armed forces, to flesh out plans for the scenarios of the **Rainbow Plans**. He outlined four plans. The one with the most potential, he believed, was Plan D, or

Plan Dog. This proposed holding operations against **Japan** while seeking the defeat of **Germany**. Plan Dog was favored by the planners. It was discussed with **Great Britain** and Canada in the ABC talks of January–March 1941 and encapsulated in the **ABC-1 plan**. This was largely approved by President **Franklin D. Roosevelt** and British Prime Minister **Winston Churchill** at their **Placentia Bay Meeting**.

PLATT AMENDMENT (1901). Introduced in the U.S. Senate in February 1901 as an amendment to a military appropriations bill, the Platt Amendment was presented by Orville Platt of Connecticut but composed by Secretary of War **Elihu Root**. It attached conditions to U.S. approval of independence for **Cuba**. The terms of the amendment were required to be written into the Cuban constitution. Most notably, Cuba was required to accept the right of the United States to "intervene for the preservation of Cuban independence, the maintenance of a government adequate for the protection of life, property, and individual liberty." Cuba also was required to "sell or lease to the United States lands necessary for coaling or naval stations at certain specified points to be agreed upon with the President of the United States." Military intervention under the measure came in 1906 and 1912.

   The Platt Amendment secured U.S. dominance of the island and was deeply resented by nationalist Cubans. In 1934, as a result of a shift in the manner in which the United States chose to exercise its hegemony, the amendment was abrogated and the treaty encapsulating it abandoned. There was one exception: the United States retained the base at Guantánamo Bay. *See also* GOOD NEIGHBOR POLICY.

POLAND. Created at the end of **World War I**, the republic of Poland became a major issue for U.S. foreign policy in the second half of **World War II**. Differences developed between the United States, **Great Britain**, and the **Union of Soviet Socialist Republics** (USSR), notably with regard to Poland's frontiers and the composition of its government. Soviet Premier **Josef Stalin** demanded that Poland concede its eastern territory to the USSR. This was agreed to at the 1943 **Teheran Conference**, with Poland to be compensated with territory from **Germany**. President **Franklin D. Roosevelt** agreed with Stalin that Poland should have a government friendly to the USSR, but he also wanted it to be selected by democratic means.

At the 1945 **Yalta Conference**, an agreement was reached to create a provisional Polish government by expanding the communist administration the USSR had established in Lublin with the addition of members of the Polish Home Army resistance organization and from the exiled Polish government in London. The failure of the USSR to keep to this agreement was a major cause of the deterioration of relations at the start of the administration of President **Harry S. Truman**. A compromise was reached by **Harry Hopkins** in Moscow in June 1945 that brought in a token representation of London Poles, and meant that Poland could become a member of the **United Nations**. Poland did not actually experience the free elections promised at Yalta until after the end of the Cold War.

POLAR BEAR EXPEDITION. *See* NORTH RUSSIA, INTERVENTION IN.

POLK, FRANK LYON (1871–1943). Lawyer Frank Polk was a counselor in the State Department who dealt with diplomatic issues arising from General **John J. Pershing**'s raid across the border of **Mexico** and from President **Woodrow Wilson**'s neutrality and **preparedness** policies during **World War I**. Polk was the first person to assume the title "undersecretary of state," and he stood in for Secretary of State **Robert Lansing** when the latter was at the 1919 **Paris Peace Conference**. Polk later became temporary head of the U.S. delegation in Paris, as the conference wound down. In 1924, he ran the convention operation for "dark horse" Democratic presidential candidate John W. Davis.

POTSDAM CONFERENCE (1945). The final summit meeting of the major Allies during **World War II** was held 16 July–2 August 1945 in Potsdam, outside Berlin. This was President **Harry S. Truman**'s only meeting with Premier **Josef Stalin** of the **Union of Soviet Socialist Republics** (USSR). Prime Minister **Winston Churchill** of

Great Britain suffered electoral defeat halfway through the conference and was replaced by Clement Attlee.

At Potsdam, Truman informed Stalin in general terms of the successful testing of the **atomic bomb** (Trinity test). No agreement was reached on the main topics of discussion: the occupation of **Germany** and **reparations**. It was agreed that the frontier of **Poland** should extend to the Oder and western Neisse Rivers. Stalin confirmed that the USSR would enter the war against **Japan**. The Potsdam Declaration was issued, demanding Japan's unconditional surrender. Truman proposed the internationalization of European waterways, notably the Danube, but this was rejected by Stalin. The United States and Britain refused to recognize the governments the Soviets had installed in Romania and Bulgaria. In order to maintain contact and to deal with the issues on which they could not agree, Truman, Stalin, and Attlee agreed that a Council of Foreign Ministers should meet regularly. No arrangements were agreed on for a formal peace conference.

PREPAREDNESS CAMPAIGN. President **Woodrow Wilson**'s response to the 1915 *Lusitania* incident during **World War I**, and to growing pressure from anti-German opinion in America, was to ask Congress to approve a massive ship construction program. The United States had far fewer ships and troops than **Germany** and **Japan**. The "preparedness" campaign caused unease among antiwar factions, who believed it to be provocative to the **Central Powers**. However, it helped Wilson gain support from interventionists such as **Theodore Roosevelt** while still enabling him to fight the 1916 election on the slogan "He kept us out of war." *See also* HUGHES, CHARLES EVANS.

PROGRESSIVISM. A reform movement in the United States during the late 19th and early 20th centuries, progressivism had its roots in efforts to "clean up" urban politics and tackle corrupt party "machines" dominating major cities such as New York and Chicago. The movement also had its roots in the crusade for Prohibition, women's rights, and labor rights and in campaigns waged simultaneously for minimum wage and child labor laws. These campaigns grew in number and strength as **immigration** and industrialization swelled city populations and increased the pressure for reform.

The progressive agenda focused on social injustice and political inequality. Progressives such as **Robert M. La Follette** advocated primaries, ballot initiatives, and referenda as means to bypass "boss control" of party nomination procedures. President **Theodore Roosevelt** adopted some aspects of progressivism during his administration (1901–9), particularly in environmental initiatives and food hygiene laws. President **Woodrow Wilson** also supported numerous progressive reforms, including direct election of U.S. senators, a national income tax, and minimum work hours laws.

Progressives were found in both the Democratic and Republican parties. During the 1920s, progressive Republican members of Congress fought running battles with Republican administrations over pro-business policies. In foreign policy, progressives did not all congregate at the liberal end of the political spectrum. Some, such as **William Borah,** endorsed reform at home but were **isolationist** in international affairs. Others, while supportive of the **League of Nations**, remained suspicious of the expansion of U.S. **trade** and global business interests. Many progressives, however, backed U.S. membership in the League of Nations and the **World Court** and later supported the creation of the **United Nations**.

PROTECTIONISM. *See* FORDNEY–MCCUMBER TARIFF ACT; SMOOT–HAWLEY TARIFF ACT; TARIFFS; TRADE.

PURPLE. The U.S. code name for the encryption machine used by **Japan** prior to and during **World War II** was Purple. The secrets of the machine were penetrated by army and navy cryptanalysts in Operation **Magic**. The Japanese never discovered that the encoding machine had been penetrated, and indeed continued to use it for a time during the postwar U.S. occupation. Decrypts of diplomatic messages sent on the Purple machine played a significant role in the conduct of U.S. operations in World War II and provided vital information about the European fronts as well as the Pacific. Purple was used by all Japanese foreign service missions overseas, and by penetrating it, U.S. cryptanalysts could read messages from Japanese embassies throughout the war, notably in Berlin, where the Japanese ambassador had access to much secret information. *See also* SIGNALS INTELLIGENCE.

– Q –

QUARANTINE SPEECH. The quarantine speech was a keynote foreign policy address delivered by President **Franklin D. Roosevelt** on 5 October 1937, in the **isolationist** stronghold of Chicago. In the speech, Roosevelt characterized aggression as a contagion and suggested that peace-loving states needed to join together to quarantine it and prevent it from spreading. The concept bore similarities to the neutrality patrols being carried out by the navies of **Great Britain** and **France** at that time to try to contain the **Spanish Civil War**. But Roosevelt did not go beyond generalities in the speech and did not follow up with any concrete proposals. It remains something of a mystery exactly what Roosevelt intended with the speech, and why he did not take any further action. He said later that he had tried to lead the nation but looked behind to find no one following. In fact, press reaction was reasonably positive. However, as a sensitive reader of public opinion, Roosevelt clearly decided that this was not a popular enough concept to pursue further at the time.

QUEBEC CONFERENCE (1943). U.S. President **Franklin D. Roosevelt**, Prime Minister **Winston Churchill** of **Great Britain**, and Prime Minister William Mackenzie King of Canada met in Quebec 19–24 August 1943, during **World War II**, for a strategic conference code-named Quadrant. The conference was concerned with plans for the invasion of France (Operation **Overlord**), the fighting in Burma, landings in Southeast Asia, and the Italian campaign.

QUEBEC CONFERENCE (1944). A joint U.S., British, and Canadian political and strategic conference code-named Octagon was held in Quebec 13–16 September 1944, during **World War II**. Participants discussed plans for moving naval forces to the Pacific after the defeat of **Germany** and assessed routes of advance for Allied forces into Germany. Politically, the principal topic was the **Morgenthau Plan** for Germany, which was accepted by President **Franklin D. Roosevelt** and Prime Minister **Winston Churchill** of Great Britain only to be later rejected.

QUOTA ACT (1921). *See* EMERGENCY QUOTA ACT.

QUOTA ACT (1924). *See* NATIONAL ORIGINS ACT.

– R –

RAINBOW PLANS. U.S. strategic contingency planning before **World War II** comprised a series of plans, each taking a different state as potential enemy, coded by colors. **Japan** was dealt with in Plan **Orange**; **Great Britain** was Red; **Germany** was Black. As crises in Europe and Asia intensified and the **Axis** powers drew together, it became more likely that the United States would be faced by coalitions of powers. The Rainbow Plans were therefore formulated, assuming various combinations. The most important was Rainbow 5, which posited an enemy combination of Germany, Italy, and Japan. The **Tripartite Pact** of September 1940 made this combination a reality, and Rainbow 5 became the main U.S. strategic concept. The Joint Planning Board then considered the implications of this, and the result was Admiral **Harold Stark**'s **Plan Dog**.

RANKIN, JEANNETTE PICKERING (1880–1973). Politician Jeanette Rankin was the first woman elected to the U.S. House of Representatives (November 1916). She represented Montana for one term (1917–19) before making an unsuccessful bid for a seat in the Senate (1918). In 1940, she was again elected a member of the House (1941–43). In 1917, she was one of 50 members of the House to vote against the request of President **Woodrow Wilson** for a **declaration of war** against **Germany**. In 1941, she was the only member to oppose President **Franklin D. Roosevelt**'s request for a **declaration of war** against **Japan** after the attack at **Pearl Harbor**. Throughout her life, Rankin was a dedicated campaigner for the causes of women's rights, child welfare, and birth control. She remained politically active after 1943, In 1968, she headed a march protesting the Vietnam War in Washington, D.C. *See also* PACIFISM.

RAPALLO, TREATY OF (1922). Signed between the **Russian Soviet Federated Socialist Republic** and **Germany** (the Weimar Republic) on 17 April 1922, the Rapallo Treaty was the first formal recognition of the communist government of the former Russian empire by a major Western power. The move caused some dissension between Germany and the United States, since the latter was still pursuing a policy of nonrecognition toward the **Union of Soviet Socialist Republics** (USSR) until the Soviets assumed responsibility for the **war debts** incurred by **Russia** in **World War I**, ceased propaganda demanding worldwide revolution, and put in place some basic domestic safeguards for life and property.

RAPIDAN CONFERENCE (1929). On 4–10 October 1929, Prime Minister Ramsay MacDonald of **Great Britain** had informal discussions with U.S. President **Herbert Hoover** in Washington, D.C., and at Hoover's country camp at Rapidan, Virginia. The press reported that at Rapidan they talked for hours sitting on a log. They discussed the need for a further naval **disarmament** conference and the implementation of the **Kellogg–Briand Pact**. Their agreement formed the basis of the discussions at the 1930 **Naval Disarmament Conference** in London. At one point, Hoover suggested the purchase of the British colonies of Bermuda, Trinidad, and British Honduras in exchange for Britain's **war debt** to the United States.

RECIPROCAL TRADE AGREEMENTS ACT. The U.S. Congress passed the Reciprocal Trade Agreements Act in March 1934, by 274–111 in the House and 57–33 in the Senate. Under the act, the president was empowered to cut **tariffs** by up to 50 percent, principally by bilateral **trade** agreements giving "most favored nation" status; each signatory would enjoy the lowest available tariff from the other. This constituted a means of lowering the high U.S. tariffs instituted under the **Smoot–Hawley Tariff** in 1930. Since the action was reciprocal, it helped restore the flow of trade damaged by the Great Depression, high tariff protectionism, and collapse of the **gold standard**. It also gave the president increased discretion in foreign economic affairs, since he could make reciprocal agreements without presenting each one for congressional approval.

Secretary of State **Cordell Hull** had long supported such arrangements, and they were his sole foreign policy initiative. He believed strongly that mutual trade was the key to international peace. While he preferred multilateral arrangements, with all nations reducing their tariffs together, economic nationalists in Congress were able to limit him to bilateral ones, in each of which the United States would receive tangible benefits.

The act was renewed in 1937, 1940, 1943, and 1945. By 1941, the State Department had negotiated 30 such agreements, mostly in the western hemisphere. This had the effect of tying the trade of the countries concerned closer to the United States, and the agreements were sometimes accompanied by warnings of the consequences should they also reduce tariffs for other nations. The effect was to preserve U.S. export markets. The measure did not lead to the spectacular increases in exports that its advocates had predicted when it was debated by Congress, but it did help to open new markets and was an important means by which the executive could offset the potential harm to foreign relations caused by the tendency of Congress at this time to favor high protectionist tariffs.

REPARATIONS. Reparations are the financial compensation from defeated powers in the aftermath of war. Delegates representing the victorious powers (chiefly **Great Britain**, the United States, Italy, and **France**) at the 1919 **Paris Peace Conference** following **World War I** demanded $6.6 billion in reparations from **Germany**. The figure was finally revised upward to $31.5 billion by the Inter-Allied Reparations Commission in 1921.

The postwar economic slump, combined with the loss of markets and raw materials imposed by the **Treaty of Versailles**, rendered it almost impossible for Germany to meet its financial obligations. The United States intervened twice (with the 1924 **Dawes Plan** and 1929 **Young Plan**) to reschedule Germany's debts and reduce the pressure of a tight repayment schedule. In 1931, with the global economic depression intensifying, the German government suspended payments in a bid to rescue its ailing economy.

A final settlement of the reparations issue was reached at the 1932 **Lausanne Conference** but was never activated. The issue of reparations was linked, at least by European politicians, to the question of repayment of **war debts**. Arthur Balfour, former prime minister of Great Britain, indicated that the pressure for reparations exerted on Germany by Britain and France reflected the pressure on them to repay U.S. loans to them during the war. The Lausanne agreement foundered on the failure of the U.S. Congress to agree to this linkage and to cancel the debts in response to the cancellation of reparations. However, no more reparations payments were made after the financial collapse of 1931. In total, Germany paid about one-eighth of the sum fixed in April 1921 and received considerably more than that in loans in 1924–29 to help its financial recovery.

The difficulties experienced with reparations led both the United States and Great Britain to oppose them at the end of **World War II**, and this became a cause of contention with the **Union of Soviet Socialist Republics** at the **Yalta** and **Potsdam conferences** in 1945.

REUBEN JAMES, **USS.** The destroyer USS *Reuben James* was the first U.S. warship sunk in **World War II**. It was on convoy protection duty near Iceland when hit by a torpedo from a German submarine on 31 October 1941. It sank with the loss of 100 lives. The loss of the *Reuben James* was a significant factor in producing a majority (albeit slim) in favor of the removal of the **cash-and-carry** provision of the **Neutrality Acts** by Congress on 13 November 1941. See also *KEARNY*, USS.

REYNOLDS, ROBERT RICE (1884–1963). A flamboyant and eccentric character, but also a skilled manipulator of class politics, Robert Rice Reynolds connected with Depression-era concerns of the lower economic classes. He was an attorney from Asheville, North Carolina, who ran unsuccessfully for lieutenant governor in 1924 and senator in 1926 before succeeding with a personality-bashing populist campaign in 1932. He served in the U.S. Senate from 1933 to 1945. Reynolds supported President **Franklin D. Roosevelt**'s New Deal programs, but uniquely among southern Democratic senators, he was also a strident advocate of **isolationism**.

Reynolds took a strong stance against all **immigration**, including that of children from Nazi **Germany**. He was characterized in the press as pro-fascist and had close relations with extreme right-wing figures like **Gerald L. K. Smith**. Roosevelt tried to run Franklin W. Hancock against him in the 1938 North Carolina Democratic primary, but Reynolds was reelected. In March 1939, Reynolds became vice chair of the **Islands for War Debts Committee**, not realizing the organization was a front for German-directed propaganda. He allowed his congressional franking privileges to be used to disseminate anti-British propaganda after having introduced into the Senate the proposal of exchanging **Great Britain** and **France**'s island colonies for remission of **war debts**, and having read the press release of the committee into the record.

Reynolds associated with openly anti-Semitic groups such as the Knights of the White Camelia and Father **Charles Coughlin**'s Christian Front. In April 1940, early in **World War II**, Reynolds supplied a German agent with information about ports in France. He was never charged with any offense and went on to become chair of the Senate Committee on Military Affairs in 1941. However, his widely known associations with people like Coughlin brought about his defeat for renomination by his party in 1944. He tried and failed to get the nomination again in 1950.

RIO DE JANEIRO CONFERENCE (1942). Foreign ministers of all 21 American republics met on 15–28 January 1942 in Rio de Janeiro, **Brazil**, to discuss the strengthening of political and economic cooperation in the western hemisphere. The main topic turned out to be methods whereby the other states would assist the United States against the **Axis** powers during **World War II**. The delegates voted to recommend to their governments that they should break diplomatic relations with the Axis. All except Chile and **Argentina** did so soon after the conference (Chile broke off relations on 20 January 1943 and Argentina on 26 January 1944). Brazil, formerly pro-German, moved away from its neutral stance. *See also* LATIN AMERICA.

ROBERTS, OWEN (1875–1955). A law professor at the University of Pennsylvania, Owen Roberts served as U.S. assistant district attorney in **World War I**. In 1924, he investigated the Teapot Dome scandal. In 1930, he was appointed to the Supreme Court by President **Herbert Hoover**. Roberts was a Republican but more moderate than some of the other conservative justices. In 1942, he chaired the investigation into the **Pearl Harbor** attack, which focused on errors made in Hawaii. Ignoring the Washington dimension, it was critical of the commanders in the field. He dissented from the Supreme Court's decision in the 1944 *Korematsu* case confirming the legality of internment of Japanese Americans in **World War II**. Increasingly at odds with more liberal justices, Roberts resigned from the Court in 1945, returning to the Pennsylvania Law School.

ROCKEFELLER, NELSON ALDRICH (1908–1979). A grandson of millionaire John D. Rockefeller, Nelson Rockefeller was director of the family oil business in Venezuela during the 1930s. He became an advocate of the **Good Neighbor policy** and supported improved cultural, scientific, and educational relations between the United States and **Latin America**. In 1940, President **Franklin D. Roosevelt** made him coordinator of commercial and cultural relations between the American republics, which later became the **Office of the Coordinator of Inter-American Affairs**. He had special responsibility for propaganda activities in the region. Rockefeller was also chair of the Inter-American Development Commission and Corporation (1940–47). In that capacity, and also as president of the Museum of Modern Art (1939–58), which he had founded, Rockefeller organized a major cultural program of exhibitions to raise the image of the United States and counter fascist influences in the region.

Rockefeller was appointed in 1944 to be assistant secretary for Latin American Affairs. He was one of the leading figures in the creation of the **Act of Chapultepec**. Concerned with possible communist penetration, Rockefeller promoted the idea of collective action. In 1945, he returned to the family's philanthropic activities but was put in charge of the International Advisory Board, part of President **Harry S. Truman**'s Point Four Program. Rockefeller supported the **United Nations** and U.S. membership in the North Atlantic Treaty Organization. A Republican, Rockefeller opposed conservative members of the party like **Robert A. Taft**.

In President **Dwight D. Eisenhower**'s administration, Rockefeller was undersecretary in the Department of Health, Education, and Welfare (1953–55). He became special assistant to the president for foreign affairs (1954–55), and was a member and subsequently head of the Operations Coordinating Board of the National Security Council (1953–58), supervising Central Intelligence Agency operations. Rockefeller was governor of New York (1959–73), defeating incumbent **Averell Harriman** in the 1958 election. After failed presidential bids in 1964 and 1968, he was vice president of the United States (1974–77) under President Gerald R. Ford.

ROGERS ACT. *See* FOREIGN SERVICE ACT.

ROOSEVELT COROLLARY (1904). A unilateral declaration claiming a U.S. prerogative of exercising "international police power" in the western hemisphere, the Roosevelt Corollary was first set forth by President **Theodore Roosevelt** on 20 May 1904 in a published letter to Secretary of War **Elihu Root**. Roosevelt was particularly alarmed in 1902 by the blockade and bombardment of Venezuela by **Germany** and **Great Britain**. As he wrote to Root, "Brutal wrongdoing, or an impotence which results in a general loosening of the ties of civilizing society, may finally require intervention by some civilized nation; and in the Western Hemisphere the United States cannot ignore this duty."

In his annual messages to Congress on 6 December 1904 and 5 December 1905, Roosevelt invoked the **Monroe Doctrine**. In March 1905, in order to forestall forced debt collection in Santo Domingo by Italy, **France**, and Belgium, he appointed a collector of customs in that indebted nation and established a de facto protectorate. Never before had the Monroe Doctrine been used to forbid temporary European intervention in order to collect debts or honor international obligations. During the presidencies of **William H. Taft** and **Woodrow Wilson**, interventions in Honduras, the **Dominican Republic**, Haiti, and **Nicaragua** were defended on the basis of the Roosevelt Corollary. *See also* CLARK MEMORANDUM; LATIN AMERICA.

ROOSEVELT, FRANKLIN DELANO (1882–1945). The 32nd president of the United States, Franklin D. Roosevelt was a distant cousin of President **Theodore Roosevelt**. He was a member of the wealthy New York elite, educated at the select Groton School, Harvard, Columbia Law School, and in **Germany**. He entered New York politics as a Democrat, and he served as assistant secretary of the navy in President **Woodrow Wilson**'s administration during **World War I**. Roosevelt ran for vice president in 1920 with presidential candidate James M. Cox, on a platform that endorsed U.S. membership in the **League of Nations**. In 1921, Roosevelt contracted infantile paralysis (polio), becoming paralyzed from the waist down, but he refused to follow his doctor's advice to quit politics.

In 1928, Roosevelt was elected governor of New York. During the Great Depression, he initiated activist reforms to help the poor and unemployed in the state, enacting proposals developed by his "brains trust" of advisors. In the 1932 election, he ran for president and beat President **Herbert Hoover** with a majority of 12 million votes. During the campaign, Roosevelt promised a "New Deal" for the American people, and this became the label given to the solutions enacted by his administration to the problems of the Depression. The New Deal was less a coherent program, more an approach of "constant, bold experimentation," as Roosevelt put it in his first inaugural address.

The New Deal's activism was not reflected in foreign policy during his first term. He sought an essentially nationalist solution to the Depression, rejected Hoover's suggestions to forge an international response, and by his indifference undermined the 1933 **London Economic Conference**. Roosevelt encouraged the investigations of the **Nye Committee**, in part because they mirrored his theme at that time of criticizing big business. However, he would have preferred that the resulting **Neutrality Act** (1935) gave him more discretion to act on his own judgment and selectively apply trade embargoes.

The neutrality policy was immediately tested when Italy invaded Ethiopia in October 1935. The embargo on sales of arms operated to the disadvantage of the victim of aggression. Roosevelt's attempt to persuade U.S. businesses, especially oil companies, to operate a voluntary "moral embargo" on Italy was unsuccessful. When the **Spanish Civil War** broke out in June 1936, Roosevelt verbally supported the efforts of the other powers to isolate the conflict with naval neutrality patrols, and he made his first cautious statements, in an address at **Chautauqua**, that the United States could be directly affected by such conflicts even though they were taking place on other continents. However, the reenacted Neutrality Act (1936) reiterated Congress's determination to avoid becoming involved in such conflicts.

Roosevelt was reelected in November 1936 in a landslide, winning all states except Maine and Vermont. The election was mainly a referendum on the New Deal, and foreign affairs played no part. They were to become increasingly urgent in Roosevelt's second term, and his actions and attitudes have been subject to much debate. The principal question is the degree to which Roosevelt regarded the rise of Nazi Germany and **Japan**'s aggression in **China** as a threat to the United States that required a more interventionist policy, or whether he shared the popular belief that the United States should isolate itself from these affairs. His **quarantine speech** in Chicago on 5 October 1937 implied the former, but his failure to follow the speech with any concrete proposals and his accommodating attitude regarding the *Panay* incident in December suggest he did not believe he could risk getting ahead of **isolationist** public opinion. His popularity was falling at that time, after a disastrous attempt to meddle with the composition of the Supreme Court, and after reductions in New Deal programs had brought an economic recession.

In the **Sino–Japanese War**, he avoided calling the aggression a war, so that the Neutrality Act was not activated. This meant aid to China could be provided, but it also meant U.S. companies continued their lucrative trade with Japan.

Roosevelt's approach to both Asian and European problems was to propose international conferences while making clear that the United States would not act as guarantor of any arrangement. To both Europeans and Asians, this appeared a signal of U.S. indifference. Roosevelt voiced some misgivings about the policy of appeasement followed by **Great Britain** and **France** but also approved attempts to solve the problems by negotiation, which was the essence of appeasement. It is likely Roosevelt believed it was against U.S. interests that the aggressors should be victorious but did not see it as a matter vital to U.S. security and did not see how to respond within the limitations of an isolationism that he at least partly shared.

After **World War II** broke out in Europe on 1 September 1939, Roosevelt announced, like Woodrow Wilson had during **World War I**, that the United States would remain neutral, but Roosevelt added that Americans could not be blind to facts. He began to deploy national security arguments to indicate that U.S. interests were best served by an Allied victory. He did this when asking Congress to revise the Neutrality Act, arguing that extending **cash-and-carry** to sales of munitions would help keep the United States out of war by aiding those whose victory was in American interest. It was at this time that **Winston Churchill**, then British First Lord of the

Admiralty, opened correspondence with Roosevelt. Once Churchill became prime minister in May 1940, his pleas for U.S. assistance increased, but Roosevelt's policy remained consistently that the United States would supply materials on a cash-and-carry basis. He did, however, press for U.S. rearmament. His critics alleged that he was deliberately edging the United States toward war, but the evidence suggests that he believed an Allied victory could be achieved without direct U.S. intervention. The fall of France in June 1940 was a shock but did not alter this attitude.

Roosevelt was prepared to support the introduction of the **Selective Training and Service Act**, once **Grenville Clark** and others had floated the idea. When Churchill pleaded that large amounts of the materials the British were buying were being lost to German submarines, he found a way around the Neutrality Act by negotiating the **destroyers-for-bases** deal in August–September 1940. Isolationist hostility picked up in response to this unneutral action. Roosevelt ran for an unprecedented third term in November 1940. His opponent, **Wendell Willkie**, was not an isolationist. Foreign policy inevitably featured in the campaign, although primarily the election was once again about the New Deal and Roosevelt's leadership. Roosevelt stated in a speech in Boston that "American boys" were not going to be sent to fight in "foreign wars." He won another convincing victory, though with a reduced majority.

Faced with an increasingly desperate British economic position, Roosevelt unveiled **Lend-Lease**, arguing that it was time to set aside the "silly, foolish dollar sign." He spelled out for the American people how he saw the world conflict and its significance for the United States in a "fireside chat" on 29 December. He said that the Allies were fighting for freedom, including that of the United States, reiterating warnings against isolation he had given in the **Charlottesville speech** in June. Despite this, the United States would not become a belligerent: it would become the **arsenal of democracy**. In his address to Congress on 6 January 1941, he reiterated the idealistic consequences of an Allied victory in his concept of the **Four Freedoms**.

Congress passed the Lend-Lease Act on 11 March. In order to protect shipments to Britain, Roosevelt extended the patrol zone of the **U.S. Navy** as far as Iceland. U.S. troops occupied bases in Greenland

and then took over from the British in Iceland. However, the navy was under orders not to shoot at German submarines and was only supposed to escort U.S., not foreign, vessels. Confrontations in the Atlantic multiplied, and at times, such as with the *Greer* and *Reuben James* incidents, Roosevelt used them as pretexts to intensify the engagement of the U.S. Navy, but at other times he allowed provocations to go unremarked, and since Germany did the same, the situation in the Atlantic reached a quasi-belligerent stand-off.

Roosevelt met with Churchill at **Placentia Bay**, where they concluded the **Atlantic Charter**. But he received a warning of the strength of antiwar feeling when selective service was extended by only one vote. Roosevelt agreed with Churchill that they would try to avoid a break with Japan, on the principle of beating Germany first. Roosevelt had generally left policy toward Japan in the hands of Secretary of State **Cordell Hull** and the State Department. In 1940, he had come to believe, in response to ambassador **Joseph C. Grew**'s recent messages, that a firm line might deter Japan from further expansion, and that this would be an easy way to assist Britain, by gaining security for the vital resources coming from the British empire in the Far East. He thus approved tightening economic pressure on Japan with embargoes. In July 1941, following the Japanese entry into southern Indochina, he ordered a freeze on Japanese assets in the United States. This was extended by **Dean Acheson** and other State Department officials to include a total embargo on exports of oil to Japan.

Once the United States entered the war following Japan's attack on Pearl Harbor, Roosevelt conducted relations with the major allies himself. He preferred either personal contacts, relying on his formidable charm to smooth over any problems, or the use of emissaries such as **Joseph Davies, Averell Harriman, Patrick Hurley,** Wendell Willkie, and **Harry Hopkins**. His main war objectives were simple: achieve complete victory over the **Axis**, and do so with as few American casualties as possible. He was publicly committed to the creation of an effective international organization, and he put major efforts into getting commitment from the **Union of Soviet Socialist Republics** (USSR) to the new **United Nations**. But his **four policemen** concept recognized the role of the great powers.

Roosevelt sought to draw Soviet Premier **Josef Stalin** into the world system by building an atmosphere of mutual trust, supplying aid without bargaining, and at the 1943 **Teheran Conference** by trying to distance himself from Churchill. With regard to Soviet territorial ambitions, he took a strong line against spheres of influence but acknowledged that the USSR needed friendly governments on its borders. At the 1945 **Yalta Conference**, Roosevelt made concessions at China's expense to get Soviet involvement in the war with Japan. Critics argue that he gave away Eastern Europe to Stalin at Yalta; however, the USSR had already gained control of this territory through the actions of the Soviet Red Army.

With regard to China, Roosevelt hoped that **Chiang Kai-shek** could unite the country, provide strong opposition to Japan, and help with the decolonization of Southeast Asia. There is evidence that by late 1944 he had become disillusioned in this regard, though public enthusiasm for Chiang prevented any alternate policy.

Roosevelt's conduct regarding the home front remained that of a bureaucratic improviser—or as he liked to call himself, a "juggler"—balancing competing interests and agencies by political skill. The results were some administrative confusion, even after the efforts of **James F. Byrnes**, but also a highly successful mobilization of the American people and economy for total war, within the context of American voluntarism and continuing party politics. From January 1944, Roosevelt's health was deteriorating, but he ran for an unprecedented fourth term in 1944, winning a convincing majority. He died of a cerebral hemorrhage at Warm Springs, Georgia, on 12 April 1945 and was succeeded by his vice president, **Harry S. Truman**.

ROOSEVELT, THEODORE (1858–1919). The 25th president of the United States, Theodore Roosevelt was a high-profile public figure as the city police commissioner and later governor of New York. He captured national attention in 1898 by quitting his post as assistant secretary of the **U.S. Navy** in the administration of President William B. McKinley to lead a cavalry regiment in **Cuba** during the Spanish–American war. Roosevelt's charge up San Juan Hill made him a public hero and facilitated his nomination as vice president of the United States in 1900. In September 1901, he became president after the assassination of McKinley.

Roosevelt was a dynamic and popular president, augmenting executive power, launching antitrust lawsuits against corporate monopolies, personally mediating a major industrial dispute in the coal industry, and advocating various **progressive** policies, including environmentalism, reform of housing, and hygiene standards. In foreign policy, he adhered to his favorite African proverb: "Speak softly and carry a big stick, you will go far." This big-stick diplomacy was used to justify interventions in **Latin America** under terms laid down by the **Monroe Doctrine**. The **Roosevelt Corollary** (1904) to the doctrine permitted U.S. intervention whenever "brutal wrongdoing" was deemed to pose a threat to the stability of a Latin American country, or where there was a risk of default on debts or of foreign aggression.

A dedicated nationalist and imperialist, Roosevelt embraced both the risks and the responsibilities accompanying the world power status which he sought for the United States. Under his administration, the United States encouraged the rebellion of Panama against Colombian rule in order to secure favorable terms for construction of the Panama Canal (the United States later paid compensation to Colombia). Roosevelt also negotiated peace between the warring powers of **Japan** and **Russia** (1905) and was consequently awarded the Nobel Peace Prize.

When his chosen successor, **William H. Taft**, won in the 1908 election, Roosevelt embarked on a year-long journey through Europe and Africa. But increasingly critical of the Taft administration, he challenged the incumbent president for the Republican Party nomination in 1912. Failing to unseat Taft, Roosevelt ran as an independent. The split in the Republican vote ensured the election of Democrat **Woodrow Wilson**. During the Wilson years, Roosevelt supported progressive causes, some of which were also espoused by the president. He supported Wilson's policy of neutrality in the early stages of **World War I** but also argued strongly for **preparedness**. His rhetoric became more strongly anti-German as unrestricted submarine warfare led to U.S. casualties, and he attacked the administration's restrained response to the sinking of the *Lusitania* (1915).

After the United States entered the war, Wilson declined Roosevelt's request for a military assignment in **France**. Roosevelt offered qualified support for U.S. membership in the **League of Nations**, but he had reservations about League influence over U.S. foreign policy similar to those of **Henry Cabot Lodge**. By the beginning of 1919, Republican Party sentiment was turning decisively toward a third term in the White House for Theodore Roosevelt, but he died suddenly in his sleep on 6 January 1919. *See also* CLARK MEMORANDUM; THOMSON–URRUTIA TREATY.

ROOT, ELIHU (1845–1937). Lawyer Elihu Root served as U.S. secretary of war under President William B. McKinley (1899–1901) and President **Theodore Roosevelt** (1901–4). He succeeded John Hay as Roosevelt's secretary of state (1905–9). Roosevelt wanted Root to succeed him as president, but Root's refusal to run forced the president to turn to **William H. Taft**. Root was instrumental in developing and improving U.S. relations with **Japan** and Central America. He was a leading proponent of the **open door policy** toward **China**.

Root became a power within the Republican Party and served as a U.S. senator for New York from 1909 to 1915. He successfully opposed a bill that sought exemptions from toll payments for U.S. shipping using the Panama Canal. Root undertook special missions at the request of President **Woodrow Wilson**, visiting **Russia** in 1917 in an effort to persuade the Kerensky government to keep Russian armies fighting in **World War I**. He became distanced from the president, however, over his mild reservationist views on membership in the **League of Nations**.

President **Warren G. Harding** considered asking Root to return to the State Department in 1921 but instead selected **Charles Evans Hughes**. Harding invited Root to be a delegate to the 1921 **Naval Disarmament Conference** in Washington, D.C., where he was instrumental in laying the foundations for the Five Power Treaty. Harding also sought Root's help in his campaign for U.S. membership in the **World Court** (Root had been one of the consultants assisting the League of Nations in devising the court). Through the 1920s, Root continued to press for U.S. membership but was unsuccessful. He was president of the Carnegie Endowment for International Peace (1910–25). In 1929, he served as the unofficial U.S. representative at the League of Nations.

ROPER, DANIEL CALHOUN (1867–1943). Daniel Roper was assistant postmaster general in 1916 and chaired President **Woodrow Wilson**'s election campaign that year. Wilson made him chair of the U.S. Tariff Commission in 1917, and he served as Commissioner of Internal Revenue (1917–21). Roper was appointed secretary of commerce by President **Franklin D. Roosevelt** in 1933 and served in that post until 1938. He was ambassador to Canada in May–August 1939, before retiring.

ROUND ROBIN. A position paper drawn up by a legislator is called a round robin if supporters add their signatures in circular fashion around the borders of the document so it is unclear who the author was or in what order it was signed. On 4 March 1919, Senator **Henry Cabot Lodge** publicized a round robin signed by 39 Republican senators and senators-elect, stating that the present form of the covenant of the **League of Nations** was unacceptable and demanding that the issue of the League be dealt with after the **Treaty of Versailles** was signed. The document was proposed by Lodge and Senator **Frank Brandegee** and drafted by Senator **Philander C. Knox**. The round robin made a strong impression, coming on the last day of the outgoing Congress and carrying the signatures of more than enough senators to prevent the ratification of the treaty. President **Woodrow Wilson**, however, declared that he would return to Paris and bring back a treaty of which the covenant was an integral part.

ROWE, LEO STANTON (1871–1946). A professor of political science at the University of Pennsylvania (1896–1917), Leo Rowe served during **World War I** as assistant secretary of the treasury. He was particularly involved with financial and economic problems in **Latin America**. He had attended the third conference of American states in 1906, and he became an expert on Latin American affairs during World War I. He was chief of the Latin American Division of the State Department (1919–20) and then was director general of the **Pan-American Union** until his death. Rowe advocated improved relations between American states and took a special interest in education in Latin America.

RUSSIA. During the last three years of tsarist rule in Russia, diplomatic relations with the United States were marked by the outbreak of **World War I**, the rapid disintegration of the 300-year-old Romanov regime, and the descent of Russia into revolutionary chaos, civil war, and totalitarianism. The last two American ambassadors were George T. Marye (1914–16) and David R. Francis (1916–18). Marye arrived in Russia during a tense period in diplomatic relations arising from a long-running dispute over Russia's refusal to relax entry and travel restrictions on Russian-born Jews who had emigrated to the United States and now carried American passports. As a result of the dispute, the 1832 treaty of commerce and navigation between the two nations had been abrogated by the U.S. Congress. Russian officials indicated, however, that the "most favored nation" status awarded to the United States under the treaty would not be withdrawn and that low **tariff** rates would continue to be applied to American goods. Ambassadors Marye and Francis attempted without success to negotiate a renewal of the treaty.

The overthrow of Tsar Nicholas II in March 1917 during the first **Russian Revolution** marked the opening of a short-lived period of warm diplomatic relations. President **Woodrow Wilson** publicly welcomed the revolution and gave Francis permission to extend diplomatic recognition to the provisional government of George Lvov. The United States thus became the first nation to formally recognize the new regime. The president showed no regret at the demise of the Romanov monarchy, despite the fact that it had fought for three years in the Allied cause. By March 1917, U.S. entry into the war appeared imminent. It is likely that the prospect of fighting alongside a newly democratic Russia, which was electing delegates to a democratic Constituent Assembly, appealed to Wilson's view of the conflict as a moral crusade. After the United States joined the war, he sought to ensure that Russia would not withdraw from a conflict that had become deeply unpopular with the Russian people. Russian forces had endured the heaviest losses of any combatant nation, and severe food and fuel shortages were generating social disorder.

In June–August 1917, Wilson sent a delegation to Russia headed by former Secretary of State **Elihu Root** to press the government, now headed by Alexander Kerensky, to remain in the war. Kerensky's pledge to fight until victory was exploited by radical socialist groups such as the Bolsheviks, led by Vladimir Ilyich Lenin, who increased their support throughout 1917 by demanding an immediate end to hostilities. But Root spoke optimistically of Russia's future, and appeared convinced that U.S. entry into the war would discourage talk of a ceasefire. Addressing journalists in Moscow in June 1917, he applauded the "self-control, restraint, and good humor" of the Russian people and pledged, "Say what Russia wants and we will come in aid."

On 7 November 1917, armed Bolsheviks seized power from the Kerensky government. Lenin closed the democratically elected Constituent Assembly after its first sitting, ending Russia's short-lived experiment with democracy. The Wilson administration, believing the new Soviet regime was unlikely to survive long, refused to extend diplomatic recognition. In January 1918, the Bolsheviks concluded the Treaty of Brest–Litovsk with Germany and withdrew Russia from the war. Civil war broke out in the summer of 1918. Ambassador Francis temporarily relocated the U.S. embassy and its staff from St. Petersburg (Petrograd) to the city of Vologda in northeastern Russia. On 7 November, he left Russia. The last U.S. personnel departed on 14 September 1919 and the embassy was closed. It did not reopen for 14 years. *See also* ARMOUR, NORMAN; BULLITT, WILLIAM C.; NORTH RUSSIA, INTERVENTION IN; SIBERIAN INTERVENTION; SOVIET ARK; UNION OF SOVIET SOCIALIST REPUBLICS.

RUSSIAN REVOLUTIONS (1917). The Russian Revolution and the overthrow of Tsar Nicholas II in March 1917 was welcomed by U.S. politicians, including President **Woodrow Wilson**. Although the Russian army had suffered millions of casualties in **World War I**, **Russia**'s Western allies had never been comfortable dealing with the autocratic Romanov monarchy. The new, moderate provisional government, headed first by George Lvov and later by Alexander Kerensky, introduced freedom of the press, abolished the death penalty, released tsarist political prisoners, and began preparing for democratic elections.

The new government's grip on the loyalties of workers and peasants weakened throughout 1917 as it refused to end Russia's involvement in the war. Leftist groups fanned social discontent and increased the power of the soviets (workers' councils) in major cities such as Moscow and St. Petersburg (Petrograd). The Bolsheviks, led by Vladimir

Ilyich Lenin, greatly increased their power after helping to end an attempted military takeover by General Lavr Kornilov in September 1917. Kerensky had approved issuing arms to workers, and after the putsch was aborted, the workers kept their guns, providing the raw materials needed for the Bolshevik Revolution on 6 November 1917. Despite seizing power in St. Petersburg and Moscow, Lenin's new Soviet government did not control the entire country. Its survival was threatened by "White" military units loyal to the old regime, as well as by disaffected socialist revolutionaries, Cossack bands, anarchists, and a revolt by Czech legions en route through Russia to their homeland. Civil war erupted in late spring 1918. Despite intervention by troops from **Great Britain**, **France**, the United States, and **Japan** on the side of the Whites, the Bolsheviks gained victory by 1920.

The U.S. government detested the Marxist doctrines of atheism, worker power, land nationalization, and state ownership of the means of production which underpinned Soviet power. Moreover, the Treaty of Brest–Litovsk, signed in January 1918, through which Russia withdrew from the war, enabled the **Central Powers** to concentrate troops and resources on the western front. These factors, together with Soviet propaganda calling for worldwide socialist revolution and the overthrow of capitalism, ensured that relations with the **Union of Soviet Socialist Republics** (USSR) would be marked by mutual hostility and suspicion. *See also* ARMOUR, NORMAN; BULLITT, WILLIAM C.; NORTH RUSSIA, INTERVENTION IN; SIBERIAN INTERVENTION; WORLD WAR II.

RUSSIAN SOVIET FEDERATED SOCIALIST REPUBLIC (RS-FSR). The Bolshevik government of Vladimir Ilyich Lenin designated **Russia** as the Russian Soviet Federated Socialist Republic in 1917. The RSFSR became part of the new **Union of Soviet Socialist Republics** (USSR), which came into existence on 1 January 1923. *See also* RUSSIAN REVOLUTIONS.

– S –

SACKETT, FREDERIC MOSLEY (1868–1941). Frederic Sackett practiced law in Ohio and Kentucky from 1893 to 1907, then moved into mining. He was director of the Louisville branch of the Federal Reserve Bank (1917–24) and during **World War I** was federal food administrator for Kentucky, which brought him into contact with national food administrator **Herbert Hoover**. He served in the U.S. Senate (R-Ky.) from 1925 to 1930. In 1930, President Hoover appointed him ambassador to **Germany**. He served from 1930 to 1933 and then returned to business.

ST. GERMAIN, TREATY OF (1919). In addition to the **Treaty of Versailles**, which dealt with **Germany**, the 1919 **Paris Peace Conference** formulated treaties with the other defeated **Central Powers**. On 10 September 1919, the treaty dealing with Austria was signed at St. Germain-en-Laye, a suburb of Paris. The new Austrian republic lost territory to Czechoslovakia and Italy, was disarmed, and was required to pay **reparations**. The treaty was not ratified by the U.S. Senate, as it included the covenant of the **League of Nations**, in common with the other Paris treaties. Instead, a separate peace with Austria was signed on 24 August 1921 and ratified on 18 October. *See also* BERLIN, TREATY OF; TRIANON, TREATY OF.

ST. PIERRE AND MIQUELON AFFAIR (1941). Situated off the coast of Newfoundland, St. Pierre and Miquelon were islands of the French empire. After the defeat of **France** in 1940 during **World War II**, the governor of the islands, Gilbert de Bournat, was loyal to the Vichy regime. There were some suspicions in Canada that the islands provided help to German submarines through radio broadcasts, but no action was taken. On 24 December 1941, Free French forces landed on the islands from the submarine *Surcouf* and took control. Free French leader **Charles de Gaulle** organized a referendum, and the result was that St. Pierre and Miquelon became the first French territories to join the Free French movement. De Gaulle had not notified the United States of the operation. It was condemned sharply by Secretary of State **Cordell Hull** as a breach of the 1940 **Act of Havana**. The United States had at that time stated its opposition to the transfer of authority over any territory held by a European power in the western hemisphere. But the implication that the islands should be returned to the collaborationist Vichy regime caused public outrage. The St. Pierre and Miquelon incident was the cause of lasting resentment and distrust toward the French leader on the part of President **Franklin D. Roosevelt**. Roosevelt sought in succeeding years to find an alternative to de Gaulle as Free French leader. *See also* CASABLANCA CONFERENCE.

SAN FRANCISCO CONFERENCE (1945). Delegates of 50 nations met at the San Francisco conference 25 April–26 June 1945 to finalize plans discussed at the 1944 **Dumbarton Oaks Conference** and modified by the **Big Three** at the 1945 **Yalta Conference**. The principal participants were Secretary of State **Edward Stettinius**, Foreign Secretary Anthony Eden of **Great Britain**, Commissar for Foreign Affairs Vyacheslav Molotov of the **Union of Soviet Socialist Republics** (USSR), and **China**'s ambassador T. V. Soong. After nine weeks of discussion, the **United Nations Charter** was signed, establishing the new **United Nations** (UN) in place of the **League of Nations**. Tensions had been greatest over the veto issue: the Soviets claimed it had been agreed at Yalta that the permanent members of the UN Security Council could veto discussion of any issues that concerned them. After President **Harry S. Truman** asked Soviet premier **Josef Stalin** to break the deadlock, the USSR agreed to allow such discussion.

Stettinius submitted the draft plan to the conference on 22 June. Dominating the UN was the Security Council, which was intended to perpetuate the **Grand Alliance**; its five permanent members could veto any actions they considered against their interests. There were six other seats on the council, occupied by states in two-year terms. The General Assembly contained all member states. Also established were the United Nations Economic and Social Council, the International Court of Justice in The Hague, and the Trusteeship Council. Administrative work would be in the hands of a General Secretariat. The UN Charter was approved unanimously on 25 June and signed the next day. *See also* ARMSTRONG, HAMILTON FISH; CONNALLY RESOLUTION; DULLES, JOHN FOSTER; EICHELBERGER, CLARK MELL; FOUR POLICEMEN; HISS, ALGER; PAZVOLSKY, LEO; SHOTWELL, JAMES T.; VANDENBERG, ARTHUR H.; YOST, CHARLES WOODRUFF.

SANTIAGO CONFERENCE (1923). The fifth pan-American conference met at Santiago, Chile, 25 March–4 May 1923. Accords were
agreed to on matters of education and health. Fact-finding commissions were to investigate disputes between states in the western
hemisphere. On 3 May 1923, the Pan-American Treaty (**Gondra
Treaty**) was signed.

SECOND FRONT. The **Union of Soviet Socialist Republics** (USSR)
proposed opening a second front in the European theater of operations during **World War II** so that the United States and **Great
Britain** would attack **Germany** in the west to relieve pressure on the
Red Army fighting in the east. Soviet Premier **Josef Stalin** began
demanding in 1942 that the main focus of western strategy should be
an early attack through northern **France**. General **George C. Marshall** and the U.S. planners supported the idea but were persuaded by
the British that losses would be prohibitive if such an operation were
carried out without adequate buildup of forces, material, and experience in large-scale landings. Consequently, the second front was not
opened until Operation **Overlord** in 1944.

The absence of the second front while the USSR was experiencing
enormous losses was a source of great tension in the **Grand Alliance**. Stalin suspected the Western powers hoped to see the Germans
and Soviets mutually exhaust themselves. But logistical issues, such
as the shortage of shipping, were probably the determining factor,
though **Winston Churchill**'s preference for avoiding a repeat of the
World War I western front was also influential. The Soviets never
accepted that operations elsewhere against the **Axis** such as Operation **Torch** (1942), Operation **Husky** (1943), the invasion of Italy,
(1943), or the **Combined Bomber Offensive** constituted a genuine
second front. *See also* BOLERO, OPERATION; CASABLANCA
CONFERENCE; TEHERAN CONFERENCE; WASHINGTON
CONFERENCE (1941–1942); WASHINGTON CONFERENCE
(1942).

SEDITION ACT (1918). The Sedition Act was passed by the U.S.
Congress on 16 May 1918 as an amendment to the 1917 **Espionage
Act**. It forbade any type of language, publication, or physical display
which could be deemed disloyal to or disparaging of the federal

government, the armed forces, or the flag of the United States. Punishments included fines of up to $10,000 and prison terms of up to 20 years. Under this act, the administration of President **Woodrow Wilson** clamped down on general antiwar dissent during **World War I**, as well as socialist and communist propaganda. Thousands were indicted, with 877 convictions secured from a total of 1,956 cases brought in 1919–20. The act was repealed in 1921.

SELECTIVE SERVICE ACT (1917). Legislation permitting the federal government to draft men into the armed services was drawn up by Brigadier General Hugh Johnson and passed by Congress as the Selective Service Act in 1917. It authorized the president to raise a volunteer infantry force of a maximum of four divisions. Registration was required of all American males age 21–30. Nearly 24 million were registered by the last months of **World War I**, although only 4.7 million were actually drafted. Roughly 2 million eventually served in Europe.

SELECTIVE TRAINING AND SERVICE ACT (1940). The Selective Training and Service Act, known also as the Burke–Wadsworth Act, was passed by Congress on 14 September 1940, by a vote of 232–124 in the House and 47–25 in the Senate. It introduced the first peacetime conscription in U.S. history. The United States had not yet entered **World War II**. The act was drafted by **Grenville Clark** of the Military Training Camps Association, a veterans group that had long been agitating for such training for young men. President **Franklin D. Roosevelt**'s administration saw it as a useful contribution to its program to increase the strength of the military but was cautious and only put its support behind the proposal once it was clear that it would gain acceptance in Congress.

Under the act, all males age 21–30 were required to register with local draft boards, and a maximum of 900,000 were to be in service at any one time. The draftees would be selected by lottery. Their period of military training and service would last 12 months, followed by 10 years in reserve. The act contained provision for conscientious objection on religious grounds. The draft began in October 1940. By spring 1941, President Roosevelt was concerned that the first cohort would return to civilian life in October 1941. He requested an extension of the period of service to 18 months, and this aroused controversy. **Iso-lationists** joined those who thought it unfair to the men who had been drafted on the basis of a one-year term. The revision narrowly passed in the House, by 203–202 on 12 August, but passed in the Senate by a wider margin. The vote was seen by Roosevelt as a warning of the continuing strength of noninterventionist feeling.

After **Pearl Harbor**, selective service was modified to make all men age 18–45 liable for military service, except conscientious objectors, and all men age 18–65 were required to register with the draft boards. By the time the act expired in 1947, over 10 million men had been drafted under its provisions.

SENATE COMMITTEE ON FOREIGN RELATIONS. The Committee on Foreign Relations is one of the oldest standing committees of the U.S. Senate, dating back to 1816. The Senate has a number of key powers in the implementation of U.S. foreign policy, and the committee is charged with leading debate and oversight of foreign policy legislation in the Senate. It debates and reports on major treaties and has the power to approve or reject diplomatic appointments. Many of the significant elements of U.S. foreign policy between 1914 and 1945 were subject to Senate approval because they were embodied in treaties or legislation, making the Committee on Foreign Relations a key player in foreign policy, notably in the debate on the **Treaty of Versailles**, the Five Power Treaty, the **Neutrality Acts**, and the **Connally Resolution**. Some powerful political figures served as chair, including **Henry Cabot Lodge** (1919–24), **William E. Borah** (1924–33), **Key Pittman** (1933–40), and **Tom Connally** (1941–47), and exercised significant influence on foreign policy making and diplomacy.

SERVICE, JOHN STEWART (1909–1999). The son of missionaries, John Service was born in Chengdu, **China**, and was fluent in Chinese. He entered the foreign service in 1933 and was sent to the U.S. consulate at Kunming, China. He rose to be second secretary at the embassy in Chungking under Ambassador **Clarence Gauss**. He was deeply critical of the nationalist **Kuomintang** and **Chiang Kai-shek**, whom he considered undemocratic and corrupt. **John Paton Davies** was then diplomatic attaché to General **Joseph Stilwell** and shared these views. Service was assigned to assist Davies, and Davies secured him the post of chief diplomatic officer on the **Dixie Mission** to the Chinese communists in June 1944.

Service wrote many reports favoring cooperation with the communists, stating that they were the future of China and were progressive and democratic. When **Patrick Hurley**'s attempt to bring the communists under the nationalist wing failed, he blamed Service and the other members of the Dixie Mission. He succeeded in getting Service and the other "China Hands" removed from China, and U.S. support remained exclusively in favor of Chiang. Service then served in Tokyo with General **Douglas MacArthur** and in India before returning to Washington, D.C., in 1946.

Service was the subject of many accusations of disloyalty in the postwar period. He was arrested in 1946 on the allegation that he had passed government documents to the editor of a pro-communist newspaper, *Amerasia*, while in China. He was acquitted but was continually subject to loyalty scrutinies and some years later was fired from the State Department by Secretary of State **John Foster Dulles** as a security risk. He took his case to the Supreme Court and was reinstated, but he was not assigned duties of any significance and left the State Department in 1962. When relations with China were normalized under President Richard M. Nixon in 1971, Service was invited back as the guest of Premier Chou En-lai. *See also* INSTI-TUTE OF PACIFIC RELATIONS.

SEVAREID, ERIC (1912–1992). Educated at the University of Minnesota, London School of Economics, and Alliance Française in Paris, Eric Sevareid worked on the *Minneapolis Journal* (1936–37) and then in the Paris office of the *New York Herald Tribune*. He was recruited in 1938 by **Edward R. Murrow** to do radio reports for the Columbia Broadcasting System (CBS). He traveled with the army of **France** in 1939–40 and was the first to report on their capitulation in **World War II**. He then moved to **Great Britain** and, as one of "Murrow's Boys," he reported on the Battle of Britain and the bombing of London (1940–41). Sevareid was in the CBS Washington News Bureau (1941–43) and then a correspondent in **China** (1943–44). He was in an airplane crash in the Burmese jungle, but **John Paton Davies** guided the party to safety. Sevareid went ashore with U.S. forces in Operation the **Dragoon** landings in southern France in August 1944 and stayed with them until victory in 1945. He continued with CBS until the 1970s, receiving three Emmys for his television work and numerous other awards.

SHANGHAI INCIDENT (1932). On 29 January 1932, Japanese naval forces attacked Shanghai, **China,** killing thousands of civilians in air raids. There was a large international settlement in Shanghai, and the event attracted considerable attention in the United States and Europe. This did not go so far as war with **Japan,** but Secretary of State **Henry Stimson** wrote an open letter to Senator **William E. Borah** reiterating U.S. commitment to the **open door policy** and the treaties of the 1921 **Naval Disarmament Conference.** In the face of international condemnation, Japanese forces were withdrawn in May 1932. They remained in Manchuria, however. The Shanghai operation had not been part of a concerted plan; it was a spontaneous act by naval officers. With its horrifying images of the impact of aerial bombardment, however, it further tarnished Japan's international image. It also strengthened the forces of **pacifism** in the United States by giving a demonstration of the potential horrors of modern warfare. *See also* MANCHURIAN CRISIS.

SHEFFIELD, JAMES ROCKWELL (1864–1938). Lawyer James Sheffield served as ambassador to **Mexico** in 1925–27 as an appointee of President **Calvin Coolidge.** Sheffield was reputedly disdainful of the turmoil of Mexican politics and society. He claimed that Mexicans understood "no argument but force" and complained that there was an absence of "white blood" in the Mexican cabinet. He was replaced by the more diplomatic **Dwight Morrow.**

SHIRER, WILLIAM L. (1904–1993). One of the foremost journalists of the 1930s and **World War II**, William L. Shirer traveled to Europe in a cattle boat in 1925 and joined the *Chicago Tribune*'s Paris office. He learned French, Spanish, Italian, and German and became a foreign correspondent. He reported on **Charles Lindbergh**'s transatlantic flight in 1927 and on **League of Nations** meetings in Geneva. He toured India and Afghanistan and struck up a close friendship with Mohandas K. Gandhi.

In 1934, Shirer moved to Berlin to work for **William Randolph Hearst**'s Universal News Service and the *International Herald Tribune*. In 1937, he was recruited by **Edward R. Murrow** to work for the Columbia Broadcasting System (CBS), making pioneering radio reports. His and Murrow's live broadcasts from Europe helped develop the interest of the American people in European affairs and lessened their visceral **isolationism**. Shirer reported on the situation in **Germany** and on the key developments that led to war, such as the annexation of Austria, the Munich Agreement, and the invasion of **Poland**.

From the summer of 1940, Shirer's reports were increasingly censored by the Nazi authorities, and in December 1940, finding it no longer possible to report effectively, he left Germany for New York. He smuggled his diaries out in a collection of radio scripts. His influential book *Berlin Diary* was published in 1941 and had an impact on growing U.S. public opinion with regard to the menace of Nazi Germany. *The Collapse of the Third Republic* gave a vivid account of events in **France** in 1940—Shirer had made the first radio announcement of France's fall. Following the war, Shirer reported on the **International Military Tribunal** (Nuremberg trials). He was blacklisted in the anticommunist witch-hunts of the early 1950s and was unable to find steady work. This gave him the time to write *The Rise and Fall of the Third Reich* (1960), one of the classic studies of Nazi Germany and World War II.

SHOOT-ON-SIGHT ORDER. On 4 September 1941, the destroyer USS *Greer* engaged in combat with a German submarine in the Atlantic Ocean although the United States had declared its neutrality in **World War II**. The *Greer* had dropped depth charges before the submarine fired a torpedo at it, but the American public was outraged. President **Franklin D. Roosevelt** declared in a fireside chat that **Germany** had been guilty of an act of piracy, and stated that "in the waters which we deem necessary for our defense, American naval vessels and American planes will no longer wait until Axis submarines lurking under the water, or Axis raiders on the surface of the sea, strike their deadly blow first." This was interpreted widely by the press as an order to "shoot on sight."

The **U.S. Navy** was thus put in a slightly clearer position with regard to its role in protecting convoys while not technically at war with Germany. Further incidents inevitably followed in this "undeclared war," but until **Japan**'s attack on **Pearl Harbor** in the Pacific in December, neither government seemed to wish to clarify the situation further. Roosevelt's action has been interpreted either as designed to push Germany into a declaration of war, thereby undercutting U.S. **isolationism**, or as an indication that he still believed the **arsenal of democracy** policy held good and that aid to **Great Britain**, so long as its delivery was assured, would be a sufficient U.S. contribution to achieve German defeat. *See also KEARNY*, USS; *REUBEN JAMES*, USS.

SHOTWELL, JAMES THOMSON (1874–1965). Canadian-born James Shotwell became a professor at Columbia University in 1908. He was managing editor of the 11th edition of the *Encyclopedia Britannica* and wrote over 250 articles for it. During **World War I**, he was a member of the National Board for Historical Service, part of the **Committee on Public Information**. In 1918, he became a leading member of the **Inquiry**, a secretive group called together by President **Woodrow Wilson**'s administration to draw on social science research and develop ideas for fostering international stability in the postwar era. Shotwell's focus was labor relations. He attended the 1919 **Paris Peace Conference** and was influential in the creation of the **International Labour Organization**.

During the 1920s, Shotwell campaigned against **isolationism** and in favor of U.S. membership in the **League of Nations**. In a meeting with French Foreign Minister Aristide Briand, he suggested there should be a treaty between **France** and the United States that outlawed war, sowing the seeds for the 1928 **Kellogg–Briand Pact**. In 1929, Shotwell was invited by President **Herbert Hoover** to assist in the effort to build "some stronger diplomatic teeth" into the pact.

Shotwell became Bryce professor of International Relations at Columbia University in 1937 and served on the Carnegie Endowment for International Peace (1942–50), becoming its president in 1949 when the incumbent, **Alger Hiss**, resigned to fight espionage charges. Shotwell was active in the **Nonpartisan Committee for Peace through Revision of the Neutrality Law**, and he attended the 1945 **San Francisco Conference** as an informal advisor to the State Department. He was involved in drawing up the social provisions in the **United Nations Charter**, though illness cut short his time at the conference.

SIBERIAN INTERVENTION (1918–1920). The United States intervened militarily in Siberia, **Russia**, in August 1918, during **World War I**. Civil war had followed the 1917 **Russian Revolution** and Bolshevik takeover of the government. Several factors motivated President **Woodrow Wilson** in approving the 1918 military operation in Siberia. The primary consideration was the rescue of the Czech Legion, which had been fighting against German forces inside Russia but was now pulling out toward the east and needed protection from the advancing Bolshevik "Red Army."

Additionally, the U.S. government worried about Japanese exploitation of the region to the detriment of U.S. business interests. A further concern, though less likely after July 1918, was intervention by the German army. President Wilson's instructions to the head of the expedition, Major General William Graves, stressed that U.S. forces should not take sides in the civil war. However, the United States and its allies had no reason to sympathize with the Bolshevik government, which had signed the Treaty of Brest–Litovsk with **Germany** in January 1918 and had withdrawn Russian troops from World War I. The Wilson administration was convinced that the Bolshevik government, which had disowned all Russian **war debts** and treaty obligations, disregarded conventional diplomacy, propagandized against the West, and was ruthlessly exterminating its opponents, constituted a menace to world stability more dangerous than that presented by Germany.

Pressure was placed on Wilson, both at home and from anti-Bolshevik "White" armies in Russia, to abandon neutrality in favor of a straightforward anti-Bolshevik intervention. Graves was frequently criticized for failing to take a harsher line against Red partisans while having to deal simultaneously with marauding bands of Cossacks and Japanese forces who, though nominally allies of the United States, were also pursuing their own material interests and territorial objectives. *See also* NORTH RUSSIA, INTERVENTION IN.

SIGNALS INTELLIGENCE. The development of electronic communications, notably the telephone and radio, created a new aspect of

intelligence gathering: signals intelligence (sigint). Although it did not entirely supersede other forms of intelligence, such as the use of agents for espionage (human intelligence, or humint), sigint significantly influenced foreign policy. It developed during the period between the two world wars and came to maturity during **World War II**. Signals intelligence often involved cryptanalysis—the decoding and interpretation of another nation's coded messages—but also embraced communications intelligence (comint), where conclusions were drawn from the extent of signals traffic and detection of its point of origin. This was important information even if the messages themselves remained unreadable.

The political significance of sigint became apparent when **Great Britain** intercepted and decoded **Germany**'s **Zimmermann telegram** in 1917, with a direct impact on U.S. entry into **World War I**. The British did not reveal the source of their interception, and a high level of secrecy was to be characteristic of sigint operations. Analyses of Japanese messages were useful for U.S. delegates during the 1921 **Naval Disarmament Conference** in Washington, D.C. However, Secretary of War **Henry Stimson** closed the U.S. Cipher Bureau, saying that "gentlemen do not read each other's mail." The U.S. Army continued with such operations.

In 1940, army and navy cryptanalysts in Operation **Magic** broke the Japanese **Purple** machine, by which Japan's diplomatic traffic was encoded. This gave vital insights into **Axis** plans and activities, particularly in the messages from **Japan**'s ambassador in Berlin. Although they cooperated to a degree in Magic, throughout World War II the U.S. Army and **U.S. Navy** ran separate sigint operations: the navy through department OP-20-G, and the army in the signals intelligence service. Coordination was limited and haphazard at first, but by 1944 it was more formalized through the Joint Army–Navy Communications Intelligence Coordinating Committee. Intelligence was supplied to the White House and to the State Department. The **Office of Strategic Services** did not gather sigint, but the **Federal Bureau of Investigation** and the Federal Communications Commission both gathered materials.

Signals intelligence made a major contribution to Allied fortunes in World War II, though there were failures, notably over the attack on **Pearl Harbor**. One of the most significant diplomatic aspects was the cooperation between the intelligence services of the United States and Great Britain. Formal liaison began in 1940, though the highly secret arrangements had been laid down as early as 1937. Initially it was over naval matters and took place through the U.S. Special Naval Observer in London. In 1941, it moved to another level with the gift of a Purple machine from the United States to Britain, and the involvement of some U.S. personnel in the British operation that was working against the German Enigma machine. The material produced was known as Ultra. These **Ultra-Magic** arrangements were formalized in the **Britain–United States of America Agreement (BRUSA)** in June 1943. From 1943, another highly significant operation was under way, the **Venona project**, which decoded messages sent from the United States by the intelligence organization of the **Union of Soviet Socialist Republics**. This provided vital information on Soviet espionage activities in the United States.

SINO–JAPANESE WAR (1937–1945). Since the 1931 **Manchurian Crisis**, militarists in **Japan** had been seeking further expansion in **China**. By 1935, all of Manchuria and Jehol were under Japan's control, and attempts had been made to move into Inner Mongolia. Following a clash between Chinese and Japanese soldiers at the Marco Polo Bridge near Peking (Beijing) on 7 July 1937, full-scale hostilities broke out. No declaration of war was made by either side. Japan called it the "China Incident," and the lack of a declaration meant that U.S. President **Franklin D. Roosevelt** could avoid invoking the **Neutrality Act**. This meant that U.S. companies could supply war materials to Chinese nationalist leader **Chiang Kai-shek**, and U.S. businesses continued their activities in China.

In December 1937, the river gunboat USS *Panay*, deployed originally to protect the interests of a U.S. oil company, was bombed and sunk by Japanese aircraft, and American sailors were killed. The U.S. government accepted Japan's apology and indemnity, and its official reaction to Japanese actions in the war was in line with the **Stimson Doctrine** of nonrecognition. This passivity was in accordance with advice from the ambassador in Tokyo, **Joseph C. Grew**, who believed the United States was too weak in the region and its interests in the **Philippines** too vulnerable to provoke Japanese retaliation. It also reflected U.S. economic interests as well, for Japan, not China, was the major U.S. trading partner in Asia.

Japan overran northern China in the fall of 1937 and occupied Shanghai in November. Japanese forces advanced up the Yangtze River and along the main railroad lines. Chiang retreated, seeking to trade space for time. His capital, Nanking (Nanjing), fell in December 1937, and a massacre known as the Rape of Nanking followed. Canton and Hankow fell in October 1938, but Chiang refused to come to terms, based now far up-country in Chungking (Chonqqing). His supply routes, except for the Burma Road through Kunming, were severed when Japan occupied northern Indochina in fall 1940, during **World War II**, cutting the last rail line. The Burma Road was cut when Japan occupied Burma in early 1942.

Chiang received help from the United States in the form of volunteers, in the **American Volunteer Group**. In an uneasy alliance with the Chinese communists based in the north (operating as the Eighth Route Army), Chiang continued resistance. He was granted extensive aid from the United States through **Lend-Lease** and a loan from Congress. A million Japanese soldiers were tied down in China throughout World War II. Most of them were involved in occupation duties, and apart from communist penetration activities, the fighting was limited, as Chiang husbanded his resources with the postwar struggle for power in China in mind, confident that the United States would defeat Japan. This attitude produced major tensions with his American chief of staff, General **Joseph Stilwell**. A major Japanese offensive, Operation Ichi-Go, seized the main strategic airfields in mid-1944. Chiang regained some of this territory in 1945. Japanese forces in China surrendered formally at Nanking on 9 September 1945. *See also* BRUSSELS CONFERENCE; CAIRO CONFERENCES; DIXIE MISSION; HORNBECK, STANLEY KUHL; HURLEY, PATRICK; LUCE, HENRY.

SMITH ACT (1940). The Alien Registration Act, commonly known as the Smith Act, was passed by the U.S. Congress in June 1940, during **World War II**. It strengthened laws governing the admission and deportation of aliens. The prime aim of the act, however, was not to control **immigration** but to combat subversive activities. It did so through adding a new definition of subversion, by making it illegal to teach or advocate the overthrow of the U.S. government by violence. By also making it illegal to become a member of any organization teaching such a doctrine, it extended the doctrine of guilt by association, as well as providing a catch-all provision for operations against fascist or communist organizations. Prosecutors did not have to show that individuals were personally involved in either activities or plots, just that they were members of a specified organization. The tone of the act reflected the views of senators like **Robert Rice Reynolds** that immigrants were the source of subversion, but also more widely held fears about infiltration of communist and fascist ideas from outside the United States, and the way that these were propagated through front organizations.

SMITH, GERALD LYMAN KENNETH (1898–1976). A minister of the Disciples of Christ in Indiana from 1916, Gerald Smith moved to Louisiana in 1928, where his pro-union and antibusiness radio broadcasts attracted the notice of Governor Huey Long. Smith became attracted to fascist causes and considered joining the ultra-right Silver Shirts, but instead, he and Long founded the Share Our Wealth Society in 1932, proposing redistribution of wealth as the answer to the Great Depression. Smith resigned as a minister when this outraged conservative parishioners.

After Long's assassination in September 1935, Smith briefly took charge of Share Our Wealth. Smith was a brilliant orator. In 1936 he formed the National Union for Social Justice with Francis Townshend and Father **Charles Coughlin**. In 1940, he became a prominent member of the **America First Committee** (AFC). After **Pearl Harbor**, the AFC was dissolved, but Smith continued to argue in favor of **isolationism**, setting up the America First Party. He published its journal, *The Cross and the Flag*. In 1944, Smith was one of the defendants in the **Great Sedition Trial**, which ended in a mistrial. He ran for president in 1944, gaining a mere 1,780 votes. After **World War II**, Smith established the anti-Semitic Christian Nationalist Party. He was responsible for erecting a seven-story statue of Jesus, the "Christ of the Ozarks," in the 1960s.

SMITH, TRUMAN (1893–1970). Graduated from Yale and Columbia Universities, Truman Smith joined the U.S. Army in November 1916 and saw service in **France** (1917–18), distinguishing himself in the Meuse-Argonne campaign. From 1919 to 1920, he was advisor to the officer in charge of civil affairs in Coblenz, **Germany**. He was then assistant military attaché in Berlin from 1920 to 1924. He was an instructor at the U.S. infantry school at Fort Benning, Georgia, under General **George C. Marshall** (1928–32).

As military attaché in Berlin from 1935 to 1939, Smith obtained important items of **intelligence** regarding the growing strength of the German air force. In 1936, Smith arranged for **Charles Lindbergh** to inspect the German aircraft industry and air force. Lindbergh returned to the United States convinced of German strength and opposed to what he regarded as weakening the United States by giving aid to the Allies. The State Department at that time preferred to avoid emphasizing any danger from Germany. Smith and Lindbergh were later criticized by those who supported aid to the Allies, on the grounds that their reports gave ammunition to those in favor of **fortress America**.

From 1939 to 1945, Smith was a German specialist at the Military Intelligence Division and personal advisor to Marshall, who was now army chief of staff. Marshall defended Smith from the criticisms. In 1946, Smith was an unsuccessful candidate for the Republican nomination to Congress representing Connecticut. He was an advisor to the Eberstadt armed forces committee in 1948. In the postwar period, he was in favor of rearming Germany against the threat from the **Union of Soviet Socialist Republics**.

SMOOT–HAWLEY TARIFF ACT (1930). Sponsored by Senator Reed Smoot of Utah and Representative Willis Hawley of Oregon, the Smoot–Hawley Tariff Act was passed by the U.S. Congress on 13–14 June 1930, raising U.S. **tariff** barriers against imported goods to unprecedented levels. Smoot–Hawley began life as another in a long line of legislative efforts to aid American farmers when agricultural prices dropped after **World War I**. The problem was exacerbated by sharp rises in farm productivity during the 1920s, leading to ever larger market gluts. By 1930, however, protectionists saw higher tariffs as the only effective way to protect jobs, bolster the nation's industrial base, and fend off foreign competition during the Great Depression. Industrial lobbyists worked aggressively on Capitol Hill during the bill's committee stages for additional tariff hikes to protect iron, steel, and chemical and textile manufacturers. The final version of the bill was therefore much broader than its authors had originally intended and caused considerable controversy. It passed the House due mainly to Republican support and scraped a narrow two-vote victory in the Senate. The bill was signed by President **Herbert Hoover**, who had supported the original version but now feared the expanded tariff would become an obstacle to economic recovery.

Smoot–Hawley is generally regarded as a natural but more severe successor to the **Fordney–McCumber Tariff Act** of 1922. Though some parts of Smoot–Hawley were diluted by the 1934 **Reciprocal Trade Agreements Act**, economic historians consider the 1930 act to have worsened the Depression by depriving hard-pressed domestic consumers of cheaper foreign imports and forcing them to choose higher-priced U.S. goods. It also provoked America's trading competitors into raising retaliatory tariff barriers against the United States, leading to a precipitate decline in the value of exports from $2,341 million in 1929 to just $784 million by 1932. Smoot–Hawley represents, to this day, the high-water mark of U.S. protectionism, a policy largely abandoned after 1933. *See also* TRADE.

SOVIET ARK. The USS *Buford* was a transport ship used to rescue U.S. citizens stranded in Europe at the outbreak of **World War I**. The American press nicknamed it the "Soviet ark" when it was later used by the U.S. government to deport 249 political detainees arrested during the war and the postwar "Red Scare" under the 1917 **Espionage Act** and 1918 **Sedition Act**. The detainees included Russian-born political agitator Emma Goldman and others who had expressed support for the new Bolshevik regime in **Russia** or opposition to U.S. participation in the war. The *Buford* took the prisoners to Finland, from where they were taken overland to Russia. *See also* RUSSIAN REVOLUTIONS.

SPANISH CIVIL WAR (1936–1939). Civil war began in Spain in June 1936, when a revolt broke out among army commanders in Spanish Morocco against the republican government in Madrid. Troops were flown to mainland Spain in transport aircraft supplied by **Germany**, and a bitter three-year war began that tore the country apart. On one side were the nationalists, who were led by General Francisco Franco and included members of the Falange (the Spanish fascist party) together with traditionalists, monarchists, and clericalists. They were united by hostility to the socialism of the government led by Manuel Azaña, the government's antipathy to the Catholic Church, and the belief that Azaña was allowing the growth of separatism in Catalonia and the Basque provinces. Against them was a coalition of socialists, communists, separatists, and anarchists with antimonarchical liberal republicans.

Franco received considerable support in munitions and 50,000 men from fascist Italy. Germany sent units of its fledgling air force in the Condor Legion, where they perfected their combat doctrine—most notoriously in the bombing of the Basque town of Guernica on 27 April 1937. The **Union of Soviet Socialist Republics** (USSR) sent munitions to the republicans and through the Communist International (Comintern) organized the International Brigades. **Great Britain** persuaded **France** and other powers to avoid involvement. Only **Mexico** joined the USSR in sending munitions to the republicans.

The Spanish Civil War became an ideological battleground for all Europe, as volunteers went to Spain to side with those with whom they sympathized. European governments adopted an official policy of nonintervention, and Britain, France, and Germany ran naval neutrality patrols to prevent foreign interference and to contain the conflict—the Germans with considerable hypocrisy, given the activities of the Condor Legion. President **Franklin D. Roosevelt** tacitly supported this policy, without committing the United States to any action. He invoked the **Neutrality Act**, which by 1937 had been amended to cover civil wars, so there was an embargo on sales of weapons to either side. This disadvantaged the republicans. U.S. merchant ships were involved in smuggling supplies and munitions to both sides.

Roosevelt's 1936 **Chautauqua speech** underlined his support for peace and his unwillingness to get involved in any collective action to preserve it. To many American liberals and socialists, the republicans were engaged in the great fight against fascism. Nearly 3,000 Americans went to Spain, mostly to participate in what became known as the **Abraham Lincoln Brigade**. The nationalists gained the upper hand during 1938, with increased German and Italian support, and divisions among the republicans, and the termination of

Soviet aid, brought the fall of Barcelona on 26 January 1939, and of Madrid and Valencia on 28 March. Franco became chief of state and remained so until his death in 1975. Despite requests by Germany, Franco kept Spain out of **World War II** on the grounds that his country was exhausted, though a division of volunteers did fight against the USSR. It has been estimated that up to 1 million lives were lost in the Spanish Civil War. *See also* STALIN, JOSEF VISSARIONOV-ICH DZHUGASHVILI.

STALIN, JOSEF VISSARIONOVICH DZHUGASHVILI (1879–1953). The son of a Georgian blacksmith, Josef Stalin was expelled from a seminary as a young man for his revolutionary views. He edited the Bolshevik newspaper *Pravda* and played a secondary role in the Bolshevik seizure of power in **Russia** in October 1917. In the subsequent civil war, he was involved in the defense of Tsaritsyn, which was renamed Stalingrad in his honor. He was commissar for nationalities under Vladimir Ilyich Lenin. Stalin progressively seized control of the machinery of the Bolshevik party under the guise of his position as general secretary. By a series of tactical alliances with other Bolsheviks, he defeated his rival Leon Trotsky and then the other leaders in turn.

By 1928, Stalin was in effective control of the **Union of Soviet Socialist Republics** (USSR) and inaugurated his policy of "socialism in one country," in which the aim of world revolution was subordinated to the growth of the industrial strength of the USSR in a series of five-year plans. This involved forced collectivization of agriculture: a massive social and economic upheaval that involved the loss of millions of lives in famine, mass murder, and deportations. Stalin turned on his own followers, purging most of the senior leaders in staged show trials in which the old Bolsheviks confessed to sabotage and treason. Stalin then purged the military, eliminating most of the officer corps of the Red Army.

Stalin used foreign communist parties as instruments of Soviet foreign policy, through the Communist International (Comintern), based in Moscow. Fearful of the rise of the virulently anticommunist Nazis in **Germany**, Stalin moved to a policy of cooperation, urging communists to form popular fronts with other antifascist groups. Through Commissar for Foreign Affairs Maxim Litvinov, he endeavored to forge a **collective security** approach at the **League of Nations** in Geneva. Stalin was not trusted in the West, and after the purges, the military potential of the USSR seemed slight. Stalin supported the republicans in the **Spanish Civil War**, which gained him credit with liberals, but this was largely lost when Spanish Stalinists purged other left-wing colleagues in Spain, and Stalin stopped arms shipments because he concluded that the nationalists would win. What was left of Stalin's reputation in the West was destroyed by his conclusion of a nonaggression Nazi–Soviet pact with German dictator **Adolf Hitler** on 22 August 1939, which allowed Germany to conquer **Poland** and divided Eastern Europe between Germany and the USSR.

As part of the attempt to improve relations with the West in the 1930s, Stalin made concessions that allowed U.S. recognition of the USSR in 1933. He welcomed U.S. expertise in the Soviet industrialization program. However, although the 1936 USSR constitution was liberal on paper, the repression of civil liberties, especially religion, reported on perceptively by **George Kennan** and others in the U.S. embassy in Moscow, led to a rapid cooling of relations. After the Nazi–Soviet pact, many Americans saw the Soviet Union to be as repugnant as Nazi Germany, and the activities of the **Communist Party of the United States** to be Soviet interference in American domestic affairs.

Stalin assumed an official position in the Soviet government only on 7 May 1941, when he became premier. When the USSR entered **World War II** against Germany, he was also commissar for defense and made himself first marshal of the Soviet Union, then generalissimo, from which positions he directed the war effort. President **Franklin D. Roosevelt** developed a policy, from mid-1942 onward, of seeking to build an atmosphere of goodwill, and when he met Stalin for the first time at the **Teheran Conference** in November 1943, he was at pains to find common ground. Stalin appears to have regarded Roosevelt as a friend but maintained his policy line on matters that were vital to himself. He pressed for a **second front**, more **Lend-Lease** supplies, and "friendly governments" on his borders. Roosevelt's readiness to concede on these matters in return for Stalin's acceptance of the plan for the **United Nations** organization, and a promise of involvement in the war against Japan, meant that relations between the two remained cordial at the 1945 **Yalta Conference**.

Stalin by this time was tightening his grip on the countries the Soviet Red Army had occupied, leading to increased tensions with President **Harry S. Truman**'s administration. Stalin suspected the Allies of doing deals with the Germans and knew they were withholding information about the **atomic bomb** and **signals intelligence**. He was still hopeful of cooperation, on his own terms, in the postwar years, but his determination to control Eastern Europe, keep Germany weak, and use communist political parties to undermine Western European economic recovery were major factors in precipitating the Cold War. Stalin continued his tyranny in the USSR with further purges. Three years after his death, the cult of his personality and his tyrannical excesses were denounced by his successor, Nikita Khrushchev.

STANDLEY, WILLIAM HARRISON (1872–1963). William Standley served in the **U.S. Navy** in the Spanish–American War (1898) and the Filipino–American War (1899–1902). From 1923 to 1926, he was chief of the war plans division in the office of the chief of naval operations and then served in positions in Washington, D.C., and at sea. Now a vice admiral, Standley was appointed chief of naval operations in 1933. He often functioned as an acting secretary of the navy because of the poor health of Secretary of the Navy Claude A. Swanson. Standley worked with **Carl Vinson** in 1934 in the formulation of the Vinson–Trammell Naval Bill that provided for maintaining the navy up to the maximum levels allowed by the naval disarmament treaties. Standley represented the United States at the 1935–36 **London Naval Disarmament Conference**. He retired in 1937.

Recalled to active duty in 1941, Standley served as naval representative on the planning board of the Office of Production Management and then was the naval member of **Averell Harriman**'s delegation to the 1941 **Moscow Conference** on supply to the **Union of Soviet Socialist Republics** (USSR). Upon his return from Moscow, Standley became a member of the Navy Board for Production Awards.

In early 1942, Standley was a member of the **Owen Roberts** Commission investigating the attack on **Pearl Harbor**. In February, he was appointed ambassador to the USSR. It was believed that as a member of the armed forces, he would be able to get on good terms with the Soviets in time of war. But Soviet officials kept foreign diplomats at arm's length, and President **Franklin D. Roosevelt** preferred to conduct relations through special envoys rather than the embassy. Standley opposed the policy of granting aid unconditionally to the Soviets and was at odds with the **Lend-Lease** officials in Moscow, notably **Philip Faymonville**. Standley's frustration caused him to make undiplomatic comments to reporters, criticizing Soviet lack of gratitude for Lend-Lease. Standley was replaced with Harriman in October 1943. From March 1944 until the end of **World War II**, Standley served in the **Office of Strategic Services**. He retired when the war ended.

STARK, HAROLD R. (1880–1972). Serving with the **U.S. Navy**, Harold Stark took part in the world cruise of the Atlantic Fleet (the "Great White Fleet") in 1907–9 and served in **World War I** on the staff of the commander of U.S. naval forces in Europe. Stark was Chief of the Bureau of Ordinance (1934–37), commanded cruiser forces, and was made chief of naval operations in August 1939, with the rank of full admiral.

Stark played a crucial part in the expansion of the U.S. Navy during 1940–41, in preparation for the war that he was certain was coming. He was responsible for updating contingency plans, and he put forward **Plan Dog** in November 1940. Stark entered secret discussions with **Great Britain** in March 1941, producing the joint **ABC-1 Plan**. He conducted the undeclared naval war in the Atlantic against German U-boats in the second half of 1941.

After the December 1941 attack on **Pearl Harbor**, the United States entered **World War II**. In March 1942, the position of chief of naval operations was merged with that of navy commander in chief in the person of Admiral **Ernest King**, and Stark was sent to London in April 1942 as commander of U.S. naval forces, Europe. He directed the naval buildup in Britain as well as U.S. naval operations on the British side of the Atlantic. He supervised U.S. naval participation in the Operation

Overlord landings in Normandy in June 1944. He forged close relations with his British and Allied counterparts and made a vital contribution to the smooth running of the war alliance. Stark served again in Washington, D.C., from August 1945 until retirement in 1946.

STATE - WAR - NAVY COORDINATING COMMITTEE (SWNCC). The State-War-Navy Coordinating Committee was formed by President **Franklin D. Roosevelt** in December 1944. It was made up of representatives, at the assistant secretary level, from the War, State, and Navy Departments. Its purpose was to provide a forum for coordination of the views of the three organizations on postwar matters, and then to formulate recommendations for the approval of the **Joint Chiefs of Staff Committee**. The SWNCC was most significant for drafting the plan for the postwar occupation of **Japan**, **Germany**, and Austria. It improved consistency in policy making across the government, particularly in the approach to international conferences. In the fall of 1947, it was renamed the State-Army-Navy-Air Force Coordinating Committee. It ceased to exist in June 1949. It has been seen as representing a significant stage in the formalization of the role of the military in the formulation of U.S. foreign policy. *See also* INTELLIGENCE; UNITED STATES NAVY.

STEINHARDT, LAURENCE A. (1892–1950). After serving in the Army Quartermaster Corps in **World War I**, Laurence Steinhardt became a career diplomat. He was minister to Sweden (1933–37) and then ambassador in Peru (1937–39), the **Union of Soviet Socialist Republics** (1939–41), Turkey (1942–45), Czechoslovakia (1945–48), and Canada (1948–50). Steinhardt, a significant contributor to **Franklin D. Roosevelt**'s election campaigns, was a capable ambassador, occupying significant posts in **World War II** and the early Cold War. He was moved from Moscow when Roosevelt wished to initiate a warmer relationship with the Soviet Union, as Steinhardt was associated with the distant and cold relations of 1939–41. While ambassador in Turkey, Steinhardt was involved in some limited rescues of Jews and helped intellectuals fleeing from Nazi-occupied Europe to settle in Turkey. He died in an airplane crash in March 1950. *See also* STANDLEY, WILLIAM HARRISON.

STETTINIUS, EDWARD R. (1900–1949). Edward Stettinius, a successful industrialist with U.S. Steel and General Motors, was involved with the National Recovery Agency under President **Franklin D. Roosevelt**'s New Deal, and he played an active role in organizing the economy during **World War II**. Roosevelt appointed him chair of the War Resources Board in 1939, and in May 1940 he became a member of the Advisory Commission to the Council of National Defense. In January 1941, he became director of priorities in the Office of War Management and in August was given the vital post of **Lend-Lease** administrator. A great success in this role, he was rewarded with appointment as undersecretary of state in place of **Sumner Welles** in September 1943. An organizer rather than an original thinker on foreign affairs, he is credited with improving the efficiency of the State Department.

Stettinius headed the U.S. delegation to the 1944 **Dumbarton Oaks Conference**. He succeeded **Cordell Hull** as secretary of state on 1 December 1944, a post he held until the end of the **San Francisco Conference** in June 1945. Stettinius accompanied Roosevelt to the 1945 **Yalta Conference**, though Roosevelt kept the conduct of relations with the **Grand Alliance** partners firmly in his own hands. Stettinius helped formulate the **Act of Chapultepec** in March 1945. After he left office with the successful conclusion of the San Francisco Conference, he served as chair of the **United Nations** preparatory commission.

STILWELL, JOSEPH (1883–1946). Joseph "Vinegar Joe" Stilwell served in the U.S. Army in **France** in **World War I**, rising to the rank of colonel. He had four tours of duty in **China** in the interwar period and became fluent in Chinese. General **George C. Marshall** considered him one of the most cultured men in the army, and in March 1942, during **World War II**, he was appointed to head the U.S. military mission to China, supervise **Lend-Lease** to China, and act as chief of staff to Chinese nationalist leader **Chiang Kai-shek**. He was given the rank of lieutenant general. His principal task was to ensure the Chinese nationalists were fully engaged in the war against **Japan**, and then subsequently to organize them as a fighting force capable of offensive action. But Stilwell grew to detest both Chiang and his allies from **Great Britain**.

Although Stilwell was chief of staff to Chiang, and commander of allied forces in China, he was unable to exercise control over Chiang or the various factions and warlords that were his followers. Stillwell also clashed with General **Claire Chennault**, who commanded U.S. air forces in China and believed the principal job of the army was to defend the air bases. Stilwell believed the large Chinese forces should act more offensively. He persuaded Chiang to approve offensives into Burma in 1944. But the Japanese Ichi-Go offensive from April 1944 swept through nationalist forces in southern China and captured many of Chennault's air bases. Aware of how much of the U.S. aid was being used corruptly, Stillwell was unable to moderate his criticisms of Chiang. He was withdrawn at Chiang's request in October 1944. *See also* DIXIE MISSION; HURLEY, PATRICK.

STIMSON, HENRY LEWIS (1867–1950). Henry Stimson first came to prominence in antitrust suits while district attorney of New York. As secretary for war (1911–13), he was responsible for modernization of the U.S. Army. He fought as a colonel of artillery in **France** in **World War I**. President **Calvin Coolidge** sent Stimson as a special envoy to **Nicaragua** in 1927, where he resolved the civil war by formulating the **Peace of Tipitapa**. He then served as governor general of the **Philippines** (1927–29).

Secretary of state under President **Herbert Hoover** (1929–33), Stimson was chief U.S. negotiator at the 1930 **London Naval Disarmament Conference** and the 1932 **Geneva Disarmament Conference**. He condemned **Japan**'s occupation of Manchuria in 1931, though his response in the **Stimson Doctrine** (1932) was limited to nonrecognition, and no action was taken to force Japan to withdraw. Stimson, with knowledge of the Far East, wished to go further but was constrained by Hoover's caution and the strength of **isolationism** in the United States.

Stimson broke with mainstream opinion in the Republican Party in 1939–40 when he became an advocate of U.S. intervention on the side of **Great Britain** during **World War II**. He joined the **Committee to Defend America by Aiding the Allies** in May 1940, and President **Franklin D. Roosevelt** appointed him to his cabinet in June, alongside another Republican interventionist, **Frank Knox**. Stimson served as secretary for war from 1940 to 1945. His experience made him an influential figure in wartime foreign and military policy, especially when **Harry S. Truman** became president in April 1945 upon Roosevelt's death. Stimson had overall responsibility for the **Manhattan Project**. He believed an invasion of Japan would be extremely costly in lives and was a strong advocate for the use of the **atomic bomb**. He saw it as a useful element in relations with the **Union of Soviet Socialist Republics** and advocated sharing atomic secrets with the Soviet Union to avoid damaging tensions. This advice was not followed. Stimson retired from office in September 1945. Stimson was the first American politician to serve in the cabinet of two Republican and two Democratic presidents.

STIMSON DOCTRINE. Also known as the Hoover–Stimson Doctrine, this was the official response of the United States to the 1931 **Manchurian Crisis**. Secretary of State **Henry Stimson** announced on 7 January 1932 that the United States would not recognize **Japan**'s conquests. The United States, he declared, would recognize no arrangements that compromised the integrity of the Chinese republic or contravened the **open door policy**. He reiterated the doctrine in a letter to the chair of the **Senate Committee on Foreign Relations**, Senator **William E. Borah**, on 25 February 1932, following the **Shanghai Incident**. Stimson himself thought the response was too weak, but he was constrained by President **Herbert Hoover**'s dislike for economic sanctions, and by his perception that U.S. public opinion would not support any policy that looked as though the United States was acting in concert with or following the lead of the **League of Nations**. *See also* CHINA; GILBERT, PRENTISS BAYLEY; SINO–JAPANESE WAR.

STONE, WILLIAM JOEL (1848–1918). Lawyer William Stone was a member of the U.S. House of Representatives (D-Mo.) in 1884–91 and governor of Missouri in 1893–97. He was elected to the U.S. Senate in 1902. Stone served as chair of the **Senate Committee on Foreign Relations** (1913–18) and voted against President **Woodrow Wilson**'s request for a **declaration of war** on **Germany** (1917).

SUN YAT-SEN (1866–1925). Chinese nationalist leader Sun Yat-sen founded the **Kuomintang**, which emerged victorious from the first democratic elections held in **China** (1913) after the collapse of the Manchu dynasty (1911). During the subsequent power struggle between rival warlords, he strengthened the party in its main bases in Canton, Nanking (Nanjing), and Shanghai, and he accepted help from Chinese communist factions in return for arms and strategic assistance from the **Union of Soviet Socialist Republics**. Sun Yat-sen believed he would be able to unite the mainland under a government based on democratic and socialist principles, avoiding the radical example of the Russian Bolsheviks. He died of cancer in Peking (Beijing) before he could bring his plans to fruition and was later succeeded by **Chiang Kai-shek**.

SUSSEX. A French passenger vessel, the *Sussex* was sunk by a German submarine on 24 March 1916, during **World War I**, in the belief that it was a mine layer. Eighty passengers were killed or wounded, including 25 Americans, prompting President **Woodrow Wilson** to threaten to cut diplomatic ties with **Germany**. Concerned at the implications of the threat, the German government issued the Sussex Pledge on 24 April 1916, promising to refrain from sinking passenger vessels and to board and search detained merchant liners before sinking them. *See also ARABIC; LUSITANIA* NOTES.

– T –

TAFT, ROBERT ALPHONSO (1889–1953). Robert Taft, son of President **William H. Taft**, trained as a lawyer at Yale and Harvard Law School. As a youth, he spent four years in the **Philippines**, where his father was governor. After being rejected for war service because of poor eyesight, Taft was counsel for the U.S. Food Administration (1917–18) and for the **American Relief Administration** (1919). In the latter, he worked with **Herbert Hoover** and became a follower of Hoover, sharing his distrust of government bureaucracies. He also distrusted the idea of the **League of Nations** and European politicians in general.

Taft served as a Republican member of the Ohio House of Representatives (1921–26), Ohio Senate (1931–32), and U.S. Senate (1939–53). One of the leading senators of his era, he was an unsuccessful candidate for his party's nomination for president in 1940, 1948, and 1952. As a conservative Republican, he opposed the New Deal and in 1946 sponsored the Taft–Hartley Act that restricted labor union activities.

An **isolationist**, he supported preparedness and strong national defense in line with **fortress America** ideas but was adamant against any intervention in foreign wars. As a libertarian conservative, he opposed the draft on the grounds that it limited draftees' freedom of choice. Taft believed a strong military, together with the Atlantic and Pacific oceans, would protect the United States during **World War II**, even if **Germany** were to control all of Europe. He opposed all attempts to aid **Great Britain**, attracting criticism from liberal Republicans such as **Thomas E. Dewey**. Taft supported the war effort after the attack on **Pearl Harbor**, but unlike fellow conservative Republican **Arthur Vandenberg**, he did not move to an **internationalist** position.

After the war, Taft opposed any U.S. involvement in alliances, including the North Atlantic Treaty Organization. He did not see the **Union of Soviet Socialist Republics** or domestic communism as a major threat. He was more concerned about the expansion of government within the United States. Taft supported the Truman Doctrine and, less enthusiastically, the Marshall Plan, but he opposed President **Harry S. Truman**'s handling of the Korean War. He also condemned the **International Military Tribunal** (Nuremberg trials) of Nazi war criminals on the grounds that they were victor's justice, with the victims of Nazi actions acting as both judge and prosecutor.

TAFT, WILLIAM HOWARD (1857–1930). The 27th president of the United States, William Howard Taft was a successful lawyer who served as governor general of the Philippines (1901–4) and secretary of war (1904–8) before serving as U.S. president (1909–13). He was a close friend and confidant of President **Theodore Roosevelt**'s, who supported Taft's election to the presidency. In foreign policy, President Taft supported the **dollar diplomacy** promoted by his secretary of state, **Philander C. Knox**. His administration encouraged U.S. banking investment in **China** as well as across the Caribbean and **Latin America**, and he was not averse to deploying military forces when necessary. Taft was instinctively more conservative than Roosevelt, and their quarrels over Taft's failure to carry out his predecessor's **progressive** agenda provoked Roosevelt to challenge him for the 1912 Republican nomination. This split led to the election of Democrat **Woodrow Wilson**. Taft continued to hold the respect of party conservatives for his pro-business views and of party moderates for his stand as a qualified **internationalist** in support of U.S. membership in the **League of Nations**. President **Warren G. Harding** made him chief justice of the Supreme Court in 1921. *See also* TAFT, ROBERT ALPHONSO.

TARIFFS. Tariffs set by the U.S. Congress as taxes on imported materials and products have been used for two purposes: to raise revenues for the government, and to protect sectors of the economy from foreign competition. The U.S. commitment to free **trade** in foreign policy, as enunciated in the **open door** doctrine, seeks the removal of protectionist or exclusionary tariffs by other states. Political tensions have existed between supporters of the open door, who wish to advantage U.S. commerce and secure the flow of cheap resources, and those who seek to protect domestic enterprises.

From 1865 to the end of the 1920s, the Republican Party favored high tariffs to protect industry. They argued that this would also protect the wages of American workers, which otherwise would be threatened by cheap foreign goods produced by lower-paid workers. In 1913, with Democrats in the majority, the proposal of **Oscar Underwood**, the Underwood–Simmons Tariff, lowered tariffs, thus favoring farmers and others primarily interested in exports. This also reflected the fact that U.S. industry was now mature and productive and less vulnerable to foreign competition.

Major problems in the farming sector after **World War I** brought calls for raises in duties on agricultural products. President Woodrow Wilson vetoed an **Emergency Agricultural Tariff Act** in 1920, but it was approved by President **Warren G. Harding** in 1921. The Republican-controlled Congress went on to enact the high **Fordney–McCumber** (1922) and **Smoot–Hawley** (1930) tariffs. The United States was now a major creditor nation as a result of other countries' **war debts** from **World War I**, and the high tariffs prevented European debtor nations earning money by exporting to the United States, which could have been used to pay the debts. Instead, more debts were incurred in loans, and international trade was harmed. This situation came to a head with the crash of Wall Street in October 1929. The Smoot–Hawley tariff, designed to protect American business, prompted retaliatory tariffs by other nations, and international trade decreased disastrously.

With the **Reciprocal Trade Agreements Act** (1934), the United States could enter into bilateral agreements with other nations to give each other the lowest available rate as "most favored nations." This gave the president some scope to reduce tariffs. The approach was extended on a multilateral basis after **World War II** in the General Agreement on Tariffs and Trade (1948). But tensions continue between those wishing to demolish trade barriers to the advantage of U.S. commerce, and those wishing to protect segments of the U.S. economy from foreign competition. *See also* BRETTON WOODS CONFERENCE.

TAYLOR, MYRON CHARLES (1874–1959). After graduating from Cornell Law School in 1894, practicing law, and working on Wall Street, Myron Taylor made his fortune in the textiles industry. In 1927, **John Pierpont Morgan Jr.** asked him to try to solve problems at U.S. Steel. As chair of the finance committee, Taylor ended U.S. Steel's indebtedness in 1929. He was therefore able to reorganize the corporation during the Great Depression without wholesale redundancies. He was chief executive and chair of U.S. Steel from 1932 to 1938. Although generally hostile to labor unions, he allowed unionization in the corporation in 1937, thereby avoiding the damaging strikes other large industrial concerns were experiencing.

Taylor retired in 1938, and President **Franklin D. Roosevelt** invited him to head the U.S. delegation to the **Evian Conference** on refugees. In 1939, diplomatic relations were opened with the Vatican, and Taylor was appointed ambassador. He served in the post until 1950. Taylor was a member of the **Council on Foreign Relations** and during **World War II** contributed to discussions on postwar planning within the State Department's **Advisory Committee on Postwar Foreign Policy** and in the Informal Political Agenda Group.

TEHERAN CONFERENCE (1943). Code-named Eureka, the Teheran Conference of 28 November–1 December 1943 was the first summit between the **Big Three** powers during **World War II**: U.S. President **Franklin D. Roosevelt**, Prime Minister **Winston Churchill** of **Great Britain**, and Premier **Josef Stalin** of the **Union of Soviet Socialist Republics** (USSR). The United States and Britain made a commitment to the Normandy landings in 1944, Operation

Overlord, and to subsidiary landings in southern France, which became Operation **Dragoon**. Stalin made a tentative commitment to join the war against **Japan** once **Germany** was defeated. He also promised a major Soviet offensive to coincide with Overlord, Operation Bagration. There was agreement on the need for a new international organization to keep the peace, and Roosevelt suggested that his **four policemen** concept should be at the center of it. There were inconclusive discussions on the dismemberment of Germany and relocating the frontiers of **Poland** so that it would gain German territory in the west to compensate for territory to be taken by the Soviet Union in the east. The Teheran Conference ushered in the period of closest and most fruitful **Grand Alliance** cooperation, which lasted until after the 1945 **Yalta Conference**. *See also* MOSCOW CONFERENCE (1943); SECOND FRONT.

THOMAS AMENDMENT (1939). In 1939, a number of **internationalist** organizations and peace societies, supported by the *New York Times* and former secretary of state **Henry Stimson**, proposed revision of the **Neutrality Act**, to allow the president discretion to ban exports to aggressors and permit exports of war materials to victims of aggression. An amendment was proposed by Senator Elbert D. Thomas (D-Utah) as Senate Resolution 67. It failed to pass but influenced revisions made to the Neutrality Act in November 1939, when the **cash-and-carry** provision was extended to include munitions, thus removing the full embargo on arms sales to belligerents. *See also* COMMITTEE TO DEFEND AMERICA BY AIDING THE ALLIES; EICHELBERGER, CLARK MELL; NONPARTISAN COMMITTEE FOR PEACE THROUGH REVISION OF THE NEUTRALITY LAW; WHITE, WILLIAM ALLEN; WORLD WAR II.

THOMAS, NORMAN MATTOON (1884–1968). Socialist leader Norman Thomas was the son of a Presbyterian minister and as a youth worked as a paperboy at the Ohio newspaper office of future president **Warren G. Harding**. He studied political science under **Woodrow Wilson** at Princeton University. Influenced by the British Christian Socialist movement, Thomas became both a socialist and a Presbyterian pastor. In 1911, he became pastor of a church in East Harlem, New York. Thomas was a **pacifist** and opposed **World**

War I on the grounds that it was a conflict of rival imperialisms. Opposition to his pacifism within the church led him to resign his pastorship and join the Socialist Party. He remained an ordained pastor, however, until 1931. With **Oswald Garrison Villard**, **Jane Addams**, **A. J. Muste**, and Scott Nearing, he founded the U.S. section of the Fellowship of Reconciliation (FOR) in 1915. In 1917, he helped establish the **National Civil Liberties Bureau** with Roger Baldwin, which developed into the American Civil Liberties Union. He was associate editor of the *Nation* (1921–22) and co-director of the League of Industrial Democracy (1922–37).

Thomas succeeded Eugene Debs as Socialist Party leader in 1926 and ran for president in 1928 and in every election up to 1948. His pacifism and socialism led him to **isolationism**. Thomas was a founding member of the **Keep America out of War Congress** in 1938 and of the **America First Committee** in September 1940. He supported the U.S. war effort in **World War II** after the **Pearl Harbor** attack. Unlike most other public figures, Thomas vigorously opposed the internment of Japanese Americans during the war. After the war, he was a strong critic of the **Union of Soviet Socialist Republics** but also denounced rearmament and the Vietnam War.

THOMPSON, LLEWELLYN E. (1904–1972). Graduating from the University of Colorado in 1928, Llewellyn Thompson entered the Foreign Service in 1929 and served in a succession of consular posts. In 1941, during **World War II**, he was appointed to Moscow as second secretary and consul. His consular role meant that he traveled fairly extensively in the wartime **Union of Soviet Socialist Republics** (USSR). In 1944, he was transferred to London. From 1946 to 1950, Thompson was in the Department of European Affairs at the State Department. He became ambassador to Austria in 1955, having helped formulate the Austrian State Treaty. He was ambassador to the USSR in 1957–62 and 1966–69, and he played a significant role in Cold War politics. He was a delegate to the Strategic Arms Limitation Talks in 1969–71. Thompson had good relations with the leaders of the USSR, who appreciated his fluency in Russian and his personal integrity.

THOMSON–URRUTIA TREATY (1921). On 6 April 1914, the U.S. minister to Colombia, Thaddeus A. Thomson, and Colombian

Foreign Minister Francisco Jose Urrutia negotiated a treaty granting Colombia $25 million. This was effectively compensation for the U.S. role in the events of 1903, when northern provinces of Colombia broke away to form Panama and provide the United States with the facilities to build the Panama Canal. Under the treaty, oil concessions were given to U.S. companies, but the U.S. Congress delayed ratification until 1921, arguing that the actions of President **Theodore Roosevelt** in encouraging the Panamanians to revolt were entirely justified. Secretary of State **Bainbridge Colby** criticized the delay as "an unmixed calamity" for its impact on the U.S. image in **Latin America**.

THUNDERCLAP, OPERATION. *See* DRESDEN.

TIPITAPA, PEACE OF (1927). Negotiated by U.S. envoy **Henry L. Stimson**, the Peace of Tipitapa was an agreement between warring liberal and conservative factions in **Nicaragua**. Under the deal, concluded on 12 May 1927, conservative Nicaraguan President **Adolfo Diaz** would remain in power until 1928, when U.S.-supervised elections would be held, with rebel liberal leader Juan Sacasa as the liberal candidate for the presidency. Both sides agreed to disarm, and a general amnesty was proclaimed. Elections took place on 4 November 1928, although it was liberal General Jose Maria Moncada, rather than Sacasa, who represented the liberals and won the presidency. *See also* MCCOY, FRANK ROSS.

TOJO, HIDEKI (1884–1948). A war college graduate, Hideki Tojo served as **Japan**'s military attaché in Germany and Switzerland (1919–22). He was more skilled as an administrator than a field commander and was known as *kamisori* ("razor") for his strictness and thoroughness. By the early 1930s, Tojo had emerged as one of the leading figures of the militarist party in Japan. In 1935, he was commander of the military police of the Kwantung Army in Manchukuo, and he suppressed the radicals of the "imperial way" faction. He became chief of staff in the Kwantung Army and played a major role in the opening campaign of the **Sino–Japanese War** in 1937. Army vice minister in 1938–39, he opposed any accommodation with **Chiang Kai-shek**, the nationalist leader of **China**.

In July 1940, Tojo became army minister in Prince Funimaro Konoye's cabinet. He favored closer relations with the **Axis** powers during **World War II** and pressed for a hard line against the Western powers and Chiang. He switched strategic planning to a focus on southward expansion, gaining **France**'s agreement to occupation of bases in southern Indochina in July 1941. On Tojo's recommendation, the Imperial Conference on 6 September 1941 agreed that Japan would go to war if no agreement was reached with the United States and Great Britain by October.

Tojo became prime minister on 16 October 1941 after Konoye failed to secure a personal meeting with President **Franklin D. Roosevelt**. Tojo set a two-month deadline for a breakthrough in negotiations with the United States, after which Japan would resort to war to resolve the oil shortage created by the U.S. embargo. On 7 December 1941 (Hawaiian time), Tojo led Japan into war with the attack on **Pearl Harbor** and against British positions in the Far East.

Tojo remained army minister while prime minister and also held the office of home minister (1941–42), foreign minister (1942), education minister (1943), and commerce minister (1943). During the war, he had wide-ranging powers, though within the framework of the constitution. He had leftists and liberals arrested (all political parties had been abolished in 1940). His education policies enforced militaristic and nationalistic indoctrination, and the police kept close watch on the population. But Tojo was not a dictator; much power, rested with the large corporations, the *Zaibatsu*, and with senior politicians and the military high command.

Tojo's standing suffered as Japan suffered defeat after defeat. He made himself chief of the Imperial Japanese General Staff in February 1944, but the loss of the Mariana Islands in June 1944 showed he had lost control of military events, and he was forced to resign in July. At the end of the war, Tojo attempted to commit suicide but failed. He was tried in the Tokyo **International Military Tribunal** for the Far East in November 1948 and found guilty of "instigating Japan's criminal attacks on her neighbors" and permitting "barbarous treatment" of prisoners of war. Tojo was held responsible for the murder of more than 8 million civilians in China, the **Philippines**, and other occupied territories, and for bacteriological experiments on live subjects by the infamous Unit 731 in China. He and six other leaders were hanged.

TORCH, OPERATION. Operation Torch was the **World War II** invasion of French North Africa by military forces of the United States and **Great Britain**, beginning 8 November 1942 and commanded by U.S. General **Dwight D. Eisenhower**. The operation was originally code-named Gymnast and was proposed by the British as an alternative to an invasion of northern **France** as a **second front** in the war. It was opposed by the U.S. **Joint Chiefs of Staff** as an unnecessary diversion. They believed in the principle of attacking enemy forces directly and aiming to defeat their strongest forces. The British preferred an indirect strategy of using naval power to attack an enemy's peripheries, with the result of stretching the enemy's resources.

President **Franklin D. Roosevelt** overrode the views of his military chiefs to agree on the operation with British Prime Minister **Winston Churchill**. His main reason was that any invasion of France in 1942 would principally involve British forces, so their opposition could not be overlooked. Torch would engage U.S. troops in the European theater in 1942 and avoid a single focus on the war in the Pacific to the detriment of the "**Germany** first" strategy agreed to at **Placentia Bay**. Torch also had the advantage that some forces could be deployed straight from the United States.

The operation and the campaign that followed, which lasted until May 1943, provided a useful combat initiation for U.S. forces and helped to develop Allied cooperation. To minimize possible fighting between Allied and French forces loyal to the collaborationist Vichy government, contacts were opened with Vichy authorities in North Africa. An arrangement was reached with Admiral **Jean François Darlan**, commander in chief of Vichy armed forces, who happened to be in North Africa at the time. This enabled most of the landings to take place unopposed but led to sharp political repercussions in the United States. The deal with a Nazi collaborator raised questions about the moral basis of the Allied enterprise. Although Darlan was assassinated by a French royalist on 24 December 1942, the issue was in Roosevelt's mind when he announced the policy of **unconditional surrender** at the **Casablanca Conference** in January 1943.

Operation Torch did not go according to plan, for the Allies had been overcautious in landing too far west. This gave Germany time to send significant reinforcements to defend Tunisia. These, strengthened by General Erwin Rommel's forces, arriving on retreat from Libya, gave the U.S. forces a sharp baptism of fire at Kasserine Pass. Useful lessons were learned, which might have been even more painful had these operations taken place in France—not only regarding modern combat techniques, but also the qualities of commanders and practices of Allied coordination. The failure to complete the conquest of Tunisia until May 1943, although it resulted in 250,000 **Axis** prisoners, had serious repercussions on the timetable of further Allied operations. It rendered impossible the American preference to open a genuine second front in France in the summer of 1943. This was replaced at the Casablanca Conference by **Operation Husky**. *See also* MURPHY, ROBERT DANIEL.

TRADE. During the 19th century, the major U.S. exports were agricultural products such as wheat and cotton. By 1914, manufactures had grown to 50 percent of American exports. Trade in both these sectors boomed after the outbreak of **World War I**. U.S. refusal to voluntarily restrict this trade can be seen as one of the causes of its eventual entry into the war.

After World War I, the United States was a major international creditor and engaged in 27 percent of the world's trade. However, a booming domestic market in the 1920s meant that exports were only 6 percent of gross domestic product (GDP). Rather than keep **tariffs** low and work to maintain the economic health of countries owing **war debts** to the United States, specific business interests, often supported by organized labor, pressed Congress to enact increasingly high protectionist tariffs**,** notably the **Fordney–McCumber** Tariff in 1922 and the **Smoot–Hawley** Tariff in 1930. U.S. industry, at the forefront of mass production techniques and mass marketing, did not actually need such protection, which only served to weaken the global economy.

The collapse of the world financial system that began with the Wall Street crash in October 1929 brought a large shrinkage in world trade. Nation-states sought to produce goods they had previously imported, and they engaged in restrictive trading blocs. The value of

U.S. exports fell by 50 percent between 1929 and 1930. Under President **Franklin D. Roosevelt**, Secretary of State **Cordell Hull** sought to improve the situation by bilateral arrangements and pushed Congress to pass the **Reciprocal Trade Agreements Act** (1934). Despite the agreements made under the act, the U.S. trade deficit disappeared only in 1940, as a consequence of **World War II**.

During World War II, U.S. trade penetrated markets formerly dominated by Great Britain. The United States acted to end trade blocs and import substitution and to advance Hull's free trade vision at the 1944 **Bretton Woods Conference**. The **International Monetary Fund** and the General Agreement on Tariffs and Trade were introduced in order to control currency fluctuations that damaged trade and to advance the reduction of tariffs. These U.S. initiatives contributed to the construction of a multinational trading system after the war and establishment of New York City as the financial capital of the world, and put the United States in a position where it could manage the economy of the liberal capitalist world.

TRADING WITH THE ENEMY ACT (1917). Passed by the U.S. Congress on 6 October 1917, this act prohibited all forms of direct and indirect trading with **Germany** or its allies during **World War I**. The law applied not only to all normal forms of commerce but also to letters and other forms of written communication. Firms with preexisting business connections were given 30 days after passage of the act to apply to the federal government for exemption licenses. The office of Alien Property Custodian was also established. All groups in possession of or having business dealings involving property of the German government or its allies were required to declare the fact by mid-December 1917. The U.S. president was empowered to "investigate, regulate, or prohibit" foreign exchange transactions, transfers of credit, and trading or hoarding of gold or silver coin or bullion, currency or securities. The act was considered to greatly enhance the power of the president and the executive branch of the federal government.

TREATY ON THE PREVENTION OF CONTROVERSIES (1936). *See* BUENOS AIRES CONFERENCE.

TREATY TO AVOID OR PREVENT CONFLICTS BETWEEN THE AMERICAN STATES (1923). *See* GONDRA TREATY.

TRIANON, TREATY OF (1919). In addition to the **Treaty of Versailles**, which dealt with **Germany**, the 1919 **Paris Peace Conference** also formulated treaties with the other defeated **Central Powers**. On 4 June 1920, a treaty was signed at the Trianon palace with Hungary. Under the Trianon Treaty, Hungary's territory was reduced, and its population fell from 21 million to 7 million. Hungary was now landlocked. It was allowed a small army. The U.S. Senate did not ratify the treaty, as it contained the covenant of the **League of Nations**. The United States signed a separate peace treaty with Hungary on 29 August 1921, and it was ratified on 18 October. *See also* BERLIN, TREATY OF; ST. GERMAIN, TREATY OF.

TRIPARTITE PACT (1940). **Germany**, Italy, and **Japan** signed the Tripartite Pact in Berlin on 27 September 1940, during **World War II**. They agreed to assist each other if attacked by a state they were not at that point at war with. This included the United States, which was still a neutral power. The United States responded to this and the simultaneous movement of Japanese troops into northern French Indo-china by imposing further embargo restrictions on U.S.–Japanese trade.

The Tripartite Pact did not lead to the establishment of alliance structures or joint planning. It was given an anti-Soviet twist by German Foreign Minister Joachim von Ribbentrop, who drew into the pact Hungary, Slovakia, and Romania in November 1940 and Bulgaria and Yugoslavia (briefly) in April 1941. Croatia joined after the German occupation of Yugoslavia, in June 1941. Japan distanced itself from the anti-Soviet direction of the pact by concluding a nonaggression pact with the **Union of Soviet Socialist Republics** in April 1941. The Tripartite Pact did not require German dictator **Adolf Hitler** to declare war on the United States in December 1941, as Japan had not been attacked. *See also* ANTI-COMINTERN PACT; AXIS POWERS.

TRUJILLO Y MOLINA, RAFAEL LEONIDAS (1891–1961). A graduate of a U.S. military training school, Rafael Trujillo rose to the top of **Dominican Republic** politics, becoming chief of staff of the Dominican army in 1928. After an election marked by violence and corruption, he served as president in 1930–38 and 1942–52. Even while not president, he was the dictatorial ruler of the country from 1930 until his assassination in 1961, calling himself the "Benefactor of the Nation." Large-scale public works programs enriched his family, and he maintained his rule by terror and corruption. He was largely responsible for the murder of 10,000 Haitian immigrants in October 1937. The United States was initially wary, fearing his methods would provoke revolutions, but came to see him as someone who brought order and stability, which meant the United States would not have to repeat its earlier military intervention. President **Franklin D. Roosevelt**, when questioned about having **Good Neighbor** relations with such a person, said, "he may be an S.O.B., but he is our S.O.B." *See also* LATIN AMERICA.

TRUMAN, HARRY S. (1884–1972). The 33rd president of the United States, Harry Truman served in the U.S. Army as an artillery captain in France during **World War I**. After the war, he set up a haberdashery business, studied law, and became a presiding judge in Jackson County, Missouri (1926–34). A nominee of the Pendergast political machine that controlled Kansas City, Truman, a Democrat, served in the U.S. Senate (1934–44). He gained a reputation as an honest, hardworking senator, critical of waste and inefficiency.

During **World War II**, Truman chaired the Senate Special Committee to Investigate the National Defense Program and was responsible for cutting waste, saving the government large amounts of money and protecting it from criticism over war production. He became President **Franklin D. Roosevelt**'s vice presidential running-mate in the November 1944 election, in place of the more radical **Henry Wallace**. Fears for Roosevelt's health meant the party wanted a more dependable person as next in line to the White House. As vice president, Truman was not involved in policy making and was thus unprepared on many issues when he became president with Roosevelt's death on 12 April 1945.

Truman resolved to continue Roosevelt's policies but sought advice from the State Department, which Roosevelt had sidelined, as well as from **William Leahy**, **Averell Harriman**, **Harry Hopkins**, and **Joseph Davies**. His approach to the **Union of Soviet Socialist Republics** (USSR) was more direct than Roosevelt's, and he criticized Foreign Commissar Vyacheslav Molotov for Soviet failures to adhere to the **Yalta** agreements. He resisted British Prime Minister **Winston Churchill**'s pressure to advance General **Dwight D. Eisenhower**'s forces in Europe as far east as possible as a bargaining counter with the USSR, and he sent Hopkins to work out a compromise deal on **Poland** with Premier **Josef Stalin** in June.

Briefed by Secretary of War **Henry Stimson** on the **Manhattan Project**, Truman delayed the **Potsdam Conference** until the successful test of the **atomic bomb** at Alamogordo. During the conference, Truman informed Stalin of the test, without revealing the nature of the weapon, and generally acted more forcefully than was Roosevelt's custom. Truman authorized the use of the atomic bombs on **Japan**. It is likely that in August 1945 he regarded the USSR more as a bully to be treated firmly than as an absolute menace with which there could be no negotiation. It was only gradually, in the following 18 months, that Truman's policy hardened into the classic Cold War policy of containment, as formulated in the Truman Doctrine (March 1947). Truman was reelected in a surprise victory in 1948 and led the United States into the North Atlantic Treaty Organization, provided economic aid to revive the democratic states of Western Europe in the Marshall Plan, and organized armed resistance against communist expansion in the Korean War (1950–53).

TWO-OCEAN NAVY ACT (1940). The possibility of a defeat of **Great Britain** by **Germany** in **World War II** prompted passage of the "11 percent" Naval Expansion Act by the U.S. Congress on 14 June 1940, sponsored by Representative **Carl Vinson**, which would increase navy aircraft carrier, cruiser, and submarine tonnage, but Admiral **Harold Stark**, chief of naval operations, pressed for $4 billion to construct a navy capable of fighting simultaneously on the Pacific and Atlantic oceans. On 19 July, the president signed a further measure, the Two-Ocean Navy Act. It ended the long-standing policy that the United States should seek parity, but no more, with the British navy. Now, the United States would seek to have a navy that could simultaneously put to sea the largest fleet in the Pacific and the largest fleet in the Atlantic.

Naval expansion was supported by many **isolationists** as a preparedness measure, because the navy was seen as a defensive weapon, designed to protect and deter. It fit with other hemispheric defense initiatives being taken by President **Franklin D. Roosevelt**, such as the **Act of Havana** and establishment of the naval neutrality patrol zone in the Atlantic. It also derived from Stark's growing belief that if the United States was drawn into war, it would be against a coalition of enemy powers, a view he later put forward strongly in the **Plan Dog** scenario.

The Two-Ocean Navy Act provided over $5.2 billion to expand the navy 70 percent by building 201 new warships. Seen as a great threat by many in the Japanese navy, it gave an urgency to **Japan**'s plans for expansion. However, the ships that came into service in 1943 provided the means by which the United States was to win its great victory in the Pacific theater. As a consequence of the Two-Ocean Navy Act, the United States became the largest naval power in the world.

TYDINGS–MCDUFFIE ACT (1934). The Philippine Independence Act, known as the Tydings–McDuffie Act, was passed by the U.S. Congress on 24 March 1934. It provided for self-government in the U.S. colony of the **Philippines** and independence after 10 years. The passage of the act came after a mission by Filipino politician Manuel Quezon to lobby Congress for a better deal than provided in the **Hare–Hawes–Cutting Act** (1933). The Tydings–McDuffie Act provided for a constitution to be drafted for the 10-year transitional government, to be known as the Commonwealth of the Philippines. In this period, U.S. forces would remain in the islands, and the U.S. president would be able to put Filipino forces under U.S. command. The **U.S. Navy** would keep its bases in the islands for two years after independence. All Filipinos in the United States would now be regarded as aliens and an **immigration** quota of 50 a year set. As a result of **Japan**'s occupation of the islands in **World War II**, independence was not actually achieved until 1946. *See also* JONES ACT.

– U –

ULTRA-MAGIC DEAL. One of the most important and highly secret aspects of relations between the United States and **Great Britain** during **World War II** was **intelligence** cooperation. General contacts began as early as 1937, and by the fall of **France** in June 1940, U.S. officials were prepared to exchange some intelligence on naval matters. The U.S. Operation **Magic** broke **Japan**'s **Purple** code machine in September 1940, and the British had made progress in breaking **Germany**'s Enigma code machine, an operation known as Ultra.

In late 1940, a delegation from the **U.S. Navy** and U.S. Army met their counterparts in Britain, at the Government Code and Cipher School at Bletchley Park. The Americans offered the Magic material, some other Japanese ciphers, the German diplomatic code, and Italian and Mexican codes. The British provided information on **Axis** and **Union of Soviet Socialist Republics** (USSR) encoding systems and some codes from **Latin America**. The British could not read Soviet diplomatic material, but by 1941 they had penetrated Soviet meteorological, naval, and army ciphers. Given the secrecy of such code-breaking activity, these contacts were developed hesitantly. Furthermore, while the British system was centralized, there was much rivalry between the U.S. Navy and U.S. Army, with the Navy sometimes refusing to provide Ultra material to the army that had already passed to the British.

It was not until June 1943 that a formal agreement was made concerning the liaison, in the **Britain–United States of America Agreement** (BRUSA). In this, they agreed to share finished intelligence, not the undecrypted raw product. Britain took prime responsibility for German communications, the United States for Japanese. The first American party arrived at Bletchley Park in April 1943, and a proper team did not begin working there until January 1944. The U.S. contingent amounted to 68 personnel: 12 or so were integrated into the British operation, and the rest operated as liaisons at U.S. field commands. The level of cooperation in such a sensitive area is indicative of the special closeness of U.S.–British relations during the war, and to a large degree it continued in the Cold War era and beyond. *See also* SIGNALS INTELLIGENCE.

UNCONDITIONAL SURRENDER. During **World War II**, U.S. President **Franklin D. Roosevelt** announced in January 1943, at the end of the **Casablanca Conference**, that the policy of the Allies was to require the **Axis** powers to surrender unconditionally. Prime Minister **Winston Churchill** of **Great Britain** may not have known that Roosevelt was going to make the announcement but knew of the idea of unconditional surrender. Churchill hoped that Italy could be drawn away from the Axis by offering terms, while Roosevelt was more concerned to restate core Allied aims unequivocally. He was motivated by the domestic political storm that had arisen over the deal made by General **Dwight D. Eisenhower** and **Robert Murphy** with Admiral **Jean François Darlan** of the Vichy government during Operation **Torch**. There was also a determination to avoid the situation at the end of **World War I**, when **Germany** surrendered on the basis of the **Fourteen Points** only to find itself faced with a postwar settlement that departed from those principles. The resentment that followed was now seen as a contributory cause of World War II.

The policy behind Roosevelt's statement was implicit in the stated war aim of achieving complete victory, and "unconditional surrender" provided a basic policy that helped to avoid contention within the **Grand Alliance**. Some argue that implying there would be harsh treatment of the Axis encouraged last-ditch resistance by them. Certainly the policy was used for propaganda purposes in Germany and **Japan**. German propaganda also cited the 1944 **Morgenthau Plan**, but the **Atlantic Charter** and **United Nations Declaration** were public statements that the Allies intended to construct a postwar order based on certain principles that would allow a place for the former Axis nations. In the end, Germany surrendered unconditionally, but Japan gained one condition, the continuation of Emperor **Hirohito** on the throne.

UNDERWOOD, OSCAR WILDER (1862–1929). Oscar Underwood represented Alabama in the U.S. House of Representatives in 1895–96 but was replaced when the election result was contested. In 1896, he ran again and was reelected. He remained in the House until 1914 (becoming House majority leader in 1911), when he was elected to the Senate. Underwood was considered as a dark horse candidate for the Democratic Party presidential nomination in 1912 and 1924. He introduced the Underwood Tariff Act (1913), which drastically reduced **tariffs** on imports, reflecting the Democrats' hostility to protectionism at this time. Underwood chaired the Senate Committee on Cuban Relations and supported the foreign policy of **Woodrow Wilson**. He served as a delegate to the 1921 **Naval Disarmament Conference** in Washington, D.C., and the 1928 **Havana Conference**.

UNION OF SOVIET SOCIALIST REPUBLICS (USSR). Following the 1917 **Russian Revolution** and rise to power of the Bolsheviks led by Vladimir Ilyich Lenin, a federation of republics was formed on 1 January 1923, bringing together **Russia**, the Ukraine, Transcaucasia, and Byelorussia. This Union of Soviet Socialist Republics was a centralized state where real power rested in the Communist Party of the Soviet Union (CPSU). The central decision-making body of the state was the Politburo of the CPSU, and individuals gained their influence from their status in it, not from their ministerial positions. After Lenin's death in 1924 and an intense power struggle, **Josef Stalin** came to power. Stalin defeated his rival Leon Trotsky by allying with other Bolsheviks but then turned on them. By the mid-1930s, he had established a totalitarian dictatorship. In show trials from 1936 to 1938, Bolshevik leaders were forced to confess to offenses against the state and were executed. Stalin went on to purge the Soviet military, eliminating over 70 percent of its officers. Stalin wielded his power from the post of general secretary of the CPSU, taking formal governmental office in May 1941, when he made himself chair of the council of people's commissars—in effect, premier.

Stalin set out to rectify the Soviet Union's industrial backwardness within 10 years. A drastic program of industrialization was set in motion in the Five Year Plans begun in 1929. A concomitant was the collectivization of agriculture, both to increase food production to feed the burgeoning urban proletariat and to drive peasants off the land and into the cities. This involved an attack on the wealthier peasants, the kulaks, and there was widespread slaughter of this section of the population. Still more were deported to the growing network of labor camps (gulags) in isolated parts of the USSR. They were joined by more and more political prisoners as Stalin's purges were extended. The collectivizations resulted in a widespread famine by 1933.

Stalin's foreign policy was subordinated to the strengthening of the USSR and the survival of his regime, under the slogan "Socialism in One Country." He used the Third, or Communist, International (Comintern), that was set up in 1919 to propagate the Bolshevik revolution, as an instrument of that policy. Foreign communists were required to follow the orders of the Comintern with no deviation. The United States had refused to recognize the legitimacy of the Soviet regime. U.S.–Soviet relations had begun badly, with the encouragement of world revolution by Lenin and U.S. deployment of troops in the **Siberian** and **North Russia** interventions from 1918 to 1920.

With the Soviet refusal to honor **war debts** to the United States that had been incurred by previous regimes, the United States continued to withhold recognition throughout the 1920s. There was also popular distaste for many aspects of the Soviet regime, especially its anticapitalism and its official policy opposing religion. However, the process of industrialization created a demand in the USSR for U.S. industrial technology, and some U.S. business people began supplying it, particularly for the oil industry. These included **Henry Ford** and **Averell Harriman**.

In 1933, President **Franklin D. Roosevelt** bowed to pressure from segments of the business community to regularize relations with the Soviet Union. In the context of the decline in world **trade** because of the Great Depression, the Soviet market was an attractive one. Informal negotiations began through **William C. Bullitt**, who had earlier attempted to broker an arrangement between the Bolsheviks and President **Woodrow Wilson** at the time of the 1919 **Paris Peace Conference**. The result was the recognition of the USSR in November 1933. Bullitt became the first U.S. ambassador.

However, trade did not grow in the amount anticipated, and no settlement was reached on the issue of war debts. The Soviets had promised not to interfere in U.S. domestic politics, but the **Communist Party of the USA** continued to take orders from the Comintern. In addition, promises of freedom of religion for Americans in the USSR were not kept. Embassy staff such as **George Kennan, Loy Henderson**, and **Charles Bohlen** reported on the purges and show trials, and the State Department Division of East European Affairs maintained a stance critical of the USSR under the direction of **Robert F. Kelley**.

The division was merged into a larger unit in 1937, and Kelley was appointed overseas.

Although **Joseph E. Davies** took a much more sympathetic line as ambassador than had Bullitt, relations did not really improve. The USSR had grown fearful of the rise of the Nazi party in **Germany** and had ordered communists to start cooperating with other left-wing groups that had previously been regarded as mortal foes. This "popular front" strategy was regarded with suspicion by many in the United States and **Great Britain** as a form of infiltration. Thus, although the USSR was overtly embracing the idea of **collective security**, and Foreign Commissar Maxim Litvinov was very active in the **League of Nations** at Geneva, it was kept at a distance. Prime Minister **Neville Chamberlain** of Great Britain thus preferred to do his own deal with German dictator **Adolf Hitler** at Munich to the exclusion of the Soviet Union.

In 1939, after Chamberlain issued a security guarantee to **Poland**, the USSR was sought as an ally by both sides. In August 1939, the great ideological foes, Nazi Germany and the USSR, concluded a nonaggression pact. They divided Eastern Europe between them, and 17 days after the Germans invaded Poland, the Soviets occupied the eastern half of the country. The Soviets annexed Latvia, Lithuania, and Estonia in June 1940, together with Bessarabia and Northern Bukovina, taken from Romania. The Red Army had invaded Finland on 30 November 1939 but suffered humiliating defeats, confirming opinions that the purges had severely weakened the Soviet military. The USSR was expelled from the League of Nations. The United States refused to recognize the Soviet annexations, and there was much sympathy for Finland, which was the only European country to pay off its war debt. U.S.–Soviet relations were very cool, and the 1940 **Smith Act** (Aliens Registration Act) was directed as much against Soviet-backed communist activity in the United States as it was against Nazi activities.

Public opinion was slow to change even after the German invasion of the USSR on 22 June 1941. However, Roosevelt recognized that the Soviets could play a crucial role in the defeat of Germany. He sent **Harry Hopkins** as a personal envoy to Stalin, and after Hopkins reported his opinion that the USSR was determined to resist, he began discreetly seeking ways to send aid. In October, Averell

Harriman was sent to negotiate arrangements in the 1941 **Moscow Conference**. **Lend-lease** for the USSR was approved by Congress in November 1941.

The United States and Soviet Union became allies when they agreed to the **United Nations Declaration** on 1 January 1942. Critics found Roosevelt overly accommodating. Roosevelt's view was that the Soviets had to be kept fighting and that good relations had to be cultivated. His tactic was to provide plentiful Lend-Lease aid, given without any of the conditions imposed in the **Master Lend-Lease Agreement** with Britain. Special envoys, such as **Wendell Willkie**, and officials independent of the State Department, such as Colonel **Philip Faymonville**, were used to implement this policy. The State Department and sections of the U.S. military remained skeptical of cooperation with the USSR, but Roosevelt simply bypassed them. His personal approach to diplomacy with Stalin was in evidence at the 1943 **Teheran** and 1945 **Yalta** conferences. His principle was to avoid contention over political issues if they could be deferred to later, and to satisfy where possible Soviet military requirements, so long as to do so did not involve high American casualties. He sought from Stalin an agreement to cooperate in policing the world after the war, as in his **four policemen** concept, and participation in the **United Nations** organization. He was also anxious that the USSR join the war against **Japan**. He achieved both of these goals, though at the cost of some concessions. He tacitly agreed that the USSR should have "friendly governments" in Eastern Europe though likely hoped that any sphere of influence would be an "open" one, from which U.S. economic activity would not be excluded.

Roosevelt died on 12 April 1945, and his successor **Harry S. Truman** knew of the public arrangements but not the tacit agreements made in private. His insistence that the Soviets keep to their public agreements struck Stalin as an unwelcome change in U.S. policy. Truman sought advice from the State Department, Harriman, and Admiral **William Leahy**, and all were inclined toward a tougher stance. The issues of the composition of Eastern European governments and the future of Germany had become impossible to defer, and the fundamental difference in U.S. and Soviet approaches to these issues meant that the 1945 **Potsdam Conference** was tense. Truman and Secretary of State **James F. Byrnes** had some hopes that the use of the **atomic**

bomb against Japan would impress a sense of U.S. strength on the Soviet leadership and cause them to be more amenable. As it turned out, it made relations more tense. After **World War II**, U.S.–Soviet relations deteriorated steadily until reaching a full-blown Cold War by the end of 1947. *See also* SOVIET ARK; STANDLEY, WILLIAM HARRISON; STEINHARDT, LAURENCE A.; THOMPSON, LLEWELLYN E.; VENONA PROJECT.

UNITED FRUIT COMPANY (UFC). The United Fruit Company was formed in 1899 and became a major actor in the political and economic affairs of Central America and the Caribbean, to a degree that it was accused of quasi-colonialism. The company had extensive plantations in Costa Rica, Colombia, **Cuba**, Jamaica, **Nicaragua**, Panama, and Santo Domingo. It owned a fleet of steamships, pioneered refrigeration at sea, was involved in railroads and postal communications, and exercised considerable influence on politicians to gain favorable conditions for its business.

United Fruit brought a great deal of development to areas of **Latin America** and paid its workers well, providing schooling and housing. On the other hand, working conditions were very hard, labor unions were suppressed, and the company maintained a paternalistic approach. It also applied U.S. patterns of racial segregation in large parts of the territory it controlled. In Guatemala in particular, United Fruit was a major influence in national politics, able to call on the U.S. government to defend its interests. This culminated in 1954 with the U.S.-backed coup against President Jacobo Arbenz. The company passed into different ownership in the 1970s and ceased to be involved in such interventionist practices. *See also* ZEMURRAY, SAMUEL.

UNITED NATIONS (UN). During **World War II**, on the basis of the **United Nations Declaration** of 1 January 1942, the Allied powers were often referred to as the United Nations. It was subsequently adopted as the name for the new international organization that replaced the **League of Nations**. The UN was officially founded at the **San Francisco Conference** of April 1945. To qualify as a founding member, a state had to have subscribed to the declaration, and therefore have been a belligerent in the war. The dominant wartime alliance of U.S. President **Franklin D. Roosevelt**, Prime Minister **Winston Churchill** of **Great Britain**, and Premier **Josef Stalin** of the **Union of Soviet Socialist Republics** (USSR) was enshrined at the heart of the UN in the permanent members of the Security Council (Great Britain, United States, Soviet Union, **China**, **France**) and their veto powers. This was also essentially an enactment of Roosevelt's **four policemen** concept. The UN includes a General Assembly, where each member state has one vote, and the Security Council, containing the permanent members and rotating membership from among the other member states. The secretary general to the council emerged as the de facto chief executive and is customarily selected from a minor state.

The UN set up its headquarters in New York, though some of the agencies that it inherited from the defunct League of Nations remained in Geneva. In contrast to the League, the United Nations was given the power to raise armed forces from among its members. It was hoped that this, and the membership of all the great powers, would make the UN a more effective guarantor of peace. This rested, as Roosevelt understood, on agreement between the great powers, but tensions between the victorious allies would render the UN incapable of fulfilling this ambitious goal. *See also* DUMBARTON OAKS CONFERENCE; HOT SPRINGS CONFERENCE; INTERNATIONAL LABOUR ORGANIZATION; UNITED NATIONS CHARTER; UNITED NATIONS RELIEF AND REHABILITATION ADMINISTRATION; WORLD BANK.

UNITED NATIONS CHARTER. The United Nations Charter is the founding document of the **United Nations** (UN). It was signed at the **San Francisco Conference** on 26 June 1945 by 50 countries. These, together with **Poland**, which signed later, were the founding members of the UN. It came into force on 24 October 1945 when ratified by the five permanent members of the Security Council: the United States, **Great Britain**, the **Union of Soviet Socialist Republics** (USSR), **France**, and **China**, together with a majority of other members.

All members of the UN are bound by the articles of the charter, and the document specifies that its provisions have precedence over all other treaties. The charter sets out the purpose of the organization: principally the maintenance of peace and international security. It describes the institutions of the UN and their powers and responsibilities, including the UN Economic and Social Council, the International Court of Justice (which replaced the **World Court**), and the Trusteeship Council. The charter invests the Security Council with power to authorize economic, military, and diplomatic sanctions, and to raise military forces. Article 51 permits the formation of regional security arrangements. *See also* INTERNATIONAL LABOUR ORGANIZATION; LEAGUE OF NATIONS; UNITED NATIONS RELIEF AND REHABILITATION ADMINISTRATION.

UNITED NATIONS DECLARATION. On 1 January 1942, the United States, **Great Britain, China**, and the **Union of Soviet Socialist Republics** issued the United Nations Declaration, which was eventually signed by 22 other nations. This was the formal basis for the Allied coalition against the **Axis** powers in **World War II**. Being multilateral and very generalized in its terms, it satisfied continuing U.S. antipathies toward formal bilateral alliances. The declaration was very simple, pledging signatories not to make a separate peace with those Axis powers with which they were at war (but not committing them to any action against those with whom they were not at war), and to make such contributions to victory as were appropriate to their means. As far as war aims were concerned, reference was made to the **Atlantic Charter**. From this point, the Allies called themselves "the United Nations," a phrase coined by President **Franklin D. Roosevelt**, but to distinguish their alliance from the later **United Nations** organization, they are customarily called "the Allies." *See also* GRAND ALLIANCE; POTSDAM CONFERENCE; TEHERAN CONFERENCE; YALTA CONFERENCE.

UNITED NATIONS RELIEF AND REHABILITATION ADMINISTRATION (UNRRA). Unlike most other **United Nations** (UN) agencies, UNRRA was established on 9 November 1943, before the UN was formed. At this time "United Nations" referred to the **World War II** Allied powers under the **United Nations Declaration**. The initial proposal for an organization to provide relief in areas the Allies were liberating was made by U.S. President **Franklin D. Roosevelt** to Congress on 9 June 1943. **Great Britain**, the **Union of Soviet Socialist Republics** (USSR), and **China** had already indicated to Roosevelt that they approved the idea. Forty other nations joined with these four to establish UNRRA.

UNRRA was organized into a general council of all members, and a central committee of the four major powers. Its original remit was extended in 1944 to include people who had been dislocated by reason of religion, ethnicity, or sympathies with the Allies, thus making it possible to extend aid to Jews from **Germany** and other persecuted groups. It was especially concerned with the plight of refugees, known as "displaced persons." General councils met in Atlantic City, New Jersey, in November 1943; Montreal, Canada, in September 1944; and London, England, in August 1945. The directors general were Americans: Herbert Lehman, former governor of New York, was followed in March 1946 by Fiorello La Guardia, former mayor of New York City, and in 1947 by Major General Lowell Ward Rooks. The headquarters was in Washington, D.C., with regional centers in London, Shanghai, Cairo, and Sydney.

Between 1943 and 1949, UNRRA spent nearly $4 billion, more than half of it provided by the United States. Each member nation not occupied by the enemy was requested to provide at least 1 percent of its national income. UNRRA had a specialized staff of about 10,000, drawn from 43 nations. It provided a reservoir of supplies and services that could be drawn on by states that demonstrated their specific needs. The major recipients were China, **Poland**, Yugoslavia, Greece, Italy, Czechoslovakia, and the Ukrainian parts of the USSR. UNRRA helped about 8 million refugees, relieved starvation in many European countries in 1945–47, was involved in reconstruction work, and helped with the revival of agriculture and industry prior to the initiation of the Marshall Plan in 1948. In the Far East, UNRRA assigned the island of Formosa (Taiwan) to the administration of China; after the Chinese nationalists were routed by the communists, **Chiang Kai-shek** based his government on the island. UNRRA ceased its operations in Europe in June 1947 and in China in May 1949. UN agencies such as the International Refugee Organization and the Food and Agriculture Organization continued certain of its activities.

UNITED STATES ARMY OBSERVATION GROUP. *See* DIXIE MISSION.

UNITED STATES NAVY. The building by the United States of an oceangoing navy of significant force in the last decade of the 19th century was a major stage in the development of U.S. foreign policy. By 1914, the United States possessed the second largest navy in the world. While many Americans saw this force as the first line of defense, it also gave the United States a capacity for power projection as well as an interest in gaining control of overseas territories as bases. The acquisition of the American empire was intimately connected with naval expansion, inspired by the writings of Alfred Thayer Mahan in the 1880s and associated particularly with the presidency of **Theodore Roosevelt** (1901–9).

During **World War I**, the United States embarked on a major building program of the latest battleships. The aim was to match the size of the British navy to guard against the possibility of **Great Britain** being defeated and losing its naval supremacy to **Germany**. Germany's ambitions were seen as more likely to impinge on U.S. interests. After World War I, this building program continued, now in direct competition with Britain and **Japan**. It was immensely costly at a time of economic retrenchment, and this was a key part of the impetus for the 1921 **Naval Disarmament Conference** in Washington, D.C. The Five Power Treaty agreed to at the conference froze the relative sizes of the world's major navies in terms of capital ships (battleships and battle cruisers). A further building race then followed, this time of cruisers, until that was somewhat restricted at the 1930 **London Naval Disarmament Conference**. The United States did not actually build up to the levels allowed in the treaties, for reasons of cost and because of prevailing attitudes of **isolationism**. The navy was the main focus of the campaigners for **disarmament**. It was not until Representative **Carl Vinson**'s 1938 **Naval Expansion Act** that the United States began to address the deficiencies in its naval strength that had resulted, and it was not done systematically until the Naval Expansion Act and the **Two-Ocean Navy Act** (1940).

In the meantime, the navy developed new weapons systems—notably aircraft and submarines. Strategic concepts were still based on a major engagement between battleships. Claims made by General William Mitchell in the 1920s that aircraft could easily sink warships had been met with hostility within the navy hierarchy. However, major progress was made in the design and use of aircraft carriers, meaning that the navy was able to adapt rapidly and effectively to the changed nature of naval warfare once it became evident in **World War II**. The navy also learned from the experience of other countries, so the Two-Ocean Navy Act not only provided for deploying superior naval forces simultaneously in the Atlantic and the Pacific, but also prioritized the kinds of ships that were to be the new war winners: aircraft carriers and submarines.

The navy was at the forefront of U.S. foreign policy after passage of the **Lend-Lease** Act in March 1941. Its activities gradually extended from neutrality patrols in the western Atlantic to increasingly close cooperation with British and Canadian vessels escorting convoys. Incidents involving the USS *Kearny*, *Greer*, and *Reuben James* drew the U.S. Navy into an undeclared war with Germany in the Atlantic. At the same time, the Pacific Fleet was used to pressure Japan, notably in the ill-fated deployment of the fleet to **Pearl Harbor** in the summer of 1940.

The massive naval buildup that followed the 1940 expansion acts gave the United States overwhelming superiority over Japan by 1944. At the end of the war, the U.S. Navy far exceeded in size and firepower the navies of all other powers combined. This was a major element in the U.S. standing as a world power. It also brought added requirements, such as the navy's desire to retain possession of island bases captured from Japan. *See also* KING, ERNEST J.; KNOX, WILLIAM FRANKLIN; NATIONAL NAVAL VOLUNTEERS; NAVAL DISARMAMENT CONFERENCE (1927); STARK, HAROLD R.

UNITED STATES V. CURTISS-WRIGHT EXPORT CORPORATION (1936). In May 1934, the U.S. Congress passed a joint resolution giving the president authority to prohibit sales of weapons by American businesses to the countries involved in the **Chaco War**. President **Franklin D. Roosevelt** then issued an embargo on sales of military equipment or materials that could be put to military use, on grounds of national security. The embargo was revoked in November 1935. In 1936, the government sued the Curtiss-Wright corporation for selling arms to Bolivia in breach of the embargo. The corporation argued in the U.S. Supreme Court case of *United States v. Curtiss-Wright Export Corporation* that Congress could not delegate the power of regulation of commerce to the president. The embargo had not been embodied in any law passed by Congress.

The Supreme Court rejected these arguments, ruling that while the Constitution did not explicitly reserve all powers in foreign policy to the president, it was done implicitly. The executive was empowered to conduct foreign policy in ways that Congress could not and should not. The president therefore was justified in exercising discretion in deciding whether application of the resolution would have a beneficial effect in bringing about peace. The ruling thus upheld the doctrine that the president could limit exports on grounds of national security, and it established the broader principle of executive supremacy in foreign affairs. Concerns that this might enable the president to lead the country into war were evident in the congressional debates on the **Neutrality Acts** and in the **Ludlow Amendment**.

– V –

VANDENBERG, ARTHUR HENDRICK (1884–1951). As editor of the *Grand Rapids Herald* in Michigan, Arthur Vandenberg endorsed an expansive U.S. foreign policy, supporting war with Spain (1898), the annexation of the **Philippines**, and the **Roosevelt Corollary**. During **World War I**, he made speeches for **Liberty bonds** and condemned **pacifism** and **isolationism** as traitorous. He supported entry into the **League of Nations**.

Vandenberg served in the U.S. Senate (R-Mich.) from 1928 to 1951, becoming Senate minority leader in 1935. He was active on the **Senate Committee on Foreign Relations** from 1929. Having supported the idea of U.S. membership in the **World Court**, the declining world situation led him to take a strongly isolationist line through the 1930s. He co-sponsored **Gerald P. Nye**'s investigations into the arms industry in 1934–35, convinced that U.S. entry into World War I had been an error, though he opposed the desire of some fellow members of the **Nye Committee** to nationalize the munitions industry. He supported the **Neutrality Acts** but wished for greater limitation of neutral rights and restriction of presidential discretion. He believed that to avoid war, the United States should sacrifice all **trade** with belligerents.

In July 1939, Vandenberg introduced legislation to nullify the 1911 trade treaty with **Japan** and urged the negotiation of a new treaty that recognized Japan's conquests in **China**. He was not happy when President **Franklin D. Roosevelt** and Secretary of State **Cordell Hull** used the proposal as a means to give notice of the termination of the treaty with the intention of pressuring the Japanese to relinquish those conquests. Vandenberg was the leading Republican isolationist after the death of **William E. Borah** in 1940. Unlike Senator **Robert A. Taft**, he opposed the extension of **cash-and-carry** in the 1939 revision of the Neutrality Act.

After the attack on **Pearl Harbor**, his position changed and he supported an active role for the United States in world affairs. He said that Pearl Harbor "ended isolationism for any realist." Vandenberg sought a bipartisan foreign policy, based on regular consultation between the president, the State Department, and senators. He played a major role in finding a suitable wording for the **Connally Resolution** that made a commitment to U.S. participation in a world organization while not conceding any Senate prerogatives. In a speech on 10 January 1945, he announced his conversion from isolationism to **internationalism** and endorsed U.S. involvement in the new **United Nations** organization, and he was a delegate to the 1945 **San Francisco Conference**. Vandenberg is more accurately described as a nationalist for whom **World War II** made clear that the United States needed to be active in world affairs, rather than an internationalist in the **Woodrow Wilson** mold.

Vandenberg chaired the Senate Committee on Foreign Relations in 1947–49. In proposing the Vandenberg Resolution in June 1948, he made a significant contribution to the process by which U.S. involvement in a peacetime alliance, the North Atlantic Treaty Organization, became acceptable to congressional opinion. Vandenberg's leadership produced a bipartisan consensus behind the emerging U.S. policy of containment of the **Union of Soviet Socialist Republics** in the early Cold War.

VENONA PROJECT. A **signals intelligence** operation begun by the U.S. Army in 1943, during **World War II**, the Venona project sought to decipher intercepted cable messages sent to Moscow by diplomatic, trade, and espionage agencies of the **Union of Soviet**

Socialist Republics (USSR) in the United States. The army began to collect the encoded cables in 1939, at the time of the pact Soviet dictator **Josef Stalin** made with German dictator **Adolf Hitler**. In 1943, Stalin was the ally of the United States, but there were rumors he was considering a separate peace with **Germany**. It was decided to try to decipher the cables, which were assumed to be solely diplomatic in content. The army Signals Security Agency (SSA) began the operation, code-named Venona, on 1 February 1943, based at Arlington Hall, Virginia.

Unlike Operation **Magic**, no technological breakthrough aided the code breakers. The USSR used double encoding and a one-time pad system, and the messages were extremely difficult to decode. By the end of World War II, there was little progress on the content, but an important discovery had been made. Nearly half of the messages concerned not diplomacy and **trade** but the Soviet **intelligence** agencies: the NKGB (secret police and foreign intelligence) and the GRU (military intelligence). Mathematical patterns and repetitions showed the range of sources of communications. Aided by information from former Soviet agent Elizabeth Bentley, defector Igor Gouzenko, and flaws in Soviet enciphering practices, the first message was decrypted in 1946. From then until Venona was closed in 1980, nearly 3,000 cables, originating from 1939 to 1948, had been at least partially decrypted.

The **Federal Bureau of Investigation** was involved in the project from 1948, and the information from Venona was important in revealing the vast extent of Soviet espionage activities in the United States. The Soviets had agents in the State Department, Treasury, Justice Department, the armed forces, **Office of Strategic Services**, and the **Manhattan Project**, as well as in many private industrial and research concerns. There continues to be disagreement over the identities of some of the agents, since they were all referred to by cover names. Venona revealed the role of the **Communist Party of the United States** in the recruitment and management of agents during the 1930s, though much of this was done by the NKGB from 1941. The USSR had an agent inside Venona itself, but that by no means undermined the importance and effectiveness of the operation, which was instrumental (though its role was kept secret) in the proceedings against **Alger Hiss** and **Harry Dexter White**, and later against the Rosenbergs, Klaus Fuchs, and the Cambridge ring of Soviet agents from **Great Britain**. A total of 349 U.S. citizens and individuals resident in the United States were revealed to be agents. Venona also gave vital insight into the USSR's espionage practices and doctrines.

VERACRUZ. The Mexican port of Veracruz was occupied by U.S. troops following an incident in Tampico, **Mexico**, during which several U.S. sailors were arrested by forces loyal to Mexican leader **Victoriano Huerta**. The Mexican soldiers were defending Tampico against the advancing rebel forces of **Venustiano Carranza** and mistook sailors from the USS *Dolphin* on 9 April 1914 as aggressors. The sailors were arrested and then released. Admiral Henry Mayo, commander of the U.S. Atlantic Fleet, demanded and received an apology from the Tampico authorities, but not from the Huerta government. A further demand that the U.S. flag be raised and a 21 gun salute fired in its honor was refused. President **Woodrow Wilson** requested permission from Congress for military action but ordered seizure of Veracruz before permission could be given, after receiving (erroneous) **intelligence** that an arms shipment from **Germany** was about to arrive at the port to assist Huerta.

Naval bombardment of the port began on 21 April 1914, with U.S. marines landing shortly afterward. U.S. control of the port lasted until late November 1914, by which time the Huerta regime had been overthrown by Carranza's armies. Although the Carranza regime was recognized by the Wilson administration, the occupation of Veracruz further soured U.S.–Mexican relations, which were already tense after the alleged collusion of a former U.S. ambassador in the overthrow of President **Francisco Madero**.

VERSAILLES, TREATY OF (1919). At the end of the **Paris Peace Conference** on 28 June 1919, the Treaty of Versailles was signed by the United States and its **World War I** allies and the defeated **Germany**. The treaty consisted of 440 articles covering major territorial issues as well as the technical aspects of **reparations**, the handling of prisoners of war and war graves, and matters related to economic and labor policy. Germany forfeited its overseas possessions and nearly 14 percent of its own territory, including Alsace-Lorraine and major territories in the east. The latter became part of the new republic of Poland. To prevent future German aggression, strict limits were placed on the size of the German army and navy, and a war guilt clause laid the blame for the war squarely with Germany. The acceptance of sole guilt for the war was the justification for the imposition of reparations to pay the victors for the cost of the war.

Although they represented a new democratic political regime that had replaced the imperial one that had taken Germany to war, the German representatives were forced to sign this agreement, which became later known in Germany as a *diktat*, or dictated peace. There was considerable resentment in Germany, shared by some in the United States, that the Versailles Treaty and the other treaties made at Paris departed in significant ways from the **Fourteen Points** enunciated by President Woodrow Wilson on the basis of which Germany had surrendered.

For the United States, the most controversial aspect of the treaty was the creation of a **League of Nations** to promote international cooperation, peace, and security. President Woodrow Wilson endorsed the idea but critics feared the United States would lose its ability to act independently in its own interests. Wilson was constitutionally obliged to submit the treaty to the U.S. Senate for ratification and was initially confident that public opinion would ensure its passage. However, a number of factors combined to block passage. The president appeared unwilling to compromise over any aspect of the treaty, contending that it would be dishonorable for him to do so since he had agreed to the original draft. In private, he hinted at the possibility that very limited changes might be acceptable, causing confusion among treaty supporters.

Wilson suffered paralyzing strokes in September and October 1919, while campaigning for the treaty. These attacks sharply curtailed his ability to participate in debates and negotiations with critics but strengthened his determination not to show weakness by compromise. Wilson's contempt for Senate Republicans was also a key factor in the debate's outcome. The aggressive partisan tone of the Democrats' 1918 midterm election campaign and the president's refusal to invite senior Republicans to join the U.S. delegation in Paris sharply reduced the chances of a bipartisan consensus.

The partisan hostility emanating from the White House was more than matched by Senator **Henry Cabot Lodge**, chair of the **Senate Committee on Foreign Relations**, who disliked and distrusted Wilson. The League debate quickly deteriorated into a battle of personalities. Despite this, ideological intransigence was a key factor. Senate **isolationists** were opposed on principle to membership, and it is unlikely that any form of treaty language would have assuaged their concerns. Wilson's contention that their conditions for acceptance would have rendered U.S. participation pointless and were based on misinterpretations of the treaty's language failed to sway the Senate's **Irreconcilables**. A working consensus could not be found in either political party. The cross-party split between Democratic and Republican **internationalists** and isolationists was complicated by additional splits between mild and strong reservationists. As a result, conventional partisanship failed to perform its usual function of balancing idealism with practicality and identifying areas of potential compromise.

On 19 November 1919, the Senate rejected the treaty version with the **Lodge reservations** by a 39–55 vote. Later that day, the treaty version with no reservations was rejected 38–53. The Senate reconsidered the treaty at the start of 1920, and the Committee on Foreign Relations recommended the Lodge reservations. But Wilson continued his opposition to reservations, though **Great Britain** and **France** indicated they were prepared to accept them. On 19 March, the Senate voted on the treaty version with the reservations: 49 voted in favor, 35 against. As it did not have the necessary two-thirds majority, the treaty was not ratified. Instead, the United States signed separate peace treaties with the former **Central Powers** and never joined the League of Nations.

Some historians claim the Versailles Treaty terms were too harsh, causing resentment and economic hardship in Germany which resulted in the rise of the Nazi regime in the 1930s. Others argue that the "stab in the back" delivered to the German army by the government's acceptance of armistice in November 1918 was the key factor in the later reappearance of German militarism. It has also been argued that the terms of the treaty were too lenient, in that they left Germany with the core of its industrial strength while its former rivals in Europe had all been greatly weakened by war. *See also* BERLIN, TREATY OF; ROUND ROBIN.

VIERECK, GEORGE SYLVESTER (1884–1962). Poet and propagandist George Viereck immigrated to the United States from **Germany** in 1896. He published his first collection of poems in 1907. He became strongly pro-German before **World War I**. In 1923, he interviewed **Adolf Hitler**. Viereck became an apologist for the Nazi regime and by 1939 was conducting propaganda in the United States on behalf of the German Foreign Ministry. His object was to encourage anti-British and anti-French sentiment, to divert attention from German actions in Europe. He thus tried to focus public attention on the **war debts** issue, creating false organizations to disseminate propaganda, such as the **Islands for War Debts Committee** and the Make Europe Pay War Debts Committee. These organizations were able to distribute propaganda under the congressional franking privilege, as a result of the contacts Viereck courted among **isolationist** members of the U.S. Congress. In 1941, he was indicted under the Foreign Agents Registration Act and served a five-year prison sentence from 1942 to 1947. *See also* REYNOLDS, ROBERT RICE.

VILLA, FRANCISCO "PANCHO" (1878–1923). Mexican revolutionary Pancho Villa (born Doroteo Arango Arámbula) supported the rebellion of Francisco Madero against the dictator Porfirio Diaz in **Mexico**'s revolution of 1910–11, and he aided **Venustiano Carranza** and **Alvaro Obregon** in the overthrow of **Victoriano Huerta** in 1913–14. He subsequently quarreled with Carranza and joined forces with Emiliano Zapata to temporarily occupy Mexico City in 1914–15 but was driven northward after several defeats. The deaths of American citizens at the hands of Mexican bandits in Chihuahua in January 1916 and Columbus, New Mexico, in March 1916 were blamed on Villa, and President **Woodrow Wilson** sent a detachment of troops, commanded by General **John J. Pershing**, across the border to capture or kill him. The mission failed, and Villa continued guerrilla operations against the Carranza government until the latter's overthrow in May 1920. Three years after reaching a peace agreement with Mexico's interim government, Villa was ambushed in his car in Parral, Chihuahua, and murdered.

VILLARD, FANNY GARRISON (1844–1928). Pacifist and social reformer Fanny Garrison Villard was the daughter of abolitionist William Lloyd Garrison. She was an active supporter of women's rights and joined the American Women's Suffrage Association in 1906. She was a founder, along with her son **Oswald Garrison Villard**, of the National Association for the Advancement of Colored People. With **Lillian Wald**, she organized a parade of 1,200 women down Fifth Avenue in New York City on 29 August 1914 to protest **World War I**. Villard helped found the **Women's Peace Party** and the **Women's International League for Peace and Freedom**. Her husband, Henry Villard, owned the liberal *Nation* magazine.

VILLARD, OSWALD GARRISON (1872–1949). Graduated from Harvard in 1893, Oswald Garrison Villard, grandson of abolitionist William Lloyd Garrison, worked as a journalist for the *New York Evening Post* and the *Nation* magazine, which were owned by his father, Henry Villard. He strongly supported free **trade** and opposed imperialism and involvement in the affairs of **Latin America**. In 1910, he played a leading role with his mother **Fanny Garrison Villard** in establishing the National Association for the Advancement of Colored People, and he served as its treasurer.

In the 1930s, Villard supported the New Deal and government intervention in the economy but came to oppose what he saw as President **Franklin D. Roosevelt**'s drift toward interventionism. Having inherited the *Nation* from his father, he sold it because of its stance on intervention. He was an early member of the **America First Committee**. Villard also criticized the growth of bureaucracy under the New Deal as potentially fascistic. During **World War II**, he condemned the strategic bombing conducted by the Allies in the **Combined Bomber Offensive**. In common with some other former liberal **progressives**, after the war he aligned himself with **Robert Taft** and other conservatives against Cold War interventionism.

VINSON, CARL (1883–1981). Lawyer Carl Vinson became a member of the U.S. House of Representatives (D-Ga.) in 1914. He was to be the first person to serve for over 50 years in Congress. He was interested in naval matters and by the 1920s was senior Democrat on the House Naval Affairs Committee. He became its chair in 1931.

In 1934, he sponsored the Vinson–Trammell Act with Senator Park Trammell (D-Fla.). The act approved the replacement of aging warships by finding a way around some of the terms agreed to at the 1930 **London Naval Disarmament Conference**. With Vinson's advocacy, the 1938 **Naval Expansion Act** and "11 percent" Naval Expansion Act of 1940 further sought to enlarge the navy, and Vinson was a leading proponent of the 1940 **Two-Ocean Navy Act**. Vinson's endeavors were crucial in providing the new warships that gave the United States naval superiority in the Pacific after 1942. After **World War II**, Vinson served on the House Armed Services Committee, chairing it when Democrats held the majority in the House. He retired in 1965. He was great-uncle to Senator Sam Nunn of Georgia. *See also* UNITED STATES NAVY.

VOLGA FAMINE RELIEF EFFORT (1921–1922). Famine struck **Russia**'s Volga basin in 1918–21 due to disruptions in farming caused by civil war following the **Russian Revolution**, the erratic policies of the Bolshevik government, and the failure of crops. Moscow appointed a committee to oversee relief efforts, and the writer Maxim Gorky appealed to world governments for assistance. U.S. President **Warren G. Harding**'s administration responded to the humanitarian crisis, despite its continuing refusal to extend diplomatic recognition to the **Union of Soviet Socialist Republics**. **Herbert Hoover**'s American Relief Administration (ARA), which was originally established to aid recovery in Europe after **World War I**, organized the distribution of food to 10 million Soviet citizens between August 1921 and July 1923, and also helped combat a severe typhus epidemic through the distribution of medical supplies. William N. Haskell, overseeing efforts on behalf of Hoover (who was now secretary of commerce), had to overcome the suspicion of the Bolsheviks that Western governments might use the ARA as a front organization for spying and propaganda.

– W –

WADSWORTH, GEORGE (1894–1958). George Wadsworth trained as a chemical engineer and in 1914–17 taught at the American University in Beirut. He took part-time work in the U.S. consulate and in 1917 entered the Foreign Service full time. He was vice consul in Nantes (1917–19), Constantinople (1919–20), Sofia (1920), and Alexandria (1920–21). He was consul in Cairo (1922–24, 1928–31) and consul general in Bucharest (1935) and Jerusalem (1936–40). In 1941, Wadsworth took over as chargé d'affaires at the embassy in Rome after Ambassador **William Phillips** left. When Italy declared war on the United States on 11 December 1941, during **World War II**, Wadsworth organized the evacuation of the embassy staff. He was appointed diplomatic agent to Syria and Lebanon in 1942, becoming minister in 1944. After the war, he was minister and then ambassador to Iraq (1947–48), and was ambassador to Turkey (1948–52), Czechoslovakia (1952–53), and Saudi Arabia and Yemen (1954–58).

WALD, LILLIAN (1867–1940). A pioneer of the settlement house movement in New York and an organizer of district nursing services, Lillian Wald campaigned for the improvement of urban living conditions and for civil rights. She was a founding member of the National Association for the Advancement of Colored People. Wald was a committed **pacifist** and led a march of 1,200 women in New York in August 1914 against **World War I**. She was a member of the **Women's Peace Party** and after the war was a founder of the **Women's International League for Peace and Freedom**. Her association with left-wing activists led to her being investigated during the 1919 "Red Scare." See also ADDAMS, JANE; VILLARD, FANNY GARRISON.

WALLACE, HENRY AGARD (1888–1965). Henry Wallace's father was secretary of agriculture in the **Warren G. Harding** administration, and Wallace himself was a renowned plant geneticist and successful agricultural businessperson. His political inclinations were Republican but he endorsed Democratic candidate Alfred E. Smith in the 1928 presidential race. **Franklin D. Roosevelt** appointed him secretary of agriculture in 1933. Presiding over the New Deal's farm reforms, Wallace was one of the most influential secretaries of agriculture in U.S. history. He resigned from the post in September 1940 to be vice presidential running mate in Roosevelt's 1940 campaign.

Wallace was selected to counter the appeal of **Wendell Willkie**'s running mate, Charles McNary, in the farming states.

Wallace was not in Roosevelt's inner circle but was sent on missions by the president to **Latin America** in 1943 and in 1944 to the **Union of Soviet Socialist Republics** (USSR) and **China**. Wallace made a point, where he could, of addressing his hosts in their own language. He brokered an arrangement with Chinese nationalist leader **Chiang Kai-shek**, whereby Chiang agreed to the **Dixie Mission** to the Chinese communists in return for a change in the status of General **Joseph Stilwell**.

Wallace was involved in the decisions that established the **Manhattan Project** and served as chair of the Supply Priorities and Allocations Board and the Board of Economic Warfare from 1941. His work on the supply board brought him up against the more conservative secretary of commerce, **Jesse Jones**, when he pressed for better conditions for labor. His May 1942 speech on the "Century of the Common Man" during **World War II** laid out a **progressive** set of war aims going beyond the defeat of Nazism, and contrasting with the nationalistic approach in **Henry Luce**'s **American Century** concept. Because of Wallace's progressive leanings, as well as fears about Roosevelt's health, Wallace was replaced as vice presidential candidate by **Harry S. Truman** for the 1944 election.

Wallace was secretary of commerce in 1945–46 but was forced to resign after making public criticisms of Secretary of State **James F. Byrnes**'s policy toward the USSR. As editor of the *New Republic* magazine (1946–48), Wallace was critical of the Truman Doctrine. He ran for president in 1948 as an independent progressive but did very badly, with many liberals in the Cold War atmosphere seeing him as "soft" on the Soviet Union. Wallace then returned to his career in agricultural science.

WAR DEBTS. Soon after the outbreak of **World War I** in 1914, the United States began to extend credit to the European powers for the purchase of U.S. goods, such as munitions, cotton, and foodstuffs, or to stabilize their own currencies. Starting in 1915, long-term loans were made, mainly to the Allied powers. After the war, loans and credits were given to both Allied and former enemy states. Approximately $10.35 billion were borrowed from the U.S. Treasury. Cash loans during the war amounted to $7.07 billion, and $2.53 billion were advanced for reconstruction after the armistice; $740 million went toward relief supplies and liquidated war stocks. Total foreign indebtedness, including interest but excluding the debts of tsarist **Russia**, which were repudiated by the new **Union of Soviet Socialist Republics**, was $11.57 billion.

President **Woodrow Wilson**'s administration allowed a three-year period of nonpayment to allow recovery from the immediate effects of the war, but indicated that it expected full repayment after that point. In February 1922, Congress formed the World War Foreign Debt Commission under the **Debt Funding Act**, which included the secretaries of state, treasury, and commerce alongside members of the Senate and House. Its stated aim was to make arrangements to amortize the principal of the debts within 25 years, with an interest rate of not less than 4.25 percent. The commission reached agreement with 15 debtor nations in the next five years, providing for repayment over 62 years.

The major debtor nations, **Great Britain**, **France**, Belgium, and Italy, paid most reluctantly, believing the debts should have been cancelled as the U.S. contribution to the common cause. They continued to pay, in order to maintain their access to U.S. markets and further loans, and in Britain's case because it was concerned about its own status as a creditor nation. To a considerable extent, the repayments were dependant on German **reparations** payments, which themselves were sustained by U.S. loans under the **Dawes** and **Young Plans**. The United States continued to resist solving the whole problem by cancellation.

In 1931, the global economic depression resulted in widespread defaulting on repayments, and President **Herbert Hoover** introduced the year-long **Hoover Moratorium** on all intergovernmental obligations. In 1932, the **Lausanne Conference** once again linked termination of reparations with cancellation of war debts, and once again Congress refused. Six countries made small repayments in 1933, but in 1934, all debtors defaulted again, this time for good, except Hungary, which paid interest until 1939, and Finland, which repaid in full. Congress responded with the Johnson **Debt Default Act**, which forbade further loans to governments in default of these debts and was of great importance when Britain and France sought U.S. aid for rearmament in **World War II**. The policy of **Lend-Lease** and, after the war, the Marshall Plan were designed to prevent the problem of war debts again distorting international economics. *See also* MELLON, ANDREW.

WAR FINANCE CORPORATION (WFC). The War Finance Corporation was created in April 1918 as a government-run agency providing financial support in the form of loans to war industries and banks. It was also intended to help with the eventual reconversion of the United States to a peacetime economy. During its short wartime operation, it made over $70 million worth of loans. Later, until its winding-up in 1939, it assisted with financing for the transport and agricultural sectors.

WAR REFUGEE BOARD (WRB). Established in January 1944, after pressure on President **Franklin D. Roosevelt** from Secretary of the Treasury **Henry Morgenthau**, the War Refugee Board was to aid victims of persecution by the **Axis** powers during **World War II**, and it was a somewhat belated recognition of the enormity of the genocidal policies being perpetrated by the Nazis in Europe. Earlier, the State Department took the line that the way to prevent Nazi atrocities was to concentrate all efforts on winning the war. Morgenthau had to bypass the department to convince the president that the United States should be more active. The WRB has been credited with rescuing as many as 200,000 Jews by working with resistance groups, Jewish organizations, and neutral diplomats—most notably Raoul Wallenberg. The WRB's director was John H. Pehle, assistant secretary of the treasury, and the board included the secretaries of state, war, and the treasury. It was dissolved at the end of World War II.

WAR RESISTERS LEAGUE (WRL). The War Resisters League was established in 1923 as a section of the War Resisters International organization based in London. The leading figure in its foundation was Jessie Wallace Hughan, a radical suffragist. Its founders had been involved in refusing military service in **World War I**. Many had been in the Fellowship of Reconciliation (FOR) and set up the WRL as a more secular organization. It attracted former suffragists and many socialists and anarchists and had a close relationship with the Socialist Party. Its **pacifist** philosophy is nonviolent opposition to all war. Members resisted the draft in **World War II** and protested against the Vietnam War in the 1960s and the 2003 U.S.-led invasion of Iraq.

WASHINGTON CONFERENCE (1941–1942). Code-named Arcadia, the 22 December 1941–14 January 1942 meeting in Washington, D.C., was President **Franklin D. Roosevelt**'s first summit with Prime Minister **Winston Churchill** of **Great Britain** after the United States entered **World War II**. The strategy of seeking the defeat of **Germany** first before turning to the Pacific theater was confirmed. The **American–British–Dutch–Australian command** (ABDA) was established to halt **Japan**'s advances in the East Indies and was the consequence of a highly significant decision to integrate the armed forces of the Allies under joint command structures, so that troops from one nation-state would serve under a supreme commander from the other. To manage joint strategic planning, a **Combined Chiefs of Staff** (CCS) was established in Washington, D.C. On 1 January 1942, Churchill and Roosevelt, together with the ambassador of the **Union of Soviet Socialist Republics**, issued the **United Nations Declaration** as the formal statement of their alliance. Roosevelt and Churchill agreed to give increased supplies to the USSR but resist demands to recognize Soviet annexations of territory in Eastern Europe made since September 1939. *See also* ABC-1 PLAN; GRAND ALLIANCE; PLACENTIA BAY MEETING.

WASHINGTON CONFERENCE (1942). When Prime Minister **Winston S. Churchill** of **Great Britain** conferred with President **Franklin D. Roosevelt** in Washington, D.C., on 18–27 June 1942, during **World War II**, their main topics were strategic. Differences had emerged between British and U.S. concepts of how to wage the war against **Germany**. At the meeting, Churchill persuaded Roosevelt that an invasion of **France** would not be possible in 1942, and that a heavy raid proposed by U.S. planners, Operation Sledgehammer, would achieve nothing. In order to engage U.S. forces in the European theater of operations as soon as possible, Roosevelt agreed to undertake landings in French North Africa, Operation **Torch**, against the preference of his own **Joint Chiefs of Staff**.

Churchill attempted to persuade Roosevelt that the main direction of advance for Allied forces should be in the Mediterranean. He claimed that Italy was the weakest Axis power, making the region the "soft underbelly" of Europe. Roosevelt's agreement to Torch did not imply, however, an acceptance of this strategy or abandonment of the U.S. desire to launch a **second front** in France in 1943. Strategic differences continued therefore and were the major bone of contention at the 1943 **Casablanca Conference**.

During the Washington meeting, when the British lost the port of Tobruk in North Africa to **Axis** forces, Roosevelt offered a consignment of 300 tanks to be rushed to the western desert front. Churchill traveled to Moscow in August 1942 to explain the Torch decision to Premier **Josef Stalin** of the **Union of Soviet Socialist Republics**. *See also* MARSHALL, GEORGE CATLETT.

WASHINGTON CONFERENCE (1943). The **World War II** strategic conference between the United States and **Great Britain** that took place in Washington, D.C., on 11–25 May 1943 was codenamed Trident. The British persuaded the Americans that there was no longer sufficient time to transfer landing craft to launch an attack on German positions in northern **France** in the summer of 1943 because of delays in capturing Tunisia. It was agreed therefore to follow the invasion of Sicily with an attack on southern Italy. Army Chief of Staff General **George C. Marshall** had misgivings about this operation, believing it an unnecessary diversion from the main task of directly attacking **Germany** by the shortest route. *See also* HUSKY, OPERATION; SECOND FRONT; TORCH, OPERATION.

WATSON, EDWIN M. (1883–1945). Edwin "Pa" Watson was a junior military aide to President **Woodrow Wilson** in 1915–17, becoming chief of the military section of Wilson's staff in 1919. From 1927 to 1931, Watson was military attaché in Brussels. When he became a member of President **Franklin D. Roosevelt**'s personal staff, one of his duties was helping the partially paralyzed Roosevelt to stand and walk. Watson was officially military aide to the president from 1 June 1933 to his death. From 1939, he was also secretary to the president. Watson provided advice on appointments, including the decision in 1944 to drop **Henry Wallace** as vice president. Watson went to overseas conferences with Roosevelt despite his own poor health. He had a heart attack at the **Teheran Conference** and another at the 1944 **Quebec Conference**. He attended the 1945 **Yalta Conference** but died on the return journey.

WEBB–POMERENE ACT (1918). In the Webb–Pomerene Act, Congress suspended the operation of antitrust regulations over U.S. corporations in order to increase their ability to compete effectively in foreign commerce. The intention was to allow U.S. firms to collaborate in foreign commerce in the same way that many European nations not applying antitrust laws already operated. *See also* EDGE ACT.

WELLES, SUMNER (1892–1961). Sumner Welles entered the Foreign Service at **Franklin D. Roosevelt**'s suggestion in 1915. His first assignment was to Tokyo (1915–17), but he subsequently became a specialist on **Latin America**, serving in Buenos Aires (1917–19). In 1920, Welles became assistant head of the Division of Latin American Affairs in the State Department, responsible for Central America and the Caribbean. In 1920, he was sent to mediate between rival parties in **Cuba**. He became chief of the division in 1921. In March 1922, he resigned in protest against the high **tariff** policy of the Republican-controlled Congress but was persuaded by Secretary of State **Charles Evans Hughes** to serve as a special commissioner to the **Dominican Republic**, where he helped prepare for the evacuation of U.S. forces. In 1924, he went to Honduras to mediate in the revolution there. While pursuing a successful career in banking, he remained interested in Latin American affairs and wrote a significant study of the region, *Naboth's Vineyard* (1928). He was a member of the **Charles G. Dawes** financial mission to the Dominican Republic (1929).

During President Franklin Roosevelt's administration, Welles was closer to Roosevelt than Secretary of State **Cordell Hull** and was a key foreign policy advisor. He played a major role, as ambassador to Cuba in April–December 1933, in the removal of the dictatorial **Gerardo Machado** and radical Ramón Grau San Martín governments, and he assisted the rise of future dictator **Fulgencio Batista**. Welles became assistant secretary of state in December 1933, and in May 1937 became undersecretary of state. Despite his activities in Cuba, he became increasingly committed to nonintervention by the United States in Latin America and helped lay the framework for the **Good Neighbor policy**. He was a delegate to the inter-American **Buenos Aires Conference** (1936), **Lima Conference** (1938), **Havana Conference** (1940), and **Rio de Janeiro Conference** (1942).

In 1940, Roosevelt sent Welles as a personal envoy to meet European leaders to try to find grounds for ending **World War II**. Unlike Hull, Welles accompanied Roosevelt to the **Placentia Bay** meeting and assisted in drafting the **Atlantic Charter**. He had a major dispute with Hull at the Rio de Janeiro Conference over the form in which the American republics should express their solidarity with the United States. Roosevelt backed Welles. Hull pressed successfully for Welles's removal when scandals surfaced in September 1943 regarding Welles's private life. Welles devoted the rest of his life to writing. *See also* MOORE, ROBERT WALTON; WHITE, FRANCIS.

WHEELER, BURTON K. (1882–1975). Lawyer Burton K. Wheeler, a member of the U.S. Senate (D-Mont.) in 1923–47, was a **progressive** and **isolationist**. He unsuccessfully sought the presidential nomination in 1940 in opposition to President **Franklin D. Roosevelt**, promising "not to send our boys outside the United States" unless the country was attacked. Wheeler's wife aided **Robert Wood** in setting up the **America First Committee** in 1940 and was instrumental in bringing Father **Charles Coughlin** into it. Wheeler opposed **Lend-Lease** and the **Selective Training and Service Act,** saying, "the draft will slit the throat of democracy." In 1941, he joined **Gerald Nye** in attacking Hollywood for being anti-isolationist. Wheeler supported U.S. entry into **World War II** only after the attack on **Pearl Harbor**. After leaving the Senate, he again practiced law.

WHITE COMMITTEE. *See* COMMITTEE TO DEFEND AMERICA BY AIDING THE ALLIES.

WHITE, FRANCIS (1892–1961). A graduate of Yale University who studied in Grenoble, Paris, and Madrid, Francis White entered the Foreign Service in 1915. He served in Peking (Beijing) (1915–18), Teheran (1918–19), Havana (1919–20), and Buenos Aires (1920–22) before becoming chief of the Division of Latin American Affairs in the State Department in 1923, succeeding **Sumner Welles**. White was a member of the U.S.–Panama Commission in June 1924 and was then posted as counselor to the embassies in Paris (1926) and Madrid (1926–27). He was made an assistant secretary of state for **Latin America** in 1927 and was a key proponent of the softer approach followed by Presidents **Calvin Coolidge** and **Herbert Hoover**.

White was a counselor to the U.S. delegation to the 1928 **Havana Conference** of American states and to the International Conference of American States on Conciliation and Arbitration in Washington, D.C., in 1928–29. He was a delegate to the 1931 Washington conference on pan-American commerce and chaired the neutral commission on the **Chaco War** (1929–33). White wanted to be ambassador to **Cuba**, but President **Franklin D. Roosevelt** appointed Welles, and White was made minister to Czechoslovakia in 1933. At the end of the year, he left the Foreign Service to join International Telephone and Telegraph (ITT). In 1934, he became vice president of the **Foreign Bondholders' Protective Council** (FBPC) and was its president in 1938–42. He then returned to ITT. White later served as ambassador to **Mexico** (1953–57) and Sweden (1957–58).

WHITE, HARRY DEXTER (1892–1948). Harry White served in **France** in **World War I** and earned a Ph.D. at Harvard University at the age of 38. In 1934, he was invited to join the Treasury Department and by 1941 was assistant to Secretary of the Treasury **Henry Morgenthau**, responsible for international issues and liaison with the State Department. White was a Keynesian economist and an **internationalist**, believing strong multilateral institutions could keep the peace and avoid economic depression. His views were **progressive** and close to those of **Henry Wallace**. During **World War II**, he was a strong believer in the **Grand Alliance**, and Soviet sources suggest that he passed classified information to the **Union of Soviet Socialist Republics** (USSR).

White is generally credited with authorship of the **Morgenthau Plan** that outlined a harsh future treatment of **Germany**. White was also a leading figure at the 1944 **Bretton Woods Conference**, along with British economist John Maynard Keynes, and was one of the principal architects of the postwar economic order. White became

U.S. director of the **International Monetary Fund** in February 1946 and left the post in June 1947. As a result of information supplied by Soviet agent Elizabeth Bentley, he was already suspected of supplying information to Soviet espionage agents. On 13 August 1948, White testified before the House Committee on Un-American Activities. He denied that he was a Soviet agent. He died of a heart attack three days later. In 1950, evidence gathered in the **Venona project** identified White as a Soviet source code-named Jurist. *See also* HOUSE COMMITTEE INVESTIGATING UN-AMERICAN ACTIVITIES.

WHITE, HENRY (1850–1927). Henry White was ambassador to Italy (1905–9). During **World War I**, he supported the neutrality policies of President **Woodrow Wilson** but backed the decision to go to war in 1917. White served as one of the U.S. government's peace commissioners in Paris (1918–19), helping to draft peace treaties with **Germany**, Austria-Hungary, and Bulgaria. He was unable to use his considerable influence to rally support for the **Treaty of Versailles**. He retired shortly after its rejection by the Senate in March 1920.

WHITE, WILLIAM ALLEN (1868–1944). Journalist and publisher William Allen White was an observer at the 1919 **Paris Peace Conference**. White was from the **internationalist** wing of the Republican Party and in 1939 helped found the **Nonpartisan Committee for Peace through Revision of the Neutrality Law**, which lobbied for changes in the **Neutrality Acts** to allow the U.S. president greater discretion to aid victims of aggression. After a remark to him by President **Franklin D. Roosevelt** during **World War II** that the public needed some education on the issues raised by the war in Europe, White and other members of the committee formed the **Committee to Defend America by Aiding the Allies** (CDAAA) in May 1940. White became chair, and it was often known as the White Committee, though he was not the most active member and at times was at odds with the other leaders. He was given prominence as a Republican so that the organization did not seem a mouthpiece for the administration. The committee lobbied in favor of aid short of war, following Roosevelt's line that aid to the powers fighting Nazi **Germany** was the best way of keeping the United States out of war.

After September 1940, it was arguing directly against the **America First Committee**. White resigned as chair in January 1941, believing the group was moving too far toward advocacy of direct intervention in the war.

WILLKIE, WENDELL L. (1892–1944). After fighting in **World War I**, Wendell Willkie practiced law in Indiana and Ohio before relocating to New York in 1929. He became legal counsel to the country's largest utility company, the Commonwealth and Southern Corporation. In 1933, he became its president. Initially a Democrat, Willkie was active at the 1932 convention as a supporter of **Newton Baker**'s candidacy. When **Franklin D. Roosevelt** received the nomination, Willkie contributed to his campaign. He turned against the New Deal with the establishment of the Tennessee Valley Authority (TVA), which intruded into Commonwealth and Southern's area of operations. In April 1933, he had testified against the TVA to Congress, but Roosevelt subsequently got the Senate to ignore the restrictions on the TVA that resulted. Willkie switched parties and began publicly campaigning against the New Deal.

Willkie ran against Roosevelt in the 1940 presidential election, attacking the economic approach of the New Deal and focusing on excessive government intervention and lack of military preparedness. He agreed early in the campaign not to criticize the **Selective Training and Service Act**, but when Roosevelt began expanding military contracts, Willkie attacked Roosevelt for war-mongering. This forced Roosevelt to make his famous pledge in Boston not to send American boys to fight in foreign wars. Willkie saw himself as a noninterventionist and supported aid to the Allies short of the war, maintaining a distance from the wing of the Republican Party that favored **isolationism**.

After Roosevelt's reelection, Willkie worked on behalf of aid to the Allies and supported **Lend-Lease**. On 23 July 1941, he urged unlimited aid to **Great Britain**. He traveled to Britain and the Middle East as Roosevelt's representative. In September 1941, he acted successfully as defense counsel for the Hollywood film studios contesting allegations of bias toward interventionism made by Senators **Gerald P. Nye** and **Burton K. Wheeler**, demolishing Nye on the stand by showing that he had not seen most of the films he was criticizing.

In 1942, Willkie served as a special envoy for Roosevelt in **China** and the **Union of Soviet Socialist Republics**, where he met Premier **Josef Stalin**. Willkie became known as a leading **internationalist** Republican, playing a significant role in reorienting U.S. public attitudes toward membership in an international organization. His book on that theme, *One World* (1943), was a major best-seller. With the president's wife, Eleanor Roosevelt, he helped found **Freedom House** in 1943. He sought nomination again in 1944 but was out of tune with the Republican Party, which was moving to the right. He did not support the party's candidate, **Thomas Dewey**. Willkie died of a heart attack on 8 October 1944.

WILSON, HUGH ROBERT (1885–1946). Educated at Yale and in Paris, Hugh Wilson joined the Foreign Service in 1911. After postings in Portugal, Guatemala, **Argentina**, **Germany**, Austria, and **France**, he was counselor to the Berlin embassy (1920–21) and Tokyo embassy (1921–23). He was chief of the State Department Division of Current Information and chief of the executive committee of the Foreign Service personnel board (1924–27). Wilson then served as minister to Switzerland (1927–37). He was a delegate to the preparatory commission for the 1927 Geneva Disarmament Conference and an advisor to the U.S. delegation to the 1930 **London Naval Disarmament Conference**. He was a delegate to the 1932 **Geneva Disarmament Conference**.

In 1937 Wilson was promoted to assistant secretary of state. He then served as ambassador to Germany (1938–39). He was recalled to the United States in protest against the *Kristallnacht* attacks on Jews in November 1938 and was then advisor to the secretary of state until his retirement in 1941.

WILSON, THOMAS WOODROW (1856–1924). The 28th president of the United States, Woodrow Wilson was a well-known scholar and academic reformer who had been president of Princeton University (1902–10), published *Congressional Government: A Study in American Politics* (regarded as a classic of American political literature), and served as governor of New Jersey (1911–13). He governed as a **progressive** reformer for two years and won the Democratic Party nomination for the presidency in 1912. Against a divided Republican Party, he won the November 1912 election with a minority popular vote but a clear electoral college majority over **Theodore Roosevelt** and President **William H. Taft.**

Wilson's administration represented a turning-point in U.S. foreign policy. The nation was forced to reexamine old assumptions and reorder priorities that had underpinned its relations with the outside world since the early 19th century. Worldwide war and international communism made it impractical for the United States to maintain its traditional distance from foreign entanglements. Wilson accepted this change more readily than some of his contemporaries but provoked opponents by refusing to compromise over his idealistic vision of a restructured world order based on international cooperation. He disliked Theodore Roosevelt's aggressive brand of nationalism, preferring to stress the nation's role as a "moral force," but shared Roosevelt's preference for conducting his own foreign policy rather than relying on the State Department or cooperating with Congress.

In **Latin America** and the Caribbean, Wilson argued, the United States should promote the principles of liberty and self-determination, which Americans regarded as the defining virtue of their own society, while protecting U.S. lives, property, and business interests wherever possible. The administration pledged peaceful cooperation to compensate for years of exploitation or aggressive intervention by the United States. Shortly after Wilson's inauguration, Congress repealed the 1912 Panama Canal Act, which had allowed American ships to avoid paying tolls for passage. The president also backed the **Thomson–Urrutia Treaty**, an agreement to compensate Colombia for America's role in the 1903 Panama Revolution. But Wilson refused to recognize the military dictatorship of **Victoriano Huerta** in **Mexico**, which came to power in 1913, and he sent arms to anti-Huerta forces. He also sent U.S. marines into combat at the port of **Veracruz** (1914) in response to a perceived attack on American naval personnel. In 1916, he dispatched General **John J. Pershing** across the U.S.–Mexican border to capture rebel leader **Francisco "Pancho" Villa**, despite protests from the Mexican government. American troops were also sent to **Nicaragua** (1914), Haiti (1915), and the **Dominican Republic** (1916). Wilson's stated aims were usually couched in altruistic terms: self-defense, the restoration of stability, or the protection of democratic rights. His use of military force, however, provoked accusations of hypocrisy from liberal and conservative critics.

On 19 August 1914, two weeks after the outbreak of **World War I** in Europe, Wilson proclaimed U.S. neutrality, believing this would enable the United States to offer "impartial mediation and speak the counsels of peace and accommodation, not as a partisan, but as a friend." However, the administration was split between advocates of strict neutrality and those quietly sympathetic to the Allied powers or **Central Powers**. In January 1915 and again in December 1915–February 1916, Wilson's personal envoy to **Great Britain**, **Edward M. House**, appeared to misrepresent the president's intentions to British diplomats, hinting that the United States might reconsider its neutral status and support the Allies if peace talks failed. Secretary of State **William Jennings Bryan** advocated strict neutrality but suspected others, including the president, of pro-British sympathies. Although Wilson had little sympathy for the Central Powers, he resented the Allied blockade of **trade** with **Germany** which, he argued, illegally obstructed American commerce. When the British released a "blacklist" of American firms trading with Germany (19 July 1916), he briefly considered banning loans and exports to Britain. He also balanced his public endorsement of the aims and activities of the neutralist **League to Enforce Peace** with a call for military **preparedness** to reduce the vulnerability of the **U.S. Navy** to sudden, unprovoked attack.

In February 1915, Germany announced that any merchant vessel, enemy or neutral, would be considered a legitimate target if it strayed within a German-defined military exclusion zone. After the sinking of the passenger liner *Lusitania* (7 May 1915), Wilson's administration found it increasingly difficult to restrain domestic anti-German sentiment. Wilson sent a strongly worded warning in response to the *Lusitania* sinking, outraging former President **Theodore Roosevelt**, who denounced the president's claim that the United States was "too proud to fight" as weak. Secretary Bryan, however, considered the note provocative and resigned in protest. Another presidential ultimatum followed the sinking of the French steamer *Sussex* (24 March 1916), with further loss of American lives. Temporarily, Germany agreed to observe conventional rules of engagement.

Wilson narrowly won reelection in November 1916, defeating Republican candidate **Charles Evans Hughes**. The Democratic slogan "He kept us out of war" attracted voters frightened by Roosevelt's saber-rattling and unconvinced by Hughes's efforts to straddle the Republican Party's interventionist and **isolationist** wings. In February 1917, Germany resumed unrestricted submarine warfare, prompting Wilson to sever diplomatic relations. In his second inaugural address (5 March 1917), he declared, "We are no longer provincials. . . . Our own fortunes as a nation are involved whether we would have it so or not." Earlier, the administration had received information from British **intelligence** of the existence of the **Zimmermann telegram,** linking Germany to a proposed conspiracy with Mexico against the United States. This revelation, combined with the renewed threat to U.S. shipping, made war inevitable. Wilson appeared before a joint session of Congress (2 April 1917) to request a formal **declaration of war** in order to "make the world safe for democracy." The United States entered the conflict on 6 April 1917.

Between April 1917 and November 1918, normal partisan politics were suspended. With congressional acquiescence, Wilson centralized economic planning and political authority in Washington, D.C., making the executive branch and the federal government more powerful than at any time since the Civil War. Coordination of wartime production was achieved through new bodies such as the War Industries Board and the **War Finance Corporation**, with government propaganda efforts handled by a **Committee on Public Information**.

In January 1918, Wilson addressed Congress and outlined the **Fourteen Points** program as the rationale for U.S. involvement in the war and guiding principles for a postwar settlement. His speech caught the imagination of liberals and progressives at home and of democratic idealists abroad, but conservatives and isolationists were disturbed at the extent to which the nation would be expected to shoulder the economic, military, and political responsibilities of postwar world leadership. In December 1918, Wilson traveled to Europe to attend the **Paris Peace Conference** (the first president to leave the American continent while in office). But Republicans had gained control of both houses of Congress in the November 1918 elections, and Senate Republican leaders now possessed the authority to amend or block ratification of any treaty arising from the Paris negotiations. Wilson made this more likely by failing to invite any leading congressional Republicans to join the U.S. delegation to Paris.

Wilson compounded the error by insisting that the **Treaty of Versailles**, which included a firm commitment to U.S. membership in the **League of Nations**, should be passed unamended. His intransigence cut the political ground from under moderate supporters, who favored compromise, and united isolationists in both parties. Senate Majority Leader **Henry Cabot Lodge** (also chair of the **Senate Committee on Foreign Relations**) proposed the **Lodge reservations** to the treaty, which he claimed were vital to protect U.S. sovereignty and freedom to act independently in its own interests. Wilson embarked on a speaking tour across the country, attacking the Republican Congress and praising the League. "Dare we reject it," he asked, "and break the heart of the world?"

Wilson suffered a stroke in Pueblo, Colorado, on 25 September 1919, and was rushed back to the White House. A second, more serious, stroke occurred on 2 October 1919. Wilson was to remain a semi-invalid for the rest of his life. In November 1919 and March 1920, the treaty failed to achieve a two-thirds majority in the Senate, ensuring its fate would lie in the hands of the winner of the 1920 presidential election. Although he appeared to have failed in his ambition to remold world politics, Wilson's idealism remained an inspirational legacy for **internationalists**, particularly Democratic liberals. It was resurrected in the 1940s when, in the aftermath of **World War II**, the United States joined the **United Nations**.

WINANT, JOHN GILBERT (1889–1947). Gil Winant worked as a teacher in Concord, New Hampshire, after graduating from Princeton in 1913. He served in **France** in **World War I**. He was elected in 1916 to the New Hampshire General Court as a Republican, and to the state senate in 1920. In 1924, he was elected governor of New Hampshire. Winant was the first person to complete more than one term as governor of New Hampshire (1925–27 and 1931–35). As a **progressive** Republican, Winant was sympathetic to labor and social welfare issues. When the Great Depression hit, he supported the measures introduced by **Franklin D. Roosevelt** as governor of New York and then president.

In 1934, Roosevelt appointed him to be a U.S. delegate to the **International Labour Organization** (ILO) at Geneva, in which the United States was participating for the first time since it was founded in 1919. Winant was talked of as a possible presidential candidate for 1936, but he was interested in the cause of international peace and economic justice, which he believed the ILO represented. He was already involved in international labor matters through his membership in the American Association for Labor Legislation (AALL). The AALL was an advocate for social insurance, and in 1935, Roosevelt asked Winant to chair the new Social Security Board, where he was responsible for initiating the new social security welfare programs. He resigned in September 1936 to speak out against the attacks against Social Security by his own party's presidential candidate, Alfred Landon. Roosevelt appointed him again after the election, and he served until 19 February 1937. He returned to the delegation at the ILO and in January 1939 was elected director.

Roosevelt appointed Winant ambassador to **Great Britain** in 1941, during **World War II**, hoping he would forge connections with ordinary British people in a way that his predecessor, **Joseph P. Kennedy**, had not, and that he would also get on good terms with the Labour Party members of Prime Minister **Winston Churchill**'s coalition government. As with other ambassadors, Winant was sometimes eclipsed by Roosevelt's preference for special envoys, notably **Averell Harriman** and **Harry Hopkins**, but he served effectively as ambassador until he resigned in March 1946. Winant did not attend the **Placentia Bay Conference** in August 1941, but his input was influential in shaping a clause of the **Atlantic Charter** regarding the improvement of labor standards and social security. He became very popular with ordinary Britons and was able to persuade striking British coal miners to return to work.

In 1947, Winant was the second American, after General **Dwight D. Eisenhower**, to receive the British Order of Merit for his services to U.S.–British relations during World War II. President **Harry S. Truman** appointed him ambassador to the United Nations Educational, Scientific, and Cultural Organization (UNESCO) in 1946, but

Winant retired shortly thereafter to write his memoirs. With his political career ruined after the attack he had made on his own party in 1936, and the death of his friend Roosevelt in 1945, Winant became subject to depression. He committed suicide on 3 November 1947.

WISE, STEPHEN (1874–1949). Born in Hungary, Stephen Wise became a rabbi and was a highly influential leader of Reform Judaism in the United States. He was an accomplished preacher, advocated social reforms, and fought political corruption in New York. Although he had opposed **Franklin D. Roosevelt**'s election for governor of New York, Wise changed his attitude and became a strong supporter of President Roosevelt's New Deal. Wise was an early convert to Zionism. A leading Jewish spokesperson on foreign affairs and a peace campaigner, he has been criticized for not pushing Roosevelt harder to respond to the Holocaust during **World War II**. *See also* EVIAN CONFERENCE; WAR REFUGEE BOARD.

WOMEN'S INTERNATIONAL LEAGUE FOR PEACE AND FREEDOM (WILPF). The WILPF is the oldest women's peace organization in the world. Its headquarters are in Geneva, Switzerland, and it has sections in 37 countries. It originated in 1915 in the activities of several groups. In the United States, the **Women's Peace Party** (WPP), was founded in Washington, D.C., in January 1915 at a meeting called by social reformer **Jane Addams** and suffragist Carrie Chapman Catt, which was attended by 3,000 women. It called for female suffrage and mediation of all conflicts by neutral states. The WPP sent representatives to the International Women's Congress for Peace and Freedom at The Hague, Netherlands, in April 1915. The Netherlands was neutral in **World War I**. The congress established the International Committee of Women for Permanent Peace (ICWPP). Addams was president, and the WPP became the U.S. branch of the ICWPP. After the 1919 **Paris Peace Conference**, the ICWPP condemned the **Treaty of Versailles** as an act of revenge that would lead to more war.

The organization became permanent as the Women's International League for Peace and Freedom, with its headquarters in Geneva, near the **League of Nations**. During the **Geneva Disarmament Conference** of 1932, the WILPF organized the Transcontinental Peace

Caravan and collected several hundred thousand signatures to send to Geneva. **Dorothy Detzer** had threatened U.S. President **Herbert Hoover** with the loss of a million female votes if he did not include Mary Woolley on the U.S. delegation to the conference. He did so. Jane Addams won a Nobel Prize for Peace for her peace efforts in the WILPF in 1931. *See also* BALCH, EMILY GREENE; PACIFISM.

WOMEN'S PEACE PARTY (WPP). On 10 January 1915, a group of women **pacifists** met in Washington, D.C., looking for a way to end **World War I**. The meeting was organized by social reformer **Jane Addams**, and 3,000 women attended. The Women's Peace Party was formed, with Addams as chair, and including **Lillian Wald**, **Jeanette Rankin**, **Emily Greene Balch**, Belle La Follette, Carrie Chapman Catt, **Fanny Garrison Villard**, and Florence Kelley. The WPP campaigned for peace, **disarmament**, and nationalized control of arms manufacturers. Members Addams, Balch, Mary Heaton Vorse, Alice Hamilton, Grace Abbott, Julia Lathrop, Leonora O'Reilly, and Sophonisba Breckinridge attended the meeting in The Hague in April 1915 where the forerunner to the **Women's International League for Peace and Freedom** (WILPF) was set up. By 1917, the WPP had 40,000 members and was headquartered in Chicago. Association with **Henry Ford**'s failed peace attempt had not helped the party's standing, and it suffered fragmentation after the United States entered the war. Rankin, the first female representative in Congress, had voted against the war, but many were caught up in the wave of patriotism, and some leaders, such as Catt, feared that opposition to the war would lose support in the quest for suffrage. Those who continued to protest U.S. involvement in the war were subject to prosecution under the 1917 **Espionage Act**. In 1919, the WPP became the U.S. section of the WILPF.

WOOD, LEONARD C. (1860–1927). General Leonard Wood was commander of the First Volunteer Cavalry Brigade ("Rough Riders") in **Cuba** during the Spanish–American War (1898), military governor of Cuba (1898–1902), and army chief of staff (1910–14). He was replaced in the latter post by General **John J. Pershing**. Wood was organizer of the **preparedness** campaign that preceded U.S. entry into **World War I**. Wood was seen by many as the natural heir of former President **Theodore Roosevelt**, who had been his second in command in the Spanish–American War. After Roosevelt's death in 1919, Wood became a leading contender for the 1920 Republican presidential nomination. The deadlock between his supporters and those of Illinois Governor Frank Lowden at the Republican convention in Chicago led to the emergence of Ohio Senator **Warren G. Harding** as a compromise candidate. After his election, Harding made Wood governor general of the **Philippines**. He died in August 1927, shortly after returning to the United States.

WOOD, ROBERT (1879–1969). A West Point graduate, Robert Wood served in the **Philippines** and the Panama Canal Zone before leaving the U.S. Army to go into business. He served as a colonel in **France** under General **Douglas MacArthur** during **World War I** and was recalled to Washington, D.C., to be acting quartermaster general, with the rank of brigadier general. After the war, Wood joined the Montgomery, Ward company and was vice president of Sears, Roebuck (1928–39) and then chair (1939–54). Although a conservative Republican, he initially supported President **Franklin D. Roosevelt**'s New Deal and cooperated with the National Recovery Agency, but he came to oppose the New Deal as it became more critical of big business. Wood also became a strong **isolationist**. Wood helped found the **America First Committee**. He was the committee's first president and agitated against U.S. involvement in **World War II**. Once the country entered the war, he combined his work at Sears with acting as a civilian advisor to the Army Ordnance Corps and Army Air Force, making two trips around the world to visit the fronts.

WORLD BANK. The International Bank for Reconstruction and Development, commonly known as the World Bank, was created at the 1944 **Bretton Woods Conference** to extend credit to **United Nations** members for rebuilding and development of economies damaged in **World War II**. As with the **International Monetary Fund**, voting rights depend on a country's capital subscription. This has meant that the president of the bank is usually from the United States. Initial funding of the bank was not sufficient to deal with the vast postwar international financial crisis, and direct U.S. loans to European countries proved necessary. Since the 1960s, the World Bank has devoted itself to development aid rather than to reconstruction. *See also* MEYER, EUGENE ISAAC; UNITED NATIONS RELIEF AND REHABILITATION ADMINISTRATION (UNRRA).

WORLD COURT (PERMANENT COURT OF INTERNATIONAL JUSTICE). The Permanent Court of International Justice, popularly known as the World Court, was a supranational judicial body established at the 1919 **Paris Peace Conference** to arbitrate international disputes following **World War I**. It was first formally convened in 1922. The court was sponsored by the **League of Nations** and grew logically out of U.S. President **Woodrow Wilson**'s concept of the League. When membership in the court threatened to become as contentious as League membership, **internationalists** transferred their energies to fighting for U.S. membership in the World Court.

Presidents **Warren G. Harding** and **Calvin Coolidge** and Secretaries of State **Charles Evans Hughes** and **Frank B. Kellogg** all supported membership as a gesture of U.S. commitment to international cooperation and stability. They were opposed by **isolationists** in Congress (such as **Hiram Johnson** and **William Borah**) who regarded World Court membership as "entry by the backdoor" to the League of Nations. Harding submitted the protocols for entry to the Senate in February 1923. His sudden death delayed an inevitable confrontation over the issue. President Coolidge was less inclined to risk reelection over the issue, although the case for membership was stated in the election platforms of both major parties in 1924.

In March 1925, the Republican-controlled House of Representatives adopted a pro-membership resolution. The Senate concurred but opposing members added amendments stipulating that League membership would not follow, that financial contribution levels would be determined by Congress not the court, that changes to court powers would not be made without U.S. consent, that the United States would have an equal role in appointing court members, and that the United States would not be "bound by advisory opinions rendered without our consent." The last stipulation, known as the **Moore–Pepper Reservation**, proved unacceptable to the court's member nations.

On 11 November 1926, President Coolidge pronounced the end of the U.S. campaign for World Court membership. The United States continued to work "with" rather than "in" the court, however, for many years, and **Charles Evans Hughes** was one of a number of prominent American public officials to sit on the court as a judge. An effort to approve U.S. membership in 1935 barely missed the necessary two-thirds vote. The World Court was dissolved in 1946, when it was replaced by the International Court of Justice, an organ of the **United Nations**.

WORLD DISARMAMENT CONFERENCE (1932). *See* GENEVA DISARMAMENT CONFERENCE.

WORLD MONETARY AND ECONOMIC CONFERENCE. *See* LONDON ECONOMIC CONFERENCE.

WORLD WAR FOREIGN DEBT COMMISSION. *See* DEBT FUNDING ACT; WAR DEBTS.

WORLD WAR I (1914–1918). World War I was the first of two global wars during the 20th century. Historians disagree over the exact origins of the conflict (some suggesting its roots lay as far back as the 1870s), but a general consensus supports the view that the complex system of public treaties, private agreements, dynastic rivalries, and shifting alliances existing from the 1880s onward between the European powers created an atmosphere of uncertainty and suspicion.

Against this backdrop, rival empires sought further territorial and material gains while smaller nations and ethnic groups struggled for recognition or independence from colonial masters. On 28 June 1914, Archduke Franz Ferdinand, heir to Emperor Franz Joseph of the Austro-Hungarian empire, and his wife were shot dead in Sarajevo by a Serbian nationalist, Gavrilo Princip. The assassination ignited the long-expected conflict between the largest European powers. Franz Joseph, encouraged by Kaiser Wilhelm II of **Germany**, imposed punitive demands on Serbia, causing the Russian empire of Tsar Nicholas II to move to Serbia's defense. Austria-Hungary declared war on Serbia on 28 July 1914. Both **Russia** and Germany then mobilized their armies, and the descent into full-scale war became inevitable.

Germany declared war on Russia on 1 August and on **France** on 3 August. **Great Britain** joined the conflict on 4 August, honoring an 1830 treaty commitment to come to the defense of Belgium, which had now been invaded by Germany.

Two rival blocs emerged. The Entente or Allied powers consisted of Russia, France, and Great Britain and later also Italy, the United States, and **Japan**. The **Central powers** were Germany and Austria-Hungary, later joined by the Ottoman empire and Bulgaria. This first world war had a catastrophic impact on Europe and changed forever the global distribution of military and economic power. As many as 45 million lives were lost between 1914 and 1918. The old monarchies of the Romanovs (Russia) and Hapsburgs (Austria-Hungary) were destroyed, together with the Ottoman empire and the Hohenzollern dynasty in Germany. Great Britain retained both its monarchy and its empire but became indebted to the United States as a consequence of the war. It never regained either the superior economic or military status it had enjoyed in 1914. The rise of communism in Russia following the 1917 **Russian Revolution** generated fresh fear and suspicion both in Europe and the United States, while totalitarian dictatorships eventually emerged in Italy (1922) and Germany (1933), capitalizing on prevailing climates of social and economic dislocation. A patchwork quilt of young republics based on groups previously bound together under the old European empires increased the instability of the postwar order and fuelled aggressive nationalism and ethnic resentments.

The United States participated in the war from 6 April 1917 until the armistice on 11 November 1918. Despite the fact that participation in the war had been a strong possibility for at least two years before 1917, the administration of **Woodrow Wilson** still had to scramble to increase the size and power of the nation's military forces after the erratic progress of expansion plans during the **preparedness** period. In April 1917, Navy Secretary **Josephus Daniels** admitted there were insufficient numbers of trained upper-grade naval officers to command the expanded destroyer and submarine fleets. In addition, the United States had only 45 naval aviators; a further 800 had to be rapidly trained to combat standard. In April 1917, the United States could muster only 200,000 combat-prepared troops. By summer 1918, it could call upon nearly 4 million.

The **American Expeditionary Force**, under the command of General **John J. Pershing**, arrived in France only gradually, the first four divisions landing in mid-1917. The first battles in which U.S. troops played a major or leading role did not occur until May–June 1918, during fighting in and around Cantigny, Vaux, Bouresches, Chateau Thierry, and Belleau Wood. In these encounters, U.S. forces suffered 10,000 casualties, including over 2,000 dead. At the Second Battle of the Marne in July–August 1918, a further 12,000 were killed in the campaign to repulse the last great German offensive. In mid-September 1918, American aircraft launched the biggest air attack of the war against the St. Mihiel salient, prior to the joint U.S.–French Meuse–Argonne offensive on 26 September, in which over 1 million American soldiers fought. During the 19 months between April 1917 and November 1918, the number of U.S. fatalities in battle was 53,402, with 204,002 wounded. A further 63,000 are estimated to have died as the result of other causes such as accidents behind the front lines and influenza (the latter accounting for a further 43,000 deaths in 1919). The total financial cost of the war to the United States has been estimated at $33 billion.

Some historians suggest the most important U.S. contribution to the Allied victory came from its financial and food resources rather than its military capabilities. German submarine warfare had failed to break Allied supply lines before U.S. troops began arriving in large numbers, thus the Central Powers did not have time to fully exploit the opportunity to redeploy troops from the eastern to the western front after the withdrawal of Russia from the war. From mid-1918, the German war machine was outgunned, outmanned, and outfinanced. There was mutiny in the High Seas Fleet at Kiel, and food shortages caused by the Allied blockade caused widespread unrest. The kaiser abdicated, and the new democratic government sued for peace on the basis of Woodrow Wilson's **Fourteen Points**, which promised a nonpunitive peace. Fighting ended on the western front on 11 November 1918, though Allied troops remained engaged in combat in Russia against the Bolsheviks well into 1919. The peace treaties were drawn up in the 1919 **Paris Peace Conference**, and the new German government was faced with demands for **reparations**.

The war had a profound long-term impact on U.S. politics and society. The centralization, albeit temporary, of administrative and economic power in Washington, D.C., boosted the already growing strength and size of the executive branch of government. The development of new, sophisticated propaganda methods and new media technology, such as radio, revolutionized politics during and after the war and ensured the presidency would remain in the political limelight. Although Congress attempted to reassert itself during the 1920s, the post-Wilson presidency never returned to its restricted late 19th-century model. Neither could the United States return to the **isolationism** of the same period. Although Senate isolationists succeeded in blocking U.S. membership in the **League of Nations** and **World Court**, they could not roll back the globalizing influence of the war and its aftermath. The United States, as the world's emerging dominant economic and military power, became increasingly involved in world affairs, from **disarmament** treaties and economic conferences to famine relief, military interventions, and mediation efforts. American corporations hastened the globalization of U.S. finance, **trade**, and culture, taking advantage of the weakened commercial power of its competitors. It gradually achieved a market dominance which strengthened as the 20th century progressed.

Militarily, the United States after 1918 could not afford to revert to the relatively lax standards and minimal levels of preparedness that existed before World War I. Pershing and other leading generals continued to push for increases in military expenditure during the 1920s to ensure the nation was capable of fighting another global war, should the need arise. To **internationalists'** frustration, the American public remained ambivalent about the country's participation in world forums such as the League and World Court. Nevertheless, World War I effectively ended the long years of American psychological and military isolation from world affairs and marked the beginning of its rise to global superpower status, a process to be completed nearly two decades later by **World War II**.

See also ARABIC; BERLIN, TREATY OF; BRYAN, WILLIAM JENNINGS; BRYCE REPORT; CLEMENCEAU, GEORGES; DECLARATION OF WAR (1917); DEVIL THEORY; GORE–MCLEMORE RESOLUTION; GREY, EDWARD; HINES PAGE, WALTER; HITCHCOCK RESERVATIONS; HOUSE, EDWARD MANDELL; INQUIRY, THE; IRRECONCILABLES; KNOX–PORTER RESOLUTION; LANSING, ROBERT; LLOYD GEORGE,

DAVID; LODGE, HENRY CABOT; LODGE RESERVATIONS; ST. GERMAIN, TREATY OF; SEDITION ACT; SELECTIVE SERVICE ACT; SIBERIAN INTERVENTION; *SUSSEX*; TRADING WITH THE ENEMY ACT; TRIANON, TREATY OF; VERSAILLES, TREATY OF; WAR DEBTS; ZIMMERMANN TELEGRAM.

WORLD WAR II (1939–1945). With **Germany**'s invasion of **Poland** in September 1939, **Great Britain, France**, and the British Dominions (Canada, New Zealand, Australia, and South Africa) declared war on Germany, in fulfillment of a security guarantee made to Poland. The invasion of Poland was the latest manifestation of German dictator **Adolf Hitler**'s assault on the **Treaty of Versailles** and his drive to achieve a greater Germany. It had been directly preceded by a nonaggression pact between Germany and the **Union of Soviet Socialist Republics** (USSR) that had partitioned Eastern Europe.

Germany defeated Poland by mid-October 1939 and invaded Belgium, the Netherlands, and France in May 1940. All three were quickly defeated. Britain fought on under a new prime minister, **Winston Churchill**. The German air force was defeated in the Battle of Britain and turned to night bombing of London and other cities. Churchill sought U.S. involvement, but President **Franklin D. Roosevelt** would only go so far as the **destroyers-for-bases deal** in September 1940 and the **Lend-Lease Act** in March 1941. In April 1941, Germany invaded Yugoslavia and Greece and in June launched a massive attack against the USSR. By December 1941, German forces were at the gates of Moscow but were held there.

Japan had embarked on further expansion into French Indochina in 1940, and relations with the United States and Britain cooled in September 1940, when Japan signed the **Tripartite Pact** with Italy and Germany, thus becoming firmly one of the **Axis** powers. Further Japanese advances in Indochina led to a full U.S. embargo, and this economic pressure eventually led militarists in Japan to decide for war with the United States. In December 1941, Japan simultaneously attacked the United States at **Pearl Harbor** and in the **Philippines** and Britain in Malaya and Hong Kong. Japan went on to seize the resources of the Dutch East Indies (Indonesia) by March 1942.

In 1942–43, the tide turned. Japan suffered significant defeats at **Midway** and in the Solomons campaign, beginning on **Guadalcanal**. Germany suffered a catastrophic defeat at Stalingrad. Britain turned the tide of its Middle Eastern campaign at El Alamein. The battle in the Atlantic against German submarines was finally won in 1943. The United States and Britain were combining their forces in Europe, though in disagreement over where to open the **second front**. U.S. forces were built up in Britain under Operation **Bolero**, but the first invasion was of French North Africa in Operation **Torch** in November 1942. This was followed by Operation **Husky** in July 1943 against Sicily and the invasion of Italy in September 1943. The **Combined Bomber Offensive** had begun against Germany but was encountering fierce opposition.

In the Pacific, a two-pronged strategy was followed, across the central Pacific beginning at Tarawa in November 1943 and in the southwest in New Guinea. Japanese forces fought tenaciously, but American productive capacity and aggressive spirit were too much for them. In **China**, the front remained stalemated, despite the attempts of General **Joseph Stillwell** to get it moving.

The **Grand Alliance** of the United States, Britain, and the Soviet Union began to function properly at the **Teheran Conference** in November 1943, though largely by setting aside any awkward political issues. It was at Teheran that Operation **Overlord** was confirmed. Germany was in retreat in the USSR, having suffered defeat at the Battle of Kursk in July, but was still very strong. Behind the front lines, Germany was exploiting European labor and enacting policies of genocide against Jews and gypsies, and Slavic peoples of Eastern Europe as well.

June 1944 saw the successful U.S.–British–Canadian landings in Normandy and a massive Soviet assault in the east. By fall, the bombing offensive was taking a heavy toll on German resources, especially oil, and the German air force was seriously reduced. Despite setbacks in the **Battle of the Bulge** (December), the Allies drove on into Germany, and the Soviets approached from the east. Berlin fell to the Soviet Red Army at the end of April, and Hitler committed suicide. On 8 May, Germany surrendered. The final **Big Three** conference took place at **Potsdam** outside Berlin in July–August, though many issues were not fully agreed upon and there was to be no final peace conference. Germany was occupied and divided into four zones, and it remained divided until the end of the Cold War.

In the Pacific, Japan refused to surrender, determined to make the cost of victory so high to the Allies that they would be prepared to negotiate terms. The Allies insisted on **unconditional surrender** and embarked on heavy bombing of the Japanese mainland. The casualty rates at **Iwo Jima** and **Okinawa** indicated how tough a job an invasion of Japan was likely to be. Roosevelt's successor, President **Harry S. Truman**, did not hesitate to use the **atomic bomb** when it became available and after Japan had not replied to the demand made at Potsdam that it surrender or face destruction. Some historians believe that Truman used the bomb to pressure the USSR. After an intervention by Emperor **Hirohito**, Japan surrendered on 14 August (formally on 2 September) following the bombings of **Hiroshima** (6 August) and **Nagasaki** (9 August) and the USSR's invasion of Manchuria (8 August). Fighting continued in some parts of Asia until September. War crimes trials were to follow in Europe and in Asia under the **International Military Tribunal**.

World War II caused immense destruction in Europe and East Asia. Fatalities were in excess of 55 million. It also spelled the end of the European empires, as well as the rise of the United States and Soviet Union as rival superpowers. Failure to agree among the Big Three over the future of Germany became a catalyst for the subsequent Cold War. In the United States, the war brought unprecedented prosperity. Pearl Harbor profoundly altered U.S. attitudes to world affairs. National security now appeared to demand engagement, not **isolation**. Americans embraced the idea of the **United Nations** and many came to believe that the **internationalist** approach of **Woodrow Wilson** had been correct. Congress said as much in the 1943 **Connally Resolution**. There remained a distaste for "entangling alliances," and possession of the atomic bomb brought a mixture of confidence in American power and uncertainty at the prospects for peace in an atomic world.

See also ABC-1 PLAN; ALLIED MILITARY GOVERNMENT; AMERICA FIRST COMMITTEE; AMERICAN SHOOTING SEASON; AMERICAN VOLUNTEER GROUP; AMERICAN–

BRITISH–DUTCH–AUSTRALIAN COMMAND; *ARIZONA*, USS; ARSENAL OF DEMOCRACY; ATLANTIC CHARTER; BACKDOOR TO WAR THEORY; BRETTON WOODS CONFERENCE; BRITAIN–UNITED STATES OF AMERICA AGREEMENT; CAIRO CONFERENCES; CASABLANCA CONFERENCE; CENTURY GROUP; CHARLOTTESVILLE ADDRESS; CHENNAULT, CLAIRE LEE; CHIANG KAI-SHEK; COMBINED CHIEFS OF STAFF COMMITTEE; COMMITTEE TO DEFEND AMERICA BY AIDING THE ALLIES; DECLARATION ON LIBERATED EUROPE; DECLARATIONS OF WAR (1941); DIXIE MISSION; DRAGOON, OPERATION; DRESDEN; DUMBARTON OAKS CONFERENCE; EUROPEAN ADVISORY COMMISSION; FIGHT FOR FREEDOM COMMITTEE; FORTRESS AMERICA; FOUR FREEDOMS; FOUR POLICEMEN; *GREER*, USS; HARRIMAN, W. AVERELL; HOPKINS, HARRY LLOYD; HULL, CORDELL; HURLEY, PATRICK; HYDE PARK AGREEMENT (1941); HYDE PARK AGREEMENT (1944); JOINT CHIEFS OF STAFF COMMITTEE; *KEARNY*, USS; KENNEDY, JOSEPH P.; KNOX, WILLIAM FRANKLIN; LIBERTY BONDS; LIBERTY SHIPS; LONDON CHARTER; MACARTHUR, DOUGLAS; MAGIC, OPERATION; MANHATTAN PROJECT; MARSHALL, GEORGE CATLETT; MASTER LEND-LEASE AGREEMENTS; MOONEY, JAMES D.; MORGENTHAU PLAN; MURPHY, ROBERT DANIEL; MURROW, EDWARD R.; NATIONAL DEFENSE RESEARCH COMMITTEE; NIMITZ, CHESTER W.; OFFICE OF STRATEGIC SERVICES; OFFICE OF WAR INFORMATION; OGDENSBURG CONFERENCE; OPPENHEIMER, JULIUS ROBERT; PANAMA DECLARATION; PLACENTIA BAY MEETING; PLAN DOG; PURPLE; QUEBEC CONFERENCE (1943); QUEBEC CONFERENCE (1944); *REUBEN JAMES*, USS; SELECTIVE TRAINING AND SERVICE ACT; MIQUELON AFFAIR AND ST. PIERRE; TOJO, HIDEKI; ULTRA-MAGIC DEAL; UNITED NATIONS DECLARATION; WAR REFUGEE BOARD; WASHINGTON CONFERENCE (1941–1942); WASHINGTON CONFERENCE (1942); WASHINGTON CONFERENCE (1943); WHITE, HARRY DEXTER; WINANT, JOHN GILBERT.

– Y –

YALTA CONFERENCE (1945). U.S. President **Franklin D. Roosevelt**'s second (and final) **Big Three** conference with Premier **Josef Stalin** of the **Union of Soviet Socialist Republics** (USSR) and Prime Minister **Winston Churchill** of **Great Britain** during **World War II** took place in Yalta, in the Crimea, on 4–11 February 1945. It was preceded by U.S.–British discussions at Malta. The high point of the wartime **Grand Alliance**, the Yalta Conference has been the subject of controversy and conflicting interpretations.

Critics have argued that Roosevelt's conduct at the conference was "appeasement" and a "selling out" of Eastern Europe to Stalin. It has also been suggested that, in ailing health, he allowed himself to be duped by the cunning Stalin. But when the conference records are examined and are considered in the context of the war, these criticisms seem weakened. While Roosevelt, like his fellow-leaders, was undoubtedly exhausted, and there are reports that he was suffering lapses of memory, his conduct at the conference did not markedly differ from that at the **Teheran Conference** in 1943. He and the other two leaders believed that while they had each had to sacrifice some aims, they had all gained their principal objectives. More importantly, it seemed that the Big Three cooperation, on which they were building the structure for postwar management of the international system, had taken place satisfactorily in an atmosphere of give and take.

Regarding the contentious agreement on **Poland**, Roosevelt apparently said to his chief of staff Admiral **William Leahy** afterward that it was certainly not perfect but was the best that could be done at the time. Roosevelt's prime concern was to keep the process of cooperation moving: if that was done, then issues could be revisited subsequently. On a number of matters that were of central importance to Roosevelt, he gained what he wanted. He got a firm commitment from the Soviets that they would enter the war against **Japan** 90 days after the defeat of Germany. Roosevelt offered Stalin concessions in the Far East, in essence the reversal of Russian losses after the Russo–Japanese War of 1904–5. This was at the expense not only of Japan (which lost Southern Sakhalin, the Kurile Islands, and rights in Manchuria) but of the American ally **China** (Outer Mongolia was recognized as a Soviet sphere, and the Soviets gained rights in Port Arthur, Dairen, and over railroads in Manchuria). China was not consulted. This was a measure, perhaps, of Roosevelt's disillusionment with **Chiang Kai-shek**, but principally a result of his concern to have the Soviet Red Army engaged with the large Japanese forces in mainland Asia, thereby preventing either their deployment against the U.S. invasion of Japan, or the reestablishment of a still defiant Japanese government on the mainland, which could happen after Japan itself was invaded. Roosevelt also obtained settlement of outstanding issues regarding the structure of the **United Nations** organization, clearing the way for the founding conference at the **San Francisco Conference** in April.

The Soviets obtained a triumph when it was agreed that the veto of permanent members of the Security Council would apply to matters in which they were themselves involved. On Poland, the Soviets agreed under pressure that their puppet Polish government would be expanded by the addition of Poles who had been based in the West during the war, along with representatives of the Polish resistance. They subsequently interpreted this to mean that they would accept a token few of these Poles into the puppet government, transferred to Warsaw. They also arrested Polish resistance leaders when they arrived in Moscow, claiming they were anti-Soviet.

All of this was in the future, however, and while Churchill certainly had misgivings, it was hard to see how he or Roosevelt could have obtained a better agreement from Stalin. On Poland's frontiers, they confirmed what they had discussed at Teheran, that Poland would move westward, losing eastern provinces to the USSR, but gaining German territory in East Prussia and up to the Oder and Neisse rivers. The exact delineation of this frontier was left for later discussion. **Germany**, apart from losing this territory to Poland, lost part of East Prussia to the USSR, and Austria was a separate nation again. There was much discussion of dismemberment as a means of dealing with a potential future German menace, but agreement could not be reached on the best form it should take, and there was concern that it would only give Germans a unifying grievance in the future. The **Morgenthau Plan** to reduce Germany to an agricultural state had by now fallen out of favor. The inclination therefore at Yalta was to leave Germany a unified and modern state.

A major Soviet goal of achieving commitment to substantial **reparations** payments to the USSR from Germany was not achieved, with the Big Three agreeing the issue should be further discussed. Churchill gained his main objective with the acceptance that **France** would have a role in the occupation of Germany and should also be on the United Nations Security Council. A State Department initiative was adopted in the **Declaration on Liberated Europe**, making an explicit commitment to democratic elections in liberated areas, but it was soon broken by Stalin, dissipating the Yalta cooperative spirit in the months that followed. *See also* POTSDAM CONFERENCE; TRUMAN, HARRY S.

YOST, CHARLES WOODRUFF (1907–1981). Charles Yost graduated from Princeton and studied at the École des Hautes Études Internationales in Paris. After traveling widely in Europe, including to the **Union of Soviet Socialist Republics**, he joined the Foreign Service in 1930 on the advice of **Robert Lansing**, a former secretary of state. Yost was a consular officer in Egypt (1930–32) and **Poland** (1932–33) but left the service in 1933 to become a foreign correspondent. He returned to the State Department in 1935 as assistant chief of the Division of Arms and Munitions Control.

In 1941, during **World War II**, Yost was State Department representative on the policy committee of the Board of Economic Warfare. In 1942 he became assistant chief of special research in the Division of European Affairs, and in 1943 was assistant chief of the Division of Foreign Activity Correlation. In 1944, he was made executive secretary of the Policy Committee. He attended the 1944 **Dumbarton Oaks Conference** and worked on drafting Chapters VI and VII of the **United Nations Charter**. At the 1945 **San Francisco Conference**, he was aide to Secretary of State **Edward Stettinius**. He was secretary general of the 1945 **Potsdam Conference**.

Following the war, Yost had a distinguished career in the Foreign Service. In 1954, he was the first U.S. ambassador to Laos. He retired in 1966 to write and teach and work with the **Council on Foreign Relations**. He was U.S. representative to the **United Nations** in 1969–71. He visited **China** in an official capacity in 1973 and 1977 and lobbied in 1979 for passage of the second Strategic Arms Limitation Treaty.

YOUNG, OWEN D. (1874–1962). Lawyer and business leader Owen Young helped draw up the **Dawes Plan** (1924), which attempted to rescue the economy of **Germany** from spiraling inflation and crippling **reparations** debts. In 1929, he drafted a replacement plan, designed to further bolster German finances. Despite the failure of the **Young Plan** due to the onset of the global economic depression, he remained an admired figure and was briefly touted for the Democratic presidential nomination in 1932.

YOUNG PLAN (1929). Successor to the **Dawes Plan** of 1924, the Young Plan, proposed by **Owen D. Young**, reduced the total payments required of **Germany** in **reparations** to $29 million, payable over a period of 58 years. A 5.5 percent interest rate was set, and the payment period was to be extended into the 1980s. The plan was undermined by the global economic depression after 1929. *See also* LAUSANNE CONFERENCE.

– Z –

ZEMURRAY, SAMUEL (1877–1951). Born in Bessarabia in the Russian empire, Samuel Zemurray relocated to the United States in 1892. His steamship company diversified, becoming a major banana producer in Central America, and was joined with the **United Fruit Company** (UFC) in 1899. Zemurray took an active interest in political affairs in the Central American states where his economic interests lay and was a key supporter of the revolution in Honduras in 1910. During the 1920s, Zemurray's Cuyamel Fruit Company became a rival to UFC. He sold it to UFC in 1930, becoming United Fruit's largest shareholder. As chief of operations, he made UFC a highly successful business in the 1930s, and he continued to exercise great influence in Central American politics and economics. He served as the UFC's president in 1938–51, with one year's break. *See also* LATIN AMERICA.

ZIMMERMANN TELEGRAM (1917). During **World War I**, German Foreign Minister Arthur Zimmermann sent a secret telegram to Heinrich von Eckhardt, German minister in **Mexico**, via the German ambassador in the United States, Johann von Bernstorff. Sent on 17 January 1917, it was intercepted by British naval **intelligence**. The Zimmermann telegram revealed a plan under consideration in Berlin whereby **Germany**, in the event the United States entered the war, would entice Mexico to invade the southwestern states in order to "reconquer the lost territory" in Texas, Arizona, and New Mexico. Zimmermann speculated that the Mexican government could also persuade **Japan** to enter the war on the side of the **Central Powers**.

The government of **Great Britain** passed the decoded message to the U.S. government, together with a further dispatch by Zimmermann dated 5 February, two days after the United States broke diplomatic relations with Germany, which sought Mexican action before the United States declared war. President **Woodrow Wilson**'s administration published the telegram in the U.S. press on 1 March 1917. It provoked widespread anger and fueled anti-German sentiment, coming as it did only a month after the German resumption of unrestricted submarine warfare, and touching on American sensibilities about European interventions in western hemisphere affairs dating back to the **Monroe Doctrine**. There was also anger in the U.S. government that Zimmermann had used a State Department cable connection that had been made available to Bernstorff on the understanding that it would solely be used for messages concerning peace negotiations. The State Department had actually therefore handled the telegram in its raw form, unsuspectingly passing it to Bernstorff undecoded. Zimmermann, seemingly unconcerned at the consequences, confirmed the telegram was genuine on 3 March. It was a major propaganda coup for Britain and a key event on the road to the U.S. **declaration of war** on 6 April 1917. *See also* SIGNALS INTELLIGENCE.

Appendix A
International Conferences

VENUE	DATE	FEATURES
Paris, France	1919	Peace conference
Washington, D.C.	1921–22	Naval disarmament
Santiago, Chile	1923	Fifth pan-American conference
Geneva, Switzerland	1925	Geneva Protocol
Geneva, Switzerland	1927	Naval disarmament
Havana, Cuba	1928	Sixth pan-American conference
Washington, D.C.	1928–29	Pan-American conciliation and arbitration
Rapidan, Virginia	1929	U.S.–British disarmament
London, England	1930	Naval disarmament
Geneva, Switzerland	1932–34	World disarmament
London, England	1933	World economic conference
Montevideo, Uruguay	1933	Seventh pan-American conference
London, England	1935–36	Naval disarmament
Buenos Aires, Argentina	1936	Maintenance of peace in Americas
Brussels, Belgium	1937	Discussion of Asian crisis
Evian, France	1938	Refugee problems
Lima, Peru	1938	Eighth pan-American conference
Panama City, Panama	1939	Pan-American foreign ministers
Havana, Cuba	1940	Pan-American foreign ministers: Act of Havana
Ogdensberg, New York	1940	U.S.–Canadian defense
Placentia Bay, Newfoundland	1941	Atlantic Charter

(continued)

VENUE	DATE	FEATURES
Moscow, USSR	1941	Allied supply protocols
Washington, D.C.	1941–42	Roosevelt–Churchill meeting
Rio de Janeiro, Brazil	1942	Defense of the Americas
Washington, D.C.	1942	U.S.–British strategic planning
Casablanca, Morocco	1943	U.S.–British strategic planning
Washington, D.C.	1943	U.S.–British strategic planning
Hot Springs, Virginia	1943	Food and Agricultural Organization
Quebec, Canada	1943	U.S.–British–Canadian planning
Moscow, USSR	1943	Foreign ministers meeting
Cairo, Egypt	1943	U.S.–British–Chinese meeting
Teheran, Iran	1943	Roosevelt–Stalin–Churchill meeting
Cairo, Egypt	1943	U.S.–British–Turkish meeting
Dumbarton Oaks, D.C.	1944	International organization
Bretton Woods, N.H.	1944	International finance
Quebec, Canada	1944	Strategic and political planning
Chicago	1944	International civil aviation
Chapultepec, Mexico	1945	Defense of the Americas
Malta	1945	U.S.–British preparation meeting
Yalta, USSR	1945	Roosevelt–Stalin–Churchill meeting
San Francisco, California	1945	Creation of the United Nations organization
Potsdam, Germany	1945	Truman–Stalin–Churchill/ Attlee meeting

Appendix B
Presidents, Secretaries of State, and Undersecretaries

PRESIDENT	SECRETARY OF STATE	UNDERSECRETARY OF STATE
Woodrow Wilson (1913–21)	William J. Bryan 1913–15	
	Robert Lansing 1915–20	Frank L. Polk 1919–20
	Bainbridge Colby 1920–21	Norman H. Davis 1920–21
Warren Harding (1921–23)	Charles E. Hughes 1921–25	Henry P. Fletcher 1921–22
		William Phillips 1922–24
Calvin Coolidge (1923–29)	Frank B. Kellogg 1925–29	Joseph C. Grew 1924–27
		Robert E. Olds 1927–28
		J. Reuben Clark 1928–29
Herbert Hoover (1929–33)	Henry L. Stimson 1929–33	Joseph P. Cotton 1929–31
		William R. Castle 1931–33
Franklin Roosevelt (1933–45)	Cordell Hull 1933–44	William Phillips 1933–36
		Sumner Welles 1937–43
		Edward R. Stettinius 1943–44
	Edward R. Stettinius 1944–45	Joseph C. Grew 1944–45
Harry Truman (1945–53)	James F. Byrnes 1945–46	Dean G. Acheson 1945–47

Appendix C
Chairs of Senate Committee
on Foreign Relations

CHAIR (PARTY AND STATE)	DATE
Augustus O. Bacon (D-Ga.)	1913–14
William J. Stone (D-Mont.)	1914–18
Gilbert M. Hitchcock (D-Neb.)	1918–19
Henry Cabot Lodge (R-Mass.)	1919–24
William E. Borah (R-Idaho)	1924–33
Key Pittman (D-Nev.)	1933–40
Walter E. George (D-Ga.)	1940–41
Tom Connally (D-Tex.)	1941–47

Appendix D
Major Ambassadorships

ARGENTINA

Frederic Jessup Stimson	1915–21
John W. Riddle	1922–25
Peter Augustus Jay	1925–26
Robert Woods Bliss	1927–33
Alexander W. Weddell	1933–38
Norman Armour	1939–44
Spruille Braden	1945

BRAZIL

Edwin V. Morgan	1912–33
Hugh S. Gibson	1933–36
Jefferson Caffery	1937–44
Adolf A. Berle	1945–46

CANADA

William Phillips	1927–29
Hanford MacNider	1930–32
Warren Delano Robbins	1933–35
Norman Armour	1935–39
Daniel C. Roper	1939
James H. R. Cromwell	1940
Jay Pierrepont Moffat	1940–43
Ray Atherton	1943–48

CHINA (ENVOYS UNTIL 1929, AMBASSADORS THEREAFTER)

Paul Reinsch	1913–19
Charles R. Crane	1920–21
Jacob Gould Schurman	1921–25
John MacMurray	1925–29
Nelson T. Johnson	1929–41
Clarence E. Gauss	1941–44
Patrick Hurley	1944–45

CUBA (ENVOYS UNTIL 1923, AMBASSADORS THEREAFTER)

William E. Gonzales (minister)	1913–19
Boaz W. Long (minister)	1919–21
Enoch H. Crowder	1923–27
Noble Brandon Judah	1927–29
Harry F. Guggenheim	1929–33
Sumner Welles	1933
Recognition was withheld by the United States between September 1933 and February 1934	
Jefferson Caffery	1934–37
J. Butler Wright	1937–39
George S. Messersmith	1940–42
Spruille Braden	1942–45
R. Henry Norweb	1945–48

FRANCE

William G. Sharp	1914–19
Hugh Campbell-Wallace	1919–21
Myron T. Herrick	1921–29
Walter E. Edge	1929–33
Jesse Isidor Strauss	1933–36
William C. Bullitt	1936–40

William D. Leahy 1941–42
Jefferson Caffery 1944–49

GERMANY

James W. Gerrard 1913–17
Ellis L. Dresel (chargé) 1921–22
Alanson B. Houghton 1922–25
Jacob Gould Schurman 1925–30
Frederic M. Sackett 1930–33
William E. Dodd 1933–38
Hugh R. Wilson 1938–39
Alexander C. Kirk (chargé) 1939–40
Leland B. Morris (chargé) 1940–41

GREAT BRITAIN

Walter Hines Page 1913–18
John W. Davis 1918–21
George Harvey 1921–23
Frank B. Kellogg 1923–25
Alanson B. Houghton 1925–29
Charles G. Dawes 1929–31
Andrew W. Mellon 1932–33
Robert Worth Bingham 1933–37
Joseph P. Kennedy 1938–40
John G. Winant 1941–46

ITALY

Thomas Nelson Page 1913–19
Robert U. Johnson 1920–21
Richard W. Child 1921–24
Henry P. Fletcher 1924–29
John W. Garrett 1929–33

Breckinridge Long	1933–36
William Phillips	1936–41
George Wadsworth (chargé)	1941
Alexander C. Kirk	1945–46

JAPAN

George Guthrie	1913–17
Roland Morris	1917–20
Charles B. Warren	1921–22
Cyrus Woods	1923–24
Edgar Bancroft	1924–25
Charles MacVeagh	1925–28
William Castle	1930
W. Cameron Forbes	1930–32
Joseph C. Grew	1932–41

MEXICO

Henry Lane Wilson	1910–13
John Lind (envoy)	1913–14
Henry P. Fletcher	1917–19
Charles B. Warren	1924
James R. Sheffield	1924–27
Dwight W. Morrow	1927–30
J. Reuben Clark	1930–33
Josephus Daniels	1933–41
George S. Messersmith	1942–46

RUSSIA

George T. Marye	1914–16
David R. Francis	1916–17

UNION OF SOVIET SOCIALIST REPUBLICS

William C. Bullitt	1933–36
Joseph E. Davies	1937–38
Laurence A. Steinhardt	1939–41
William H. Standley	1942–43
W. Averell Harriman	1943–46

Bibliography

CONTENTS

This bibliography offers a selection of recommended readings on aspects of U.S. diplomacy between the start of World War I and the end of World War II. This era saw the transformation of the United States and its place in the world and therefore has attracted a great deal of attention from writers. Such is the extensive nature of this literature that only texts in the English language are listed here, and the focus is limited to the conduct of U.S. foreign policy. There is no attempt to list texts on the diplomacy and politics of other states with which the United States interacted.

It is often asserted that the historiography of U.S. foreign relations has gone through distinct periods, and that in each period, one school of thought was predominant. The realist approach dominated scholarship after World War II. It was challenged in the 1960s by revisionist scholars who substituted an emphasis on economic and expansionist motives for the realist focus on security and national interests. Subsequently, postrevisionism offered a synthesis of the two approaches, demonstrating a greater sense of objectivity that came with increased access to archives. This simple typology is deceptive, however, for there have always been divergent voices that presented alternative viewpoints. Thus, realists engaged in fierce discourse with idealists, who shared a strong affinity with the liberal internationalism of President Woodrow Wilson. Some postrevisionists inclined more toward a realist perspective, and some accepted a greater primacy for economic motivations in U.S. foreign policy. Since the 1970s, corporatists have drawn attention to the links between private business interests and the makers of policy, without the sometimes crude determinism of some 1960s revisionists. In the late 20th century, issues of gender and race and an increased focus on culture and ideology enriched the field, while making it harder to categorize, since they exist alongside, rather than replacing, older realist, idealist, and revisionist perspectives. Historical debate continues unabated, therefore, on many of the key issues that arose during this crucial era.

While there has been less writing on this period than on the post-1945 years, readers looking for a broad overview of U.S. foreign policy from World War I to World War II have a good range of choices. For a realist approach, George Kennan, *American Diplomacy 1900–1950*, is an acknowledged classic. By contrast, William Appleman Williams, *The Tragedy of American Diplomacy*, offers a radically revisionist perspective. Lloyd Gardner, *American Foreign Policy: Present to Past*, gives a more measured revisionist analysis. For more depth on the key themes of the 1914–45 period, see Selig Adler, *Uncertain Giant: American Foreign Policy between the Wars*, and Akira Iriye's volume of the Cambridge History of American Foreign Relations, *The Globalizing of America*. A good introduction to the various historiographical approaches to the issues of this era can be found in Michael Hogan, ed., *Paths to Power: The Historiography of American*

Foreign Relations to 1941, while two useful essays questioning traditional interpretations of key periods in U.S. foreign policy (1900–21 and 1920–42) can be found in Barton Bernstein, ed., *Towards a New Past: Dissenting Essays in American History*. Justus Doenecke has written widely and insightfully on peace movements and noninterventionism and provides an excellent survey of the literature in *Anti-intervention: A Bibliographical Introduction to Isolationism and Pacifism from World War I to the Early Cold War*.

The historiography of the diplomacy of the Woodrow Wilson presidency (1913–21) is dominated by two issues: the entry into World War I, and the negotiation of and subsequent failure to ratify the 1919 Treaty of Versailles. A good overall introduction to the diplomacy of the whole period is D. M. Smith, *The Great Departure: The U.S. and World War I*. A readable account of the 1914–17 neutrality period is Patrick Devlin, *Too Proud to Fight: Woodrow Wilson's Neutrality*. Insightful in-depth studies are provided in Kendrick Clements, *Woodrow Wilson: World Statesman*; John Milton Cooper, *The Warrior and the Priest: Woodrow Wilson and Theodore Roosevelt*; and Lloyd Ambrosius, *Wilsonian Statecraft: Theory and Practice of Liberal Internationalism during World War I*. Clements and Cooper bring out the complexity of Wilson's character and challenge the standard description of Wilson as wholly a visionary idealist. John Thompson, *Woodrow Wilson*, emphasizes the particularly American style of Wilson's war leadership.

There have been many fine studies of Wilson's involvement in framing the Treaty of Versailles and of the subsequent fight over the treaty and the League of Nations in the U.S. Senate. Once again excellent studies are provided by Lloyd Ambrosius, *Woodrow Wilson and the Diplomatic Tradition: The Treaty Fight in Perspective*, and John Milton Cooper, *Breaking the Heart of the World: Woodrow Wilson and the Fight for the League of Nations*. An older but still excellent study is Thomas A. Bailey, *Woodrow Wilson and the Lost Peace*. Like Cooper's and Bailey's works, Thomas Knock's *To End All Wars: Woodrow Wilson and the Quest for a New World Order* finds Wilson's approach to postwar peacemaking to be essentially correct. While these accounts acknowledge that Wilson's refusal to compromise doomed the treaty, they tend to criticize strongly his main senatorial opponent, Henry Cabot Lodge. Bailey's *Woodrow Wilson and the Great Betrayal* (intended as a sequel to *Lost Peace*) is characteristic of many post-1930s works in its negative representation of anti-League forces in the United States. For a more positive view of Lodge, see William C. Widenor, *Henry Cabot Lodge and the Search for an American Foreign Policy*.

In view of the subsequent significance of U.S. relations with the Union of Soviet Socialist Republics in the Cold War period, historians have devoted a great deal of attention to American responses to the Bolshevik Revolution. Betty Miller Unterberger's "Woodrow Wilson and the Bolsheviks: The 'Acid Test' of Soviet–American Relations" is a useful study by a major authority on the subject. Arthur S. Link, *Woodrow Wilson: Revolution, War, and Peace*, considers Wilson's approach to revolution. N. Gordon Levin, *Woodrow Wilson and World Politics: America's Response to War and Revolution*, also considers the issue in the context of Wilson's broader attitude toward revolution and takes a revisionist approach. Lloyd C. Gardner, *Safe for Democracy: The Anglo–American Response to Revolution, 1913–1923*, also fits the Russian Revolution into a broader thesis, which sees Wilson (and the subsequent Warren G. Harding administration) supporting revolutions but only when believing them to be following the principles of American liberal capitalism. On the specific response to events in Russia, see David S. Fogelsong, *America's Secret War against Bolshevism: U.S. Intervention in the Russian Civil War, 1917–1920*, for an approach that sees Wilson's policy as both anti-German and anti-Bolshevik, and Linda Killen, *The Russian Bureau: A Case Study in Wilsonian Diplomacy*. David W. McFadden, *Alternative Paths: Soviet–American Relations, 1917–1920*, sees Wilson essentially undecided whether to confront the Bolsheviks or seek accommodation with them.

For an overview of the foreign policy of the Republican adminstrations (1921–33), see Warren I. Cohen, *Empire without Tears: America's Foreign Relations, 1921–1933*. Historians have challenged in various ways the traditional depiction of the policy of this era as uniformly isolationist. A landmark text in this process is Joan Hoff Wilson, *American Business and Foreign Policy, 1920–1933*. Hoff Wilson coined the term "independent nationalism" to describe the overall thrust of U.S. policy under Warren Harding, Calvin Coolidge, and Herbert Hoover which, despite congressional resistance to U.S. membership in the League of Nations and World Court, was marked by an increase in global commercial activism and innovative approaches to Latin American and Caribbean affairs. Eugene P. Trani and David L. Wilson note the trend to revisionism in *The Presidency of Warren G. Harding*, as does Kenneth J. Grieb in *The Latin American Policy of Warren G. Harding*. For a detailed overall assessment of Harding's foreign policy, see Robert K. Murray, *The Harding Era*. A challenge to revisionist perspectives on the Harding period can be found in Robert Accinelli's treatment of the World Court debate, "Was There a 'New' Harding?" Chapters detailing foreign policy approaches in the Coolidge years can be found in Donald McCoy, *Calvin Coolidge: The Quiet President*, and Robert Ferrell, *The Presidency of Calvin Coolidge*.

For nationalism in Republican policy, see Karen A. J. Miller, *Populist Nationalism: Republican Insurgency and American Foreign Policy Making, 1918–1925*. William Appleman Williams, in "The Legend of Isolationism in the 1920s," had earlier sharply contested the use of the term "isolationism" from a radical revisionist perspective. The term is still useful in describing some cultural attitudes and in characterizing the political approach of the government to issues outside the western hemisphere. In this context, see Leroy Rieselbach, "The Basis of Isolationist Behavior," and Richard N. Current, "The Stimson Doctrine and the Hoover Doctrine."

The focus of much scholarship has been on the naval disarmament conferences. See Thomas Buckley, *The United States and the Washington Conference, 1921–1922*, and Richard W. Fanning, *Peace and Disarmament: Naval Rivalry and Arms Control, 1922–1933*. A significant influence on disarmament policy was exercised by newly enfranchised women, as discussed in Rhodri Jeffreys-Jones, *Changing Differences: Women and the Shaping of American Foreign Policy, 1917–1994*.

The roles of other significant individuals in the shaping of foreign policy during the interwar years are examined in Harold Josephson, *James T. Shotwell and the Rise of Internationalism in America*, and Betty Glad, *Charles Evans Hughes and the Illusions of Innocence: A Study in American Diplomacy*. The increasing importance of economic ties between the United States and Europe and the growing influence of the U.S. Department of Commerce as a foreign policy actor are examined in Michael J. Hogan, *Informal Entente: The Private Structure of Cooperation in Anglo–American Economic Diplomacy, 1918–1928*, and Joseph Brandes, *Herbert Hoover and Economic Diplomacy: Department of Commerce Policy, 1921–1928*. For individual case studies of the influence of economic policy, see N. Stephen Kane's analysis of U.S.–Mexican relations, "American Businessmen and Foreign Policy," and Melvyn Leffler's examination of war debt and reparations issues, "The Origins of Republican War Debt Policy, 1921–1923."

The phenomenon of peace movements in the interwar years is discussed in Cecelia Lynch, *Beyond Appeasement: Interpreting Interwar Peace Movements in World Politics*. Carrie A. Foster has extensively explored the Women's International League for Peace in *Women for All Seasons: The Story of the Women's International League for Peace and Freedom* and *The*

Women and the Warriors: The U.S. Section of the Women's International League for Peace and Freedom, 1915–1946. The peace progressives were an influence on Woodrow Wilson but criticized his interventions in Central America: see Robert David Johnson, *The Peace Progressives and American Foreign Relations.* For the continuing influence of the peace movements in the 1930s, see Robert D. Accinelli, "Militant Internationalists: The League of Nations Association, the Peace Movement, and U.S. Foreign Policy, 1934–38," and Lawrence S. Wittner, *Rebels against War: The American Peace Movement, 1933–1983.*

There is an extensive literature on U.S. foreign policy during the 1930s. For a generally positive account of Franklin D. Roosevelt's diplomacy, see Robert Dallek, *Franklin D. Roosevelt and American Foreign Policy, 1932–1945.* Among Roosevelt's early critics was historian Charles A. Beard; see his *American Foreign Policy Making 1932–1940.* A later critical account is Frederick W. Marks, *Wind over Sand: The Diplomacy of Franklin Roosevelt.* Two conflicting viewpoints are set out in Justus D. Doenecke and Mark Stoler, *Debating Franklin D. Roosevelt's Foreign Policies, 1933–1945.* There is much discussion of the various strands of isolationism in the 1930s. For a good overview, see Manfred Jonas, *Isolationism in America, 1935–41,* and for the president's approach to isolationism, see Wayne S. Cole, *Roosevelt and the Isolationists, 1932–1945.* For the Nye Committee and neutralism, see John E. Wiltz, *In Search of Peace: The Senate Munitions Inquiry, 1934–36,* and Matthew W. Coulter, *The Senate Munitions Inquiry of the 1930s: Beyond the Merchants of Death.* There has been much controversy over American involvement in the appeasement of Germany. Generally critical is Arnold Offner, *American Appeasement; United States Foreign Policy and Germany, 1933–1938.* For a range of different perspectives, see David F. Schmitz and Richard D. Challener, eds., *Appeasement in Europe: A Reassessment of U.S. Policies.*

Herbert Hoover's own account of his administration's foreign policy priorities and decisions, with particular reference to tariff reform and world disarmament, can be found in *The Memoirs of Herbert Hoover, 1920–1933: The Cabinet and the Presidency.* Hoover's private papers and memoranda also form the basis of William Starr Myers, *The Foreign Policies of Herbert Hoover, 1929–1933.* A classic account focusing on economic elements in Roosevelt's diplomacy is Lloyd C. Gardner, *Economic Aspects of New Deal Diplomacy.* Roosevelt's secretary of state was principally interested in trade, as discussed in Michael A. Butler, *Cautious Visionary: Cordell Hull and Trade Reform.*

Two useful introductory articles with regard to the historical debates on the motivations of U.S. policy toward Latin America in the interwar years are D. M. Pletcher, "United States Relations with Latin America: Neighborliness and Exploitation," and Jules R. Benjamin, "The Framework of U.S. Relations with Latin America in the Twentieth Century: An Interpretative Essay." Walter LaFeber, *Inevitable Revolutions: The United States in Central America*, contests the traditional view that the United States acted in Latin America to defend it against European intrusions; he argues that policy makers and business interests sought to relieve U.S. domestic tensions and problems with industrial and agricultural overproduction by seeking to control markets in the regions. Thus the U.S. imposition of protectorates kept out European intrusions but did not protect from U.S. incursions. Jules Benjamin, *The United States and Cuba: Hegemony and Dependent Development, 1880–1934*, and David Healy, *Drive to Hegemony: The United States in the Caribbean, 1898–1917*, see a complexity of motives and point out how elites in these countries cooperated with U.S. interventionists. For intervention across the region, see also Whitney T. Perkins, *Constraint of Empire: The United States and Caribbean Interventions*, and John J. Johnson, *A Hemisphere Apart: The Foundations of United States Policy toward Latin America*.

For individual countries, notable studies include Karl Berman, *Under the Big Stick: Nicaragua and the United States since 1848*; Bruce Calder, *The Impact of Intervention: The Dominican Republic during the U.S. Occupation of 1916–24*; Linda B. Hall, *Oil, Banks, and Politics: The United States and Postrevolutionary Mexico 1917–1924*; William Kamman, *A Search for Stability: United States Diplomacy toward Nicaragua, 1925–1933*; and Joseph Smith, *Unequal Giants: Diplomatic Relations between the United States and Brazil, 1889–1930*. Republican policies are now seen as precursors for the 1930s Good Neighbor policy. See Earl R. Curry, *Hoover's Dominican Diplomacy and the Origins of the Good Neighbor Policy*; for an earlier but still useful account, see Alexander deConde, *Herbert Hoover's Latin American Policy*.

For Franklin D. Roosevelt's policy on Latin America, see the more general studies listed for Roosevelt above, and more specifically, Irwin Gellman, *Good Neighbor Diplomacy*; Randall Bennett Woods, *The Roosevelt Foreign Policy Establishment and the Good Neighbor: The United States and Argentina, 1941–1945*; and Eric Paul Roorda, *The Dictator Next Door: The Good Neighbor Policy and the Trujillo Regime in the Dominican Republic, 1930–1945*. Two contrasting interpretations of the Good Neighbor policy can be found in Frederick B. Pike, *FDR's Good Neighbor: Sixty Years of Generally Gentle Chaos*, and Michael Grow, *The Good Neighbor Policy and Authoritarianism in Paraguay: United States Economic Expansion and Great-Power Rivalry in Latin America during World War II*. Pike's cultural analysis shows security and economic objectives to be so entwined as to be inseparable. Grow sees the policy as liberal imperialism, with the objective being informal U.S. hegemony rather than mutually beneficial security and economic activities.

For good overviews of U.S. relations with the two most significant Asian powers in this period, see Warren I. Cohen, *America's Response to China: A History of Sino–American Relations*, and Walter LaFeber, *The Clash: U.S.–Japanese Relations throughout History*. For the 1920s, an essential text is Akira Iriye, *After Imperialism: The Search for a New Order in the Far East, 1921–1931*. For the crisis-ridden 1930s, the majority of texts tend to view events merely as a prelude to the outbreak of war between the United States and Japan in 1941. A solid account of the period in its own right is Dorothy Borg, *The United States and the Far Eastern Crisis of 1933–1938*. For two important individuals, see Joseph Stilwell, *The Stilwell Papers*, and Stanley K. Hornbeck, *The Diplomacy of Frustration: The Manchurian Crisis of 1931–1933 as Revealed in the Papers of Stanley K. Hornbeck*. On Hornbeck, see Hu Shizhang, *Stanley K. Hornbeck and the Open Door Policy, 1919–1937*, and for another important lobbyist in favor of China, see Robert E. Herzstein, *Henry R. Luce, Time, and the American Crusade in Asia*. For the road to war in Asia, see the essays in Akira Iriye and Warren I. Cohen, eds., *American, Chinese, and Japanese Perspectives on Wartime Asia, 1931–1949*; Akira Iriye, *The Origins of the Second World War in Asia and the Pacific*; and You-Li Sun, *China and the Origins of the Pacific War, 1931–1941*. For the wartime period, see Michael Schaller, *The U.S. Crusade in China, 1938–1945*, and Akira Iriye, *Power and Culture: The Japanese–American War, 1941–1945*, together with texts noted later under World War II.

The expansion of U.S. interests and influence after World War I brought the United States increasingly into interaction with the European imperial powers, notably Great Britain, an economic and naval rival. Broad themes are discussed in David Reynolds and David Dimbleby, *An Ocean Apart: The Relationship between Britain and America in the Twentieth Century*. For clashes over empire, see Anne Orde, *The Eclipse of Great Britain: The United States and British Imperial Decline,1895–1956*, and William Roger Louis, *Imperialism at Bay: The United States and the Decolonization of the British Empire.* John E. Moser, *Twisting the Lion's Tail: American Anglophobia between the World Wars*, explores negative American views of Britain. For the 1920s, see Brian J. C. McKercher, ed., *Anglo–American Relations in the 1920s: The Struggle for Supremacy*, and for the impact on U.S. relations with Europe, see Patrick O. Cohrs, *The Unfinished Peace after World War I: America, Britain, and the Stabilisation of Europe, 1919–1939.* For a treatment of tensions with Britain over naval armaments, see Stephen Roskill, *Naval Policy between the Wars: The Period of Anglo–American Antagonism, 1919–1929.*

U.S. relations with Germany have also attracted great attention from scholars, notably with reference to the economic rescue packages of the 1920s, and concerning U.S. responses to the rise of Nazism in the 1930s. For an overview, see Manfred Jonas, *The United States and Germany: A Diplomatic History.* For the economic issue, see Frank Costigliola, "The United States and the Reconstruction of Germany in the 1920s," and Patricia M. Clavin, *The Failure of Economic Diplomacy: Britain, Germany, France, and the USA, 1931–36.* On the issue of appeasement, see Arnold Offner, "Appeasement Revisited: The United States, Great Britain, and Germany, 1933–1940," as well as Callum MacDonald, *The United States, Britain, and Appeasement 1936–1939*, and David F. Schmitz and Richard D. Challener, eds., *Appeasement in Europe: A Reassessment of U.S. Policies.* For U.S. involvement in European reconstruction in the 1920s, see Melvyn P. Leffler, "Political Isolationism, Economic Expansionism or Diplomatic Realism: American Policy toward Western Europe 1921–1933," and Frank Costigliola, *Awkward Dominion: American Political, Economic, and Cultural Relations with Europe, 1919–1933.* U.S. policy toward one of the key events in Europe in the 1930s, the Spanish Civil War, is analyzed in Douglas Little, *Malevolent Neutrality: The United States, Great Britain, and the Origins of the Spanish Civil War*, and Richard P. Traina, *American Diplomacy and the Spanish Civil War.*

An overview of U.S. relations with the Union of Soviet Socialist Republics is provided by Peter Boyle, *American–Soviet Relations: From the Russian Revolution to the Fall of Communism.* Both a participant and a scholar, George F. Kennan provides an analysis of relations between 1917 and 1953 in *Russia and the West under Lenin and Stalin.* Kennan was one of the young diplomats trained as experts on the USSR and whose views on that state profoundly shaped U.S. policy; their development is analyzed in Frederic Propas, "Creating a Hard Line toward Russia: The Training of State Department Soviet Experts, 1927–1937," and Hugh De Santis, *The*

Diplomacy of Silence: The American Foreign Service, the Soviet Union, and the Cold War, 1933–1947. The debate over U.S. recognition of the USSR is covered in Joan Hoff Wilson, *Ideology and Economics: United States Relations with the Soviet Union, 1918–33,* and Edward Bennett, *Recognition of Russia: An American Foreign Policy Dilemma.*

The first two U.S. ambassadors to the USSR were contrasting figures; see Beatrice Farnsworth, *William C. Bullitt and the Soviet Union,* and Elizabeth Kimball MacLean, *Joseph E. Davies: Envoy to the Soviets.* David Mayers considers all of the U.S. ambassadors in *The Ambassadors and America's Soviet Policy* and gives an alternative take on Davies in "Ambassador Joseph Davies Reconsidered." Two views on U.S. diplomacy toward the USSR in the period leading up to World War II are given in Douglas Little, "Antibolshevism and American Foreign Policy, 1919–1939: The Diplomacy of Self-Delusion," and T. R. Maddux, "Watching Stalin Maneuver between Hitler and the West: American Diplomats and Soviet Diplomacy, 1934–39." The transformation in relations leading to the World War II alliance is traced in Edward M. Bennett, *Franklin D. Roosevelt and the Search for Victory: American–Soviet Relations, 1939–1945.* For the effect on U.S. public opinion of this changing relationship, see Ralph B. Levering, *American Opinion and the Russian Alliance, 1939–1945.* General John Deane was head of the military mission in Moscow in the second half of World War II and gives an insider's account in *The Strange Alliance: The Story of Our Wartime Efforts at Collaboration with Russia.* More texts on wartime diplomacy are considered below.

The diplomatic events leading up to U.S. entry into World War II have been subject to more exhaustive study than any other period covered by this book. Public and scholarly attention has been focused on two main issues: President Franklin D. Roosevelt's attitudes regarding entering war with Nazi Germany, and the extent to which the administration bears responsibility for the outbreak of war with Japan. The back door to war interpretation, and associated conspiracy theories, continue to generate much writing, most of it of poor quality. The more considered approach can be found in the work by Charles A. Beard, one of Roosevelt's fiercest contemporary academic critics, *President Roosevelt and the Coming of the War, 1941: A Study in Appearances and Realities.* Robert A. Divine gives a short, sharp overview from a more sympathetic perspective, in *The Reluctant Belligerent: American Entry into World War II.* Taking a longer perspective is Justus D. Doenecke and John E. Wiltz, *From Isolation to War, 1931–1941.* Roosevelt's developing policies toward Great Britain and Germany are examined in Waldo Heinrichs, *Threshold of War: Franklin D. Roosevelt and American Entry into World War II*. Patrick Hearden, *Roosevelt Confronts Hitler: America's Entry into World War II*, puts a different emphasis on Roosevelt's policies, seeing his motivation in confronting Germany to be the advancement of American hegemony. Justus Doenecke has done extensive work on the anti-interventionists and has succeeded in removing some of the opprobrium attached to them as "isolationists" in the wake of Pearl Harbor, when most Americans converted to some form of internationalism. See in particular his *Storm on the Horizon: The Challenges to American Intervention 1939–41*.

For the breakdown in relations with Japan and the events leading to Pearl Harbor, two classic texts are Dorothy Borg and Shumpei Okamoto, eds., *Pearl Harbor as History: Japanese–American Relations, 1931–1941*, and Roberta Wohlstetter, *Pearl Harbor: Warning and Decision*. These should be read with the following more recent works: Jonathan G. Utley, *Going to War with Japan, 1937–1941*; Gordon Prange, *Pearl Harbor: The Verdict of History*; and Hilary Conroy and Harry Wray, eds., *Pearl Harbor Reexamined: Prologue to the Pacific War*. More conspiratorial works, which should be read with care, are Bruce M. Russett, *No Clear and Present Danger: A Skeptical View of the U.S. Entry into World War II*; James Rusbridger and Eric Nave, *Betrayal at Pearl Harbor: How Churchill Lured Roosevelt into World War II*; and Robert B. Stinnett, *Day of Deceit: The Truth about Pearl Harbor*. By contrast, the superbly illustrated account by H. P. Willmott, *Pearl Harbor*, is highly recommended.

The literature for the period of U.S. involvement in World War II is vast. Issues of diplomacy and foreign policy were intimately connected with politics, strategy, and economics. The bibliography gives selected readings to enable a reader to gain a good grounding in these areas and to gain insight into the multiple connections between them. For an overview of the war itself, Gerhard Weinberg's *A World at Arms: A Global History of World War II* is recommended. Overviews of all the interconnecting issues, including social developments and American cultural responses, are in Martin Folly, *The United States and World War II: The Awakening Giant*, and William O'Neill, *A Democracy at War: America's Fight at Home and Abroad in World War II*. Robert Cowley, ed., *No End Save Victory: Perspectives on World War II*, is a blend of useful primary materials and contributions from major scholars. For the cultural and ideological issues central to the war against Japan, see John W. Dower, *War without Mercy: Race and Power in the Pacific War*. A groundbreaking study on U.S. strategic planning during the war, with connections to future diplomatic developments, is Michael Sherry, *Preparing for the Next War: American Plans for Postwar Defense, 1941–45*. Mark Stoler sets out the strategic debate over the key issue of the European theater in *The Politics of the Second Front: American Military Planning and Diplomacy in Coalition Warfare, 1941–43*. On the bureaucratic war in Washington, D.C., see George Hooks, *Forging the Military-Industrial Complex: World War II's Battle of the Potomac*.

The relationship of the United States with its major allies, Great Britain and the USSR, has been the subject of a great deal of controversy, and the viewpoints taken by scholars have been reflective of the significance of the subject to the subsequent Cold War. Early but still valuable studies are Herbert Feis, *Churchill, Roosevelt, Stalin: The War They Waged and the Peace They Sought*, and William Hardy McNeil, *America, Britain, and Russia: Their Co-operation and Conflict, 1941–1946*. These studies see the alliance with the USSR as having been undermined by Soviet leader Josef Stalin's expansionist ambitions. Later revisionist works emphasized U.S. ambitions and ideology: see especially William Appleman Williams, *The Tragedy of American Diplomacy*; Walter LaFeber, *America, Russia, and the Cold War*; and Gabriel Kolko, *The Politics of War: The World and United States Foreign Policy, 1943–1945*. President Franklin D. Roosevelt conducted relations with the major allies himself, and there have been numerous studies of his policies. Warren Kimball, *The Juggler: Franklin Roosevelt as Wartime Statesman*, is excellent. Kimball is the foremost authority on the relationship with Prime Minister Winston Churchill of Great Britain; see his *Forged in War: Roosevelt, Churchill, and the Second World War*. Robin Edmonds covers the relations between Roosevelt, Churchill, and Stalin in *The Big Three: Churchill, Roosevelt, and Stalin in Peace and War*. Highly critical of Roosevelt's policies is Amos Perlmutter, *FDR and Stalin: A Not So Grand Alliance 1943–1945*. Richard Beitzell also emphasizes the elements of conflict in the relationship, in *The Uneasy Alliance: America, Britain, and Russia, 1941–1943*. Mary Glantz, however, sees Roosevelt to have been battling elements in his own administration as he sought to build a constructive relationship with the USSR, in *FDR and the Soviet Union: The President's Battles over Foreign Policy*. Daniel Yergin, in *Shattered Peace: The Origins of the Cold War and the National Security State*, had earlier outlined the differing assessments of the USSR's foreign policy in the administration, contrasting what he called the "Yalta axioms" of Roosevelt with the "Riga axioms" of anti-Soviet officials like George Kennan and Loy Henderson.

The close but often difficult wartime relationship with Great Britain has been the subject of many excellent studies. Recommended especially are Mark Stoler, *Allies in War: Britain and America against the Axis Powers 1940–1945*; Keith Sainsbury, *Churchill and Roosevelt at War: The War They Fought and the Peace They Hoped to Make*; David Reynolds, "Competitive Cooperation: Anglo–American Relations in World War Two"; Theodore A. Wilson, *The First Summit: Roosevelt and Churchill at Placentia Bay 1941*; and Randall Bennett Woods, *A Changing of the Guard: Anglo–American Relations, 1941–1946*. For the controversial subject of U.S. policy toward the Holocaust, see Verne Newton, ed., *FDR and the Holocaust*, and for a critical treatment, see David Wyman, *The Abandonment of the Jews*. Roosevelt had a poor relationship with General Charles de Gaulle, leader of the Free French, as recounted in Simon Berthon, *Allies at War: The Bitter Rivalry among Churchill, Roosevelt, and De Gaulle*. A growing area of World War II studies is intelligence. Bradley F. Smith has written two excellent books on this subject that connect to key foreign policy issues: *The Ultra-Magic Deals and the Most Special Relationship, 1940–1946*, and *Sharing Secrets with Stalin: How the Allies Traded Intelligence, 1941–1945*. For the war in Asia, in addition to the books by Michael Schaller and John W. Dower referred to above, a fine study is Christopher Thorne, *Allies of a Kind: The United States, Britain, and the War against Japan, 1941–1945*.

No subject in this period raises greater passion than the dropping of the atomic bomb on Japan. Originally seen as a purely military action to end the war as quickly as possible (and subsequently justified in those terms by President Harry S. Truman and Secretary of War Henry L. Stimson), revisionists in the 1960s presented it as primarily an act of foreign policy, designed to intimidate the USSR. The leading protagonist of this viewpoint has been Gar Alperovitz, in his *Atomic Diplomacy: Hiroshima and Potsdam, the Use of the Atomic Bomb and the American Confrontation with Soviet Power*, and in *The Decision to Use the Atomic Bomb and the Architecture of an American Myth*. The political themes and bureaucratic politics are explored in varying ways by Martin Sherwin in *A World Destroyed: Hiroshima and the Origins of the Arms Race*, and in many works by Barton J. Bernstein. Bernstein's perceptive "Understanding the Atomic Bomb and the Japanese Surrender: Missed Opportunities, Little-Known Near Disasters, and Modern History" is particularly useful. The revisionist viewpoint has been countered from a veteran's point of view in Paul Fussell, *Thank God for the Atom Bomb and Other Essays*, and Robert J. Maddox, ed., *Hiroshima in History: The Myths of Revisionism.* J. Samuel Walker gives a useful overview in *Prompt and Utter Destruction: Truman and the Use of Atomic Bombs against Japan.* An excellent account of the development of the bomb is Richard Rhodes, *The Making of the Atomic Bomb.* Lawrence Lifschultz and Kai Bird have compiled *Hiroshima's Shadow: Writings on the Denial of History and the Smithsonian Controversy,* which takes a revisionist perspective but is also useful for presenting a whole range of materials on the use of the bomb, including Truman's original statement defending it.

The reader is well served by memoirs and diary material of participants in the events covered in this book, and by the high quality of many of the biographies of influential figures in U.S. diplomacy. Particularly recommended are Averell Harriman's memoir, *Special Envoy to Churchill and Stalin, 1941–1946;* Joseph C. Grew, *Turbulent Era: A Diplomatic Record of Forty Years, 1904–1945;* and George F. Kennan, *Memoirs, vol. 1, 1900–1950.* Ambassador William Dodd's diary is a vital record of an American scholar-diplomat's encounter with Nazi Germany; see *Ambassador Dodd's Diary 1933–1938.* Spruille Braden, *Diplomats and Demagogues: The Memoirs of Spruille Braden,* is the account of one of the more controversial ambassadors. For biographies of major policy makers, see Julius Pratt's magisterial *Cordell Hull* in the *American Secretaries of State and Their Diplomacy* series, and David F. Schmitz, *Henry L. Stimson: The First Wise Man.* For Stimson, see also Godfrey Hodgson, *The Colonel: The Life and Wars of Henry Stimson, 1867–1950.*

For highly influential figures in the early part of the period covered by this book, see especially Kendrick A. Clements, *William Jennings Bryan, Missionary Isolationist;* David J. Danelski and Joseph S. Tulchin, *The Autobiographical Notes of Charles Evans Hughes;* and the study of Hughes by Betty Glad discussed earlier. Scholars interested in the deployment of special envoys during the 1920s will find an interesting perspective in Andrew J. Bacevich, *Diplomat in Khaki: Major General Frank Ross McCoy and American Foreign Policy, 1898–1949.* For a study of a key relationship by a privileged insider, see Robert E. Sherwood, *Roosevelt and Hopkins.* Two major congressional figures are examined in Robert J. Maddox, *William E. Borah and American Foreign Policy,* and Richard Coke Lower, *A Bloc of One: The Politics and Career of Hiram W. Johnson.* For insights into another dissenting figure, see Michele Stenehjem Gerber, *An American First: John T. Flynn and the America First Committee.*

Readers wishing to access primary sources in print are well served by the multiple volumes of the State Department's *Foreign Relations of the United*

States series, which contain secret internal departmental memoranda, position papers, and correspondence with ambassadors, together with extensive material from the White House. For each year, there are a number of volumes, arranged by region. In addition, there are special volumes devoted to the major international conferences during World War II. There are also edited collections of the papers of the presidents, and special mention must be made of the 69-volume collection edited by Arthur S. Link, *The Papers of Woodrow Wilson.* For Franklin D. Roosevelt's presidency, there are the 30 volumes edited by George McJimsey, *The Documentary History of the Franklin D. Roosevelt Presidency.* Essential reading for the wartime period is Warren Kimball's 3-volume *Churchill and Roosevelt: The Complete Correspondence.*

Official documents can be found not only in printed volumes but also on the World Wide Web. Presidential libraries mount special exhibitions from time to time, as does the Library of Congress (at www.loc.gov). The best materials are to be found in the collections of documents made available by Yale University Law School's Avalon project and by Mount Holyoke College. The documents published by the State Department in the *Foreign Relations of the United States* series are also now available online; for the period covered by this book, they are hosted at the University of Wisconsin. For debate on recent publications and new trends in scholarship, the interactive site h-diplo is highly recommended. The journals *Foreign Affairs* and *Diplomatic History* can also be found online. Information and links for the two world wars can be found at firstworldwar.com and secondworldwarhistory.com. The full text of Roosevelt's fireside chats is at www.mhric.org/fdr/fdr.html. There are Web sites devoted to many of the figures and institutions featured in this book, but they are of varying quality and authority. Particular favorites of the authors are the Polar Bear Expedition site at the University of Michigan and the meticulous League of Nations timeline hosted by Indiana University. There are also, of course, many sites advancing a biased, polemical, and prejudiced viewpoint, and readers are advised to use the Web widely but with care.

GENERAL HISTORICAL STUDIES

Adler, Selig. *The Uncertain Giant: American Foreign Policy between the Wars.* New York: Macmillan, 1965.

Ambrose, Stephen, and Douglas Brinkley. *Rise to Globalism: American Foreign Policy since 1938.* 8th ed. New York: Penguin, 1997.

Buckley, T., and E. Strong. *American Foreign Policy and National Security Policies, 1914–1945*. Knoxville: University of Tennessee Press, 1987.

Burk, Kathleen. "The Lineaments of Foreign Policy: The United States and a 'New World Order,' 1919–1939." *Journal of American Studies* 26 (1992): 377–91.

Carr, E. H. *International Relations between the Two World Wars, 1919–39*. New York: Macmillan, 1948.

Ferrell, Robert H. *American Diplomacy: The Twentieth Century*. Rev. ed. New York: Norton, 1988.

Gardner, Lloyd C. *American Foreign Policy: Present to Past*. London: Collier Macmillan, 1976.

———. *A Covenant with Power: America and World Order from Wilson to Reagan*. New York: Oxford University Press, 1984.

Graebner, Norman A. *America as a World Power: A Realistic Appraisal from Wilson to Reagan*. Wilmington, Del.: Scholarly Resources, 1984.

Hoff Wilson, Joan, ed. *The Twenties: The Critical Issues*. Boston: Little, Brown, 1972.

Hunt, Michael H. *Ideology and U.S. Foreign Policy*. New Haven, Conn.: Yale University Press, 1987.

Iriye, Akira. *The Cambridge History of American Foreign Relations, vol. 3, The Globalizing of America*. Cambridge: Cambridge University Press, 1993.

Kennan, George F. *American Diplomacy 1900–1950*. Chicago: University of Chicago Press, 1957.

May, E. R. *"Lessons" of the Past: The Use and Misue of History in American Foreign Policy*. Oxford: Oxford University Press, 1973.

Noggle, Burl. *Into the Twenties: The United States from Armistice to Normalcy*. Urbana: University of Illinois Press, 1974.

Parrish, M. E. *Anxious Decades: America in Prosperity and Depression, 1920–1941*. New York: Norton, 1992.

Paxson, Frederic L. *American Democracy and the World War: Postwar Years, Normalcy 1918–1923*. Berkeley: University of California Press, 1948.

Powaski, Ronald E. *Toward an Entangling Alliance: American Isolationism, Internationalism, and Europe, 1901–1950*. New York: Greenwood, 1991.

Schmitz, David F., and T. Christopher Jespersen, eds. *Architects of the American Century: Individuals and Institutions in Twentieth-century U.S. Foreign Policy-making*. Chicago: Imprint, 2000.

Schulzinger, Robert. *American Diplomacy in the Twentieth Century*. Oxford: Oxford University Press, 1990.

Smith, Robert. F. "American Foreign Relations 1920–1942." In *Towards a New Past: Dissenting Essays in American History*, ed. Barton Bernstein. New York: Pantheon, 1968.

Smith, Tony. *America's Mission: The United States and the Worldwide Struggle for Democracy in the Twentieth Century*. Princeton, N.J.: Princeton University Press, 1995.

Williams, William A. *The Tragedy of American Diplomacy*. Rev. ed. New York: Dell, 1972.

Wright, Chester W. *Economic History of the United States*. New York: McGraw-Hill, 1941.

HISTORIOGRAPHICAL AND BIBLIOGRAPHICAL STUDIES

Barnhardt, Michael. "The Origins of World War II in Asia and the Pacific." *Diplomatic History* 20 (1996): 241–60.

Bernstein, Barton J. "An Analysis of 'Two Cultures': Writing about the Making and Using of the Atomic Bombs." *Public Historian* 12 (1990): 83–107.

——, ed. *Towards a New Past: Dissenting Essays in American History*. New York: Knopf, 1969.

Carroll, F. M. "A Double-Edged Sword: Anglo–American 'Special Relations,' 1936–1981." *International History Review* 6 (1984): 454–64.

Doenecke, Justus D. *Anti-intervention: A Bibliographical Introduction to Isolationism and Pacifism from World War I to the Early Cold War*. New York: Garland, 1987.

Gatell, Frank Otto, and Allen Weinstein, eds. *American Themes: Essays in Historiography*. London: Oxford University Press, 1968.

Hammersmith, Jack L. "In Defense of Yalta: Edward R. Stettinius's *Roosevelt and the Russians*." *Virginia Magazine of History and Biography* 100 (1992): 429–54.

Hogan, Michael J., ed. *Paths to Power: The Historiography of American Foreign Relations to 1941*. New York: Cambridge University Press, 2000.

Steigerwald, David, "The Reclamation of Woodrow Wilson." *Diplomatic History* 23 (1999): 79–99.

PRESIDENT WOODROW WILSON
AND WORLD WAR I

Ambrosius, Lloyd. "The Orthodoxy of Revisionism: Woodrow Wilson and the New Left." *Diplomatic History* 1 (1977): 199–214.

——. *Wilsonian Statecraft: Theory and Practice of Liberal Internationalism during World War I.* Wilmington, Del.: Scholarly Resources, 1991.

Buehrig, Edward, ed. *Wilson's Foreign Policy in Perspective.* Bloomington: Indiana University Press, 1957.

Burk, Kathleen. *Britain, America, and the Sinews of War, 1914–1918.* Boston: Allen and Unwin, 1985.

Calhoun, Frederick S. *Power and Principle: Armed Intervention in Wilsonian Foreign Policy.* Kent, Ohio: Kent State University Press, 1987.

Clements, Kendrick A. *The Presidency of Woodrow Wilson.* Lawrence: Kansas University Press, 1992.

——. *William Jennings Bryan, Missionary Isolationist.* Knoxville: University of Tennessee Press, 1982.

——. *Woodrow Wilson: World Statesman.* Boston: Twayne, 1987.

Clements, Kendrick A., and Eric A. Cheezum. *Woodrow Wilson.* Washington D.C.: CQ Press, 2003.

Cohen, Warren I., ed. *Intervention, 1917: Why America Fought.* Englewood, N.J.: Heath, 1966.

Cooper, John M. *The Vanity of Power: American Isolationism and World War I, 1914–1917.* Westport, Conn.: Greenwood, 1969.

——. *The Warrior and the Priest: Woodrow Wilson and Theodore Roosevelt.* Cambridge, Mass.: Harvard University Press, 1983.

Cooper, John M., and Charles E. Neu, eds. *The Wilson Era: Essays in Honor of Arthur S. Link.* Wheeling, Ill.: Harlan Davidson, 1991.

Devlin, Patrick. *Too Proud to Fight: Woodrow Wilson's Neutrality.* New York: Oxford University Press, 1974.

Esposito, David M. *The Legacy of Woodrow Wilson: American War Aims in World War I.* Westport, Conn.: Praeger, 1996.

Ferrell, Robert H. *Woodrow Wilson and World War I, 1917–1921.* New York: Harper and Row, 1985.

Gelfand, Lawrence E. "Where Ideals Confront Self Interest: Wilsonian Foreign Policy." *Diplomatic History* 18 (1994): 125–33.

Hoover, Herbert. *The Ordeal of Woodrow Wilson.* New York: McGraw-Hill, 1958.

James, D. Clayton, and Anne S. Wells. *America and the Great War, 1914–1920*. Wheeling, Ill.: Harlan Davidson, 1998.

Kennedy, Ross A. "Woodrow Wilson, World War I and American National Security." *Diplomatic History* 25 (2001): 1–31.

Link, Arthur S. *Wilson the Diplomatist: A Look at His Major Foreign Policies*. Baltimore, Md.: Johns Hopkins University Press, 1963.

Mamatey, V. S. *The United States and East Central Europe, 1914–1918: A Study in Wilsonian Diplomacy and Propaganda*. Princeton, N.J.: Princeton University Press, 1957.

Peterson, Horace C., and Gilbert C. Fite. *Opponents of War, 1917–1918*. Madison: University of Wisconsin Press, 1957.

Schaffer, Ronald. *America in the Great War: The Rise of the War Welfare State*. New York: Oxford University Press, 1991.

Schmitt, Bernadotte E., and Harold C. Vedeler. *The World in the Crucible, 1914–1919*. New York: Harper and Row, 1984.

Smith, D. M. *The Great Departure: The U.S. and World War I, 1914–1920*. New York: Wiley, 1965.

Stevenson, David. *The First World War and International Politics*. New York: Oxford University Press, 1988.

Thompson, John A. *Reformers and War: American Progressive Publicists and the First World War*. New York: Cambridge University Press, 1996.

———. "Woodrow Wilson and World War I: A Reappraisal." *Journal of American Studies* 19 (1985): 325–48.

———. *Woodrow Wilson: Profiles in Power*. London: Longman, 2002.

PRESIDENT WOODROW WILSON
AND THE PEACE SETTLEMENT

Ambrosius, Lloyd. "Wilson, the Republicans, and French Security after World War I." *Journal of American History* 59 (1972): 341–52.

———. *Woodrow Wilson and the Diplomatic Tradition: The Treaty Fight in Perspective*. Cambridge: Cambridge University Press, 1987.

———. "Woodrow Wilson's Health and the Treaty Fight, 1919–20." *International History Review* 9 (1987): 73–84.

Bailey, Thomas A. *Woodrow Wilson and the Great Betrayal*. New York: Macmillan, 1945.

———. *Woodrow Wilson and the Lost Peace.* Chicago: Quadrangle, 1963.

Bassett, John S. *The League of Nations.* New York: Longmans, Green, 1928.

Cooper, John M. *Breaking the Heart of the World: Woodrow Wilson and the Fight for the League of Nations.* Cambridge: Cambridge University Press, 2001.

Egerton, G. W. "Britain and the 'Great Betrayal': Anglo–American Relations and Struggle for the United States Ratification of the Treaty of Versailles." *Historical Journal* 21 (1978): 885–911.

Finch, George A. "The Treaty of Peace with Germany in the United States Senate." *American Journal of International Law* 14 (1920): 155–206.

Fleming, Denna Frank. *The United States and the World Court.* Garden City, N.Y.: Doubleday, Doran, 1945.

Knock, Thomas. *To End All Wars: Woodrow Wilson and the Quest for a New World Order.* Princeton, N.J.: Princeton University Press, 1995.

Lazo, Dimitri D. "A Question of Loyalty: Robert Lansing and the Treaty of Versailles." *Diplomatic History* 9 (1985): 35–54.

Lentin, A. *Lloyd George, Woodrow Wilson, and the Guilt of Germany: An Essay in the Pre-history of Appeasement.* Baton Rouge: Louisiana State University Press, 1985.

Lodge, Henry Cabot. *The Senate and the League of Nations.* New York: Charles Scribner's Sons, 1925.

Lovin, Clifford R. *A School for Diplomats: The Paris Peace Conference of 1919.* Lanham, Md.: University Press of America, 1997.

Margulies, Herbert F. *The Mild Reservationists and the League of Nations Controversy in the Senate.* Columbia: University of Missouri Press, 1989.

Mervin, David. "Henry Cabot Lodge and the League of Nations." *Journal of American Studies* 4 (1970–71): 201–14.

Schwabe, Klaus. *Woodrow Wilson, Revolutionary Germany, and Peacemaking, 1918–1919: Missionary Diplomacy and the Realities of Power.* Trans. Rita and Robert Kimber. Chapel Hill: University of North Carolina Press, 1985.

Sharp, Allan. *The Versailles Settlement: Peacemaking in Paris, 1919.* New York: St. Martin's, 1991.

Vinson, J. Chalmers. "The Parchment Peace: The Senate Defense of the Four-Power Treaty of the Washington Conference." *Mississippi Valley Historical Review* 39 (1952): 303–14.

Walworth, Arthur. *Wilson and His Peacemakers*. New York: Norton, 1986.

Widenor, William C. *Henry Cabot Lodge and the Search for an American Foreign Policy*. Los Angeles: University of California Press, 1980.

U.S. POLICY TOWARD THE RUSSIAN REVOLUTION

Calhoun, Frederick. *Power and Principle: Armed Intervention in Wilsonian Foreign Policy*. Kent, Ohio: Kent State University Press, 1986.

Fic, Victor M. *The Collapse of American Policy in Russia and Siberia, 1918: Wilson's Decision Not to Intervene*. New York: Columbia University Press, 1995.

Fogelsong, David S. *America's Secret War against Bolshevism: U.S. Intervention in the Russian Civil War, 1917–1920*. Chapel Hill: University of North Carolina Press, 1995.

Gardner, Lloyd C. *Safe for Democracy: The Anglo–American Response to Revolution, 1913–1923*. New York: Oxford University Press, 1984.

Killen, Linda. *The Russian Bureau: A Case Study in Wilsonian Diplomacy*. Lexington: University Press of Kentucky, 1983.

Levin, N. Gordon. *Woodrow Wilson and World Politics: America's Response to War and Revolution*. New York: Oxford University Press, 1968.

Link, Arthur S. *Woodrow Wilson: Revolution, War, and Peace*. Wheeling, Ill.: Harlan Davidson, 1979.

——, ed. *Woodrow Wilson and a Revolutionary World, 1913–1921*. Chapel Hill: University of North Carolina Press, 1982.

Long, J. W. "American Intervention in Russia: The North Russian Expedition, 1918–19." *Diplomatic History* 6 (1982): 45–68.

McFadden, David W. *Alternative Paths: Soviet–American Relations, 1917–1920*. New York: Oxford University Press, 1993.

Rhodes, Benjamin. *The Anglo–American Winter War with Russia, 1918–1919: A Diplomatic and Military Tragicomedy*. Westport, Conn: Greenwood, 1988.

Schild, Georg. *Between Ideology and Realpolitik: Woodrow Wilson and the Russian Revolution, 1917–1922*. Westport, Conn.: Greenwood, 1995.

Unterberger, Betty Miller. *American Intervention in the Russian Civil War*. Lexington, Mass.: D. C. Heath, 1969.

——. *America's Siberian Expedition, 1918–1920.* Durham, N.C.: Duke University Press. 1956.

——. *The United States, Revolutionary Russia, and the Rise of Czechoslovakia.* Rev. ed. College Station: Texas A&M University Press, 2000.

——. "Woodrow Wilson and the Bolsheviks: The 'Acid Test' of Soviet–American Relations." *Diplomatic History* 11 (1987): 71–90.

ISOLATIONISM, DISARMAMENT, AND NATIONALISM, 1921–33

Accinelli, Robert D. "Was There a 'New' Harding? Warren G. Harding and the World Court Issue, 1920–1923." *Ohio History* 84 (1975): 168–81.

Adler, Selig. *The Isolationist Impulse: Its Twentieth Century Reaction.* New York: Abelard-Schuman, 1957.

Bagby, Wesley M. *Road to Normalcy: The Presidential Campaign and Election of 1920.* Baltimore, Md.: Johns Hopkins University Press, 1962.

Boyle, Peter. "The Roots of Isolationism: A Case Study." *Journal of American Studies* 6 (1972): 41–50.

Brandes, Joseph. *Herbert Hoover and Economic Diplomacy: Department of Commerce Policy, 1921–1928.* Pittsburgh, Penn.: University of Pittsburgh Press, 1962.

Buckingham, Peter H. *International Normalcy: The Open Door Peace with the Former Central Powers, 1921–1929.* Wilmington, Del.: Scholarly Resources, 1983.

Buckley, Thomas H. *The United States and the Washington Conference, 1921–1922.* Knoxville: University of Tennessee Press, 1970.

Buell, Raymond L. *The Washington Conference.* New York: D. Appleton, 1922.

Cohen, Warren I. *Empire without Tears: America's Foreign Relations, 1921–1933.* New York: Knopf, 1987.

Current, Richard N. "The Stimson Doctrine and the Hoover Doctrine." *American Historical Review* 59 (1954): 513–42.

DeWitt, Howard A. "The 'New' Harding and American Foreign Policy: Warren G. Harding, Hiram W. Johnson, and Pragmatic Diplomacy." *Ohio History* 86 (1976): 96–114.

Dingman, R. *Power in the Pacific: The Origins of the Naval Arms Limitation, 1914–1922.* Chicago: University of Chicago Press, 1976.

Doenecke, Justus D. *When the Wicked Rise: American Opinion-Makers and the Manchurian Crisis of 1931–1933.* Lewisburg, Penn.: Bucknell University Press, 1984.

Driggs, Don W. "The President as Chief Educator on Foreign Affairs." *Western Political Quarterly* 11 (1958): 813–19.

Dunne, Michael. *The United States and the World Court, 1920–1935.* New York: St. Martin's, 1988.

Ellis, L. Ethan. *Republican Foreign Policy, 1921–1933.* New Brunswick, N.J.: Rutgers University Press, 1968.

Epstein, Mark. "The Historians and the Geneva Naval Conference." In *Arms Limitation and Disarmament: Restraints on War, 1899–1939,* ed. Brian J. C. McKercher. Westport, Conn.: Praeger, 1992.

Fanning, Richard W. "The Coolidge Conference of 1927: Disarmament in Disarray." In *Arms Limitation and Disarmament: Restraints on War, 1899–1939,* ed. Brian J. C. McKercher. Westport, Conn.: Praeger, 1992.

———. *Peace and Disarmament: Naval Rivalry and Arms Control, 1922–1933.* Lexington: University Press of Kentucky, 1995.

Feis, Herbert. *The Diplomacy of the Dollar: First Era, 1919–1932.* Baltimore, Md.: Johns Hopkins University Press, 1950.

Ferrell, Robert H. *American Diplomacy in the Great Depression: Hoover–Stimson Foreign Policy, 1929–1933.* Hamden, Conn.: Archon, 1957.

———. *Peace in Their Time: The Origins of the Kellogg–Briand Pact.* Hamden, Conn.: Archon, 1952.

———. *The Presidency of Calvin Coolidge.* Lawrence: University Press of Kansas, 1998.

Glad, Betty. *Charles Evans Hughes and the Illusions of Innocence: A Study in American Diplomacy.* Urbana: University of Illinois Press, 1966.

Goldstein E., and J. Maurer, eds. *The Washington Conference, 1921–22: Naval Rivalry, East Asian Stability, and the Road to Pearl Harbour.* London: Frank Cass, 1994.

Guinsburg, Thomas N. *The Pursuit of Isolationism in the United States Senate from Versailles to Pearl Harbor.* New York: Garland, 1982.

Hall, C. *Britain, America, and Arms Control, 1921–37.* London: Macmillan, 1987.

Hoff Wilson, Joan. *American Business and Foreign Policy, 1920–1933.* Lexington: University Press of Kentucky, 1971.

Hogan, Michael. *Informal Entente: The Private Structure of Cooperation in Anglo–American Economic Diplomacy, 1918–1928.* Columbia: University of Missouri Press, 1977.

Jeffreys-Jones, Rhodri. *Changing Differences: Women and the Shaping of American Foreign Policy, 1917–1994*. New Brunswick, N.J.: Rutgers University Press, 1995.

Jennings, David H. "President Harding and International Organization." *Ohio History* 75 (1966): 149–65.

Josephson, Harold. *James T. Shotwell and the Rise of Internationalism in America*. Madison, N.J.: Fairleigh Dickinson University Press, 1974.

———. "Outlawing War: Internationalism and the Pact of Paris." *Diplomatic History* 3 (1979): 377–90.

Kaufman, Robert Gordon. *Arms Control in the Pre-Nuclear Era: The United States and Naval Limitation between the World Wars*. New York: Columbia University Press, 1990.

Kennedy, Gregory C. "Depression and Security: Aspects Influencing the United States Navy During the Hoover Administration." *Diplomacy and Statecraft* 6 (1995): 342–72.

———. "The 1930 London Naval Conference and Anglo–American Maritime Strength, 1927–1930." In *Arms Limitation and Disarmament: Restraints on War, 1899–1939*, ed. Brian J. C. McKercher. Westport, Conn.: Praeger, 1992.

Kneeshaw, Stephen. *In Pursuit of Peace: The American Reaction to the Kellogg–Briand Pact, 1928–1929*. New York: Garland, 1991.

Koistinen, Paul A. C. *Planning War, Pursuing Peace: Tlie Political Economy of American Warfare, 1920–1939*. Lawrence: University Press of Kansas, 1998.

Leffler, Melvyn. "The Origins of Republican War Debt Policy, 1921–1923: A Case Study in the Applicability of the Open Door Interpretation." *Journal of American History* 59 (1972): 585–601.

Louria, Margot. *Triumph and Downfall: America's Pursuit of Peace and Prosperity, 1921–1933*. Westport, Conn.: Greenwood, 2001.

Lovin, Clifford R. "Herbert Hoover, Internationalist, 1919–1923." *Prologue* 20 (1988): 248–67.

McCoy, Donald R. *Calvin Coolidge: The Quiet President*. New York: Macmillan, 1967.

Miller, Karen A. J. *Populist Nationalism: Republican Insurgency and American Foreign Policy Making, 1918–1925*. Westport, Conn.: Greenwood, 1999.

Murfett, Malcolm H. "Look Back in Anger: The Western Powers and the Washington Conference of 1921–22." In *Arms Limitation and Disarmament: Restraints on War, 1899–1939*, ed. Brian J. C. McKercher. Westport, Conn.: Praeger, 1992.

Murray, Robert K. *The Harding Era: Warren G. Harding and His Administration.* Minneapolis: University of Minnesota, 1969.

Myers, William Starr. *The Foreign Policies of Herbert Hoover, 1929–1933.* New York: Scribner's, 1940.

Nash, George H. *The Life of Herbert Hoover, vol. 2, 1914–17.* New York: Norton, 1988.

———. *The Life of Herbert Hoover, vol. 3, 1917–18.* New York: Norton, 1996.

Nevins, Allan. *The United States in a Chaotic World: 1918–1933.* New Haven, Conn.: Yale University Press, 1950.

O'Connor, Raymond G. *Perilous Equilibrium: The United States and the London Naval Conference of 1930.* New York: Greenwood, 1962.

Palmer, Niall A. *The Twenties in America: Politics and History.* Edinburgh: Edinburgh University Press, 2006.

Pusey, Merlo J. *Charles Evans Hughes.* New York: Macmillan, 1951.

Rieselbach, Leroy. "The Basis of Isolationist Behavior." *Public Opinion Quarterly,* 24 (1960): 645–57.

Sobel, Robert. *Coolidge: An American Enigma.* Washington, D.C.: Regnery, 1998.

Toth, Charles W. "Isolationism and the Emergence of Borah: An Appeal to American Tradition." *Western Political Quarterly* 14 (1961): 555–68.

Trani, Eugene P., and Donald K.Wilson. *The Presidency of Warren G. Harding.* Lawrence: University Press of Kansas, 1977.

Van Meter, R. "The Washington Conference of 1921–22: A New Look." *Pacific Historical Review* 66 (1977): 603–24.

Williams, William Appleman. "The Legend of Isolationism in the 1920s." *Science and Society* 18 (1954): 1–20.

PEACE MOVEMENTS

Accinelli, Robert D. "Militant Internationalists: The League of Nations Association, the Peace Movement, and U.S. Foreign Policy, 1934–38." *Diplomatic History* 4 (1980): 19–38.

Alonso, Harriet Hyman. *Peace as a Women's Issue: A History of the U.S. Movement for World Peace and Women's Rights.* Syracuse, N.Y.: Syracuse University Press, 1993.

Bartlett, Ruhl J. *The League to Enforce Peace.* Chapel Hill: University of North Carolina Press, 1944.

Bussey, Gertrude, and Margaret Tims. *Pioneers for Peace: Women's International League for Peace and Freedom 1915–1965*. Oxford: Alden, 1980.

Chatfield, Charles. *For Peace and Justice: Pacificism in America, 1914–1941*. Knoxville: University of Tennessee Press, 1971.

Foster, Carrie A. *The Women and the Warriors: The U.S. Section of the Women's International League for Peace and Freedom, 1915–1946*. Syracuse, N.Y.: Syracuse University Press, 1995.

——. *Women for All Seasons: The Story of the Women's International League for Peace and Freedom*. Athens: University of Georgia Press, 1989.

Johnson, Robert David. *The Peace Progressives and American Foreign Relations*. Cambridge, Mass.: Harvard University Press, 1995.

Kuehl, Warren F., and Lynne K. Dunn. *Keeping the Covenant: American Internationalists and the League of Nations, 1920–1939*. Kent, Ohio: Kent State University Press, 1997.

Lynch, Cecelia. *Beyond Appeasement: Interpreting Interwar Peace Movements in World Politics*. Ithaca, N.Y.: Cornell University Press, 1999.

Wittner, Lawrence S. *Rebels Against War: The American Peace Movement, 1933–1983*. Philadelphia: Temple University Press, 1984.

FRANKLIN D. ROOSEVELT'S FOREIGN POLICY, 1933–39

Adamson, Michael R. "The Failure of the Foreign Bondholders Protective Council Experiment, 1934–1940." *Business History Review* 76 (2002): 479–514.

Beard, Charles A. *American Foreign Policy in the Making 1932–1940: A Study in Responsibilities*. Hamden, Conn.: Archon, 1968.

Berg, Meredith W. "Protecting National Interests by Treaty: The Second London Naval Conference, 1934–1936." In *Arms Limitation and Disarmament: Restraints on War, 1899–1939*, ed. Brian J. C. McKercher. Westport, Conn.: Praeger, 1992.

Borg, Dorothy. "Notes on Roosevelt's 'Quarantine' Speech." *Political Science Quarterly* 72 (1957): 405–33.

Burns, James McGregor. *Roosevelt: The Lion and the Fox*. New York: Harcourt Brace Jovanovich, 1956.

Butler, Michael A. *Cautious Visionary: Cordell Hull and Trade Reform*. Kent, Ohio: Kent State University Press, 1998.

Cohen, Warren I. *The American Revisionists: the Lessons of Intervention in World War I.* Chicago: Chicago University Press, 1967.

Cole, Wayne S. *Determinism and American Foreign Relations During the Franklin D. Roosevelt Era.* Lanham, Md.: University Press of America, 1995.

——. *Roosevelt and the Isolationists, 1932–1945.* Lincoln: University of Nebraska Press, 1983.

Coulter, Matthew W. *The Senate Munitions Inquiry of the 1930s: Beyond the Merchants of Death.* Westport, Conn.: Greenwood, 1997.

Dallek, Robert A. *Franklin D. Roosevelt and American Foreign Policy, 1932–1945.* Rev. ed. New York: Oxford University Press, 1995.

Dickinson, Matthew J. *Bitter Harvest: FDR, Presidential Power, and the Growth of the Presidential Branch.* Cambridge: Cambridge University Press, 1997.

Doenecke, Justus D., and Mark Stoler. *Debating Franklin D. Roosevelt's Foreign Policies, 1933–1945.* Lanham, Md.: Rowman & Littlefield, 2005.

Feis, Herbert. *1933: Characters in Crisis.* Boston: Little, Brown, 1966.

Freidel, Frank. *Franklin D. Roosevelt: A Rendezvous with Destiny.* Boston: Little, Brown, 1990.

Gardner, Lloyd C. *Economic Aspects of New Deal Diplomacy.* Madison: University of Wisconsin Press, 1964.

Jablon, Howard. *Crossroads of Decision: The State Department and Foreign Policy 1933–1937.* Lexington: University Press of Kentucky, 1983.

Jonas, Manfred. *Isolationism in America, 1935–41.* Ithaca, N.Y.: Cornell University Press, 1966.

——. "The United States and the Failure of Collective Security in the 1930s." In *Twentieth-century American Foreign Policy,* ed. John Braeman, Robert H. Bremner, and David Brody. Columbus: Ohio State University Press, 1971.

Langer, William L., and S. Everett Gleason. *The Challenge to Isolation, 1937–40.* New York: Harper, 1952.

Marks, Frederick W. *Wind over Sand: the Diplomacy of Franklin Roosevelt.* Athens: University of Georgia Press, 1988.

Nevins, Allan. *The New Deal and World Affairs: A Chronicle of International Affairs, 1933–1945.* New Haven, Conn.: Yale University Press, 1950.

Offner, Arnold. *American Appeasement: United States Foreign Policy and Germany, 1933–1938.* Cambridge, Mass.: Harvard University Press, 1969.

———. "Appeasement Revisited; The United States, Britain, and Germany, 1933–1940." *Journal of American History* 64 (1977–78): 373–93.

Roberts, John W. *Putting Foreign Policy to Work: The Role of Organized Labor in American Foreign Relations, 1932–1941.* New York: Garland, 1995.

Schmitz, David F. *The Triumph of Internationalism: Franklin D. Roosevelt and a World in Crisis, 1933–1941.* Washington, D.C.: Potomac, 2007.

Schmitz, David F., and Richard D. Challener, eds. *Appeasement in Europe: A Reassessment of U.S. Policies.* New York: Greenwood, 1990.

Seheer, Arthur. "Louis Ludlow's War Referendum of 1938: A Reappraisal." *Mid-America* 76 (1994): 133–55.

Smith, Geoffrey S. *To Save a Nation: American Countersubversives, the New Deal, and the Coming of World War II.* Rev. ed. Chicago: Elephant, 1992.

Wiltz, John Edward. *In Search of Peace: The Senate Munitions Inquiry, 1934–36.* Baton Rouge: Louisiana State University Press, 1963.

U.S. RELATIONS WITH LATIN AMERICA AND THE CARIBBEAN

Adler, Selig. "Bryan and Wilsonian Caribbean Penetration." *Hispanic American Historical Review* 20 (1940): 198–226.

Becker, William H., and William M. McClenahan. *The Market, the State, and the Export-Import Bank of the United States, 1934–2000.* New York: Cambridge University Press, 2003.

Bemis, Samuel Flagg. *The Latin American Policy of the United States.* New York: Harcourt, Brace, 1943.

Benjamin, Jules R. "The Framework of U.S. Relations with Latin America in the Twentieth Century: An Interpretative Essay." *Diplomatic History* 11 (1987): 91–112.

———. *The United States and Cuba: Hegemony and Dependent Development, 1880–1934.* Pittsburgh, Penn.: University of Pittsburgh Press, 1977.

Berman, Karl. *Under the Big Stick: Nicaragua and the United States since 1848.* Boston: South End, 1986.

Bethell, Leslie, and Ian Roxborough, eds. *Latin America between the Second World War and the Cold War: Crisis and Containment, 1944–1948.* Cambridge: Cambridge University Press, 1992.

Calder, Bruce. *The Impact of Intervention: The Dominican Republic during the U.S. Occupation of 1916–24.* Austin: University of Texas Press, 1984.

Child, John. "From 'Color' to 'Rainbow': U.S. Strategic Planning for Latin America, 1919–1945." *Journal of Interamerican Studies and World Affairs* 21 (1979): 233–59.

Clements, Kendrick A. "Woodrow Wilson's Mexican Policy, 1913–1915." *Diplomatic History* 4 (1980): 113–36.

Coletta, Paolo E. "William Jennings Bryan and the United States–Colombia Impasse, 1903–1921." *Hispanic American Historical Review* 47 (1967): 486–501.

Curry, Earl R. *Hoover's Dominican Diplomacy and the Origins of the Good Neighbor Policy*. New York: Garland, 1979.

deConde, Alexander. *Herbert Hoover's Latin American Policy*. Stanford, Calif.: Stanford University Press, 1951.

Dosal, Paul. *Doing Business with the Dictators: A Political History of the United Fruit Company in Guatemala, 1899–1944*. Wilmington, Del.: Scholarly Resources, 1993.

Gellman, Irwin F. *Good Neighbor Diplomacy*. Baltimore, Md.: Johns Hopkins University Press, 1979.

——. *Roosevelt and Batista: Good Neighbor Diplomacy in Cuba, 1933–1945*. Albuquerque: University of New Mexico Press, 1973.

Gilderhus, Mark. *Pan-American Visions: Woodrow Wilson in the Western Hemisphere, 1913–1921*. Tucson: University of Arizona Press, 1986.

Grieb, Kenneth J. *The Latin American Policy of Warren G. Harding*. Fort Worth: Texas Christian University Press, 1976.

——. "Warren G. Harding and the Dominican Republic U.S. Withdrawal, 1921–1923." *Journal of Inter-American Studies* 11 (1969): 425–40.

Grow, Michael. *The Good Neighbor Policy and Authoritarianism in Paraguay: United States Economic Expansion and Great-Power Rivalry in Latin America during World War II*. Lawrence: Regents Press of Kansas, 1981.

Guerrant, E. O. *Roosevelt's Good Neighbor Policy*. Albuquerque: University of New Mexico Press, 1950.

Haines, Gerald K. "The Roosevelt Administration Interprets the Monroe Doctrine." *Australian Journal of Politics and History* 24 (1978): 332–45.

——. "Under the Eagle's Wings: The Franklin Roosevelt Administration Forges an American Hemisphere." *Diplomatic History* 1 (1977): 373–88.

Hall, Linda B. *Oil, Banks, and Politics: The United States and Postrevolutionary Mexico 1917–1924*. Austin: University of Texas Press, 1995.

Hanson, Gail. "Ordered Liberty: Sumner Welles and the Crowder–Welles Connection in the Caribbean." *Diplomatic History* 18 (1994): 311–32.

Harrison, Richard A. "A Neutralization Plan for the Pacific: Roosevelt and Anglo–American Cooperation, 1934–1937." *Pacific Historical Review* 57 (1988): 47–72.

Healy, David. *Drive to Hegemony: The United States in the Caribbean, 1898–1917.* Madison: University of Wisconsin Press, 1988.

Johnson, John J. *A Hemisphere Apart: The Foundations of United States Policy toward Latin America.* Baltimore, Md.: Johns Hopkins University Press, 1990.

Kamman, William. *A Search for Stability: United States Diplomacy toward Nicaragua, 1925–1933.* Notre Dame, Ind.: University of Notre Dame Press, 1968.

Kane, N. Stephen. "American Businessmen and Foreign Policy: The Recognition of Mexico, 1920–1923." *Political Science Quarterly* 90 (1975): 293–313.

Krenn, Michael L. *U.S. Policy toward Economic Nationalism in Latin America, 1917–1929.* Wilmington, Del.: Scholarly Resources, 1990.

LaFeber, W. *Inevitable Revolutions: The United States in Central America.* New York: Norton, 1983.

Langley, Lester. *The Banana Wars: An Inner History of American Empire, 1900–1934.* Lexington: University Press of Kentucky, 1985.

——. *Mexico and the United States: The Fragile Relationship.* Boston: Twayne, 1991.

McCann, Frank D. *The Brazilian–American Alliance 1937–1945.* Princeton, N.J.: Princeton University Press, 1974.

Munro, D. G. *The United States and the Caribbean Republics, 1921–1933.* Princeton, N.J.: Princeton University Press, 1974.

Perkins, Whitney T. *Constraint of Empire: The United States and Caribbean Interventions.* Oxford: Clio, 1981.

Pike, Frederick B. *FDR's Good Neighbor: Sixty Years of Generally Gentle Chaos.* Austin: University of Texas Press, 1995.

Pletcher, D. M. "United States Relations with Latin America: Neighborliness and Exploitation." *Hispanic American Historical Review* 82 (1977): 39–59.

Pope Atkins, G., and Larman C. Wilson. *The Dominican Republic and the United States: From Imperialism to Transnationalism.* Athens: University of Georgia Press, 1998.

Roorda, Eric Paul. *The Dictator Next Door: The Good Neighbor Policy and the Trujillo Regime in the Dominican Republic, 1930–1945.* Durham, N.C.: Duke University Press, 1998.

Salisbury, Richard V. *Anti-Imperialism and International Competition in Central America, 1920–1929.* Wilmington, Del.: Scholarly Resources, 1989.

Sater, William F. *Chile and the United States: Empires in Conflict.* Athens: University of Georgia Press, 1990.

Schmitz, David F. *Thank God They're on Our Side: The United States and Right-wing Dictatorships, 1921–1965.* Chapel Hill: University of North Carolina Press, 1999.

Smith, Joseph. *Unequal Giants: Diplomatic Relations between the United States and Brazil, 1889–1930.* Pittsburgh, Penn.: University of Pittsburgh Press, 1991.

Smith, Robert F. *The United States and Revolutionary Nationalism in Mexico, 1916–1932.* Chicago: University of Chicago Press, 1972.

Trani, Eugene P. "Harding Administration and Recognition of Mexico." *Ohio History* 75 (1966): 137–48.

Tulchin, Joseph S. *The Aftermath of War: World War I and U.S. Policy toward Latin America.* New York: New York University Press, 1971.

———. *Argentina and the United States: A Conflicted Relationship.* Boston: Twayne, 1990.

Vazquez, J. Z., and L. Meyer. *The United States and Mexico.* Chicago: University of Chicago Press, 1985.

Walker, William O., III. "Crucible for Peace: Herbert Hoover, Modernization, and Economic Growth in Latin America." *Diplomatic History* 30 (2006): 83–117.

Williams, William A. "Latin America: Laboratory of American Foreign Policy in the Nineteen-Twenties." *Inter-American Economic Affairs* 11 (1957): 3–30.

Woods, Randall Bennett. *The Roosevelt Foreign Policy Establishment and the Good Neighbor: The United States and Argentina, 1941–1945.* Lawrence: Regents Press of Kansas, 1979.

U.S. RELATIONS WITH ASIA

Bagby, Wesley M. *The Eagle-Dragon Alliance: America's Relations with China in World War II.* Newark: University of Delaware Press, 1992.

Borg, Dorothy. *The United States and the Far Eastern Crisis of 1933–1938.* Cambridge, Mass.: Harvard University Press, 1964.

Burns, Richard Dean, and E. M. Bennett, eds. *Diplomats in Crisis: United States–Chinese–Japanese Relations, 1919–1941.* Santa Barbara, Calif.: ABC-Clio, 1974.

Cohen, Warren I. *America's Response to China: A History of Sino–American Relations.* 4th ed. New York: Columbia University Press, 2000.

Craft, Stephen G. "John Bassett Moore, Robert Lansing, and the Shandong Question." *Pacific Historical Review* 66 (1997): 231–49.

Dingman, R. *Power in the Pacific: The Origins of the Naval Arms Limitation, 1914–1922.* Chicago: University of Chicago Press, 1976.

Esherick, Joseph W., ed. *Lost Chance in China: The World War II Dispatches of John S. Service.* New York: Random House, 1974.

Haight, John McVickar, Jr. "Franklin D. Roosevelt and a Naval Quarantine of Japan." *Pacific Historical Review* 40 (1971): 203–26.

Haines, Gerald K. "American Myopia and the Japanese Monroe Doctrine, 1931–41." *Prologue* 13 (1981): 101–14.

Herzstein, Robert E. *Henry R. Luce, Time, and the American Crusade in Asia.* New York: Cambridge University Press, 2005.

Hornbeck, Stanley K. *The Diplomacy of Frustration: The Manchurian Crisis of 1931–1933 as Revealed in the Papers of Stanley K. Hornbeck.* Comp. Justus D. Doenecke. Stanford, Calif.: Hoover Institution, 1981.

Iriye, Akira. *After Imperialism: The Search for a New Order in the Far East, 1921–1931.* Cambridge, Mass.: Harvard University Press, 1965.

———. *The Origins of the Second World War in Asia and the Pacific.* London: Longman, 1992.

———. *Power and Culture: The Japanese–American War, 1941–1945.* Cambridge, Mass.: Harvard University Press, 1981.

Iriye, Akira, and Warren I. Cohen, eds. *American, Chinese, and Japanese Perspectives on Wartime Asia, 1931–1949.* Wilmington, Del.: Scholarly Resources, 1990.

LaFeber, Walter. *The Clash: U.S.–Japanese Relations throughout History.* New York: Norton, 1997.

Linn, Brian McAllister. *Guardian of Empire: The U.S. Army and the Pacific, 1902–1940.* Chapel Hill: University of North Carolina Press, 1997.

Lytle, Mark H. *The Origins of the Iranian–American Alliance, 1941–1953.* New York: Holmes and Meier, 1987.

Miller, Edward S. *War Plan Orange: The U.S. Strategy to Defeat Japan, 1897–1945*. Annapolis, Md.: Naval Institute, 1991.

Papachristou, Judith. "Soviet–American Relations and the East-Asian Imbroglio, 1933–1941." In *Essays in Twentieth Century American Diplomatic History*, ed. C. L. Egan and A. W. Knott. Washington, D.C.: University Press of America, 1982.

Pugach, N. "American Friendship for China and the Shantung Question at the Washington Conference." *Journal of American History* 64 (1977–78): 67–86.

Sbrega, John J. *Anglo–American Relations and Colonialism in East Asia, 1941–1945*. New York: Garland, 1983.

Schaller, Michael. *The United States and China in the Twentieth Century*. Rev. ed. Oxford: Oxford University Press, 1990.

——. *The U.S. Crusade in China, 1938–1945*. New York: Columbia University Press, 1979.

Shizhang, Hu. *Stanley K. Hornbeck and the Open Door Policy, 1919–1937*. Westport, Conn.: Greenwood, 1995.

Spector, Ronald H. *Eagle against the Sun: The American War with Japan*. New York: Free Press, 1985.

Stilwell, Joseph. *The Stilwell Papers*. Ed. Theodore White. New York: Sloane, 1948.

Storry, R. *Japan and the Decline of the West in Asia, 1894–1943*. London: Macmillan, 1979.

Sun, You-Li. *China and the Origins of the Pacific War, 1931–1941*. New York: St. Martin's, 1993.

Thorne, Christopher. *The Limits of Foreign Policy: The West, the League, and the Far Eastern Crisis of 1931–1933*. London: Macmillan, 1972.

Tuchman, Barbara. *Stilwell and the American Experience in China, 1911–1945*. New York: Macmillan, 1971.

Van Alstyne, R. *The United States and East Asia*. London: Thames and Hudson, 1973.

Waldron, Arthur. *How the Peace Was Lost: The 1935 Memorandum—Developments Affecting American Policy in the Far East*. Stanford, Calif.: Hoover Institution, 1992.

Young, Arthur N. *China and the Helping Hand, 1937–1945*. Cambridge, Mass.: Harvard University Press, 1963.

Yu, Maochun. *OSS in China: Prelude to Cold War*. New Haven, Conn.: Yale University Press, 1997.

U.S. RELATIONS WITH EUROPE

Bailey, Fred Arthur. "A Virginia Scholar in Chancellor Hitler's Court: The Tragic Ambassadorship of William Edward Dodd." *Virginia Magazine of History and Biography* 100 (1992): 323–42.

Burke, Bernard V. *Ambassador Frederic Sackett and the Collapse of the Weimar Republic, 1930–1933: The United States and Hitler's Rise to Power.* New York: Cambridge University Press, 1994.

Clavin, Patricia M. *The Failure of Economic Diplomacy: Britain, Germany, France, and the USA, 1931–36.* New York: St. Martin's, 1996.

Cohrs, Patrick O. *The Unfinished Peace after World War I: America, Britain, and the Stabilisation of Europe, 1919–1939.* Cambridge: Cambridge University Press, 2006.

Costigliola, Frank. *Awkward Dominion: American Political, Economic, and Cultural Relations with Europe, 1919–1933.* Ithaca, N.Y.: Cornell University Press, 1984.

———. "The United States and the Reconstruction of Germany in the 1920s." *Business History Review* 50 (1976): 477–502.

Dayer, R. A. "The British War Debts to the United States and the Anglo–Japanese Alliance, 1920–23." *Pacific Historical Review* 45 (1976): 569–95.

Dobson, Alan P. *Anglo–American Relations in the Twentieth Century.* London: Routledge, 1995.

Harper, John Lamberton. *American Visions of Europe: Franklin D. Roosevelt, George F. Kennan, and Dean G. Acheson.* Cambridge: Cambridge University Press, 1994.

Harrison, R. A. "A Presidential Demarche: Franklin D. Roosevelt's Personal Diplomacy and Great Britain, 1936–37." *Diplomatic History* 5 (1981): 245–72.

Hogan, Michael J. *Informal Entente: The Private Structure of Cooperation in Anglo–American Economic Diplomacy, 1918–1928.* Chicago: Imprint, 1991.

Hurstfield, Julian G. *America and the French Nation, 1939–1945.* Chapel Hill: University of North Carolina Press, 1986.

Jonas, Manfred. *The United States and Germany: A Diplomatic History.* Ithaca, N.Y.: Cornell University Press, 1984.

Leffler, Melvyn P. "American Policy Making and European Stability, 1921–33." *Pacific Historical Review* 46 (1977): 207–28.

——. "Political Isolationism, Economic Expansionism, or Diplomatic Realism: American Policy toward Western Europe 1921–1933." *Perspectives in American History* 8 (1974): 413–61.

Little, Douglas. *Malevolent Neutrality: The United States, Great Britain, and the Origins of the Spanish Civil War.* Ithaca, N.Y.: Cornell University Press, 1985.

Louis, William Roger. *Imperialism at Bay: The United States and the Decolonization of the British Empire.* Oxford: Oxford University Press, 1977.

MacDonald, C. *The United States, Britain, and Appeasement 1936–1939.* London: Macmillan, 1981.

Marks, S. *The Illusions of Peace: International Relations in Europe, 1918–33.* London: Macmillan, 1976.

McKercher, Brian J. C., ed. *Anglo–American Relations in the 1920s: The Struggle for Supremacy.* London: Macmillan, 1991.

——. "'Our Most Dangerous Enemy': Great Britain Pre-eminent in the 1930s." *International History Review* 13 (1991): 751–83.

McNeil, William C. *American Money and the Weimar Republic: Economics and Politics on the Eve of the Great Depression.* New York: Columbia University Press, 1986.

Miller, James E. *The United States and Italy, 1940–1950: The Politics and Diplomacy of Stabilization.* Chapel Hill: University of North Carolina Press, 1986.

Moser, John E. *Twisting the Lion's Tail: American Anglophobia between the World Wars.* New York: New York University Press, 1999.

Offner, Arnold. "Appeasement Revisited: The United States, Great Britain, and Germany, 1933–1940." *Journal of American History* 64 (1977–78): 373–93.

——. "Influence without Responsibility: American Statecraft and the Munich Conference." In *Appeasing Fascism: Articles from the Wayne State University Conference on Munich after Fifty Years*, ed. Melvin Small and O. Feinstein. Lanham, Md.: University Press of America, 1991.

Orde, Anne. *The Eclipse of Great Britain: The United States and British Imperial Decline, 1895–1956.* New York: St. Martin's, 1996.

Reynolds, David, and David Dimbleby. *An Ocean Apart: The Relationship between Britain and America in the Twentieth Century.* New York: Random House, 1988.

Roskill, Stephen. *Naval Policy between the Wars: The Period of Anglo–American Antagonism, 1919–1929.* London: Collins, 1968.

Rossi, Mario. *Roosevelt and the French*. Westport, Conn.: Praeger, 1993.

Schmitz, David F. *The United States and Fascist Italy, 1922–1940*. Chapel Hill: University of North Carolina Press, 1988.

Schmitz, David F., and Richard D. Challener, eds. *Appeasement in Europe: A Reassessment of U.S. Policies*. Westport, Conn.: Greenwood, 1990.

Traina, Richard P. *American Diplomacy and the Spanish Civil War*. Bloomington: Indiana University Press, 1968.

van Everen, Brooks. "Franklin D. Roosevelt and the Problem of Nazi Germany." In *Essays in Twentieth Century Diplomatic History*, ed. C. Egan, and A. Knott. Washington, D.C.: University Press of America, 1982.

Wandycz, Piotr S. *The United States and Poland*. Cambridge, Mass.: Harvard University Press, 1980.

Wittner, Lawrence S. *American Intervention in Greece 1943–1949*. New York: Columbia University Press, 1982.

U.S. RELATIONS WITH RUSSIA AND THE UNION OF SOVIET SOCIALIST REPUBLICS

Bennett, Edward. *Franklin D. Roosevelt and the Search for Security: American–Soviet Relations, 1933–1939*. Wilmington, Del.: Scholarly Resources, 1985.

———. *Franklin D. Roosevelt and the Search for Victory: American–Soviet Relations, 1939–1945*. Wilmington, Del.: Scholarly Resources, 1990.

———. *Recognition of Russia: An American Foreign Policy Dilemma*. Waltham, Mass.: Blaisdell, 1970.

Boyle, Peter. *American–Soviet Relations: From the Russian Revolution to the Fall of Communism*. London: Routledge, 1993.

Deane, John. *The Strange Alliance: The Story of Our Wartime Efforts at Collaboration with Russia*. New York: Viking, 1947.

De Santis, Hugh. *The Diplomacy of Silence: The American Foreign Service, the Soviet Union, and the Cold War, 1933–1947*. Chicago: Chicago University Press, 1980.

Farnsworth, Beatrice. *William C. Bullitt and the Soviet Union*. Bloomington: Indiana University Press, 1972.

Filene, Peter G. *Americans and the Soviet Experiment, 1917–1933*. Cambridge, Mass.: Harvard University Press, 1967.

Herring, George C. *Aid to Russia, 1941–1946: Strategy, Diplomacy, and the Origins of the Cold War*. New York: Columbia University Press, 1973.

Hoff Wilson, Joan. *Ideology and Economics: United States Relations with the Soviet Union, 1918–33*. Columbia: University of Missouri Press, 1974.

Kennan, George F. *Russia and the West under Lenin and Stalin*. London: Hutchinson, 1961.

Levering, Ralph B. *American Opinion and the Russian Alliance, 1939–1945*. Chapel Hill: University of North Carolina Press, 1976.

Little, Douglas. "Antibolshevism and American Foreign Policy, 1919–1939: The Diplomacy of Self-Delusion." *American Quarterly* 35 (1983–84): 376–90.

MacLean, Elizabeth Kimball. *Joseph E. Davies: Envoy to the Soviets*. Westport, Conn.: Praeger, 1992.

Maddux, T. R. "Watching Stalin Maneuver between Hitler and the West: American Diplomats and Soviet Diplomacy, 1934–39." *Diplomatic History* 1 (1977): 140–54.

Mayers, David. "Ambassador Joseph Davies Reconsidered." *Society for Historians of American Foreign Relations Newsletter* 23 (1992): 1–16.

———. *The Ambassadors and America's Soviet Policy*. New York: Oxford University Press, 1995.

Morris, M. Wayne. *Stalin's Famine and Roosevelt's Recognition of Russia*. Lanham, Md.: University Press of America, 1994.

Propas, Frederic. "Creating a Hard Line toward Russia: The Training of State Department Soviet Experts, 1927–1937." *Diplomatic History* 8 (1984): 209–26.

Smith, Walter Bedell. *My Three Years in Moscow*. Philadelphia, Penn.: Lippincott, 1950.

van Tuyll, Hubert P. *Feeding the Bear: American Aid to the Soviet Union, 1941–1945*. Westport, Conn.: Greenwood, 1989.

Westad, Arne. *Cold War and Revolution: Soviet–American Rivalry and the Origins of the Chinese Civil War, 1944–1946*. New York: Columbia University Press, 1993.

ROAD TO WORLD WAR II

Bailey, Thomas A., and Paul B. Ryan. *Hitler vs. Roosevelt: The Undeclared Naval War*. New York: Free Press, 1979.

Beach, Edward L. *Scapegoats: A Defense of Kimmel and Short at Pearl Harbor*. Annapolis, Md.: Naval Institute, 1995.

Beard, Charles A. *President Roosevelt and the Coming of the War, 1941: A Study in Appearances and Realities.* New Haven, Conn.: Yale University Press, 1948.

Borg, Dorothy, and Shumpei Okamoto, eds. *Pearl Harbor as History: Japanese–American Relations, 1931–1941.* New York: Columbia University Press, 1973.

Brune, Lester H. "Considerations of Force in Cordell Hull's Diplomacy, July 26 to November 26 1941." *Diplomatic History* 2 (1978): 389–406.

Butow, R. J. C. "Backdoor Diplomacy in the Pacific." *Journal of American History* 59 (1972): 48–72.

Chadwin, Mark L. *The War Hawks of World War II.* Chapel Hill: University of North Carolina Press, 1968.

Clausen, Henry C., and Bruce Lee. *Pearl Harbor: Final Judgement.* New York: Crown, 1992.

Cole, Wayne S. *America First: The Battle against Intervention 1940–1941.* Madison: University of Wisconsin Press, 1953.

Compton, James V. *The Swastika and the Eagle: Hitler, the United States, and the Origins of World War II.* Boston: Houghton Mifflin, 1967.

Conroy, Hilary, and Harry Wray, eds. *Pearl Harbor Reexamined: Prologue to the Pacific War.* Honolulu: University of Hawaii Press, 1990.

Divine, Robert A. *The Reluctant Belligerent: American Entry into World War II.* New York: Wiley, 1979.

Doenecke, Justus D. "Non-Intervention of the Left: The Keep America out of the War Congress, 1938–41." *Journal of Contemporary History* 12 (1977): 221–36.

———. *Storm on the Horizon: The Challenges to American Intervention 1939–41.* Lanham, Md.: Rowman & Littlefield, 2000.

———. "U.S. Policy and the European War, 1939–1941." *Diplomatic History* 19 (1995): 669–98.

———, ed. *In Danger Undaunted: The Anti-interventionist Movement of 1940–1941 as Revealed in the Papers of the America First Committee.* Stanford, Calif.: Hoover Institution, 1990.

Doenecke, Justus D., and John E. Wiltz. *From Isolation to War, 1931–1941.* 2nd ed. Wheeling, Ill.: Harlan Davidson, 1991.

Drummond, Donald F. *The Passing of American Neutrality, 1937–1941.* Ann Arbor: University of Michigan Press, 1955.

Farnham, Barbara Rearden. *Roosevelt and the Munich Crisis: A Study of Political Decision-Making.* Princeton, N.J.: Princeton University Press, 1997.

Feis, Herbert. *The Road to Pearl Harbor: The Coming of War between the United States and Japan*. Princeton, N.J.: Princeton University Press, 1950.

Friedlander, Saul. *Prelude to Downfall: Hitler and the United States 1939–1941*. London: Chatto and Windus, 1967.

Haglund, D. "George C. Marshall and the Question of Military Aid to England, May–June 1940." *Journal of Contemporary History* 15 (1980): 745–60.

Hearden, Patrick. *Roosevelt Confronts Hitler: America's Entry into World War II*. DeKalb: North Illinois University Press, 1986.

Heinrichs, Waldo L. "President Franklin D. Roosevelt's Intervention in the Battle of the Atlantic, 1941." *Diplomatic History* 10 (1986): 311–32.

———. *Threshold of War: Franklin D. Roosevelt and American Entry into World War II*. Oxford: Oxford University Press, 1988.

Herzstein, Robert E. *Roosevelt and Hitler: Prelude to War*. New York: Paragon House, 1989.

Keiichiro, Komatsu. *Origins of the Pacific War and the Importance of Magic*. New York: St. Martin's, 1999.

Kimball, Warren F., and Bruce Bartlett. "Roosevelt and Prewar Commitments to Churchill: The Tyler Kent Affair." *Diplomatic History* 5 (1981): 291–311.

Kinsella, William E. *Leadership in Isolation: FDR and the Origins of the Second World War*. Boston: G. K. Hall, 1978.

Kirkpatrick, Charles E. *An Unknown Future and a Doubtful Present: Writing the Victory Plan in 1941*. Washington, D.C.: U.S. Army, Center of Military History, 1990.

Langer, William L., and S. Everett Gleason. *The Undeclared War, 1940–41*. New York: Harper, 1953.

Love, Robert W., ed. *Pearl Harbor Revisited*. New York: St. Martin's, 1994.

Lowenthal, Mark M. "Roosevelt and the Coming of the War: The Search for United States Policy 1937–42." *Journal of Contemporary History* 16 (1981): 413–40.

McEnaney, Laura. "He-Men and Christian Mothers: The America First Movement and the Gendered Meanings of Patriotism and Isolationism." *Diplomatic History* 18 (1994): 47–57.

Moser, John E. "'Gigantic Engines of Propaganda': The 1941 Senate Investigation of Hollywood." *Historian* 63 (2001): 731–51.

Offner, Arnold A. *The Origins of the Second World War: American Foreign Policy and World Politics, 1917–1941.* New York: Praeger, 1975.

———, ed. *America and the Origins of World War II.* Boston: Houghton Mifflin, 1971.

Prange, Gordon W. *At Dawn We Slept: The Untold Story of Pearl Harbor.* New York: McGraw-Hill, 1981.

———. *Pearl Harbor: The Verdict of History.* New York: McGraw-Hill, 1986.

Reynolds, David. *The Creation of the Anglo-American Alliance, 1937–41.* Chapel Hill: University of North Carolina Press, 1981.

———. *From Munich to Pearl Harbor: Roosevelt's America and the Origins of the Second World War.* Chicago: Ivan R. Dee, 2001.

Rusbridger, James, and Eric Nave. *Betrayal at Pearl Harbor: How Churchill Lured Roosevelt into World War II.* New York: Summit, 1991.

Russett, Bruce M. *No Clear and Present Danger: A Skeptical View of the U.S. Entry into World War II.* New York: Harper, 1972.

Smith, Geoffrey S. "Isolationism, the Devil, and the Advent of the Second World War: Variations on a Theme." *International History Review* 4 (1982): 55–89.

Steele, Richard W. "The Great Debate: Roosevelt, the Media, and the Coming of the War, 1940–1941." *Journal of American History* 71 (1984): 69–82.

Stinnett, Robert B. *Day of Deceit: The Truth about Pearl Harbor.* New York: Touchstone, 2000.

Tansill, Charles C. *America Goes to War.* Boston: Little, Brown, 1938.

———. *Back Door to War: The Roosevelt Foreign Policy, 1933–1941.* Westport, Conn.: Greenwood, 1952.

Toland, John. *Infamy: Pearl Harbor and Its Aftermath.* Garden City, N.Y.: Doubleday, 1982.

Utley, Jonathan G. *Going to War with Japan, 1937–1941.* Knoxville: University of Tennessee Press, 1985.

Weinberg, Gerhard. "Why Hitler Declared War on the United States." *MHQ: The Quarterly Journal of Military History* 4 (1992): 18–23.

Willmott, H. P. *Pearl Harbor.* New York: Cassell, 2001.

Wohlstetter, Roberta. *Pearl Harbor: Warning and Decision.* Stanford, Calif.: Stanford University Press, 1962.

WORLD WAR II: STRATEGIC DIPLOMACY AND POLITICS

Costello, John. *The Pacific War.* New York: Rawston, Wade, 1983.

Cowley, Robert, ed. *No End Save Victory: Perspectives on World War II.* New York: Putnam, 2001.

Dower, John W. *War without Mercy; Race and Power in the Pacific War.* New York: Pantheon, 1986.

Drea, Edward J. *MacArthur's Ultra: Codebreaking and the War against Japan, 1942–1945.* Lawrence: University Press of Kansas, 1992.

Eisenhower, Dwight D. *Crusade in Europe.* New York: Doubleday, 1948.

Greenfield, Kent R. *American Strategy in World War II: A Reconsideration.* Baltimore, Md.: Johns Hopkins University Press, 1963.

Higgins, Trumbull. *Soft Underbelly: The Anglo–American Controversy over the Italian Campaign, 1939–1945.* New York: Macmillan, 1968.

Hooks, George. *Forging the Military-Industrial Complex: World War II's Battle of the Potomac.* Urbana: University of Illinois Press, 1991.

Hoyt, Edwin P. *Japan's War: The Great Pacific Conflict.* New York: Da Capo, 1986.

James, D. Clayton, and Anne S. Wells. *From Pearl Harbor to V-Day: The American Armed Forces in World War II.* Chicago: Ivan R. Dee, 1995.

———. *A Time for Giants: Politics of the American High Command in World War II.* New York: Franklin Watts, 1987.

Larrabee, Eric. *Commander-in-Chief: Franklin Delano Roosevelt, His Lieutenants, and Their War.* New York: Simon and Schuster, 1987.

Leighton, R. "Overlord Revisited: An Interpretation of American Strategy in the European War, 1942–1944." *American Historical Review* 68 (1963): 919–37.

Lewin, Ronald. *The American Magic: Codes, Ciphers, and the Defeat of Japan.* New York: Farrar, Straus and Giroux, 1982.

Overy, Richard. *Why the Allies Won.* New York: Norton, 1995.

Parrish, Thomas. *The Ultra Americans: The U.S. Role in Breaking the Nazi Codes.* New York: Stein and Day, 1986.

Prange, Gordon W. *Miracle at Midway.* New York: McGraw-Hill, 1982.

Rose, Lisle A. *Dubious Victory: The United States and the End of World War II.* Kent, Ohio: Kent State University Press, 1973.

Sainsbury, Keith. "'Second Front in 1942': A Strategic Controversy Revisited." *British Journal of International Studies* 4 (1978): 47–58.

Schaffer, Ronald. *Wings of Judgment: American Bombing in World War II.* New York: Oxford University Press, 1985.

Sherry, Michael. *Preparing for the Next War: American Plans for Postwar Defense, 1941–45.* New Haven, Conn.: Yale University Press, 1977.

———. *The Rise of American Air Power: The Creation of Armageddon.* New Haven, Conn.: Yale University Press, 1987.

Sigal, Leon V. *Fighting to a Finish: The Politics of War Termination in the United States and Japan.* Ithaca, N.Y.: Cornell University Press, 1988.

Smith, Bradley F. *The Shadow Warriors: OSS and the Origins of the CIA.* New York: Basic, 1983.

Stoler, Mark. "The 'Pacific-First' Alternative in American World War II Strategy." *International History Review* 2 (1980): 432–52.

van der Vat, Dan. *The Pacific Campaign in World War II: The U.S.–Japanese Naval War, 1941–1945.* London: Hodder and Stoughton, 1992.

Weinberg, Gerhard L. *A World at Arms: A Global History of World War II.* Cambridge: Cambridge University Press, 1994.

Weingarten, Stephen, ed. *The Greatest Thing We Have Ever Attempted: Historical Perspectives on the Normandy Campaign.* Wheaton, Ill.: Cantigny, 1998.

WORLD WAR II: SIGNIFICANT ISSUES IN DOMESTIC POLITICS

Blum, John M. *V Was for Victory: Politics and American Culture during World War II.* New York: Harcourt Brace Jovanovich, 1976.

Brinkley, David. *Washington Goes to War.* New York: Knopf, 1987.

Burns, James McGregor. *Roosevelt: The Soldier of Freedom.* New York: Harcourt Brace Jovanovich, 1970.

Cashman, Sean D. *America, Roosevelt, and World War II.* New York: New York University Press, 1989.

Folly, Martin H. *The United States and World War II: The Awakening Giant.* Edinburgh: Edinburgh University Press, 2002.

Gellman, Irwin F. *Secret Affairs: Franklin Roosevelt, Cordell Hull, and Sumner Welles.* Baltimore, Md.: Johns Hopkins University Press, 1995.

Hess, Gary R. *The United States at War, 1941–1945.* 2nd ed. Wheeling, Ill.: Harlan Davidson, 2000.

Leigh, Michael. *Mobilizing Consent: Public Opinion and American Foreign Policy, 1937–1947.* Westport, Conn.: Greenwood, 1976.

Levine, Ellen. *A Fence away from Freedom: Japanese Americans and World War II*. New York: Putnam, 1995.

MacDonnell, Francis. *Insidious Foes: The Axis Fifth Column and the American Home Front*. New York: Oxford University Press, 1995.

O'Neill, William L. *A Democracy at War: America's Fight at Home and Abroad in World War II*. New York: Free Press, 1993.

Steele, Richard W. "American Popular Opinion and the War against Germany: The Issue of Negotiated Peace, 1942." *Journal of American History* 65 (1978): 704–23.

Stoler, Mark. *Allies and Adversaries: The Joint Chiefs of Staff, the Grand Alliance, and U.S. Strategy in World War II*. Chapel Hill: University of North Carolina Press, 2000.

——. *The Politics of the Second Front: American Military Planning and Diplomacy in Coalition Warfare, 1941–43*. Westport, Conn.: Greenwood, 1977.

Vatter, Harold G. *The U.S. Economy in World War II*. New York: Columbia University Press, 1985.

Winkler, Allan M. *The Politics of Propaganda: The Office of War Information, 1942–1945*. New Haven, Conn.: Yale University Press, 1978.

Young, Roland A. *Congressional Politics in the Second World War*. New York: Columbia University Press, 1956.

WORLD WAR II: POLITICAL DIPLOMACY

Aglion, Raoul. *Roosevelt and De Gaulle: A Personal Memoir of Allies in Conflict*. New York: Free Press, 1988.

Armstrong, Anne. *Unconditional Surrender: The Impact of the Casablanca Policy on World War II*. New Brunswick, N.J.: Rutgers University Press, 1961.

Beitzell, Robert. *The Uneasy Alliance: America, Britain, and Russia, 1941–1943*. New York: Knopf, 1972.

Bercuson, David J., and Holger H. Herwig. *One Christmas in Washington: The Secret Meeting between Roosevelt and Churchill That Changed the World*. New York: Overlook, 2005.

Berthon, Simon. *Allies at War: The Bitter Rivalry among Churchill, Roosevelt, and De Gaulle*. New York: Carroll and Graf, 2001.

Brinkley, Douglas, and David R. Facey-Crowther, eds. *The Atlantic Charter*. New York: St. Martin's, 1994.

Buckley, Thomas H., and Edwin B. Strong. *American Foreign and National Security Policies, 1941–1945.* Knoxville: University of Tennessee Press, 1988.

Buhite, Russell D. *Decision at Yalta: An Appraisal of Summit Diplomacy.* Wilmington, Del.: Scholarly Resources, 1986.

Casey, Steven. *Cautious Crusade: Franklin D. Roosevelt, American Public Opinion, and the War against Nazi Germany.* New York: Oxford University Press, 2002.

Chalou, George C., ed. *The Secrets War: The Office of Strategic Services in World War II.* Washington, D.C.: National Archives and Records Administration, 1992.

Clemens, Diane S. *Yalta.* New York: Oxford University Press, 1970.

Cull, Nicholas J. *Selling War: The British Propaganda Campaign against American "Neutrality" in World War II.* New York: Oxford University Press, 1995.

Dietrich, John. *The Morgenthau Plan: Soviet Influence on American Postwar Policy.* New York: Algora, 2002.

Divine, Robert A. *Roosevelt and World War II.* Baltimore, Md.: Johns Hopkins University Press, 1969.

Dunn, Dennis J. *Caught between Roosevelt and Stalin: America's Ambassadors to Moscow.* Lexington: University Press of Kentucky, 1998.

Edmonds, Robin. *The Big Three: Churchill, Roosevelt, and Stalin in Peace and War.* New York: Norton, 1991.

Eubank, Keith. *Summit at Teheran.* New York: Morrow, 1985.

Feingold, Henry. *Bearing Witness: How America and Its Jews Responded to the Holocaust.* Syracuse, N.Y.: Syracuse University Press, 1995.

Feis, Herbert. *Churchill, Roosevelt, Stalin: The War They Waged and the Peace They Sought.* Princeton, N.J.: Princeton University Press, 1957.

Ferrell, Robert H. *Harry S. Truman and the Cold War Revisionists.* Columbia: University of Missouri Press, 2006.

Gaddis, John L. *The United States and the Origins of the Cold War, 1941–47.* New York: Columbia University Press, 1972.

Gardner, Lloyd C. *Architects of Illusion: Men and Ideas in American Foreign Policy, 1941–1949.* Chicago: Quadrangle, 1970.

———. *Spheres of Influence: The Great Powers Partition Europe—From Munich to Yalta.* Chicago: Ivan R. Dee 1993.

Glantz, Mary E. *FDR and the Soviet Union: The President's Battles over Foreign Policy.* Lawrence: University Press of Kansas, 2005.

Gormly, J. *The Collapse of the Grand Alliance, 1945–1948*. Baton Rouge: Louisiana State University Press, 1987.

Harper, J. L. *American Visions of Europe: Franklin D. Roosevelt, George F. Kennan, and Dean G. Acheson*. Cambridge: Cambridge University Press, 1994.

Hart, Justin. "Making Democracy Safe for the World: Race, Propaganda, and the Transformation of U.S. Foreign Policy during World War II." *Pacific Historical Review* 73 (2004): 49–84.

Hildebrand, Robert C. *Dumbarton Oaks: The Origins of the United Nations and the Search for Postwar Security*. Chapel Hill: University of North Carolina Press, 1990.

Hindley, Meredith. "The Strategy of Rescue and Relief: The Use of OSS Intelligence by the War Refugee Board in Sweden, 1944–45." *Intelligence and National Security* 12 (1997): 145–65.

Kimball, Warren F. *Forged in War: Roosevelt, Churchill, and the Second World War*. New York: Morrow, 1997.

——. *The Juggler: Franklin Roosevelt as Wartime Statesman*. Princeton, N.J.: Princeton University Press, 1991.

——. *The Most Unsordid Act: Lend-Lease, 1939–1941*. Baltimore, Md.: Johns Hopkins University Press, 1969.

Kolko, Gabriel. *The Politics of War: The World and United States Foreign Policy, 1943–1945*. Rev. ed. New York: Random House, 1990.

Lacey, M. J., ed. *The Truman Presidency*. Cambridge: Cambridge University Press, 1989.

LaFeber, Walter. *America, Russia, and the Cold War, 1945–2002*. 9th ed. Boston: McGraw-Hill, 2004.

Lane, Ann, ed. *The Rise and Fall of the Grand Alliance, 1941–45*. London: Macmillan, 1995.

Langer, William L. *Our Vichy Gamble*. New York: Knopf, 1947.

Leffler, Melvyn P. *The Specter of Communism: The United States and the Origins of the Cold War, 1917–53*. New York: Hill and Wang, 1994.

Mark, Eduard. "American Policy toward Eastern Europe and the Origins of the Cold War, 1941–46: An Alternative Interpretation." *Journal of American History* 68 (1981): 313–36.

——. "'Today Has Been a Historical One': Harry S. Truman's Diary of the Potsdam Conference." *Diplomatic History* 4 (1980): 317–26.

Marrus, Michael R. *The Holocaust in History*. Hanover, N.H.: University Press of New England, 1987.

Mayers, David. "Nazi Germany and the Future of Europe: George Kennan's Views 1939–45." *International History Review* 8 (1986): 550–72.

Mayle, Paul. *The Eureka Summit*. Newark: University of Delaware Press, 1987.

McNeill, William H. *America, Britain, and Russia: Their Cooperation and Conflict, 1941–1946*. Oxford: Oxford University Press, 1953.

Mee, Charles L. *Meeting at Potsdam*. London: Deutsch, 1975.

Messer, Robert L. *The End of an Alliance: James F. Byrnes, Roosevelt, Truman, and the Origins of the Cold War*. Chapel Hill: University of North Carolina Press, 1982.

Miner, Steven M. *Between Churchill and Stalin: The Soviet Union, Great Britain, and the Origins of the Grand Alliance*. Chapel Hill: University of North Carolina Press, 1988.

Newton, Verne, ed. *FDR and the Holocaust*. New York: St. Martin's, 1995.

Perlmutter, Amos. *FDR and Stalin: A Not So Grand Alliance 1943–1945*. Columbia: University of Missouri Press, 1993.

Reynolds, David. "Competitive Cooperation: Anglo–American Relations in World War Two." *Historical Journal* 23 (1980): 233–45.

———. "Roosevelt, the British Left, and the Appointment of John G. Winant as United States Ambassador to Britain in 1941." *International History Review* 4 (1982): 393–413.

Sainsbury, Keith. *Churchill and Roosevelt at War: The War They Fought and the Peace They Hoped to Make*. New York: New York University Press, 1994.

———. *The Turning Point: Roosevelt, Stalin, Churchill, and Chiang Kai-shek, 1943—The Moscow, Cairo, and Tehran Conferences*. Oxford: Oxford University Press, 1985.

Shogan, Robert. *Hard Bargain: How FDR Twisted Churchill's Arm, Evaded the Law, and Changed the Role of the American Presidency*. New York: Scribner, 1995.

Smith, Bradley F. *Sharing Secrets with Stalin: How the Allies Traded Intelligence, 1941–1945*. Lawrence: University Press of Kansas, 1996.

———. *The Ultra–Magic Deals and the Most Special Relationship, 1940–1946*. Novato, Calif.: Presidio, 1993.

Smith, Gaddis. *American Diplomacy during the Second World War 1941–1945*. 2nd ed. New York: Knopf, 1985.

Stoler, Mark. *Allies in War: Britain and America against the Axis Powers 1940–1945*. New York: Oxford University Press, 2005.

Thorne, Christopher. *Allies of a Kind: The United States, Britain, and the War against Japan, 1941–1945*. Oxford: Oxford University Press, 1978.

Tillapaugh, J. "Closed Hemisphere and Open World? The Dispute over Regional Security at the U.N. Conference 1945." *Diplomatic History* 2 (1978): 25–42.

Weiss, Steve. *Allies in Conflict: Anglo–American Strategic Negotiations, 1938–1944.* New York: St. Martin's, 1996.

Wilson, Theodore A. *The First Summit: Roosevelt and Churchill at Placentia Bay 1941.* Rev. ed. Lawrence: University Press of Kansas, 1991.

Woods, Randall Bennett. *A Changing of the Guard: Anglo–American Relations, 1941–1946.* Chapel Hill: University of North Carolina Press, 1990.

Wyman, David S. *The Abandonment of the Jews.* New York: Pantheon, 1984.

Yergin, Daniel. *Shattered Peace: The Origins of the Cold War and the National Security State.* Rev. ed. Harmondsworth, England: Penguin, 1990.

ATOMIC BOMB

Allen, Thomas B. *Code-named Downfall: The Secret Plan to Invade Japan and Why Truman Dropped the Bomb.* New York: Simon and Schuster, 1995.

Alperovitz, Gar. *Atomic Diplomacy: Hiroshima and Potsdam, the Use of the Atomic Bomb, and the American Confrontation with Soviet Power.* Rev. ed. London: Pluto, 1994.

———. *The Decision to Use the Atomic Bomb and the Architecture of an American Myth.* New York: Knopf, 1995.

Bernstein, Barton J. "The Alarming Japanese Buildup on Southern Kyushu, Growing U.S. Fears, and Counterfactual Analysis: Would the Planned November 1945 Invasion of Southern Kyushu Have Occurred?" *Pacific Historical Review* 68 (1999): 561–609.

———. "The Challenges and Dangers of Nuclear Weapons: Foreign Policy and Strategy, 1941." *Maryland Historian* 9 (1978): 73–99.

———. "The Perils and Politics of Surrender: Ending the War with Japan and Avoiding the Third Atomic Bomb." *Pacific Historical Review* 46 (1977): 1–27.

———. "The Quest for Security: American Foreign Policy and International Control of Atomic Energy 1942–46." *Journal of American History* 60 (1974): 1003–44.

———. "Reconsidering the 'Atomic General': Leslie R. Groves." *Journal of Military History* 67 (2003): 883–920.

———. "Roosevelt, Truman, and the Atomic Bomb: A Reinterpretation." *Political Science Quarterly* 90 (1975): 23–69.

———. "Seizing the Contested Terrain of Early Nuclear History: Stimson, Conant, and Their Allies Explain the Decision to Use the Atomic Bomb." *Diplomatic History* 17 (1993): 35–72.

———. "Understanding the Atomic Bomb and the Japanese Surrender: Missed Opportunities, Little-Known Near Disasters, and Modern History." *Diplomatic History* 19 (1995): 227–73.

Feifer, George. *Tennozan: The Battle of Okinawa and the Atomic Bomb.* New York: Houghton Mifflin, 1992.

Fussell, Paul. *Thank God for the Atom Bomb and Other Essays.* New York: Summit, 1988.

Hersey, John. *Hiroshima.* New York: Knopf, 1946.

Hogan, Michael, ed. *Hiroshima in History and Memory.* Cambridge: Cambridge University Press, 1996.

Kurzman, Dan. *Day of the Bomb: Countdown to Hiroshima.* New York: McGraw-Hill, 1986.

Lifschultz, Lawrence, and Kai Bird. *Hiroshima's Shadow: Writings on the Denial of History and the Smithsonian Controversy.* Stony Creek, Conn.: Pamphleteer's, 1998.

Maddox, Robert J., ed. *Hiroshima in History: The Myths of Revisionism.* Columbia: University of Missouri Press, 2007.

Newman, R. P. "Hiroshima and the Trashing of Henry Stimson." *New England Quarterly* 71 (1998): 5–32.

Rhodes, Richard. *The Making of the Atomic Bomb.* New York: Simon and Schuster, 1986.

Sherwin, Martin J. *A World Destroyed: Hiroshima and the Origins of the Arms Race.* Rev. ed. New York: Random House, 1987.

Takaki, Ronald. *Hiroshima: Why America Dropped the Bomb.* Boston: Little, Brown, 1995.

Wainstock, Dennis D. *The Decision to Drop the Atomic Bomb.* Westport, Conn.: Praeger, 1996.

Walker, J. Samuel. *Prompt and Utter Destruction: Truman and the Use of Atomic Bombs against Japan.* Chapel Hill: University of North Carolina Press, 1997.

BIOGRAPHIES, DIARIES, MEMOIRS, AND AUTOBIOGRAPHIES

Abramson, Rudy. *Spanning the Century: The Life of W. Averell Harriman.* New York: Morrow, 1992.

Acheson, Dean. *Present at the Creation: My Years in the State Department.* New York: Norton, 1969.

Ambrose, Stephen. *Eisenhower.* Vol. 1. New York: Simon and Schuster, 1983.

Bacevich, Andrew J. *Diplomat in Khaki: Major General Frank Ross McCoy and American Foreign Policy, 1898–1949.* Lawrence: University Press of Kansas, 1989.

Berg, A. Scott. *Lindbergh.* New York: G. P. Putnam, 1998.

Berle, Adolf A. *Navigating the Rapids, 1918–1971: From the Papers of Adolf A. Berle.* Ed. Beatrice Bishop Berle and Travis Beal Jacobs. New York: Harcourt Brace Jovanovich, 1973.

Blum, John M., ed. *From the Morgenthau Diaries: Years of War, 1941–1945.* Boston: Houghton Mifflin, 1967.

———, ed. *The Price of Vision: The Diary of Henry A. Wallace, 1942–1946.* Boston: Houghton Mifflin, 1973.

Bohlen, Charles E. *Witness to History, 1929–1969.* New York: Norton, 1973.

Braden, Spruille. *Diplomats and Demagogues: The Memoirs of Spruille Braden.* New Rochelle, N.Y.: Arlington House, 1971.

Brands, H. W. *Inside the Cold War: Loy Henderson and the Rise of the American Empire, 1918–1961.* New York: Oxford University Press, 1991.

Bryn-Jones, David. *Frank B. Kellogg: A Biography.* New York: G. P. Putnam's Sons, 1937.

Byrnes, James F. *Speaking Frankly.* New York: Harper, 1947.

Castle, Alfred A. *Diplomatic Realism: William R. Castle Jr. and American Foreign Policy, 1919–1953.* Honolulu: Samuel L. and Mary Castle Foundation, 1998.

Clements, Kendrick A. *William Jennings Bryan, Missionary Isolationist.* Knoxville: University of Tennessee Press, 1982.

Cooper, John M. *Walter Hines Page: The Southerner as American, 1855–1918.* Chapel Hill: University of North Carolina Press, 1977.

Danelski, David J., and Joseph S. Tulchin. *The Autobiographical Notes of Charles Evans Hughes.* Cambridge, Mass.: Harvard University Press, 1973.

Dodd, William E., Jr., and Martha Dodd, eds. *Ambassador Dodd's Diary 1933–1938.* New York: Harcourt, Brace, 1941.

Ellis, L. Ethan. *Frank B. Kellogg and American Foreign Relations: 1925–1929.* New Brunswick, N.J.: Rutgers University Press, 1961.

Forrestal, James. *The Forrestal Diaries*. Ed. Walter Millis and E. F. Duffield. New York: Viking, 1951.

Garraty, John A. *Henry Cabot Lodge: A Biography*. New York: Knopf, 1953.

Gazell, James A. "Arthur H. Vandenberg, Internationalism, and the United Nations." *Political Science Quarterly* 88 (1973): 375–94.

Gerber, Michele Stenehjem. *An American First: John T. Flynn and the America First Committee*. New Rochelle, N.Y.: Arlington House, 1976.

Grew, Joseph C. *Turbulent Era: A Diplomatic Record of Forty Years, 1904–1945*. Vol. 2. Ed. Walter Johnson. Boston: Houghton Mifflin, 1952.

Hamby, Alonzo. *Man of the People: A Life of Harry S. Truman*. New York: Oxford University Press, 1995.

Harriman, W. Averell, and Elie Abel. *Special Envoy to Churchill and Stalin, 1941–1946*. New York: Random House, 1975.

Heinrichs, Waldo. *American Ambassador: Joseph C. Grew and the Development of the United States Diplomatic Tradition*. Oxford: Oxford University Press, 1986.

Hodgson, Godfrey. *The Colonel: The Life and Wars of Henry Stimson, 1867–1950*. New York: Knopf, 1990.

Hoover, Herbert C. *The Memoirs of Herbert Hoover 1920–1933: The Cabinet and the Presidency*. New York: Macmillan, 1952.

Hull, Cordell. *The Memoirs of Cordell Hull*. 2 vols. New York: Macmillan, 1948.

Kennan, George F. *Memoirs, vol. 1, 1900–1950*. Boston: Little, Brown, 1967.

Lansing, Robert. *War Memoirs of Robert Lansing, Secretary of State*. New York: Bobbs-Merrill, 1935.

Leahy, William. *I Was There: The Personal Story of the Chief of Staff of Presidents Roosevelt and Truman*. New York: Whittlesey House, 1950.

Lower, Richard Coke. *A Bloc of One: The Politics and Career of Hiram W. Johnson*. Stanford, Calif.: Stanford University Press, 1993.

MacArthur, Douglas. *Reminiscences*. New York: McGraw-Hill, 1964.

Maddox, Robert J. *William E. Borah and American Foreign Policy*. Baton Rouge: Louisiana State University Press, 1969.

Mayers, David. *George Kennan and the Dilemmas of U.S. Foreign Policy*. New York: Oxford University Press, 1988.

McLellan, David S. *Dean Acheson: The State Department Years*. New York: Dodd, Mead, 1976.

Morison, Elting E. *Turmoil and Tradition: A Study of the Life and Times of Henry L. Stimson*. Boston: Houghton Mifflin, 1960.

Mugridge, Ian. *The View from Xanadu: William Randolph Hearst and United States Foreign Policy.* Montreal: McGill-Queen's University Press, 1995.

Pogue, Forrest C. *George C. Marshall: Order and Hope, 1939–42.* New York: Viking, 1965.

——. *George C. Marshall: Organizer of Victory, 1943–45.* New York: Viking, 1973.

Pratt, Julius W. *Cordell Hull.* Vols. 12 and 13 of the *American Secretaries of State and Their Diplomacy.* New York: Cooper Square, 1964.

Salzman, Neil V. *Reform and Revolution: The Life and Times of Raymond Robbins.* Kent, Ohio: Kent State University Press, 1991.

Schmitz, David F. *Henry L. Stimson: The First Wise Man.* Wilmington, Del.: Scholarly Resources, 2001.

Sherwood, Robert E. *Roosevelt and Hopkins.* New York: Harper, 1948.

Smith, Amanda, ed. *Hostage to Fortune: The Letters of Joseph P. Kennedy.* New York: Viking, 2001.

Steel, Ronald. *Walter Lippmann and the American Century.* Boston: Little, Brown, 1980.

Stimson, Henry L., and McGeorge Bundy. *On Active Service in Peace and War.* New York: Harper, 1948.

Truman, Harry S. *Memoirs.* 2 vols. New York: Doubleday, 1955.

DOCUMENTARY COLLECTIONS

Butler, Susan, ed. *My Dear Mr. Stalin: The Complete Correspondence Between Franklin D. Roosevelt and Joseph V. Stalin.* New Haven, Conn.: Yale University Press, 2005.

Kimball, Warren F., ed. *Churchill and Roosevelt: The Complete Correspondence.* 3 vols. Princeton, N.J.: Princeton University Press, 1984.

Link, Arthur S., et al., eds. *The Papers of Woodrow Wilson.* 69 vols. Princeton, N.J.: Princeton University Press, 1966–93.

Loewenheim, Francis L., Harold L. Langley, and Manfred Jonas, eds. *Roosevelt and Churchill: The Secret Wartime Correspondence.* New York: Saturday Review/Button, 1975.

McJimsey, George, ed. *The Documentary History of the Franklin D. Roosevelt Presidency.* 30 vols. Washington, D.C.: University Publications of America/Lexis-Nexis, 2001–06.

United States Department of State. *Foreign Relations of the United States.* Multiple volumes for each year, 1914–45, divided by region. Special volumes for World War II conferences.

SELECTED ONLINE MATERIALS

American Academy of Diplomacy, www.academyofdiplomacy.org

American Diplomacy online journal, www.americandiplomacy.org

American History Documents for the Twentieth Century, www.cc.ukans
.edu/carrie/docs/texts/33wils2.htm

American Presidency Project, www.presidency.ucsb.edu/index.php

Association for Diplomatic Studies and Training, www.adst.org

Atlantic Charter meeting: *USS Augusta*, www.internet-esq.com/ussaugusta/
atlantic/index.htm

Avalon Project of the Yale Law School, www.yale.edu/lawweb/avalon/
avalon.htm

Bentley Historical Library, University of Michigan, Polar Bear Expedition
Digital Collections, polarbears.si.umich.edu

Charles Lindbergh and America First, www.charleslindbergh.com/american
first/index.asp

Cordell Hull Museum, www.cordellhullmuseum.com/history.html

Council on Foreign Relations, www.cfr.org

Documents of the Interwar Period, www.mtholyoke.edu/acad/intrel/interwar
.htm

Foreign Affairs magazine, www.foreignaffairs.org

Franklin D. Roosevelt fireside chats, www.mhric.org/fdr/fdr.html

Franklin D. Roosevelt Library, www.fdrlibrary.marist.edu

h-diplo discussion forum for U.S. diplomatic history, www.h-net.org/~diplo/

Herbert Hoover Library, www.presidency.ucsb.edu/herbert_hoover.php

Institute on World War II and the Human Experience, Florida State University, www.fsu.edu/~ww2/links.htm

League of Nations Timeline, www.indiana.edu/~league/timeline.htm

Schoenherr, Steven E., *The Versailles Treaty of June 28, 1919*, history.
sandiego.edu/gen/text/versaillestreaty/vercontents.htm

Second World War History, www.secondworldwarhistory.com

University of Wisconsin Digital Collections, *Foreign Relations of the
United States* series, 1861–1960, digital.library.wisc.edu/1711.dl/FRUS

U.S. Department of State Office of the Historian, www.state.gov/r/pa/ho

U.S. Diplomacy Association for Diplomatic Studies and Training, www
.usdiplomacy.org/exhibit/ambivalent.php

World War I information and articles, www.firstworldwar.com

About the Authors

Martin H. Folly is senior lecturer in U.S. and international history at Brunel University, London, England. He is an expert in U.S. foreign policy in the 1930s, World War II, and the Cold War. His publications include *The United States in World War II: The Awakening Giant* (2002) and *The Palgrave Concise Historical Atlas of World War II* (2004). He has published articles on the Grand Alliance during World War II and on the international diplomacy that led to the creation of the North Atlantic Treaty Organization. He has presented papers at the annual meeting of the Society of Historians of American Foreign Relations and was an invited speaker at a joint Anglo–Russian symposium in the British Foreign and Commonwealth Office in 2002.

Niall A. Palmer is a lecturer in politics and history at Brunel University, London, England. He is the author of *The New Hampshire Primary and the American Electoral Process* (1997) and *The Twenties in America: Politics and History* (2006). He has written for *BBC History* magazine and holds a permanent visiting scholarship at the New Hampshire Institute of Politics, St. Anselm's College, New Hampshire. In 2007, he was invited by the Ohio Historical Society to give guest lectures on the Warren G. Harding administration. His most recent publication is "The Veterans' Bonus and the Evolving Presidency of Warren G. Harding," *Presidential Studies Quarterly* 38, no. 1 (2008).

Breinigsville, PA USA
15 March 2010
234155BV00003B/2/P